Introduction to Recreation and Leisure

HUMAN KINETICS

Editor

Human Kinetics

Library of Congress Cataloging-in-Publication Data

Introduction to recreation and leisure.
      p. cm.
Includes bibliographical references and index.
ISBN 0-7360-5781-1 (hard cover)
1. Recreation. 2. Leisure. I. Human Kinetics (Organization)
GV14.I68 2006
790--dc22

                              2005012483

ISBN: 0-7360-5781-1

Copyright © 2006 by Human Kinetics, Inc.

The Web addresses cited in this text were current as of June 28, 2005, unless otherwise noted.

Acquisitions Editor: Gayle Kassing, PhD; **Developmental Editor:** Melissa Feld; **Assistant Editors:** Michelle M. Rivera and Derek Campbell; **Copyeditor:** Annette Pierce; **Proofreader:** Erin Cler; **Indexer:** Marie Rizzo; **Permission Manager:** Dalene Reeder; **Graphic Designer:** Robert Reuther; **Graphic Artist:** Dawn Sills; **Photo Manager:** Sarah A. Ritz; **Cover Designer:** Keith Blomberg; **Photographers (cover):** Dan Wendt, Kelly Huff, © Photodisc, and © Comstock; **Photographer (interior):** © Human Kinetics, unless otherwise noted; © Comstock (p. 1 [left]); courtesy of San Jose Parks, Recreation and Neighborhood Services (pp. 1 [bottom right] and 65 [top left]); courtesy of Craig Ross (p. 251 [top left]); © Eyewire/Photodisc/Getty Images (p. 251 [top right]); courtesy of Gaylene Carpenter (p. 251 [bottom]); **Art Manager:** Kelly Hendren; **Illustrators:** Al Wilborn, Stuart Cartwright, and Andrew Tietz; **Printer:** Sheridan Books

Printed in the United States of America   10   9   8   7   6   5   4   3   2   1

Human Kinetics
Web site: www.HumanKinetics.com

United States: Human Kinetics
P.O. Box 5076
Champaign, IL 61825-5076
800-747-4457
e-mail: humank@hkusa.com

Canada: Human Kinetics
475 Devonshire Road Unit 100
Windsor, ON N8Y 2L5
800-465-7301 (in Canada only)
e-mail: orders@hkcanada.com

Europe: Human Kinetics
107 Bradford Road
Stanningley
Leeds LS28 6AT, United Kingdom
+44 (0) 113 255 5665
e-mail: hk@hkeurope.com

Australia: Human Kinetics
57A Price Avenue
Lower Mitcham, South Australia 5062
08 8277 1555
e-mail: liaw@hkaustralia.com

New Zealand: Human Kinetics
Division of Sports Distributors NZ Ltd.
P.O. Box 300 226 Albany
North Shore City
Auckland
0064 9 448 1207
e-mail: info@humankinetics.co.nz

Contents

PART II — Leisure and Recreation As a Multifaceted Delivery System — 65

Chapter 5 — Delivery Systems — 67

Betty van der Smissen

Chapter 6 — Parks in Canada and the United States — 75

Stephen M. Holland and Paul F.J. Eagles

Chapter 7 — Public Recreation — 109

Sara Hensley, Susan Markham-Starr, Ellen Montague,
and Jane Hodgkinson

Chapter 8   Nonprofit Sector 143
Robert F. Ashcraft

Chapter 9   Commercial Recreation and Tourism 163
Lynn M. Jamieson

Chapter 10   Therapeutic Recreation 177
Frances Stavola Daly and Robin Kunstler

Chapter 11   Unique Groups 197
Robin Mittelstaedt, Brenda Robertson, Kelly Russell, John Byl, Jeff Temple, and Laurie Ogilvie

Chapter 12 Leisure and Recreation Across the Life Span 229

Laura L. Payne and Lynn A. Barnett

PART III Recreation and Leisure Service Areas 251

Chapter 13 Program Delivery and the Many Modes of Recreation . .253

Maureen Glancy

Chapter 14 Recreational Sport Management 271

Craig M. Ross

Chapter 15 Health, Fitness, Wellness, and Livability 289

Kathy Spangler and Ellen O'Sullivan

Chapter 16 Outdoor and Adventure Recreation 307

Randy J. Virden

Chapter 17 Arts and Culture 333

Gaylene Carpenter

Chapter 18 The Nature of Recreation and Leisure As a Profession . . 353

Mary G. Parr, Mark E. Havitz, and Andrew T. Kaczynski

Appendix: Accreditation Standards 377

Preface

Welcome to recreation and leisure studies. This introductory course textbook provides you with a broad view of one of the top industries for the 21st century. Recreation and leisure programs serve people 24/7/365 and are part of a global economy. These services are vital to the lives of individuals, families, and communities and can provide you with a challenging career path.

This book invites you to take an amazing journey as you explore the world of recreation and leisure. Your escorts are 34 professors and professionals in the field from throughout the United States and Canada. Their careers and passions mirror the various aspects of this profession. From rising stars, experts, leading thinkers, and icons in the field, the contributing authors serve as your personal guides as you begin your undergraduate studies of this exciting field. Their unique viewpoints provide a foundation for understanding the field upon which your undergraduate studies will build.

Introduction to Recreation and Leisure showcases the authors who have made incredible contributions in providing this unprecedented view of recreation and leisure. The goal of this book is to illustrate the wealth of opportunities within this diverse profession.

For students pursuing a career or considering recreation or leisure as a potential career choice, this book offers vital information from which you can begin to make informed choices. We want to provide you with a big picture of this diverse profession so that in your later studies you can explore specific areas in depth to gain an understanding of recreation and leisure as the following:

- A profession that offers lifetime career satisfaction or maybe an entry-level start on a career path with many options
- A contemporary industry that provides employment opportunities in a wide variety of fields
- A worldwide phenomenon that drives most of the world's economies

ORGANIZATION

Introduction to Recreation and Leisure is divided into three parts. Part I, Foundations of Recreation and Leisure, provides the foundation of this industry, including an introduction, history, and philosophical concepts. Part II, Leisure and Recreation As a Multifaceted Delivery System, introduces you to different sectors and areas of the field. Part III, Recreation and Leisure Service Areas, presents the different types of programming found in recreation and leisure services. These interest areas include recreational sports; fitness, health, and wellness; outdoor and adventure; and culture and the arts. The final chapter addresses the nature of the profession and what it takes to become a professional.

FEATURES

Several unique and useful features are included in the book.

- **Chapter objectives.** Each chapter lists the many important concepts you will learn and understand.
- **Outstanding graduates.** Students who have graduated from recreation and leisure programs and gone on to successful careers have been highlighted. They share insights and advice on recreation and leisure as a career.
- **Web sites.** Each chapter includes a list of Web sites that provide additional information for you to explore.
- **Glossary.** Important terms are printed in boldface in the text, and the definitions are included in the glossary at the end of the book.
- **NRPA standards.** You will find a list of competencies in the appendix.

ANCILLARIES

Three types of ancillaries are available to supplement the information presented in the textbook:

- **Instructor guide.** The instructor guide includes chapter overviews, chapter objectives, discussion questions, and learning activities.
- **Test package.** The test package includes a variety of questions, from true/false to short answer. Instructors can create their own tests.
- **Presentation package.** A Microsoft® PowerPoint presentation package includes key points from the chapters. Instructors may use the presentation package to supplement their lectures. The presentation package may be adapted to suit each instructor's lecture content and style.

Introduction to Recreation and Leisure presents a comprehensive view of the multifaceted, expansive field of recreation and leisure. It is hoped you enjoy learning about recreation and leisure, reading what the principal thinkers and leaders have to say about the field, and meeting outstanding graduates from universities across the United States and Canada who share their career experiences. Let's enter the world of recreation and leisure.

Textbook
Advisory Board

PART I

Foundations of Recreation and Leisure

CHAPTER 1

Power, Promise, Potential, and Possibilities of Parks, Recreation, and Leisure

Ellen O'Sullivan

Photo courtesy of San Jose Parks, Recreation, and Neighborhood Services

You can tell more about a society by how it plays rather than by how it works.

A. Bartlett Giamatti, president of Yale University (1978-1986), commissioner of Major League Baseball (1989)

CHAPTER OBJECTIVES

After reading this chapter, you should be able to do the following:

- Appreciate the role that parks, recreation, and leisure plays in all facets of life for all people
- Identify the different types of benefits associated with parks, recreation, and leisure
- Appreciate the unique qualities and opportunities afforded by this professional field

WHAT IF?

What if there were an aspect of life with promise and potential to empower people to grow and thrive; provide communities with facilities and services that enhance quality of life; connect people both locally and globally; preserve and protect our natural, historic, and cultural heritage; and contribute to a prosperous economy? What if there was an aspect of life so central to human existence that people spent more time engaged in this critical life pursuit than working or attending school combined? What if there was a category of the economy that accounted for substantial expenditures and appeared to be an ever growing economic force? What if there were a variety of career opportunities associated with this essential aspect of behavior and major component of the economy that created opportunities for personal growth, professional flexibility, sense of purpose, and resourcefulness on the part of the professionals in that field?

WELCOME TO THE WORLD OF PARKS, RECREATION, AND LEISURE

Welcome to the opportunities, options, pursuits, and possibilities of parks and recreation. The shortened term for this profession, which encompasses myriad pursuits and passions such as sports, tourism, health and wellness, adventure recreation, environmental preservation and management, is generally *parks, recreation, and leisure*.

The challenge in learning more about this field as a personal pursuit, professional career, or a combination of both is to grasp the size and significance of the world known as parks, recreation, and leisure. This field is powerful because its activities and pursuits are truly everywhere, touching the lives of all human beings, and occur 24 hours a day, seven days a week, for the 52 weeks of a year. The potential and promise of parks, recreation, and leisure are simultaneously challenging to grasp and critical to the well-being of individuals, communities, societies, and the world. The benefits of this field ensure that we have sufficient clean air and water to sustain life, opportunities to live purposeful and pleasurable lives, memories of happy times with friends and family, and options and opportunities for health and well-being throughout our lives.

PARKS, RECREATION, AND LEISURE: EVERYWHERE, EVERYONE, ALL THE TIME

Well-worn soccer balls skirt the streets of villages around the world, whether the villages are wracked with strife or disaster or support manicured fields and youth and adult teams in matching uniforms. The five rings of the Olympic Games burn brightly every four years as tens of thousands of athletes representing hundreds of countries from around the world gather in the spirit of competition and unity. Street merchants in Bangkok play a checker-like board game hastily constructed of cardboard and discarded bottle caps. Visitors from around the world marvel at the migration of wildlife across the plains of the Serengeti while other visitors admire the exceptional beauty and unique geological features of Gros Morne National Park in Newfoundland. People travel great distances to snorkel in Belize, fish in New Zealand, explore the Louvre, or observe the changing of the guard in Ottawa or at the Tomb of the Unknown Soldier in Washington, DC. Historic sites and natural areas around the world are preserved and protected so that people can engage firsthand in a natural, cultural, or historic awareness and appreciation.

Parks, recreation, and leisure is everywhere—in the far reaches of the Sahara, the crowded seashores of California, the Broadway theaters and museums of New York City, the Hell's Gate Airtram, and the Classic Chinese Garden of Vancouver. Leisure pursuits take place in cities and towns, small villages, the countryside, and mega-urban centers. Leisure experiences occur inside buildings or outside and sometimes in either location. For example, basketball is played either indoors or out, and band concerts, too, take place in buildings or in parks. The array of places is extensive, including auditoriums, zoos, churches, and casinos. There are even health clubs and spas located in airports, rock-climbing walls in retail establishments, and, of course, play areas at fast-food restaurants and even some furniture stores. Parks and recreation can be and is found everywhere—all the places and spaces in which people gather to play, enjoy, and relax.

Another dimension of the "everywhere" quality of parks and recreation is illustrated in the fact that a variety of organizations provide park, recreation, and leisure services. The delivery of services is not limited to just one type of organization. For example, one golf course might be under the governance of a city or state, and another similar course might be a private country club for members only, while a third course might be managed by a corporation. Organizations offering adventure pursuits can run the gamut from outdoor leadership training by a nonprofit organization such as a local YMCA to travel companies designing and offering adventure experiences around the globe. Parks and recreation services and facilities are provided by all types of organizations and businesses.

It's for Everyone

Consider the ways in which parks, recreation, and leisure touches the lives of everyone, all ages, life stages, cultures, social classes, and genders. Recall personal experiences or observations and identify the people participating in a recreation activity or spending time in a natural setting. These might include the following:

- College students playing coed volleyball in the school's intramural league
- A 10-year-old taking beginning drawing lessons at the community center

© Photodisc

© Comstock

Recreation can take place indoors or outdoors, at home or in a park, and at any time of day.

- A parent and toddler enrolled in the movement class at the local YMCA
- Female friends spending time together at a day spa
- Families picnicking while enjoying an outdoor band concert
- A youth hockey team practicing in the early morning on the same rink where up-and-coming young pro players ready themselves for the NHL at evening events
- A 12-year-old going away to camp for the first time
- Guys playing pickup basketball at the local park
- An adolescent testing self-sufficiency on an Outward Bound trip
- Grandparents taking grandchildren on a trip to the Grand Canyon
- A teen group teaching retirees how to surf the net
- A stressed-out adult watching the sunset
- Employees attending the annual company outing to a theme park
- Special Olympic athletes crossing the finish line with elation that brings smiles to the faces of participants and spectators alike
- The over-60 softball team exhibiting a desire to win similar to that of the youth soccer league players
- Both fledgling and gifted artists displaying work in the same community art show

An adage often used by park and recreation professionals employed in the community sector is that parks and recreation takes people "from the cradle to the grave," and while that is not the most appealing description, it does reinforce the presence of parks, recreation, and leisure in everyone's life.

All the Time

Although the pursuits of open space, physical activity, and social outings happen all the time—any month of the year, any day of the week, and throughout all the life stages of human existence. Some recreation activities are associated mainly with the summer or the winter, and holidays sometimes serve as an impetus. For example, the New Year with its emphasis on resolutions moti-

vates people to become more physically active or seek out new experiences. Independence Day celebrations are commonly accompanied by picnics, concerts, fireworks, trips, and other outings, and Halloween brings out the childlike spirit in young and old alike with parties and parades.

The physical characteristics of different seasons provide opportunities for year-round activity. The first thaw finds people tending lawns and starting gardens. Summer draws people to mountains, lakes, streams, or seashores. Winter gives way to skiing, skating, curling, and snowboarding. People's passions for certain activities have influenced the "all the time" approach to parks and recreation. At one time, tennis or soccer could only be played in warm weather, just as ice-skating and hockey once required cold weather. Indoor facilities and lighted playing fields and trails expand the opportunity for parks and recreation services to "all the time."

Recreation is pursued 24 hours a day as well. Ski areas open at first light to give would-be lift ticket purchasers the chance to check out snow conditions. Health clubs open at 4:30 a.m. enabling early risers to work out before heading to work. Heavily industrialized communities offer adult leagues and activities to accommodate the traditional three shifts of factory work. The city of Las Vegas with its "Beyond the Neon" slogan offers unusual times for programs and activities because many residents work shifts in the casinos, which, of course, operate around the clock. YMCAs and community centers offer sleepovers, which provide not only fun and excitement for children but also leisure time for parents. Midnight basketball continues to put recreation on the 24-hour timetable.

Parks, recreation, and leisure is "all the time" in an additional way. Play is essential for children. From infancy and through adolescence, they acquire important life skills through recreation and leisure activities and experiences. The peek-a-boo games so popular with babies and the Duck, Duck, Goose of almost everyone's early childhood teach important social connections and interactions. The same holds true at the other end of the life cycle, as recreation provides stress reduction for overworked adults and social support for older people living on their own.

Parks and Recreation: It Makes Up Most of Our Time

People sometimes discount the role and the importance of unobligated, or discretionary, time and the role it plays in their quality of life. They focus on attending school, getting a good night's sleep, and going to work, but those activities don't take up all of their time.

If people living in industrialized nations sleep between six and eight hours every day and work or go to school for another eight hours during the week, how much unobligated time do they have? Although the number of hours consumed by sleep, work, and the requirements of daily living such as housework, commuting, and so on varies from person to person, one thing is certain, unobligated time accounts for well over one-third of most people's lives. To see how this can be true consider the following:

- **Life span.** People born today in the United States or Canada can expect to live at least 70 years, and school attendance and work do not occur during all 70 of those years.

- **Sleep.** Approximately one-third, or 8 hours, of every day is spent sleeping.

- **Infants and toddlers.** Children from birth to 4 years old spend a minimum of 6 hours per day exploring, learning, and growing through play.

- **Formal schooling.** Young people start school at 5 years of age and complete formal schooling between the ages of 18 and 25; therefore, only 13 to 20 of their 70-plus years are occupied with school. School and related activities such as homework might consume 8 hours per day, and a school year lasts 30 to 36 weeks. This leaves a substantial amount of time for nonacademic and nonsleeping activities.

- **Working world.** Full-time work will claim the years from 18 or 25 to 55 or 65. Most people work 40 hours per week, whether it is 8 hours for five days or 10 hours for four days per week, and have a minimum of two weeks of vacation plus holidays.

- **Third age.** Retirement, when every day is a Saturday and people are not restricted to two weeks of vacation, typically lasts at least five years and could be longer depending on longevity.

Play around with the years and hours cited in the previous list to see how much time in a person's life is available after you account for sleeping, eating, schooling, and working. The remaining hours available for leisure, or unobligated time, just might surprise you. Depending on individual variations, leisure time could amount to more than one-third of a person's life.

Beyond Everywhere and Everyone

Although we know that parks, recreation, and leisure facilities and services are everywhere and available to everyone most of the time, their presence alone isn't enough to prove their value to the lives of individuals, families, work groups, neighborhoods, communities, and society. Just being everywhere all of the time is not necessarily a valuable or positive attribute.

The obesity epidemic or an outbreak of the flu may be everywhere, but that doesn't make these occurrences positive for individuals or society. Cable television operates 24 hours a day, 365 days a year, but that does not mean that the programs or offerings are positive or of value or interest to the viewer. So we need to explore the depth of values and benefits that lie beneath the surface of parks and recreation. A review of the "everyone" list of people participating in recreation activities included earlier in this chapter begins to uncover the values of parks and recreation.

- Why would a university student choose to join the intramural coed volleyball team? Is it a chance to be physically active, a time to hang out with friends, an opportunity to meet new people, a change of pace from classes and study time, or all of these reasons or a combination of them?

- Why would a 12-year-old look forward to leaving family and friends behind venturing to a residential camp for a month? Could it be the chance to acquire new skills, practice being independent, and make new friends, or is it a way to be recognized as self-reliant?

- What motivates a single mother with a very long day ahead of her to rise at 5:30 a.m. to sit with a cup of tea and watch the sun rise? Might it be the opportunity to relax, reflect, and regroup before the nonstop demands of her day?

It is these values and benefits that an individual or a family or a community derives from the park setting, the recreation activity, or the leisure experience that imbues parks and recreation with its inherent value. Incorporating parks and recreation into people's lives, whether it was the Olympics of ancient Greece or is the sand gardens of Boston, Massachusetts, or the 39 national parks in Canada, reflects those benefits. The unusual list of questions titled "Guess Who I Am?" from an issue of *Parks & Recreation* published by the National Recreation and Park Association can serve as a springboard for the various ways parks and recreation can be viewed and the diverse roles it can play (Corwin, 2001) (see figure 1.1).

Guess Who I Am?

1. I keep you in good health and prevent you from heart disease, but I'm not a *doctor* or *cardiologist*.
2. I host parties and events of all sizes, but I'm not a *meeting planner*.
3. I put a smile on your face, but I'm not a *dentist* or *orthodontist*.
4. I often raise lots of money for charity, but I'm not a *professional fundraiser*.
5. I provide an outstanding forum for you to learn about many things, but I'm not a *teacher* or *professor*.
6. I have often introduced couples who meet and begin long-term relationships, but I'm not a *matchmaker*.
7. I often bring music to your ears, but I'm not a *musician* or a *singer*.
8. I have lots of friends in the animal world, but I'm not a *veterinarian*.
9. I have tons of friends in the insect world, but I'm not an *entomologist*.
10. I am often surrounded by birds of many types, but I'm not an *ornithologist*.
11. I enjoy the company of trees and shrubs, but I'm not a *nursery manager*.
12. I am very photogenic, but I'm not a *fashion model*.
13. My brethren and I have been in many movies, but I'm not a *movie star*.
14. I'm often on your local television news, but I'm not a *news anchor*.
15. I often appear in your local newspaper, but I'm not a *reporter* or a *photographer*.
16. I work around lots of sneakers, but I'm not an *athletic shoe salesperson*.
17. I'm a good friend to many of you on the Fourth of July, but I'm not a *fireworks technician*.
18. I make the value of your house as great as possible, but I'm not a *real estate agent*.
19. I often entertain children, but I'm not a *baby sitter*.
20. I often prevent crime, but I'm not a *police officer*.

Okay that's 20 clues, can you guess who I am?

FIGURE 1.1   The answer, of course, is parks and recreation.

Reprinted courtesy of *Parks & Recreation*, National Recreation and Park Association.

VALUES AND BENEFITS OF PARKS, RECREATION, AND LEISURE

When you start to develop a list of the range of benefits that can be attributed to state and provincial parks, community centers, historic sites, and fitness clubs, just to cite a few alternatives within the greater parks and recreation family, the list can become cumbersome. A more organized way to consider these benefits is to incorporate two different levels. A broader, more general, category consists of three different types of benefits as identified by Bev Driver (1998), an early proponent of this approach. These three types of benefits are **improved condition, prevention of a worse** condition, and **realization of a psychological experience.** Originally, the benefits consisted of improving or preventing conditions, but the benefit attributed to psychological experiences was added when it became apparent that important benefits could be gained in more internal, and certainly less tangible, ways such as awareness, appreciation, and sense of self. The three conditions incorporate the following:

1. Improved condition. If a human, natural, or economic factor is not functioning at full capacity or is functioning in a deleterious manner, the benefit of recreation would be to ameliorate this condition.

2. Prevention of a worse condition. Not every instance of poor performance or threatening

conditions can be improved, so in this case, the value of parks and recreation would be to stem further erosion or deterioration of a human, natural, or economic condition.

3. Realization of a psychological experience. This category represents the leisure pursuits that people select for the intrinsic values they gain through the experience. Stress reduction, sense of control, and spirituality are examples of these benefits.

Each of the three types of benefits can be further divided into four different categories of values and benefits: individual, social, environmental, and economic. The Canadian Parks and Recreation Association took a lead in this effort with its publication of *The Benefits Catalogue* in the early 1990s. This valuable effort was augmented by the National Recreation and Park Association's approach to a similar set of values and benefits a short time later. Although in many instances, there is evidence of overlap between and among the four different categories, there are indeed specific values and benefits within each.

Individual and Personal Benefits of Parks and Recreation

The first category is **individual and personal benefits of parks and recreation.** This category encompasses the many different avenues in which a person's life can be enriched and enhanced or even extended by various leisure pursuits. The various individual benefits and the range of outcomes associated with these benefits are extraordinary as are the potential impact they have on one's life (see figure 1.2).

The benefits attributed to parks and recreation can be observed in people at play and in pursuits such as the following:

- An overstressed adult sitting on a beach quietly enjoying the serenity of the sunset
- A child the first time he or she manages to ride a bicycle without external support
- A Saturday hiking group that challenges itself to longer, steeper treks over time
- A 78-year-old who learns to use the Internet at the community center as a way of keeping pace with the changes in the world around him

In more recent years, parks and recreation professionals have collected data and statistics that

---

Individual and Personal Benefits of Parks and Recreation

Broad Benefits

Full and meaningful life

Balance between work and play

Life satisfaction

Quality of life

More-Specific Benefits

Physical health

- Muscle strength
- Flexibility
- Cardiovascular conditioning
- Weight control

Emotional well-being

- Sense of self
- Sense of control
- Problem-solving ability

Lifelong learning

- Independent living
- Personal growth
- Adaptation to change

Quality of life

- Awareness and appreciation of the arts, history, and nature

FIGURE 1.2   Individual and personal benefits of parks and recreation.

Joe Abraham "Pepito" Gil, Age 5, and His Mom, Sanjua

"Tee-ball is my favorite sport. I'm 5 now. I can run all the way around the bases, and I'm a lot faster. I'm in tee-ball again this year, and then I'm going to be in kindergarten."—Pepito.

"One important thing that I've noticed since he started tee-ball is that he can tell the difference between left and right. In preschool he was confused about right and left, but since he's been in tee-ball, he knows that he's left-handed. When he first started he was afraid of the other kids. He opened up and made good friends that he invites home with him. Getting better at the sport has given him confidence." —Sanjua, Pepito's mother.

Reprinted courtesy of *Parks & Recreation*, National Recreation and Park Association.

better document the role their services play in a person's well-being as well as conducting specific studies. Some of the studies that reveal the benefits of parks and recreation include the following:

• Children, adolescents, and adults reported adopting healthier behaviors—such as choosing heart-healthy food more often—after participating in Hearts N' Parks programs that incorporate heart-healthy behaviors into regular activities offered by parks and recreation departments (National Institutes of Health, 2003).

• Savanna-like settings are associated with self-reports of peacefulness, tranquility, or relaxation as well as decreased fear and anger; enhanced mental alertness, attention, and cognitive performance as demonstrated through proofreading tasks and psychological testing (R.S. Urich, 2001, as cited in Frumkin, 2001).

• Significant research indicates that participation in after-school programs is positively associated with more positive attitude toward schoolwork, higher aspirations for college, finer work habits, better interpersonal skills, reduced dropout rate, higher-quality homework completion, less time spent in unhealthy behaviors and improved grades (National Institute on Out-of-School Time, 2003).

Social and Community Benefits of Parks and Recreation

The second category is **social and community benefits of parks and recreation** (see figure 1.3). This subset of values and benefits is characterized by the many opportunities for success and enjoyment that are afforded by interacting with others; these encounters can be positive and enriching for individuals, small groups, and society overall.

Photo courtesy of Gaylene Carpenter

Photo courtesy of Gaylene Carpenter

Recreation and leisure brings social and community benefits. Adolescents can explore arts and dance at their community center, providing an outlet for stress.

Social and Community Benefits of Parks and Recreation

Broad Benefits

Social bonds and sense of belonging

Strong, vitally involved groups and communities

Ethnic and cultural understanding and goodwill

More-Specific Benefits

Sense of community

- Community pride
- Community cohesiveness
- Reduced alienation
- Involvement in issues

Awareness and appreciation

- Tolerance and understanding
- Outlets for conflict resolution
- Cooperation

Social support

- Lifeline for elderly
- Support for youth
- Cultural identity

FIGURE 1.3   Social and community benefits of parks and recreation.

Mark Nabarro

"I moved to Santa Barbara three years ago. I knew nobody, I had no job and no place to live, but I love sports. I joined the parks and rec softball league as soon as I got here, and I began to have friends immediately. One of the guys I met helped me get a room to rent and offered me a job. Now, I have a good job in town and a two-bedroom apartment. My girlfriend grew up in Santa Barbara and she's always amazed that I know more people than she does, and it's all through parks and recreation. I'm a counselor at a juvenile facility, and by bringing some of the kids to the game with me, it's actually helped my work. Now the kids I work with are all excited about sports and it gives us a special relationship. I'd have to say that being part of a team has improved just about every relationship in my life." —Mark Nabarro

Reprinted courtesy of *Parks & Recreation*, National Recreation and Park Association.

The social and community benefits attributed to parks and recreation can be exhibited through the following:

- A newly widowed gentleman who receives a hot meal and the social support of others through his daily visit to the senior center
- The family photo albums replete with treasured memories rekindled by the candid shots of family and friends while on vacation, picnics, holidays, special events, and other social gatherings
- A young Latino child experiencing firsthand the art, food, and songs of his parents' homeland at the community Latino festival
- A newcomer to the community who doesn't know anybody in town and welcomes the open format of drop-in basketball at the local YMCA as a way to meet others who live in the area

- A child frightened during her first stay in the hospital finding comfort by playing familiar games with newly acquired friends
- The sense of belonging and community that envelops the crowd gathered at the annual Fourth of July picnic and fireworks display

Similar to the data and statistics presented for the individual benefits of parks, recreation, and leisure, there is evidence of the value human contact and group interactions can contribute to the social and community well-being of all. Some of the community benefits that can be attributed to parks and recreation include the following:

- A study by the Human-Environment Research Laboratory at the University of Illinois at Urbana-Champaign found that more green space within inner-city neighborhoods resulted in greater use of the public common spaces and that the relationship between neighbors was stronger because of the presence of vegetation (Kuo, Sullivan, Coley, & Brunson, 1998).
- A police-documented 28 percent drop in juvenile arrests and significant improvement in grades occurred after the start of the Success Through Academics and Recreation Support (STARS) program was created in Fort Myers, Florida (Witt & Crompton, 1996).

• Neighborhoods with community gardens in St. Louis, Missouri, a city that lost approximately 50,000 residents between 1990 and 2000, were more stable than those without community gardens. The population in neighborhoods without gardens dropped by 6 percent compared to 13 percent for the overall city (Tranel, 2003, as cited in Sherer, 2003).

Environmental Benefits of Parks and Recreation

The third category, **environmental benefits of parks and recreation,** addresses the wide-ranging and critical role of the environment in quality of life (see figure 1.4). An interesting difference between this category and the others is that the environmental benefits sustain human life by protecting the ecosystem in addition to providing other more pleasurable benefits.

The environmental benefits attributed to parks and recreation can be exhibited through the following:

• Setting aside public lands as natural watersheds for preservation allows local residents

---

Environmental Benefits of Parks and Recreation

Broad Benefits
  Clean air and water
  Environmental protection
  Preservation of natural and historic areas

More-Specific Benefits
Health and well-being
  • Reduced stress
  • Venues for physical activity

Education
  • Improved science and math skills
  • Natural life cycle knowledge
  • Environmental ethic

Economic impact
  • Catalyst for relocation
  • Reduced cost of utilities
  • Increased tourism

FIGURE 1.4   Environmental benefits of parks and recreation.

---

to pay less for drinking water and provides them access to hiking trails.

• The natural desert environment surrounding Tucson, Arizona, makes it a desirable location for the many spas and resorts that take advantage of the natural desert environment, and residents and business owners alike benefit from reduced tax base and increased business.

• Urban dwellers flock to the city parks to reconnect with nature.

• Fourth graders calculate the speed of the water in the streambed during outdoor classroom sessions.

Some of the studies that reveal the benefits of environmental activities conducted through parks and recreation include the following:

• Health studies have shown that contact with plants, animals, pleasing landscapes, and wilderness areas offers a wide range of health benefits including lower blood pressure and reduced cholesterol levels (Frumkin, 2001).

• In a survey conducted in Missouri by Active Living by Design, 55.2 percent of people using trails reported an increase in the amount that they walked since starting to use the trails. This study also found that trail walking might promote physical activity among women and people in lower socioeconomic groups (Active Living by Design, n.d.).

Economic Benefits of Parks and Recreation

The fourth and final category is **economic benefits of parks and recreation** (see figure 1.5). While other values and benefits are often underrecognized, this category of benefits tends to be more visible and seemingly more important. The adage "money talks" certainly comes into play in this instance.

The economic benefits attributed to parks and recreation can be exhibited through the following:

• The owners of small stores and restaurants adjacent to national parks who make a living providing services to park visitors

• The corporations that increase productivity through fewer sick days by implementing recreation and wellness programs

• The older adults who lower their cholesterol levels by exchanging costly medications for daily walks

By setting aside land for recreation, governments benefit individuals and the environment.

Economic Benefits of Parks and Recreation

Broad Benefits

Cost reduction

Funds generation

Catalyst for development

More-Specific Benefits

Cost reduction

- Health care
- Decreased vandalism and crime
- Less stress

Increased financial resources

- Enhanced land values
- Neighborhood revitalization
- Increased worker productivity

Catalyst for economic growth

- Favorable business climate
- Increased tourism

FIGURE 1.5   Economic benefits of parks and recreation.

- Today's knowledge workers seek to live, work, and play in communities with access to the natural environment and public places to meet, gather, and socialize. It is these amenities that companies employing today's knowledge workforce seek as a way of attracting and retaining a highly skilled workforce.

Some of the information and studies that reveal the economic benefits of parks and recreation include the following:

- Physically active people had lower annual direct medical costs than did inactive people. The cost difference was $330 U.S. per person (Pratt, Macera, & Guijing, 2000).

- Recreational sporting events can positively affect a community's economy. For example, an annual soccer tournament in Tempe, Arizona, has added $1 million U.S. each year of operation to that city's economy (Sosteck, 2004).

- A review of 25 studies examining the impact of parks and open space on property values found that in 20 of the cases, the presence of parks and open space resulted in higher local property taxes (Crompton, 2000).

What Recreators Can Do

It costs approximately $30,000 to incarcerate a juvenile offender for one year. If that money were available to Parks and Recreation, we could do the following:

Take him swimming twice a week for 24 weeks,

And give him four tours of the zoo, plus lunch,

And enroll him in 50 community center programs,

And visit the nature center twice,

And let him play league softball for a season,

And tour the gardens at the park twice,

And give him two weeks of tennis lessons,

And enroll him in two weeks of day camp,

And let him play three rounds of golf,

And act in one play,

And participate in one fishing clinic,

And take a four-week pottery class,

And play basketball eight hours a week for 40 weeks,

After which we could return to you: $29,125 and one much happier kid.

Reprinted courtesy of *Parks & Recreation*, National Recreation and Park Association.

Another way of looking at the economic relationship between supporting the health, safety, and growth of a child is succinctly presented in the sidebar "What Recreators Can Do" by Bob Jennings, a naturalist in Oklahoma.

PARKS AND RECREATION: A PASSION, A PURSUIT, A PROFESSION

For the thousands of people who never pass up an opportunity to collect mineral specimens or plan vacations around the Major League baseball schedule or sport bumper stickers that read "backstrokers keep their faces dry," parks, recreation, and leisure is indeed their passion. For those who play golf every couple of weeks or try to catch new exhibits at the local gallery or look forward to planning their various weekend adventures, parks, recreation, and leisure is a life pursuit.

Yes, parks, recreation, and leisure assumes many roles in people's lives. It can be either a passion or a life pursuit or a bit of both. However, you may recall the series of questions at the start of this chapter; one of the queries was this:

What if there were a variety of career opportunities associated with this essential aspect of behavior and major component of the economy that created opportunities for personal growth, empowerment, sense of purpose, and resourcefulness on the part of the professionals in that field?

There is! It's the profession of parks and recreation. The everywhere, everyone, most-of-the-time characteristics of this field as well as the values and the benefits cited previously transform parks and recreation into a profession with the potential for both making a living and being enriched personally by the many alternatives within careers associated with this field. These career options enable a person to work in the following situations:

• With almost any segment of society—age groups from cradle to grave, rich, not so rich, those with disabilities and those without, highly proficient, rank beginners, well and ill, and everything in between

• With a wide range of interest areas such as art, music, dance, drama, sports from Little League up, games, nature, environmental protection, therapeutic settings, fitness, wellness, arts, culture, travel, tourism, and additional areas that are discussed in later chapters

• In a variety of settings such as parks, nature centers, hospitals, correctional facilities, resorts, college campuses, military installations, corporations, hotels, and communities and housed within various organizational patterns such as public, nonprofit, private, commercial, or corporate entities and independent contractors

The array of career options and opportunities presents a challenge when attempting to share information and insight into a diverse and dynamic field such as parks and recreation. One way in which you can secure greater insight into this field is by engaging in conversations with people employed in the profession. Throughout the book you will find Outstanding Graduates—profiles of graduates of recreation and leisure programs and their career paths.

A Professional Career Choice

These interviews are a great beginning for learning about this field; however, you can gain additional insight. In the event that you find yourself with extra time and in the company of professionals working in parks and recreation, ask them how they found themselves in this particular career category. The majority of them will share personal stories about their road to becoming a park and recreation professional. It could that a passion for swimming, golf, gymnastics, ceramics, the outdoors, or some other leisure activity set them down this path. Or maybe the positive influence that a coach, camp counselor, theater director, park ranger, or recreation therapist had on their life spurred their career choice. Naturally, some professionals are drawn to the field because they want to work with a certain group such as children, dancers, or active adults, just to cite a few.

Qualities and Characteristics of the Profession

If the situation presents itself, try to discover the characteristics of their work world that make the field of parks and recreation particularly worthwhile for them. It is virtually impossible to identify every characteristic of such a diverse field because spas and stadiums don't appear to have a great deal in common. However, it would be enlightening to attempt to discern those attributes of the working world of parks and recreation that might resonate with others exploring career options. Some of those attributes and characteristics include the following:

• **Variety of settings.** Park and recreation activities take place indoors, in the woods, on the sea, close to home, and around the globe; therefore, this profession provides the opportunity to accommodate shifts in your career goals.

• **Burnout prevention.** Often professionals who work with people have a tendency to burn out from the continual challenges of one group or another. The number and diversity of people from cradle to grave, the rich and the poor, and the healthy and less healthy provide ample opportunity to transport your skills and knowledge to a different population.

• **Less formal settings.** Although not true of all parks and recreation career settings, it is true that many activities, programs, and services take place in a less formal setting than in other professional alternatives.

• **Creativity in approaches.** Although parks and recreation professionals must adopt specific practices, consider safety issues, and meet focused goals, the flexibility to creatively meet these requirements helps many practitioners pursue their own growth and development.

• **Continual change.** Another asset of the parks and recreation field is that no two days are exactly the same. The rain changes the forest, a child learns to float, and a new exhibit opens at the museum. Part of the attraction of this profession is the continual change that keeps professionals alert and retooled.

• **Responsibility.** Many of the entry-level positions in parks and recreation come with the opportunity to assume responsibility almost right from the start. Whether it be responsibility for a park area, tour group, or swimming pool, new parks and recreation professionals often are in charge.

• **Resourcefulness.** The less formal nature of the programs and settings combined with the challenges of working with a variety of participants with individual goals and abilities spells the need to be resourceful. One of the many things that parks and recreation professionals comment on is the ongoing challenges of their positions.

Making a Difference

When you ask several parks and recreation professionals who have spent several years working in this field why they stayed in the profession, you will hear a variety of responses. However, you may find a thread that holds the various responses together. That theme most often reflects "making a difference." These professionals might talk about making a difference in the life of one person or a group. Or they could mean their contribution to the vitality and viability of a community or the far-reaching difference that will result from their effort to protect nature or preserve cultural or historic sites.

The common "making a difference" response will be ever present in conversations with parks and recreation professionals. A quote attributed to Socrates perhaps sums up the essence of a career in parks and recreation: "Leisure is the best of all professions." Socrates was most likely suggesting that being at leisure is the best way to occupy time, but based on some of the attributes and characteristics of the field, the "best" connotation could be applied to the professions within parks, recreation, and leisure as well.

Unique Quality of Parks and Recreation

Aristotle believed that a good life is predicated on engaging in activities that are intrinsically valuable. Recreation activities and leisure pursuits generally fall within this parameter. Other disciplines can create and support activities that are intrinsically valuable, and other employment areas involve working with children or adults or in the outdoors or nonprofit sector. What then makes parks and recreation unique in its own right?

The one quality that makes parks, recreation, and leisure both unique and valuable while setting the field apart from other endeavors is the voluntary nature of participation along with the promise or potential of fun and enjoyment. Our bodies compel us to eat and sleep. There are societal norms that contribute to time spent in schooling and work. However, this is not the case with participation in parks, recreation, and leisure activities. The common elements that draw people to choose from an extensive array of alternative opportunities within their leisure time are the power, promise, potential, and possibility that those choices hold for fun, pleasure, or meaning. That statement may seem a bit misleading when we consider the teenagers who submit to family vacation under duress or the people training to run marathons or even the people involved in less-than-positive activities in their free time. It is important to note that some recreational pursuits such as vandalism and gang activity are usually voluntary choices made during a person's unobligated time and as such can be considered recreation. The common element that enables a teenager to enjoy a family trip and the long-distance runner to venture outside in inclement weather is the power, promise, potential, and possibility that the vacation, the training, or even the vandalism holds for fun, pleasure, or meaning.

Yes, fun is fundamental; fundamental to attracting people to activities and options that will be valuable to them and possibly to friends, families, neighborhoods, communities, or society overall. There are numerous instances when the concept of fun can and is dismissed as having no value, but it is the element of fun that attracts people to particular activities and motivates them to remain committed and involved. A concise explanation of the role that "fun" can and does play might include the following:

> FUN is FUNdamental to valuable life experiences. Fun attracts attention, sparks an interest, engages participation, creates motivation, fuels repeated involvement, and supports results. FUN is FUNdamental = Positive results for individuals and society.

MOVING ON

This chapter begins our discussion of the profession. However, it barely scratches the surface of the unique qualities and characteristics of the profession and only touches on the diverse values and benefits that parks, recreation, and leisure hold for individuals, groups, communities, the environment, and the economy. The rest of the book serves as a road map to guide your journey that starts by exploring the history and background of this field as well as identifying the various organizations that provide leisure-related services for people. Other sections and chapters provide an overview of the variety of settings and populations that make up this unique profession. This book offers you a depth of information about the various career choices in recreation and leisure.

Web Sites to EXPLORE

Project for Public Spaces: www.pps.org
The Wallace Foundation: www.wallacefoundation.org
American Planning Association: www.planning.org
The Trust for Public Lands: www.tpl.org

CHAPTER 2

History of Recreation

*Douglas Kennedy, Jerome Singleton,
and M. Rebecca Genoe*

© Associated Press

Those who cannot remember
the past are condemned to
repeat it.

*George Santayana, Spanish and
American philosopher*

If history repeats itself and the
unexpected always happens,
how incapable must Man be of
learning from the experience.

George Bernard Shaw, playwright

CHAPTER OBJECTIVES

After reading this chapter, you should be able to do the following:

- Identify and explain the historical development of recreation and leisure in prehistoric societies
- Identify and explain the historical development of recreation and leisure in ancient Rome and Greece
- Identify and explain the historical development of recreation and leisure in Europe
- Identify and explain the historical development of recreation and leisure in the United States
- Identify and explain the historical development of recreation and leisure in Canada
- Identify and explain how government and professional organizations impacted the development of recreation and leisure in Canada and the United States

INTRODUCTION

History shapes what we understand today. To understand how recreation and leisure services are delivered in the United States and Canada today, you must understand the historical periods and their societal expectations that have influenced the development of these services. Societies in both Canada and the United States have been affected by the generations of immigrants that have landed, settled, and influenced recreation and leisure. By understanding how leisure has emerged, it is possible to see how history often repeats itself, and what we see today is often similar to what happened long ago. Whether lessons can be learned from the past undoubtedly requires an appreciation and understanding of our history.

TRACING THE ROOTS OF LEISURE IN CANADA AND THE UNITED STATES

Because past definitions of leisure influence our understanding of leisure today, we will trace the development of leisure from prehistoric societies to the Protestant Reformation.

Prehistoric Societies

People in prehistoric societies were primarily concerned with survival (Shivers & deLisle, 1997). Hunting and gathering were the primary activities and provided resources to maintain life. There was little "free time" as we know it today. Work, survival, and rest melded to become one life-sustaining activity. Once prehistoric people could create tools and were able to store information in a larger brain, more time became available. This free time was used for ritualization, or ceremonial acts (Ibrahim, 1991). These acts often focused on celebrations of successful hunts, offerings for bountiful harvests, and beseeching the gods for their favor. It is believed that playlike activities were also critical to the needs of emerging tribes. These activities depicted historical events, transportation practices, war games, and the use of farm tools. Play prepared children for their responsibilities as youth and adults and became a way of achieving solidarity and morality. It also became a healing experience and a means of communication and provided pleasure and entertainment. As societies emerged, playlike activities were also a means to relax, recover, and replenish strength after working (Kraus, 1971). These emerging societies also developed structures that allowed people an opportunity to focus on specific work roles. One person could focus on being a hunter, while another could be a builder. With these roles established, greater cooperation provided people with the resources for activities that did not relate to sustaining life. Thus, for the first time, greater opportunities for leisure were experienced. This is no different from today when people "specialize" in a particular vocation needed by society, while relying on the specialties of others for their own well-being.

Ancient Greece

Ancient Greece (1200-500 B.C.) is an excellent example of how societal structure influenced the development of leisure. Greek citizens, who could vote and participate in state affairs, sought to become the well-rounded ideal of that era.

They embraced what was known as the **"Athenian ideal,"** which was a combination of soldier, athlete, artist, statesman, and philosopher. Rather than focusing on one area of expertise as is valued today, developing all areas was valued. This was only possible because the tasks of everyday living were provided by laborers or slaves (Shivers & deLisle, 1997) who outnumbered the citizens approximately three to one. Those who were freed from everyday activities had the opportunity to pursue the range of activities necessary to become the Athenian ideal.

Leisure was very important in Greek society. The Greek philosopher Plato and his student, Aristotle, supported this in their beliefs that virtuous and constructive leisure activities were the route to happiness and fulfillment. Contemplation, which involved the pursuit of truth and understanding, was thought to be the highest form of leisure (Dare, Welton, & Coe, 1987). Athenian philosophers strongly believed in the unity of mind and body and valued each. Play was perceived to be essential to the healthy growth of children from both a physical and social perspective (Ibrahim, 1979). Citizens regarded leisure as an opportunity for intellectual cultivation, music, theater, and poetry as well as political and philosophical discussions. The concept **"schole"** meant to cease and have quiet or peace. It meant having time for oneself and being occupied in something for its own sake, such as music, poetry, the company of friends, or the exercise of speculative faculties (Ibrahim, 1991). Schole embraced the experience and not the outcome. How different this is from today where the pursuit of an activity is often valued only if something tangible like a victory, mastery of a skill, or a specific expectation is gained.

An important part of ancient Greek culture, and perhaps at odds with the notion of schole, was its passion for games. Athletic games were held to celebrate religious rites and heroes, for entertainment, and for pleasure. Only men played sport, and women were often excluded from public life (Shivers & deLisle, 1997). Four Panhellenic games were very popular among the spectators and athletes. These included the Olympic Games, the Pythian Games, the Nemian Games, and the Isthmian Games and are thought to be held in honor of the gods, although others suggest that they commemorated the death of mythic mortals and monsters (Ibrahim, 1979; Mendelsohn, 2004). When athletic games were held, wars often ceased so that participants could compete (Poliakoff, 1993). The early Olympic Games, honoring Zeus included chariot races, combat events, boxing,

wrestling, footraces, and the pentathlon—a five-sport event embracing the Athenian ideal. Athletes also competed individually, not on teams, and represented their home villages (Ibrahim, 1991). This is similar to the modern Olympic Games, in which participants represent their countries. The early Olympics were an extremely serious event as well. It was not uncommon for participants in aggressive sports such as pankration (a combination of boxing and wrestling) to be encouraged to fight to the death. This fate was seen as especially noble because it would immortalize the competitor in story for generations to come as having sacrificed his life in the pursuit of victory. So important were the Olympics that Athenians would place an olive wreath on their door when a boy was born, thus signaling the hope that he would become an Olympian (Mendelsohn, 2004). This seriousness of purpose and the use of leisure time to develop sport-specific skills are still found today. We "work" at getting better so we can "play" a sport well. Like the ancient Greeks, we claim to value well-rounded people, yet parents increasingly encourage their children to specialize in one particular sport, often played year-round, so that they have the greatest opportunity to become better than their peers. It should be of no surprise then that at a time when success in sports rivals that of the adulation shown to the earliest Olympic victors, the world finds itself facing an epidemic of cases in which competitors turn to illegal performance-enhancing drugs to assure victory.

Ancient Rome

The emergence of Rome as a dominant society influenced how leisure was perceived at that time. Rome conquered the majority of Europe and Asia after about 265 B.C. and emerged as a dominant power in the Mediterranean (Shivers & deLisle, 1997). The Roman Empire influenced the judicial systems and societies it conquered by attempting to overwrite with its own culture what had come before. The Roman government was based on distinct classifications of citizens. These included senators, who were the richest and owned most of the land and power; curiales, who owned 25 or more acres (10 hectares) of land and were office holders or tax collectors; plebes, or free common men, who owned small properties or were tradesmen or artisans; coloni, who were lower-class tenants on land; and finally, indentured slaves. Early Roman slaves were captured in war and served as agricultural laborers. Much later, large numbers of captives from Asia, Greece, and central Europe became slaves and were exploited by their owners (Shivers & deLisle, 1997). Like in societies that came before it, the opportunity to participate in leisure during the Roman era was limited to those who had the appropriate resources. The greater one's standing at this time, the greater the opportunity for freedom from the daily requirements necessary to live a comfortable life. Senators enjoyed almost unlimited leisure, while coloni struggled to make a comfortable life. This is not unlike the present day where distinct economic classes enjoy varying degrees and types of leisure.

Unlike the ancient Greeks, who saw leisure as an opportunity for well-rounded development, Romans perceived leisure to be primarily rest from work. Considering that the Romans were on an almost constant crusade to dominate foreign cultures, this viewpoint was necessary and allowed recuperation before the next crusade. Play then served utilitarian rather than aesthetic or spiritual purposes (Horna, 1994). As the Roman Empire grew and the increasing availability of slaves decreased the amount of daily work people were required to do, leisure time increased and was increasingly used as a way to control the masses. During Emperor Claudius' reign (41-54 A.D.) Rome had 59 public holidays and 95 game days, and by 354 A.D., there were more than 200 public holidays and 175 game days. The reason for this was simple: As Romans became less occupied with work, they became increasingly bored and critical of the government. The government then attempted to pacify unrest by providing pleasurable experiences through spectacle and celebrations of holidays. "Bread and circuses," free food and entertainment, provided the framework for Roman society (Horna, 1994).

To hold people's attention, leisure activities became increasingly hedonistic and shocking. When battles between gladiators became less interesting, animals from foreign lands were brought in to become part of the savagery seen in the great coliseums. When the scale of those battles became ordinary, artificial lakes were created by slaves who were then used to re-create bloody sea battles depicting a successful conquest. This focus on the entertainment of the masses, instead of their participation, has lead some historians to argue that one of the reasons for the fall of the Roman Empire was its inability to deal with mass leisure (McLean, Hurd, & Rogers, 2005). This concern is often heard today in reference to current leisure

habits. Increasingly, it appears that people are more content to be spectators than participants. Some sporting events such as football and boxing also take on the appearance of a spectacle similar to that seen in ancient Rome. In fact, it isn't uncommon to hear the participants in these events referred to as "gladiators." Should this be a concern? Well, with the rate of obesity increasing greatly in Canada and the United States, it's worth considering whether the focus on mass leisure seen during the Roman era (and perhaps the eventual outcome) is being repeated.

Middle Ages

When the Roman Empire eventually collapsed, the Catholic Church became the dominant structure in Europe (Shivers & deLisle, 1997). The Catholic Church rejected the activities that the Roman Empire had accepted, including its hedonistic ways (Horna, 1994). One example of this was the fact that people involved in theater could not be baptized. The concept that "idleness is the great enemy of the soul" emerged, and doing nothing was thought to be evil. The church wielded great influence during this time over the social order, consisting of nobility and peasants. The clergy dictated societal values, whose adoption would lead to saving souls, the highest goal at the time. Although the Catholic Church influenced what were acceptable and unacceptable leisure activities, so strict were many rules that during the end of this period the church went through a period of renaissance where individuals within the church developed different perspectives. This renaissance saw a renewed appreciation for a variety of leisure activities.

Renaissance

Spreading from the 14th century in Italy to the 16th century in northern Europe, this era saw power shift from the church to the nobility. Previously ostracized by the church, artists were now supported and encouraged by the nobility to express their art (Horna, 1994). Play was perceived to be an important part of education. During the 16th century, Francois Rabelais (1490-1553) emphasized the need for physical exercise and games. Michel Eyquem de Montaigne (1533-1592) supported the concept of unity of mind, body, and spirit, opposing the medieval ideal of separation, or dualism, of the mind and body. John Locke (1632-1704) was so concerned with play as a medium of learning that he made the distinction between play and recreation: Recreation was not being idle, it provided a specific benefit by easing and helping to recover the people wearied by their work. Jean-Jacques Rousseau (1712-1778) advocated for the full freedom of physical activity rather than constraint. It was during the Renaissance that an increased interest in play, both as a form of popular entertainment and as a medium of education, developed.

Three types of parks emerged during the late Renaissance under the nobility:

1. royal hunting preserves providing wild-game hunting,
2. formal garden parks where participants viewed their surroundings much as you would experience a museum, and
3. English garden parks with a greater emphasis on interacting with the environment through activities such as picnics and other restful pursuits.

These parks, developed by the nobility for their own use, were often seen as symbols of status. People caught hunting in a royal hunting preserve who were not nobility were often killed. Still, the growth of parks within the nobility provided other classes an understanding of what was possible and led to the first thoughts of parks for the masses.

Protestant Reformation

During the Protestant Reformation (16th century), Martin Luther and others questioned the accepted practices of the Catholic Church and split off into other Protestant religions. Each religious group governed the perception of what was acceptable as leisure. Play was frowned on as evil by certain churches during this transition. The reformer John Calvin believed that success on earth determined your place in heaven. With that in mind, extraordinarily hard work and lack of leisure time were signs of great success. The influence of the Protestant and Catholic churches in Europe was critical to the earliest development of leisure in Canada and the United States because settlers came primarily from Europe, bringing these values and social structure to the New World. This was no different than what we see today with immigrant groups in Canada and the United States participating in different recreation activities, having different perspectives on leisure, and helping to expose others to different beliefs.

DEVELOPMENT OF RECREATION IN THE UNITED STATES AND CANADA

Recreation developed over time in the United States and Canada. Exploration in Canada began in the 11th century and in the United States in the 15th century. It continued to develop as the populations in both colonies grew. By the late 19th century, governments in both countries began to play a role in providing recreation and leisure services. This role changed and developed throughout the early part of the 20th century. Never static, recreation and leisure continued to evolve through wars and the depression, longer and shorter workweeks, and other periods in the United States. In Canada the post–World War II era brought renewed interest in recreation services, but later declines in resources meant a lack of funding for recreation. One consequence of this ever changing face of recreation and leisure was the emergence of **professional organizations** that addressed the needs of both countries' citizens.

Early Settlement of the United States

To fully understand leisure during the settlement period, it's important to recognize the purpose of the earliest inhabitants and visitors. Christopher Columbus opened up the Americas in a time when exploration for the purposes of trade, profit, and control resulted in circumnavigation of the world (Shivers & deLisle, 1997). Europeans seeking adventure, wealth, or freedom from persecution arrived later in the United States bringing with them their traditions and beliefs. Two early colonies founded in the United States were in Virginia and New England (Shivers & deLisle, 1997). Preceding this period, Native Americans had developed their own unique forms of recreation. Although these activities often celebrated great religious rituals, they were also often highly competitive. One of the most well-known recreation activities, which is still growing in popularity, is the game of lacrosse. Given its common name by French settlers, this activity was common throughout Native American tribes in the east, Great Lakes region, and south with each having variations of the same activity. The game itself was often filled with great traditions and ceremony, used to release aggression or settle disputes, and often included wagering (Vennum, 2005). Other Native American tribes developed their own unique activities. The

Men of the Choctaw tribe playing the traditional ball game with rackets and tall goalposts. Hundreds of players can take part in one game, while other members of the tribe lay extravagant bets on the outcome.

Illinois developed a straw game in which wagering revolved around who could guess the correct number of straws after a large pile was divided. Although this was often a male-dominated game, women were known to participate in their own game involving plum stones, which were used like modern dice (Illinois State Museum, 2000).

Virginia

The settlement in Virginia, established in Jamestown in the 17th century, was composed of aristocracy, adventurers, and traders. These people loved sports games, theater, books, music, and exercise and continued to pursue these activities once they arrived. However, with little free time available as they tried to survive, the governors banned recreational activities (Shivers & deLisle, 1997). One of the primary reasons for the strict control over these activities was the harsh conditions the colonists faced and the need for diligence to ensure survival. So difficult were the conditions, that of the 8,000 colonists who arrived in Virginia by 1625, only 1,200 survived an additional 10 years

(Edgington, Jordan, DeGraff, & Edgington, 1998). The Virginia Assembly enforced observance of the Sabbath, prohibited gambling, and regulated drinking (Ibrahim, 1991). Penalties for partaking in Sunday amusements or failure to attend church services included imprisonment. Activities common to the weekend, including dancing, fishing, hunting, and card playing, were among those strictly prohibited (Kraus, 2001). However, these restrictions were lifted once survival became easier in Virginia and a "leisure class" began to emerge through the benefit of indentured servants and slaves. This societal arrangement mirrored that of those discussed previously in which the absence of a significant and identifiable middle class suggested the development of a developing leisure class. With laws and social mores relaxing in response to a social class seeking new ways to take advantage of its free time, many activities such as cockfighting, dice games, football, forms of bowling, and tennis (all of which were illegal) became more common among the privileged while still unavailable to the working class (Kraus, 2001).

New England

Although the settlement in New England also had to fight for its survival, its settlers were Calvinists escaping persecution in Europe. All forms of recreation were illegal, and the Puritan ethic restricted social activities. This philosophy valued frugality, hard work, self-discipline, and observance of civil and religious codes. Pleasure was considered to be the devil's work, and time not spent in worship or productive labor was considered wasteful (Shivers & deLisle, 1997). People were expected to behave religiously all of the time, thus work became a holy task. If daily activities belonged to God, then "God's time" should not be wasted in trivial pursuits. This Protestant work ethic often removed pleasure from lives. Leisure was considered a lure to sin and a threat to godliness. Puritans believed that they should avoid pleasures in their own lives and struggle against pleasure in the community (Cross, 1990). New England Puritans banned labor, travel, and recreation on Sundays. However, recreation was tolerated if it could help with work, such as quilting bees and barn raisings (Cross, 1990). The restrictions on Sunday activities continue today with "blue laws" that restrict the sale of items such as liquor that may not be purchased on Sundays.

Eventually, the strict control over the masses could not be sustained. Towns saw construction of meeting houses and taverns. The love of games and sport was rediscovered in these taverns. Later, bees, or working groups, emerged as a form of leisure. These provided a chance for dancing and horseracing (Ibrahim, 1991). Hunting became a popular leisure activity among the men because game was abundant. Training days, where young men learned how to serve in the militia, were held in Boston, and these were celebrated at the local tavern. Taverns were also used for cockfighting, animal baiting, dances, and orchestras. The church during this period of the 18th century, while increasingly concerned with these activities, was content to allow its participation in the relatively controlled setting of these public facilities. On the other hand, acceptable leisure activities included public readings and moral lectures. Amateur musical performances were occasionally tolerated. Plays were eventually accepted in Boston and Philadelphia. New York City had its own theater. The mercantile class enjoyed many leisure activities, including sleigh rides, horse races, balls, and card parties (Ibrahim, 1991). The trend of allowing questionable activities to occur behind closed doors, while encouraging acceptable activities to be held in public is still seen today. Laws often prohibit activities such as drinking in public, while taxes may support community events such as picnics and parades that are seen as more wholesome.

During the American Revolution, theaters, music halls, and horse tracks were closed until the end of the war (Ibrahim, 1991). Western expansion led to new leisure pursuits. Settlers were no longer solely European, but increasingly were born in America. Because physical survival was needed in the West, shooting matches were popular, as were wrestling matches, jumping contests, footraces, tomahawk hurling, and rail flinging (Ibrahim, 1991). Free time for frontier families had to be useful, and laboring activities were turned into recreation. Plowing competitions, horse and oxen pulls, and cooking contests were enjoyed (Shivers & deLisle, 1997).

Early Park Development

An important development during the early colonial period was the realization that open space was important to growing communities. The Boston Common, a 48-acre oasis of nature in the middle of the city was established in 1634 and is viewed as the first municipal park (Kraus, 2001). This in turn influenced the creation of laws in Massachusetts requiring that bodies of water larger than 10 acres (4 hectares) be open to the public for fishing and hunting (Edgington et al., 1998). As communities grew and the first organized urban planning efforts took shape, further efforts were undertaken to ensure open space was provided. The center of Philadelphia, Pennsylvania, is a prime example. Several north–south streets are intersected by streets named after species of trees. Within each of the resulting quadrants is park area providing a touch of nature within the metropolis. The creation of Central Park in New York City is probably the best-known example of early urban open-space provision.

Frederick Law Olmsted, considered the founder of American landscape architecture, was hired to design New York's Central Park in 1858, as well as municipal parks in Brooklyn, Philadelphia, Detroit, Chicago, and other areas in the late 19th century. He adapted the English style of a natural park to the rectangular restrictions of American parks (Ibrahim, 1991). He also established the initial purpose for city parks throughout the United States: providing a space for contemplative leisure (Ibrahim,

1991). Organized and structured sports so common in parks today were not permitted. Instead, the parks were initially intended to soothe the minds of newcomers to North America who were facing an increasingly industrial age and limited amount of open space (Kraus, 2001). Olmsted felt that parks should be large enough to shut out the city and that green spaces could inspire courtesy, self-control, and temperance. Olmsted's parks involved walkways, natural vistas, and landscaping to create a feeling of nature in the middle of the city (Cross, 1990). According to Goodale and Godbey (1988), parks developed by Olmsted were an attempt to regain the countryside in the city. They had artificial lakes, regularly mowed grass, and pathways for carriages. Goodale and Godbey note that although the parks existed for passive use, they were full of people enjoying activities such as baseball, cycling, skating, and horseback riding. Refreshment stands and restrooms were included for people spending the day at the park.

Above, women and men ice-skate in New York's Central Park in 1893. Below, Central Park today. Notice how few buildings adjoined the park in 1893 compared to today.

Playground Movement in the United States

The **playground movement** in the United States was first adopted by New York City when land was allocated for Central Park in 1855 (Ibrahim, 1991). Its purpose was to provide passive rest and aesthetics. In Chicago, however, Washington Park was opened in 1876 for more active sport. In Boston, Dr. Maria Zakrzewska promoted the concept of a "sand garden," which would eventually shape the idea of playgrounds for generations to come. In 1868, city leaders determined that an ever increasing number of children without constructive free-time pursuits needed more constructive outlets, so they developed the first organized playground program. It grew until 1886 when the addition of a pile of sand changed the notion of playgrounds. Started by school leaders and well-meaning citizens, a "sand garden" was created in Boston solely for use by children. Although this may seem commonplace today, it was for most children the first time they had ever played in sand or experienced a space designed for the active use of children only. So successful was the first Boston sand garden that city leaders produced 21 more playgrounds of the type by 1889. The popularity of this effort grew until many more playgrounds were created in New York City, Chicago, and other areas (Kraus, 2001; Edgington et al., 1998).

In 1906, a small group of dedicated citizens involved with schools and parks and recreation boards founded the Playground Association of America. These representatives from across the United States selected Luther Halsey Gulick as the organization's first president. Gulick, a physician, held strong religious beliefs, as did many of the earliest leaders in recreation and leisure. Besides his involvement with the Playground Association of America, he was active in the Young Men's Christian Association (YMCA) in the United States and Canada, was the first president of the Camp Fire Girls (now Camp Fire USA), and served as an instructor in what would eventually become Springfield College (Kraus, 2001). Perhaps the following quote of Gulick's best summarizes the prevailing belief at the time that play was extremely serious, a view shared by developing cultures throughout time:

> The boy who is playing football with intensity needs recreation as much as does the inventor who is working intently at his invention. Play can be more exhausting than work, because one can play much harder than one can at work. No one would dream of pushing a boy in school as hard as he pushes himself in a football game. If there is any difference in intensity between play and work, the difference is in favor of play. Play is the result of desire; for that reason it is often carried on with more vigor than work. (Gulick, 1920, p. 125)

Government Involvement: United States

As the United States expanded in population and size, the government became increasingly concerned with the national quality of life. In 1880 President James Garfield stated, "We may divide the whole struggle of the human race into two chapters: first, the fight to get leisure; and then the second fight of civilization—what shall we do with our recreation when we get it" (Kraus, 1990, p. 154). One major issue confronting government leaders was the amount of natural resources that would be available for future generations. Forests were being eliminated at breakneck speed to support massive amounts of construction. Out of this concern, the conservation movement was born and was intended to protect the national heritage of America, not to influence specific leisure behavior of Americans (Ibrahim, 1991). Mindful of what many thought was a perilous decline in available natural resources, the Forest Service was created in 1906, with the creation of the National Park Service following in 1916. Yosemite Valley and the Mariposa Grove were granted to California to protect and preserve for future generations. Yellowstone National Park in Wyoming was the first national park, and Yosemite was taken back by the federal government and became the second (Ibrahim, 1991).

While the conservation movement sought to preserve natural resources typically far from the centers of the population, recreation participation within urban areas steadily increased in number and variety. Perhaps no era of American history so embraced the free-spirited notion of leisure than the Roaring '20s. This era saw the widespread increase in commercial recreation, disposable income, and the use of recreation as a sign of status. However, the economic pendulum of the time swung back quickly and in a shocking reversal of fortune: The crash of the stock market and ensuing Great Depression quickly ended the lifestyle of the Roaring '20s. The stock market crash led to never-before-seen levels of unemployment, poverty, and inadequate housing. With local governments struggling, the federal government assumed a larger role in the provision of parks and recreation (Goodale & Godbey, 1988). Massive unemployment stimulated a growing concern for the mass leisure that was now thrust on the unemployed. This sparked a new discussion of how people defined "free time." Studies showed that people were humiliated by unemployment and that leisure was meaningless without a job (Cross, 1990).

During this period in the United States, the American federal government tried a variety of actions to combat the economic peril that befell many. One effort included an attempt to spread jobs through the population by implementing a 34-hour workweek (Ibrahim, 1991). Making the biggest impact on recreation for generations to follow was the creation of the Works Progress Administration (WPA). This massive organization sought to put citizens back to work through a variety of methods. One of the most important to parks and recreation was the branch of the WPA known as the Civilian Conservation Corps (CCC). The CCC was responsible for countless construction projects providing a variety of recreation areas never before seen, many of which are still in use today. To get an idea of the scale of the CCC's work, consider that it employed enough workers to complete the following: the building of 800 state parks, 46,854 bridges, 28,087 miles (45,200 kilometers) of trails, 46,000 campground facilities, and 204 lodges and museums and the planting of more than three billion trees (Edgington et al., 1998).

The increase in facilities provided by the federal government spurred state and local governments to establish and enhance their own agencies responsible for recreation. After six CCC camps were created in Virginia in 1933, the state created its first state parks from the original camps and opened them all on the same day in 1936 (Virginia State Parks, 2005). In Missouri, after 4,000 men were employed by the CCC to construct facilities, the state developed in 1937 an independent state park board (Missouri State Parks and Historic Sites, 2005). Other states, such as Delaware, Florida, and Georgia, also created state park systems during this time to address the increasing popularity of the new sites provided by the federal government.

Professional Organizations: United States

Professional organizations emerged early in the United States. In 1906, Jane Addams, Joseph Lee, and Luther Gulick among others organized the Playground Association of America. In 1911, the name was changed to Playground and Recreation Association of America. In 1926, the name was changed again to the National Recreation Association. As employment in leisure-related agencies grew and professional preparation and competence continued to be of interest, additional professional organizations were formed. Initially acting independently, the National Recreation Association, American Institute of Park Executives, National Conference on State Parks, American Association of Zoological Parks and Aquariums, and the American Recreation Society merged in 1965 to become the National Recreation and Park Association (NRPA). With the addition shortly afterward of the National Association of Recreation Therapists and the Armed Forces Section of the American Recreation Society, and even after the American Association of Zoological Parks and Aquariums left to form its own organization, NRPA had become the largest organization in the United States to serve the needs of the general public and professionals in the promotion of parks, recreation, and leisure-related opportunities (Ibrahim, 1991). The mission of the NRPA is "To advance parks, recreation and environmental conservation efforts that enhance the quality of life for all people" (NRPA, n.d. paragraph 2). Affiliate park and recreation associations within each state further address this mission. These affiliates such as the Virginia Recreation and Park Society, Florida Recreation and Park Association, and Texas Recreation and Park Society serve their members through local outreach that meets the demands of professionals serving unique populations.

American Alliance for Health, Physical Education, Recreation and Dance (AAHPERD) was founded in 1885 when William Gilbert Anderson invited a group of people who were working in the gymnastics field to discuss their profession. AAHPERD is the largest organization for professionals involved in physical education, leisure, recreation, dance, health promotion, fitness, and education. The organization provides resources, support, and education to professionals to enhance their skills and improve the health and well-being of Americans (AAHPERD, n.d.a). It is an alliance of six national organizations and six district organizations. The mission of AAHPERD is to promote and support healthy lifestyles with high-quality programs in health, physical education, recreation, dance, and sport (AAHPERD, n.d.b).

Post–World War II Growth: United States

After World War II, recreation and leisure saw changes, challenges, and growth in several areas. Among those were the following:

• **Therapeutic recreation.** The extraordinary increase in the number of citizens who faced disabling injuries from their wartime fighting provided a challenge. The use of recreation as a therapy and the birth of therapeutic recreation as a distinct discipline occurred largely from its provision in government-sponsored Department of Veteran's Affairs (VA) hospitals. As recreation therapy grew and expanded from VA facilities to services provided in the community, a growing need for training and education evolved. Colleges and universities filled this need by creating a distinct body of knowledge, while professional organizations such as the National Therapeutic Recreation Society and American Association for Therapeutic Recreation were formed in 1966 and 1984, respectively. Lastly, professional certification of recreation therapists was provided by the National Council for Therapeutic Recreation Certification in 1981.

• **Concern for youth fitness.** A critical development in recreation and leisure came about in 1956. A battery of physical fitness tests comparing American youth to their peers in Europe produced shocking results that showed European children to be in much better condition. Having been involved in two world wars within the last half-century, the government, under President Eisenhower, created the President's Council on Youth Fitness in 1956. Eventually changing its name in 1966 to the President's Council on Physical Fitness and Sports, this initiative promotes health and wellness for all ages by first introducing physical skill testing and awards in schools, and also offering Active Lifestyle awards for all ages. In 1983, Congress declared May National Physical Fitness and Sports month. These initiatives mirrored a growth in mandatory physical education classes throughout the school year. Unfortunately, as time passed, the concern

Today, recreation has taken on a different form. The Mall of America in Minnesota contains over 500 stores, over 13,000 employees, 12,000 parking places, and 50 restaurants as well as Camp Snoopy—a theme park within the mall.

for youth fitness and the need for physical education were eclipsed by the concern for academic achievement in other areas. Perhaps it is worth considering whether this decreased emphasis on physical education in schools is just one factor in the sedentary American lifestyle that many see as contributing to a growing obesity epidemic.

- **Economic challenges and the impact on national affluence.** The end of the 20th century saw swift changes in the American economic landscape. The pendulum of affluence swung quickly from the relative comfort in the 1950s and 1960s, to times of great difficulty as the Arab oil embargo and stock market corrections affected the decades that followed. One way in which recreation and leisure addressed decreased government funding during tough times was the reliance on fees and charges. Following a marketing model for the first time to provide recreation programs, many agencies assessed charges to offset program cost or in some cases to produce a profit that would support other programs. These fees and charges, including membership fees, subsidized many programs but have been criticized for potentially excluding those with less income.

While some decades saw economic struggle, others enjoyed relative prosperity. During that time, the American thirst for consumer spending was in evidence as an ever increasing number of opportunities evolved to use recreation and leisure as a method to demonstrate one's social class. Private-club memberships grew, second homes were purchased, and increasingly expensive pieces of recreation equipment were within reach. This was not a new theme. In his 1899 book *The Theory of the Leisure Class,* Thorstein Veblen first introduced the notion that the use of leisure was an important way for people to define who they were. His term "conspicuous consumption" was as true at the beginning of the century as it was at the end. People increasingly embraced recreation activities and their associated equipment and lifestyle as a way to create their identity and compete with others (Veblen, 1998 [1899]). So true was the recurrence of this use of leisure that "shopping fever" became a term used in 2001 to describe other issues such as "mall mania," "home shopping," "cyber shopping," and "shopping as therapy," all of which related to the "dogged pursuit of more," a condition known as "affluenza" (DeGraff, Wann, & Naylor, 2001, p. 2).

How did recreation emerge in Canada? The following sections provide insights into the development of recreation in Canada.

Early Settlement of Canada

Canada, a frontier settlement, consisted of a few homesteads and resource-dependent rural communities (Harrington, 1996). The communities' economic well-being were based on natural resources such as fishing, logging, and agriculture. The first European explorers arrived in Canada in the 11th century. The first permanent European settlements were founded in the 1600s (Francis, Jones, & Smith, 1988). However, before the Europeans began to explore and settle, there were many different nations and languages among Canada's aboriginal peoples (LaPierre, 1992). The origin of Canada's first people is uncertain. Some argue that the aboriginal peoples emerged on the continent, while others argue that they migrated from Siberia. Regardless of their origin, Native Canadians were living in North America at least 10,000 years before the arrival of the Europeans (Francis et al., 1988). The aboriginal peoples in southern Canada enjoyed games, music, and storytelling for entertainment. Games were often based on hunting and fishing skills (Karlis, 2004). The Inuit, who lived in the Arctic, played many games including Nalukatook, involving bouncing on a walrus hide held by others, and Ipirautaqurnia, which involved flipping a whip accurately. Baggataway, played by the Algonquins and Iroquois, involving a curved netted stick, is now referred to as lacrosse (Karlis, 2004).

Early Settlers

The first Europeans who arrived in Canada appear to be the Norse, who explored the west Atlantic coast in approximately 1,000 A.D. The Norse settled on the northern coast of Newfoundland, but did not stay very long, which is evidenced by the lack of bones and debris left behind (Francis et al., 1988). Five hundred years after the first Norse settlement, other European explorers followed. The Europeans wanted expansion, which led to the conquest of the Americas for three reasons. The first was a combination of curiosity and the desire to find better land. Second, they sought a route to Asia for spices to preserve meat, and finally, they wanted to convert the aboriginal peoples to Christianity (Francis et al., 1988).

In 1497, the British sponsored John Cabot's expedition to North America. Cabot saw Newfoundland, but he fished off the coast instead of continuing further exploration. He did, however, discover the Gulf of St. Lawrence. The Portuguese followed in 1500. Portuguese fishermen fished the Grand Banks and the coastal waters of Newfoundland. In 1524, Francois I, the king of France, became involved in exploration, with passage to Asia his goal. In 1534, Jacques Cartier embarked to find passage to Asia and entered the Gulf of St. Lawrence. He led two more explorations, setting the stage for France's claim to Canada.

Colonization

Between 1604 and 1607, the first Acadian settlement was formed when Champlain and his men explored the coastline of the Maritimes and wintered at Port Royal, the first agricultural settlement in Canada. In 1606, Champlain's men took part in Canada's first theatrical production, and in 1607, Champlain founded the Order of Good Cheer, which was the first social club in Canada. However, the colony was abandoned in 1607 due to lack of money (Francis et al., 1988). In 1608, Champlain constructed a habitation, or wooden buildings forming a quadrangle, which became the center of the first permanent French settlement. The French colony existed only for the purpose of trading fur and grew very slowly. By 1620, there were only 60 people in Quebec. However, by the 1650s, the French colony began growing steadily, and by the late 1700s, the language was altered by settlers to reflect traditions of the emerging country, thus the identity of Canadiens emerged.

While the French were settling New France, the British were settling colonies in Newfoundland, Virginia, New York, and Massachusetts. They also sponsored expeditions north of New France, and in 1610 and 1611, Henry Hudson discovered Hudson Bay. Fifty years later, British fur-trading posts were established around the bay (Francis et al., 1988).

The Acadians, who spoke French, were among the first settlers on Canada's East Coast. The Treaty of Utrecht in 1713 ended the War of Spanish Succession. The French were driven out of Spanish Netherlands by the British and their allies, and relinquished mainland Acadia (Nova Scotia and New Brunswick) to the British (Hiller, 1998). Following the Treaty of Utrecht in 1713, the Acadians refused to pledge allegiance to the British Crown. Consequently, from 1755 to 1759, an estimated 10,000 Acadians were deported, mostly to American colonies such as Louisiana (Daigle, 1982). From 1760 to 1800, many of these deported Acadians returned to eastern Canada, mostly to New Brunswick (Daigle, 1982).

The British colony in Newfoundland was a fishing station, and by 1775, the population was greater than 10,000 people (Finlay & Sprague, 2000). After the British expelled the Acadians from the Maritimes in the 1750s, British settlers arrived in Prince Edward Island. Much of the Nova Scotia settlement was British born at that time (Finlay & Sprague, 2000).

During the American Revolution, 45,000 British Loyalists left the 13 American colonies and moved north. Nineteen thousand settled in Nova Scotia, 15,000 settled north of the Bay of Fundy, in New Brunswick, while others settled in Quebec (Finlay & Sprague, 2000). The Loyalists also settled in southern Ontario (Harrington, 1996).

Because early settlement in Canada focused on the fur trade, and farming in Canada required a great deal of hard labor and preparation for winter, recreation opportunities were limited for the early settlers (Harrington, 1996). However men and women enjoyed activities such as curling, skating, ice hockey, snowshoeing, and tobogganing in the winter. Drama and music were also popular leisure activities at that time (McFarland, 1970).

Park Development

The first park in Canada, the Halifax Common, was established in 1763. Two hundred forty acres (97 acres) were designated for exercise for the militia in the early years (McFarland, 1970). Later the park was used for skating, lawn tennis, croquet, and archery (Wright, 1983). Municipal parks and public squares were established throughout the 19th century (McFarland, 1970; Searle & Brayley, 1993). For example, 14.9 acres (6 hectares) of land in London, Ontario, was deeded from the federal government for Victoria Park in 1869. Also, 200 acres (81 hectares) of land on the Halifax peninsula was leased from the federal government for 999 years for Point Pleasant Park, where all members of the community could enjoy exercise and recreation in 1875. However, much like in the United States, games were often prohibited in the parks, as was walking or lying on the grass. Parks were largely used for walking, sitting, horse drawn carriage driving, bird watching, and enjoying the plant life (McFarland, 1970).

As transportation improved in Canada and the railway was built, it became possible to travel for pleasure. This led to the formation of national parks. In 1885, the Canadian Pacific Railway suggested the establishment of Rocky Mountain Park, in Banff (Wetherell & Kmet, 1990). Although the difficult work required of the early settlers to build the country meant that there was little time for leisure, recreation eventually became a part of the lives of Canadians.

Photo courtesy of Paul F.J. Eagles

The early development of the national park system of Canada was stimulated by political pressure fomented by the railway companies. This early linkage of tourism and national parks provided strong stimulus for Canadian travel to explore these unique places.

Playground Movement in Canada

In Canada, the playground movement developed supervised playgrounds for children. Similar to its development in the United States, the playground movement in Canada was born from an increasing sense that recreation and leisure had an important role to play in the betterment of its citizens' quality of life. In the 1800s, municipal parks were used by the upper classes, and the lower classes did not have access to open areas. However, concern for those who lived in overcrowded areas with high crime and disease led to the creation of safe places for play (McFarland, 1970). Searle and Brayley (1993) note that this movement was based on the notion that play was the only appropriate method for physical development for children and was necessary for their health, strength, and moral character. There was a belief that children required encouragement to play and that the playground could be used to teach health and social customs in a play environment (McFarland, 1970). In 1893,

the National Council of Women was formed, and the council and its local groups played a major role in initiating the playground movement (McFarland, 1970).

According to McFarland (1970), there were two different justifications for the playground movement. The first was the prevention of delinquency and drunkenness, and the second was the belief that all people had the right to opportunities for leisure. However, the emphasis on preventing delinquency and drunkenness was necessary for receiving funding and to justify giving time to the playground movement. School grounds were selected for the playgrounds, and in 1908, the Toronto school board was the first to develop summer playground programs. In general, playground programs were initiated by local branches of the National Women's Council, followed by the formation of a playground association, and finally, a civic department responsible for playgrounds and recreation programming was established. In the beginning, teachers were chosen for playground supervisors, and programs included games, stories, reading, sewing, and music. Eventually, summer and winter programs merged, and indoor programs were developed, which led to the hiring of full-time supervisors for public playgrounds. The playground movement led to the concept of a comprehensive parks system (McFarland, 1970).

Government Involvement: Canada

Federal, provincial, and municipal governments have long been involved in providing recreation opportunities for Canadians. The land for the first parks in Canada was often deeded or leased to municipalities from the federal or provincial governments. For example, the Canadian government authorized Saint John, New Brunswick's, horticultural society to establish gardens, a park, and a pleasure resort with 1,700 acres (688 hectares) for Rockwood Park (McFarland, 1970). Also, the city of Vancouver received permission from the federal government to establish Stanley Park on part of the local harbor peninsula. In 1865, a Montreal city bylaw designated 13 open spaces for citizens to enjoy, although games and walking on the grass were prohibited (McFarland, 1970).

In 1883, the province of Ontario passed the first legislation that affected the development of provincial parks. The Public Parks Act established parks in cities and towns with the consent or petition of the electors. The local government could appoint park management boards that included the mayor of the municipality and six board members. These park boards could purchase land for parks not more than 1,000 acres (405 hectares) in cities and 500 acres (202 hectares) in towns. In 1892, the province of Manitoba passed a similar act (McFarland, 1970); thus, the provincial governments played an important role in the development of parks in Canada.

In the 1940s, the federal and provincial governments, under the National Physical Fitness Act, provided recreation services that influenced municipal recreation (McFarland, 1970). In Ontario in 1945, 18 municipalities passed recreation bylaws, and one year later, 70 had passed bylaws (Markham, 1992). The governments focused on leadership development in schools and the community and increased awareness of the possibilities of public recreation programs. The act was repealed in 1954 (Westland, 1979). The Ontario provincial government gave grants to municipalities and encouraged the local provision of recreation opportunities for all. In the 1950s, British Columbia and Alberta supported local governments in developing municipal grant structures suitable for social and economic situations (McFarland, 1970).

All three levels of government continue to be involved in providing recreation services. The Interprovincial Sport and Recreation Council (ISRC) developed the National Recreation Statement in 1987. The statement defines the roles of each level of government. In 1978, the provinces and territories agreed that recreation was within their jurisdiction; thus, their role in recreation became significant. Once local volunteers make decisions about recreation services, provincial governments are responsible for providing the assistance, leadership, and recognition necessary to deliver these services. They provide support to community volunteers who manage recreation clubs and societies and provide leadership and instruction, raise money, and coordinate programs. The interprovincial council agreed that it is the role of the provincial governments to state policy outlining the goals and objectives and stress the importance of recreation as a social service. Some of their other roles include observing and analyzing trends and issues to update policy; providing municipal governments with resources to enhance the quality of life of a community through grants for conferences and training; providing programs and services to build a delivery system that links the three levels of government and voluntary, private, and commercial sectors; and planning and supporting recreation research.

The role of the municipality in providing recreation services is to ensure a wide range of opportunities for all community members. Municipalities are responsible for establishing a recreation authority to provide opportunities, be aware of resources and opportunities and ensure that information is available to the public, provide incentives and services to develop opportunities based on needs, conduct regular assessments of needs and interests that are not being met, and develop a council to determine the best use of community resources (Interprovincial Sport and Recreation Council [ISRC], 1987).

Finally, the Interprovincial Sport and Recreation Council outlined the federal government's role in providing recreation services. The council agreed that the federal government must take action to influence the scope of recreation and work closely with all recreation agents in implementing programs that affect recreation services. The federal government should provide recreation through national organizations and ensure Canadian representation in activities that serve a national purpose. The federal government should contribute to the development of recreation services through provision of resources to support public, voluntary, and commercial sectors. And finally, the federal government should provide promotional materials to encourage recreation participation (ISRC, 1987).

Parks Canada is one federal agency that provides recreation opportunities for Canadians. The mandate of Parks Canada is to protect and present examples of Canada's natural and cultural heritage as well as to foster understanding, appreciation, and enjoyment to ensure this heritage (Parks Canada Agency, n.d.). The agency serves as the guardian of parks, historic sites, and national marine conservation. The agency guides visitors to national parks and serves as partners in building on the traditions of Native Canadians, diverse cultures, and international commitments. Parks Canada recounts the history of the land and people and is committed to protecting heritage, presenting the beauty and significance of the natural world, and to serving Canadians (Parks Canada Agency, 2002).

Professional Organizations: Canada

Professional recreation groups began to emerge in Canada in the first half of the 20th century. Both national and provincial associations serve recreation professionals and volunteers. The Canadian Parks and Recreation Association (CPRA) was founded in 1945 (CPRA, n.d.a). It developed from the expanding mission and influence of the Ontario Parks Association in the later years of the war. During postwar discussions, the Ontario Parks Association called on the government to consider parks, playgrounds, and recreation a separate reconstruction project after the war. On July 11, 1944, in Windsor, Ontario, the CPRA started as a means of broadening the mandate of the Ontario Parks Association for Ontario and Quebec. Formal creation of CPRA occurred one year later (Markham, 1995). At that time it was known as the Parks and Recreation Association of Canada. Its purpose was to deal with changes that occurred after World War II, including the need to provide parks and recreation services. The name was changed in 1970 to the Canadian Parks and Recreation Association, and the society has responded to and will continue to respond to social, economic, and political changes within the country (CPRA, n.d.a). The mission of CPRA is to build healthy communities and enhance the quality of life and environment. The association serves as a national voice for parks and recreation, and it advocates on behalf of parks and recreation as essential for health and well-being of Canadians. CPRA communicates and promotes the values and benefits of parks and recreation, responds to diverse and changing needs, and provides educational opportunities (CPRA, n.d.b).

Another national organization for recreation professionals is the Canadian Association for Health, Physical Education, Recreation and Dance (CAHPERD). CAHPERD is a national, charitable, voluntary organization that focuses on the healthy development of children and youth by advocating for physical and health education. CAPHERD began as the Canadian Physical Education Association in 1933. The name changed in 1948 to the Canadian Association of Health, Physical Education and Recreation, and in 1994, "dance" was added to the name to recognize its value (CAHPERD, n.d.).

Provinces also have recreation associations. For example, the Saskatchewan Parks and Recreation Association (SPRA) is a nonprofit volunteer organization that promotes, develops, and facilitates parks and recreation opportunities throughout the province (SPRA, n.d.a). In the 1940s, 10 communities in Saskatchewan had recreation boards. The Saskatchewan recreation movement was established and later renamed the SPRA. The association converted military units to recreation facilities after the war. The society emphasized physical activity at that time. In the 1950s, the first library was opened and community halls and curling rinks were built (SPRA, n.d.b).

Recreation Nova Scotia, another provincial organization, promotes the values and benefits of recreation toward a healthier future. Recreation Nova Scotia began as the Recreation Association of Nova Scotia in 1972 and in 1998, merged with the Recreation Council on Disabilities in Nova Scotia and Volunteer Nova Scotia (Recreation Nova Scotia, n.d.).

A third provincial organization, Parks and Recreation Ontario (PRO), is a not-for-profit group whose history goes back to 1945 (PRO, n.d.). PRO is open to all who are interested in recreation, parks, fitness, sport and facilities, aquatics, therapeutic recreation, arts, and culture. Membership includes more than 1,000 recreation professionals, volunteers, educators, students, citizens, elected officials, and commercial organizers.

OUTSTANDING *Graduates*

Background Information

Name: Jim King

Education: Bachelor of arts, honors recreation, University of Waterloo, Ontario, department of human kinetics and leisure studies; master's degree in public administration, University of Western Ontario

Special Affiliations: Canadian Association of Municipal Administrators, past president

Career Information

Position: Commissioner of Community Services Department, Cambridge, Ontario

Organization: Municipal government with 110 full-time staff and 150 part-time staff serving 118,000 people.

Job Description: Provide overall responsibility for parks, forestry, horticulture, cemeteries, arenas, pools, and community center. Provide consultation, through staff, with about 100 organizations.

Courtesy of Jim King

Career Path: I have worked for the city of Cambridge since graduation in 1976. I have held 10 different positions including director of administrative services, director of personnel, director of recreation, and commissioner.

Likes and Dislikes About the Job: I like the contact with people in the community and having an opportunity to have a positive influence on the lifestyle of the community. There have been times in my career when I felt my family took a secondary role as a result of the demands of the work environment.

Advice to Undergraduates

This can be a very gratifying career path, but remember to keep your career and personal life as balanced as possible.

Post–World War II Growth: Canada

Like the United States, Canada also experienced a host of challenges related to recreation and leisure after World War II, some similar and some different. Included in these challenges were the following:

- **Concern for fitness.** The 1960s were characterized by renewed concern for physical fitness (Searle & Brayley, 1993). The Fitness and Amateur Sport Act, which was passed in 1961, redefined the role of government in sport, recreation, and leisure. In the 1960s all levels of government became involved in financial assistance to promote recreation development. Much of this money was dedicated to building facilities (Searle & Brayley, 1993). ParticipACTION was established in 1971 as a nonprofit organization to promote a healthy, physically active lifestyle (Canadian Public Health Association [CPHA], 2004). The program was started by Pierre Trudeau in order to battle rising health care costs (Canadian Broadcasting Corporation, 2000). ParticipACTION pioneered the use of social marketing and health communication techniques and produced one of the longest-running (1971-2000) communication campaigns to promote

physical activity in the world (CPHA, 2004). The media campaign suggested to Canadians that a 60-year-old Swede was as fit as, or more so, than a 30-year-old Canadian (ParticipACTION, n.d.). The program continued until 2000, when the federal government refused ParticipACTION's funding request (CBC, 2000).

- **Economic challenges.** In 1973, the Arab oil embargo ended the rapid development of recreation resources and opportunities. High energy costs led to empty arenas and poorly maintained parks. The oil embargo also affected pleasure travel when gas was rationed and higher jet fuel costs made flying expensive. Provincial and municipal governments were forced to limit the growth of recreation. They needed to adopt a new style of leadership. Municipal recreation agencies became less involved in directly providing services and started playing a facilitative role instead (Searle & Brayley, 1993).

- **Changing demographic trends.** The changing nature of the family throughout the 1980s and 1990s influenced recreation service delivery, causing service providers to respond to different needs, opportunities, and constraints. Various family structures had to be considered, including blended families, single-parent families, childless families, multiple generation families, and traditional nuclear families, to name a few (Searle & Brayley, 1993). The majority of single-parent families were headed by women in the 1980s, and these families had lower incomes than two-parent families (Harrington, 1996). Common-law relationships became more common throughout the 1980s and 1990s, and marriage rates were lower. The age of first marriage rose during the 80s and 90s, divorce rates also rose, and fertility rates declined (Harrington, 1996). All of these trends have had an impact on leisure services delivery.

People living in poverty also posed a new challenge for service providers. The new poor were of particular concern and included children living in poverty, the working poor, and the frail elderly community members. Leisure services were needed to help build self-esteem, develop social support networks, and teach self-reliance skills. Focus was on satisfying needs and delivering programs in the most appropriate way for clients (Searle & Brayley, 1993).

Multiculturalism was another issue arising in the 1980s and 1990s and continues today. Canadian public policy defends the idea that differences in a nation are good for it, and the government protects the cultures of new Canadians. The fact that two differing cultural groups participate in the same activity does not mean that the nature and/or meaning of the activity is the same for each of these groups (Allison, 1988; Karlis & Dawson, 1990; Malloy, Nilson, & Yoshioka, 1993; Reid, 1993; Karlis & Dawson, 1995). Differences in participation pattern are more a result of culturally transmitted norms, values, and expectations of the subcultural group (Allison, 1988). Studies indicate that leisure is part of culture (Karlis & Dawson, 1990, 1995, 1996). Often recreation professionals do not understand cultural differences in perceptions of what leisure is (Karlis & Dawson, 1990, 1995, 1996). Leisure can help to sustain a community's cultural mosaic, and ethnospecific recreation is important for recreation service delivery (Searle & Brayley, 1993; Karlis & Dawson, 1990, 1995, 1996).

• **Unique leisure needs of women.** Women's leisure has been studied during the past 30 years in order to understand how women's leisure experiences are different from men's. After World War II, women continued to be denied equal access to sport and recreation facilities and resources. According to Harrington (1996), the majority of

Canadian women engage in domestic-based leisure instead of physical activity. Women's time away from paid work and housework is used to care for family members. Women find it difficult to disengage from domestic obligations and become involved in personal leisure or leisure outside of the home. Instead, women derive happiness from facilitating the happiness of others. In the 1990s, it was argued that women spent their leisure time on call for others' needs (Harrington, 1996). Women in isolated communities and small villages especially face obstacles because their communities' recreation resources are often limited to just a hockey arena and a library. Often in such communities, leisure opportunities and services are directed toward men (Harrington, 1996).

• **Enhanced recreation services for people with disabilities.** Witt's 1973 study of recreation services for people with disabilities indicated that these services needed to be enhanced. Lyons (1983) replicated Witt's study and found that services for people with disabilities needed to be further enhanced. The rights of people with disabilities within Canada was emphasized in the Obstacle report (Witt & Ellis, 1982). Canadian society recognizes that services for people with disabilities need to be enhanced, and individual's rights are protected under the Charter of Rights. Issues around advocacy for access to recreation services for persons with disabilities and inclusion of persons with disabilities in recreation have confronted recreation professionals in Canada since the 70s (Lyons, 1981). Recreation professionals providing services for people with disabilities in Canada have been called leisure integrators, leisure facilitators, activity directors, and therapeutic recreation professionals. Currently, 12 different professional organizations in Canada represent professionals in this area. The Canadian Therapeutic Recreation Association is in the process of forming links with provincial therapeutic recreation organizations to enhance the professional development of people working in this field.

SIMILARITIES BETWEEN CANADA AND THE UNITED STATES

Recreation has developed similarly in the United States and Canada. For example, both countries developed playgrounds in similar ways at about the same time. The following are among the trends that have been identified:

- Expansion of activities for children to activities for all ages
- Expansion of summer programs to yearlong programs
- Provision of indoor and outdoor activities
- Expansion of playgrounds into rural areas
- Shift from philanthropic to community financial support of playground programs
- Increased importance of organized play over unorganized play
- Shifting philosophy to include use of leisure and not just provision of facilities by communities
- Increased importance of community and group activities over individual interests (Rainwater, 1992)
- Creation of play spaces
- More opportunities for child development through play
- Growing belief in the importance of outdoor play for young
- Increased opportunities for public recreation
- Quest for a better balance between work and play
- Appreciation of the value of play in the life of a child

What's clear is that the playground movement in Canada and the United States continued the path of the pendulum that had long before started swinging toward a greater appreciation for recreation and leisure. Like in ancient Greece, economic class separation in Canada and the United States was a growing reality, class structure in Western society since the industrial revolution has been structured related to economic wealth, and the upper classes were demonstrating a growing concern for those in the lower classes. Recreation and leisure was no longer seen as a privilege, but was increasingly considered an important part of life and a way for those who were well off to help those who were less so. This sense of obligation helped ensure the value of recreation and leisure, and in this case the playground movement, as a way to address life's challenges.

Government has played an important role in providing recreation and leisure opportunities in both the United States and Canada. In the United States, the government began to play a role in providing social services during the Great Depression when the lack of jobs increased the amount of time available (most likely more than was wanted) to pursue leisure activities. The federal government also developed organizations to protect natural resources and preserve them for future generations. This continued a trend of governments tackling societal problems through concern for the leisure-related issues facing their citizens.

SUMMARY

Leisure in the United States and Canada has been influenced by past definitions of leisure. Primitive societies had little time for leisure as they fought for survival. However, as their tools became more sophisticated, they gained more free time. Play was used to teach children about their roles as adults, as an opportunity for ritualization, and for rest and relaxation in prehistoric societies. Among the ancient Greeks, contemplation, education, philosophy, and athletics were important leisure activities and helped in reaching the "Athenian ideal." However, only full Greek citizens had opportunities for leisure. In ancient Rome, leisure was considered to be time away from work, and recuperation was of great importance. Leisure was also used as a method of social control. After the fall of the Roman Empire, the Catholic Church, which restricted leisure participation, controlled what people perceived to be leisure by placing values on activities. Further restrictions were placed on leisure and social activity during the Protestant Reformation, as new churches emerged. These strict rules were relaxed during the Renaissance when artists were supported and play was considered important for education.

Early settlers in the United States and Canada brought these perceptions of what was acceptable leisure to their new countries. These views and the environmental conditions they faced have influenced leisure today. The first colonies in the United States restricted leisure as settlers, like members of prehistoric civilizations, fought for survival and had time for little else. However, as restrictions were lifted, work bees, hunting, and going to the tavern became popular pastimes. As time passed, exploration and settlement resulted in increasing recreation opportunities for European settlers. As governments established parks as early as the 1700s, participation started to grow and a concern for the appropriate use of leisure time emerged.

The playground movement in both the United States and Canada began in the late 1800s and early 1900s. The first sand garden was founded in

Boston, and more playgrounds followed in New York and Chicago following Boston's success. The movement was started in Canada by the National Council of Women to give children opportunities for supervised play in order to prevent delinquency and promote healthy development.

All levels of government in both countries are involved in recreation. Governments provide facilities, funding, support, policy, information, and training for recreation services. The growth of organizations concerned with recreation program provision and the workers responsible for it emerged in the United States at the same time as the playground movement. These organizations evolved to become the two main national organizations found today: the National Recreation and Park Association and the American Association for Health, Physical Education, Recreation and Dance. In Canada, professional organizations emerged on the national level with the Canadian Parks and Recreation Association and the provincial level in the 1940s with Recreation Nova Scotia. Like in the United States, these agencies provide support for recreation programs and promote the importance of recreation and leisure for health and well-being. In Canada after World War II, leadership styles changed from direct service to facilitative assistance due to decreases in funding for recreation. The ParticipACTION program was developed in

Web Sites to EXPLORE

Parks Canada: www.pc.gc.ca/
Canadian Parks and Recreation: www.cpra.ca/
Lifestyle Information Network: www.lin.ca
Office of Health Promotion Nova Scotia: www.gov.ns.ca/ohp/
CAHPERD: www.cahperd.ca
Canadian Therapeutic Recreation Association: www.canadian-tr.org/
NRPA: www.nrpa.org
National Therapeutic Recreation Society: www.nrpa.org/
American Therapeutic Recreation Association: www.atra-tr.org/atra.htm
National Council on Therapeutic Recreation Certification: www.nctrc.org/

the 1970s to encourage Canadians to become fit, and the President's Council on Physical Fitness and Sports was formed in the 1960s to address fitness in the United States. Finally, as the new millennium unfolded, it became clear that many themes of the past including how best to serve a changing society, the appropriate use of mass leisure, government's role, and the importance of professional organizations were again as important as ever.

CHAPTER 3

Philosophy and Leisure

Donald J. McLean

Happiness is thought to depend on leisure; for we are busy that we may have leisure, and make war that we may live in peace.

Aristotle, Greek philosopher

CHAPTER OBJECTIVES

After reading this chapter, you should be able to do the following:

- Understand how philosophic reasoning can help solve ethical problems and dilemmas that you will encounter as a leisure services professional
- Understand that philosophy can help clarify your leisure values and provide a way to evaluate the worthiness of leisure services
- Use ethical theories to help you find solutions to particular ethical dilemmas
- Understand the importance of being able to rationally justify your decision

INTRODUCTION

This chapter explains how the methods of philosophy can be put to good use in the delivery of leisure services. We will see that philosophic inquiry is important to leisure services providers in two ways. The first way that philosophy helps us be better services providers is that it helps us to more clearly understand our leisure values. The ancient Greek philosopher Socrates lived by the dictum that one should "know thy self." He was painfully aware of how people can fancy themselves as experts on all sorts of topics if they never take the time to seriously question their beliefs. Similarly, as leisure services providers, it is easy enough for us to think that we know what types of leisure experiences people need. But if we have not critically examined our leisure values, we may end up providing leisure opportunities that are convenient and amusing, but which may not improve people's quality of life. Philosophical analysis can help us rationally evaluate the worthiness of various leisure opportunities. We will see that there are good reasons for believing that many of our modern-day leisure practices are not conducive to a fulfilling style of life. The second way philosophy helps us to be better leisure services providers is that it gives us a method for solving the practical ethical dilemmas that all leisure services providers face during their careers. While philosophy does not promise a simple solution to every ethical problem that we encounter, it can structure and guide our thinking so we can explain and justify to other people the particular courses of action that we have chosen.

WHY DOES PHILOSOPHY MATTER?

For many people, the subject of **philosophy** appears to have little relevance to recreation and leisure. Our stereotype of philosophers suggests that they are deep thinkers who are uninterested in practical matters relating to relaxation, pleasure, or fun. This "highbrow" image of philosophy is spoofed in the old Monty Python skit of the philosophers' soccer game: Aristotle, Kant, Hegel, and other great thinkers from the past stand like statues deep in thought on a soccer field. The ball just sits there for the whole match until Archimedes suddenly has a revelation and kicks the ball to Socrates who then fires it into the net while the other players look on in bewilderment.

Like the immobilized philosophers in the skit, many recreation students become frozen in their seats, their eyes glazed over, when their instructor announces that the week's topic is the "philosophy of leisure." Typically, students have chosen recreation and leisure studies because they prefer active, hands-on experiences to abstract thinking. What use, students ask, is there in learning what some dead white guy from long ago thought about leisure and recreation? Wouldn't their time be better spent learning how to program activities, create budgets, and market events?

Because the philosophy of leisure is often taught as a history lesson, or as part of the "intellectual foundations" of leisure and recreation, it is understandable that students are doubtful that philosophy has any real application to leisure services. However, if leisure philosophy is approached from an applied-ethics perspective, then it is essential that students have a grounding in philosophical reasoning to help them become ethical leisure services providers.

The suggestion that recreation students need to study applied **ethics** may puzzle some people. After all, doesn't leisure services provide nice things in life such as fun, pleasure, and enjoyment? Why would people working in recreation need to worry about moral issues? Unfortunately, leisure services providers are likely to encounter many vexing ethical dilemmas during their careers. Just consider the context in which leisure services occur. Leisure services is very much a people-oriented business, and when people interact, there is always the chance that things may go awry. Leisure services providers are often put in positions of trust. Park rangers are charged with protecting both the natural environment and the safety of park visitors. Therapeutic recreation specialists are often entrusted with the care for vulnerable populations. Supervisors and program leaders of youth programs are expected to exercise a high degree of responsibility and provide healthful activities for their young charges. And the list goes on. It is clear that the provision of organized leisure services is not simply fun and games, but is a serious undertaking that imposes significant ethical responsibilities on services providers.

So how does philosophy help leisure service providers solve ethical issues? Philosophical analysis can be useful in two ways. The first is that philosophizing can clarify our leisure values. The second thing philosophy can do for us is to provide a method to resolve specific **ethical dilemmas.** These two functions of philosophic inquiry—values clarification and ethical dilemma solving—can complement each other. We might think of leisure values clarification as a macro, or big picture, approach to solving ethical issues in leisure services, and ethical dilemma solving as the micro approach, or the detailed analysis of a particular ethical dilemma involving certain people at a certain time and place. To deal effectively with ethical issues in leisure services, our thinking needs to be consistent enough that we can move between the macro issues regarding our leisure values and the micro issues of solving a particular ethical dilemma without making contradictory judgments.

Philosophical analysis can help us to organize and rationally justify our values and also provide us with a method for resolving particular ethical dilemmas. Using philosophy, we can articulate and refine our preferences into a coherent system of values regarding leisure and recreation, and we can provide persuasive justifications for our actions when we face ethical dilemmas. In fact, applying philosophic analysis to issues of leisure values and ethics is exactly what ancient Greek philosophers such as Plato and Aristotle did more than 2,000 years ago. They began their philosophic inquiry by asking themselves what an ideal lifestyle for human beings should be like. Let's first see how Plato handled this question, and then we can compare it to how his student Aristotle refined his master's teachings on the value and ethics of leisure.

PLATO'S PHILOSOPHY OF LEISURE

Plato wrote several great dialogues to answer the practical question of how people should best live their lives. His dialogues read like the script of a play. In them, various characters debate with each other about a particular question or issue. Plato's greatest dialogue, *The Republic,* lays out his vision of a utopian society. He reasons that a perfectly ordered society would maximize the happiness of its citizens. To achieve such an ideal state Plato argues that people's thoughts and actions must be strictly controlled. He proposes a harsh censorship of playful leisure activities that he believes would disrupt the order of a perfect society:

> We must begin, then it seems, by a censorship over our story makers, and what they do well we must pass and what not, reject. And the stories on the accepted list we will induce nurses and mothers to tell their children and so shape their souls by these stories. . . . (Plato, Republic II 377c cited in Hamilton and Huntington, 1961, p. 624)

Plato is taking aim at the telling of various Greek myths and the epics of the poet Homer. Anyone familiar with Greek mythology knows that the residents of Mount Olympus were hardly good role models. Their chief god Zeus is depicted as a philandering husband who is taken with the seduction of both mortal and divine females. His jilted wife Hera hatches various plots for revenge on her hapless rivals. The rest of the Olympian gods are no more admirable and are portrayed with all sorts of human failings, vices, and weaknesses. Plato believed that telling these stories of debauched and corrupt gods would harm both individuals and society, so he wanted them banned.

As well as controlling storytelling, Plato believed that other types of leisure activities should be censored. He thought some musical instruments, such as flutes, should not be allowed in his ideal society because their sound would stir the passions of listeners. Similarly, music that was either dirgelike or effeminate should not be allowed because it would make people weak or sad (Plato, Republic II 398e, 399d cited in Hamilton and Huntington, 1961).

Plato carefully separated good leisure activities from bad ones based on his theory of what an ideal society should be like. According to his political philosophy, leisure activities are tools to be used to shape the character of citizens of his utopian society. Only those types of leisure activities that he judged to be virtuous were allowed. He saw many forms of leisure and recreation as threats to his perfectly ordered society. He was most fearful of playful forms of recreation that excited the emotions. Plato thought an ideal society should be ruled by reason alone. The citizens of his ideal Republic were expected to behave as somber, sober rationalists. Perhaps the metaphor of an anthill would best describe his vision of how society should be structured. The workers, soldiers, and rulers who were the citizens of Plato's utopia would all go about doing their assigned **work** with the greatest seriousness. **Leisure, recreation,** and **play** would only be encouraged if it had educational or developmental value (Hunnicutt, 1990).

We can still see a legacy of Plato's political philosophy in present-day leisure services. For example, a lot of recreational programming for youth is based on the notion that activities should contribute to positive character development (Johnson & McLean, 1994). And, like Plato, many

Detail from Raphael's "School of Athens." © Time Life Pictures/Getty Images

Plato and Aristotle began their philosophic inquiry by asking themselves what an ideal lifestyle for human beings should be like. What do you think?

adults are concerned about the influence of music and stories on children. Even though modern-day democracies permit many freedoms, V-chips are used in televisions, sales of "adult" books and magazines are restricted, and filters are used on computers to try to prevent young minds from being exposed to the images and ideas that parents and community leaders believe harmful.

Plato's philosophy makes it clear that leisure and recreation is an important tool for influencing individuals and society. He does not regard leisure and recreation as mere fun and games, but instead treats it as a critical component of a properly functioning society. Yet his vision of leisure emphasizes repression and control. Who would really want to live in his dreary, regimented utopia? Where is the notion that freedom is an integral part of experiencing leisure? To put the freedom back into leisure we need to turn to Plato's student, Aristotle.

ARISTOTLE'S PHILOSOPHY OF LEISURE

In many ways Aristotle followed Plato's political teachings. Aristotle was willing to advocate the repression of the majority of people living in his society. Women and slaves were not allowed the luxury of leisure. That privilege was reserved for the male citizenry. But Aristotle did not picture this leisured class as the idle rich. Rather, the leisured elite was expected to strive for self-perfection. For Aristotle, living the ideal lifestyle was a practical matter. It required following those habits of living that were virtuous and avoiding those that were vices (Hemingway, 1988).

Aristotle defined virtue as a midpoint between the vices of excess and deficiency (Aristotle cited in [Nicomachean Ethics 1107a] McKeon, 1941). Take, for example, the virtue of courage. It is an excellence of character that results from neither being cowardly (a deficiency) nor foolhardy (an excess). He recognized that every person's situation varies according to personal circumstances. However, each should live his or her life to maximize virtue—in other words, each person should try to be his or her very best. To excel in one's life requires a continual commitment to self-improvement. Aristotle therefore argues that one needs to develop habits of living that lead to excellence. It is instructive that the Greek word for ethics is derived from the word *ethos*, which means "habit"—a behavior or practice we continually engage in throughout our lifetime.

But what is the ultimate purpose of developing virtuous habits? Aristotle says that happiness results from being the best we can be. The sort of happiness that Aristotle is thinking of should not be equated with simple pleasure. Amusing ourselves can be pleasant, but he says it is childish and has the potential to cause us harm. **Amusement** for sheer pleasure degrades rather than improves us. Aristotle admits that amusement is helpful if it refreshes us from work. But amusement is never as good as true leisure, which provides a life of deep fulfillment rather than fleeting bodily pleasures (Aristotle cited in [Nicomachean Ethics 1176b] McKeon, 1941).

By using leisure to become our best, Aristotle is not simply thinking of moral goodness, but also those characteristics that make us uniquely human. And what did he think were our most noble qualities? Because he is a philosopher, perhaps it is not surprising that Aristotle says that it is people's ability for rational thought that is most admirable. Therefore, he concludes that the person who has the most rewarding lifestyle is the philosopher who is at leisure to develop his intellect to its highest capacity (Aristotle cited in [Nicomachean Ethics 1178a] McKeon, 1941).

We may disagree with Aristotle that being an intellectual is the most rewarding life people can live. It could be plausibly argued that excelling at other human activities such as food preparation, athletics, or art could produce equally satisfying lifestyles. But perhaps it is not important to quibble over which human activity is best. Instead, the important feature of Aristotle's theory of happiness is that it is based on the idea that human fulfillment results from achieving excellence from things we choose to do when we use our leisure appropriately.

Aristotle's philosophy of leisure, which emphasizes discipline and commitment rather than the freedom and choice we associate with our modern-day leisure experiences, may seem demanding. Nonetheless, freedom is an important element of Aristotle's concept of virtuous leisure. First, we need freedom from material wants so that we can have time for leisure. This means that we cannot be enslaved to our work. We need a sufficient level of material comfort (food, shelter, clothing, and so on) so that at least during part of our day we can have time for leisure. Second, we need intellectual freedom to understand why virtuous leisure activities are good. When we are children we can be trained to practice virtuous habits without knowing why those things are desirable. For example, we learn

at a very young age not to lie. But it is only when we are older that we fully understand why lying is wrong (e.g., it is hurtful to others). So it is with the practice of virtuous leisure activities. If you are an ancient Greek freeman, you choose certain activities to excel at not because someone has trained you to do them, but because you understand and appreciate that these activities are noble. Third, freedom is the essential characteristic of any virtuous leisure activity. These activities are simply worthy in themselves; we do not do them because they will bring fame, wealth, or other extrinsic rewards. In other words, virtuous leisure activities are intrinsically good.

CONTEMPORARY PHILOSOPHY OF LEISURE

We might ask whether Aristotle's elitist definition of leisure has much relevance to our modern lifestyles. Perhaps we can relate to Aristotle's refined version of leisure when we think of the high level of accomplishment of professional athletes, cordon blue chefs, and concert pianists. These people live lives devoted to perfecting their talents. But these examples are not leisure activities. Instead, they refer to occupations—ways of making a living. It is difficult for us to think of excellence apart from working. Typically, when we are very good at something, we want to find ways to turn it into a career. We tend to value activities that can be made productive. We are very work oriented, whereas the ancient Greeks were work averse. It was not that the Greeks thought that work was something evil, but rather they regarded it only as a necessity of life. They worked so that they could enjoy life. According their value system, it was leisure that gave meaning and purpose to their life, not work (DeGrazia, 1963).

For most of us, it is typically our work, our career, and our occupation that give us our sense of self-worth. If you do not believe this is true, think back to the last time you met someone at a social occasion. When making new acquaintances, was it your leisure activities or your work that you primarily used to describe yourself to others? In our modern culture the question "So what do you do?" implicitly assumes that you will respond by describing your occupation and workplace. Extolling the virtues of work would seem very odd to the ancient Greeks. We, however, with our modern lifestyles appear to have reversed that equation.

Why do we value work over leisure? Contemporary philosophers and social scientists have argued that in the last several hundred years there has been a fundamental shift in the values of Western society. We no longer define the good life in terms of leisure. Instead, it is the activities connected with working and consuming that are thought to make life worthwhile. Ironically, being a worker and being a consumer are often not the opposite roles that we suppose. Instead, working tends to promote consumption, and vice versa. Thus working and consuming are activities that mutually reinforce each other. Traditional notions of leisure are irrelevant to this production–consumption cycle where the good life is more and more being defined in terms of the "goods life." How did we get on this working and consuming treadmill?

Weber's Analysis of the Work Ethic

Have you ever heard someone being praised for having a strong work ethic? The term is derived from Max Weber's influential book *The Protestant Ethic and the Spirit of Capitalism* (Weber, 1958 [1930]). The **Protestant work ethic** refers to a cultural ideal that regards work as *the* most important activity in an individual's life. Weber believed that a new reverence for work arose from the Protestant Reformation, when Christian religious leaders such as Martin Luther and John Calvin rebelled against the Catholic Church. Both Luther and Calvin saw the medieval church as a corrupt institution in which the upper echelons

of the clergy lived a life of wealth and leisure. Up until the time of the Reformation, the church had followed Aristotle's teachings concerning leisure and the good life. The clergy and the nobility comprised the leisured class—both educated and wealthy enough to have the free time to engage in refined intellectual and cultural activities. The great mass of ordinary, uneducated peasants were little more than slaves who provided brute labor for the upper classes. In their radical break from the church, Luther and Calvin turned Aristotle's conception of the good life on its head, making work—not leisure—the foundation of a worthy life. Both Luther and Calvin believed in the notion of a "calling" whereby everyone had been assigned by God a certain task or occupation, which they should perform throughout their life. Answering one's calling in life was considered a virtue because you would be doing the work God intended for you. Conversely, ignoring your calling was a vice and would lead to an empty, directionless life. Thus, since the time of the Reformation, it has been work rather than leisure that culturally defines our conception of the good life.

Russell's Critique of the Work Ethic

Some modern philosophers have taken great exception to the notion that work can make our lives truly happy. Bertram Russell penned a tongue-in-cheek essay in the early 1930s titled "In Praise of Idleness" in which he criticizes the idea that work is virtuous. Russell argues that

Photo courtesy of San Jose Parks, Recreation and Neighborhood Services

© Photodisc

Weber's work ethic changed our view of the good life to one that valued hard work over leisure.

preindustrial societies were based on a "slave morality" used to justify the subjugation of large numbers of manual laborers so that a privileged aristocracy would have leisure to pursue spiritual, cultural, and intellectual activities. However, with the coming of the industrial revolution, modern technology has created such an abundance of goods that it is now possible for everyone to have sufficient resources for a leisured lifestyle. But rather than using technology to give everyone adequate leisure, Russell says we have continued to support the idea that leisure should be reserved for the upper crust of society and denied to the working class:

> The idea that the poor should have leisure has always been very shocking to the rich. In England, in the early nineteenth century, fifteen hours was the ordinary day's work for a man; children sometimes did as much, and very commonly did twelve hours a day. When meddlesome busy bodies suggested that perhaps these hours were rather long, they were told that work kept adults from drink and children from mischief. When I was a child, shortly after urban working men had acquired the vote, certain public holidays were established by law, to the great indignation of the upper classes. I remember hearing an old Duchess say: 'What do the poor want with holidays? They ought to work.' (Russell, 1960, p. 14)

Russell argues that it would be more rational to replace the traditional, but outmoded, slave morality with a leisure ethic that distributes work evenly. Rather than having a leisure class that does no work at all and a working class that is either overworked or unemployed, Russell proposes that a work-sharing arrangement that would reduce people's working time to four hours per day and still provide the "necessaries and elementary comforts" of life (Russell, 1960, p. 17). Russell believes that with these greatly reduced work hours, humanity would enter a new golden age of leisure, giving people the freedom to pursue cultural and intellectual interests. Perhaps Russell is naive to think that everyone would use their liberation from work for ennobling leisure activities. Would not many people choose to waste their free time engaged in frivolous amusements? Nonetheless, even if many people would not use their leisure wisely, we can still ask if that is a good enough justification for keeping people busy with work. Maybe what is really needed is not only sufficient free time, but also the availability of attractive and meaningful leisure opportunities that professionalized leisure services can provide.

Pieper's Critique of the Work Ethic

Josef Pieper, a Catholic theologian, also strongly criticizes our allegiance to the work ethic in his book *Leisure: The Basis of Culture* (1998). Pieper, who is writing of Europe in the aftermath of World War II, says that we no longer know what leisure is because we live in a totally work-oriented culture. Pieper argues that our fixation on work is so complete that even liberal arts disciplines such as philosophy are now treated as a type of "intellectual labor" and are only valued for their usefulness for solving practical problems. (And isn't this why many people ridicule philosophy and leisure studies—because these disciplines are thought to be "useless"?) According to Pieper, knowledge for knowledge's sake is devalued by our culture of work, and our leisure time is only thought to be useful if it refreshes us so that we can then resume our work with renewed vigor. Ironically, Pieper observes, our worship of work produces a meaningless, unsatisfying lifestyle. We live to work well, rather than working so that we can live well.

Veblen's Critique of Consumption

Although many people believe that being a success entails working hard to achieve enough financial independence to be able to retire to a life of luxury, could our worship of work actually sabotage our leisure lives? Many critics argue that our economic system actually works against our aspirations for a truly leisured lifestyle.

Modern economies encourage ever expanding growth in the production and consumption of products and services. As individuals, we live in a consumer culture where our success is measured by how much we can purchase. The more luxurious and expensive the goods we can own, the higher our social status. The American economist Thorstein Veblen termed the ostentatious displays of wealth as "conspicuous consumption" (Veblen, 1998 [1899]). Veblen criticized the superrich of his era—the Vanderbilts, Carnegies, and Rockefellers—as status seekers who used the great wealth they had amassed from their 19th-century business empires to give themselves an air of nobility. Their mansions, yachts, and lavish parties were symbols that these American industrialists "had arrived" at the good life.

Of course, most of us are not billionaires. We cannot hope to own executive jets, hand-built sports cars, or vacation homes on private Caribbean islands. Yet compared to the standard of

OUTSTANDING *Graduates*

Courtesy of Sherri Hildebrand

Background Information

Name: Sherri A. Hildebrand

Education: Master of science, Western Illinois University, department of recreation, park, and tourism administration

Special Awards: Outstanding Graduate Student (2003), William L. Lakie Scholarship (2004)

Special Affiliations: Rho Phi Lambda, honorary recreation fraternity (2002)

Career Information

Position: Adjunct professor at Black Hawk College, Moline, Illinois

Organization: Community college

Job Description: Teach the following courses in the department of health, physical education, and recreation: personal health, introduction to physical education, introduction to community recreation, leadership in leisure activity, first aid and CPR, physical education for grades 1 through 6, lifesaving, and beginning, intermediate, and advanced swimming.

Career Path: I received a bachelor of science in education from Drake University, Des Moines, Iowa, in 1979 and master's of education degree from the University of Toledo in 1982. My major in both instances was physical education.

I began teaching at Black Hawk College in 1984 in the health and physical education department. In 2001, I began pursuing a degree in recreation, and began my second master's program at Western Illinois University.

I am so blessed to have finally found an area that I belong in. The area of recreation and leisure is me! I have valued recreation and leisure experiences most of my life but did not realize how important they were to my quality of life until recently. My teaching has a passion it never used to have since I discovered how strongly I can relate to the ideals of recreation and leisure—and I want others to experience the same.

Likes and Dislikes About the Job: I love everything about my job, but my greatest love is being in a classroom. My relationship with the students I teach is the most important and most exciting part of my job. The only thing I can say I dislike about my job is feeling unappreciated by the full-time faculty as a part-time instructor.

Advice to Undergraduates

Get as much experience as possible in your field, whether you acquire it through volunteering or a paid position. This will not only serve to communicate to your future employer your level of experience but will also give you the chance to see if this is the field you belong in. One of the greatest gifts in life is to get up every morning and go to work at a job you love. I am lucky to have achieved this.

---

living of ancient Greek freemen, the lifestyle of the average person living in postindustrial societies is opulent. We have at our disposal a vast array of consumer products and services that Aristotle and his compatriots could not have imagined.

Other Critiques of Consumption

Unfortunately, to be able to afford these products and services means that most of us must devote a huge portion of our adult lives to work. The flip side of a highly consumptive lifestyle is that we must also be highly productive to pay for it. During our working lives, many of us find our time for leisure limited. Our careers require us to put in long days at work, leaving little time or energy for family and friends.

The consumerist lifestyle that most of us have adopted encourages us to think of leisure as a basket of commodities from which we pick and choose. Instead of being participants in unique and personal recreation activities, we are consumers of leisure experiences designed and mass produced by others (Hemingway, 1996). In this market-driven context, the concept of freedom is inextricably tied to the act of purchasing: the more leisure products and services there are for sale, the greater our freedom to choose.

It is undeniable that this free-market model of leisure services and products is attractive to most people. The "leisure industry" is one of the biggest and fastest growing sectors of the economy. Yet this apparent success masks several drawbacks to our commercialized leisure. As social economist Juliet Schor (1998) argues in her aptly titled book *The Overspent American,* the most obvious problem with the idea that we can buy happiness is that many of us spend more on our leisure than we can afford. In the United States, the number of personal bankruptcies is at an all-time high. One reason for the growth of people's personal financial problems stems from an abundance of easy credit. Consumers are constantly encouraged to increase their discretionary spending on leisure-related items and services. Using credit to finance otherwise unaffordable spending on vacations, entertainment, and recreational equipment can quickly lead to a buildup of bad debt (compared to good debt such as mortgages and student loans, which are investments in your future well-being). Yet many people still go ahead and borrow money to finance their consumptive leisure lifestyles. It is as though consumerism promotes immature behavior. Like young children, many of us are impatient and unwilling to delay our gratification, so we go ahead and borrow so that we can have what we want now.

The commodification of leisure may also discourage our personal growth by making our recreation experiences too convenient. Commercial providers of leisure services typically want to make their offerings as attractive as possible to their potential clientele. Competitive advantage can be gained by making the consumption of leisure services and products as effortless as possible. The examples are many: golf manufacturers advertise

These frenzied shoppers hope to find happiness from the products they can purchase. The consumerist lifestyle demands that we work more to afford more goods. As a result, shopping has become a major leisure-time activity for many people.

that their clubs alone will lower your handicap, therefore, you don't have to improve your swing; resort operators provide familiar fast-food items at exotic destinations so that guests will not have to adjust to the local cuisine; movie and television producers "dumb down" the content of popular entertainment lest audiences be made to think; and the list goes on.

Although our modern leisure services and products may be convenient, we might ask whether most of them are worthy of our time, not to mention our money. Aristotelian leisure is based on the idea that we should devote our free time to being the best we can be. The ancient view of leisure emphasized commitment and accomplishment. In contrast, as philosopher Albert Borgmann notes, commodified leisure appeals to our desire for comfort (Borgmann, 1984). Often, our modern leisure practices do not result in self-improvement. In fact, many of our recreational activities may cause us harm. Watching television, our most popular leisure pastime, has been linked to several modern maladies including obesity, depression, and paranoia (Kubey & Csikzentmihalyi, 1990; Gerbner, 1999). But it is attractive because of its easy access—you simply turn on the TV, then sit back and enjoy. But even our more active forms of recreation tend to cater to our desire for creature comforts. When practical and affordable, we often choose to motorize outdoor recreation activities. Why climb up a slope when you can use a chairlift? Why paddle or row when you can simply twist the throttle on an outboard engine? Why carry your clubs when you can ride in a cart? These uses of machines are said to enhance our leisure experiences, yet they may also disengage us from our environment and ourselves. Harvard sociologist Robert Putnam (2000) argues in his book *Bowling Alone* that Americans are becoming increasingly isolated socially. He cites a wealth of statistics showing that membership in community organizations dropped dramatically at the end of the 20th century. As a result, Putnam believes that Americans have become less satisfied with their lives because they have experienced a decline in their **social capital**—the social connections that support people in times of difficulty and make life more enjoyable in times of leisure. He attributes diminishing social capital to the changes in society that alter our work and leisure values:

> Over the last three decades a variety of social, economic and technological changes have rendered obsolete a significant stock of America's social capital. Television, two-career families, suburban sprawl, generational changes in values—these and other changes in American society have meant that fewer and fewer of us find that the League of Women Voters, or the United Way, or the Shriners, or the monthly bridge club, or even a Sunday picnic with friends fits the way we have come to live. (Putnam, 2000, p. 365)

A similar decline in social capital may be happening in Canadian society, although the data are more mixed. For example, a study of the "social cohesion" found that Canadians perceived themselves as having a high level of personal social support ("someone they can confide in, count on in a crisis situation, obtain advice from when making important decisions, and someone who makes them feel loved and cared for"), but they had a low level of social involvement ("frequency of participation in associations or voluntary organizations and frequency of attendance at religious services") (Jackson et al., 2000, pp. 66, 68).

Putnam compares the malaise in community involvement to the problems that faced American society at the end of the 19th century when rapid industrialization created a host of social problems in large cities. He notes that people responded to these social ills by becoming more involved in civic activities and voluntary organizations, and he argues that we need to find ways to use our leisure time to actively participate together in civic activities.

Perhaps it is because we are at least subconsciously aware that many of our leisure activities are unworthy experiences that we devise various rationales to justify our modern leisure lifestyles. We interpret shopping to be an exciting recreational activity rather than a mundane necessity of life. We tell our employees that we value wellness, but what we are really worried about are rising absenteeism and medical expenses. We take mini-vacations that cause the least disruption of our work schedules, taking along our laptop computers to avoid falling behind. At home, rather than spending unstructured, spontaneous time with our kids, we plan infrequent special activities and call it *quality time*. Unfortunately, this list goes on as well.

What we seem to lack is a sense that our leisure activities can be self-justifying. Our view of leisure as a commodity is based on the implicit premise that our leisure activities are a means to achieving some other goal. Perhaps that is not a surprising mindset, given that we live in a commercialized culture, constantly bombarded with messages about products and services that promise this or that benefit. But this lifestyle is ultimately unsatisfying for many of us because it keeps us focused on our leisure as a means to something else, rather than a worthy end in itself. The ancient Greeks understood very well that leisure should be reserved for activities that were good in and of themselves. Aristotle did not recommend philosophic inquiry as the best leisure activity because it made him more productive at work. Rather, he simply argued that it was the most intrinsically worthy activity that human beings could do.

Aristotle, of course, did not face the challenges to leisure that we do today. His social environment was far less complex than what we must deal with as leisure services providers. Of course, it may seem that there is little we can do to influence the quality of people's lives, given the strong cultural and economic forces that encourage people to be workers and consumers. But we are not completely powerless. As leisure services providers, we can make a difference in the lives of the people and communities that we serve. It all begins with a clear understanding of our own leisure values. For example, if we know that people are stressed by a culture that overvalues work, then we have an obligation as leisure services providers to advocate for the value of leisure. If we see that people are stressed by an economic system that encourages the overconsumption of products, then we can offer alternative leisure activities that encourage social interaction and community building. Surely, if we think of ourselves as quality-of-life specialists, then we need a philosophical understanding of some of the major problems that people and communities face, or else we may unwittingly become part of the problem, rather than part of the solution.

SOLVING ETHICAL DILEMMAS IN LEISURE SERVICES

So far, we have used philosophical analysis to help us evaluate our leisure lifestyles. In our role as socially responsible leisure services providers, we need this macro, or big-picture, understanding of the broad social and ethical issues affecting the quality of people's leisure lives. But is there another way that philosophical analysis can help us solve problems relating to the delivery of leisure services? Consider the following scenario.

Tanning-Bed Case

You are the recreation supervisor at a multipurpose community recreation center. The mission of the center is to promote the well-being of the citizens in the local community by providing a wide variety of high-quality recreation activities. Since the center opened, the fitness area has played an important role in satisfying the recreation center's mission. The fitness equipment and programs are popular and benefit participants' physical health and well-being. Recently, however, some of the patrons have asked the recreation center to install tanning beds. Many of these requests are from teenagers and young adults who say they like to work out at the center, but also want to be able to get a deep tan. You have never wanted to install tanning beds, because you have read research that indicates that the exposure to UV rays that these beds produce increases the likelihood of skin cancer, including the most deadly form of the disease, malignant melanoma. You announce that the center will not purchase the beds because of the possible negative health effects. Unfortunately, your decision is met with dismay and even outright hostility. Many of the young people who want the beds installed say they are not worried about cancer. Some say they will drop their membership and join a nearby private health club that has the beds. Several of the middle-aged members have contacted their representatives on city council (to whom you report) to lobby for purchasing the beds. And a few have threatened to go to the local media and "raise a stink" about how adults should be allowed to choose whether they can tan and should not be treated like children by the recreation center staff.

Dealing effectively with the tanning-bed problem just presented requires more than having a big-picture understanding of the situation. After all, the big picture tells us that skin cancer is a serious health problem, and as socially responsible leisure services providers we shouldn't provide equipment or services that are potentially dangerous. Yet many of the people we serve don't agree with our point of view; therefore, we are left in an uncomfortable position in which a lot of people may be angry or unhappy. What we need is a way to deal with these thorny situations that offers a win–win solution. Fortunately, philosophical analysis can help us decide the proper course of action in cases where we are confronted with an ethical conflict involving particular people at a particular time and place.

To deal effectively with ethical dilemmas we need an ethical decision-making method we can use to justify our decisions. And as responsible leisure services providers we are obligated to provide the people who are affected by our decisions

© AP/Wide World Photos

Philosophical analysis can help solve the problem of whether or not tanning beds should be used at a recreation center.

with reasonable explanations for our actions. Not everyone will agree with our decisions, but we need to demonstrate that our decisions are not made arbitrarily. Skepticism about the wisdom of our decisions is likely to be stronger when we are dealing with ethical dilemmas, and emotions tend to run high when moral points of view come into conflict. Although it is a common belief that ethical issues are based on opinion rather than fact, in reality we can nonetheless apply ethical theories to help us create a rationale for our actions.

Ethical Analysis: Three Approaches

Let's consider how we might apply ethical theory to help us determine what to do in the tanning-bed case. Three basic ethical theories can help us decide whether to install the beds: (1) **consequence-based ethics,** (2) **duty-based ethics,** and (3) **virtue-based ethics.** Using the first approach, we weigh the consequences of installing or not installing the tanning beds. If we install the beds we will make many people who use the recreation center happy. We will also not lose members to the private health club because of a lack of tanning beds. We also will not have to deal with client

complaints to the city council or the newspapers. From a consequence-based ethics perspective, the only downsides would be the initial cost of the equipment and the possibility that some recreation center clients might eventually develop skin cancer. Because there seems to be several definite, immediate benefits to installing the beds, based on a review of the likely consequences, it would be reasonable to conclude that we should go ahead and spend the money on the tanning beds.

The second way we can determine the most ethical course of action is to use a duty-based ethics perspective to evaluate our duties and obligations. One important duty we have is to carry out the mission of the recreation center. We are there to serve the public, so we have an obligation to provide services that people want. But we also have an obligation to provide services that benefit people's well-being. Given that public recreation organizations receive tax monies to provide leisure services that serve the public good, it is reasonable to assume that protecting the community's well-being is a more important duty than simply providing services that people want. Therefore, from a duty-based ethics perspective we should not install the tanning beds because that would betray our obligation to provide healthy leisure services.

At this point in our moral deliberations we see that we have come to opposing conclusions. Analysis from consequences-based ethics indicates that we should install the tanning beds, while duty-based ethics argues that we should not install them. How do we break this moral deadlock? Well, we might want to turn to the third way of analyzing ethical dilemmas: virtue-based ethics. With virtue-based ethics, moral decisions are made by consulting one's conscience. Instead of comparing outcomes or weighing duties, virtue-based ethics resolves ethical dilemmas on the basis of our personal integrity. For example, would we feel guilty if we installed the tanning beds in the fitness center? If the users of the beds are mature adults aware of the dangers of UV exposure, then we may not be bothered. These adults have simply made a choice to engage in an activity that endangers their health. But what about the teenagers who also want to use the beds? Will we find it hard to look at ourselves in the mirror before we go to work knowing we have helped expose teenagers to health risks that they might not be willing to take if they were mature adults? Therefore, from a virtue-ethics perspective we might install the tanning beds only if we had an effective way to prohibit teens from using the beds and if we could ensure that the adults at the center were well educated about the risks of UV exposure.

We can see from the application of the three ethical theories to the tanning bed scenario that solutions to ethical dilemmas are not always obvious. Some of us may think that tanning beds should be installed, while others may be opposed to placing this type of equipment in a community recreation facility. Furthermore, we may disagree on which ethical theory is best for solving the dilemma. Some people may think consequences should decide the issue, others may believe duties are paramount, while a third group may believe that conscience should dictate what to do. The important point is not that we might disagree about the proper solution to the ethical dilemma, but instead that our moral deliberations help us justify and explain our decision to people who disagree with us. For example, suppose the people who want the tanning beds are thinking in terms of the consequences. They want the beds because they are after certain outcomes such as what they believe to be a healthy look or a sexier body. Now we can talk to them on their wavelength by pointing out negative outcomes such as skin cancer and premature aging. If they still insist that the benefits outweigh the costs, then we can also explain that we have a duty to uphold the mission of the agency to provide healthy recreation, and that according to our own professional standards, we would not feel right about providing equipment that could cause serious health problems. Of course, it is completely possible that people still will not be persuaded that we are making the right decision, but at least we have provided them a reasonable, well-thought-out explanation for our decision. And we have accomplished this very practical task by using philosophy to justify our decision!

SUMMARY

We now see that philosophy is important to the provision of leisure services. Contrary to popular opinion, working in leisure services is not all fun and games. Serious social and ethical issues are bound to arise as we work to help people improve their leisure lifestyles. If we are unable to critically assess the worthiness of various leisure activities, then we run the risk of providing leisure opportunities that may not enhance the quality of people's lives. Philosophical analysis can give us a "macro" understanding to judge the worthiness of the various leisure and recreation activities that we might choose to provide. And we have seen that there is reason to believe that most of our current leisure experiences seem to be geared toward the worlds of work and commerce rather than providing us with opportunities to engage in intrinsically satisfying activities and personal growth. But as well as providing us with a "big picture" of some of the social issues facing leisure services, philosophical analysis can also help us deal with "micro" issues arising from the ethical dilemmas we will inevitably encounter during our careers as leisure service providers. Without an awareness and understanding of the ethical issues arising from leisure and recreation activities, we run the risk of causing unintended harm to the people we serve and the resources that we have been entrusted with. Rather than having to rely solely on our intuition, we can use methods of philosophical and ethical analysis to help us justify and explain our solutions to difficult moral dilemmas. Neither leisure services nor philosophy is a frivolous subject. Leisure services have great potential to affect the quality of people's lives. Philosophical analysis can help us ensure that the leisure opportunities we provide are beneficial rather than harmful.

CHAPTER 4

Leisure and Recreation for Individuals in Society

Daniel G. Yoder

© Comstock

People live in groups. From the earliest known history, people have lived together in families, clans, and tribes, have assembled in neighborhoods, communities, villages, towns and cities and have operated in gangs, clubs, unions, associations, and congregations and innumerable other groups. The person and the group are not separable phenomena, but are simply the individual and collective aspects of the same thing.

Loran David Osborn and M.H. Neumeyer, sociologists

CHAPTER OBJECTIVES

After reading this chapter, you should be able to do the following:

- Understand that leisure and recreation is a complex human endeavor that takes place within society
- Explain how leisure and recreation, whether as a solitary activity or undertaken with friends, family, or larger groups, affects and is affected by society
- Understand how gender, ethnicity and race, religion, and socioeconomic class affect leisure and recreation and how leisure and recreation in turn affects these factors
- Understand that the value of "goodness" or "badness" can be applied to leisure and recreation
- Understand the implications of a social perspective for leisure and recreation professionals

INTRODUCTION

This chapter considers the leisure of the individual *in* society, not the leisure of the individual *and* society. Although this may seem trivial, it is an important distinction. Individuals and societies do exist as separate entities in concept, but on a practical level, neither can exist independent of the other. Societies are composed of men, women, and children of various ages, races, classes, and so on. Without these essential parts, there could be no whole. Nor do individuals exist isolated from society; human beings are social animals by nature. All human existence (including leisure and recreation) takes place at the intersection of the individual and the diverse social structures that make up our world. Even the act of thinking, seemingly the quintessential individual activity, is impossible without the use of mental cultural symbols. These mental images are possible only within the borders of a common cultural context.

We begin this chapter with a general discussion of how leisure and recreation activities take place against a social backdrop and that even when people are physically alone in their activities, **society** influences them, and their activities may in turn influence society. We also discuss the relationships between leisure and primary groups of family and close friends, secondary groups, and four social institutions: gender, ethnicity, religion, and social class. Because the moral value of a leisure activity (its goodness or badness) is determined by both leisure participants and the world in which they live, we consider good and bad leisure. Finally, we discuss the implications of leisure and recreation in society for the professional practitioner.

LEISURE AS A COMPLEX SOCIAL PHENOMENON

Leisure is a wonderfully complex social phenomenon, affected by many social institutions including economics, politics, work, technology, and war. But we must be careful in thinking that leisure and recreation is a trivial pastime, influenced and even dictated by these social structures. In fact, leisure and recreation significantly affects the social forces we have just listed. Consider, for example, Las Vegas, Nevada. Without the leisure and tourism industries that pour billions of dollars into Las Vegas each year, the town would be much different, if it even existed at all. Examples like this, while perhaps not as obvious, play out every day in thousands of communities across North America and the globe.

Solitary Leisure and Society

A few leisure activities are entirely solitary, some are purely social, and most can be either private or communal. Reading is almost always undertaken alone, and playing a game of tennis always requires interaction with others. Playing cards is an example of an activity that can be either solitary or social, which characterizes the majority of leisure activities. Some people spend hours playing the classic solo card game, solitaire. On the other hand, you cannot play bridge without other players to compete against.

Although we might be inclined to think that our **solitary leisure** is ours and ours alone, it does not take place in a social vacuum. Indeed, other people and groups of people profoundly affect our solitary leisure activities. Furthermore, the leisure activities we undertake while we are alone have an influence—sometimes significant and sometimes not so significant—on the people and the world around us. The world around us affects our private leisure in three ways: by supporting it, by infringing on it, and by forcing us into it.

Other peoples' actions may support solitary leisure. Five-year-old Hannah gets a doll and a dollhouse for her birthday. She plays with the gifts by herself a great deal for the first few weeks. She uses her imagination and dreams of having her own home and family someday. This particular type of play would have been impossible without someone (in this case her parents) supporting Hannah by purchasing the dolls and the dollhouse. In another example, Argyle State Park recently constructed 6 miles (10 kilometers) of new hiking trails, and Tom cannot wait to get out and use them. Occasionally Tom hikes with his girlfriend, but most often he walks by himself. He finds it relaxing after a long day of school and work. In this instance, the construction of a walking and hiking trail affects Tom's solitary leisure.

Certainly, others can infringe on our private leisure. For example, Leann loves to watch television, particularly the different survival shows. Unfortunately, it seems that every Wednesday at 8:00 when Leann is settling in to watch her favorite program, her children need something. Bridget has to have her volleyball uniform washed, and Johnny needs help with his homework. It becomes almost impossible for her to keep up with the show. Or consider the case of Jacob, who loves nothing more than to jump on his motorcycle and take an exhilarating ride on the back roads in the mountains near his house. But Jacob has been stopped several times by local law enforcement agents, and they have cited him for traffic violations. Last week, he learned that his driving privileges had been suspended for six months. So much for Jacob's favorite solitary leisure activity!

In some situations, others can actually force people into solitary leisure. For example, teenage girls report that one of their favorite places to spend leisure time is their bedroom. Although they may spend a great deal of time on the telephone with friends, they also spend time just "hanging out" reading or writing in journals. They perceive this as a place that is safe from the scrutiny and criticism of peers and parents. In addition, some people in our society are deemed too dangerous to be with others; they may be confined and isolated as a means of punishment, or they may be prisoners of war. Even when the traditional resources and settings for leisure are denied, some are able to creatively use what is available. Prisoners of war in Vietnam reportedly caught rats, mice, and even insects and kept them as pets to fill their time. Others spent their time memorizing songs or poems.

Next let's consider how a person's leisure activities can directly and indirectly affect those around them, either positively or negatively, causing either minor or profound consequences. Take for example, Bob Feller, a Hall of Fame baseball player who pitched for 18 years for the Cleveland Indians. Feller played from 1936 to 1941 and from 1945 to 1956. His illustrious career was interrupted by a four-year stint in the United States Navy during World War I. Considered by many to be the greatest right-handed pitcher of all time, "Rapid Robert" struck out 2,581 batters. Feller was born and raised on an isolated farm outside of Van Meter, Iowa. Because few youngsters his age lived in the vicinity, Bob spent countless hours throwing

© AP/Wide World Photos

Bob Feller is shown here after pitching his 250th victory in May 1954. His solitary leisure influenced fans for years to come.

a baseball against his father's barn. Those hours of private leisure eventually led Feller to be the most popular baseball phenomenon of his day, indirectly providing entertainment for the additional 10,000 fans who showed up to cheer for him each time he was scheduled to pitch (CMG Worldwide, n.d.).

In contrast to the positive influence of Bob Feller's solitary leisure on others, the results of a person's private leisure can have serious negative consequences not just for themselves but also for those around them. Let's use Georgia, who, at the completion of a painting she had worked on for several weeks, decided she had earned a private celebration party. After mixing and drinking a few too many of her favorite drinks, she ran out of pineapple juice. Since she wanted just one more, she determined to drive six blocks to the convenience store and get the necessary ingredient. On the way she failed to see a car stopped at a stop sign, ran into it, and severely injured the occupants. The lives of the people in the car, their friends, family, and, of course, Georgia herself, were changed forever.

A single act of solitary leisure can even have both a negative and a positive influence. Even if you don't recognize the name, nearly everyone is familiar with the story of Aron Ralston, the young climber in Utah who was forced to cut off his arm after it became trapped between two boulders. Thousands of dollars were spent by state and county agencies in the effort to find and save Ralston. Hundreds of volunteers sacrificed days for the search. The tragedy could have been averted if Ralston had hiked with a companion. But Ralston chose to go it alone on this adventure. On the other hand, this story has been a tremendous inspiration to a lot of people—not just outdoor enthusiasts. It is impossible to measure the positive consequences of this single act of courage on a solo hike in the Utah desert.

Leisure and Primary Groups

Although some leisure activities can be solo endeavors, most directly involve others. Moreover, the others involved in the leisure activity are not merely bystanders, but essential components of the activity. Kelly (1987) has noted, "In general, people are more important in leisure than the form of the activity" (p. 158). Especially significant are those who are part of the participant's **primary group.** Sociologists have defined primary groups, as "small groups in which there are face-to-face

relations of a fairly intimate and personal nature. Primary groups are of two basic types, families and cliques. In other words, they are organized around ties of either kinship or friendship" (Lenski, Nolan, & Lenski, 1995, p. 48). We examine leisure activities with family and close friends only briefly here because this topic is more thoroughly considered in chapter 12.

Social custom and societal expectations profoundly affect leisure when activities are undertaken with family members and close friends. Defining the term **family** is not as simple as it may seem at first glance. Because different cultures use various forms of kinship groupings, and even the same culture may change its notion of family over time, a definition that all can agree on has been elusive. But no matter how it is defined, the family profoundly influences leisure. Kelly's (1999) concept of core plus balance is particularly helpful in understanding these dynamic relationships. A particular core of activities persists through a person's life, especially his or her adult years. A person may participate in various hunting and fishing pursuits throughout her life, or a person may have a lifelong interest in music. General types of leisure also tend to be common for many members of the same age group. For example, many young male adolescents participate in sports, and many elderly adults watch a great deal of television. But there is also variation, or balance, among and between the age groups. An older woman may have sung children's songs in her early years, played the flute as a high school student, sung in the church choir in her middle years, and listened to classical music later in life.

Leisure activities play a vital role in a person's physical, emotional, intellectual, and social development, even in the earliest stages. In childhood (birth to age 12), play and leisure contribute greatly to the socialization process. In play, children learn how to express and later how to control their emotions. Especially before formal schooling begins, children learn how to live in the world with others through a variety of play settings.

Henslin (1993) notes that **adolescence** (ages 13 through 19) is a relatively recent social creation. Until the 16th century, most cultures did not recognize adolescence as a period in life. And some cultures, such as hunter/gatherers and those engaged in prolonged warfare, still don't (Jensen, 1985). Some cultures used initiation rites to clearly mark when a person became a young adult with all the trappings—responsibilities as well as

A person may participate in various fishing pursuits throughout his life because of experiences fishing with his father as a child.

privileges. But the industrial revolution, with its increased materialism and a higher standard of living, allowed teenagers to remain outside of the workforce longer. This puts adolescents in an interesting and somewhat contradictory position. While they attempt to escape the limitations of childhood and strive toward the apparent freedoms of adulthood, they also appreciate the safety of being children and fear some of the expectations of being adults. The leisure lifestyle of adolescence clearly shows the effect of two occasionally competing forces—family and friends. Let's consider clothing as an example. Kelsey is a typical 16-year-old from Montreal. Like many teenagers, she considers her parents to be too conservative, especially when it involves how she dresses. As she comes down the

stairs on her way out to meet her friends for the evening, her father notices that her blouse is small and very revealing and her jeans are torn in several places. His comment, "There is no way you are going out in public in that shirt and those pants!" is met with, "Oh, Dad! That's the way we dress now. Do you want me to be covered from head to toe?" Most people—certainly older mainstream parents—do not wear such revealing clothing nor do they wear clothing that is badly worn and torn. However, that is the norm for this particular group of young people.

Families typically move through a series of somewhat predictable stages. Not all families go through every stage, but most do or aspire to do so. These stages are not distinct; instead, each stage merges into the one before and after it. Each phase of a family's development includes typical leisure activities, roles, and patterns. For example, many new families without children have a great deal of flexibility. Leisure activities can be spontaneous. Couples may be able to throw a few items together and get away for a weekend vacation in an hour or so. This is not the case for a family with children. Work and school schedules must be coordinated. Perhaps child care must be arranged. Considerably more clothing and equipment must be organized. Child safety must be considered. Even the destination of the vacation is affected. A quick trip to Las Vegas is more common for a family without children, while a trip to visit grandparents is common for families with children.

Leisure and Secondary Groups

Secondary groups affect a person's leisure activities, and in turn, the leisure activities of an individual have the potential to affect the secondary group. Henslin (1993) defines a **secondary group,** compared with a primary group, as "a larger, relatively temporary, more anonymous, formal and impersonal group based on some interest or activity, whose members are likely to interact on the basis of specific roles" (p. 150). Some secondary groups, such as a college classroom, a political party, and a labor union, are not related to leisure, but many are. Examples of these include a pottery class, the National Rifle Association, a travel club, and a Texas Hold 'Em poker league.

A few examples show the obvious influence a secondary group can have on its members. Jane has dedicated Wednesday evenings to attending her pottery class at the local park district. Instead

As a member of a pottery class, the individual has an influence on the group as much as the group influences the individual.

of returning home after work on Wednesdays to spend time with her family, Jane grabs a quick bite to eat and heads straight to the pottery class. Nick is a member of the National Rifle Association (NRA), and with a particularly contentious national election coming up he receives promotional material from this organization nearly every week. In part because of this, Nick decides to vote for a candidate who supports the NRA and opposes gun control. Jim and Margaret, recently retired and fairly affluent, love to travel. They have joined a local group that organizes trips for its members. They benefit from the reduced group rates and the opportunity to interact with people with similar travel interests. Rusty has been involved with a poker league that plays Texas Hold 'Em every Friday night. Not only does he enjoy playing, but he also sees a great deal of potential for this activity as a fund-raiser. When the board of the local food pantry (of which Rusty is a member) discusses fund-raisers, Rusty volunteers to organize a poker tournament for the community.

Although we can see how a secondary group influences the actions of individuals, the influence an individual may have on the group is not quite so obvious. It is nevertheless very real. For example, Jane, the fledgling potter, has had a very bad week. When she attends the week's pottery session, she gets into an argument with the instructor about the schedule for firing her pottery pieces. Their heated conversation is overheard by several other class members, and it casts a pall on the evening's class. Although Nick believes in most of the positions

taken by the NRA, he cannot support the right of Americans to own assault rifles. It is one thing to have a rifle or a shotgun for hunting, but assault rifles are just too dangerous, he believes. Thus, he begins to encourage other members to write letters to the national organization to put pressure on it to change its stance on this issue. Jim and Margaret believe that the local travel club has been a little too conservative in planning trips. At a meeting they ask why the club cannot plan a trip to an exotic location such as Tahiti. Although some of the members balk at the idea, some become convinced that this is a good idea, and they assign a subcommittee to look into the possibility of such a trip. Finally, Rusty has convinced the food pantry's board to take on the poker tournament as its primary fund-raiser. The organization needs to discontinue two other fund-raising events to have enough volunteers for this activity. Moreover, one of the board members has to resign from the board because he has been convicted of a felony and the state will not issue a license for the poker tournament as long as a convicted felon is on the board of directors.

As the examples illustrate, members of secondary leisure groups are not only influenced by the groups, but they can in turn affect the group itself. The possibility of significantly affecting the group is more likely if the secondary group is local, such as the pottery class. Although it is difficult for an individual to change a national organization such as the National Rifle Association, it is possible.

In addition to primary and secondary groups, another type of social structure affects a person's leisure activities: social categories. Lenski and Lenski (1987) note that human beings can be grouped into a variety of societal classifications. We become members of some of these groups voluntarily, and we are born into others. For instance, we can choose to become a member of a cooking and dining club, but our gender is largely predetermined. Next we examine how gender, ethnicity and race, religion, and socioeconomic class influence leisure and recreation.

LEISURE, RECREATION, AND GENDER

Before venturing further into this topic it is important to discuss the difference between gender and sex. **Sex** refers to the biological component of being either male or female. **Gender,** on the other hand, is a social category that includes attitudes, expectations, and expressions of masculinity and femininity. Gender is one of the most defining characteristics human beings possess. Because of that, it is linked to leisure in myriad complex relationships.

Historically, men have enjoyed a privileged position in all Western cultures. Although patriarchy has been most evident in politics, industry, the arts, and many professions, male superiority has also been expressed and fortified in leisure and recreation. In the 1800s many recreation activities were reserved for men only. At that time, no "self-respecting" female would have gone to a tavern. And segregation of the genders for no apparent logical reason was common. For example, men rode bicycles, and women rode tricycles in the early years of cycling in the United States. It simply was not proper to do otherwise.

The traditional roles within the family have also affected the leisure activities and recreation of men and women. Males were assigned the role of the breadwinner who earns the family's financial resources. Women were assigned the tasks of caring for her children and husband and maintaining the home. Thus, many recreation activities for women took place in the home and included a domestic component like cooking, decorating, or supervising activities for children.

The roles and expectations of men and women in Western society have changed significantly over the past century. Robinson and Godbey (1997) have noted, "Perhaps the most important ongoing social revolution in the United States is the change in women's roles" (p. 13). However, many authors and researchers caution that although change has been made, androgyny, the balance of both male and female characteristics, has not yet fully arrived. Sociologists have pointed out that one of the barriers to a more androgynous society is that parents and other people in nurturing roles have a tendency to treat children in a gender-biased fashion. This can be seen in the actions of the father who invites his son to go hunting with him but never considers that his daughter might want to go as well. Teachers may also show similar biases when it comes to recreation activities. They may discourage young boys from playing with dolls and little girls from playing with toy trucks because it is not acceptable in their eyes. Such behaviors, although not intentionally meant to harm children, have long-term effects, in many cases continuing to

deny rewarding and self-enhancing activities to millions of Americans (Eschleman, Cashion, & Basirico, 1993).

Women are still responsible for the majority of duties involved in maintaining home and family. Newman (1999) writes that on average women spend 50 hours each week on family work, while men average 11 hours. This affects leisure by limiting how much time is available for it. Although, the apparent imbalance in leisure time between men and women is somewhat offset by the fact that men still average more working hours outside the home than women do. Kelly and Godbey (1992) note the following:

> Most large studies of participation in many forms of recreation and leisure, which take place outside of the home, find that females are less likely to participate (in the different forms) and, when they do, to participate less often than do males. This is generally true in participation in most forms of outdoor recreation and sport. (p. 311)

As mentioned previously, sport has been almost entirely a male arena. However, progress has been made. No longer is the old adage true that boys perform and girls cheer. One of the most important steps in the process was adoption of **Title IX** in 1972, legislation that directed educational institutions to develop parity between men's and women's sports in the United States. As evidence of its effectiveness, in 1971, 300,000 females took part in high school sports in the United States; in 1994 that number had risen to 2.24 million (Online Newshour, 1997). This increase in sport participation by girls and women shows that the gap in participation rates between men and women is narrowing.

In Canada, progress has also been made to provide gender equity in sports opportunities. However, Beaubier (2004) notes that a policy to govern the process has been only recently enacted. Canadian Interuniversity Sport, the leading national organization to control sports at the university level, developed a policy statement that included 12 goals to achieve gender equity. Some in Canada believe that the policy is incomplete and encourage Canadian sports organizations to look to the Title IX legislation in the United States for further development on this issue. Russell (2002) offers five conclusions about gender, recreation, and leisure:

1. Although the disparity has decreased over the past century, men continue to experience more leisure in terms of its breadth and depth. A

Today, boys and girls participate in sports together. The boy, third from left, is a member of the girls' volleyball team. His school did not have a boys' team. Presented with the option of playing boys' volleyball for his sister school or playing on the girls' team, he opted to stay put.

© AP/Wide World Photos

greater diversity of recreation activities is available to men and boys, and it is easier for males to devote more time and effort to activities that are especially important to them. (These activities are often referred to as **serious leisure**.)

2. Long-entrenched roles for the different genders significantly affect recreation. Especially in older and more traditional families, women typically assume the complex and time-intensive task of caring for others. It is not uncommon for the mother in the family to plan, purchase, prepare, and serve the food, then clean up after a Saturday evening barbeque with neighbors. The values and benefits of this leisure activity will likely be different for the mother than for the father in this family. The mother values her ability to provide her neighbors a meal and enjoyable evening, despite the amount of work involved, while the father values spending time with the neighbors in a relaxing atmosphere.

3. Because men tend not to be the primary caregivers in the family, their recreation more often takes place outside the home. Women, on the other hand, more often spend leisure time in the home. Often their leisure activity is blended with, or at least compatible with, caring for the home.

4. The burden of family care has a greater impact on females; thus, women's leisure and recreation are often quite fragmented. Men, as a result, may have more opportunity to block out an entire afternoon or even a few days exclusively for leisure. Although a woman may plan an afternoon of relaxing reading, she may be interrupted by children who need clothes washed or a husband that needs her help.

5. Older women especially might labor under the false belief that leisure must be earned or that they are not entitled to leisure at all. If they do not do work outside the home, they may not feel like they work and therefore are unworthy of leisure.

LEISURE, ETHNICITY, AND RACE

Race and ethnicity are sometimes used interchangeably, but there are important differences. **Race** refers to biological characteristics, whereas **ethnicity** refers to cultural characteristics. Henslin (1993) notes that people of the same ethnicity "identify with one another on the basis of common ancestry and cultural heritage. Their sense of belonging centers on country of origin, distinctive foods, dress, family names and relationships, language, music, religion and other customs" (p. 311). Leisure and recreation is part and parcel of these various cultural qualities. Some social scientists and politicians argue that more equity exists among racial and ethnic groups today, while others contend that stereotyping, prejudice, discrimination, and racial inequality are every bit as prevalent as they ever were, but they simply are more difficult to detect. Others operate under the assumption that, even if race and ethnicity are issues that must be attended to, they have little relation to leisure. Phillip (2000) however, disputes this line of thinking: "Perhaps, nowhere else does race matter as much as during leisure. While schools and workplaces have been integrated over the past three decades by force of law, no similar laws have been enacted to secure the racial integration of leisure spaces" (p. 121).

Leisure participation rates vary according to race and ethnicity. For example, Bultena and Field (1978) found that African Americans use national parks and participate in some outdoor recreation activities significantly less than Anglo ethnic groups do. Furthermore, even if participation rates by minorities are not significantly different, use patterns may vary. For example, Irwin, Gartner, and Phelps (1990) note that although Hispanics visit most recreation areas at rates similar to those of Anglo groups, they tend to do so in larger groups that are "more varied in their composition than typical Anglo groups" (p. 16). Recently, racial gaps have increased for some leisure activities. Robinson and Godbey (1997) note that African Americans now spend more time watching TV and listening to the stereo and less time reading than whites do.

Beyond recognizing differences, attention has been devoted recently to the issue of *why* leisure is different for racial and ethnic groups. Two general explanations have come to the forefront: the marginality hypothesis and the ethnicity explanation. The marginality hypothesis explains lower participation in some activities as the consequence of a history of discrimination, resulting in fewer socioeconomic resources. To explain why fewer African American children than white children join swim teams, this theory holds that historically African American children were denied access to quality aquatics facilities and coaches. On the other hand, the ethnicity explanation suggests that different rates and patterns of participation are the result of different norms, beliefs, and social organizations.

According to this theory, Amish adults do not gamble at as high a rate as other groups because their culture rejects this activity as unwholesome and creating problems for individuals, families, and their communities. Floyd (1998) argues that these two approaches to accounting for differences in leisure and recreation may be only a beginning. He suggests that each has serious weaknesses and that leisure researchers must continue to research in this area. According to the ethnicity theory, one of the reasons African Americans do not participate on swim teams is that they see less value and benefit from participation in organized swimming than in some other sports. Aspiring African American athletes can see professionals similar to themselves on pro football, basketball, and baseball teams. On the other hand it is extremely rare for them to see black swimmers.

LEISURE, RECREATION, AND RELIGION

Although religion is fundamentally related to ethnicity, it warrants further attention. For our purposes, we must differentiate between two related concepts. **Spirituality** is a personal belief system that may, but most often does not, have a strong social component. **Religion,** on the other hand, is a thoroughly and universally social institution. According to Eschleman, Cashion, and Basirico, "Religion has always been the anchor of identity for human beings. Religious beliefs give meaning to life, and the experiences associated with them provide personal gratification, as well as release from the frustrations and anxieties of daily life" (1993, p. 344). In all of its wonderfully diverse forms, religion pervades nearly every human endeavor, from presidential elections to child rearing, from marriages and funerals to hairstyles and the length of skirts. Even the recreation activities of those who do not consider themselves to be religious are affected by religion. For example, Norman and Arlene are a middle-aged couple who haven't attended church for the past 20 years. One of their favorite leisure activities since their oldest daughter started high school is watching her participate in athletic events. Because of Arlene's work schedule, she has had difficulty getting time off on Saturdays for her daughter's volleyball games. It would be much easier for her if some of them were played on Sunday afternoons. However, that's not likely because their community, like many others, does not hold school events on Sundays to avoid conflict with the local churches. Also, the mascot for the sports teams was changed a few years ago as a result of vocal and influential Christian parents. No longer do Norman and Arlene cheer for the Fighting Blue Devils. They now cheer for the Lightning. One of the biggest tournaments of the season is held at the local YMCA. Norman and Arlene did not realize however that the Young Men's Christian Association of the United States of America, a national organization with its roots in the Christian faith, was one of the pioneers in developing the sport of volleyball. It is possible that the games they now enjoy watching would not exist if it were not for this Christian-based organization.

We must be careful not to portray religion as simply a constraint on leisure and recreation. In fact, churches use recreation as a method of maintaining its sense of community, to attract new members, and to keep its members from activity it perceives as harmful. For example, instead of promoting traditional Halloween events like trick or treating, churches across the country offer parties that emphasize other types of fun and worship. Many churches and synagogues have athletic teams that participate either in community leagues or in leagues with other churches and synagogues. Moreover, many children attend summer camps operated by religion-related organizations. Even the traditional potluck after Sunday morning service is a leisure activity that serves to maintain the sense of community of the church people.

Nowhere is the relationship with religion in the United States and Canada more complex and intriguing than in the special arena of sports. This should come as no surprise given the fact that this country not only has the greatest diversity of sports but also has the greatest diversity of religions. Many athletes have had to struggle with the demands of their faith and their desire to participate in sports. One of the classic examples of this struggle is depicted in the 1981 movie, *Chariots of Fire,* in which devout Christian Eric Liddell must choose between the biggest race of his life and honoring his faith's admonition about running on the Sabbath.

Recently, much attention has been given to the theory that sport has replaced religion in the lives of many North Americans. Edwards' seminal work on the topic of sport as religion continues to influence sport sociologists. According to Edwards (1973) sports and religion have 13 important similarities. Four of them follow:

- Just like religion, sports have their saints. These are the great athletes of previous eras that serve as examples for current athletes and fans.

- The world of sports has its "gods," those superstars that transcend time and culture and dominate the lives of individuals and even countries.

- Sport has its hallowed shrines. These range from the widely recognized Hall of Fame sites to the trophy rooms of colleges and high schools.

- Sports have powerful symbols of faith. The bat that Ruth hit his record home run with and the ball that Dwight Clark caught to win the 1982 National Football League playoffs are examples. And who can argue that there is not a certain sacred quality of an Olympic gold medal?

One of the similarities between sport and religion can be seen in this high school trophy case, a hallowed shrine at many high schools.

In writing about the similarity between religion and sport, Prebish noted that "religion is the raft that ferries from profane reality to the realm of the sacred, that enables us to transcend ordinary reality and directly apprehend the extraordinary" (1993, p. 3). He goes on to make the case that for some people, sport does the same thing. When we watch the Super Bowl, we make a mental and emotional journey from everyday life to a world of fantasy.

LEISURE, RECREATION, AND SOCIOECONOMIC CLASS

The individuals of nearly all societies are categorized according to some combination of wealth, power, party affiliation, life chances, and prestige. Some systems, like the **caste system** in India, are very rigid. The boundaries are distinct and movement between the different categories is nearly impossible. A **class system,** like that in many developed countries including the United States and Canada, is much more fluid with overlap between classes and the possibility of movement up and down among the classes. In many countries, classes are designated according to a combination of income, education, and occupation. This classification system is referred to as socioeconomic status, SES.

Newman (1999) documents four classes in contemporary industrialized societies. The upper class consists of owners of vast property and wealth. Some estimate that one-half percent of the upper class owns more than 25 percent of the country's wealth (Henslin, 1993). The middle class is made up of managers, small-business owners, and professionals. The working class is made up predominantly of laborers who make modest wages and own little property. Finally, the people of the lower, or poor, class are those who either work for minimum wages, are often unemployed, or are unemployable.

There is general agreement that socioeconomic status affects leisure. There is, however, less agreement on exactly *how* it affects it. Addressing a particular leisure category, Gruneau wrote, "Recent research on sports and social equality in the United States demonstrates a general pattern of under-representation of people from the lowest income levels among active participants in organized sports and physical recreation" (1999, pp. 52-53). Recognizing some of the disagreement about the relationship between socioeconomic status and leisure, Kelly noted, "Economic stratification is at least a filter,

with low incomes simply eliminating the majority of the population from cost-intensive activity" (1996, p. 78).

Research supports the notion that class affects travel and tourism. Mill (1986) determined that economic standing, one of the key elements of SES, affected several aspects of tourism. Not surprisingly, people in the upper and middle classes traveled more often through commercial providers, while the working class tended to travel by some form of public transportation. The destinations for travel were also different. The upper classes tended to travel internationally more often than other classes. The higher on the SES scale, the longer the time spent at a destination. And as might be expected, the upper and middle classes spent more money when they traveled for leisure purposes.

We should not overlook the fact that although class affects leisure, the reverse may also be true—leisure may affect class. Thorstein Veblen, in his classic 1899 treatise, *The Theory of the Leisure Class,* argued that the upper class, which he called the leisure class, used leisure as a way to display and maintain their prized position in society (1998 [1899]). Elegant and exclusive social gatherings and highly consumptive activities sent a clear message to those in lower social positions that class did indeed matter. At the same time, many of the lower classes emulated the upper classes and tried to match their leisure styles. When a sufficiently large group from the middle class was able to participate in activities that resembled those of the rich, the upper class found even more expensive and elaborate leisure activities to maintain their status. The recent remarks at a polo game in the Hamptons in New York provide proof that although Veblen wrote at the turn of the 20th century, his theory may still be true today: "It (the Hamptons) used to be a destination for people living a certain lifestyle. Now it's a destination for people who *want* to live a certain lifestyle" (Bernard, 2002, p. 22).

GOOD AND BAD LEISURE AND RECREATION

If we're not careful, we may assume that leisure and recreation is unequivocally good. Who can argue that an exercise program for seniors or making parks available for picnics are not admirable and decent efforts? Certainly no one could be opposed to arts and crafts classes and family vacations. But some activities are not wholesome, and some seem to be just downright wrong. We could list the bad activities, but that wouldn't be especially helpful because the list would be in a constant state of flux with leisure activities being struck from the list and new ones being added all the time. It may be more productive for us to consider how to determine the goodness or badness of an activity.

Participation in recreation cannot be forced upon us. We decide to participate because we think it will be fun and possibly rewarding. In fact, the defining quality of leisure and recreation is the freedom to participate or not. But the same freedom in leisure and recreation can be problematic when considering the moral value of an activity. We might think that our leisure is just that— entirely and completely *our* leisure. How dare anyone tell us that our chosen activity is wrong and then try to stop us from doing it! Although that may be our initial reaction to placing moral value on recreation and leisure, we must go beyond that if we are to truly understand our society and ourselves. Let's take a moment and consider how we determine good and bad in contemporary culture.

Goodness has been discussed by every culture since the ancient Greeks. Today we have several different and competing theories about what is good and bad, right and wrong. Although there are a lot of diverse ideas, nearly all agree that goodness is not a concept simply left up to the individual to determine. Even proponents of **hedonism,** a philosophy in which individual pleasure is the chief good, recognizes that our consequences have actions that affect our pleasure seeking; thus we have to consider our behaviors in light of those around us. Other ethical theories place concerns for others at the middle of the debate about good and evil. The point is that the individual actor and the various societies of which he or she is a part jointly determine goodness in all things, including leisure and recreation.

Let's briefly consider a couple of contemporary theories about good and bad leisure. Nash (1953) was one of the first to tackle the issue. His model of good and bad recreation resembled a pyramid with the very best activities at the peak. These activities not only provided satisfaction to the actor but also contributed to making a better society. In the middle of the pyramid were activities that were merely entertaining to the participants. They were not harmful to anyone, but they did not affect society either. Near the bottom were activities that, although freely chosen, were harmful to the individual. Finally, at the bottom of the diagram, were activities that not only hurt the participant

but damaged society as well. Curtis (1979) devised an even simpler continuum with "good" recreation activities on one end and " bad" recreation activities on the other end. Curtis labeled bad activities as **"purple leisure"** and defined them as activities that might bring pleasure to the individual but would cause harm to society.

Let's look at various recreation activities in light of this discussion of goodness and badness. Activities at the top and bottom of Nash's model and at either end of Curtis' continuum are pretty easy to understand. Most of us would agree that writing and performing a beautiful song would be good and vandalizing a playground would be bad. But it is much more difficult to reach consensus on the goodness of many other activities. Where would we put hunting? How about alcohol use? Marijuana use? Cocaine? Television viewing? Playing violent video games? Or how about ultimate fighting? Is it wrong or bad to go to a strip club? Then there is the thorny issue of gambling. At one time in the United States almost every type of gambling was banned. Then it became available only in certain states and locations like Nevada and American Indian reservations. Now, some form of gambling is available in just about every state and county. Many states have horse and dog races to bet on. Casinos are floating on almost every major body of water in the United States, and there are only three or four states that do not have a legal lottery. In Canada, gambling is legal to anyone over the age of 18. Options include scratch tickets (similar to the lotteries in the United States), horse races, bingo, betting on sports events, and gambling at one of the 106 casinos scattered across Canada. So, is gambling good or bad? It's legal and widespread, provides jobs and resources for schools and (whatever else governments do with the money), and provides entertainment for many. But it is also associated with addiction, corruption, and other negative aspects—possibly the diminution of the work ethic. As you can see, determining whether a leisure activity is good or bad is not easy. But as a society, we must attempt to because leisure activities affect us all.

IMPLICATIONS FOR PROFESSIONALS

Charged with the task of providing leisure and recreation opportunities, leisure and recreation professionals must first understand how leisure and recreation takes place. Who participates? How

OUTSTANDING *Graduates*

Background Information

Name: Debbie Rubenstrunk

Education: Bachelor of science, Arizona State University, department of leisure studies, American Humanics program, College of Public Programs

Credentials: American Humanics certification

Special Awards: George F. Miller Outstanding Student Award (1987-1988)

Career Information

Position: Development director at Body Positive, Phoenix, Arizona

Organization: Body Positive, an HIV/AIDS community-based research and resource center, is working on a preventive vaccine and other promising therapies in the treatment of HIV and AIDS. Body Positive also provides vital services and support to the HIV community in Arizona, serving more than 7,000 people with 45 employees.

Organization's Mission: Body Positive aims to provide the community with the knowledge, resources, and collective strength necessary for people to live long and well with HIV and prevent the spread of the disease.

Job Description: Serve as one of the five members on the agency's management team. Supervise staff. Develop and direct the development plan for the agency. Board development. Oversee and conduct special events, such as Night for Life Gala, An Evening of Positive Energy, Positive Share annual giving campaign, and An Exquisite Home Tour. Cultivate and solicit donors. Oversee Body Positive Foundation and Body Positive Advisory Council.

Career Path: In 1979, I had the pleasure of meeting the late singer-songwriter and social activist Harry Chapin. I became involved with the organization he had founded, World Hunger Year (WHY). Because of my eagerness to address the issue of hunger in our community, I started the first pilot program for developing a national chapter for WHY. I learned about the power of the media, the difference that one person can make, and that working together as a community makes change possible. After Harry's death, I realized that if I wanted to continue working in the nonprofit arena, I needed to get a degree. Arizona State University (ASU) offered the American Humanics (AH) program, and I was able to earn my degree in an area that I was already fully engaged in: nonprofit management. While at ASU, I served as the AH Student Association president and fund-raising chair. During my senior year, the student association awarded me the George F. Miller Outstanding Leadership award. I performed my senior internship with Camp Fire Boys and Girls and was hired as the public relations director in 1988. Over the 13 years that I worked with the local Camp Fire council, my role evolved into the development director and assistant executive director for the agency. Wanting to move away from youth development and back into an area that had global impact, I accepted the position as the development director for Body Positive.

Likes and Dislikes About the Job: I love being a part of making a difference in the lives of people. I dislike having to bug people for answers—but I'm really good at it.

Advice to Undergraduates

While you are in school get to know the professionals working in the community. They are the ones who will hire you when you graduate. It is never too soon to make connections.

> Working in the nonprofit field brings you in contact with an incredibly diverse group of individuals. You will spend time with the richest and poorest and with celebrities and average Joes. You will touch the lives of all these people for a common cause and you will make a difference and you will know that you did good work.

do they participate? What are their motivations? What are their constraints and limitations? What are the benefits of recreation? Are there direct consequences or indirect consequences that will not be evident for years? Armed with the answers to these questions, we can design programs, facilities, and open spaces that make it possible for human beings to flourish.

For example, knowing the demands and limitations placed on single mothers, recreation and parks professionals must offer programs that allow them the opportunity to participate. Perhaps that means that some fitness programs take place in the middle of the morning and the agency offers a toddler play period at the same time. Given the fact that money is in short supply for this population, the agency must also subsidize the program so that the mothers do not have to choose between their own physical fitness and paying the utility bills. This must all be accomplished without perpetuating the stigma that single-parent households are inferior and a societal burden that must be dealt with as conveniently as possible.

But even these efforts, as challenging as they are, are not enough. On another level, leisure and recreation professionals must be educators. They must continue to drive home the point that leisure and recreation is essential—so important that people, regardless of their lot in life, have it by right, not because they are of a particular color, age, ethnicity, gender, religion, or class. Showing the current benefits and extolling the future benefits of leisure and recreation for all will strengthen the case. The world really can be better today and tomorrow for all of us through equal leisure and recreation opportunity.

SUMMARY

As we have seen, leisure is a wonderfully complex human phenomenon that is never undertaken in a social vacuum—it is absolutely inseparable from society. A multitude of social institutions including stratification, religion, ethnicity, gender, family, and friendships thoroughly influence leisure. But the causation arrow goes both ways. Leisure often profoundly affects the society in which it takes place. Thus, contrary to the thinking of previous eras, leisure is not a trivial pursuit relegated to the realm of leftover time and energy. Rather, it is an essential ingredient of the lives of individuals, communities, nations, and humankind. Into this rich boiling stew of the human experience venture leisure and recreation professionals.

PART II

Leisure and Recreation As a Multifaceted Delivery System

CHAPTER 5

Delivery Systems

Betty van der Smissen

Those who decide to use leisure as a means of mental development, who love good music, good books, good pictures, good plays, good company, good conversation—what are they? They are the happiest people in the world.

William Lyon Phelps, American educator, literary critic, and author

CHAPTER OBJECTIVES

After reading this chapter, you should be able to do the following:

- Understand the four ways, or systems, in which recreation and leisure is delivered
- Describe the facets of each of these four systems
- Explain how the four systems encompass the whole of recreation and leisure and are interrelated but not mutually exclusive
- Understand how a person making a professional decision chooses one facet from each system to determine for which position in the recreation and leisure profession he or she is best suited

INTRODUCTION

Because recreation and leisure is pervasive throughout society, individual perspective on recreation and leisure delivery systems is varied depending on their experience with the field. Those who have participated in recreation at a community recreation center, at a Boys and Girls Club or YMCA, or at a private theme park will think of recreation delivery primarily in terms of the **sponsoring sector**—the public agency, the nonprofit association, or the private for-profit enterprise. Those individuals who do everything outdoors, participate in community-wide activities, or "live" at the athletic club, the Boys and Girls Club facility, or YMCA building will see recreation and leisure delivery as the **setting**—the natural environment, the community as a whole, or the building. Individuals who are active in or volunteer to work with the senior citizen club, participate in or give leadership to activities for teenagers, or are involved in special programs for people with disabilities think of recreation and leisure delivery in terms of age or type of **population segment,** regardless of who the sponsor might be. However, other individuals participate in a sport league, a fitness program, or the theater, regardless of sponsor or population group, and they think of recreation and leisure delivery in terms of these organized programs or activities, which are the **service modality** of the sponsor.

So, indeed, recreation and leisure services are delivered in a multifaceted system. The four basic delivery systems are sponsoring sector, setting, population segment, and service modality. When planning recreation and leisure for a community or inventorying opportunities, we usually think in terms of one of these systems. For example, who is the sponsoring sector? In what setting do the services take place? Are services delivered to all ages and types of people? Do the services include all of the modalities? However, these systems are not independent or mutually exclusive. Instead, predominant characteristics distinguish the different facets within each delivery system. Refer to table 5.1 for a summary of facets for each system. Each system is described in the following sections.

SPONSORING SECTOR

All organized recreation and leisure is sponsored by an entity. The three primary sectors are public agencies, nonprofit associations, and private for-profit enterprises. This is perhaps the most common approach to delivery systems. Each sector is distinguished by its predominant characteristics, including governing authority, philosophy, and funding.

Public agencies are sponsored by all jurisdictional levels—local (cities, townships, counties), state, provincial, and federal—and schools. They also include institutions sponsored by the government. The governing authority is a body elected by the citizens within that jurisdiction. Public agencies focus on community services to their jurisdictional constituency, who pay taxes, which is the primary funding source for these services. There are two types of services:

1. Natural environment areas, such as parks, forests, water bodies, (see chapter 6)
2. Recreation, including services for special groups, such as the military, correctional institutions, and hospitals (see chapters 7 and 11)

TABLE 5.1 Delivery Systems and Facets

Sponsoring sector	Setting	Population segment	Service modality
Public agencies • Governments (local, state, federal) • Schools • Institutions	Natural environment • Parks • Forests • Water bodies • Other natural areas	Ages • Children • Youths • Young adults • Adults • Seniors • All ages across life span	Program fields • Fitness and wellness • Recreational sports • Arts and culture • Social recreation • Outdoor (nature oriented) and adventure
Nonprofit associations • Human-service agencies (e.g., YMCA, YWCA, Boy Scouts, Girls Scouts, Boys and Girls Clubs, 4-H) • Private, nonprofit agencies (e.g., athletic clubs, country clubs, social clubs)	Institutional • Hospitals • Correctional institutions • Colleges • Churches • Military bases	Types • Youth at risk • People with disabilities • Ethnic and cultural groups • Lower-economic groups • All types	Operational management fields • Risk management, safety, and security • Public relations and marketing • Business and financial management • Facility design and operation
Private for-profit enterprises • Business and commercial enterprises • Tourism related	Building centered • YMCA, YWCA • Boys and Girls Clubs • Athletic clubs • Recreation centers • Museums General community • Community centers • Other public recreation and park settings		

This activity is building centered, is specific to seniors, and is sponsored by a nonprofit association.

The second primary sponsoring sector is **non-profit associations,** of which there are two types, each with a different focus and membership structure: human-service agencies and private nonprofit agencies. The **human-service agencies** include the YMCA, YWCA, Boy Scouts, Girl Scouts, Boys and Girls Clubs, and 4-H. They often are referred to as voluntary agencies, and most receive United Way funds as well as receive limited membership fees and donations. Services are offered to members, but membership is widely available to targeted populations with specific needs. They rely heavily on volunteers. The **private nonprofit associations,** including country clubs and athletic clubs, provide specific services to members who pay to join and receive these services (see chapter 8).

The third sponsoring sector is the **private for-profit enterprise,** which includes business and commercial enterprises and tourism. The focus is on profit, and this sector emphasizes marketing and consumerism, offering a product or service to customers for a price (see chapter 9).

The foregoing sectors are the most common; however, unique **closed** or special groups, a fourth sector of sponsorship, could be added, although the groups may fall within one of the other three sectors. This sector focuses on colleges for their students, industries for their employees, and religion-affiliated organizations not only for members but also for those whom they are seeking to gain as members.

The objectives of services include health and fitness and enjoyment (see chapter 11).

SETTING

Recreation and leisure service modalities can take place in one of four types of settings:

1. The **natural environment,** of course, is the setting for local, state, provincial and national parks; forests; and water bodies. Resident camps and adventure and challenge activities and trips also take place in the natural environment.

2. **Institutional settings** include facilities for "closed" populations such as mental and rehab hospitals and correctional institutions or "special" populations such as colleges, industries, churches, and military.

3. **Building-centered settings** include YMCA and YWCA, Boys and Girls Clubs, athletic clubs, recreation centers, museums, and commercial businesses.

4. **General community** settings include community centers and other public recreation settings such as parks.

Although these are the principal settings, services can be provided in other types of settings.

POPULATION SEGMENT

Providers in this delivery system offer programs and activities to different homogeneous population segments. Some of these segments are related to age, such as children, youths, young adults, adults, and seniors, while others are inclusive across the life span (see chapter 12). Other segments are categorized by the type of group such as youth at risk, various ethnic and cultural groups, people of lower-economic status, and people with disabilities; the services are targeted toward the special needs of each group (see chapter 10). The services may be provided in institutions or in a community setting.

People are usually more comfortable with and relate better to certain groups and find certain services more gratifying than others. For example, some people prefer working in youth

Courtesy of Craig Ross

Fitness and wellness is just one program field that can be delivered in any setting by any sector. The commonality of all sponsoring sectors, settings, and population segments is activity.

development programs, others enjoy providing rehabilitation to a particular group, and others would rather provide entertainment and enjoyment. Because population segments are diverse, recreation and leisure service professionals have the opportunity to work with the group and services that they find most gratifying.

SERVICE MODALITY

To the participant, the most important aspect of recreation and leisure is the activity in which he or she is engaged, regardless of its objective. In fact, the service modality of *all* sponsoring sectors, settings, and population segments is activity. These activities link the different systems. All activities, when properly conducted, can be provided by any sector in any setting to any segment. These include **program fields** such as recreational sports, arts and culture, fitness and wellness, social recreation, and nature-oriented and adventure recreation (see chapters 13-17).

Two functions must be fulfilled when offering an activity: direct leadership and supervision. Direct leadership is conducting the actual activity, while supervision is helping develop the service modality or program field (aquatics supervisor, fitness supervisor, and trip coordination are all types of supervision). Some professionals may perform both functions. Recreation and leisure professionals must be aware of the importance and difficulty of providing direct leadership and understand the relationship between the service modality (activities) and different population segments.

A second aspect of the service modality is **operational management.** Recreation and leisure professions concerned with operational management include risk management, safety, and security; public relations and marketing; business management; and facility facilitation, design, and operation. These important professional positions are essential to the proper administration of service modalities and are well suited to people who want to work in the recreation and leisure environment but do not want to conduct

One aspect of the service modality is operational management where a professional is involved in facility design and operation.

(direct leadership) activity or supervise the service modality.

THE PROFESSION

The multifaceted delivery systems provide unparalleled professional opportunity to people wanting to serve in the recreation and leisure profession. Career decisions should embrace life philosophy, professional goals, the nature of the people with whom you wish to work and in what setting, enjoyment of an activity, and gratification in rendering service. In selecting your desired professional position, you will select a facet for each delivery system. Figure 5.1 depicts the choices within each of the four delivery systems.

1. In which sponsoring sector do you wish to be employed? The sponsorship choices provide opportunities in accord with your philosophy, for example, public service, nonprofit human service, business for profit.

2. In which setting would you prefer to work?

3. With which population segment are you comfortable and able to work? With which groups do you find it gratifying to work?

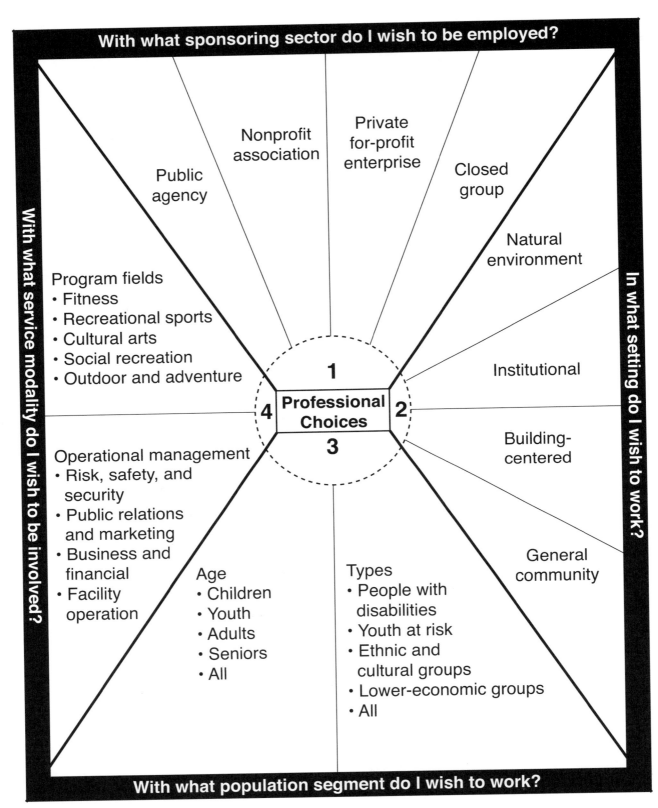

FIGURE 5.1 Professional choices.

4. What type of service modality do you particularly enjoy—a program field or operational management field?

After answering these four questions, you should have a good idea of what sort of position in the recreation and leisure profession you'd like to pursue. Table 5.2 illustrates several combinations. For example, a school may serve the youth at risk in the community through service projects. Or, a local government may have a recreation center in which it provides social recreation activities for senior citizens. Or, a nonprofit YMCA may have a pool in its building with swimming activities for all ages.

The professional position opportunities are wide open, and you can move within a delivery system. For instance, a person skilled in aquatics can use that service modality in any facet of other systems. For example, nonprofit human-services agencies like the YMCA may have a pool that services all membership (children, adults). Similarly, local government may have a swimming pool also serving all of its constituency, and may also have special therapeutic sessions for seniors with heart conditions. A hospital may have a pool for therapy and rehabilitation purposes. Remember that no delivery system is exclusive and that each usually involves aspects of others.

Professional organizations can help you get started and then help you develop professionally. You will want to participate actively in a professional organization to enhance your profession. Professional organizations may focus on a sponsoring sector, a setting, a population segment, or a service modality. See table 5.3.

SUMMARY

With the great diversity in the delivery of recreation and leisure, individuals interested in the profession have many choices—choices within each delivery system—and thus should be able to find a combination to meet their interests. The rest of part II covers the sponsoring sector and population segments in detail to help you determine your interests. Part III covers the service modalities and ends with a chapter on being a professional to help you make decisions about your career path.

TABLE 5.2 Facet Combinations From the Four Delivery Systems

Sponsoring sector	Setting	Population segment	Service modality
School	Community	Youth at risk	Service projects
Local government	Building (recreation center)	Seniors	Social recreation
Government institution (military base)	Building and fields	Military and families	Recreational sports and social recreation
Nonprofit (human services) YMCA	Building with pool	All ages	Swimming
Private, nonprofit (athletic club)	Building	All ages	Health and fitness
Private, for profit: commercial (white-water rafting)	Natural environment (river)	All (groups and individuals)	Outdoor (natural) rafting
Private, nonprofit hospital	Building	Individuals with disabilities	Rehabilitation therapy
Federal government	Parks	All	Interpretive services (nature-oriented activities)
Nonprofit (churches)	Building and natural area (camp)	All	Nature-oriented activities, social recreation, religious activities
State institution (college)	Recreation center and fields	College age	Recreational sports, fitness and wellness
For profit: tourism	Community	Community and visitors	Festival, cultural, historical, points of interest

TABLE 5.3   Professional Organizations

Focus by system	Association	Web site
SPONSORING SECTOR		
Public agency [government] (local)	American Park and Recreation Society (APRS), a branch of NRPA	www.nrpa.org/content/default.aspx? documentId=525
Public agency (institutions)	American Zoo and Aquarium Association (AZA)	www.aza.org
Nonprofit association	Society for Nonprofit Organizations	www.snpo.org
Private, for profit: tourism	Travel and Tourism Research Association (TTRA)	www.ttra.com
SETTING		
Natural environment (parks)	National Association for Interpretation (NAI)	www.interpnet.com
Institution (industry)	Employee Services Management Association (ESM)	www.esmassn.org
POPULATION SEGMENT		
Age (children)	Child Life Council, Inc. (association for child life and therapeutic recreation professionals)	www.childlife.org
Type (individuals with disabilities)	National Therapeutic Recreation Society (NTRS), a branch of NRPA	www.nrpa.org/content/default.aspx? documentId=530
SERVICE MODALITY		
Intramural and recreational sports	National Intramural-Recreational Sports Association (NIRSA)	www.nirsa.org
Adventure and challenge programs	Association for Experiential Education (AEE)	www.aee.org
Fitness and wellness	International Health, Racquet and Sportsclub Association (IHRSA)	www.ihrsa.org

For a detailed look at professional organizations, please see Betty van der Smissen, 2005, *Recreation and parks: The profession*, Champaign, IL: Human Kinetics.

CHAPTER 6

Parks in Canada and the United States

Stephen M. Holland and Paul F.J. Eagles

Courtesy of Paul F.J. Eagles

I would feel more optimistic about a bright future for man if he spent less time proving he can outwit Nature and more time tasting her sweetness and respecting her seniority.

E.B. White, Pulitzer Prize–winning 20th-century American writer

The day will come when the population of Canada will be ten times as great as it is now but the national parks ensure that every Canadian…will still have free access to vast areas possessing some of the finest scenery in Canada, in which the beauty of the landscape is protected from profanation, the natural wild animals, plants and forests preserved, and the peace and solitude of primeval nature retained.

James Harkin, 1912, Dominion Parks Commission for Canada, director of the first national park agency in the world

CHAPTER OBJECTIVES

After reading this chapter, you should be able to do the following:

- Understand the history and development of Canadian and American park systems, as well as their similarities and differences
- Know the distinctions between different levels of parks
- Know the names and accomplishments of a few of the most prominent individuals who promoted and created parks through history
- Understand current issues and trends in park resources management
- Understand distinctions between preservation, wilderness, conservation, multiple use, and wise use of natural resources and parks
- Understand a few career opportunities in park settings

INTRODUCTION

Parks are important parts of the cultures of Canada and the United States. Just mentioning a national park, wildlife refuge, or wilderness evokes strong feelings among citizens and foreign tourists. This chapter presents the history and description of the major park systems in the United States and Canada.

Three of the earliest parks in the United States and Canada were developed around hot springs: Hot Springs National Park in Arkansas in 1832, Yellowstone National Park in 1872, and Banff National Park in 1885. In each case, the government developed hot springs for the purpose of public bathing, a practice with roots in ancient Rome. These parks illustrate the link between health and government actions in early park development in North America. Today, parks are still places for people to retain and renew physical, emotional, and spiritual health.

This chapter contains two major discussions. First is an outline of the situation in Canada. Second is a similar outline for the United States. This is followed by a summary and comparison between the countries.

HISTORY OF PARKS IN CANADA

Canada is a large country composed of 10 provinces and three territories. It was created when four British colonies came together to form a country through confederation in 1867. Over time, other colonies joined to create new provinces, and other provinces were created from territories. As the country grew, the provinces retained considerable land management responsibility. One important power was the ownership and management of all crown land, or public land as it is called in the United States. Because the provinces legally owned the crown land within the provincial boundaries, it was relatively easy for them to create parks (see table 6.1). Conversely, it was difficult for the federal government to create parks within provinces, because it required provincial cooperation. Therefore, it is important to note that some of the **provincial park** systems in Canada are as large and prominent as the **national park** system in the United States.

First Parks in Canada

The first parks created in Canada were in cities. The movement to form city parks was strongly influenced by the British experience in England. The large, green central parks of London, for example, were well known to the populace of Canada and became a model for park creation in British North America.

In 1763 the lieutenant governor of the British colony of Nova Scotia granted the Halifax Common, former military land, to the city of Halifax. It was first used as community pasture and for military exercises. The Halifax Common later became city parkland and is now located in the heart of the city. It is recognized as the first park in Canada.

Toronto was the first city in British North America to formally create urban parks and a public agency to manage these parks. After eight years of operation, Toronto's Committee on Public Walks and Gardens, the name of Canada's first park management agency, took political action in front of the elected city council to promote the idea of urban parks. The chairman of the committee spoke at a Toronto City Council meeting in 1859 and stated the following:

TABLE 6.1   Land Ownership in Canada

Province	Total area*	Federal**	Provincial**	Private**
Newfoundland	371,690	0.7	94.9	4.4
Prince Edward Island	5,660	0.8	12.1	87.1
New Brunswick	72,090	3.0	42.9	54.1
Nova Scotia	52,840	2.9	29.8	67.3
Quebec	1,356,790	0.2	92.1	7.7
Ontario	891,190	0.9	88.0	11.1
Manitoba	548,360	0.8	78.0	21.2
Saskatchewan	570,700	2.4	57.7	37.9
Alberta	644,390	9.6	62.6	27.8
British Columbia	929,730	0.9	93.3	5.8
Yukon Territory	478,970	99.9	0.1	0.03
Northwest Territories	3,293,020	99.9	0.08	0.002
TOTAL				
Canada	9,215,430	40.3	50.0	9.7

* Area in square kilometers

** Federal, provincial, and private land in percentages. Much of the land designated as crown land is owned and used by aboriginal peoples.

In the first place, they furnish to the wealthy places of agreeable resort, either for driving or walking, and free from exposure to the heat and dust of an ordinary road . . . thus enabling them to enjoy the inestimable blessing of the free open air of the Country—so conducive to the promotion of health and morality.

In the second place, to the mechanic and working classes, Public Grounds are of incalculable advantage. How much better it is for the families of such to have these places of recreation and healthful exercise, than to have them exposed on the crowded streets of the city? (as cited in McFarland, 1982, p. 16)

As seen in this speech, the committee assumed the responsibility for providing "public grounds" for all classes of society, and especially for the working class who badly needed access to "places of agreeable resort," free of charge. This public-spirited and socialistic approach to parks—public use subsidized by community taxes—became a fundamental aspect of park management in Canada. Over the next 150 years virtually every city and town in Canada created parks for the welfare, use, and health of their citizens. The municipalities funded these parks from income earned by **land taxes** and provided most of the parks and their facilities free to the local citizens.

In the initial days, city parks were managed by volunteers. Starting in the early decades of the 20th century some staff members were hired to manage special facilities, such as agricultural fairs and sports grounds. It was not until the 1960s that universities and colleges in Canada started to train people specifically for working in parks and recreation in cities. The first program of this type in Canada was the Department of Recreation at the University of Waterloo, which admitted its first students in 1968.

The origin of national and provincial parks can be traced to the 1880s and occurred simultaneously in Niagara Falls in Ontario and on the remote mountain pass of the Bow Valley in the Northwest Territories of western Canada.

From the beginning of European settlement, Niagara Falls attracted tourists. Because the Niagara River and Niagara Falls are located in both the United States (New York) and Canada (Ontario), cross-border discussions were necessary for determining how to manage this wild but promising tourism development. The Canadian side of the river had the best view of the falls, and by 1885 every possible view was privately owned, with entrepreneurs charging fees for visitors to enter their premises to look out windows at the magnificent waterfalls and cataracts. One planning idea proposed by parties in New York in the early 1880s was to create reserves and organize tourism management institutions to develop public parks and foster cooperation between the two countries. Ontario adopted the idea and asked the Canadian government to fund and operate the Canadian portion of a park and tourism reserve. The idea was to create a national park on the Canadian side of the river by buying out all of the private properties and replacing them with a properly designed park and tourism facility to replace the ad hoc and exploitive private development. The vast expense of the proposed land purchase and park development incited opposition from members of Parliament from the province of Quebec and the Maritime Provinces. They objected to potentially large amounts of federal money being spent in Ontario on this development. In 1885 Ontario moved alone to create a major park and tourism facility along the Niagara River and Niagara Falls (Seibel, 1995). This involved the purchase and removal of thousands of buildings on the lip of the falls and the gorge and the creation of a green parkway available for all to use. The Ontario Parliament also passed legislation for the creation of the Niagara Parks Commission, a park and tourism management body.

The Ontario provincial government actions at Niagara set precedents in three important areas. First, Niagara was the first park created by a provincial government in Canada and had the first stand-alone park management agency with its own legislation and mandate. Second, it stimulated the creation of future parks in Ontario by the provincial government, not the national government. Third, it set a tone of American–Canadian cooperation in park management. All three movements continued and strengthened in subsequent years—this textbook is just one example of the ongoing sharing of ideas and cooperation in park management.

Simultaneous to the debates over Niagara in Ontario, the government of Canada pushed the first national cross-country railway through the Rocky Mountains. When hot springs were discovered near the railway tracks in the Bow Valley in the eastern Rockies, the potential for tourism was quickly recognized. The national government acted through a cabinet order in 1885 to reserve the hot springs for public use. This was followed in 1887 by formal federal legislation to create Rocky Mountains Park, Canada's first national park, later renamed Banff National Park. This national government activity started the federal government of Canada in the parks business. Rocky Mountains Park in Canada became the third national park in the world, after Yellowstone National Park in the United States, created in 1872, and Royal National Park in the British Colony of New South Wales, now a state of Australia, created in 1879 (Marty, 1984).

In 1887, Canada's federal government created North America's first wildlife conservation reserve at Last Mountain Lake in the Northwest Territories, now Saskatchewan. This small reserve was established to protect the nesting and migration habitat of wildlife in the Canadian prairies (Foster, 1978). This reserve became the first of many national wildlife areas and migratory bird sanctuaries created by the national government in Canada.

In 1893, Ontario made the next important move by creating Algonquin National Park. This huge area of forested and rocky hills, lakes, and rivers became a forest conservation area and park. The government wanted to better manage the logging industry in this area, wanted to protect the headwaters of five important rivers, and wanted to stop the movement of farmers into the Algonquin highlands. This creation of a large conservation park by a provincial government was a first for Canada. It set a precedent for Ontario and for other provinces (Killan, 1993; Saunders, 1998). The name was changed to Algonquin Provincial Park in 1913, giving notice that the parks operated by provinces were unique and separate from those operated by the national government.

By 1900, the die was cast in Canada, the initial debates and decisions coalesced into precedents that would guide future park creation and management across the country. After this date, cities and towns throughout the country saw park creation as a normal and expected activity. Provincial governments created regional parks for specific tourism and resource management concerns in regional geographical areas. Provincial parks were increasingly created for **conservation** and tourism purposes. Two types of federal reserves were established: national parks and national wildlife areas. The signing of the Migratory Bird Treaty with the United States in 1916 gave the federal government a powerful tool to regulate waterfowl and bird hunting. The treaty also gave this government the power to deal with wildlife management all over the country.

Over the next century, these emerging approaches strengthened and deepened. Many more parks and reserves were created. Management institutions were created. Canadians used and appreciated these areas in increasing numbers. In the 20th century, parks became a central part of the life of all Canadians and were to become a major part of the culture of the country.

In Canada, the provincial governments do not have formal roles in the creation or management of long-distance hiking trails. However, Canada has a large number of long-distance hiking trails, all of which are operated by nongovernmental organizations, typically called trail clubs. The oldest trail is the Bruce Trail in southern Ontario. It runs along the Niagara Escarpment from Niagara Falls in the south to Tobermory in the north on the Bruce Peninsula. This trail was opened in 1967—Canada's centennial. Initially the trail was almost entirely on private land. However, over time many landowners have denied public use of their land, so the trail is now on a combination of private land, park land, and land owned by trail clubs. The Canadian long-distance trail movement was heavily influenced by earlier trail activities in the United States.

The most ambitious trail effort in Canada is the Trans Canada Trail. The creation of this trail is ongoing and the goal is to have a national trail from Newfoundland across Canada to the west coast, including a branch north to the Yukon, for a total length of 18,078 kilometers (11,234 miles). The trail also includes a water route from central Alberta to the Arctic Ocean.

Canada has a system of national heritage rivers. This system is cooperatively managed by the provinces and by the federal government. The system contains 38 rivers, 4 of which are in the process of designation. The goal of the system is to promote, protect, and enhance Canada's river heritage and to ensure that Canada's leading rivers are managed in a sustainable manner. The system has no legal mandate and is entirely cooperative among governments.

Wilderness in Canada: 1600-2005

In Canada, the concept of establishing large areas of uninhabited area as wilderness is largely restricted to national and provincial parks. This situation is markedly different from that in the United States. In summary, in Canada aboriginal land rights are respected, meaning that the creation of parks or wilderness sites involves negotiation with aboriginal peoples. In Canada, outside of some parks, all land is owned and managed by people—aboriginal people. There is very little land that is considered vacant. A summary of the history of this situation follows.

For political and military reasons, the British government formed alliances with many of the aboriginal groups that lived in the area that is now Canada. One of the major reasons for these alliances was the concern shared by the British government and the aboriginal peoples of the expansionist nature of the United States to the south. Shared actions were in both their interests in order to preserve independence. Since the British needed the military prowess of the many aboriginal people, their land rights were recognized and supported. Therefore, the wilderness in Canada contains aboriginal people. It was a living landscape composed of forests, rivers, wildlife, and native people. In the United States, the situation was much different: Native people were removed from the land and placed into reservations, thereby creating the misconception that the area was wilderness, land without people. Therefore, there was never widespread support in Canada for the classical American view of wilderness, large expanses of land without people. Canada's wilderness contains people. These are the substantive reasons that the American concept of wilderness, out of national parks, has never gained much traction in Canada.

Important People in Canadian Parks

During the 1870s and 1880s, Sir Sandford Fleming was the engineer in charge of the construction of the Canadian Pacific Railway, which was built to link the industrial eastern provinces through the open prairies to the west coast province of British Columbia. In an attempt to increase the use of his developing railway, Fleming proposed a series of national parks across Canada for the purpose of creating tourism demand and railway use. The discovery of thermal springs in the Bow Valley in the Rocky Mountains in 1883 provided an opportunity for the national government of Prime Minister John A. Macdonald to create the first of Fleming's proposed parks. Therefore, Sir Sanford Fleming, a railway engineer, and Prime Minister John A. Macdonald, a powerful politician, were central figures in the creation of Canada's first national park in 1885, now known as Banff National Park.

In 1887, the federal government of Canada created the first bird sanctuary in North America. Areas around Last Mountain Lake in the Northwest Territories, now Saskatchewan, were withdrawn from settlement and set aside for the breeding of waterfowl. The creation of this reserve was the work of Edgar Dewdney, then the lieutenant governor of the Northwest Territories. He feared that the extension of the railway into this area would destroy the wildlife habitat. The creation of this wildlife reserve set the precedent for the national government to set aside areas for wildlife conservation.

Starting in 1885, Alexander Kirkwood, a clerk in the Ontario Department of Crown Lands, lobbied

Courtesy of Paul F.J. Eagles

During the construction of the Canadian National Railway through the Rocky Mountains in 1885, hot springs were discovered. The railway encouraged the national government of Canada to create a national park in order to better stimulate and manage the hoped-for tourism boom. These hot springs were developed for tourism and represent the birth of the national park idea in Canada.

In 1911, the government of Canada created the Parks Branch and appointed James Harkin as the Dominion Parks commissioner, the first national park management agency in the world and Harkin the first director. Harkin was an aggressive supporter of park creation and management. He was a strong supporter of parks, wilderness values, and tourism. He set out to attract Canadians to national parks and to ensure that national parks were as important cultural icons as historic sites and art were in Europe. He was famously successful in his goals, and as a result, is recognized as the person who started the movement to make national parks the cultural icons that they are today.

These five people, Fleming, Macdonald, Dewdney, Kirkwood, and Harkin, set in motion ideas that resulted in Canada's national and provincial park systems. Two of these people were politicians and three were government employees. Although many of their ideas can be traced to England and the United States, they adapted them to Canadian reality. It is important to note the influence of politicians and government employees in this movement. This reflects that Canadian style of government, largely borrowed from Britain, involving a powerful and professional civil service reporting to elected politicians. Notably absent from the Canadian experience are writers, artists, and scholars. A possible exception to this rule is Sir Sandford Fleming, the railroad engineer, who was also a planner, author, and civil servant.

PARK SYSTEMS OF CANADA

By 1900, the form of the emerging park systems in Canada was set with four types of parks: city parks, regional parks, provincial parks, and federal national parks and wildlife areas. All over the country towns and cities made park creation and management a normal role of government. In some provinces special regional park agencies were set up to manage parks, usually around geographical features such as rivers or lakes. All provincial governments moved forward in creating provincial park systems, often in active competition with the emerging national park system. The government of Canada worked slowly but diligently to add to the two major federal systems, the national parks and the national wildlife areas.

for the creation of a national forest and park in the Algonquin Highlands of southern Ontario. His idea slowly gained the support of other government officials, influential members of the community, and ultimately elected officials. In 1893, the government of Ontario created Algonquin National Park, later renamed Algonquin Provincial Park. This action created the first large provincial park in Canada based on the emerging American model of large, uninhabited wilderness reserves. This action set in motion events that resulted in the creation of thousands of provincial parks in all Canadian provinces.

City Parks

Parks are located in virtually every village, town, and city in Canada. They fulfill many functions, sport, recreation, and health being particularly important. In the 1980s, some cities added conservation of natural lands to these functions. Today, city parks are a mixture of recreation, parks, and green space.

Most city parks are managed by a parks and recreation agency that is part of the municipal government. This agency is responsible for facility construction, park maintenance, and recreation programs. Advisory groups, sports bodies, and volunteers are hallmarks of municipal parks and recreation management. Park management at the municipal level is operated by professional managers, specialized part-time employees, and many volunteers.

Land taxes pay for most municipal park management. Some recreation service fees are used for special-purpose activities, such as renting a community hall or paying for sport lessons. Therefore city park management is funded from a combination of taxes and use fees.

No national inventory of the number and size of municipal parks in Canada exists. However, the amount of land used for parks in cities varies from a small percentage of the city land area to nearly 40 percent. Examples include Stanley Park in Vancouver, a large natural park on the ocean near the downtown of the city; Victoria Park in Kitchener, a traditional city park of trees, lawns, gardens, and statues located downtown in the city; and Pleasant Point Park in Halifax, a park with impressive lawns and gardens.

Regional Parks

In Canada provincial governments often create regional park agencies to fulfill both conservation and recreation mandates. The province of Ontario has the most extensive system of regional parks in the country. Over many decades the Parliament of Ontario passed legislation to create regional park agencies to create and manage park systems in specific areas of the province. The Niagara Parks Commission manages parks in the Niagara River and Falls area, the St. Lawrence Parks Commission in the St. Lawrence River area, and the Lake St. Clair Parks Commission in the Lake St. Clair area. The Niagara Parks has one of the highest park visitation rates in the world, up to 16 million visitors per year. More recently the Ontario Parliament passed legislation to create regional planning bodies that coordinate the conservation and management of specific landscape features. The best example of this is the Niagara Escarpment Commission that coordinates planning and conservation over the Niagara Escarpment that runs through southern Ontario from Niagara Falls in the south to the Bruce Peninsula in the mid-north.

Unique in Canada, Ontario provincial legislation encourages and provides for the creation of 36 conservation authorities that manage watersheds in the populated areas of the province. Each of these local government authorities oversees a park system, largely composed of water management projects such as dams, river valley protection areas, and wetlands. Many of these conservation areas are close to large cities and are therefore important for providing outdoor recreation near urban areas. Ontario conservation authorities serve about five million **visitor days** of outdoor recreation each year.

Provincial Parks

Every province and territory in Canada has a provincial or territorial park system. However, the size and use of the systems vary considerably. Some provinces, for example British Columbia, Alberta, and Ontario, developed large and well-used provincial park systems. Other provinces such as New Brunswick, Newfoundland, and Prince Edward Island oversee small systems. These differences are due to the history and political cultures of each province.

The wealthier and more heavily populated provinces created large provincial park systems for the use of the middle- and upper-middle class members of their society, while concurrently discouraging federal efforts to create parks in their provinces. The poorer provinces encouraged the national government to meet the demand for parks by funding, creating, and managing national parks in their provinces. This ensured that federal tax dollars rather than provincial tax dollars were spent on parks in these provinces.

National Parks and Wildlife Areas

The national park system in Canada is large, popular, well funded, and growing. Because most Canadians have grown up visiting Canada's national parks or at least hearing about them and seeing them in the media, national parks in Canada have become national cultural icons. In the 1930s and 1940s, the mountain parks were backdrops for many popular Hollywood movies. This exposure created a positive profile in the minds of both

Canadians and Americans that helped create a boom in tourism that continues today.

As of 2005 Canada had 44 national parks and national park reserves. More national parks are proposed and are under land-claim discussions with aboriginal groups; therefore, more parks will be created in the coming years. Parks Canada, the federal park management agency, is responsible for four major park and reserve systems: national parks and reserves, national historic parks and sites, national canals, and national marine conservation areas. The Canadian Wildlife Service is responsible for two major park and reserve systems: national wildlife areas and migratory bird sanctuaries.

National parks in Canada are created according to a **system plan** that calls for at least one national park in each major biogeographic region of the country (see figure 6.1). This plan divides the entire country into 39 easily recognizable biogeographic regions, such as the Pacific Coast Mountains, the Prairie Grasslands, and the Hudson-James Bay Lowlands, to illustrate three examples. This approach is ecologically sound in that the park creation is based upon the existing biogeography of the country. This ensures that national parks are created in all regions of the country. Parks Canada was one of the first park agencies in the world to develop such a system plan. The system plan idea subsequently spread all over the world.

The number of national parks continues to increase in Canada as the demands of the system plan are fulfilled. Most of these new national parks are in the arctic and subarctic, but substantial new parks have recently been created in the populated southern area of British Columbia and Ontario.

The national parks attract approximately 26 million **person visits** per year. Because national park visitors tend to stay for more than two days each visit, the total number of visitor days is more than 50 million per year. The highly popular mountain parks of Banff, Jasper, Kootenay, and Yoho attract the most visitors. These four parks combined serve approximately 7 million person visits per year, or more than 15 million visitor days. Some of the remote northern parks receive very few visitors, with some recording less than 1,000 per year.

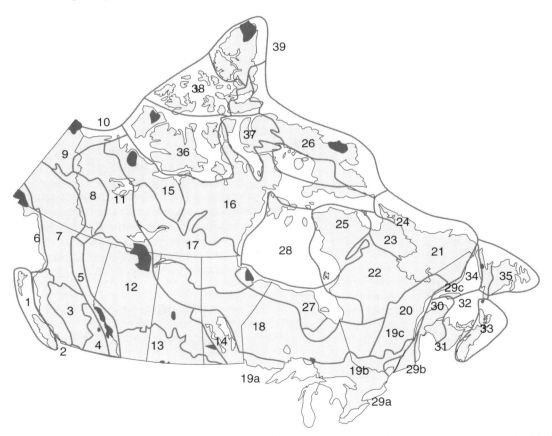

FIGURE 6.1   The Canadian National Park System plan divides the entire country into 39 easily recognizable biogeographic regions, such as the Pacific Coast Mountains (Natural Region 1), the Prairie Grasslands (National Region 13), and the Hudson James Bay Lowlands (Natural Region 27).

Canada also has an extensive system of national historic parks and sites. Historic sites are chosen according to a system plan of national historic sites. The goal of this plan is to represent the country's important historic and cultural themes within the park and site system. The plan has five themes:

1. Peopling the land
2. Developing economies
3. Building social and community life
4. Expressing intellectual and cultural life
5. Governing Canada

All historic sites and parks are commemorated within one of those broad themes. To be recommended for designation, a site, person, or event must have had a nationally significant effect on, or illustrate a nationally important aspect of, the history of Canada. Places designated as national historic sites are occasionally acquired by the federal government for protection and interpretation. Of the 849 national historic sites, Parks Canada administers 150 and contributes money to an additional 71 managed by other governments or organizations. Parks Canada serves approximately 10 million visitors per year at the 150 sites it manages. The number of yearly visitors to these sites varies dramatically, from 3.6 million person visits to the historic fortifications of Quebec City to a few hundred people visiting historic sites in the far north of the country.

Parks Canada also manages a series of historic canals. These canals were originally built for military purposes but are now used for recreation and are very popular with boaters. For example, the Trent-Severn Waterway in southern Ontario serves approximately 1.5 million person visits per year.

Recently, the Canadian Parliament passed legislation to create a system of national marine conservation areas. Parks Canada was given the responsibility to establish and manage these marine conservation areas off the Atlantic, Arctic, and Pacific coasts of Canada. Major reserves are also planned in the Great Lakes area. As of 2005, this system has only two such reserves, but many more are planned.

The Canadian Wildlife Service manages two large national systems: national wildlife areas and national migratory bird sanctuaries. The national wildlife area system in Canada is large, poorly funded, and not well known by the Canadian public. Fifty-one national wildlife areas are scattered across Canada. These sites are important for migratory birds, both for nesting and migratory stopover. The national wildlife areas have just

Courtesy of Paul F.J. Eagles

The Louisbourg Fortress National Historic Site interprets the colonial struggle between France and Great Britain for the possession of northeastern North America. This restored French city is the largest historic reconstruction in history. Canada, like the United States, manages national cultural sites within its national park management agency.

100,000 visitor days of use per year. The visitation rates at the 92 sites in Canada's national migratory bird sanctuary system are not documented and therefore cannot be reported.

Summary

The differences between the Parks Canada systems and the Wildlife Service systems are vast. The national parks, national historic parks, and heritage canals focus on both conservation and tourism. Canadians are encouraged to visit through excellent information sources, tourism facilities, and programs. As a result, the public profile is high, visitation is high, and the government responds with substantial funds. The wildlife areas, in contrast, focus on wildlife conservation. Recreation is not encouraged, with the exception of some hunting and fishing. As a result, the public profile is low, visitation is low, and the government provides very few management funds. This situation suggests that for a park system to obtain sufficient government funds to be managed effectively, it must have a positive public profile and must have a clientele that is mobilized to support the parks politically. Many people argue that a park or reserve with low visitation has fewer management stresses and therefore has more effective conservation. This position ignores the many stresses that occur in such a reserve besides recreation, including poaching, nearby resource extraction, illegal logging, destructive farming, all-terrain vehicle use, and many other resource-damaging activities. Such stresses can only be effectively curtailed if the reserve receives sufficient funds, staff, and political support. This example from Canada shows that without tourism the political support does not build up and therefore the government funds are not allocated, resulting in few or no management staff.

Canada has tremendous diversity in the approaches used in park management. The following are the institutions used:

1. A government agency funded largely from taxes (e.g., Parks Canada)

2. A stand-alone government agency that functions as a private corporation (e.g., the Niagara Parks Commission)

3. A government agency that has a few supervisory staff but uses private corporations to provide most of the public services (e.g., British Columbia Provincial Parks)

4. A nonprofit organization that functions as a private corporation and provides all park services (two national historic parks and some provincial parks in Ontario are operated using this approach)

5. A mixture of public agencies and private operations that use both public funding and tourism fees and charges (e.g., Ontario Provincial Parks)

This range of approaches in management is an important area of park management that requires further investigation by scholars in the parks and recreation field. This diversity of activity reveals that park managers of the future in Canada need to have a broad background in business as well as in cultural and natural resource management.

Over the last decade in Canada, park funding has varied amongst jurisdictions. For example, major reductions occurred in the budgets for provincial parks in Alberta and British Columbia. The large system in Ontario saw budget increases in accordance with large increases in parkland area and visitation (Eagles, 2005). The national parks saw major increases in budget along with substantial increases in the numbers of national parks. In all jurisdictions, there was a trend toward increased use of tourism fees and charges to fund part of the costs of parkland management.

It is important to understand that parks, reserves, and other types of protected areas exist because of the acceptance and approval of society and therefore of government. Therefore, for the sites to exist and to be effectively managed, there must be enough political support to counter the many societal forces that would see these lands used for other purposes. It is vital for parks to be used and appreciated by substantial numbers of citizens.

Canada has a large number of trails on abandoned railway lines. These function through local initiative and occasionally have weak support from the provincial governments. Nevertheless, as with the long-distance hiking trails, the rails-to-trails movement is very active and expanding entirely because of the initiative of hikers and other trail users.

HISTORY OF PARKS IN THE UNITED STATES

The history of parks in the United States illustrates a combination of concern for the social and psychological well-being of children and adults, the conservation and **preservation** of natural areas as the country developed and resource extraction and urbanization accelerated, and the evolution of natural areas as attractions that spurred opportunities for tourism business. Improvements in transportation, the rise of the middle class, the recognition of the need for workers to renew and refresh themselves, and the fascination with the natural world also increased the demand for parks and protected natural areas (Sears, 1980).

City Parks and Playgrounds: 1850 to 1930

Established in 1634, the Boston Common set a precedent that was later copied by cities all over the emerging United States of America. As the early American cities began to grow with the influx of immigrants, awareness grew of a need for public parks in the bustling, increasingly congested, and hygienically challenged cities such as Boston, New York, Chicago, and Philadelphia. Thus began a period from about 1850 to the 1930s when American cities built city parks and playgrounds for the public (Cavallo, 1981; Young, 2004). Most notable among these was Frederick Law Olmsted and Calvin Vaux's plan to landscape Central Park in New York City. Olmsted felt strongly about the concept of park access for people as a demonstration of democratic principles. Olmsted believed that parks, unlike other developed spaces in cities that were highly stratified by social class, could serve as meeting grounds for people of different backgrounds and classes. He also believed that great parks and open space in cities were evidence of the progressiveness of American democracy (Rybczynski, 1999). Olmsted went on to play a role in designing, planning, and building major city parks in or around Boston; Atlanta; Riverside, Illinois; Chicago; Buffalo; and Niagara Falls, New York. Through his sons and students, Olmsted had an influence on hundreds of city parks and college campuses. By 1905, spurred by the writings and actions of Joseph Lee and Luther Gulick, 24 cities had installed 87 playgrounds, and by 1917, 481 cities had created 3,940 playgrounds. In conjunction with this was the "muscular Christianity" movement (Putney, 2001), which loosened the Christian restrictions on physical activity for men, the YMCA movement (starting in 1845 in the United States), and the YWCA movement (starting in 1858 in the United States).

Federal Conservation Initiatives: 1900 to 1925

Early federal protection of natural areas dates back to 1832 when the federal government created the Hot Springs Reservation in Arkansas as a protected area for the use of native Americans, people traveling through on their way west, and local residents. It was later redesignated as a national park in 1921. Although the first national park in the world, Yellowstone, was designated by President Grant in 1872 in the territories of Montana and Wyoming, it was clearly an idea ahead of its time, made possible by the incredible confluence of natural features present at Yellowstone and the prescience of citizens such as Cornelius Hedges, Nathaniel

Langford, Ferdinand Hayden, Henry Washburn, and David Folsom, who led expeditions into the area in 1869 through 1871 and proposed creating a park. The idea also received considerable support from the corporate leaders of the Northern Pacific Railroad, who understood the park's potential to attract tourists (Runte, 1998). The seed of the idea for national parks had been sown but needed time and leadership to grow. Progress was at first slow; by the turn of the century, there were only five national parks and three of those were related to California redwood or sequoia forests.

Until the 1960s, the federal government purchased no national park areas. Before that, all national park areas had been designations from existing federal land (General Land Office public domain lands), transfers from other agencies (usually from national forest lands or in the case of historic sites, the army), or gifts from state lands (e.g., Everglades National Park). National parks had also been created through private-, citizen-, or state-funded purchases of private lands from lumber companies (e.g., Redwood National Park) or private owners to create parks such as Shenandoah, Great Smoky Mountains, and Grand Teton National Parks and deeded to the National Park Service.

Leadership came in the form of President Theodore Roosevelt, who launched federal leadership in conservation. In less than eight years as president he created the U.S. Forest Service; set aside 148 million acres (60 million hectares) as national forests, some of those against the wishes of powerful senators and timber interests; established the first federal **wildlife refuge** in the United States (Pelican Island, Florida, in 1903); created six national parks; and supported the passage of the Antiquities Act of 1906, which created 16 national monuments (including the Grand Canyon). Over the years presidents have used this Act to take bold conservation action. Although national forests were primarily viewed as a harvestable timber resource, more accessible and scenic areas were opened to outdoor recreation use. Two major figures were advisors to President Roosevelt: Gifford Pinchot, scientific conservationist and head of what became the USDA Forest Service and founder of the Society of American Foresters, and John Muir, ardent preservationist, Sierra Club founder, writer, and lobbyist for wilderness and parks (Ehrlich, 2000; Keene, 1994; Miller, 2004; Zaslowsky and Watkins, 1994).

Although the utilitarian conservation movement had become institutionalized by 1910 in the form of the Forest Service, Geological Survey, and the Bureau of Reclamation, there was no federal park agency to lead the charge for preservation of parklands or outdoor recreation. There were national parks but no organized effort or agency to manage them. The few federal parks were "managed" by the U.S. Army Cavalry and local park boards, usually made up of dedicated volunteers. C.S. Ucker, a chief clerk of the U.S. Department of the Interior, and James Harkin, the Dominion Parks commissioner for Canada, carried on a steady correspondence, consulting each other on mutual problems in park administration. The Canadian commissioner sent Ucker a copy of the 1911 Canadian Forest Reserves and Parks Act as well as copies of debates on the Forest Reserves bill, believing they would be of some help to the Americans in drafting their own national park legislation (Foster, 1978). After two years of lobbying for the creation of a National Park Service, Stephen Mather, a Chicago businessman, was named the first director of the National Park Service (NPS) after Congress passed the law creating the NPS in August 1916, which had been advocated for years by Frederick Law Olmsted, Horace McFarland, and Henry Barker (National Park Service, 2003). Over time, Congress had created historic sites, army forts, battlefields, cemeteries, and monuments, many managed by the military branches. Congress transferred the management of these sites to the newly created National Park Service as well as the existing national parks and national monuments. Slow and steady growth in the number of sites occurred, but use waned during the Great Depression (1929-1939) and U.S. involvement in World War II (1941-1945). The Civilian Conservation Corps (1933-1941) employed about 3 million young men in many public works projects such as planting trees; stocking fish hatcheries; fighting forest fires; and building hundreds of park roads, trails, campgrounds, visitor centers, and water systems.

One other realm of conservation, wildlife, also benefited from federal action during this time. Historically, wildlife management had been the purview of the states, and by 1880 all states had passed some form of game laws. In 1894, the federal government passed the Yellowstone Park Protection Act, which made it a crime to hunt or remove wildlife from the park. In 1900, the Lacey Act prohibited the interstate transportation of any wild animals or birds killed in violation of state law. Teddy Roosevelt used executive orders to create 51 bird reservations during his presidency, and in 1905 also designated the Wichita Game Preserve

in Oklahoma. The signing of the Migratory Bird Treaty with Great Britain (on behalf of Canada) in 1916 gave the federal government a powerful tool to regulate waterfowl and bird hunting. In 1924, Congress acquired 194,000 acres (78,507 hectares) of Mississippi River wetlands, stretching for 284 miles (457 kilometers) in four states along the migratory bird route known as the Mississippi flyway (Vileisis, 1997; Zaslowsky and Watkins, 1994).

All of these efforts at creating protected natural areas, along with the increasing urbanization of the country, the increasing popularity of automobiles, and the expansion of the roads associated with them, starting in about 1910, gradually increased the pressure on national park and national forest managers to provide access, accommodations, campgrounds, and information for an increasing number of visitors (Belasco, 1979). The "See America First" patriotic movement generated public interest in America's natural wonders (Shaffer, 2001), and rangers began to expand their focus from protecting resources to accommodating and educating larger numbers of recreationists and visitors. This foreshadowed the massive expansion in travel and outdoor recreation that took place after the end of World War II.

State Park Initiatives: 1880 to 1925

Several states initiated efforts to protect natural areas for public use: Massachusetts' Great Pond Act (1641); Georgia's Indian Springs (1825); New York's off-and-on attempts to protect the scenic attributes of Niagara Falls, culminating in state acquisition in 1885; and California's failed attempt to support a Yosemite State Park, starting in 1864. In the 1800s the concept of natural-area parks was new, the mechanisms and skills to manage them were still forming (mostly through trial and error), and the support of Congress or state legislatures was often unsubstantial and sporadic as the years passed. According to Landrum (2004), in addition to Niagara Falls, other early **state parks** that have remained successful are Texas' San Jacinto Battleground State Historic Site (1883), Minnehaha Falls Park (1885) and Itasca State Park in Minnesota (1891), Miller State Park in New Hampshire (1891), and New York's Adirondack State Park (1892). The story of each state park typically involved local proponents who were persistent and creative in garnering support. Stephen Mather, as the new director of the National Park Service in 1916, saw one of his challenges to be maintaining the quality of the national park system. He was concerned about attempts to designate parks of little national significance as national parks, and he became a prime sponsor of a national conference in 1920 that promoted the idea of a system of parks that would come under the domain of each state. Although it is unclear who proposed it, the idea of creating a park every 100 miles (the distance that automobiles at that time typically traveled in a day) for the public to enjoy and camp in appeared, and it was suggested that this goal was clearly more appropriate for state parks to fulfill (Landrum, 2004). The idea developed that state parks should preserve representative environments, preferably scenic or historical and cultural sites, typical of each state to provide outdoor recreation areas closer to home for local residents and for tourists.

Trail Initiatives: 1930s, 1960s, and 1970s through 1990s

Native American, wagon train, and cattle drive trails are an important part of U.S. history. In 1921,

Benton MacKaye, a forester and planner, proposed a foot trail along the Appalachian ridges from the highest mountain in the north, Mount Katahdin in Maine, to the highest peak at the southern end, Springer Mountain in Georgia, passing through 12 other states along the way. The approximately 2,150-mile (3,460-kilometer) Appalachian Trail was completed in 1937.

Public interest in outdoor recreation waned some in the 1930s and 1940s because of the Depression and World War II, but interest began to grow again in the 1950s and 1960s with the baby boom generation. Interest in visiting America's parks, camping, hiking, boating, canoeing, and rafting grew dramatically. This affected almost every aspect of the growing park movements discussed so far, but in this context, led to the National Trails Systems Act of 1968, which gave the National Park Service the responsibility of overseeing the Appalachian Trail and provided funds to start the process of purchasing the entire trail and buffering it where possible with federal land. It also designated three types of trails: national recreation trails; national scenic trails; and connecting, or side, trails. The

© AP/Wide World Photos

The Appalachian Trail is a U.S. national scenic trail. Hikers walk part of the Appalachian Trail atop Mount Greylock in Lanesboro, Massachusetts, the state's highest peak at 3,491 feet (1,064 meters).

Act designated the Appalachian Trail and the Pacific Crest Trail, approximately 2,350 miles (3,782 kilometers) from the Mexican to Canadian borders along the mountain ranges of the Pacific Coast states, as national scenic trails. It also listed 14 other trails to be further studied as potential national scenic trails. In 1976, an amendment to the Act added nine more trails for consideration. In 1978, another amendment added a new category of trails: national historic trails. As of 2005, there were 8 national scenic trails (including Continental Divide Trail, Florida Trail, Ice Age Trail, Natchez Trace National Scenic Trail), 11 national historic trails (including Iditarod Trail, Lewis and Clark

National Historic Trail, Mormon Pioneer National Historic Trail, Oregon Trail, Santa Fe Trail) (see figure 6.2), and about 900 national recreation trails, most in or near urban areas.

Another form of "trail parks" is located along rivers. On the same day in October 1968 that the National Trails System Act was passed, President Lyndon Johnson signed the Wild and Scenic Rivers Act. For the first time, protected status could be given to free-flowing (not dammed) rivers, thereby assuring that white-water recreational opportunities could be protected. Three categories of rivers were established: wild rivers, scenic rivers, and recreational rivers. The differences were based

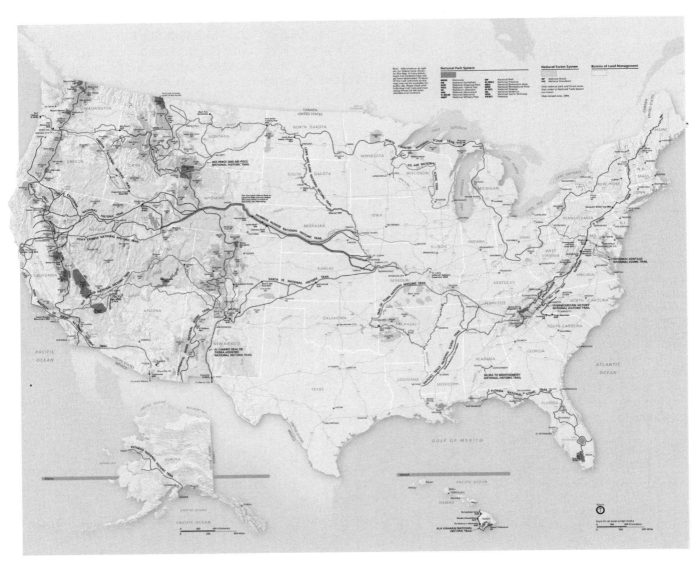

FIGURE 6.2   United States National Trails map.

Reprinted, by permission, from National Trails Partnership. Available: www.nationaltrailspartnership.org/map.asp

on different levels of access, primitiveness, and shoreline development, with wild rivers being the most pristine. In 2005, there were about 5,350 miles (8,610 kilometers) of wild rivers (more than half in Alaska), 2,480 miles (5,637 kilometers) of scenic rivers, and 3,503 miles (5,637 kilometers) of recreational rivers, all in 156 river units. Most rivers are managed by the agency that manages the land through which the river flows, usually the USDA Forest Service, National Park Service, Bureau of Land Management, or U.S. Fish and Wildlife Service (National Park Service, 2005c).

In 1983, Congress passed the Rails to Trails Act to facilitate the conversion of abandoned or unused railroad tracks and corridors into public trails. In the 1980s, President Reagan's Commission on Americans Outdoors (1987) recommended that communities and states promote "corridor" parks, and the Intermodal Surface Transportation Efficiency Act (ISTEA) of 1991 (and its successors, TEA-21 and TEA-3) provided funds for alternative transportation routes such as bicycle trails. These actions invigorated the rails-to-trails movement and other local trail-oriented programs that produced thousands of shorter walkways, bicycle–skateboard trails, and hiking trails, most in or near urban areas or connecting urban areas or previously unconnected parks (Rails to Trails Conservancy, 2005).

Wilderness: 1930s to 1970s

In the 1930s, farsighted pioneers detected that the American **wilderness** was a rapidly diminishing resource. A paradox was becoming apparent. Protecting an area by declaring it a national park virtually assured that roads would be built to and within that park, eventually thousands of people would visit it, and the characteristics of "wilderness" would be diminished or lost. In the 1960s, an oft-repeated phrase was that "Americans were loving their parks to death" as congested roads and campgrounds became the norm, at least in the summer vacation season or autumn leaf-color season. Early proponents of creating protected wilderness areas include Aldo Leopold, U.S. Forest Service scientist and the father of wildlife ecology; Robert Marshall, an environmental lawyer; Howard Zahniser, president of the Wilderness Society; and Hubert Humphrey, senator from Minnesota who sponsored four versions of the Wilderness Act over eight years. The forth amended version eventually passed Congress and was signed into law by President Lyndon Johnson in 1964 (Nash, 1982).

Because wilderness designation would permanently prohibit development, roads, timber removal, and motorized activities, this bill caused considerable concern among lumber interests, off-road-vehicle enthusiasts, and real estate developers. However, the Wilderness Act passed (in a compromise needed to pass the bill, previously existing grazing, mining, and a few administrative roads would still be operated and motor boats permitted in a few previously existing areas, and hydroelectric projects could be authorized by the president). The process of designating new wilderness areas has provided some of the most heated environmental battles in the second half of the 20th century. Especially controversial were the USDA Forest Service Roadless Area Review and Evaluation (RARE) process and the Endangered American Wilderness Act of 1978 and the 1980 Alaska National Interest Lands Conservation Act. The two acts were signed and engineered by President Jimmy Carter, doubling the size of the National Park Service and National Wildlife Refuge lands and tripling the size of designated wilderness. In 2000, there were about 662 wilderness areas. There are about 106 million acres (43 million hectares) of designated federal wilderness; 54 million of those acres (22 million hectares) are in Alaska. California, Arizona, Washington, and Idaho have the next largest area.

Era of Fiscal Restraint: 1970s to the Present Day

Starting in the 1970s, after the rapid growth in participation in outdoor recreation and the expansion of federal programs to accommodate this growth, a series of developments led to a leveling off and even decline of federal actions. A few initiatives were associated with the nation's bicentennial celebration in 1976: adding bicentennial parks around the country and the Urban Park and Recreation Recovery (UPARR) program, which provided federal assistance to counteract the decline in many urban areas by rehabilitating critically needed recreation and park facilities. Also during this time more female rangers and managers were hired to work in the federal parks. However, several factors such as the Watergate scandal, opposition to America's participation in the Vietnam war, and high inflation rates caused the public to become more skeptical of federal initiatives, including the management of federal lands. The increase in oil prices in 1973 and 1979 resulted in many park agencies experiencing tight budgets when dollars appropriated for conservation or visitor services needed to be spent on higher utility and fuel costs instead. In addition, with fuel costs increasing across the entire federal budget (e.g., military, agriculture, airline ticket prices, and so on), monies that might have been allocated to parks were shifted to other higher-priority agencies. This led to hiring freezes and program cuts. Many park visitor and nature centers undertook major efforts in energy conservation to save money as well as to act as demonstration areas to teach the public about energy conservation. With more of their budgets going to pay for energy costs and educational

efforts focusing on conservation, national parks had less money for traditional environmental educational programs or visitor recreation programs.

In 1978, Proposition 13 passed in California; it was a popular ballot initiative that placed a cap on property taxes. Initially, this had a substantial impact on funding for state and local parks in California, because it reduced local property tax revenues by approximately $6 billion (53%) virtually overnight by capping property tax rates at 1 percent and it made raising taxes more difficult by requiring state tax increases to receive the approval of two-thirds of the legislature and by imposing restrictions on the taxing authority of local governments. As has become typical in government priority lists, parks bore the brunt of budget cuts in deference to education, emergency services, and roads. Proposition 13 also sparked a taxpayer revolt nationwide, which assisted the election of President Ronald Reagan, who advocated similar reductions in tax rates in other states and within the federal government. President Reagan and his supporters believed that there was an adequate amount of federal parklands and that future parks should be acquired by state and local governments. However, with the tax revolt movement spreading across the country, it was impossible for local governments to increase taxes to acquire more parks or to increase services or facilities in existing parks. The practice of hiring private companies to perform some park jobs once done by park employees (privatizing), such as trash collection, vehicle maintenance, lawn care, and Web page development, became popular. The recent proposal to downsize the National Weather Service so that private companies can make a profit in providing weather predictions is a continuation of these efforts. President Reagan appointed James Watt to the position of secretary of interior. Watt was controversial and led a series of retrenchments of federal conservation actions such as eliminating the Bureau of Outdoor Recreation, greatly reducing the rate at which new federal lands were purchased for parks (proposing that it was more important to take better care of the parks we already had), and supporting the continuation of mining and drilling for oil on federal lands. During this time, a grassroots backlash, the Sagebrush Rebellion, began. Local proponents of private land rights and public access performed actions of civil (and

Parks are successful when competent, dedicated, and innovative employees manage them.

Courtesy of Paul F.J. Eagles

occasionally criminal) disobedience in opposition to various conservation actions on federal lands. The Reagan administration (1980-1988) instituted staff reductions in the land agencies and advocated state and local conservation initiatives, many of which were suggested by the 1987 President's Commission on American Outdoors report.

In the 1990s, there were few federal conservation initiatives or new park acquisitions because federal budgets were fairly tight. One bright spot was the Transportation Efficiency Act of 1991, and its successors the Transportation Equity Act for the 21st Century (1998) and the Efficient Transportation Equity Act of 2005, which designated that 10 percent of the allocations for highway construction be set aside for alternative transportation options such as mass transit and walking, biking, and horse trails. Many localities used these funds for rails-to-trails initiatives for corridor park trail system developments. In the 1990s, many federal agencies became better connected to and appreciated by local and state tourism promoters, and now partnerships abound between what used to be separate entities. Local tourism businesses began to understand better how their livelihood in ecotourism was based on quality parks (because they attracted tourists and their money) and became partners in supporting parks in Congress or state legislatures and in volunteering labor and services to assist parks. In 1996, Congress authorized the Recreation Fee Demonstration Program for the Forest Service, National Park Service, Bureau of Land Management, and U.S. Fish and Wildlife Service. The program allowed federal lands charging entrance fees to increase their fees and retain the additional funds to improve their recreation facilities and services. President Clinton, in the late 1990s, designated seven new national monuments. In 2001, a report titled "Rethinking the National Parks for the 21st Century" was released that recommended seven areas that the NPS should focus on for the next 25 years, including being more involved in education, especially of American history and native cultures, adopting biodiversity and sustainability as core principles, and collaborating with regional, state, and local parks to make an outdoor recreation network available to everyone (National Park Service, 2005a).

After the September, 11, 2001, terrorist attacks most federal parks had to divert a segment of their tight budgets to homeland security efforts, especially the National Park Service, which manages many high-profile monuments that could present symbolic targets for possible future attacks. The

cost of additional security patrols and adding law enforcement officers and metal detectors to the entrance of many park buildings often put a strain on other operations. Another area of concern is parks on national borders, such as Big Bend National Park in Texas and Organ Pipe Cactus National Monument in Arizona. Some believe that illegal aliens or terrorists could sneak into the country through these areas. Because of these concerns, some visitors stay away, park rangers have to be trained in law enforcement and border patrol strategies for 24-hour guarding, and time and money are spent more on security and less on visitor services or programs (National Geographic News, 2004). By 2005, with federal budget deficits growing and gasoline prices remaining higher than in the past, funding for park agencies and programs had decreased or remained level. President George W. Bush proposed not providing Land and Water Conservation grant funds to individual states. These funds have been used since 1965 to purchase parklands and develop facilities such as campgrounds, playgrounds, trails, and visitor centers (National Park Service, 2005b). And after several years, efforts by Congress to pass a Conservation and Reinvestment Act (CARA) to find a more permanent source of funding for outdoor recreation programs, with Congress and the outdoor industry proposing various changes, had still not passed. Some discussions have apparently occurred suggesting expanding privatization efforts in some additional National Park Service sites.

PARK SYSTEMS OF THE UNITED STATES

Most parks have been created on undeveloped lands and waters that the government has held since the land was taken from native peoples and reserved for public use or created on land not desired by private developers. Therefore, most publicly owned parks are managed by some level of the government. Similar to schools, public water supplies, or airports, parks are services that local, state, and federal governments provide their citizens for their benefit and enjoyment.

City Parks

Historically, city parks were created to address social problems by providing safe areas for children to play and soothing islands of green in which to escape from urban crowding, congestion, and concrete. Most city parks are smaller, closer to home, and more sport oriented than other kinds of parks. City parks, by definition, are owned, managed, and staffed by the city government they are located in, although there are exceptions such as the Illinois park districts, a few county-operated parks in urban areas, and some federally operated urban parks. City parks are frequently used in more varied ways than traditional resource-based state or federal parks. For example, city parks might provide swimming pools, concerts in the park, and concession stands, and they might allow dogs. Some even have small zoos, botanical gardens, or carnival-type rides. City parks usually are not concerned with maintaining natural resources in an undisturbed state; in most cases, the natural environment has already been heavily altered and the area artificially landscaped or designed. Therefore, the grounds are often heavily modified to provide amenities such as tennis courts, golf courses, swimming pools, fountains, paved walkways, ice-skating rinks, skateboard ramps, soccer fields, and playgrounds. Despite the less-than-pristine environment, city parks often provide inner-city children their first taste of a "natural" area (American Planning Association, 2003; Harnick, 2000; Taylor, Kuo, & Sullivan, 2001; Wals, 1994). The earliest academic programs in the United States to offer classes in recreation and playground management, primarily for city settings, were Springfield College in Massachusetts; George Williams College in Chicago in the 1880s; a series of professional training courses in recreation leadership offered by the Playground Association of America, starting in 1909; and Northwestern University in 1911 (VanDoren and Hodges, 1975).

City parks vary greatly depending on the size of the city. Some New England towns, such as Guilford and New Haven in Connecticut, have classic "greens." Town greens are common areas that were the first examples of urban planning in the United States in the 1600s, in which communally owned lands in the center of town are used as a meeting area, militia parade grounds, grazing area for livestock, marketplace, and burying grounds (Connecticut Trust for Historic Preservation, 2005). Some of the more classic, well-known, or unique city parks are Central Park in New York City; Boston Commons; Jackson Square in New Orleans; the Riverwalk in San Antonio, Texas; the town squares of Savannah, Georgia; Grant Park in Chicago; Phoenix's unusual mountain parks (including the largest city park in the United States, South Mountain Park and Reserve); and Water Gardens Park, in Ft. Worth. Several urban,

or city, parks are managed by the National Park Service, notably Rock Creek Park, the National Mall and famous monuments in Washington, DC, and Golden Gate Park in San Francisco.

City parks also play an important nonrecreational role in times of crisis. When hurricanes struck Florida in 1992 and 2004 and during some California earthquakes, city and county parks were widely used as food, shelter, and ice distribution points; information tables were set up in parks; and people reunited with each other in parks. This scenario has been repeated numerous times in many locations when wildfires, earthquakes, tornadoes, or floods have occurred; often city parks serve as staging or assistance centers. It has been said that there are no great cities without great parks, and when you think about locations like Washington, DC, Paris, London, New York, Sydney, Rio de Janeiro, Los Angeles, Boston, Vancouver, Chicago, and San Francisco, this does seem to be true (Tate, 2001).

County Parks, Regional Parks, and Park Districts

County parks are usually larger, more natural, less congested, and quieter. They are typically more oriented to activities such as swimming, hiking, boating, fishing, and sometimes camping that require a more natural setting than city parks. They are owned and managed by county governments and usually operated by county employees, although a recent trend for some counties is to subcontract park operations to a private operator or group such as the YMCA. County parks are larger and less oriented to urban uses than city parks but are not as environmentally sensitive, as restrictive in uses, or as large as most state parks. Some county parks have larger sport facilities than those found in city parks. Local school systems often conduct lessons in environmental education at county parks because they are typically close by, are easily accessible, and have parking. Fishing, sailing, canoeing, or water safety lessons are also conducted in county parks. In coastal states, many "beach parks," especially the more developed ones, are county parks.

Regional parks are similar to county parks, except that they may be managed by a partnership between a city and county government or by several counties. For example, if the shore of a reservoir or lake crosses into two or three different counties, cooperation among those counties is necessary for planning, financing, staffing, and programming activities that occur in the lake park. Rivers frequently serve as county boundaries; therefore, parks that span both sides of the river, boat launch ramps, or swimming areas may be located within a regional park. Regional parks typically serve residents of more than one county.

Illinois has set up park districts and forest preserve districts. These districts are specially designated areas (typically they do not follow city or county boundaries) with taxing authority. They function very much as a system of regional parks, often with a city at its core. Park districts operate facilities such as community centers, fitness centers, swimming pools, ball fields, indoor tennis courts, tracks, and basketball courts as well as natural areas. Another example of a park district is the Huron-Clinton Metropolitan Authority in the Detroit area. Five counties cooperate to manage regional preserves associated with the Huron and Clinton rivers as well as many more urban sport-related parks (Chubb & Chubb, 1981).

State Parks

State parks are typically more focused on preserving the natural characteristics of an area than on building facilities such as swimming pools, sport fields, or indoor recreation centers. Usually, they are more distant from urban population centers than most city or county parks, although in a few cases, the population centers have grown out to and around state parks that were remote when they were created. And in general, state parks are larger than most city or county parks. In 2002, there were 5,655 state parks in the United States (Landrum, 2004). New York had the most with 830, and Alabama, Kansas, and Nevada had the fewest with 24 each. Often state parks are associated with water bodies, have substantial wildlife populations, and are representative of key environmental ecosystems that characterize that state, such as beaches in Florida, deserts in Arizona, prairie in Illinois and Kansas, and mountains in California, Colorado, and New Hampshire. However, most state parks generally are not unique enough, scenic enough, or large enough, or they are not filled with enough features to qualify as a national park. In addition to highlighting natural areas, state parks also promote the state's historical figures or important events.

The character of state parks varies substantially. Some are similar to a large city park in a more natural setting and others are as wild or wilder than some national parks or forests. Adirondack State Park and Forest Preserve in New York, which has several small cities and many farms, private camps, and residential developments within its boundaries is the largest park in the lower 48 states (6 million acres [2.4 million hectares]), larger than even Yellowstone National Park (Adirondack State Park Agency, 2003). In contrast, the variety of amenities in Eugene T. Mahoney State Park, in a rural area south of Omaha, Nebraska, is more typical of a city park. It has a mechanical wave-generating outdoor swimming pool with water slides, a large indoor playground area with play equipment, well-furnished cabins, an ice-skating rink, a theater where dramatic plays are presented, a restaurant, a souvenir store, a conference center, a tower providing access to a scenic view over the tree canopy, and environmental programs on 690 acres (279 hectares) (Nebraska Game and Parks Commission, n.d.). Although this is a state park, it is not typical. Most state parks are of modest size, usually ranging from a few hundred to a few thousand acres, and provide basic facilities such as campgrounds, picnic areas, trails, visitor centers, and environmental education programs.

Several states have created what are called resort state parks. These are park destinations that provide the services you would expect at a resort, but they are located on state parklands and managed and funded by the state park service or corollary association, often with subcontracts to concessionaires. The Lake Barkley State Resort Park in Kentucky has a golf course, aerobic fitness center, swimming pool, tennis courts, small airport, cabins, lodge hotel, restaurant, and a marina (Kentucky State Parks, 2005). The resort state park idea has expanded to at least 12 states, many of them in the South (Alabama State Parks, 2005; West Virginia Division of Natural Resources, 2005).

In addition to state parks, most states, especially those in the East, also have state forests. Many of the forest areas have camping areas, hiking trails, and hunting areas. Many states, mostly in the Midwest and West, operate state fish and game or state wildlife management areas, which are usually available for various forms of outdoor recreation.

Federal Parks, Forests, and Refuges

Tracts of land not delegated to the states or claimed by private owners have been retained in federal ownership since the creation of the United States government in 1776. Much of this land was not suitable for agriculture or residential development or was eventually recognized as land that the public should have access to (public domain land). Rather than sell off all the land for private development, Congress considered it the government's duty to serve the people by protecting areas for uses such as parks, wildlife habitat, lumber production, flood control, and watershed protection. Although most of these areas were conserved for reasons other than recreation, recreational opportunities were often a side benefit. A variety of agencies were created to manage national parks, national forests, national resource lands, and waters and national wildlife areas (Zaslowsky and Watkins, 1994; Zinser, 1995).

National Parks

The National Park Service (NPS) has been a world leader in establishing the policies and operating procedures and in maintaining the character of unique and outstanding areas. The NPS operates under a principle of preservation and is funded by the U.S. Department of the Interior. The NPS manages both natural and historical areas that are of national or international importance and does its best to preserve them for the enjoyment of future generations while allowing some contemporary use. Maintaining a balance between allowing use and protecting and preserving resources is a constant challenge. Providing recreational opportunities that do little or no permanent harm to the park or its wildlife is one of NPS's prime missions. Many believe that the national park idea is one of the best ideas the United States has contributed to the world, and countries around the world have used the NPS as a model for their park systems (National Park Service, Office of International Affairs, 2005; Sellars, 1999).

With 388 National Park Service units, the national park system encompasses approximately 83.6 million acres (33.8 million hectares) and manages many categories of parks (see table 6.2).

With such diversity of areas, almost any imaginable form of outdoor recreation occurs in the national park system. These include mountain climbing, horseback riding, boating, camping, history reenactments at the sites where they occurred, hiking, white-water rafting, and driving and "windshield" sightseeing, especially during spring wildflower or fall leaf-changing seasons. The 270 million visitors annually to the national parks

TABLE 6.2 U.S. National Park Service Categories and Examples

Categories	Total number	Examples
National parks	57	Yellowstone, Grand Teton, Yosemite, Smoky Mountains, Grand Canyon, Rocky Mountain, Shenandoah
National monuments	74	Grand Portage, Bandelier, Craters of the Moon, Coronado, Fort Sumter
National preserves	17	Big Thicket, Big Cypress, Timucuan, Gates of the Arctic
National historic sites	77	First Ladies, Fort Davis, McLoughlin House, Carl Sandburg Home, Lincoln Home
National historical parks	41	Minute Man, Women's Rights, Valley Forge, Chaco Culture, Cumberland Gap
National memorials	30	Chamizal, African American Civil War, USS Arizona, Mount Rushmore, World War II, Flight 93
National military parks	9	Shilo, Gettysburg, Horseshoe Bend, Pea Ridge
National battlefields	15	Manassas, Fort Donelson, Cowpens, Antietam
National recreation areas	18	Gateway, Santa Monica Mountains, Golden Gate
National reserves	2	New Jersey Pinelands, City of Rocks
National seashores	10	Gulf Islands, Padre Island, Canaveral, Cape Cod, Point Reyes
National lakeshores	4	Pictured Rocks, Sleeping Bear, Apostle Islands, Indiana Dunes
National rivers	5	Buffalo, Big South Fork, New River Gorge, Mississippi
Wild and scenic rivers	10	Obed, Ozark, Rio Grande, Farmington, Salmon
National parkways	4	Baltimore-Washington, George Washington
National scenic trails	4	Natchez Trace, Potomac Heritage, Appalachian
International historic site	1	Saint Croix Island
No Designation	11	National Mall, Rock Creek Park, Catoctin Mountain, Wolf Trap National Park for the Performing Arts

make a significant contribution to the economy of the nation and especially to many rural areas that depend on the tourism that the national parks attract. Considerable adaptability and creativity are needed to manage these diverse areas, and expertise from many disciplines is needed across the system of parks. These disciplines include ecology, geology, archeology, military history, national history, fisheries, wildlife and resource management, forestry, outdoor recreation management, interpretation, business management, marketing, public relations, urban recreation programming, environmental education, alternative energy, public works, transportation management, tourism, law, and political science. The NPS also coordinates the Land and Water Conservation Fund, which is a program in which federal funds are distributed to the states and federal agencies for new or continuing park or conservation projects.

National Forests and Grasslands

The Forest Service was created in 1905 (although a Division of Forestry had been created in 1876 and Forest Reserves were authorized in 1891) and is an agency of the Department of Agriculture. The USDA Forest Service manages large forests and grasslands, mostly in the western states, and follows a basic conservation and **wise-use philosophy.** The agency's mission is to achieve quality land management under the sustainable multiple-use concept to meet the diverse needs of people. **Multiple-use management** means the USDA Forest Service areas should be used for outdoor recreation, range grazing, timber, watershed management, and wildlife and fish habitat. Providing recreational opportunities, which the agency tries to balance with the other uses, is a major focus of the Forest Service. Historically, the Forest Service gave priority to timber management but was induced over time through court cases, political pressure, and debates on wilderness to increase the outdoor recreation opportunities in the forests, especially since the 1960s. In 2002, more than 214 million people visited USDA Forest Service lands, waters, and recreation sites (USDA Forest Service, 2005).

Courtesy of Paul F.J. Eagles

In 1872, Yellowstone National Park was designated the first national park in the world.

There are 177 USDA Forest Service units (155 national forests and 22 national grasslands), totaling 192 million acres (78 million hectares) in 42 states (USDA Forest Service, 2002). National forests constitute 98 percent of USDA Forest Service lands. These include 403 national wilderness areas (35.2 million acres [14.2 million hectares]), 20 national recreation areas, 7 national monuments and preserves, and 9 national scenic areas; these last three designated areas total more than 7 million acres (3 million hectares). About 160 million acres (42.9 million hectares) are in the western United States, 47.5 million acres (19.2 million hectares) in the eastern United States, and 24 million acres (9.7 million hectares) in Alaska. The Forest Service also manages 136 scenic byways (9,126 miles [1,469 kilometers]), 95 wild and scenic rivers (4,418 miles [7,110 kilometers]), 133,087 miles (214,177 kilometers) of trail, 4,300 campgrounds, 135 alpine ski areas, 1,200 boating areas, and 1,500 picnic areas (USDA Forest Service, 2001; Zinser, 1995).

Wildlife Refuges

The U.S. Fish and Wildlife Service (USFWS) is part of the U.S. Department of the Interior. Its mission is to work with others to conserve, protect, and enhance fish, wildlife, and plants and their habitats for the continuing benefit of the American people. The service originated with the U.S. Commission on Fish and Fisheries in the Department of Commerce in 1871 and the Division of Economic Ornithology and Mammology in the Department of Agriculture in 1886. Renamed the Fish and Wildlife Service in 1940, its programs are among the oldest in the world dedicated to scientific wildlife conservation, though Canada had a wildlife conservation reserve in 1887. As of 2004, the service manages a 96-million-acre (39-million-hectare) national system of more than 545 national wildlife refuges (made up of 92.6 million acres) and thousands of small wetlands and other special management areas. Under the fisheries program it also operates 69 national fish hatcheries, 64 fishery resource offices, and 78 ecological services field stations (U.S. Fish and Wildlife Service, 2004a).

Most wildlife refuge areas are water related, either freshwater or saltwater, and therefore are often found along rivers, marshlands, or coastal areas. The primary focus of refuges and fish hatcheries is wildlife and fish habitat protection, promotion of breeding, and provision of safe refuge to animals. However, refuges permit secondary recreational activity as long as it is compatible with the primary purpose of the refuge and funds are available to administer it. Some may think it strange that hunting or fishing is permitted in wildlife refuges, but this is deeply rooted in the history of the service where much of the funding and support of wildlife refuges came from hunters and anglers when Congress expressed little interest in spending money on wildlife, birds, and fish. The hunting and fishing that occur are regulated, and in some areas control the populations of animals whose natural predators have been long removed. The primary recreational uses in wildlife refuges are day-use areas, visitor centers, **walk-in areas,** hiking trails, wildlife viewing sites, archaeological sites, wilderness areas, and motorized and non-motorized boating, hunting, and fishing. About 30 percent of refuges are not open to recreation; these are mostly in Alaska.

Key programs that facilitate the survival of wildlife and fish in the United States and around the world are enforcing federal wildlife laws, protecting endangered species, managing migratory birds, restoring nationally significant fisheries, conserving and restoring wildlife habitat such as wetlands, and helping foreign governments with international conservation efforts.

Other Areas Managed by Federal Agencies

In addition to the parks, forests, and refuges just discussed are other federal areas that are less well known, many types existing only in certain regions of the United States and usually providing fewer recreation programs and facilities. The Bureau of Land Management, U.S. Army Corps of Engineers, Tennessee Valley Authority, Bureau of Reclamation, and American Indian reservations manage these areas. They also include national wilderness areas and international peace parks.

National Resource Lands

The Bureau of Land Management (BLM) manages 264 million acres (106 million hectares) of land, about one-eighth of the land in the United States, more than any other federal agency (Bureau of Land Management, 2003). Most of the lands the BLM manages are located in the western United States, including Alaska, which contains 34 percent of BLM-managed land, and are dominated by extensive grasslands, forests, high mountains, arctic tundra, and deserts. The BLM manages a variety of resources and uses, including energy and mineral mining; timber; grazing; wild horse and burro habitats; fish and wildlife habitat; wilderness areas; and archaeological, paleontological, and historical sites.

BLM recreation management areas fall into three primary classifications. Extensive recreation areas are generally backcountry areas with minimal development of recreation facilities; BLM manages 180 areas totaling about 194 million acres (78.5 million hectares). Special recreation areas provide specific recreation facilities such as campgrounds, boat launch ramps, cabins, and environmental education centers. BLM manages 338 areas on 29 million acres (12 million hectares) of land or water. BLM manages 147 designated wilderness areas, totaling 6.2 million acres (4.9 million hectares). BLM reports about 68 million visitor days per year (Bureau of Land Management, 2002). Most of the land managed by BLM is desert and barren; however, some of the land contains lakes, rivers, and mountains, and some of it is very scenic. BLM lands contain trails, campgrounds, picnic areas, boating areas, visitor centers, horse-riding trails, and **ORV sites,** sustaining a variety of recreational pursuits (Top4x4sites, 2005), although uses in designated wilderness areas are restricted.

Wilderness Areas

Areas created under the 1964 Wilderness Act and the 1973 Eastern Wilderness Act are managed by the four federal agencies discussed earlier: Bureau of Land Management, U.S. Fish and Wildlife Service, USDA Forest Service, and National Park Service. These areas are open to the public for nonmotorized day or overnight recreation. Permits are usually required, and it's wise to get one so that a ranger will know to look for people if they fail to return when expected. These are truly wild areas; many have spotty cell phone service, if any at all; and there's little likelihood that a ranger will just happen to come across a party unless they are in a heavily used camp or on a popular trail. Here is a summary of the federal wilderness areas:

National Park Service—55 sites, approximately 43.7 million acres (17.7 million hectares) (85 percent in Alaska)

Forest Service—406 sites, approximately 34.9 million acres (14.1 million hectares) (17 percent in Alaska)

Fish and Wildlife Service—71 sites, approximately 20.7 million acres (8.4 million hectares) (90 percent in Alaska)

Bureau of Land Management—175 sites, approximately 7.3 million acres (2.83 million hectares) (none in Alaska)

Total national wilderness—677 sites, approximately 106 million acres (43 million hectares) (Wilderness Society, 2005a); only about 2.57% of the continental United States is designated wilderness (Wilderness Society, 2005b; Zinser, 1995).

These national wilderness areas are subareas of existing national parks, national monuments, national preserves, national forests, national grasslands, natural resource lands, or fish and wildlife refuges. For example, 86 percent of Everglades National Park is designated wilderness. Some states also have state-designated wilderness areas that are smaller than federal wilderness areas and tend to follow the same principles of "no development or motorized access."

U.S. Army Corps of Engineers Waterways

The Army Corps of Engineers is the steward of the lands and waters at corps water resources projects. The Army Corps of Engineers manages thousands of dams and flood-control projects across the country. Historically, the army has been involved in the defense of harbors and the prevention of invasion through rivers. This agency is part of the Department of Defense, but most of its employees are civilians. Its natural resources management mission is to manage and conserve natural resources consistent with principles of ecosystem management while providing public outdoor recreation experiences to serve the needs of current and future generations (U.S. Army Corps of Engineers, 2002).

The Army Corps of Engineers is the nation's largest provider of outdoor recreation, operating more than 2,500 recreation areas at 463 projects (mostly lakes and reservoirs) and leasing an additional 1,800 sites to state or local park and recreation authorities or private interests. The Corps hosts about 360 million visitors a year at its lakes, beaches, and other areas, and estimates that 25 million Americans (1 in 10) visit a Corps project at least once a year. Recreationally, the Corps manages campgrounds, boat launch ramps, fishing piers, marinas, bathrooms, and swimming areas. The Corps also manages the intracoastal waterway that provides boating opportunities across many states, including the operation of many drawbridges and locks (U.S. Army Corps of Engineers, 2002).

Tennessee River Valley

The Tennessee Valley Authority (TVA) is a federal agency but with a limited service area encompassing only seven states: Tennessee, Alabama, Georgia, Kentucky, Mississippi, North Carolina, and Virginia. President Franklin Roosevelt created the TVA during the Depression in 1933 as an innovative way to bring electrification, flood control, and economic development to an underdeveloped region. TVA is the United States' largest public power company, and because it manages a major river (650 miles long [1,046 kilometers]), many recreation opportunities are available on TVA-managed areas. Millions of people enjoy recreational activities on TVA reservoirs or rivers and adjacent land each year. The reservoirs and the 290,000 acres (117,357 hectares) of land surrounding them offer opportunities for recreational activities, including water skiing, canoeing, sailing, windsurfing, fishing, swimming, hiking, nature photography, picnicking, bird-watching, and camping. Recreation management has not been a major priority of TVA, and recently, it has begun minimizing the amount of active recreation management it does (Tennessee Valley Authority, n.d.). However, because of the water-related resources, millions of people still engage in recreational activities on areas managed by TVA.

Large Western Reservoirs

Across the arid western states, water management became a critical focus as the population in these areas grew. In 1902, Teddy Roosevelt established the Bureau of Reclamation (BOR). This agency is part of the U.S. Department of the Interior and is best known for the dams, power plants, and canals it has constructed in 17 western states. These water projects led to homesteading and promoted the economic development of the West. The mission of BOR is to manage water and water-related resources in the western United States in an economically and environmentally sound manner for the American people. The bureau has constructed more than 600 dams and reservoirs, including massive Hoover Dam on the Colorado River and Grand Coulee on the Columbia River. It is also the second largest producer of hydroelectric power in the western United States, serving 6 million homes.

As a recreation provider, BOR serves a major role in providing water recreation opportunities to the rapidly growing western states. Without the reservoirs created by this agency and the marinas managed by concessionaires, the boating, water-skiing, bird-watching, fishing, camp-ing near water, house boating, and swimming in natural areas would be a rare event for millions of residents in the dry western states (Bureau of Reclamation, 2005).

American Indian Reservations

The Bureau of Indian Affairs (BIA) is responsible for administering and managing 55.7 million acres (22.5 million hectares) of land held in trust by the United States for American Indians, Indian tribes, and Alaska natives. Most of the land is in Arizona, New Mexico, Montana, and South Dakota, although 31 states have some Native American lands. The BIA is an agency within the U.S. Department of the Interior. Developing forestlands, leasing assets on these lands, directing agricultural programs, protecting water and land rights, developing and maintaining infrastructure, and promoting economic development are all part of the agency's responsibility. As part of its economic development efforts, many tribes attract tourists to their lands by offering guided tours, camping, hunting, fishing, museums, lodges, and alpine skiing. Since the passage of the Indian Gaming Act (1988), many tribes have opened casinos and associated resorts, hotels, shopping areas, and restaurants that attract visitors to American Indian lands (U.S. Department of the Interior, n.d.).

Coastal Areas

Coastal lands and waters are difficult to categorize because they fall under multiple ownership, include sea animals, and are a natural resource that extends around the world. The effort to protect and sustain coastal and ocean-related resources is a recent extension of the park idea.

Beaches and Coastal Wetlands

Coastal areas, including sandy beaches, barrier islands, and coastal salt marsh wetlands, are some of the most heavily used natural resources in the United States and around the world. The number of visits to coastal beaches on a summer day in the United States dwarfs the number of visitors to all national park areas combined on the same day. Coastal areas are owned and managed by every conceivable entity: many federal, state, and local government agencies and hundreds of thousands of private companies or individuals. Approximately 50 percent of the American public lives within 100 miles (161 kilometers) of the coast. Coastal population in the United States is projected to increase by 28 million people from 1994 to 2015.

Many coastal areas are becoming increasingly urbanized. The public, in particular, often considers sand beaches as "parks" even when there is no designated government-owned park nearby. Coastal areas are also multiple-use areas where the same short stretch of coast may be used for commercial fishing, shore-based outdoor recreation, water-based outdoor recreation, private homes or resorts, restaurants, bars or ice-cream stands, umbrella rental stands, wildlife management, and military defense. Coastal areas, especially the lagoon wetland areas, are incredibly rich biological resources for crustaceans, insects, birds, fish, and other wildlife and important breeding and migratory routes for waterfowl and migratory birds. Local city or county park departments manage most beaches; however, there are also some larger state and federal beach parks.

Hundreds of city, county, or state beach parks and several national seashore parks have been established, most since 1950. In 1937, Cape Hatteras was designated as the first national seashore; today, there are 10. The national seashores (operated by the National Park Service) are some of the only substantially undeveloped stretches of shoreline left in the lower 48 states and allow a glimpse at what the American coastline looked like before the increase in coastal zone development started in the 1970s. Two federal agencies, both part of the U.S. Department of Commerce's National Oceanic and Atmospheric Administration (NOAA), manage ocean-area "parks": the National Marine Sanctuary Program and the National Marine Fisheries Service.

National Marine Sanctuaries

During the 1970s, when many environmental acts were passed, the Marine Protection, Research, and Sanctuaries Act of 1972 created the sanctuaries program, partially in response to oil spills and reports of toxic dumping in the ocean. Today, 13 national marine sanctuaries protect 18,618 square miles (48,221 square kilometers) of ocean and coasts (National Marine Sanctuaries, 2005).

The system's first sanctuary, Monitor, the wreck site of the USS Monitor (a famous civil war ship), was designated in 1975. The Channel Islands, Monterey Bay, Thunder Bay, Cordell Bank, Gulf of the Farrallones, and the Florida Keys are a few of the other sanctuaries. The act to create these underwater sanctuaries was passed 100 years after the legislation to create the first national park on land. These sanctuaries provide underwater environmental education and opportunities for snorkeling or scuba sightseeing, fish and coral watching, and photography.

Ocean Fishing and Boating

Many people enjoy boating or deep-sea fishing, either on private boats, **charter boats,** or party **(head) boats.** If the fishing occurs within 3 miles (5 kilometers) of shore (or 9 miles [14 kilometers] off the Florida and Texas Gulf of Mexico coasts), then it is in "state waters," and the state controls the fishing that occurs there. However, if the recreational or commercial fishing occurs beyond state waters, out to 200 miles (322 kilometers) from shore, then it is in an area known as the exclusive economic zone (EEZ), and fishing that occurs there is managed and regulated in conjunction with regional fishery management councils of the National Marine Fisheries Service (NMFS) or NOAA Fisheries. NOAA Fisheries are responsible for the management, conservation, and protection of living marine resources within the United States' exclusive economic zone. NOAA Fisheries work to promote sustainable fisheries and to prevent the lost economic potential associated with overfishing, declining species, and degraded habitats. NOAA Fisheries strives to balance competing public needs and interests in the use and enjoyment of the oceans' resources.

INTERNATIONAL TREATIES AND PROTECTED AREA DESIGNATIONS AND PARKS

Protected natural areas that transcend national borders are known as transboundary protected areas. Because the world's natural resources and parks are best managed on an ecosystem scale, some believe that national borders should not interfere with good conservation practice.

Transboundary protected areas, which are located in more than one country, have been created around the world. These areas were largely created to facilitate the movement of wildlife and birds between two countries in order to protect a certain type of ecosystem. In 1997, 136 protected areas were located in 98 countries that represent 112 international borders (Zbicz, 1999). A few of the world's transboundary protected areas have been designated as "peace parks." A peace park is a casual term adopted by the United Nations Environment Programme (UNEP) in the 1980s to describe a region that embraces the land of more than one nation, unifying fragmented ecological

Sunrise is reflected in the waters of Bowman Lake in Glacier National Park, Montana. The Waterton-Glacier International Peace Park is made up of two parks that straddle the U.S.–Canadian border: Glacier National Park in Montana and Waterton Lakes National Park in Alberta. The park is the world's first international peace park and was designated a World Heritage Site by the UN in 1995.

habitats and promoting environmental and political stability (United Nations Environment Programme, 2004). North America's first international peace park was founded in 1932, the Waterton-Glacier International Peace Park World Heritage Site, in Alberta, Canada, and Montana in the United States. Also, an International Peace Garden crosses the U.S.–Canadian border north of Dunseith, North Dakota, and south of Brandon, Manitoba. This 2,300-acre (930.7-hectare) garden has 100,000 flowers, an 18-foot (5.5-meter) floral clock, a peace tower, and a peace chapel to celebrate the tradition of peace between the two nations (International Peace Garden, 2005). Another peace park has been proposed on the U.S.–Mexican border.

In addition, the United Nations Educational, Scientific and Cultural Organization (UNESCO) designates international **biosphere reserves,** which are terrestrial and coastal areas representing the main ecosystems of the planet in which plants and animals are to be protected and where research, monitoring, and training on ecosystems are carried out. Many of the larger national parks in the United States and Canada have been designated as international biosphere reserves. Canada has 13 biosphere reserves and the United States has 47 (Canadian Biosphere Reserve Association, 2005; UNESCO, 2005a). Examples of biosphere reserves in Canada include Long Point in Ontario and Waterton in Alberta. Examples in the United States include the Mammoth Cave Area in Kentucky and the California Coast Ranges. Similarly, UNESCO designates **World Heritage Sites** to encourage countries to ensure the protection of their natural and cultural heritage (UNESCO, 2005b); most of these sites are major national parks. For example, Canada contains 13 world heritage sites (Parks Canada, 2005) and the United States contains 20 sites (UNESCO, 2005b). Some sites were designated for world-class natural features, such as Dinosaur Provincial Park in Alberta, the Rocky Mountain National Parks in Alberta and British Columbia, Nahanni National Park in the Northwest Territories, Redwood National Park in California, and Everglades National Park in Florida. Other sites were designated for world-class cultural and historic values, such as L'Anse aux Meadows National Historic Site in Newfoundland, the Old Town of Lunenburg in Nova Scotia, the Statue of Liberty in New York, and Independence Hall in Massachusetts. Another international designation for wetland areas is the **Ramsar Convention,** which designates internationally important wetlands (Wetlands International, 2005). In 2005, there were 1,459 Ramsar Wetlands worldwide.

COMPARING CANADA AND THE UNITED STATES

Table 6.3 shows the current status as of 2002 of the parks and protected areas in Canada and the United States according to the United Nations List of Protected Areas (Chape et al., 2003). Urban parks are not included in the list because of their small size, and historic parks are not included because of their cultural focus.

Similarities Between Canada and the United States

The park systems in both countries are similar and have often designated the same types of lands for protection. This is not surprising because both countries developed their park systems with constant communication and friendly competition. The United States and Canada are similar in geographic size, so directly comparing areas dedicated to various types of parks and protected areas is possible (see table 6.3). Both countries have similar amounts of area designated as nature reserves and habitat and species management areas. Canada has much more national parkland, in part because the very large provincial parks are of national-park stature and size and are recognized as such in the international classification of parks. The data in table 6.3 come from the 2003 version of the United Nations List of National Parks and Protected Areas. The data on this list are presented according to the IUCN (**World Conservation Union**) categories of protected areas, not according the official titles of the parks. For example, many provincial parks in Canada are classified in the UN list as Category II parks, national parks. Therefore, table 6.3 shows 1,100 national parks in Canada. However, there are only 44 such parks owned and operated by the national government; the rest are owned and managed by provincial governments. Additionally, neither the national historic sites nor the historic canals are included in the database used for the table. The UN does not recognize cultural or historic sites in its classification system.

The similarity in the form and function of parks in Canada and the United States is caused by several factors. The government structures are similar, including cities, towns, counties, provinces or states, and a federal government. Each of these levels of government develops and manages parks. Both countries have cultural roots in England, which transferred the English love of nature, outdoor recreation, and the use of specialized reserves for conservation and recreation to North America

TABLE 6.3 Parks and Protected Areas in Canada and the United States

IUCN* category	Number in Canada	Number in the United States	Area in Canada in million acres	Area in United States in million acres
Ia: Nature reserve	724	74	5.7 (2.3 ha)	9.1 (3.7 ha)
Ib: Wilderness	112	586	25.9 (10.5 ha)	89 (36 ha)
II: National park	1,110	210	106 (43 ha)	64 (26 ha)
III: Natural monument	287	277	0.310 (0.125 ha)	17.5 (7.1 ha)
IV: Habitat & species management area	571	788	77 (31 ha)	106 (43 ha)
V: Protected landscape	765	1,319	3.0 (1.2 ha)	30 (12 ha)
VI: Managed-resource protected area	941	287	18 (7.6 ha)	272 (110 ha)
Unclassified	789	4,442	8.4 (3.4 ha)	5.9 (2.4 ha)
Total	5,299	7,983	245 (99 ha)	593 (240 ha)

Founded October 5, 1948, as the International Union for the Protection of Nature (IUPN) following an international conference in Fontainebleau, France, the organization changed its name into International Union for Conservation of Nature and Natural Resources (IUCN) in 1956. In 1990 it was shortened to IUCN-The World Conservation Union.

(Glendening 1997; Hudson, 2001; Ritvo, 2003). The green parks in the central areas of English cities were a model widely emulated across the various British colonies in North America. As the park movement in Canada and the United States deepened and strengthened through increasing activities by cities, provinces or states, and national governments, there was an ongoing communication of ideas between the two countries. It is remarkable how many government precedents and management details and how much wording in legislation moved back and forth between agencies in both countries over a 200-year period. Therefore, it is expected that both countries have national parks, national historic sites and parks, national wildlife reserves and areas, provincial or state parks, regional parks, and municipal parks. And it is not surprising that parks in both countries have been created for everyone's use and funded primarily by taxes.

Academic programs in the United States started offering courses in natural resource and forest recreation through some workshops by the New England Association of Park Superintendents (which later became the American Institute of Park Executives), starting in 1898, and the New York State College of Forestry at Syracuse, starting in 1912 (VanDoren and Hodges, 1975). By the 1930s, the University of Massachusetts, Utah State College, and Colorado State University had added courses in recreation land use or park management. Canada followed suit with academic programs in the 1960s. Colleges and universities in both Canada and the United States developed specialized college and university programs to provide training for leisure, parks, recreation, and resource management professionals. Park managers in both countries are now viewed as professionals, with training appropriate to the challenging tasks of conservation and recreation.

Canada and the United States both play a large role in park management internationally. Both countries have influenced the types and forms of park management that have developed around the world. United States government officials and academic scholars were particularly influential in spreading the concept of the U.S. model of national parks worldwide. The U.S. model is typically seen as consisting of very large areas of natural area in which aboriginal people had been removed. The management is by a government agency that concentrates on conservation and outdoor recreation. Canadian officials have been influential in international activities such as creating biosphere reserves and managing the world heritage convention. Scholars in both countries have written abundant literature that has distributed the concepts of park planning and management as well as outdoor recreation planning and management. The United States and Canada have consistently shown international leadership in park planning and management.

Differences Between Canada and the United States

Although the park systems in both countries are similar, there are important differences (Eagles, McLean, and Stabler, 2000). The wilderness concept is more popular in the United States than in Canada; therefore, the United States has much more designated wilderness. The United States has a much larger national monument designation by a president's executive order because this type of designation is not used in Canadian park law. However, the biggest differences occur in the amount of land comprising protected landscape and managed resource-protected areas. In the United States the federal government manages these lands and has designated large areas as national forests, and the lands managed by the Bureau of Land Management are considered managed-resource protected areas. However, in Canada, the provinces manage the forestlands, and Canada does not include all undesignated crown lands managed by the provinces, territories, and the national government in its tabulation of protected areas.

One major difference between Canada and the United States is the constitutional structure of land-ownership. In the United States, the federal government owns most of the public land. Therefore, the national government of the United States has the capacity to create parks and reserves on this land. As a result, a large number of land management agencies have developed to manage the variety of reserves created on federal land. The United States has more diverse management institutions and reserves than Canada. For example, the following systems exist in the United States but not in Canada: national forests, national parkways, national scenic rivers, national wilderness areas, U.S. Army Corps of Engineer waterways, and BLM national resource lands.

Another difference between the two countries is that in Canada the provincial parks are much larger and more fully developed than the state park systems in the United States. For example, the provincial park system in Ontario is larger in land area than all 50 of the U.S. state park systems combined. In essence, many provincial park systems in Canada are of the stature of national parks. This is because in Canada, the provincial governments own most of the crown land within their borders. Therefore, the provincial governments found it relatively easy to create provincial parks on land they already owned and managed. And many preferred that to having the national government involved in land management activities within their province. Some provinces blocked national park creation while putting the best lands into their own provincial park system. Others welcomed national park creation because the federal government would then pay the cost of land management.

In Canada within the territories, the federal government holds crown land. Therefore, national parks and wildlife areas were most easily created by the national government in territories. This is why the major concentration of national parks occurs in the western mountains and in the high north. In the West, the parks were created before the provinces had been created. In the North, park creation is ongoing. However, a few provinces have gone in a different direction. Some of the poorer provinces, such as the Maritime Provinces in the East, encouraged the federal government to create national parks and to subsequently pay for their management. In these provinces the national parks are prominent and the provincial park systems smaller and less developed.

CAREER OPPORTUNITIES

Traditionally, the operation of most public natural areas occurs within the federal, state or provincial, or municipal levels of government. City parks and recreation departments, however, also rely on parks and recreation specialists. Thus, employment opportunities are available with agencies such as the national park agencies, the national wildlife agencies, and forest services, as well as the many regional, local, and municipal parks and recreation agencies. In the United States, opportunities are available with the AmeriCorps program. Many different job positions are available at parks, forests, and refuges. These positions encompass areas such as administration and support services, finance, maintenance, law enforcement, biology, history, and lifeguarding. Generally, park rangers supervise, manage, and perform work in the conservation and use of resources in parks. Specifically, park rangers carry out various tasks associated with forest or structural fire control; protection of

property; gathering and dissemination of natural, historical, or scientific information; development of interpretive material for the natural, historical, or cultural features of an era; demonstration of folk art and crafts; enforcement of laws and regulations; investigation of violations, complaints, trespassing and encroachment, and accidents; search and rescue; and management of historical, cultural, and natural resources, such as wildlife, forests, lakeshores, seashores, historic buildings, battlefields, archeological properties, and recreation areas. They also operate campgrounds, including such tasks as assigning sites, replenishing firewood, performing safety inspections, providing information to visitors, and leading guided tours. Differences in the exact nature of duties depend on the grade of position, the size of the site, and specific needs of the site (National Park Service, 2004). Educational requirements vary depending on the position, but for permanent employment, a college degree is preferred for most positions. In many areas seasonal employment is available so that those interested can gain experience while in college or after graduation. Educational training should relate to the position sought (e.g., history degree for historians; parks, recreation, and tourism degree for visitor management; biology, ecology, forestry, geology, or wildlife management degree for natural resource management positions). Except for some maintenance positions (e.g., electricians, plumbers), law enforcement, or lifeguard positions, certifications are generally not required, though some organizations in the United States may prefer or give preference to candidates that have Certified Park and Recreation Professional (CPRP) status. Information on obtaining that certification is available from the National Recreation and Park Association in Ashburn, Virginia, USA.

Those interested in pursuing park-related careers have many options in terms of professional organizations to join. Many organizations have student membership rates, and most have annual conferences that are good opportunities for networking and exploring internship or employment opportunities. Some of the better-known ones are the National Recreation and Park Association (especially the National Society for Park Resources branch), the Canadian Parks and Recreation Association, the National Parks and Conservation Association, Society of American Foresters, National Association of Recreation Resource Planners, National Association for Interpretation, state and provincial park and recreation associations, the George Wright Society, and the Wilderness Society.

Courtesy of Paul F.J. Eagles

In Canada and the United States, there is a positive relationship between universities and park managers. Many parks rely heavily on student employees for many activities, such as biological inventories, campground management, law enforcement, and environmental education. Most park managers and planners are university graduates.

The World Playground Industry (2005) maintains a Web site with a partial list of park and recreation associations (and employment opportunities) in the United States, Canada, and the rest of the world.

Opportunities for employment in recreation also exist in the private sector, both the profit-making sector and the nonprofit sector. These jobs include program planning, direct program delivery, resort-park concessionaire or lodging operations, and the sale of specialized recreation merchandise. Opportunities in small businesses providing outdoor programs and services for activities such as rafting, birding, bicycling, and canoeing are growing, as a glance in the classified ads section of most recreational, vacation, or conservation magazines will demonstrate or on Web sites such as those for Cool Works, GORP, or American Outdoors. Some resorts recognize the need for a staff naturalist or recreation employees to answer guests' questions and offer tours and lead sightseeing trips. Some commercial theme parks such as Walt Disney World, Silver Springs, zoos, Busch Gardens, and Marineland seek employees

with park and recreation resources, marketing, and leadership or management training to lead environmental education programs, interpretation talks, or children's programs or to perform duties at information desks. Summer camps; ski resorts; tour boat companies; bed and breakfasts; park or beach concessionaires; park lodges; canoe, kayak, and bicycle rental companies; water parks; marinas; and outdoor equipment stores are a few more examples of potential job sites.

CHALLENGES AND TRENDS FOR THE 21ST CENTURY

Parks are an important part of the culture of Canada and the United States. Virtually every citizen uses, knows about, and supports the creation and management of parks. Public demand has resulted in increasing amounts of land reserved for parks and removed from other types of land use. Across North America park usage is increasing. However, this leads to two increasingly complicated problems.

How can the cultural and ecological values of the parks be conserved and interpreted while at the same time actively used by large numbers of tourists? How can the management of all this parkland and visitor use be financed? We are fortunate to have thousands of park resources available to us because of the farsightedness, willingness to sacrifice, and the ethos of preservation of previous generations. However, those resources face challenges and trends that current generations must respond to:

• **International tourism.** In both countries, the impact of international tourists is becoming increasingly important as large numbers, especially those from Europe, Japan, and other Asian countries, visit high-profile parks. The increase in visits to national parks by international tourists can be attributed to a greater awareness of environmental concerns, scarcity of natural land at home, and higher levels of travel by some foreign populations. As international tourism increases, so does the demand for a higher quality of service management and park staff with advanced education in tourism management, cultural sensitivity, and language skills.

• **Funding.** Over the years, government funding for public parks became increasingly limited, and the number of park agencies that must compete for these funds grew. Some of the causes of the shortage in funding are rising land prices and energy and fuel costs and a trend toward reducing taxes. Insufficient funding hinders the provision of environmental and historical interpretation programs and the ability to retain enough park rangers or staff to maintain facilities, manage resources, and serve the public. Not only must parks compete with each other for funding, but they must also compete with other large and popular public institutions such as education and health care for these limited public funds.

Innovative responses to the problem of funding include increasing the use of tourism fees and charges, relying more on volunteer efforts such as friends groups, and encouraging park agencies to function as businesses by tapping all possible streams of income. Many park agencies are aggressively moving into a business model of management, in which they have the ability to set prices, retain funds, hire staff, and operate programs with flexibility similar to that of a private business. Traditional income sources continue to include government grants, campsite rentals, and day-use fees. Innovative income sources include

souvenir sales, grocery sales, recreation equipment rental, specialized clothing and equipment sales, specialized accommodation rental, money exchange bureaus, soft drink sales, firewood sales, fees for using parks as movie-filming sites, art sales, and interpretive program charges. Friends groups are also entrepreneurial. Examples of fund-raising activities include providing specialized festivals; developing aboriginal-themed activities; encouraging film, art, and cultural development; staffing book or gift stores and donating a portion of sales income to the park; and encouraging donations of time and money. Advanced training in the business of leisure and tourism is needed in all park agencies in the 21st century.

Major debates on park management revolve around the types of activities that should be encouraged and allowed, the management structures used, and the source of the funding. The proportion of funding that should come from taxes or from user fees also produces heated debate. In recent years, there has been a trend toward increasing the use of various types of fees and charges to fund park management. There is an urgent need for park managers with specialized training in finance and business management. Many universities train resource managers. Too few train business managers for parks.

• **Market specialization.** Over the years the various park agencies have increasingly specialized in providing services to a particular segment of the population. For example, youth and people without much discretionary income most heavily use city parks. Conversely, well-educated and wealthy older people who have the time and money to travel far from home most heavily use national parks. The baby boom generation is another target market. Today's park managers must plan and manage for the needs of this largest, healthiest, wealthiest cadre of retirees in world history. For example, the picturesque landscapes of North American parks attract older travelers, but the services and facilities are usually more appropriate for young, physically active visitors. Aging baby boomers seem to be shifting to a preference for what has been labeled "soft camping," in which they hike and sightsee in the parks in the daytime but retire to nearby lodges, bed and breakfasts, restaurants, and cabins at night. Resolving this discrepancy poses a challenge to parks.

• **Increasing demand.** The biggest problem on the horizon for parks is one inherent in the growth of this important cultural activity of outdoor recreation and conservation. As demand grows for more parks, some governments respond with campaigns to create new parks, which have been more successful in recent years in Canada but not as successful in the general anti-new-tax political climate in the United States. However, even if new parks are acquired, the money available for park management is not increasing at the same rate as the amount of land that needs to be managed. As a result, funding for land management is decreasing on a unit-area basis. With rising populations; increased air travel; increased interest in health, exercise, and weight control; more people living in higher-density housing; and increasing demand for tourism with ever-disappearing natural open space nearby, more people are relying on park areas for stress reduction, family time, and leisure pursuits. The legacy of past generations of planning for future population growth with systematic growth management strategies including new park areas should be continued.

- **Encroachment.** As development of private land encroaches on park borders, it limits the ability of wildlife to move across natural areas. It also increases the temptation for government to use public parklands for public services such as roads, power lines, cell phone towers, and pipelines.

- **Environmental threats from outside the park.** Problems originating elsewhere can affect park resources. For example, polluted river water originating in a populated area but flowing through a park, or air pollution from outside a park, can spoil the fresh air and views within the park. Seeds from exotic plant species are dispersed by wildlife or wind and result in non-native plants flourishing inside park boundaries, which may crowd out native species.

- **Antisocial behavior.** In urban parks, vandalism, drug use, public sexual behavior, crime, and gang activity make many people (especially women) afraid to visit parks (especially in the evening). Approaches to addressing these problems include zero-tolerance zones for crimes committed within 100 yards (91.4 meters) of a park and adding special fines or sentences for doing so and monitoring parks with cameras. Another strategy is national night-out events to encourage large numbers of people to use the parks, which usually discourages crime.

- **Motorized vehicles.** Inappropriate use of motorized vehicles such as snowmobiles, personal watercraft, and off-road vehicles (ORVs) scars fragile lands and harasses wildlife.

- **Coastal development.** On many coastlines, condominiums and high-rise buildings with thousands of residents are being built, greatly increasing the use of nearby coastal parks. Coastal lands have become so expensive that few areas can afford to expand existing coastal parks. Coastal property is so lucrative that water access areas such as marinas or private boat ramps are being sold to developers who convert them to private condo-owner-only marinas or privately owned water access routes.

- **Multiethnic cultural changes.** It is projected that an amalgam of minorities will make up more than 50 percent of the U.S. population by 2050. Because of immigration from a diverse set of countries, the Canadian and American populations are becoming more diverse in cultures and ideas. This creates an issue of concern for park managers because some cultures have little tradition of visiting parks or participating in traditional outdoor recreational activities (Chavez, 2002; Johnson et al., 1997; Virden and Walker, 1999). As the ethnic balance in North America shifts, park, forest, and refuge agencies at all levels must understand the preferences and outdoor recreational behaviors of various minority groups and work to introduce them to activities that they may have little experience with or adapt facilities or programs to their cultures. This will be necessary in order to continue the legacy of public service that makes park resources available to all citizens and guests in the United States and Canada.

SUMMARY

The parks in Canada and the United States contain some of the most significant and attractive natural landscapes in North America. Each year they illustrate for millions of people the ecological and cultural values of both countries. Canada's and the United States' parks are highly valued not only by their citizens but also by an increasing number of international visitors. These parks have become icons representing the strong political, social, and cultural ideas that formed each country. While European countries have many castles and cathedrals marking centuries of their cultural history, in North America, the beauty of the wilderness (its mountains, deserts, prairies, rivers, and lakes) celebrates a major aspect of the culture and its people of the past millennium on this continent.

Those who work in park settings feel strongly about the value of their role, and many consider their job a positive lifelong endeavor. In an increas-

Web Sites to EXPLORE

America Outdoors: www.americaoutdoors.org

American Trails: www.americantrails.org

Biosphere Reserves: www.unesco.org/mab/wnbr.htm

Bureau of Land Management: www.blm.gov; monitor the "News" or various program links

Bureau of Reclamation: www.usbr.gov/newsroom

Canadian Biosphere Reserves Association: www.biosphere-canada.ca/biosphere_reserves.htm

Center for the National Institute for the Environment: www.cnie.org/nle/info-7/InternetRes/natres.htm

Coastal Channel Web site: www.coastalnews.com

Cool Works: www.coolworks.com; lists 75,000 jobs in great places such as U.S. National Parks, ski resorts, ranches, theme parks, and so on

Forest Service Employees for Environmental Ethics: www.fseee.org; click on the "Stay Informed" link

Global Heart: www.peacepoles.org

GORP: http://gorp.away.com/gorp/eclectic/jobs.htm

Indian Country Today: www.indiancountry.com

International Institute for Peace Through Tourism: www.iipt.org

International Peace Garden: www.peacegarden.com

National Marine Sanctuaries: www.sanctuaries.nos.noaa.gov; monitor the "Sanctuary News" link

National Park Service: www.nps.gov; check the "News & Information" link and read the "Morning Report"; this provides a daily list of news releases, incidents, and events from the last few days occurring across the national park system

National Parks Conservation Association: www.npca.org

National Wilderness Areas: www.wilderness.net

National Wilderness Preservation System map: www.wilderness.net/index.cfm?fuse=NWPS

National Wildlife Federation: www.nwf.org

Native American Times: http://nativetimes.com

NOAA Fisheries Service Web site: www.nmfs.noaa.gov

Ontario Parks: www.ontarioparks.com/

Parks Canada: http://parkscanada.pch.gc.ca/progs/np-pn/index_E.asp

Peace Parks Foundation: www.peaceparks.org

Ramsar Convention on Wetlands: www.ramsar.org/

Recreation.gov (lists many federal parks that offer recreational opportunities): www.recreation.gov

Sierra Club: www.sierraclub.org; type "BLM" in the search window to monitor the Bureau of Land Management; type "Corps of Engineers" to monitor the U.S. Army Corps of Engineers; type "TVA" in the search window to monitor the Tennessee Valley Authority; type "Bureau of Reclamation" in the search window to monitor the Bureau of Reclamation; type "Bureau of Indian Affairs" in the search window to monitor the Bureau of Indian Affairs

Tennessee Valley Authority: www.tva.gov/news/releases

U.S. Army Corps of Engineers: www.usace.army.mil/news.html

U.S. Fish and Wildlife Service: www.fws.gov; monitor the "News" or various program links

United Nations Education, Scientific and Cultural Organization: www.unesco.org/mab/wnbr.htm; to learn more about biosphere reserves

University of Waterloo (the most important park-related Web sites in Canada are found at the University of Waterloo): www.ahs.uwaterloo.ca/rec/parksoption/parkslinks

USAJobs: www.usajobs.com; click on "Search Jobs" under the "Keyword Search" window, type the word "Park," then click "Search for Jobs" at the bottom of page to see the federal agency park jobs currently available. If you locate your state park agency Web page, you can often do a similar search.

USDA Forest Service: www.fs.fed.us; monitor the "Newsroom" link

Wilderness Society: www.wilderness.org; read the "News Room" or "Our Issues" links

World Commission on Protected Areas: http://iucn.org/themes/wcpa/

World Heritage: http://whc.unesco.org/

---

ingly urbanized, technology filled, overstimulated, and fast-paced culture, people seek opportunities to connect with nature. Public parks, forests, rivers, mountains, beaches, lakes, deserts, and oceans can provide inspiration, fascination, and education. These natural resources, gifts from earlier generations, can provide escape from work and social challenges, peace and relaxation, and a place to spend quiet times with family and friends or by oneself. They are living schools for ecology, wildlife, nature, and self-discovery.

Not many places endure unchanged over a lifetime. Over the past 50 years, North America has lost many farms and natural areas to development. Yet, most parks remain more or less unchanged over the years: your first visit as a child to swing or slide in a local park; swimming or camping with your family as an adolescent;

strolling hand in hand or sharing a kiss on a park bench; celebrating anniversaries in park lodges; taking your children hiking, fishing, canoeing, or camping; and watching sunsets and moonrises across a scenic natural landscape during your retirement years. Parks are invaluable for creating personal memories as well as a national heritage and culture. Visit your parks, make memories in them, celebrate your natural roots and connections to the animal and plant kingdoms, and play your role in protecting and sharing existing parks and creating new ones.

CHAPTER 7

Public Recreation

*Sara Hensley, Susan Markham-Starr,
Ellen Montague, and Jane Hodgkinson*

Courtesy of San Jose Parks, Recreation and Neighborhood Services

Public sentiment is everything.
With public sentiment,
nothing can fail. Without it,
nothing can succeed.

*Abraham Lincoln, 16th president
of the United States*

CHAPTER OBJECTIVES

After reading this chapter, you should be able to do the following:

- Identify the groups and individuals that helped to create public recreation services in Canada and the United States
- Describe the responsibilities of each of the three levels of government for providing recreation services
- List the five roles that governments can play in providing recreation services
- Understand why and how partnerships are formed between agencies that deliver recreation services
- Identify current issues and trends facing public recreation professionals
- Understand the political realities in which public recreation professionals work
- Identify the two people who most influenced the beginning of community education in the United States and Canada
- Describe the differences between community education and community schools
- Discuss the primary difference between community education and recreation
- Explain why schools were selected as the common site for community education activities
- Describe the philosophy of community building that was initiated by the community education movement
- List and describe the six components of community education
- Describe the origins of national community education legislation
- Identify examples of community education partnerships
- Understand how community-based recreation for the disabled came about
- Explain factors that led to the deinstitutionalization of people with disabilities
- Identify significant American legislation that has led to services in the community
- Describe the philosophy of community-based recreation approaches
- Identify the continuum of special recreation
- List and describe three types of community-based recreation programs for people with disabilities

INTRODUCTION

This chapter includes three sections that cover different types of public recreation: public parks and recreation, school-based recreation and community schools, and special recreation. All three sections were written by practicing professionals in the field, who provide unique and valuable insights into their professions. A common thread runs through all three sections: Public recreation depends on community partnerships to be successful. All three types of recreation also grew from the philosophy that public recreation is essential for the well-being of young people and communities.

Public Recreation in the United States and Canada

Susan Markham-Starr and Sara Hensley

"I am not concerned with our inability to nail down the specifics of what we do in parks and recreation. As I see it, our strength lies in our diversity. We can do anything. More specifically, I believe our job is to help people improve their quality of life through recreation and parks."

Robert F. Toalson, Champaign, Illinois, Park District

Picture a community without a public swimming pool, community center, playground, park, or recreation programs. Can you imagine? The connections to many, if not all, of these opportunities are found in our everyday life. For example, a family outing to a neighborhood park may uncover what recreation and leisure means to you. Close your eyes and think about a family outing to a local park or community center. Remember the excitement when you discussed which park you wanted to visit because of certain play areas, trails, and open space? What about that special community center that offered programs, activities, and special events for the entire family? For many of us, these places become an important part of our life. In a recent study by the National Recreation and Park Association (NRPA), 75 percent of the American public uses park and recreation services. It seems that public recreation is popular and valued by our communities.

In the abstract, the challenge and the role of public recreation is to serve all of us. But does this really happen? And who is "us"? Is it realistic to believe that the public recreation system *can* serve all? Who takes up the challenge to try to serve all? And can they succeed? Is recreation really a "public good"? To whom do we listen? From whom do we solicit input? Much of the work that we do involves members of the community either as individuals or as organized groups. Each group has its own mission and agenda. Each group is convinced that it has the correct solution to any issue. Your agenda must be to facilitate the discussions that will help these groups fulfill their agenda without creating conflict between competing groups. Now there is a daunting task!

This section provides a realistic picture of the diverse areas in public recreation and leisure as a profession and career. It describes contemporary public recreation and leisure services against the backdrop of the Canadian and American social, economic, and political environment; partnerships; the role of recreation professionals; ever changing social issues; and some of the political realities of life in the public sector.

HISTORICAL OVERVIEW OF CANADIAN PUBLIC RECREATION

When you consider the development of recreation and leisure services in Canada, you most often turn your attention first to the services that are closest to you—services at the local level, primarily municipal services. In the early 21st century, these municipal services are both supported by and driven by a range of provincial and federal programs operating in a system propelled by professional, community, and political initiatives. Local recreation and leisure services began as a set of independent initiatives aimed at solving problems (real or perceived) or creating opportunities for local residents. The roots of today's integrated recreation, park, and leisure services system were parks established for civic beauty and to promote a healthy environment, playgrounds established to provide wholesome play opportunities for children, and physical-activity programs to build the fitness levels of young people to make them fit for work or for war.

Influences on recreation and leisure services in Canada have come from Great Britain, Europe, and the United States. Readily identifiable links are those between British and Scandinavian proponents of physical fitness such as the Young Men's Christian Association (YMCA) that came to Canada from England; the British Columbia Provincial Recreation (BC Pro-Rec) program, whose first director was from Denmark; and the American advocates of supervised playgrounds and urban recreation programs. Each of these groups helped plant ideas and provide information to Canadians, but the version of each idea evolved according to the social, economic, and political influences in Canada. The expansion of eastern Canadian cities in the mid- and late-19th century, the rapid expansion of the West in the early 20th century, the depression of the 1930s, the post–World War II urban growth, and the role of government as the provider of a social safety net all contributed to the Canadian solution.

One of the essential building blocks of any profession is its understanding of its roots—its reasons for being, its historical development. By understanding the beginnings and the development of the profession, students entering this profession can gain a sense of why we do what we do, can have confidence in the actions that we take, and can take pride in the contribution that the broad field of recreation has made to Canadian society. Elsie McFarland made her mark in the mid-20th century, first as a practitioner and then as an academic. In all of her work she was a champion of public recreation. Although she focused on the youth of the profession (which in itself is a relevant note in parks and recreation history), her 1970 statement of her belief in the value of recreation history continues to give guidance to the profession. Her broad review in her book, *The Development of Public Recreation in Canada*, which is the base from which most historians of recreation and leisure services in Canada have embarked, sprang from her belief in the following:

The young people entering the field of recreation will need considerable faith in themselves and in their profession. Knowledge of earlier development, of the progress that has been made, and of the men and women who made it possible may provide future leaders with roots from which to grow in strength and wisdom to face the challenges that lie ahead. (McFarland, 1970, p. 1)

Although not all those entering the field are "young," the viewpoint certainly continues to be valid as practitioners and students continue to encounter challenges to beliefs about the value of recreation and leisure services.

The recreation profession comes from many roots. It comes from parks, from playgrounds, from fitness, and from employment initiatives. It has come from those who wanted to reform the "sorry condition of Canada's big cities" (Rutherford, 1974, p. xv); from those who wanted to enhance the physical, mental, and moral health of all; and from those who wanted to enhance investment growth and prosperity in cities. In summary, it has come from those who wanted to create a better environment—although each proponent of recreation might define what "better" is in a different fashion.

Playgrounds Came First, Then Recreation

The rather narrowly defined field of municipal recreation in Canada can trace its roots to the National Council of Women's Vacation Schools and Supervised Playgrounds Committee that began work in 1901. But, the notion of recreation in cities was certainly prevalent in the 19th century as the philanthropic, volunteer-based Young Men's Christian Association (YMCA) and Young Women's Christian Association (YWCA) established themselves in Canadian cities. Founded to promote uplifting educational and recreational programs for men and women, the YMCA and YWCA provided working-class men and women with community-based recreation programs. Within a decade of its foundation in London, England, in 1844 (Cross, 1990, p. 96), the YMCA began in Montreal in 1851 and soon after in Toronto in 1852. The Canadian YWCA began in 1870 in Saint John, New Brunswick, and within five years there were YWCAs in Toronto, Montreal, and Quebec City (Strong-Boag, 1976, p. 63). As the municipal recreation programs began in the early 1900s, the YMCA and the YWCA often contributed moral support and staff support to the

local playgrounds associations or recreation commissions, for example, in Halifax, Saint John, Winnipeg, Regina, Calgary, and Edmonton (McFarland, 1970; Markham, 1988).

The National Council of Women of Canada, the group most active in the promotion of organized, supervised playgrounds, began its support of them in 1901 after lobbying from the ladies of the Saint John Local Council of Women led by Miss Mabel Peters (McFarland, 1970, pp. 19-20). Mabel Peter's work and that of the National Council through its committees and local councils focused on "'prevention' as its guiding principle" (Strong-Boag, 1976, p. 268). The local councils of women were frequently responsible for establishing and operating supervised playground programs in eastern Canadian cities. By 1913, the National Council of Women's Committee on Vacation Schools and Supervised Playgrounds was able to state firmly its mission and successes, using ideas familiar to us today:

> Its work is formative as opposed to reformative. It seeks to eventually dispense with the curfew, the juvenile court, the jail and the reform school for the young of our land. Educationists are now agreed that the public supervised playground and recreational Social Center stimulates and guides a child's life in a way which no other factor of modern living can do. (Peters, 1913, p. 48)

We no longer have reform schools and we seldom have curfews, but we now speak of "at-risk youth." The ideas of a century ago are still with us.

The ideas influencing the National Council of Women to promote vacation schools and supervised playgrounds originated in the United States. You may not be familiar with the phrase "vacation schools," but that is what the early advocates called playgrounds. They were a place, often at a school, that children went during their vacation. Links between eastern Canada and New England were strong, and influential members of the National Council of Women such as Mabel Peters traveled and were exposed to the work of like-minded social reformers in the United States (Markham, 1998).

Although the National Council of Women and its local councils were advocates for playgrounds and the catalysts for their development, they were not committed to their long-term operation. In many cities they helped establish local playgrounds associations, whose broad base could include representation from the following: the Council of Women, who aided in fund-raising; the city council, who provided grants and parkland; the school board, who provided school sites; and local service

A local playgrounds association's advocacy work, promoting playground development in the early 20th century. The sign reads "Try and secure one for your neighbourhood."

clubs, who raised funds. The photo above shows one playgrounds association's publicity efforts as they urged visitors to try to get a playground in their neighborhood. The Council of Women's role was finished when they handed off the responsibility for playgrounds to another agency.

Development of Recreation and Leisure in Canada

In many Canadian cities the development of what we now call recreation and leisure services systems began with volunteers in the local councils of women and playgrounds associations and progressed to become a responsibility of municipal government. This progression often proceeded through the following pattern. The responsibility for playgrounds would be taken over by a playgrounds commission or a recreation commission, which meant that there was a more secure, ongoing commitment from the municipal government to provide funding and space for playgrounds. Increasing commitment from the municipal government would come when a civic department of recreation was created; this occurred in many Canadian cities in the 1940s, although there were notable exceptions such as Halifax where this did not occur until the late 1960s. Amalgamation of recreation services with park services often occurred in the 1950s, although advocates of amalgamations were evident long before then. Through the 1990s we saw further mergers between municipal parks and recreation and other units with similar mandates or client groups, for example, merging agencies that provided recreation, parks, and other social services and culture or tourism services into a local department of community services.

Federal and Provincial Governments

The federal government's involvement in recreation and sport can be attributed to the work of a few individuals and groups. The most often cited are Charlotte Whitton and the Canadian Council on Child Welfare, Ian Eisenhardt and the British Columbia Provincial Recreation movement, and Arthur S. Lamb and the Canadian Physical Education Association.

The Canadian Council on Child Welfare and its recreation division were involved in promoting recreation and sport services throughout Canada. Correspondence of the Council's executive director, Charlotte Whitton, and the chair of the recreation division, Major Bowie of the Montreal Parks and Playgrounds Association in the early 1930s, shows that the Council attempted to promote recreation throughout Canada and communicated with those who were working in recreation in Canada in the United States. Correspondence shows that the United States–based Playground and Recreation Association of America had staff members who gave assistance to fellow recreation advocates in Canada. The successor to that organization, the National Recreation and Parks Association, continues to have Canadian members but no longer acts in a consulting role. The Canadian Council on Child Welfare (now known as the Canadian Council on Social Development) has worked to promote the need for recreation opportunities for children and families.

The involvement of provincial governments and the federal government can be attributed primarily to the search for antidotes to unemployment during the depression of the 1930s. Two threads lead us to the solutions adopted by provincial and federal governments. One thread developed in British Columbia. The other thread included the efforts of the federal government. They were intertwined.

In British Columbia, the government began its Provincial Recreation Program, Pro-Rec, to provide physical recreation for unemployed young men and women in 1934 as an effort to deal with "the large number of unemployed youth . . . who are exposed to the demoralizing influences of enforced idleness" (Schrodt, 1979, appendix A). The first director was Ian Eisenhardt, a staff member of the Vancouver Parks Board who had been trained in Denmark. When, in 1936, the federal government established the National Employment Commission to investigate the needs of the unemployed, it was searching for solutions that addressed not only employment but also leisure needs. As the commission consulted experts such as Eisenhardt and devised programs to alleviate the problems of unemployment, programs similar to the British

Columbia program emerged. Through the Federal Unemployment and Agricultural Assistance Act of 1938 and the Youth Training Act of 1939, assistance was given to provinces to create training programs that would prepare young people to work in physical training and health education in local communities and then provide recreation opportunities for trainees in other programs such as forestry, agriculture, mining, industrial apprenticeships, and domestic and household work (Canada, 1938). Responsibility for these training programs, including recreation workers, was delegated to the various provincial governments. Provinces that established training programs frequently relied on expert advice from Eisenhardt and staff from British Columbia.

Federal involvement in recreation had an impact on the municipal level through its programs of assistance in partnerships with most of the provinces. In 1943, the National Physical Fitness Program was established. The mandate of this program was to "encourage, develop and correlate all activities related to physical development of the people through sports, athletics, and similar pursuits" (Canada, 1943). This program ended in 1954 and after seven years was succeeded by the Fitness and Amateur Sport Act (1961-2003) and later by the Physical Activity and Sport Act (2003). As the federal government's involvement in recreation and leisure services evolved, various government programs such as Recreation Canada came in 1971 and went in 1980 (Westland, 1979, p. 30; MacIntosh, Bedecki, & Franks, 1988, p. 81). The role of the federal government in recreation in Canada was to support sport governing bodies, health concerns, the provinces, recreation-related associations, and ParticipACTION, a private initiative to promote fitness through physical activity. By 2001, the federal government, while still espousing the ideals represented by ParticipACTION, withdrew adequate support and the agency closed (Canadian Public Health Association, 2004).

HISTORICAL OVERVIEW OF PUBLIC RECREATION IN THE UNITED STATES

Organized efforts to provide recreation and leisure services began in the United States in the late 1890s. Shortly after moving to Pittsburgh, Pennsylvania, Beulah Kennard realized that the busy industrial city provided no play activities for children. So, with the help of the local civic club, she opened Pittsburgh's first playground in the Forbes School yard on July 6, 1896. In the early 1900s professional leadership in the area of recreation and parks emerged. For instance in 1904, the first playground commission was formed in Los Angeles.

Jane Addams, Luther H. Gulick, Joseph Lee, and others met on April 12, 1906, in Washington, D.C., and founded the Playground Association of America. They were concerned about the safety and moral welfare of city children. In 1911, the association's name changed to Playground and Recreation Association of America. Also in 1911, New Jersey became the first state to pass an act permitting the formation of local recreation agencies.

In 1915, as the United States entered World War I, the Playground and Recreation Association of American (PRAA) and War Camp Community Service provided recreation for new recruits in towns near training camps. PRAA promoted programs for urban African Americans in 1920, and in 1926 was reorganized and named the National Recreation Association (NRA). The association established a National Recreation School to train college graduates as municipal recreation executives to fill positions created by the growth of public recreation. The Society of Recreation Workers was formed in 1938, then later changed its name to American Recreation Society.

In 1958, the United States Congress authorized an Outdoor Recreation Resources Review Commission to examine the nation's recreation needs. The National Recreation and Park Association became a reality on August 14, 1956, with the merger of the National Recreation Association, the American Recreation Society, the American Recreation Society, the American Institute of Park Executives, the National Conference on State Parks, and the American Association of Zoological Parks and Aquariums. The Community Services Act of 1975 provided summer recreation for low-income families.

PUBLIC RECREATION DELIVERY SYSTEMS

Public recreation depends on government involvement and responsibilities. Both the Canadian and American delivery systems can be discussed by looking at different levels of government. However, the delivery systems are different based on the philosophies of each government.

Canadian Delivery Systems

The issue of the various levels of governments' jurisdiction over matters of recreation and leisure services has often been a source of debate. As a result, the National Recreation Statement of 1987 jointly signed by the Canadian federal and provincial and territorial governments laid out the following broad principles to guide the respective responsibilities of the three levels of government as follows:

1. The federal government will do the following:
   - "Primarily involve itself in those activities that are national in scope."
   - "Provide for the development and maintenance of recreation programs and services appropriate to those facilities and institutions under the jurisdiction of the federal government." (Interprovincial Sport and Recreation Council [ISRC], 1987, p. 11)

2. The provincial and territorial governments have substantial responsibilities related to recreation. These responsibilities are primarily at the level of coordinating programs, providing information and financial resources to program delivery agencies, planning and supporting research. They are very rarely the direct delivery agent for recreation and leisure services (ISRC, 1987, pp. 8-9).

3. Municipal governments are deemed to be the suppliers of services:
   - "Municipal governments are closest to the people; they are likely to respond more flexibly, more quickly and more effectively to the needs of the community in matters of recreation. For this reason the municipality is the primary supplier of direct recreation services" (ISRC, 1987, p. 9).
   - The basic role of the municipality is to ensure the availability of the broadest range of recreation opportunities for every individual and group consistent with available community resources (ISRC, 1987, p. 10).

But, what does this division really mean? Who does what? Who has legislative authority? At first glance it might appear that the federal government has an overall constitutional responsibility for recreation and leisure, but it does not. Nowhere in the

Canadian Constitution Act (1982) is there mention of federal responsibility for recreation or leisure. The closest that the Constitution Act of 1982 comes is to guarantee the following through the Charter of Rights and Freedoms:

Everyone has the following fundamental freedoms:

- Freedom of conscience and religion
- Freedom of thought, belief, opinion, and expression, including freedom of the press and other communication media
- Freedom of peaceful assembly
- Freedom of association

Thus, while the Constitution Act does not allocate legislative responsibility for recreation and leisure or state how recreation and leisure services are delivered, it does guarantee the freedoms that are considered to be essential elements of leisure. Individual professionals and the agencies in which they operate must uphold the Charter of Rights and Freedoms.

In keeping with the emphasis on "activities that are national in scope," the federal responsibility for recreation-related matters is governed by the Physical Activity and Sport Act of 2003. This act is not under the jurisdiction of one department but two. The responsibility for physical activity is allocated to the minister of health, with the responsibility for sport being under the minister of Canadian heritage. That latter assignment is in keeping with that department's mandate for programs that "promote Canadian content, foster cultural participation, active citizenship and participation in Canada's civic life, and strengthen connections among Canadians" (Canadian Heritage, 2004). Sport is viewed as part of several programs that contribute to Canadian identity through high-performance sport and international sport. To the Canadian federal government, recreation is a physical activity that enhances health, and international sport solidifies Canada's identity. This often seems far removed from recreation professionals' day-to-day operation.

The various provinces' and territories' views of recreation vary. All have some type of government unit responsible for recreation, but the labels differ. Over the past half-century, provincial governments have committed themselves to assisting recreation and leisure services through various government departments such as Education and Health and Public Welfare

(McFarland, 1970, p. 60). Yet, not until 1972 did a provincial government, Nova Scotia, establish a department whose sole mandate was recreation. Most provinces carried out similar actions in the 1970s. However, just as a province can establish a recreation department, it also can change it, as evidenced by Nova Scotia, which changed the Department of Recreation to the Department of Culture, Recreation, and Fitness in 1978, to the Sport and Recreation Commission in 1987, to the Department of Tourism, Culture and Recreation in early 1993, then back to the Sport and Recreation Commission in mid-1993 after an election, and finally to the Sport and Recreation Commission within the Office of Health Promotion. Other provinces have gone through similar amalgamations and disintegrations with partners that include departments for community services, tourism, culture, parks, environment, agriculture, forestry, and so on, all in the interest of efficiency, effectiveness, and political expediency. Table 7.1 shows the names of provincial and territorial departments responsible for recreation.

The previous discussion looked at the legislation and the labels for the government agencies responsible for some form of recreation. But how do government departments carry out their responsibility? Tim Burton, former University of Alberta professor, created an explanatory model that explains the five roles that governments can take in delivering public services:

1. Direct provider
2. Enabler and coordinator
3. Supporter and patron
4. Arm's length provider
5. Legislator and regulator (Burton & Glover, 1999)

As you move down the list of the five roles, the amount of direct involvement on the part of government agencies decreases. Many recreation students will be most familiar with the **direct-provider** role, which "describes the situation in which a government department or agency develops and maintains leisure facilities, operates programs, and delivers services using public funds and public employees" (Burton & Glover, 1999, p. 373). If you have been a town playground supervisor or a city swimming pool instructor, you have been part of the direct-provider role. The facility was owned by the municipality that developed the program, ran the program, and paid you.

TABLE 7.1   Canadian Provincial and Territorial Agencies Responsible for Recreation (2005)*

Province or territory	Department or ministry	Division	Web site
British Columbia	Ministry of Small Business and Economic Development	Sport and Physical Activity Branch	www.cse.gov.bc.ca/SportBranch/
Alberta	Ministry of Community Development	Sport and Recreation Branch	www.cd.gov.ab.ca/building_communities/sport_recreation/index.asp
Saskatchewan	Department of Culture, Youth and Recreation	Sport and Recreation Branch	www.cyr.gov.sk.ca/
Manitoba	Department of Culture, Heritage and Tourism	Recreation and Regional Services Branch	www.gov.mb.ca/chc/rrs/
Ontario	Ministry of Tourism and Recreation	Sport and Recreation Branch	www.tourism.gov.on.ca/english/
Quebec	Ministère de la Culture et des Communications	Culture et loisir	www.mcc.gouv.qc.ca/loisir/loisir.htm
New Brunswick	Culture and Sport Secretariat		www.gnb.ca/0131/index-e.asp
Nova Scotia	Office of Health Promotion	Sport and Recreation Commission	www.gov.ns.ca/ohp/srd/
Prince Edward Island	Department of Community and Cultural Affairs	Sport and Recreation Division	www.gov.pe.ca/commcul/sar-info/
Newfoundland and Labrador	Department of Tourism, Culture and Recreation	Recreation and Sport Division	www.gov.nf.ca/tcr/
Yukon	Department of Community Services	Sport and Recreation Unit	www.community.gov.yk.ca/
Northwest Territories	Department of Municipal and Community Affairs	Sport, Recreation, Youth and Volunteerism Division	www.maca.gov.nt.ca/sport/index.html
Nunavut	Department of Community and Government Services	Recreation and Leisure Division	www.gov.nu.ca/Nunavut/English/departments/CGT/

*Information gleaned from the various provincial and territorial Web sites, May 2005

The next three roles involve decreasing amounts of direct involvement by the government. When a government department acts as an **enabler and coordinator,** it will "identify organizations and agencies which produce leisure services for the public and help coordinate their efforts, resources and activities" (Burton & Glover, 1999, p. 374). If you have worked for a local community group that received funds and services such as leadership training from a recreation department, you have seen a government unit acting as an enabler and coordinator. When a government department acts as a **supporter and patron,** it "recognizes that existing organizations already produce valuable public leisure services and can be encouraged to do so through specialized support" (Burton & Glover, 1999, p. 374). If your local community festival received a government grant to assist in the production of a special event or to develop a facility, that would have been the government acting as a supporter and patron. Furthest away from government's direct influence is the role of **arm's length provider.** "This requires the creation of a . . . special purpose agency which operates outside the regular apparatus of government (Burton & Glover, 1999, p. 373). Arts and culture organizations such as museums or galleries operate in this relationship. In theory the government unit does not interfere with the internal operation of such an organization; however, theory and practice occasionally conflict when political decision makers object to an organization's decisions to acquire a controversial piece of art or mount a controversial play using public funds to do so.

The last role of government, **legislator and regulator,** affects many of our actions as both

Courtesy of San Jose Parks, Recreation and Neighborhood Services

Different delivery systems exist for providing public recreation. In this photo we can see the role of direct provider.

providers and consumers of recreation opportunities. This role operates in the background of many parts of our work and leisure lives because we must abide by laws passed by various levels of government. When a government agency requires you to obtain a permit to put on an event or have a fireworks display, it is acting in this role. When you as a consumer must get a fishing license or be of a certain age to enter a facility that serves alcohol, you are also experiencing these powers of government.

The municipal, provincial and territorial, and federal levels of government do not all engage in each of these five roles to the same degree. Municipal governments traditionally have operated using a direct-provider role; however, as cities and towns have faced financial stresses, many have shifted to a model in which they have transferred services to community groups while providing financial or in-kind support to those groups, thus moving toward an enabler and coordinator or a supporter

and patron model. Provincial and federal government departments have historically used the latter two models. Provincial and federal governments have also created arm's length agencies to carry out cultural programs. Many provincial agencies' mandates require that they operate in a legislator and regulator model.

American Delivery Systems

In the United States, the recreation and leisure industry encompasses many organizations that offer programs and services. Over the last 15 years, recreation and leisure services have become more important and more widely recognized as an avenue for meeting the physical, social, and emotional needs of community members. These services are created to benefit the community of people living within the designated areas. Public park and recreation opportunities are provided through local, state, and federal agencies, each serving a different purpose.

Municipal Recreation Leisure Services

Local park and recreation departments are usually municipal programs. Counties and special districts also provide local recreation and leisure services. These local departments receive their power from the state, and they function within a framework established by state legislation. In various states, cities and counties have combined to form regional departments or authorities. Examples are Prince William County Park Authority, headquartered in Manassas, Virginia, and East Bay Regional Park District, headquartered in Oakland, California.

Special districts are another type of local organization that provides park and recreation services. These are formed by legislation at the state level. These districts are independent from park districts, with their own governing bodies. Many districts have been established in Illinois, Ohio, Michigan, Oregon, California, and Washington. (Illinois maintains two types of special districts: park districts and special recreation districts.) Examples of special districts are the Cleveland Metroparks in Cleveland, Ohio, and Tacoma Metropolitan Park District in Tacoma, Washington. The programs offered within these organizations vary from recreation classes, sports, aquatics, camps, clinics, therapeutic recreation, golf course operations, special events, and water park operations to nature-based programs, marketing and volunteer programs, camping, and parks and trails. As you can see, the field encompasses a wide variety of areas that rely on diverse programming and leadership skills.

State Recreation Leisure Services

State recreation and leisure services are varied. They include maintaining state parks and forests, operating fish and wildlife agencies, and providing programs at state hospitals and correctional institutions. The authority for these agencies comes from the U.S. Constitution, Article X, which grants to the states all powers that are not reserved for the federal government. The state establishes and authorizes the oversight of state parks and forests through legislation. Similarly, the state authorizes an entity to administer the recreation and leisure services in state correctional facilities and hospitals.

All 50 states have established state parks, mainly for the purpose of preserving natural areas, and all but three states—Kansas, Nebraska, and Oklahoma—have state forests. Alaska has the most state parks, and California parks have the highest visitation rates. State forests are multiuse areas containing recreation, resource management, watershed, and fish and wildlife areas. Fish and wildlife agencies are primarily responsible for managing wildlife areas such as reserves, hatcheries, and game farms. In 2001, 735 million people visited state parks; 5,842 state park areas covered 13 million acres (5.3 hectares); and state parks included amenities such as golf courses, ski slopes, stables, marinas, and more than 43,000 miles (69,200 kilometers) of trails with 208,849 campsites.

Federal Recreation and Leisure Services

The federal government authorizes recreation services for the health and welfare of certain groups of people for which it is responsible, for example, people in federal prisons, military personnel and their families, and patients in Department of Veterans Affairs hospitals. In addition, numerous federal agencies such as the USDA Forest Service; National Park Service; Bureau of Land Management; U.S. Fish and Wildlife Service; Bureau of Indian Affairs; U.S. Army Corps of Engineers; Morale, Welfare and Recreation and Services; and National Endowment for the Arts provide public multiuse services. Functions under their leadership include managing outdoor recreation resources, restoring land, acquiring and developing property, providing direct

The municipal leisure services offer programs such as sports camps and track meets as shown here.

Courtesy of San Jose Parks, Recreation and Neighborhood Services

recreation services, providing technical advice and financial assistance, promoting tourism, and setting and regulating quality standards.

PARTNERSHIPS: CONNECTIONS TO THE COMMUNITY

"Without partnerships things wouldn't happen!" That was the phrase a municipal recreation director used during an interview for a 1991 *Recreation Canada* article about the role of partnerships in rural recreation. The municipality in which she worked included about 21,000 people spread over about 965 square miles (2,500 square kilometers). More than 88 percent of the municipality was rural (Markham, 1991b). Who forms the partnerships in municipalities like that one? The town, the county, the provincial government, community groups, sport groups, arts groups, ethnic groups, schools, police, social service agencies, private clubs, commercial operations, businesspeople, and the list goes on.

Forming partnerships, cooperative ventures, and collaborative agreements or alliances has long been practiced by recreation and leisure professionals in the public sector. However, the emphasis and encouragement to review, revise, and renew partnering efforts are more critical now than ever before. No one agency or entity can thrive alone. It is imperative to seek out the new, inclusive, innovative, flexible, and commonly focused opportunities. Why? Because in forming partnerships, you may be able to reduce the duplication of existing services, save dollars, and streamline the organizations. Inevitably, you will increase the visibility of the organization, gain a better network, and develop a more viable resource pool. In addition, personnel will have the opportunity to grow along with the community.

Several of the five roles that governments take in recreation service delivery that Burton described involve partnerships (Burton & Glover, 1999). Public recreation staffs would suggest that partnerships are more important today than they ever were. When a government agency acts as an enabler and coordinator or a supporter and patron, they are involved in a partnership. Partnerships are mutually beneficial arrangements in which the partners share the resources, share the costs, and receive a benefit for their efforts. But who ultimately benefits? Not the agency and not the staff, but the recipients of the services: the community members who would otherwise not have the service. The 1991 *Recreation Canada* issue noted earlier began with an editorial:

> Partnerships are essential in the generation of ideas, the discussion of approaches, the planning of strategies and the delivery of services. Partnerships can range from informal discussions to formal legal agreements. Partnerships are a key ingredient in any approach to parks and recreation whether it be direct or indirect service delivery. (Markham, 1991a, p. 4)

Courtesy of San Jose Parks, Recreation and Neighborhood Services

Public recreation departments can partner with outside agencies to provide health services. As you discover the various aspects of recreation and leisure, community involvement with a variety of interest groups will be one of your most frustrating, yet rewarding experiences.

Partnerships come in a variety of shapes and sizes. For example, it is not uncommon for park districts and departments to work together to provide services and share resources. In addition, many partnerships are formed within a municipal government. Parks and recreation departments work with police and fire departments on safety protocol and camps and on programs such as bicycle or fire safety. Ongoing partnerships with other departments such as public works and planning address building needs and general maintenance operations.

Local neighborhood groups work with parks departments to provide events and develop facilities and cleanup programs. Not only do these partnerships benefit the park and recreation department, but they also bring families and friends closer together by working toward a common goal. One of the most common cooperative efforts is between park and recreation departments and local school districts. These partnerships provide wonderful opportunities to work on joint facility development, share existing facilities, and implement after-school programs. What better way to share facilities that are funded by taxpayers?

Every community can provide examples of successful partnerships. Look for examples of the following in your community:

- Programs that strengthen families such as Big Brothers and Big Sisters
- Business relationships such as a public and private partnership in developing or operating a facility
- Law enforcement agencies involved in community youth programs such as Night Hoops
- School systems that share their resources in a community school (see pages 132-139)
- Volunteer groups such as community leagues or neighborhood recreation associations that are advocates for their community and also deliver programs

The future of partnerships is bright. As agencies and communities realize the many benefits of working together, there will be more and more opportunities to develop partnerships.

THE MANY FACES OF PUBLIC RECREATION

If you enjoy working with community members of all ages and abilities and working in diverse areas such as community and senior programs, sports, aquatics, golf, social service programs, arts, early care and education, and parks, then parks and recreation may be your field!

Public Recreation Professionals

It seems that no other field incorporates as many different professions as public recreation does. In public recreation and leisure, you may focus on a specialized area such as parks, therapeutic recreation, or sport management, or you may focus on a more general field such as recreation administration. Professionals in public recreation use a variety of skills:

- Planning and developing programs form the hub of recreation and leisure services responsibility as professionals create and place into action a variety of programs, activities, and events.
- Gaining knowledge of the world around you, including the local social, political, and economic environment; individual and social aspects of leisure and recreation; and all sectors of the recreation delivery system, is important for service providers.
- Understanding how political systems, political processes, organizations, financial systems, accounting, and auditing work is necessary.
- Fiscal services such as forecasting, setting priorities, and developing policies related to recreation and leisure services are critical, as staff members develop budgets and set revenue and expenditure projections. These services surround the actual program work.
- Effective two-way communication between different staff levels and between staff and community members and other stakeholders is essential. Effective written communication is equally important. Tact and diplomacy are essential.
- The ability to manage a complete and accessible information technology system allows professionals to store data that help them make decisions, develop policy, track inventory, and retain records. Information technology can help store information such as number of programs offered, sections of the community in which participants live, revenues and expenditures of specific program areas, facility usage, and much more.

OUTSTANDING *Graduates*

Courtesy of Maddie Kelly

Background Information

Name: Maddie Singler Kelly

Education: Bachelor's degree in leisure studies, University of Illinois (1978); master of arts in recreation management, Michigan State University (1980)

Credentials: Certified park and recreation professional (CPRP)

Special Awards: Joseph Bannon Practitioner Award

Special Affiliations: Illinois Park and Recreation Association (IPRA), National Recreation and Park Association (NRPA), and South Suburban Parks and Recreation Professional Association (SSPRPA) member

Career Information:

Position: Executive director, Oak Lawn Park District, Oak Lawn, Illinois

Organization: Oak Lawn Park District serves 56,000 residents and numerous non-residents. Fifty-six full-time and 300 part-time employees operate 22 parks and 14 facilities.

Organization's Mission: Oak Lawn Park District is a service-oriented organization dedicated to enhancing the quality of life for the citizens of Oak Lawn. It is the park district's goal to promote a strong sense of community by providing diverse recreational and cultural opportunities for all ages and abilities. The park district is committed to establishing and maintaining beautiful and safe parks and facilities and preserving open space.

> You will never regret a career in this field, and you must never forget our mission of providing quality leisure services. We do make a profound impact on people's lives!

Job Description: Administer and direct the operations and activities of the director's office, recreation department, parks department, revenue facilities department, and business department.

Career Path: I have held the positions of facility manager, aquatics manager, athletic and recreation supervisor, and superintendent of recreation.

Likes and Dislikes About the Job: I love the diversity and constant challenges. In 18 years in this field, I can honestly say that I have never had a boring day on the job. Issues in a typical day can run the gamut from complaints about a fox on the golf course stealing golf balls to cutting $100,000 out of the budget. The satisfaction I receive from providing quality leisure experiences for our patrons is immeasurable. I dislike it when local politics rears its ugly head in park district operations.

Advice to Undergraduates

Get experience working in as many leisure service organizations as possible and keep an open mind about where you are willing to begin your career. I had no intention of working for a park district upon completion of my master's degree, and I have now devoted almost 20 years of my life to the public sector. I could not have asked for a better career choice.

- Marketing "focuses on individuals before they become customers and has as its primary objective 'selling' an organization's facilities and service" (Ipson, Mahoney, & Adams, 1999, p. 403).

Many skills are needed to ensure that recreation and leisure professionals are well rounded. Therefore comprehensive professional training and preparation are detailed, yet practical. In addition to program development classes, recreation and leisure students take courses in environmental design and planning, leadership, and management. And because the field of parks and recreation continues to expand rapidly, new skills are always required. For example, in the past 10 years, public recreation professionals have become involved in prevention efforts in health and wellness and have undertaken antigang, antigraffiti, and prevention of elder abuse efforts. Each of these focuses requires additional training.

Any job in public recreation will involve meetings, meetings, and more meetings! The job will involve reports, reports, and more reports! You will be accountable to your boss, to your staff, to your community, to your clients, and to your elected officials—which one gets highest priority? You will have to answer this question often in your professional career.

Most people today still believe that the field of parks and recreation encompasses sport, fun, and games. Although, certainly, these are part of the profession, they do not begin to cover all the diverse areas and links to other professions.

Public Recreation Management

Managers and leaders in recreation and leisure services plan, organize, direct, and control in order to oversee the agency and various areas of the agency. Managers fall into three categories: top, or executive managers; middle managers; and frontline, or supervisory managers. Within these categories are other positions that may report to them.

Managers must possess three types of skills:

1. Technical skills require specialized knowledge in operations, techniques, and procedures.
2. Human skills require understanding and the ability to motivate and work with employees.
3. Conceptual skills allow the development and organization of a philosophy, a mission, goals, and objectives.

In addition to organizational and administrative functions within an organization, managers are also involved in strategic planning, which encompasses community involvement and coordination with municipalities and other agencies. Most important is working with community members to plan the many activities and facilities that are needed. It is important to work with the community so there is "buy in" and they have a sense of ownership. Successful collaboration draws on all the skills required of recreation and leisure professionals.

Professional must ask themselves the following: What do we do as professionals in public recreation? Whom do we serve? Do we serve our career? Do we serve the public? Do we serve the politicians? Whom do the politicians serve? Coming to your own answers to those questions is a major step in your professional career.

Canadian Professional Organizations

The previous section showed the structure and mandate of the various sectors of the public recreation delivery system. It is within this framework of public and governmental jurisdictions that many recreation and leisure service professionals work. Just as these professionals have established or worked in organizations to deliver services, they have also joined together in associations to promote the cause of recreation and leisure services. From the roots of the Ontario Parks Association grew the Parks and Recreation Association of Canada (PRAC) in 1945. PRAC's mandate was "the Dominion-wide stimulation of recreation, [and] the Dominion-wide extension of parks including municipal, provincial and national parks and recreation activities" (Parks and Recreation Association of Canada, 1947). As the organization adapted to changes in the environment in the 1960s, it changed its name first to the Canadian Parks/Recreation Association (CP/RA) in 1969 and later refined it to the Canadian Parks and Recreation Association (CPRA). CPRA promotes itself as an organization of both professionals and volunteers involved in parks and recreation. Today CPRA provides services through its affiliation with 13 provincial or territorial organizations, each of which is autonomous and offers services in keeping with its local requirements. Table 7.2 lists the national, provincial, and territorial associations.

As part of CPRA's 1969 changes, the Recreation Institute of Canada was formed as the result of pressure to form an organization reflecting the needs and interests of professionals in the field. The institute had a short life. Interest by professionals was not as high as expected, and the institute ceased operation after four years, in 1973. Therein lies one of the essential, enduring debates in the recreation and leisure services field: Is it a profession? If it is, how does it deal with the thousands of volunteers who guide policy and deliver services? If it is not, how does it attain the status and profile that it needs both to ensure the competence of those leading the field and to endure in the face of policy and funding priority debates with other professions?

American Professional Organizations

As early as 1926, the need to fill professional positions in recreation and leisure existed. With that effort followed the development of professional associations that could assist with the ever changing profession. Today, the largest association of park and recreation professionals in the United States is the National Recreation and Park Association. In addition, there are numerous affiliates within the national organization (see table 7.3).

TABLE 7.2 Canadian National, Provincial, and Territorial Associations (2005)*

Association	Description	Web site
Canadian Parks and Recreation Association	CPRA is the national voice for a vibrant grassroots network with partnerships that connect people who build healthy, active communities and impact the everyday lives of Canadians.	www.cpra.ca/cpra-new/en/Welcome.htm
British Columbia Recreation and Parks Association	BCRPA is a not-for-profit organization dedicated to building and sustaining active, healthy lifestyles and communities in BC.	www.bcrpa.bc.ca/
Alberta Recreation and Parks Association	ARPA believes that "A province, and communities within, that embrace and proactively use recreation and parks as essential means for enhancing individual well-being and community vitality, economic sustainability and natural resource protection and conservation."	www.arpaonline.ca/
Saskatchewan Parks and Recreation Association	SPRA is a nonprofit volunteer organization whose purpose is to promote, develop and facilitate parks and recreation opportunities throughout the province. SPRA is recognized as the provincial umbrella organization representing parks and recreation in Saskatchewan. SPRA manages the recreation division of the Saskatchewan Lotteries Trust Fund for Sport, Culture and Recreation.	www.spra.sk.ca/
Recreation Connections Manitoba	Recreation Connections Manitoba membership is open to all volunteers and professionals in the recreation, parks, and leisure delivery system in Manitoba. Recreation Connections Manitoba has three strategic directions: networking and partnerships, education/professional development, and advocacy.	www.recconnections.com/
Parks and Recreation Ontario	PRO is an all-inclusive, not-for-profit corporation dedicated to enhancing the quality of life of the people of Ontario. PRO fulfills this mandate by collaborating with stakeholders to influence decisions and policies that support the benefits of recreation through information, advocacy, and the research and development of innovative and relevant products and services.	http://216.13.76.142/PROntario/about.html
Association Québécoise du loisir municipal	AQLM est la voix unifiée du loisir municipal au Québec et vise l'atteinte d'objectifs majeurs, tout en se portant à la défense des intérêts de ses membres.	www.loisirmunicipal.qc.ca/index.html
Association des travailleuses et travailleurs en loisirs du Nouveau-Brunswick	L'ATLNB est une association relativement jeune et très dynamique qui a su s'adapter, au cours des dernières années, aux nombreux changements socio-économiques ou autres dont nous sommes tous témoins et qui nous affectent tous comme travailleurs ou travailleuses en loisir. Ces changements reflètent très bien le dynamisme et la volonté de progression qui existent au sein de l'ATLNB.	http://atlnb.ca/
Recreation and Parks Association of New Brunswick	RPANB is a not-for-profit organization dedicated to advancing the recreation and parks field by broadening the knowledge and experience base of its members and by advocating for the value and benefit of leisure and recreation opportunities for all people.	www.rpanb.nb.ca
Recreation Nova Scotia	RNS is a vibrant new, province-wide, not-for-profit organization established in 1998 to promote the values and benefits of recreation and leisure resulting from a merger of the Recreation Association of Nova Scotia, the Recreation Council on Disability in Nova Scotia, and Volunteer Nova Scotia. In partnership with the volunteers and professional recreation community, Recreation Nova Scotia advocates on behalf of all Nova Scotians for high-quality recreation and leisure opportunities.	www.recreationns.ns.ca/
Prince Edward Island Recreation and Facilities Association	The PEIRFA's mandate is to promote excellence in the provision of recreation services and facilities.	www.gov.pe.ca/infopei/index.php3?number=10773&lang=E
Newfoundland and Labrador Parks/Recreation Association	NLP/RA works to improve the quality of recreation for Newfoundlanders and Labradorians. NLP/RA members are the leaders in recreation and are the link between Newfoundlanders and Labradorians and the recreation decision makers.	www.nlpra.ca/
Recreation and Parks Association of the Yukon	RPAY is a nonprofit organization that works in partnership with Yukon groups, agencies, and individuals to promote and support healthy, active lifestyles in the Yukon.	www.polarcom.com/~rpay/
Northwest Territories Recreation and Parks Association	NWTRPA is a nonprofit organization that works with communities across the territory to promote healthy living through active recreation.	www.nwtrpa.org/

*Information gleaned from various national, provincial, and territorial association Web sites, May 2005

TABLE 7.3 U.S. Agencies Responsible for Parks and Recreation

National	Description	Web site
National Recreation and Park Association (NRPA)	For more than 100 years, NRPA has advocated the importance of thriving, local park systems; the opportunity for all Americans to lead healthy, active lifestyles; and the preservation of great community places.	www.nrpa.org/
Armed Forces Recreation Society (AFRS)	AFRS represents NRPA members working in military settings worldwide.	www.nrpa.org/content/default.aspx?documentId=526
American Park and Recreation Society (APRS)	APRS serves more than 7,000 members. The APRS goals include the following: To be advocates for parks and recreation in the United States and Canada To foster professional growth and development of parks and recreation personnel, thus improving the delivery of leisure services To provide advice to NRPA in achieving overall organizational goals To gather and disseminate information on significant parks and recreation issues	www.nrpa.org/content/default.aspx?documentId=525
NRPA Citizen Branch	The NRPA Citizen Branch represents members nationwide. The Citizen Branch's goals include the following: Promotion and organization of a statewide citizens board-commission association in every state Legislative action programs, materials, and resources at all levels Special institutes, forums, and workshops, especially designed for board-commission members National awards and recognition programs Expansion of the branch information and education program	www.nrpa.org/content/default.aspx?documentId=527
National Aquatic Branch (NAB)	NAB represents NRPA members working in aquatic settings. The NAB serves aquatic professionals, including pool managers to executive staff. Approximately 205,000 swimming pools and 5,000 beaches are owned, operated, managed, and maintained by NRPA-represented park and recreation systems.	www.nrpa.org/content/default.aspx?documentId=528
National Society for Park Resources (NSPR)	NSPR represents NRPA members working in natural resources, parks, and conservation.	www.nrpa.org/content/default.aspx?documentId=529
National Therapeutic Recreation Society (NTRS)	NTRS provides therapeutic recreation services for people with disabilities in clinical facilities and in the community. NTRS members include practitioners, administrators, educators, volunteers, students, and consumers.	www.nrpa.org/content/default.aspx?documentId=530
Society of Park and Recreation Educators (SPRE)	SPRE members are NRPA members working in educational settings.	www.nrpa.org/content/default.aspx?documentId=531
Student Branch	The Student Branch represents NRPA members attending post-secondary institutions.	www.nrpa.org/content/default.aspx?documentId=532
Commercial Recreation and Tourism Section (CRTS)	CRTS represents NRPA members working in commercial recreation and tourism settings. CRTS membership comprises individuals and businesses who are involved in the management, operation, and recreational programming of, among other areas, resorts, health and fitness clubs, country clubs, campgrounds, theme parks, tour and travel businesses, and corporate employee service programs.	www.nrpa.org/content/default.aspx?documentId=533
Leisure and Aging Section (LAS)	LAS represents NRPA members working in settings that focus on leisure and aging issues.	www.nrpa.org/content/default.aspx?documentId=534
National Recreation and Park Association regions*	**Description**	**Web site**
Great Lakes	The Great Lakes Region supports the Great Lakes region. It consists of Illinois, Indiana, Iowa, Michigan, Minnesota, Missouri, Ohio, Wisconsin, and two Canadian provinces.	www.nrpa.org/content/default.aspx?documentId=536

(continued)

TABLE 7.3 *(continued)*

National Recreation and Park Association regions* *(continued)*	Description	Web site
Mid-Atlantic	The Mid-Atlantic Region consists of Delaware, District of Columbia, Maryland, New Jersey, New York, and Pennsylvania.	www.nrpa.org/content/default.aspx?documentId=537
Midwest	The Midwest Region consists of Colorado, Kansas, Nebraska, North Dakota, South Dakota, and Wyoming.	www.nrpa.org/content/default.aspx?documentId=538
New England	The New England Region consists of Connecticut, Maine, Massachusetts, New Hampshire, Rhode Island, Vermont, New Brunswick, Newfoundland, Nova Scotia, and Prince Edward Island.	www.nrpa.org/content/default.aspx?documentId=539
Pacific Northwest	The Pacific Northwest Regional Council supports the Pacific Northwest region. It consists of five states, three Canadian provinces, and one Canadian territory.	www.nrpa.org/content/default.aspx?documentId=540
Pacific Southwest	The Pacific Southwest Regional Council supports the Pacific Southwest region. It consists of five states and Guam.	www.nrpa.org/content/default.aspx?documentId=541
Southern	The NRPA Southern Region consists of 10 southeastern states, Puerto Rico, and the Virgin Islands. A regional council of 70 members represents the 5,200 NRPA members and gives advice, counsel, and direction to NRPA.	www.nrpa.org/content/default.aspx?documentId=542
Southwest	The NRPA Southwest Region consists of Arkansas, Louisiana, Oklahoma, New Mexico, and Texas.	www.nrpa.org/content/default.aspx?documentId=543
NRPA national affiliates	**Description**	**Web site**
Park Law Enforcement Association (PLEA)	PLEA was established in 1984 to improve law enforcement and visitor protection services in parks and recreation areas through professional development, thus better assuring quality of life and leisure opportunities in local, state, and national parks and recreation areas.	www.parkranger.com/
National Association of County Park and Recreation Officials (NACO)	The purpose of NACO is to cooperate with all parks and recreation professional bodies and organizations with similarly related objectives and to encourage cooperation and coordination between agencies and organizations concerned with the provisions of parks, open spaces, and recreation services.	www.nacpro.org/
NRPA national affiliates	**Description**	**Web site**
Please see United States state parks listing on the NRPA Web site.	NRPA has 52 state affiliates—think of them as your *local* parks and recreation associations.	www.nrpa.org/content/default.aspx?documentId=497

*The NRPA's eight regions represent the geographically diverse interests of the association's 22,000 members. These regional organizations provide effective outreach and education and help to extend NRPA's service from the organization's national headquarters in Ashburn, Virginia.

CHAMELEON PROFESSION: EVER CHANGING SOCIETAL ISSUES AND NEEDS

Sometimes being a chameleon is viewed in a negative sense, perhaps as selling out to external influences, but in the case of the public recreation profession, it is not. We must be adaptable. We must respond to changes in the environment, whether those changes are in the physical, economic, political, or social parts of the environ-

ment. But, we must not lose sight of our founding roots, our reasons for being, and our desire to contribute to the public good. What is the future of public-sector recreation and leisure? To discover where we are headed, we must understand the current reality.

Current Themes

Recent labor, leisure, and longevity trends affect how much unobligated time people have and how they use it. This in turn affects recreation and leisure services and professionals that provide them. In *Leisure and Leisure Services in the 21st Century,* Geoffrey Godbey (1997), a professor at Pennsylvania State University in the recreation, park, and tourism management program, summarizes that most workers today do not work a standard workday from 9 to 5. Godbey also states that 40 percent of North Americans reported always feeling rushed, yet they average approximately 40 hours of free time per week. Today, two-thirds of the public have lived the last 15 to 20 years of their life without participating in the labor force. This is due to our aging, retired population, and people older than 50 have more free time today than they did in 1965. People are working mixed schedules that vary based on the needs of the different communities.

As leisure patterns in North America continue to change, one of the best predictors of change is our aging citizens, who are more active than ever before. In addition, our urban areas are becoming more diverse. More people are pursuing higher levels of formal education with an eye toward increasingly diverse roles for women. The gap between the haves and have-nots is widening. And, citizens expect government to do more, but they want to pay less. People are obsessed with health, but citizens of the United States are now more obese than ever, especially the young. All of this means that recreation and leisure service professionals must deal with a wide set of issues when creating programs, making plans, and obtaining resources and funding.

Statistics Canada's 2001 census yields the following insights into the current population and the trends that affect employees of Canadian recreation agencies and the people they serve:

- The median age in Canada has reached an all-time high: 37.6 years.
- The population gain is fastest among the oldest age groups: The 80-and-over age group grew by 41.2 percent between 1996 and 2001. Statistics Canada predicts that by 2011 this group will number 1.3 million.
- The working-age population is increasingly made up of older workers: One-quarter of Canada's population is in the 45 to 64 age group.
- Senior women outnumber senior men: For every 100 women over age 65, there are 75 men of similar age.

- There are questions about whether Canada can maintain its population growth without substantial immigration (Statistics Canada, 2002).

But what do these insights tell us about how recreation services will have to change to accommodate the changing population? David Foot's 1998 analyses of population growth or lack of it in *Boom, Bust and Echo* provide us with insights on how Canadian demographics affect many social, economic, and political issues such as real estate, investing, jobs, retail, leisure, urban development, education, health care, and family structure. Even though Foot was basing his analyses on the 1996 census data, he identified trends that continued between 1996 and 2001, and will continue for the foreseeable future. Regarding leisure activities for the declining younger population and the increasing older population, Foot (1998) projected the following:

- "There is no excuse for a community to spend money on hockey rinks at the millennium that are likely to be empty in 2005, while neglecting to provide the parks and walking trails that an aging population needs" (p. 148).
- "A nation of young people is a society of hockey and tennis players. A nation of older people is a society of walkers and gardeners" (p. 151).
- "New [hockey] rinks should be built sparingly and selectively, and they should be easily adaptable to curling" (p. 155).
- ". . . activities like birdwatching, . . . will grow two and a half times as much as skiing" (p. 155).
- "Golf is growing" (p. 160).
- "The movement to make the countryside more accessible will intensify. The most spectacular example is the Trans-Canada Trail" (p. 165).
- "Volunteering is one of those rare activities that people do more of as they get older" (p. 173).

David Foot's detailed projections may be subject to debate as the interests of individuals and specific communities are taken into account, but his macro-level analyses such as the population pyramids shown at www.footwork.com/pyramids.html give us a stunning view of the future.

In addition to affecting the type of leisure services that must be provided, an aging population also affects funding for recreation services. Many key questions come out of Foot's analyses. For example, in a 2002 *Globe and Mail* article, Foot noted the following:

> Over the 1950s and 1960s, when most of the boomers were born, annual rates of population growth were much higher. Since people are customers, taxpayers and workers, slower population growth suggests slower growth in consumer spending, tax revenues, and the work force. (March 21, 2002, p. A17)

If there is lower growth in tax revenues, and because much of the public recreation sector depends on tax revenues for its support, what does that mean for recreation agencies?

In that same article Foot addressed population growth caused by immigration:

> As the gap between births and deaths narrows, domestic sources become a smaller component of population growth and net immigration (immigrants minus emigrants) becomes relatively more important. Over the past five years, international sources surpassed domestic sources of population growth for the first time in Canada's postwar history. (March 21, 2002, p. A17)

What does this mean to the multicultural makeup of Canada? Where do these immigrants settle? Mostly they settle in the major urban centers such as Montreal, Toronto, and Vancouver. What does that mean for public recreation services in those cities? Are we in recreation prepared to serve this diverse mosaic of traditions, needs, interests, and expectations? There are numerous examples of diverse recreation programs in cities with a substantial multicultural makeup. One example is the Sunset Community Centre in Vancouver. This Centre "serves a multi-cultural population of over 33,000 with a high proportion of Chinese and Punjabi residents, young families and children" (Vancouver Board of Parks and Recreation, 2005).

The Changing Profession

The future of the public leisure and recreation profession seems to lead us to a decline in most forms of sport participation and greater interest in the environment. People seem to now be more interested in the quality of the experience and a sense of place. It also seems that there will be more diversity of leisure expression because our population is much more diverse.

Because state and federal funding of recreation and leisure services is declining, these services will be more locally focused than federally. Citizens want local assistance in forming their "quality of life." Providing parks and recreation services for all ages and diverse populations is critical. For example, citizens want the local parks and recreation agency to provide parks, various programs, and facilities. Therefore recreation departments need to be flexible and innovative in their work efforts, including staff assignments, decision making, training programs, and the knowledge, skills, and abilities needed to do the job.

Finally, outsourcing may become the norm instead of the exception. Recreation and leisure service agencies may become more "enterprising" than in the past. The "customization" of leisure programs will be necessary to retain community consumers, treating people appropriately, not equally. For instance, more strategic planning will be necessary to place appropriate, applicable facilities and programs in a community based on numbers and needs. This means that the squeaky wheel may not get the grease. In the past, areas of a community were often treated as though their needs were all the same. This effort created more amenities but not necessarily a strategic approach to what may really be needed.

The future of this profession lies in your hands. As the members of diverse communities request more and different services, it is the responsibility of recreation and leisure professionals to address emerging trends and issues to meet the ever changing needs and expectations of their clientele. As services continue to evolve, parks and recreation professionals will create the future.

POLITICAL REALITIES: NO PAIN, NO GAIN

One of the most telling comments on the realities of working in public recreation is the title of George Cuff's article "First on the Agenda: Last on the Budget" that appeared in *Recreation Canada* (1990). Based on his personal experiences as a recreation director and later as a mayor, he describes the "challenges, difficulties and competing influences which Council members face the moment they assume public office" (p. 34).

To many novices in recreation, the words "politics" and "politicians" are incredibly negative. Why? What would make you think that? The reality of public recreation is that the ultimate decision makers are often elected officials. Who elects them? We do: we, the public! So here we are right back to the questions at the beginning of this section: In the abstract, the challenge and the role of public recreation are to serve all of us. But does this really happen? And who is "us"? Is it realistic to believe that the public recreation system *can* serve all? Who takes up the challenge to try to serve all? And can they succeed? Is recreation really a "public good"?

Public recreation is about creating a sense of inclusion. Are you prepared to listen to and assist everyone in your community? You should be. How will you deal with competing interests? Think about a small community park. How many groups with competing interests can you imagine that want to use that park: how about the young soccer players and their parents, the older aggressive soccer players, the baseball players of all ages, the parents of small children, the dog walkers, the neighbors who want peace and quiet, the neighbors who want a pretty park to enhance their property values, the kids who want a place to splash in the hot summer, the teenagers who want a place to hang out, the musicians who want a place to jam, the skateboarders who want a place to practice stunts, the pacifists who want a place to protest against a war, the theater group that wants a place to perform, the religious group that wants to perform a religious play, the homeless who want a place to hunker down at night?

There will always be a need for balance between the requests of communities and the other desires or actions that political powers believe need attention. Somewhere in the middle of the issue are the parks and recreation staff members trying to once again resolve the situation or create the "win-win." It is what we do.

Leaders in the recreation profession need to realize that political responsiveness becomes a more difficult and complex task as the size and diversity of the population they serve increase. Problems of political responsiveness are most likely found in one of two different types of settings. The first, and most widely recognized, is that in which a new group either moves into a community or rapidly increases its percentage of the community's members. One example of this is the growth of youth soccer and parents' desire for more fields and amenities. Difficulties are frequently encountered in accommodating the views and attitudes of the new group in policy-making processes. The second setting is one in which the community experiences rapid population growth, growth that outpaces the ability to provide resources and facilities. This setting further identifies the city with the "haves" and "have-nots."

What role can interest groups play in obtaining recreation services? Interest groups can be powerful, vocal advocates for recreation services, or they can be adversaries. They can publicly address issues that a recreation staff member cannot. They can provide a public face for those who need services. They can provide the political face for your agency. Each recreation professional must decide how he or she will work with interest groups. That brings us right back to the question "Whom do we serve?"

The public recreation profession in the United States began with the advocacy work of Joseph Lee, the father of the playground movement. He helped to create in the late 1800s the first model playground in a dejected Boston neighborhood. Lee was convinced that all young people needed a place to play. He promoted a bill in the Massachusetts state legislature that required towns and cities with populations of more than 10,000 to develop playgrounds. Joseph Lee's actions set the stage for future actions by other state and local governments. This is an example of how powerful a citizen with a cause can be and what a difference it can make.

When we think about developing the work we do, we must begin with our community members. We work with many members of diverse communities to help them experience, in some form or fashion, a better quality of life. That is why we provide services, activities, and events. That is why we build facilities. That is the very reason we exist as a profession.

BENEFITS OF RECREATION

Since the foundation work of Joseph Lee in the United States and the National Council of Women in Canada more than a century ago, we have intuitively known that recreation benefits people and their communities. But we must go beyond intuition to research. The Benefits Project collected past research about how parks and recreation helps people, their communities, and the environment. The product of this collecting was *The Benefits Catalogue* (Canadian Parks and Recreation Asssociation, 1997), which moved the exercise from collecting research studies to packaging them into a form that can be used in the political arena. *The Benefits Catalogue* summarized 44 statements of benefits, each with substantial background research, and focused them into eight marketing messages:

- Recreation and active living are essential to personal health.
- Recreation is a key to balanced human development.
- Recreation and parks are essential to quality of life.
- Recreation reduces self-destructive and anti-social behavior.
- Recreation and parks build strong families and healthy communities.
- Recreation reduces health care, social service, and police and justice costs.
- Recreation and parks are significant economic generators in the community.
- Parks, open spaces, and natural areas are essential to ecological survival.

The *Benefits Catalogue* was created to address a substantial political issue—the perception, more real than imagined, that recreation services, although important to our communities, are not considered to be essential by the decision makers. This is our biggest challenge as we strive to contribute to the public good.

SUMMARY

Public recreation and leisure is a diverse area of the recreation and leisure field. As a professional you serve many different types of people and can work in a wide variety of areas. It was originally conceived as a way of solving real or perceived problems and as a way of creating opportunities for communities. The role of public recreation is to serve everyone, but this mission can be difficult due to political realities. Because of political pressures, it is important to remember the founding roots of public recreation when deciding how to work with interest groups. Public recreation is an exciting profession with challenges, benefits, and opportunities for those who choose to pursue it as a career.

School-Based Recreation and Community Schools

Ellen Montague

Education has no more serious responsibility than making adequate provision for enjoyment of recreative leisure; not only for the sake of immediate health, but . . . for the sake of its lasting effect upon habits of mind.

John Dewey, professor of philosophy at Columbia University (1904–1930)

The introduction to and instruction in recreation activities have long been considered essential elements of a well-rounded kindergarten through grade 12 (K-12) curriculum. Not only have recreation activities been vital to nurturing strength, flexibility, and self-esteem in young people, they also have contributed to educational achievement. In 1968, Indiana University recreation professors Carlson, Deppe, and MacLean wrote of the school's recreation responsibilities:

There is no conflict between teaching the fundamental processes or attaining the highest intellectual achievement and teaching the arts of leisure. The latter may contribute to intellectual achievement. Some of our best learning takes place in relaxed leisure hours when we turn to books, nature lore, scientific experiment or discussions because we choose to do so. Inspiration to use in leisure the basic skills and knowledge that must be learned anyway is often the teachers' greatest contribution. (p. 116)

The integration of recreational activities into the school-day curriculum was indeed an inspiration. Also born of inspiration, originally by the need to provide young people with constructive activities when they were not engaged in school, was the concept of **community education.** Through participation in community education—after-school and evening classes and activities and programs at the local school—students could further enhance their strength, flexibility, self-esteem, and academic performance.

The contributions to intellectual achievement that Carlson, Deppe, and MacLean ascribed to recreation in 1968 continue in 2005 to be practiced in schools across North America. One example of this link is found in research through the **cause-related marketing** activities of the VH1 Save the Music

Foundation. Their studies prove that students who engage in 30 minutes of music education, practiced three times a week, significantly increase their ability to learn (VH1 Save the Music Foundation, n.d.). In the world of education, this research and the positive impact that music education and other recreative activities have on student success continue the positive association with recreation and leisure activities.

CONDENSED HISTORY OF COMMUNITY EDUCATION

Although recreation activities have generated student success for years, many of the factors and conditions in communities that have created barriers to learning have remained constant as well. Many of the barriers that were present at the beginning of the 20th century are still present a century later.

> In 1906, the following conditions were identified that stimulated the unification of the recreation movement: Depletion of natural resources; Effects of the industrial (now technological) revolution; Urbanization; Rise in crime and delinquency; Increase in population; Rise in incidence of mental illness; Unwholesome commercial recreation; Increasing mobility of the population; and the Need for unification of individual efforts in recreation. (Carlson et al., 1968, p. 41)

Education alone, even with the assistance of recreation integrated into the curriculum, could not completely stem the tide of these factors for communities. Something more was needed.

In the United States, several national movements were established in the early 1900s in response to needs of young people. The Boy Scouts of America (1910); the Campfire Girls (1910); the Girl Guides, later named the Girl Scouts (1912); and the National Recreation Association, established in 1911 as the Playground and Recreation Association of America, provided activities and social interaction opportunities for youngsters. Still, there remained young people who were not part of these organizations and had a great deal of unstructured time on their hands. In Milwaukee, Wisconsin, an influx of immigrant factory workers with limited English-speaking skills gave rise to the development of daytime and evening English as a second language classes at local schools. Dorothy Enderis, known as the "Lady of the Lighted Schoolhouse," led this effort, which branched into additional programs for adults and youth at school sites. She promoted legislation, which passed in 1911, opening the schools to public use as long as this use did not interfere with the prime purpose of the buildings (Wisconsin Department of Public Instruction, 2004).

In 1935, Frank Manley, a city recreation leader from Flint, Michigan, visited the Wisconsin program and returned with a proven method for addressing the needs created by unstructured time among the youth of his town. Manley developed the lighted schoolhouse model, and it did not take long for communities across the country to adopt it as an answer to their growing needs.

Manley believed that using public school facilities to hold activities after the regular school day was the way to effectively engage young people in constructive activities and thus reduce the incidence of delinquency that was growing in his town. He believed that because the public paid taxes to build and maintain the schools, the public deserved ownership for the buildings and the right to use them during nonschool hours.

He put the idea into practice, and the idea worked. Young people began attending organized activities in school gyms in the evenings and on weekends. Adults helped to coach and provide building security. Although these activities met an obvious need, it soon became apparent that this idea held more potential than simply the constructive use of free time for youth. To harness this potential, Manley developed the "Four Is" and encouraged his staff to use them when working with people using the school (see figure 7.1).

- **In:** Get the people of the community into the school, primarily by means of recreation and education.
- **Interested:** Get them interested by explaining problems and asking their help in solving them.
- **Involved:** Ask people to help. They are willing and able (to help) when given the opportunity.
- **Informed:** An informed person is a responsible citizen concerned with improvement.

FIGURE 7.1 Frank Manley's Four *Is* of community participation.

Reprinted, by permission, from L. Decker, *The evolution of the community school concept: The leadership of Frank J. Manley.*

The original concept of the community school as Manley conceived it was intended to tackle a practical, intuitively obvious problem with an immediate and tangible cure, for example, to provide boys who have too much unconstructive time on their hands the opportunity to play basketball. But Frank Manley's work and his passion for it went deeper than that and proved critical to the further development of schools as vehicles for community activities and gatherings, be they for fun, recreation, learning, or community problem solving. As a neutral, local gathering place in most communities, the **community school** offered the capacity to expand the school's role and extend it further into the community to serve the needs of more people. No longer was it just about opening the school doors and letting youth in. Manley believed that organized activity and community-building needed to be equal parts of the equation for what was fast becoming the model community school. Others grabbed hold of the concept as well. In 1939, Elsie Clapp described the community school as ". . . a place used freely and informally for all the needs of living and learning" (Parson, 1999). W. Fred Totten defined the role of the community school as that of "enlisting the services of all citizens to provide education for the total community" (1970).

Charles Stewart Mott was another person who found merit in Manley's work. A wealthy industrialist from Flint, Michigan, Mott had established the C.S. Mott Foundation in 1926 and, through it in 1935, assisted the city of Flint in its efforts to expand the community education program that Manley was developing. As it became apparent that more and more communities desired guidance in initiating their own community education programs, the C.S. Mott Foundation introduced the Mott intern training program for community educators to train those who would take a leadership role in establishing community education programs in their own school districts around the country.

RESPONDING TO NEEDS

Quickly, the philosophy of community education, and the community school with it, evolved into a catalytic and holistic delivery system—one that implemented a refreshingly new, collaborative approach to problem solving. Rather than providing communities with programs that professionals thought they would want, this model was based on asking the community for its thoughts, ideas, and suggestions. Once this information was collected, the community school coordinator and advisory council then acted on what the community had requested and enlisted the help of other community members in creating, teaching, supervising, and otherwise being involved in the delivery of activities that met the needs expressed.

This concept of community-driven program identification was a new approach to governance, requiring practitioners to make a paradigm shift from the former autocratic system of top-down, "we know best" leadership, which was common at the time. The timing for such a change was right, and the new model easily gained popularity. To support the concept as it flourished around the country, training centers and associations were developed. The National Center for Community Education was established in Flint in 1964, originally to provide short-term training, then expanding into longer workshops and internship opportunities. The National Community School Education Association (now the National Community Education Association) began in 1966. State professional community education associations also arose during this time and provided conferences and in-service training for aspiring professionals at the state level.

Developing Community Response

Noted recreation professors Meyer and Brightbill (1956, p. 46) outlined five principles for establishing recreational programs in a community:

1. Anything and everything that is done should have its base in the community.

2. Ample recreational opportunities should exist for all the people: children, youth, and adults in all economic and social strata.

3. The talents of people and the natural resources of the community should be used to the fullest extent.

4. The program should function through all types of agencies: public, private, and commercial.

5. Recreation should be recognized as an essential force in the life of the people for what it contributes to social well-being.

Not so different from these five principles are the six components that comprise the philosophy of community education. Developed as an inclusive system, each component is vital to an effective, comprehensive community school.

1. **Community involvement:** Building a feeling of inclusion among community members by providing encouragement and opportunities for involvement and leadership in the development of community school activities

2. **Facility use:** Making use of existing school facilities, which are owned by the taxpayers

3. **Adult programming:** Organizing and implementing classes and activities that are requested and designed by and that appeal to the needs of adults in the community

4. **Youth programming:** Organizing and implementing classes and activities that are requested and designed by and that appeal to the needs of young people in the community

5. **Classroom enrichment through community resources:** Augmenting and enriching classroom curriculum and lessons by requesting the expertise and passion of knowledgeable speakers who live in the community and scheduling hands-on learning opportunities during the school day through field trips to community sites

6. **Coordination and cooperation and delivery of community services:** Bringing people to the table who are involved in similar pursuits to benefit the entire community, avoiding duplication of effort, and resolving issues

Leadership to Cooperation to Collaboration

The defining principles of recreation and components of community education overlap in several areas: the availability of activities for all members of the community, the encouragement of inclusion, and the use of community resources to the fullest extent. Although it was expected that these similarities in philosophy would enhance the services to cities and towns where recreation and community education professionals both worked, the overlap in philosophy at times caused disagreement. In fact, recreation staff and community education staff ran the risk of misunderstanding each other's intentions and falling prey to what former professor of recreation Dr. Effie Lu Fairchild described as the "Three Terrible Ts" (personal communication July 1978). The Three Terrible Ts referred to the difficulties that could occur when arguments over *turf*, "this is our town," "that's my instructor"; *territory*, "we were here first," "this section of town is where our participants come from"; and *tradition*, "we've always done it this way," "folks are used to our organization offering this service," affected programming and marketing for classes and activities. Ultimately, the staffs of recreation and community education programs operating in the same communities often had to work hard to understand each other's philosophies, practices, and motivations for serving the community and to identify cosponsored services as well as the separate activities offered by each organization. Recreation and community education staffs still risk falling prey to the Terrible Ts and need to work together.

In their book *Community Education: From Program to Process to Practice,* Jack Minzey and Clyde LeTarte caution community educators to continue this collaboration.

> Community educators must understand that there is often a broader more encompassing view of recreation than their own and that they must be willing to accept and respect this as they begin planning recreational programs for the entire community. The best recreation programs are those incorporating as many agencies as possible. Great diversity and choice in recreational offerings is best achieved through diversity in the groups and agencies providing the services, each coordinating its efforts with the others. (Minzey & LeTarte, 1979)

The impact of the Three Terrible Ts was a barrier to service; however, resolving this issue ultimately provided a positive outcome. The communication necessary to overcome differences between local community education and recreation providers mirrored the practice of community education at the institutional level. Successful conflict resolution served to deepen cooperative relationships among educators, recreators, and community service providers, which in turn further encouraged and deepened the new model of providing integrated community services. In this way community schools played a role in helping to expand the recreation and leisure service opportunities in a community by working collaboratively with recreation professionals to develop program schedules that included recreation activities too. Recreation programs also helped to promote the activities of community schools. At times, both organizations developed and presented programs together. Partnership activities such as these expanded the use of school district and community facilities and the promotion of available programs, meeting community needs in a way that neither group could have done as effectively alone.

Community schools took up the mantle of this collaborative approach in their program development approach as well. Community school staff encouraged community residents to come forward as instructors and volunteers, thereby promoting the natural bank of talent in a community that previously had been largely untapped. The resulting classes and activities fostered a cooperation that broadened the connections between community adults and youth and between local businesses, organizations, and the school.

The community education concept was originally grounded in involvement and participation, and that tenet has been the hallmark of its extended success. The practice of community education invited a new, collaborative spirit to the old model of program development. It promoted a process in which people could become involved, rather than simply an event in which they could participate.

This application in the development of community school services offered a seat at the table for all members of the community, including adults, youth, senior citizens, people with disabilities, males, females, and citizens of all cultural backgrounds and faiths.

CURRENT CONDITIONS OF COMMUNITY EDUCATION

Over the years, community education has continued to provide programs and activities that are driven by expressed community need and involve community members in meaningful leadership roles that enrich community living. Community school advisory councils and advisory boards have become important components of successful community schools, providing the foundation, voice, and representation for community members and community organizations—individuals, schools, businesses, and public and private organiza-

Community school classes and activities encourage participation from people of all ages and abilities.

Courtesy of Willamette ESD/Steve Lamb

tions—to become partners in addressing community needs.

Community school advisory councils and boards took the first component of community education seriously and began developing community response to local needs and concerns in addition to developing programs of activities. "Community educators have reached beyond traditional . . . concerns and have begun to define a role for themselves in broader community problem-solving activities . . ." (Moore, 1992, p. 76).Through the leadership of small groups of dedicated community members, crosswalks and streetlights were installed to make communities safer for children, school foundations were developed to provide needed revenue for instructional improvement projects, and land was developed into zoned parks to preserve nature and provide leisure space for neighborhood residents.

Community education advisory councils and boards became incubators for site-based leadership, a model used across the country in school reform efforts. And the influence did not end there. Community participation in education issues and school reform has been embraced by school districts from shore to shore and become part of the institutional culture of those organizations. In the United States, education reform's influence has been seen in federally funded programs such as Immigration Goals 2000, Education 2000 (see www.ed.gov/G2K/index.html for more information), 21st Century Community Learning Centers, and the No Child Left Behind Act, all of which highlight activities that enhance academic achievement, literacy, and the unique needs of urban and rural communities.

The original community education model was founded on components that provide for the delivery of quality programs, activities, and services; the development of leadership; the shared use of school and community facilities; the integration of resources into the K-12 classroom curriculum; and the conversations necessary to achieve collaborative and inclusive relationships, all driven by the desire to respond to identified needs. When all of these components are given equal voice in a community school, the result is a balanced program that invites participation and welcomes diverse activities that meet the comprehensive needs of the community. When attention is cast on just one or two of these elements, a threat to the full capacity of the model arises.

The desire to produce results that will satisfy funding sources is one example of focusing on a single aspect of community education to the detriment of other objectives. Scientific, research-based evidence of proven practices and outcome-oriented achievement in regard to the ways in which we respond to identified needs is one potential model. In the eyes of many grant-funding sources, a program gains or retains merit if a direct, tangible outcome can be identified and proven. And a program must have merit before it receives, or continues to receive, resources. However, rather than allowing the attention to such singular considerations become a threat, community educators across the country found that the drive for research-based results posed a unique and stimulating challenge, and they set about to meet that challenge. In 1998, Senator Jim Jeffords of Vermont introduced the **21st Century Community Learning Centers** (21st CCLC) legislation. Jeffords crafted the language of the bill with the help of the National Community Education Association (NCEA) and its former executive director Starla Jewell-Kelly. The intent of the bill was to provide a stable base of funding from which community school programs could flourish. The original legislation agreed to provide grants to fund 13 different types of programs. The program activities focused on community-based education, reflecting services that community schools had traditionally provided:

- Literacy education programs
- Senior citizen programs
- Child care services
- Integrated education, health, social services, recreational, or cultural programs
- Summer and weekend school programs in conjunction with recreation programs
- Nutrition and health programs
- Expanded library service hours to serve community needs
- Telecommunications and technology education programs for all ages
- Parenting-skills education programs
- Support and training for child care providers
- Employment counseling, training, and placement
- Services for people who leave school before graduation
- Services for people with disabilities

Although the original intent of the legislation was to help fund all six components of "traditional community education," the national politics surrounding education demanded that student academic progress become the primary outcome of after-school or community school programs. Due to this influence, the 21st CCLC legislation underwent significant changes, ultimately relegating successful grant applicants to the development of academically focused after-school programs for a specifically defined sector of the community, students who were at risk of underachieving. Still, communities throughout the country have increased their capacity to obtain other funding and develop programs and partnerships of merit that maintain the community education philosophy.

In Portland, Oregon, community education partnerships are stronger than ever because of the collaboration of recreation departments, county funding agencies, the Portland City Council, and the Portland Public Schools (Decker & Decker, 2004, pp.13-15). In St. Louis Park, Minnesota, community education partnerships remain a vital part of the community, a testimony to the foundational belief in the development and nurturing of strong relationships (Decker & Decker, 2004, pp. 22-24). The state of Minnesota passed its community education legislation in 1972, allowing school districts with community education advisory councils to increase their taxes by one dollar per resident, providing for a state match of half the amount raised, and setting up a governor's advisory council on community education (Department of Health, Education and Welfare, 1980). Charleston, South Carolina, attributes its 27 years of successful community education to the collaborative partnerships between the Parks and Recreation Commission and the school district (Decker & Decker, 2004, p. 28).

In Anchorage, Alaska, programs that have served the community since the mid-1970s and are in jeopardy because of funding shortfalls have sought and received funding through new streams that offer a stronger collaboration between the state, the school district, and federal programs. Across the state of Oregon, the Rural Community School Partnerships Program, a collaborative partnership between The Ford Family Foundation, the Oregon Community Education Association, and the Willamette Education Service District, has funded and supported the establishment of 16 community school programs that are making a direct and positive impact on the vitality of rural communities. Conversations have begun with partners and organizations at the state level to determine what contribution community schools can make to the current and future educational climate.

Careers in Community Education

Skills needed for professional entry-level positions in community schools:
   Volunteer management; publicity, promotion, and marketing; programming; funding and resource development; demonstrated leadership ability; group-process skills; customer service skills; positive attitude; sense of humor; and ability to build, maintain, and deepen relationships with community members, businesses, and organizations

Types of community education positions available:

   Community college continuing education coordinator or director, community school coordinator or director, community education agent, school business partnership director, service learning coordinator, volunteer manager, facilities scheduling manager, community resources center manager or director, community school or community learning center grant manager

Professional organizations:
   National Community Education Association (NCEA): www.ncea.com; National Center for Community Education (NCCE): www.nccenet.org; Local State Community Education Associations: www.ncea.com/StateAssociations.html for state links; National Association of Partners in Education (NAPE): www.napehq.org; National Council of State Community Education Associations (NCSCEA): www.ncea.com

SUMMARY

Dorothy Enderis' original concept and Frank Manley's further development of community education have played influential roles in shaping the way citizens engage in community development. Conceived at a time in U.S. history when communities were ripe for change, the concept and practice of community education helped to affirm the importance of asking communities for advice and feedback in the development of programs and activities that addressed actual rather than perceived community needs. The support of the C.S. Mott Foundation in funding the training of community education professionals and lay leaders offered the strength of leadership necessary to help communities walk into the new era with confidence and expertise. Through the work of community education professionals across America, the concept of community education has encouraged education for people of all ages through class instruction and the infusion of additional community resources to the classroom, encouraged leadership through advisory councils and community development activities, fostered the wise and economical use of public facilities through the extended use of school buildings, and fostered and encouraged creative, collaborative partnerships among community agencies, organizations, and businesses that have enriched community strength, pride, ability, and confidence.

Special Recreation

Jane Hodgkinson

A person who is severely impaired never knows his hidden sources of strength until he is treated like a normal human being and encouraged to shape his own life.

Helen Keller, American author, activist, and lecturer

By the second half of the 20th century, people with disabilities no longer resided in large institutions such as mental hospitals. Developments in medications and technology, changes in public school practices, acceptance by the general public, and passage of enabling legislation helped people return and live in their homes. When communities recognized a void in recreational programming focused on the interests of people with special needs, the special recreation movement was started. **Special recreation** is a recreational service that takes place in a public community setting to provide enjoyment and to challenge and enrich people rather than to serve as a treatment modality.

Organized efforts extend beyond parks and recreation departments to schools, YWCAs, libraries, service clubs, and nonprofit organizations. According to various sources (U.S. Census and Harris Poll), people with special needs make up 5 to 10 percent of the general public and most of them live within communities. Varying from state to state and province to province, a wide range of arts, sports, camping, and day camping experiences exist. For example, accessible camps provide residential camping opportunities to people with disabilities. The first Special Olympics was offered in 1968. The first Paralympics was held in 1956. These international programs are available in most areas. It is estimated that more than a million people worldwide participate in special recreation programs today.

Before 1960, many children born with disabilities lived in institutions. President John F. Kennedy, who had a sister with intellectual disabilities and a psychiatric disability, actively championed the movement of children out of large state institutions with the Mental Health Act of 1962. This was the beginning of "**deinstitutionalization,**" in which people moved from large hospitals and back into the community. During this time, large institutions that had held as many as 25,000 residents with mental disabilities released them to live with their families and in community homes. Parents, who had been encouraged to place children with severe disabilities into institutions, began to keep them at home. As the number of people with disabilities living in homes and community apartments increased, schools, parks and recreation agencies, and community agencies began receiving requests to provide services. This section provides a short history of the disability movements of the 20th century and explores community-based opportunities for recreation.

SPECIAL RECREATION ASSOCIATIONS

When communities seek to provide special recreation services by joining other communities, they form **special recreation associations,** an intergovernmental agreement between two or more communities or park districts, established to provide recreational services to people with special needs. In 1969, Illinois park districts took the lead in forming special recreation associations (SRA).

History of Special Recreation Associations

Communities with park districts and city recreation departments recognized that few if any programs were available for children and adults with disabilities. Summer day camps for children with cognitive or mental disabilities were the first to be recognized and offered. Twelve communities outside Chicago formed the first SRA, Northern Suburban Special Recreation Association (NSSRA), in 1969. Illinois passed legislation that allowed communities to form intergovernmental agreements for special recreation, levy a property

Basketball is one of the more than 25 sports offered by the Special Olympics program. Sports allow people with disabilities to compete with others of like abilities and to gain all the benefits from athletic competition.

Courtesy of Jane Hodgkinson

tax to fund the programs, provide transportation, and share special recreation staff. The benefits for the consumers were immediate. Families were offered as wide a range of recreation programs as those offered to people without disabilities. The participating communities shared staff, adapted equipment, and accessible vehicles.

Starting in the late 1960s and early 1970s, urban communities joined forces to provide special recreation services to children and adults with disabilities. These early programs typically included day camps, social clubs, bowling, and swimming. Early special recreation programs expanded to include day camps, trips, scouting, wheelchair sports, leisure education in school settings, nature activities, dramatics, and other activities. During these programs, participants would learn sports, arts, crafts, music, and other skills.

The United States Education for All Children Act of 1975 declared that states must require local school districts to provide special education services for children with disabilities. States that did not offer these services lost their federal funding. Children, who before the act might have been placed in an institution, were now encouraged to remain in their homes and attend school. Frequently, these services were offered in separate schools away from other students. As school districts moved special education students into regular classrooms, the **mainstreaming** movement was born. Students with special needs would participate in classrooms with their nondisabled peers.

Benefits of Special Recreation Associations to Communities

The greatest benefits to communities that provide services through SRAs are the efficiencies and economies gained by sharing facilities and staff. For example, rather than each community hiring and training staff and purchasing accessible vehicles, communities pool their resources to create a central group that serves all the communities. A second benefit is the ability to share facilities. For example, a community without a swimming pool could obtain swimming services for its residents from a neighboring community. A third benefit of the cooperative approach is the

ability to combine the relatively small number of people with disabilities in each community to create a population large enough to make programming feasible. For example, if a community wants to offer tandem bicycle riding for its residents who are visually impaired, there may be too few participants to make the program worthwhile. However, if residents from four or five communities register for the program, it stands a better chance of being successful. Another benefit is in the area of staff training. Certain disability groups require staff with extensive training: People with hearing impairments require staff who use sign language, or some people with physical disabilities require staff who can lift or move them safely. By pooling staff, an SRA provides staff trained in diverse specialties.

SPECIAL RECREATION CONTINUUM OF SERVICES

High-quality special recreation services should provide people the opportunity to participate in a variety of activities on a continuum from most restrictive to least restrictive settings (table 7.4). As medical advances help to prolong life and technology makes it easier for people to live in the community, opportunities continue to increase for full participation in community life. The extent to which this process of **inclusion** can be achieved depends on the needs of the person with a disability.

Special recreation associations offer recreation opportunities in all four of the areas of the recreation

TABLE 7.4   Continuum of Special Recreational Services

	LEAST RESTRICTIVE ⟶ TO ⟶ MORE RESTRICTIVE			
	Independent inclusion	Supported inclusion	Parallel inclusion	Segregated programs
Settings	Paralympics Senior program Special recreation association	Special Olympics Unified Sports Parks and recreation inclusion program School inclusion Special recreation association	Separate school Special Olympics Special recreation association Leisure education	Residential facility Hospital Workshop Prison Special recreation association
Residential environment	People independently register and participate in programs	People reside in homes and communities and participate in programs with people without disabilities but with support	People reside in homes and communities and participate in programs with other people with disabilities	People reside in sheltered settings away from communities and natural families

continuum. Services are sometimes provided in specific residential facilities solely for the enjoyment of their residents; segregated programs in a prison or hospital might help ready a person for life in the community. Parallel programs such as Special Olympics are offered to groups with special needs, and staff or volunteers support the participants. Special recreation associations offer inclusion services such as providing adaptive equipment so that people with disabilities can use community services. Special recreation associations also help families pursue independent recreation opportunities.

The Americans with Disabilities Act of 1990 requires governmental entities to make their services available to people with disabilities by removing architectural barriers, providing aids to help include people in recreational programs, providing communication devices if necessary, helping people with physical disabilities to use public transportation, and prohibiting employers from discriminating against people with disabilities based on the disability. This act was so significant that it is sometimes referred to as the "Civil Rights Act for the Disabled."

Some communities offer programs exclusively in a supported-inclusion setting. They make all of their programs available through services such as sign language interpreters, adaptive equipment, or hiring of inclusion aides. Inclusion aides are staff who assist the individual in "fitting in" with the group. Other supported inclusion strategies are to build accessible parks and playgrounds, translate written materials such as brochures into alternate formats, provide program buddies, and train staff in how to integrate people into programs. However, how extensively a person can take advantage of supported-inclusion services depends on the nature of his or her disability. For example, it can be more difficult to provide supported-inclusion services to adults with cognitive disabilities than to children with physical disabilities.

SPECIALIZED RECREATION PROGRAMS

Many types of recreational programs are available to people with disabilities. Some of these programs are specific to a disability and programming area; for instance, the Special Olympics provides sport opportunities to people with intellectual disabilities (and autism), and the Paralympics provides sport opportunities to people with physical challenges. Very Special Arts is an art program offered to people with intellectual disabilities (a disability and

a skill area such as the Paralympics). Still others, like Outward Bound, are offered to people with and without disabilities. These programs are generally provided or supported by nonprofit agencies that rely on fund-raising to carry out programs.

Special Olympics

In 1968, the first Special Olympics was held in Chicago's Soldier Field. Sponsored by the Joseph P. Kennedy Jr. Foundation, these games were the first organized sporting opportunities for people with developmental disabilities. Special Olympics is an international organization dedicated to helping people with intellectual disabilities to become physically fit through sports training and competition. Modeled after the Olympics, competition includes standard track and field events, swimming, winter and team sports, as well as wheelchair events. Led by the athlete oath, "Let me win, but if I cannot win, let me be brave in the attempt," Special Olympics has spread through many of the countries of the world and, in many areas, is the only recreation or sport program available to people with developmental disabilities (www.specialolympics.org).

The roots of the Special Olympics date back to 1962 when Eunice Kennedy Shriver conducted a camp for 35 kids paired with volunteers who helped them with arts and crafts, sports, and other recreational activities. Mrs. Shriver had received camp training from Dr. William Freeberg, who employed college students at a summer camp program and a modified "Olympics." Mrs. Shriver believed that communities should open schools and public places for these programs to encourage those with intellectual disabilities to develop to their full potential. She persuaded the Joseph P. Kennedy Jr. Foundation to offer grants to universities, camps, and recreation centers to begin programs.

Paralympics

The Paralympic Games are the largest sporting event in the world for people with physical disabilities. The multisport competition showcases the talents and abilities of the world's most elite athletes with physical disabilities. Currently, Paralympics features 21 sports, 18 of which are also included in the Olympics. Athletes are divided into six classifications depending on their disability: visual impairments, intellectual disabilities, amputation, spinal-cord injuries, cerebral palsy, and a group that includes all those that do not fit into one of the aforementioned groups, les autres.

Before the Paralympic Games, however, were the wheelchair games started in 1948 by Dr. Ludwig Guttmann and held in Stoke Mandeville, England. Dr. Guttmann hoped to help the thousands of people injured in World War II to return to sports. By the early 1950s, many wheelchair basketball teams had been organized. The first Paralympics were held in 1960 in Rome, Italy, with 400 wheelchair athletes competing. By 1976 other athletes besides those using wheelchairs were added. At the 1988 Paralympics in Seoul, Korea, the practice of the Olympic host also hosting the Paralympics began. Today more than 5,000 athletes compete in the Summer and Winter Paralympics.

Special Recreation Camping and Adventure Programs

Special recreation camping is now available in most American states and Canadian provinces. Camping opportunities include accessible day camps offered by local parks and recreation agencies, specialty camps (camps geared to a specific disability), and camps located in the natural environment. Accessibility varies in each of these settings. One notable program is the National Sports Center for the Disabled (NSCD). The NSCD was founded in 1970 in Winter Park, Colorado, when children with amputations were brought from the Children's Hospital in Denver to ski. The NSCD now offers a wide range of winter sports, traveling on mountain trails, and golf links. The center provides trained staff and adaptive equipment.

Wilderness Inquiry, an organization based in Minneapolis, Minnesota, that helps people experience the natural world, started in 1977 with a trip to Minnesota's Boundary Waters Canoe Area Wilderness by two people who used wheelchairs and two who were deaf. Today the backcountry trips are available to people of all abilities. Participants use canoes, kayaks, dogsleds, and horse packs or hike. Trip locations included the Rocky Mountains, Grand Canyon, Yukon's Big Salmon River, Yellowstone National Park, and Alaska's Queen Charlotte's Island (www.wildernessinquiry.org).

The Outward Bound School, developed by Kurt Hahn and Lawrence Holt, opened in 1941 in Wales after earlier programs in Germany, Britain, and Scotland were discontinued. The core mission of Outward Bound is the education of the youth of the world, ages 16 to 24. Outward Bound International (OBI) believes that young men and women must face increasingly complex situations in which self-esteem and confidence are at a premium. OBI trains and prepares people to face difficult natural environments by focusing on four pillars: physical fitness, an expedition that provides challenge and adventure, a project that develops self-reliance and self-discipline, and a sense of compassion through service. In the 1950s, Outward Bound programs expanded in the United Kingdom, Asia, Germany, and Australia. By the 1960s, Outward Bound Schools had spread to the United States and Canada. Programs for those with special needs have been developed in 1970 with increasing focus on helping those with physical and mental challenges discover their strengths and build their confidence (www.outward-bound.org).

In addition to organized camping and adventure programs, people with disabilities can also use parks on their own. Most public and private parks publish the accessible features of their park areas so that potential users can make travel and usage plans. These are often included on local Web sites. Travel agencies, airlines, and railway companies can provide extensive resources for people with disabilities.

Arts

Perhaps no area of recreational programming offers more opportunities for people with disabilities than the arts. Unlike sports that have winners and losers, art represents how the artist feels or views life and is not measured by points, time, or distance. There are no right or wrong ways to create art opportunities. Many communities offer creative outlets, and individual agencies encourage participation in the arts. Two national programs provide art opportunities.

- **VSA arts.** VSA arts is an international nonprofit organization founded in 1974 by Jean Kennedy Smith. VSA arts is dedicated to creating a society in which people with disabilities can learn through, participate in, and enjoy the arts. VSA arts offers diverse programs and events and innovative lifelong learning opportunities at the international, national, and local levels. These range from training institutes and artist-in-residence projects to arts camps and emerging-artist award programs (www.vsarts.org).

- **National Theater for the Deaf.** David Hays in Waterford, Connecticut, founded the National Theater for the Deaf (NTD). The mission of the NTD is to produce theatrically challenging work at a world-class level, drawing from as wide a range of the world's literature as possible; to perform these original works in a style that links American Sign Language with the spoken word; to seek, train, and employ deaf artists to offer their work to as culturally diverse audiences as possible; and to provide community outreach activities that educate and enlighten the general public.

FUTURE OF SPECIAL RECREATION ASSOCIATIONS

As more communities recognize the need to provide recreational opportunities to people with disabilities, as medical developments continue to expand the life expectancies of people who are seriously ill, and as the baby boomer generation ages, increasing the number of people who need assistance with their recreation, the special recreation association movement will continue to grow. The development of accessible recreational facilities will aid involvement. Populations that remain unserved or underserved by recreational opportunities include the homeless and people with conditions such as cancer, diabetes, arthritis, and multiple sclerosis and people undergoing dialysis. Funding for programs to serve these people provides a major challenge, but as those hurdles are cleared, program opportunities will increase through partnerships between agencies.

SUMMARY

Public recreation programs continue to recognize that a well-rounded diverse offering of programs means that niche programs will be more successful than a "one size fits all" approach. In every group of people, there are wide ranges of abilities and skills. Programs that are revenue driven must still take this range into consideration. In the United States, the Americans with Disabilities Act requires that public services be made available to people with disabilities by removing physical barriers to participation and supplying assistance where needed. Medical science developments continue to help people to live longer, and better diagnostic tests keep identifying more people who will need help to recreate in the community.

CHAPTER 8

Nonprofit Sector

Robert F. Ashcraft

© 2001 Boys & Girls Clubs of America

Nonprofit activity is everywhere. It is hard to find a neighborhood without visible nonprofit presence . . . and impossible to find a neighborhood untouched by nonprofit work . . .

Michael O'Neill, professor of nonprofit management, founder and former director of the Institute for Nonprofit Organization Management, University of San Francisco

CHAPTER OBJECTIVES

After reading this chapter, you should be able to do the following:

- Describe the overall role and characteristics of the nonprofit sector in society
- Identify the types of national and community-based nonprofit recreation organizations
- Explain the role of the professional in nonprofit organizations
- Describe challenges and opportunities for the future

INTRODUCTION

An understanding of recreation and leisure services is incomplete without examining the role of **nonprofit sector** organizations. In neighborhoods and communities across North America, millions of people are served by, and give service to, entities that are organized for public and **quasi-public** purposes.

It is hard to imagine that anyone goes through life without being touched by a **nonprofit organization.** Yet only in recent years have nonprofits received the attention expected for an organizational form with such a large societal impact. Historian and scholar David Mason notes the evidence of the influence of nonprofits. On receiving the Distinguished Lifetime Achievement Award from the Association for Research on Nonprofit Organizations and Voluntary Action, Mason made the following remarks to the luncheon group assembled in his honor:

> My values, attitudes, and behaviors, like most of yours, have been profoundly influenced by nonprofits . . . My parents met when they were students in a nonprofit. I was born in one. I learned about God in one, my ABCs in another, how to play ball and be a team player in another, and met my first girlfriend in another. I prepared for my career at a nonprofit university, met my wife in a nonprofit church, went on to several nonprofit graduate schools, joined numerous nonprofit professional groups, brought two newly born sons home from nonprofit hospitals, and on and on it goes, including what I read, how I vote and my avocations. It weaves its way like a golden thread through the tapestry of my life. (Mason, 1999)

Similar stories can be told by millions of citizens who have been affected in comparable ways. The nonprofit sector is ubiquitous, so it is often taken for granted. Yet an examination of the sector reveals countless examples of how nonprofit organizations affect human lives. While both complementing and contrasting recreation and leisure services provided by business (the economic/market sector) and by government (the political sector), the nonprofit form (the social sector) is growing in numbers as part of a **three-sector model** of service delivery. Whether people organize to serve their personal self-interests or to promote a broader public good, nonprofits are one way in which citizens operate outside the government and business apparatuses to improve the quality of life in communities. In addition, as a growing career field, the nonprofit sector has emerged as a vocational choice for increasing numbers of recreation professionals.

This chapter reveals the characteristics of nonprofit organizations in the United States and Canada, including their goals and functions, size and scope, and resource base. The significance of the nonprofit sector is considered in ways that differentiate service delivery approaches from those found within government or business recreation providers. A variety of types of nonprofit organizations are discussed, as are the professional opportunities that exist within such entities. Finally, the factors that influence the future of nonprofit organizations is addressed, providing insight into collaborative ventures developing among organizations, the impact of the nonprofit sector in the United States and Canada, and the challenges and opportunities ahead for this important dimension of recreation and leisure service delivery systems.

NONPROFIT SECTOR IN THE UNITED STATES AND CANADA

Although examples of nonprofit sector activities exist across all regions and countries of North America, it is difficult to make direct comparisons from one country to another. There are enormous variations in how nonprofit organizations are structured, how they are registered, and how they operate within the cultural, political, civic, and economic contexts of community life. There are also major differences in the terms used to describe entities that comprise the nonprofit sector. Different terms are found in nonprofit literature such as "voluntary sector," "charitable sector," "quasi-public sector," "independent sector," "third sector," "civil society sector," "social sector," "nongovernmental organization sector," "tax-exempt sector" and "nonprofit sector." The terms underscore why understanding the nonprofit sector is a challenging task, given the variety of interpretations noted. However, these variations also suggest a robust and vibrant sector that accommodates diverse forms and expressions. In this chapter, the term "nonprofit" is used, while fully acknowledging the diversity of terms available.

Nanus and Dobbs (1999) identify three primary sectors of society: economic, political, and social. As noted in figure 8.1, these sectors are inextricably linked, and together they represent the variety of ways to organize and deliver recreation and leisure

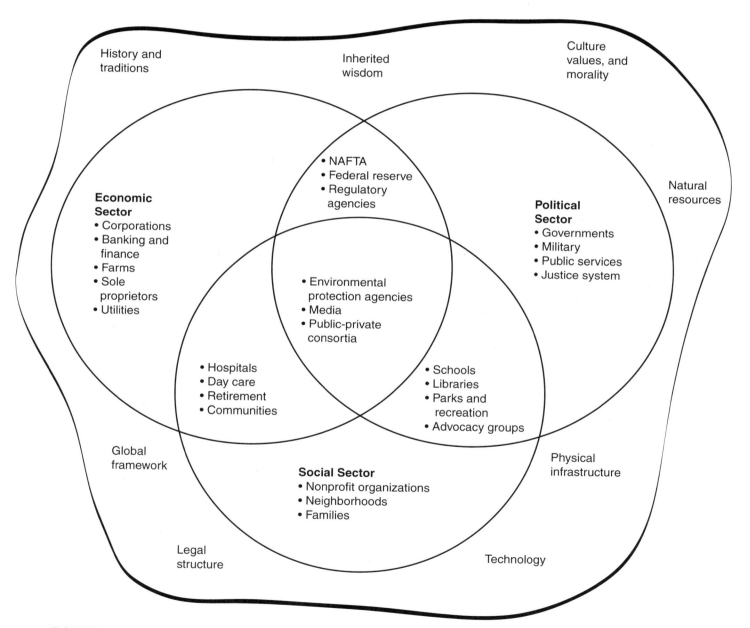

FIGURE 8.1   Three main sectors of society.

services. The sectors exist within a milieu of forces and forms that shape society.

Some nonprofits are widely recognized and provide ready access to their programs, financial statements, governance policies, and so on. However, thousands of small, grassroots, and community-based organizations are lesser known and go largely unexamined. So to fully appreciate the nonprofit sector's role one must consider this segment of recreation and leisure services in all of its vastness and vagueness. One way to understand the range of the nonprofit form is to review what nonprofit organizations hold in common.

Common Characteristics of Nonprofit Organizations

Despite enormous variations, several characteristics apply generally to nonprofit organizations whether found in Canada, the United States, or other countries around the world. According to nonprofit scholars such as Lester Salamon (1999), Michael O'Neill (2002) and others, nonprofit entities share six common features:

1. **Organized.** They have an institutional presence and structure; there is an identifiable entity.
2. **Private.** They are separate from the state. While following laws established by legislative bodies, these entities determine their own policies, programs, and services.
3. **Nonprofit distributing.** They do not return profits to their managers or to a set of "owners." Whereas publicly traded corporations have shareholders, and government entities have voting constituents, nonprofit organizations consider a range of stakeholders when making decisions and providing services.
4. **Self-governing.** They are fundamentally in control of their own affairs.
5. **Voluntary.** Membership in them is not legally required, and they attract some level of voluntary contribution of time and money.
6. **Beneficial to the public.** They contribute to the public purpose and public good.

These characteristics apply to a wide range of recreation and leisure entities found within the nonprofit sector. Therefore, a small running club organized and financed by and for its members in a remote New England community in the United States is as much a part of the nonprofit sector as is the Red Cross, a large multiservice, social service agency with operating units in Canada and the United States. Nonprofit organizations, therefore, are organized to serve public purposes or mutual-benefit purposes that improve the quality of life in communities.

The nonprofit organizational form is found throughout the recreation field, from sports clubs to professional associations, to direct service providers. Interestingly, nonprofit organizations and their activities affect people across the range of individual life-span development from "cradle to grave." Often the introduction to nonprofit organizations occurs through recreation programs, as children and youth become involved in Boy Scout and Girl Scout programs, YMCAs, Boys and Girls Clubs, Little League, and other recreation-based programs. As interests and skills are developed through outlets such as camping programs, appreciation often grows for the outdoors. The Sierra Club, The Nature Conservancy, and The Trust for Public Land, among other environmental organizations, are nonprofit entities that advance specific mission-driven purposes that often appeal to those concerned about outdoor recreation. These youth development and environmental entities are just two examples of recreation-based nonprofits that are part of a much larger collection of hundreds of thousands of organizations operating throughout North America to advance both special-purpose and broadly based public benefit goals.

Goals and Functions

Given the vast array of activities and people that comprise the sector, it is not surprising that the goals and functions of nonprofit organizations are also varied. Such organizations often serve widely different needs and at times conflicting values. For example, one nonprofit may organize to protect a wilderness area by calling for the elimination of off-road vehicle use, while another organizes to open the same area to such activity. Often, however, nonprofit recreation and leisure services organizations share similar values between themselves and among government and business entities. After-school child care programs offer examples where overall goals regarding the education, safety, and recreation needs of children are similar even though their delivery systems (programs, clientele, fee structure, and so on) are organized in different ways for various reasons.

Despite these variations, Salamon (1999) and others suggest that the following two primary goals frame the orientation of most nonprofits:

1. **Public benefit.** Some nonprofits are organized specifically for social outcomes that appeal across a wide spectrum of population groups. Educational organizations, hospitals, museums, and community recreation centers are examples of public benefit nonprofits.

2. **Mutual benefit.** These nonprofits exist primarily to provide services exclusively to a limited number of members with common

interests. Examples include business and professional associations, social clubs, and some golf clubs.

Nonprofits, therefore, are organized to serve both individual needs and broader community goals. Some are organized to conserve and preserve historical, cultural, environmental, and other traditions. Others are developed to advance social change with a focus on improving the condition of disadvantaged and disenfranchised people who do not feel a part of mainstream community life. Figure 8.2 shows examples of nonprofit organizations across these various domains.

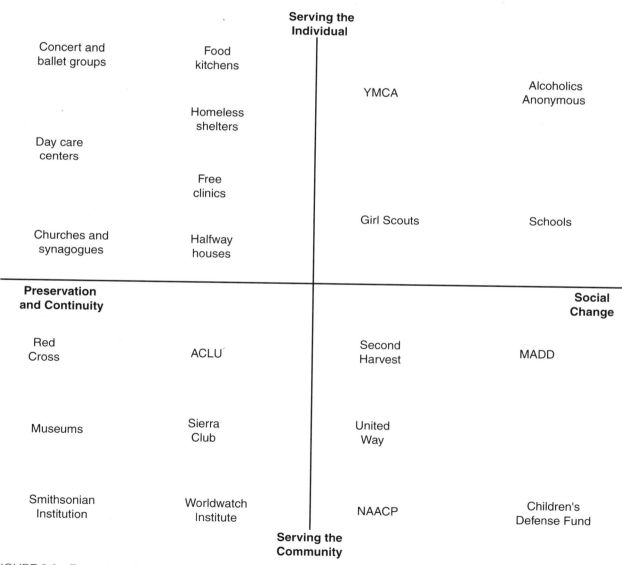

FIGURE 8.2   Examples of nonprofit organizations.

Organizing Framework

Because the nonprofit sector is so diverse and it encompasses such a wide array of types and sizes of organizations, studying its structure and impact can be difficult. A typology developed by researchers at Johns Hopkins University, known as the International Classification of Nonprofit Organizations (ICNPO) facilitates understanding of the sector (Salamon & Anheier, 1996). ICNPO divides nonprofits into 12 major activity groups and 24 subgroups according to the primary type of goods or services each one provides (e.g., recreation, environment, health). The following are the major activity groups:

1. **Culture and recreation.** Includes organizations and activities in general and specialized fields of culture and recreation

2. **Education and research.** Includes organizations and activities administering, providing, promoting, conducting, supporting, and servicing education and research

3. **Health.** Includes organizations that engage in health-related activities, providing health care, both general and specialized services, administration of health care services, and health support services

4. **Social services.** Includes organizations and institutions providing human and social services to a community or target population

5. **Environment.** Includes organizations promoting and providing services in environmental conservation, pollution control and prevention, environmental education and health, and animal protection

6. **Development and housing.** Includes organizations promoting programs and providing services to help improve communities and promote the economic and social well-being of society

7. **Law, advocacy, and politics.** Includes organizations and groups that work to protect and promote civil and other rights, advocate the social and political interests of general or special constituencies, offer legal services, and promote public safety

8. **Philanthropic intermediaries and voluntarism.** Includes philanthropic organizations and those promoting charity and charitable activities including grant-making foundations, voluntarism promotion and support, and fund-raising entities

9. **International.** Includes organizations promoting cultural understanding between peoples of various countries and historical backgrounds and also those providing relief during emergencies and promoting development and welfare abroad

10. **Religion.** Organizations promoting religious beliefs and administering religious services and rituals; includes churches, mosques, synagogues, temples, shrines, seminaries, monasteries, and similar religious institutions, in addition to related organizations and auxiliaries of these organizations

11. **Business and professional associations and unions.** Includes organizations promoting, regulating, and safeguarding business, professional, and labor interests

12. **Groups not classified elsewhere.**

Reprinted from the International Classification of Nonprofit Organizations.

Size and Scope

Determining the size and scope of the nonprofit sector in North America is difficult for several reasons as previously noted. However, what is known suggests that nonprofits have played a larger role in the United States than in Canada or other countries. This fact in no way minimizes the importance of nonprofits outside the United States. However, given the size and scope of the sector in the United States, spawned from a nation whose laws and culture have encouraged such activity, it is not surprising that nonprofit literature on recreation and leisure organizations frequently accentuates U.S. examples when examining nonprofit organizations and their purposes and approaches to service delivery.

Nonprofit Sector in Canada

Despite an increasing number of studies on the topic, there is still a great deal that is not known about the nonprofit sector and the role it plays in Canada (Hall & Banting, 2000). Because there is no central registry for nonprofits in Canada, what is known comes from charities, as a subset of the overall nonprofit sector, that register with Revenue Canada (the government agency similar to the Internal Revenue Service in the United States).

As of 2000, there were approximately 200,000 nonprofits operating in Canada with 80,000 of them registered as official charities (Wagner, Orva-nanos de Rovzar, & Imdieke, 2003). According to Revenue Canada, a nonprofit organization (NPO) is, "an association [that] must be both organized and operated exclusively for social welfare, civic improvement, pleasure or recreation or for any other purpose except profit" (Revenue Canada, 2004, paragraph 5 at http://www.cra-arc.gc.ca/E/pub/tp/it496r/it496r-e.html). Revenue Canada details these four categories as follows:

1. Social welfare nonprofits assist disadvantaged groups for the common good and for the general welfare of the community.

2. Civic improvement nonprofits are organized to enhance the value or quality of community or civic life.

3. Pleasure or recreation nonprofits are organized to provide a state of gratification or a means of refreshment or diversion.

4. The final category, which can serve any purpose except profit, is a generic grouping of associations that are organized for other noncommercial reasons.

Categories of nonprofits in Canada are found in table 8.1.

As noted in table 8.1, several categories account for the array of Canadian nonprofits that work to advance community life by providing services that address core social needs while advancing overall community well-being. They range from nonprofits that organize parks and museums for general community betterment to sport clubs involving special interests such as golf, curling, and badminton that are organized and operated to provide recreational facilities for the enjoyment of members and their families.

One of the primary sources of information about the Canadian nonprofit sector is Imagine Canada, a nonprofit that was launched in 2005 from a strategic alliance of the Canadian Centre for Philanthropy and the Coalition of National Voluntary Organizations. Imagine Canada works with charities, governments, and corporations to advance the role and interests of the charitable sector for the benefit of Canadian communities. The organization conducts and disseminates research, develops public policy, promotes public awareness, shares tools and standards, and encourages businesses to be more community-minded.

Nonprofit Sector in the United States

As previously noted, the nonprofit sector in the United States is pervasive and robust. Salamon (1999) estimates that more than 1.6 million nonprofit organizations exist in the United States. Of these, 400,000 are member-serving nonprofits and more than 1.2 million are public-serving nonprofits. The U.S. Internal Revenue Service provides 27 types of tax-exempt organizations under Section 501(c) of the federal tax code. The organization BoardSource (2002) examines the major subcategories of the U.S. nonprofit sector as follows:

- **Charities.** Perhaps the most readily identifiable form of nonprofits are those known as charities. The majority of nonprofits in the United States (approximately 600,000) are classified as public charities and are exempt under **Section 501(c)(3)** of the U.S. Internal Revenue Service tax code. They represent diverse organizations from those that provide free services in soup kitchens and homeless shelters to vulnerable populations to those that provide wide community development and cultural enhancement activities such as hospitals, museums, and recreation centers. Many "friends" organizations are organized within this category to support parks and recreation efforts. For example, the Friends of Buford Park and Mt.

TABLE 8.1   Categories of Nonprofit Organizations in Canada

Category	Purpose
Social welfare	Provides assistance for disadvantaged groups or for the common good and general welfare of citizens
Civic improvement	Provides for the enhancement of civic life through efforts such as the establishment of parks, museums, and so on
Pleasure of recreation	Provides a state of gratification or a means of refreshment or diversion through social clubs, golf clubs, curling clubs, for example, that are organized and operated to provide recreational facilities for the enjoyment of members and their families
For any other purpose except profit	A catchall for all other associations that are organized and operated for reasons other than commercial or financial gain

Pisgah in Eugene, Oregon, was founded in 1989 to support the ecological integrity of the nearly 2,400 acres (971 hectares) that comprise the Howard Buford Recreation Area. Although working in conjunction with the Lane County Parks Department, this friends group is organized separately. Thousands of such friends groups exist across the United States.

- **Foundations.** One way that individuals, organizations, and communities support causes that benefit society is through private, corporate, operating, or community foundations. These also operate as 501(c)(3) nonprofits, and their purposes and operating systems are as varied as those of public charities. Some foundations make grants to a range of community causes. These types of foundations encourage grant proposals from many different areas of the community, including recreation and cultural causes. Other types of foundations, however, serve as a conduit for amassing resources to support their own programs and activities. Creating an operating foundation is one way that government parks and recreation programs generate private support for their public goals. There are several other structural variations of this complex nonprofit form.

- **Social welfare organizations.** Some nonprofits advocate for specific issues by lobbying legislators to advance social causes and by actively campaigning for political candidates. These nonprofits are recognized in the Internal Revenue Service code as 501(c)(4) organizations. They are exempt under the tax code, but donations to these causes are not tax deductible. The National Rifle Association and the National Organization for Women are two examples of such organizations.

- **Professional and trade associations.** Nonprofits that promote business or professional interests comprise a collection of nonprofits known as professional or trade associations. They usually qualify for tax exemption under Section 501(c)(6) of the tax code, and they focus on the interests of specific industries or professions. They also may have broader community interests such as chambers of commerce or business leagues. Similar to advocacy organizations, donations to these associations are not tax deductible.

Reprinted from BoardSource.

Hundreds of thousands of nonprofits are registered as associations in the United States and, depending on their specific mission, they fall within one of the 501(c) categories listed earlier.

Nonprofits formed as associations are of particular interest to the recreation professional and are worthy of expanded discussion in this chapter for two reasons. The first is that some professional associations benefit the recreation professional by providing training, certifications, and a network of colleagues that assist in career success and advancement. The second is that the association format is one way citizens organize around mutual interests. Frequently, these interests involve recreation, leisure, and sport pursuits.

According to the American Society of Association Executives, more than 147,000 associations exist in the United States (American Society of Association Executives, 2004). Approximately 1,000 new associations are created each year. Figure 8.3 shows the five largest membership associations—several of these associations are directly applicable to recreation, sport, and leisure pursuits. Figure 8.4 provides examples of associations with direct recreation ties.

Resource Base

The resource base of a nonprofit includes all the sources of support that make offering its programs and services possible. Nonprofits derive their revenue from a combination of one or more sources. The following are the most common sources:

- **Membership fees.** These are fees charged to members, usually annually, in return for programs provided by the nonprofit in service to its members.

- **Program fees.** Participants pay fees for participating in specific programs. Depending on

---

1. American Automobile Association, 43,000,000
2. American Association of Retired Persons, 33,000,000
3. YMCA of the USA, 16,900,000
4. The National Geographic Society, 9,500,000
5. National Parent-Teacher Association, 6,500,000

FIGURE 8.3 The top five U.S. national associations by membership.

From American Society of Association Executives.

American Alliance for Health, Physical Education, Recreation and Dance
American Association for Active Lifestyles and Fitness
American Association for Health Education
American Association for Leisure and Recreation
American Association for Nude Recreation
American Park and Recreation Society
American Recreation Coalition
American Therapeutic Recreation Association
Americans for Our Heritage and Recreation
Association of Outdoor Recreation and Education
Disabled Sports USA
Employee Services Management Association
International Council for Health, Physical Education, Recreation, Sport, and Dance
National Association for Girls and Women in Sport
National Association of County Park and Recreation Officials
National Association of Recreation Resource Planners
National Association of State Outdoor Recreation Liaison Officers
National Council for Therapeutic Recreation Certification
National Recreation and Park Association
National RV Dealers Association or Recreation Vehicle Dealers Association
National Therapeutic Recreation Society
Native American Recreation and Sport Institute
Outdoor Industry Association
Recreation Vehicle Industry Association
Recreation Vehicle Rental Association
Resort and Commercial Recreation Association
Society of Park and Recreation Educators
Society of State Directors of Health, Physical Education and Recreation

FIGURE 8.4   United States–based associations with direct recreation ties. There are several Canadian associations with similar titles.

the nonprofit, program participants may or may not be members of the organization.

- **Private philanthropy.** Fund-raising from individuals, corporations, and foundations provides revenue to nonprofit organizations. The skills associated with cultivating donors, developing proposals, and securing gifts from a range of philanthropic stakeholders require increased sophistication because contributed income has grown to become an essential revenue source for many nonprofits.

- **Government grants.** Many nonprofits compete for and receive government grants from local, state, and federal agencies to provide

services based on targeted community needs and priorities.

- **Interest income.** Nonprofits receive income from cash reserves and other unspent monies that are actively managed to maximize earnings until used for expense purposes. Some nonprofits have developed endowment funds that build assets so that the mission of the organization may continue into perpetuity.

- **Earned income.** For nonprofits that own facilities, earned income can occur through rental arrangements, admission fees, and other agreements that turn physical assets into revenue streams.

- **Sales income.** For many youth development organizations, sales from cookies, candy, and other products provide a dual benefit to the organization: a program in which young people learn to organize, implement a plan, and reach goals and revenue for the organization.

- **Social enterprise.** A new and growing trend for some nonprofits is the creation of for-profit companies that channel profits back into their social cause.

Philanthropy in Nonprofit Organizations

Nonprofit organizations often intersect with our lives in deep and abiding ways through philanthropy. **Philanthropy** is the promotion of common good through voluntary action, voluntary association, and voluntary giving (Payton, 1988). Philanthropy is expressed in a variety of forms by people who freely give their money and time to the causes of their choice.

One way in which our sense of belonging and identification of feelings are attached to nonprofit organizations is through acts of philanthropy. Mason (1999), whose quote introduced this chapter, notes that, "when people describe their relationship to their employer, they state, 'I work for Exxon. I am with Intel.'" However, he continues, "We reserve the 'belonging' for our voluntary enterprises," the nonprofit organizations that we intersect with in our lives. Consider the following statements:

I *belong* to the YMCA.

I *am* a Boy Scout.

I *belong* to the Camelback Mountain Hiking Club.

I *am* a volunteer at the teen center.

The philanthropic tradition in the United States has been well documented. According to research by the national organization Independent Sector (2004), in 2001, 83.9 million American adults (44 percent of the population) volunteered, representing the equivalent of more than 9 million full-time employees at a value of $239 billion U.S. Giving money is no less impressive; nearly 90 percent of all U.S. households contributed to charities, with an average annual contribution of $1,620 U.S.

In recent years, the growing philanthropic tradition in Canada has been studied as well. According to 2000 research by the Canadian Centre for Philanthropy, 6.5 million Canadians volunteered through a charitable or nonprofit organization (27 percent of the population). This represents the equivalent of 549,000 full-time jobs. Nearly 8 of 10 (78 percent) Canadians made direct financial donations at an average annual donation amount of $259 Canadian. When considering in-kind contributions such as clothing and food, then 91 percent of Canadians contributed to philanthropies.

Contributors of time (volunteers) and money (financial donors) provide important human and financial resources that nurture, sustain, and bolster nonprofit recreation organizations. For example, in many nonprofit youth development organizations, volunteers serve as coaches, mentors, teachers, camp counselors, troop leaders, and board members. As financial donors they support cookie sales, donate to annual support campaigns, organize special events, and otherwise contribute income that is a vital part of organizational budgets.

Given the importance of philanthropy to nonprofit organizations, the recreation professional in the United States with responsibility for coordinating volunteer programs or raising funds can benefit from a nationwide network of volunteer centers. The Volunteer Center National Network (VCNN), in partnership with the Points of Light Foundation, helps connect interested volunteers with organizations and activities. More than 350 volunteer centers exist across the United States and are a resource to any recreation professional interested in developing or expanding his or her volunteer program capacity.

In addition, two professional organizations advance competencies for volunteer management and fund-raising. The Association for Volunteer Administration (AVA)—www.avaintl.org—provides training and other resources that support volunteer managers. AVA's performance-based credentialing program enables people to become certified in volunteer administration (CVA). Similarly, the Association of Fundraising Professionals (AFP)—www.afpnet.org—is a national association that provides training, research, and other support to those involved in fund-raising. Through AFP's credentialing program, qualified fund-raisers can earn the designation of certified fund-raising executive (CFRE) that attests to a development professional's knowledge, skill, and achievements.

OUTSTANDING *Graduates*

Background Information

Name: Annette Keep (nee Bax)

Education: Honors bachelor of arts, Redeemer University College, Ancaster, Ontario, department of physical education, major in honors kinesiology and psychology

Credentials: Social service worker–gerontology program, Sheridan College, Ontario, diploma

Career Information

Position: Program coordinator at Alzheimer Society of Peel Brampton Day Centre, Region of Peel, Mississauga, Ontario

Organization: The Alzheimer Society of Peel was incorporated in 1984 as a charitable organization. Since that time, the chapter has diligently worked to support families and individuals affected by Alzheimer's disease. The society serves the Region of Peel through two offices in Mississauga and one in Brampton. The chapter promotes public and professional awareness of Alzheimer's disease and related dementias and offers a variety of programs and services. All services and programs operate either free of charge or for a nominal fee. People do not need a diagnosis or a referral to gain access to these services. Twenty-five people are served daily at each location. There are 43 employees in the society.

Organization's Mission: The Alzheimer Society of Peel exists to alleviate the personal and social consequences of Alzheimer's disease and other dementias and to help find the prevention and cure.

Job Description: Lead feedback sessions with program workers every two to eight weeks depending on their needs and goals. Oversee staff orientation and education, payroll and schedule, and preventive maintenance. Perform programming work such as distributing caseloads to prime workers to update client level and interests. Set and chair seasonal change meetings to discuss program ideas and client needs.

Review seasonal change plans to ensure that they are complete and client focused. Chair planning meeting and therapeutic recreation service plan (TRSP) meeting. Serve as liaison with Meals on Wheels. Receive initial calls and forward information to the manager for follow-up and to the administrative assistant to complete an introductory mail-out package and letter.

Career Path: After graduating from university, I knew I wanted to work with seniors in a recreational setting, so I began the social service worker–gerontology program at Sheridan College to help me get my foot in the door. A requirement of the program was completion of a student placement, which I carried out at the Alzheimer Society of Peel Brampton Day Centre. Shortly into my placement with the society, in November of 2001, I began to work part-time as a program worker in addition to my student placement hours. After obtaining my diploma from Sheridan, I obtained a contract position, which led to a full-time position as a program worker in August of 2002. In May of 2003, I applied for and received a four-month contract as acting program coordinator, which led to my current permanent position as program coordinator of the Brampton Day Centre.

Likes and Dislikes About the Job: I like the variety of tasks and interaction with staff and clients. There is great flexibility within a routine because you're dealing with people and no two days are alike, and I am able to learn something new each day. A lot of problem solving is required within this type of position (e.g., finding solutions to behaviors, scheduling solutions to meet the needs of clients and staff, creating program ideas), which forces me to find creative solutions and remain current in my knowledge of dementias and items relating to recreation and the centre. It would

> Be fearless . . . always be willing to try something new and don't be afraid to think outside of the box. There is no such thing as a failed program, event, or activity. You can always learn something from what occurred and use the information gained to improve or build on the idea for the future.
>
> No matter what aspect of the recreation and leisure field you decide to work in, your creativity and problem-solving skills will be put to work, so never stop being willing to learn.

(continued)

Outstanding Graduates *(continued)*

be nice to have more regular contact with caregivers and the clients themselves; sometimes I am unable to do so because I am ensuring that the logistics of running the centre are smooth so that staff is better able to serve the seniors.

Advice to Undergraduates

Be willing to pursue avenues you may not have considered before, such as working with special popula-tions and the organizations that exist to serve these populations. These organizations often evolve to meet the needs of their clients and as such tend to be dynamic. Different positions relating to the recreation and leisure field often exist and include tasks such as planning activities, coordinating events, coordinating roles, and fund-raising through events. You may find something you truly love to do and help those in need in the process!

TYPES OF NATIONAL AND COMMUNITY-BASED NONPROFIT RECREATION ORGANIZATIONS

As previously noted, more than a million organizations—large and small, formal and informal—exist within the U.S. and Canadian nonprofit sector. Nonprofit organizations play a critical role in the recreational and cultural life of the United States. Salamon notes that, "Many of the central recreational institutions of local communities—swimming clubs, tennis clubs, Little Leagues, country clubs—are nonprofit in form. Even more importantly, nonprofit organizations form the backbone of the nation's cultural life, producing most of the live theater, symphonic music, and opera, and providing venues for art and for cultural artifacts" (1999, p. 131).

Interestingly, the nonprofit form is often most potent when it is organized around individual special interests in collaboration with government and business to advance mutually agreed-on goals. Instances of these occurrences in the recreation field abound. One example is that of Kartchner Caverns State Park located outside Benson, Arizona. First discovered in 1974 by Gary Tenen and Randy Tufts, the cave was kept secret for years in order to protect its natural and fragile beauty. The discoverers worked through several people and organizations to realize their dream of preserving forever their unique geological find. In particular, they worked through a nonprofit, The Nature Conservancy, and with a government entity, the Arizona State Parks Department, to preserve the site. Following years of study and design, Kartchner Caverns opened in 1999 as a state park. Today, three sectors work together to sustain the caverns including *government* (Arizona State Parks, which owns the land and administers the park), *business* (Aramark Sports and Entertainment Services, which holds the contract for concessions at the park), and *nonprofit* (Friends of Kartchner Caverns State Park, which raises funds to support educational, scientific, and conservation programs). Thousands of examples exist whereby nonprofit organizations help to nurture and sustain recreation settings in collaboration with government agencies and business enterprises.

Whether organized in direct collaboration with government and business or as largely independent entities, various types of national and community-based nonprofit recreation organizations produce significant social benefits. Some of these organizations are identified clearly by their mission, purpose, logo, and other features, and they have a history as a successful entity. Many are part of the essential delivery system of the recreation movement.

Nonprofits that are part of the recreation and leisure services arena can be generally organized as follows:

1. Voluntary youth-serving organizations
2. Religious and faith-based organizations
3. Social service and relief organizations
4. Special populations–serving organizations
5. Environmental and conservation organizations
6. Associations
7. Membership or service clubs and fraternal organizations

The mission and programs of some nonprofits cut across more than one category. The Salvation Army, for example, serves youth, is faith based, provides wide-ranging social services, and often serves special populations. In some communi-

©AP/Wide World Photos

Kartchner Caverns State Park is an example of the success of individual special interests working through non-profits in collaboration with government and business.

ties, the local affiliate of Boys and Girls Clubs of America resides inside a Salvation Army unit. It is helpful to consider these varied categorizations when thinking about the core mission of organizations and their targeted client or customer populations. A sampling of these organizations follows. Descriptions are derived directly from organization Web sites and materials provided by these organizations.

Voluntary Youth-Serving Organizations

More than 49 leading nonprofit youth and human services organizations across the United States serve more than 40 million young people, reports the National Assembly of Health and Human Service Organizations (2004). These organizations enlist more than 6 million volunteers to provide services and employ more than 100,000 paid staff.

Many of the organizations use sport and recreation activities, community service, youth and adult partnerships, and other programming features as a means to instill core values in their youth members. Some of these organizations are also organized with affiliates in Canada. A sampling of nonprofits with specific youth development goals include the following:

• **Big Brothers Big Sisters of America.** Founded in 1904, Big Brothers Big Sisters of America is the oldest and largest youth-mentoring organization in the United States. In 2002, the organization served more than 200,000 youth ages 5 through 18, in 5,000 communities across the country through a network of 470 agencies. Big Brothers Big Sisters promotes one-on-one mentoring relationships between capable adult volunteers and youth. Research studies show that mentoring relationships between positive adult role models and youth have a lasting impact on children's lives.

Big Brothers Big Sisters of Canada was organized in 1921 and, similar to its U.S. counterpart, is organized to provide high-quality volunteer-based mentoring programs to more than 300 Canadian communities.

- **Boy Scouts of America.** The Boy Scouts of America was founded in the United States in 1910 with the mission of preparing young people to make ethical and moral choices during their lifetimes by instilling important values. Ranging from 7-year-old Tiger Cubs to teenage Varsity Scouts, Boy Scouts of America strives to build character, foster citizenship, and develop mental, moral, and physical fitness in young people. In 2003, the Boy Scouts of America had more than 3.2 million

Boy Scouts march in a parade. Boy Scouts of America is an example of a voluntary youth-serving organization.

youth members and 1.2 million adult members and had a paid staff of approximately 4,000. The Boy Scouts organization serves more than 300 councils in 28 areas and four regions in the United States. Scouts Canada shares a similar purpose—forming the character of boys and imparting patriotic and civic values among members.

- **Boys and Girls Clubs of America.** Since 1906, Boys and Girls Clubs of America has served 3.6 million children, particularly boys and girls from disadvantaged circumstances, encouraging them to realize their full potential as productive, responsible, and caring citizens. In facilities stocked with game rooms, learning centers, and gymnasiums, trained professionals help young people learn to solve conflicts, develop study skills, and work as part of a team. Boys and Girls Clubs also offers programs aimed at developing leadership, career, health, and overall life skills. The organization planted strong roots in Canada, serving nearly 150,000 children and youth in 101 clubs since its inception in 1929.

- **Camp Fire USA.** Founded in 1910, Camp Fire USA is committed to building caring, confident youth and future leaders through its educational programs. The organization serves 735,000 children and youth annually, with the help of nearly 18,000 volunteers and 620 paid staff through 120 councils in 40 states and the District of Columbia. Camp Fire is organized primarily as a club with age-appropriate programs for younger children. For older children, Camp Fire offers self-reliance classes aimed at building the skills necessary to resist peer pressure and cultivate healthy relationships. It also offers service-learning courses intended to instill the importance of community service and offers camping and environmental education programs for children of all ages.

- **Girl Scouts of the USA.** Girl Scouts of the USA was founded in 1912 with the purpose of helping today's girls become tomorrow's leaders. For 90 years, the Girl Scouts program has served girls locally, nationally, and internationally and encouraged them to develop integrity, good conduct, financial literacy, and health so that they can become fulfilled and responsible citizens. In addition to an emphasis in expression through the arts, Girl Scouts encourages girls to explore their potential in math, science, and technology. In nearly 300,000 troops throughout the United States, Girl Scouts of the USA has more than 3.8 million youth members, 986,000 adult members, and 9,800 paid staff. Girl Scouts has a very strong North American presence though the Canadian organization Girl Guides.

- **Girls Incorporated.** Girls Incorporated was founded as Girls Clubs of America in 1945. There is formal history and informal history of many of these organizations. Technically, the very first organization of its kind in the United States that was a precursor was in the 1860s. But the national Girls Clubs of America was founded in 1945 and then changed to Girls Incorporated in 1990, with the goal of inspiring all girls to be strong, smart, and bold. Local affiliates of Girls Incorporated work to help girls and young women overcome the effects of discrimination and develop their capacity to be self-sufficient, responsible citizens, and they serve as vigorous advocates for girls. The organization also works to build girls' skills and interest in science, math, and technology and works to prevent girls from falling victim to peer pressure. With 525,000 members in the United States, Girls Incorporated has 116 affiliates in 37 states and five affiliates in Canada. Most Girls Incorporated centers are located in low-income areas and provide a weekly average of 30 hours of after-school, weekend, and summer activities.

- **Little League Baseball.** The Little League program owes its history to the 1880s when leagues for preteen children were formed in New York. In the 1920s and 1930s an organization began to emerge, and in 1939 the first Little League game was played. Little League baseball stakes a claim to being the largest organized youth sports program in the world with 180,000 teams in all 50 U.S. states and scores of countries. Through proper guidance and exemplary leadership, the Little League program assists youth in developing the qualities of citizenship, discipline, teamwork, and physical well-being. By espousing the virtues of character, courage, and loyalty, the Little League Baseball program develops superior citizens rather than superior athletes.

Religious and Faith-Based (Church and Synagogue) Organizations

Some nonprofits have grown to become nonsectarian organizations with historical roots in faith-based communities. The YMCA and YWCA are two examples. Other nonprofits are created and administered by faith-based or church communities. The Catholic Youth Organization (CYO), Young Men's Hebrew Association (YMHA), and Young Women's Hebrew Association (YWHA) are examples.

- **YMCA of the USA.** The first Young Men's Christian Association (YMCA) of the USA was established in 1851, with the initial purpose of meeting the spiritual needs of young men. Today, that philosophy has expanded to include multiple services directed toward a much broader cross section of the population, with an emphasis on families. The mission statement, "to put Christian principles into practice through programs that build healthy spirit, mind and body for all," reflects the organization's commitment to its Christian roots and its global perspective. YMCA programs are family based. Purchased memberships for individuals and families cover the use of basic services such as gymnasiums, game rooms, swimming pools, locker rooms, and lounges. Members are also eligible for reduced fees on other programs such as resident and day camp programs for children and youth sports. YMCA's program offerings are virtually endless and serve members nationwide in 972 member YMCAs and 1,568 branches, units, and camps. The YMCA has a strong volunteer program, with more than 550,000 volunteer program leaders and 54,000 volunteer policy makers, and more than 100,000 part-time and full-time staff.

- **YMCA Canada.** YMCA Canada was founded in 1851 and is dedicated to the growth of all people in spirit, mind, and body and in a sense of responsibility to each other and the global community. YMCA Canada provides health, fitness, and recreation programs that encourage people of all abilities to pursue healthy lifestyles. Disease prevention and health promotion continue to be mainstays of the YMCA. Program offerings are similar to those in the United States. There are 48 YMCAs and 13 joint YMCA–YWCAs across Canada.

- **YWCA of the USA.** The Young Women's Christian Association (YWCA) of the USA was established in 1858, and now has more than 4 million members and more than 300 associations. The program, rooted in Christianity, is a women's membership movement sustained by the richness of many beliefs and values. Strengthened by diversity, the YWCA draws together members who strive to create opportunities for women's growth, leadership, and power in order to attain a common vision: peace, justice, freedom, and dignity for all people. The YWCA seeks to empower women and eliminate racism. Programs include services for women in crisis, refugee women, single parents, homeless women, women in prison, women coping with substance abuse, and other women in the general population.

- **YWCA Canada.** The YWCA in Canada was established in 1870 with the tagline: A voice for equality—a strong voice for women. The YWCA movement in Canada has provided many of the same services as the YWCA of the USA, with an emphasis on women's shelters and camping programs. YWCA Canada consists of 36 member associations serving 1 million women, teen girls, and their families through operations in more than 200 communities across Canada.

Social Service and Relief Organizations

Some of the most recognizable names and logos in the nonprofit sector belong to organizations that provide social and relief services. These organizations are difficult to categorize because some are nonsectarian and others are part of faith-based communities. Each has a mission to improve the quality of individual lives in communities, and they intersect in ways that bolster the goals of recreation service providers or they provide direct recreation services themselves by either joining forces with recreation service providers to meet mutual goals or by providing direct recreation services themselves. The American Red Cross is perhaps one of the best known of any organization in this category.

- **American Red Cross.** The Red Cross was organized internationally in 1863, and the American Red Cross was founded in 1881 as a humanitarian organization to provide relief to victims of disasters and help people prevent, prepare for, and respond to emergencies. Through a network of more than 1,400 chapters in the United States, the American Red Cross provides numerous services to meet its mission. These include disaster relief services; international services; blood, tissue, and plasma services; services to military members and families; community services; and health and safety services. Ninety-seven percent of Red Cross staff members are volunteers. Local Red Cross chapters assist recreation professionals by providing water safety, CPR, and first aid training and certification.

- **Canadian Red Cross.** The Canadian Red Cross was founded in 1909, and its work is organized through 370 chapters and supported by more than 63,000 volunteers. Services of the Canadian Red Cross include disaster relief, international services, first aid/water safety education, and

home-care services in some communities (e.g., meals and general assistance for seniors, etc.).

Special Populations– Serving Organizations

Although otherwise similar in structure to other types, some nonprofits are organized to meet the needs of specific population groups. For example, the United Service Organization (USO) was created in 1941 to support the needs of enlisted military personnel. Many services provided by the USO are oriented toward the leisure and recreation pursuits of its clientele. Other nonprofits work with people with specific disabilities. The Arc of the United States and Special Olympics are two examples.

- **The Arc of the United States.** The Arc of the United States works to include all children and adults with cognitive, intellectual, and developmental disabilities in every community through 1,000 chapters nationwide. Founded in 1950, the Arc is the national organization of and for people with mental retardation and related developmental disabilities and their families. It is devoted to promoting and improving support and services for this group. The association also supports research into and education about the prevention of mental retardation in infants and young children.

- **Special Olympics.** Special Olympics was founded in 1968 to provide year-round sport training and athletic competition in 26 Olympic-type sports for children and adults with intellectual disabilities. With the help of its more than 500,000 volunteers, Special Olympics gives athletes ages 8 years or older opportunities to develop physical fitness, demonstrate courage, experience joy, and participate in a sharing of gifts, skills, and friendship with their families, other Special Olympics athletes, and the community. Through the Family Leadership and Support initiative, Special Olympics offers families not just opportunities for sport, social interaction, and fun but also a much-needed support system. Special Olympics served more than 1.7 million athletes in 2004 worldwide.

Environmental and Conservation Organizations

Environmental organizations are primarily involved in lobbying and education activities for specific concerns such as wildlife protection, global warming, and safe water. They are worthy of consideration because their efforts often make possible the places and spaces in which recreational activities occur. The Sierra Club and The Trust for Public Land are two examples.

• **Sierra Club.** Founded in 1892, the Sierra Club's purpose is to explore, enjoy, and protect the wild places of the earth; to practice and promote the responsible use of the earth's ecosystem and resources; to educate and enlist humanity to protect and restore the quality of the natural and human environment; and to use all lawful means to carry out these objectives. From grassroots campaigns to environmental law programs, the Sierra Club seeks to spread the word about the importance of protecting the planet. The Sierra Club has more than 700,000 members and 560 field staff throughout 28 field offices and 63 chapters in the United States. The U.S. Sierra Club has created the Mexico Project to help support and strengthen Mexican grassroots environmental and community organizations. The Sierra Club of Canada was founded in 1963 to develop a diverse, well-trained network to protect the integrity of the global ecosystems.

• **The Trust for Public Land.** The Trust for Public Land (TPL) uses its more than 400 paid staff and 400 volunteers to accomplish its mission of conserving land for people to enjoy as parks, gardens, and other natural places, ensuring livable communities for generations to come. Operating in 37 offices across the United States since its inception in 1972, TPL runs several national programs, such as the Working Lands Program (WLP) and Tribal Lands Program (TLP). The WLP responds to threats such as urban sprawl, poor urban and municipal planning, and nonsustainable management of precious natural resources, while the TLP expands partnerships with tribes to assist them in reversing a history of dispossession.

Associations

Several nonprofit professional associations concern the recreation field and are a resource to students and practitioners in the field.

• **American Alliance for Health, Physical Education, Recreation and Dance.** The American Alliance for Health, Physical Education, Recreation and Dance (AAHPERD) is the largest

©AP/Wide World Photos

The Nature Conservancy, an environmental and conservation organization, has partnered with Great Northern Paper to protect more than 240,000 acres of forestland around Mount Katahdin, Maine, shown here.

organization of professionals, supporting and assisting those involved in physical education, leisure, fitness, dance, health promotion, education, and all specialties related to achieving a healthy lifestyle. Founded in 1885, the association represents an alliance of six national associations and enjoys a membership of more than 26,000.

• **American Camp Association.** The American Camp Association (ACA) is a diverse community of camp professionals dedicated to enriching the lives of children and adults through the camp experience. For nearly 100 years, the ACA has used camp programs to impart powerful lessons in community, character building, and skill development. With more than 6,600 members, the ACA works to preserve, promote, and improve the camp experience.

- **American Therapeutic Recreation Association.** With approximately 5,000 members, the American Therapeutic Recreation Association (ATRA) is the largest membership organization representing the interests and needs of health care providers who use recreational therapy to improve the functioning of people with illness or disabling conditions.

- **Canadian Association for Health, Physical Education, Recreation and Dance.** Canadian Association for Health, Physical Education, Recreation and Dance (CAHPERD) is a national, charitable, voluntary-sector organization with 2,500 members whose primary concern is to influence the healthy development of children and youth by advocating for quality, school-based physical and health education.

- **Canadian Parks and Recreation Association.** Canadian Parks and Recreation Association (CPRA) is "the national voice for the parks and recreation field." CPRA provides a national network of 2,500 members and advances its belief that parks and recreation is essential to the well-being of individual and community life. There are also provincial and territorial parks and recreation associations operating across Canada.

- **National Recreation and Park Association.** For more than 100 years, the National Recreation and Park Association (NRPA) has advocated the importance of thriving, local park systems; the opportunity for all Americans to lead healthy, active lifestyles; and the preservation of great community places. Its mission is "to advance parks, recreation and environmental conservation efforts that enhance the quality of life for all people." NRPA enhances professional development and provides services that contribute to the development of its 21,000 members. Competency guidelines form the curricular content of NRPA-accredited colleges and universities that offer degrees in parks and recreation.

Membership or Service Clubs and Fraternal Organizations

Although we do not always think of service clubs and fraternal organizations as a part of the recreation and leisure services community, we should consider them for two reasons. The first is that many of these organizations support parks and recreation programs through their donations of time and money. The second is that they provide a personal and professional development networking opportunity for the recreation professional who becomes a member. Two of the better-known service clubs are Kiwanis International and Rotary International.

- **Kiwanis International.** Founded in 1915, Kiwanis International has a membership of professional business people dedicated to serving their communities. In 2000, the organization had nearly 300,000 members and 108 paid staff in 5,795 clubs throughout the United States. The organization evaluates both children's issues and community needs and conducts service projects that respond to those identified needs. In Canada, Kiwanis International operates in 297 clubs and promotes the same standards of leadership and community awareness and involvement.

- **Rotary International.** Rotary is a worldwide organization of business and professional leaders who provide humanitarian service, encourage high ethical standards in all vocations, and help build goodwill and peace in the world. The organization was founded in 1905. In the United States, more than 7,500 Rotary clubs encourage their nearly 400,000 members to become actively involved in hands-on projects in which their vocational skills are put to use. Rotary International operates in Canada with more than 29,299 members and 720 clubs.

Differences and Similarities Among Organizations

Organizations share differences and similarities according to several distinguishing variables (Hansmann, 1987). These variables include (1) the beneficiaries of their services, such as youth, seniors, or animals; (2) their function, such as service delivery or political advocacy; and (3) their primary source of revenues, distinguishing between nonprofits that rely primarily on sales of goods or services and those that rely largely on donations. Two additional distinctions regarding service delivery are evident within nonprofit recreation organizations. They are (4) whether the organization is facility or nonfacility based and (5) the extent to which volunteers deliver services.

Facility-based recreation organizations attract participants to programs that occur at specific locations. These include Boys and Girls Clubs, YMCAs, and similar organizations. Other nonprofits, such as Big Brothers Big Sisters, are not facility based and therefore rely on community-based facilities for their program delivery. Still other nonprofits, such as Camp Fire USA, Boy Scouts, and Girl Scouts, rely in part on their own place-based facilities, such as summer camps owned by these agencies. However, for other programming they rely on community-based facilities, such as schools, churches, and neighborhood centers.

Another distinction is the role of volunteers in service delivery. Volunteers provide an essential human resource to many nonprofits. In fact, in organizations such as Big Brothers Big Sisters and in Boy Scouts and Girl Scouts programs, volunteers are the delivery system. Without them, there would be no services delivery, and the mission of each organization could not be carried out. Other organizations such as Boys and Girls Clubs rely more on paid staff to deliver their core programs. However, in every case, volunteers serve in a variety of governance roles, such as boards of directors and task groups, and in support roles, such as fund-raising.

THE PROFESSIONAL IN NONPROFIT ORGANIZATIONS

About 6 percent of all organizational entities in the United States are nonprofits, and 1 in 15 people works for one (Salamon, 1999). Career opportunities for nonprofit professionals are growing rapidly across all subsectors, including recreation and leisure services providers. Nonprofits hire people with diverse skills, just as business or government entities do, because there are as many different job functions as those found in other industries. However, many recreation and leisure nonprofits have relatively small numbers of paid staff in relation to their number of volunteers. Thus, the professional is often given broad responsibility for a variety of duties within the organization.

Given the unique nature of philanthropy in many nonprofits, staff members who demonstrate skills in raising financial resources and working with and through volunteers to accomplish organizational goals are particularly successful. In youth development nonprofits, some practitioners work directly with children. More likely, however, they are responsible for a geographic territory with responsibility for assuring that financial and human resources are acquired and deployed within the mission of the organization.

A variety of job and career resources are available for those interested in pursuing careers in nonprofit recreation and leisure organizations. The national organization Action Without Borders (www.idealist.org) is one of several entities that provides career guidance and posts job openings. Trade publications such as *The NonProfit Times* and *The Chronicle of Philanthropy* are also helpful tools.

Students pursuing degree programs in recreation who have an interest in nonprofit careers may benefit from earning national certification through American Humanics (www.humanics.org). American Humanics (AH) is a national alliance of colleges, universities, and nonprofit partners preparing undergraduate students for careers in nonprofit organizations. Campus affiliates of AH offer curricular and cocurricular offerings leading to national certification for students pursuing nonprofit professional careers. The program was founded in 1948 and is offered in the United States at more than 70 colleges and universities nationwide.

CHALLENGES AND OPPORTUNITIES FOR THE FUTURE

Several trends serve as both challenges and opportunities for the nonprofit sector. These include the effect of commercialization, the changing shape of government and nonprofit relations, public trust issues, and the effect of changing demographics (Salamon, 2002). Three of these have direct implications for nonprofit recreation and leisure services providers.

The first is the issue of trust and accountability. If nonprofits depend on the charitable giving of time and money to assure the success of their missions, then it is imperative that such organizations be led and managed effectively. Although other sectors also face accountability issues, the special trust held by nonprofits as stewards of philanthropy makes this issue especially important.

The second is the opportunity for collaboration in response to marketplace challenges. It is a rare nonprofit that can afford to operate its programs

Web Sites to EXPLORE

Action Without Borders: www.idealist.org
American Alliance for Health, Physical Education, Recreation and Dance: www.aahperd.org
American Camp Association: www.acacamps.org
American Red Cross: www.redcross.org
American Therapeutic Recreation Association: www.atra-tr.org
Big Brothers Big Sisters of America: www.bbbsa.org
Boys and Girls Clubs of America: www.bgca.org
Boy Scouts of America: www.scouting.org
Camp Fire USA: www.campfire.org
Canadian Association for Health, Physical Education, Recreation and Dance: www.cahperd.ca
Canadian Parks and Recreation Association: www.cpra.ca
Canadian Red Cross: www.redcross.ca

Girls Incorporated: www.girlsinc.org
Girl Scouts of the USA: www.girlscouts.org
Imagine Canada: www.imaginecanada.ca/languagePreference.asp
Kiwanis International: www.kiwanis.org
Little League Baseball: www.littleleague.org
National Recreation and Park Association: www.nrpa.org
Rotary International: www.rotary.org
Sierra Club: www.sierraclub.org
Special Olympics: www.specialolympics.org
The Arc of the United States: www.thearc.org
The Trust for Public Land: www.tpl.org
The Volunteer Center National Network (VCNN): www.pointsoflight.org/centers
YMCA Canada: www.ymca.ca
YMCA of the USA: www.ymca.net
YWCA Canada: www.ywcacanada.ca
YWCA of the USA: www.ywca.org

without regard for the other providers of similar services, be they government, nonprofit, or business providers. Issues of pricing, marketing, and consumer choice suggest that the successful nonprofit of the future must use businesslike principles without abandoning the core public service mission that earns its tax-exempt privilege.

The third is demographic challenges and opportunities. As communities change and grow, many will find that the majority of their citizens are from ethnic minorities. Sweeping demographic changes also mean that nonprofit providers must make adjustments to stay relevant if they want to make a broad-based impact. Honoring their historic traditions as they change structures, processes, and programs to welcome new and diverse populations to their organizations presents both a challenge and an opportunity. This tension between exclusion and inclusion cuts across many demographics including race, ethnicity, culture, sexual orientation, and physical abilities. Using history as a predictor of the future, the nonprofit sector in North America will be composed of organizations that change, some that remain static, and some that are created anew.

SUMMARY

Understanding the role of nonprofit organizations is important if recreation and leisure services are to be thoroughly understood. The nonprofit form is one way in which services are organized and delivered. There are enormous variations in how nonprofits are organized across North America. The extent to which the nonprofit form is used in one country compared to another is largely based on the economic, social, and political differences found among different nations.

The career field for graduates of recreation and related degree programs who seek professional opportunities is growing. A number of trends are influencing the organizations of society that deliver recreation services as a blurring of the lines of the three sectors (business, government, and nonprofit) occurs. Successful nonprofit managers will be those who are skillful across a range of competencies. In particular, the ability to raise philanthropic resources and to work with and through volunteers to achieve organizational goals are hallmarks of the successful nonprofit professional.

CHAPTER 9

Commercial Recreation and Tourism

Lynn M. Jamieson

© Getty Images

The finest workers in stone are not copper or steel tools, but the gentle touches of air and water working at their leisure with a liberal allowance of time.

Henry David Thoreau, American author, poet, and philosopher

CHAPTER OBJECTIVES

After reading this chapter, you should be able to do the following:

- Define types of commercial recreation
- Describe the leisure industry model and note examples in each category
- Define a tourist and understand the different reasons for travel
- Identify the market segments within the tourism sector
- Understand the organizational aspects of commercial recreation and tourism enterprises
- Identify career opportunities in commercial recreation and tourism
- Articulate the challenges and trends in the leisure industry
- Understand why businesses fail and what makes them successful

INTRODUCTION

Welcome to 90 percent of the leisure industry! In this chapter, we explore the many opportunities for and characteristics of private for-profit enterprises, also known as commercial recreation and tourism. **Commercial recreation and tourism** is the umbrella term for the industries that deal with leisure services conducted predominantly for profit. Under this umbrella are a host of businesses and agencies that provide services for those who are willing to pay for them. Commercial recreation is a large industry whose businesses compete for a customer's discretionary dollars.

Although the umbrella term is commercial recreation and tourism, implying that the businesses operate primarily for profit and financial self-sustainability, tourism organizations may be organized as nonprofits as well as operate for profit. However, in this chapter, we deal with those aspects of the commercial recreation and tourism industry that are chiefly for-profit operations.

DEFINING TYPES OF COMMERCIAL RECREATION AND TOURISM

To understand the vastness of the commercial recreation and tourism field, let's look at definitions of several aspects of the industry.

- **Commercial recreation** provides recreation-related products and services by private enterprise for a fee with the long-term intention of being profitable. For example, an owner-opera-tor of a white-water rafting business charges a fee for a river-rafting adventure to a customer who is willing to pay for it. Fees must be sufficient to maintain the operation and cover all expenses, as well as gain a profit.

- **Commercialized public recreation** is similar to commercial recreation, except that instead of a private owner providing services, a government or nonprofit organization provides the services with much or all of the costs covered by fees, charges, or other nontax revenues. For example, a city golf course runs as a for-profit operation under contract with a city. Fees and charges must cover all aspects of the operation, and revenue bonds must pay for facilities and land over time.

- **Entrepreneurial recreation** provides new recreation-related services and products through new businesses that take advantage of emerging trends and changes in recreation habits. These endeavors require creativity and the willingness to take a risk. For example, a landowner notices that tourists like to walk along her private farm trail. Rather than posting no-trespassing signs, this entre-preneur develops a guide service to ensure safety and enjoyment during planned walks through her private property.

- **Intrapreneurial recreation** provides new recreation-related services and products within an organization. Opportunities exist within public agencies, nonprofit associations, and private for-profit enterprises; however, new programs must support the goals of the organization. An example is company-sponsored employee recreation programs.

Six Flags

Many recreational activities are seasonal. A successful tourism or recreation enterprise needs to capitalize on high-season usage and find innovative ways to increase off-season usage. Six Flags is a large U.S.-based corporation that operates 30 themed amusement parks that emphasize thrilling rides. Six Flags Kentucky Kingdom offers some of the world's oldest and most thrilling roller coasters. In addition to the original year-round operation, the company also offers a full-service water park during the summer season. Six Flags Kentucky Kingdom relies on a strong seasonal and shoulder season response, high visitor rates during the summer season and the periods leading into and out of it, in order to maintain profits all year. However, the company has developed special events and themes to attract visitors during the winter.

LEISURE INDUSTRY MODEL

The three components of the commercial recreation and leisure industry are local commercial recreation, hospitality, and travel. Some businesses fall neatly into one category or another, but often the distinctions are subtle. Crossley, Jamieson, and Brayley (2001, p. 17) have developed a leisure industry model to illustrate where the services of commercial recreation, travel and transportation, and hospitality overlap. Figure 9.1 offers a simplified version of this model.

Local commercial recreation refers to businesses that are available to residents and tourists and provide entertainment. **Hospitality** refers to businesses that cater to travelers and the special needs of residents by providing accommodations, food and beverages, and other amenities. And finally, the travel component consists of businesses that move people and services. Crossley, Jamieson, and Brayley (2001) also refer to facilitators, which are businesses that must be in place before the main commercial and tourism enterprises can function. These support enterprises consist of travel information services, transportation providers, and equipment manufacturers.

UNDERSTANDING TOURISM

Tourism is an integral part of the commercial recreation and leisure industry and sometimes it's difficult to determine if a recreation service falls into the commercial recreation category or tourism. Services targeted to tourists can serve local customers and vice versa. Therefore, what sets the tourism industry apart is the fact that tourists, rather than residents, use these services.

Leisure Industry Model

Local commercial recreation

Entertainment such as theaters, concerts, and sport arenas

Activities and programs such as golf courses, skating rinks, and fitness clubs

Retail products such as fishing, sporting goods, and arts and crafts

Hospitality

Accommodations such as hotels and motels

Food and beverages such as restaurants and bars

Amenities such as recreation communities and resort condominiums

Travel and transportation

Move people and services such as airlines, rental cars, and railroads

FIGURE 9.1   A simplified version of the leisure industry model. Casinos, theme parks, resorts, and major entertainment events overlap all three segments of the industry.

Modified from Crossley, Jamieson, and Brayley, 2001.

The involvement of the community, including businesses, government, and various organizations, has become important in attracting tourists. Although some community members may view tourism as a necessary evil, many realize the economic necessity of a diversified economy that includes tourism. Even though many tourist-oriented businesses also cater to local residents, the tourist experience may be the lifeblood of the community's economy, and therefore, it is considered a necessity.

Characteristics of Tourists

A **tourist** is someone who travels for business or pleasure and spends at least one night away from home. After spending a year in one place, a tourist becomes a resident. Tourists travel for many reasons, but they all spend at least one night away from home. This distinguishes the tourism industry from other suppliers of leisure services.

Tourists consume leisure services in various ways. Mass tourists prefer to travel with large groups. They follow the crowds to events and attractions and are happy being bussed, carted, fed, and thrilled with throngs of others. Individual tourists, on the other hand, enjoy pursuits away from the crowd. It is sometimes difficult for both

types of tourists to share resources. For example, a skilled canoeist may feel that her river experience is spoiled by the masses of beginners coming down the river. And a mass tourist may dislike being alone outdoors fending for himself. Therefore, tourism professionals must be sensitive to the desires and expectations of various types of tourists and identify experiences that will satisfy a variety of needs, which can be difficult, given the diversity among tourists.

Types of Travel

Tourists travel for many reasons: for pleasure to a specific destination for entertainment, relaxation, cultural enrichment, or some other purpose; for pleasure mainly to visit family or friends but perhaps also working in a trip to a tourist destination; and for business. Each type of travel presents a variety of needs that the tourism and support industries must meet.

A majority of tourists travel for recreation and pleasure. Trips for pleasure require accommoda-

Tourists from all over the world came to New York City's Central Park to view *The Gates* for an arts and cultural experience. *The Gates* promoted tourism to New York City and brought a tremendous economic impact to the city.

tions, food, entertainment, and transportation. And travelers expect these services to be convenient. Services must be organized so that all members of a group may access them. For example, a cruise for families should include children's activities and activities targeted to adults as well as activities appealing to the whole family. Because people sometimes try to do things while traveling that they would not ordinarily do, service providers must consider their customers' safety and well-being. Tourist tries rock climbing and climbing company provides education and experienced belayers.

A smaller segment of the traveling population visits family and friends and uses very few services from the tourism industry. However, educating residents about tourist attractions may attract this group of travelers.

Business travel makes up another large piece of the tourism pie. Business travel can range from a single salesperson flying to another city to make a presentation to a large group of doctors attending a convention. In this category, it is essential to provide services that support business needs as well as provide convenient visits to sites that will fit into the business day or a specific time period such as Internet capability, support services, conferencing opportunities, and similar services.

Services Within the Tourism Industry

The tourism portion of the leisure industry caters to people traveling to many locations for many purposes. Because these people are away from home, they require an enormous amount of service provided by a collection of public, private, and commercial operations working together to deliver a positive tourism experience.

Shelter and food are two of the most important aspects of the tourist experience. The accommodations industry refers to the myriad lodging opportunities available to tourists. These range from primitive campgrounds to five-star hotels. Food service can range from a hot dog at the ballpark to a posh restaurant serving haute cuisine. Moving people from place to place, or **travel services,** can be one of the most complicated aspects of the industry because it requires the coordination of a specific attraction, transportation, food, and accommodations. Tourists use planes, boats, trains, automobiles, buses, and even horses and carriages to get where they want to go when they want to get there.

The opportunity to engage in a wide range of leisure activities attracts travelers in the first place.

Although there are more food, shelter, and transportation providers within the tourism industry and they generate the most revenue, in the tourists' mind, it's the recreation and amenities services (such as travel kits, discounts, special offers, and memorable experiences) that create the vacation.

Services that manage and coordinate travel for tourists make up another segment of the tourism industry. The two major management systems are destination management organizations (DMOs) and meeting management organizations (MMOs). DMOs coordinate an array of services at a particular destination. Examples are a convention and visitors bureau or chamber of commerce, a resort, and a real estate firm that provides concierge services that may factor in discounts to local restaurants or lodging facilities. MMOs arrange meeting services in a variety of settings: hotels, company conference rooms, and the convention and visitors bureau, among other places. Services include preconvention and postconvention tours and visits to area attractions.

Types of Tourism

Now that we understand the components of tourism, we can discuss the various categories within the industry.

- **Ecotourism** provides people an opportunity to visit natural areas to study biodiversity, improve the well-being of the local people, build environmental and cultural awareness, and provide direct financial benefits for conservation (The International Ecotourism Society, 2004). These locations have been made available through substantial efforts by local government and environmental groups to protect them.

- Agrotourism provides people the opportunity to view farm and agricultural operations, pick their own produce, and live on a working property to learn more about their operation. These businesses allow tourists to learn about our agricultural heritage while giving agricultural operations another source of income.

- Sport tourism provides sporting events and programs that attract tourists to an area. In addition to providing entertainment, sport venues can improve the local economy.

- Cultural tourism provides people the opportunity to experience the cultural heritage of a locale.

Ecotourism provides individuals an opportunity to visit natural areas and study biodiversity.

COMMERCIAL RECREATION AND TOURISM MARKET SEGMENTS

Consumers of commercial recreation and tourism services can be divided into various market segments. It is highly essential for those involved in tourism and commercial recreation to understand the needs and expectations of these segments in order to capitalize on the financial health of a business.

Singles are one segment of the leisure services market. These individuals and groups are interested in activities that allow them to interact with other singles in order to form social bonds and relationships. Club Med and other resorts and camps are examples of businesses that target this group. This is a growing market for all commercial recreation and tourism enterprises.

Another growing segment is families with or without children; this group is traveling and consuming commercial recreation resources at a rapid rate. More and more leisure services providers are catering to this group by providing family retreats and reunions and including child care as part of their services. Many hotels develop programs with a variety of activities that family members can participate in together or separately.

The power of the student as a consumer is evident from the marketing efforts aimed at the "affluent teen." This group is increasingly courted by the leisure industry. For example, youth hostels and Eurail passes are available for youth traveling on a budget. At the other end of the age spectrum, people age 55 and older are considered to have more discretionary income than most of the other segments, and this group is more active than ever before. Commercial recreation and tourism enterprises increasingly cater to the wide range of interests of this group. Many cruise lines, attractions, hotels, spas, and entertainment events cater to this age category.

Diversity of culture and ethnic origin is prevalent in many messages regarding commercial recreation and tourism. The multicultural nature of most larger cities in Canada and the United States is a part of many marketing pursuits within the leisure industry. Ethnic festivals may attract a diverse group of attendees.

Another way to categorize commercial recreation and travel consumers is by their interests. Golfers, opera buffs, surfers, and quilters, for example, are small but easily targeted market segments. Market segments may also be categorized by a special need. For example, people with disabilities require certain accommodations and aids in order to participate in recreation and tourism programs. The Americans with Disabilities Act has provided guidelines for making all leisure programs and services available to those who want to participate, and commercial recreation and tourism providers are marketing to this segment more and more.

OPERATING A COMMERCIAL RECREATION OR TOURISM ENTERPRISE

The business of providing leisure services presents many of the challenges and joys common to any business operation. These include the ability to answer to yourself, create a new attraction,

Marine World Africa USA

In attracting customers to a new venue, marketing and favorable publicity, created in an unusual way, can be very effective. Maybe one of the most unique publicity campaigns for a recreation facility was conducted when Marine World Africa USA put itself up for auction in the mid-1980s. The park decided to move from its site in Redwood City, California, because investors wished to convert the area to condominiums. It offered local cities the chance to bid for the right to house the park. At issue was a potential loss of a customer base in exchange for a new base. When the city of Vallejo won, the park and its animals sailed across San Francisco Bay in an arklike structure to their new home. The media attention surrounding this move was enormous. This ingenious marketing ploy ensured that the park was instantly one of the most popular themed animal parks in the state. (The photo on the first page of this chapter is from Marine World Africa USA.)

respond to increases in profit, and other opportunity. However, because the leisure industry provides a service rather than something tangible, many operational aspects are considerably different from those encountered in a product-driven business. This section identifies those differences. It also outlines the process and various options for planning, starting, and operating a successful for-profit commercial recreation business.

Government Involvement

Government provides the infrastructure for all commercial recreation and tourism enterprises. They assist businesses by creating a positive business environment through support for tax relief, zoning and planning, marketing, and providing services and resources to help launch start-up businesses. Governments may provide inclusion in long-range plans, land, and other services. Government and businesses collaborate in many ways. For example, a city might build the shell for an office building and lease it to a business that improves it. Or a county government could provide infrastructure improvements by building access roads to a new facility. Governments might also provide tax breaks for new businesses or grant permission to use land or other public resources. These practices help businesses become profitable.

The Nature of the Leisure Experience

Leisure experiences are produced and consumed simultaneously with no residual evidence. For example, when hiking on a marked trail in a national park, you consume the product—a safe,

enjoyable hike through a protected wildlife area—while you walk on the trail, but once you leave the trailhead, you're left with nothing but memories of the experience. The activity-based nature of commercial recreation makes this industry unique in the following ways:

- Leisure services providers produce intangible experiences rather than products that can be touched and owned; therefore leisure products are hard to measure.

- The chief value of the leisure experience is in doing and reliving.

- It is difficult to predict what someone will do with his or her spare time. Customers can be fickle. People often move from activity to activity without developing loyalty to a set of experiences. This means that successful business owners must anticipate changes in trends and leisure habits and be ready to provide new or different services.

- It is difficult to measure someone's satisfaction with the leisure experience because it is hard to determine if someone is really happy with their experience.

- The factors of the leisure experience often are not figured into the marketing plan. If not factored in, a business owner may miss opportunity to attract customers.

- Although long-term profitability is desired within the leisure industry, people often enter it for reasons other than making a profit. Perhaps they enjoy the activity the business provides, or maybe they are attracted to the seasonality of the business. For whatever reason, it is estimated that a commercial recreation business has a longer

Commercial recreation providers furnish boats, guides, and food to white-water rafters, but they produce no tangible product, only the tourists' memories.

profit window compared to the one to two years for businesses that provide a tangible product.

- Because the cost of travel can be high, visitors may be disappointed if their experience is less than perfect. Those in the travel industry are under constant pressure to organize services that will bring travelers maximum enjoyment.

Although the experiential component of the leisure activity presents several challenges, it also provides an opportunity for success. Because people anticipate, participate in, and then finally reminisce about these experiences, the more successful a business owner is in providing the memories and the ability to relive the experience, the greater the chances that a commercial recreation and tourism business will succeed.

Elements of Success

Regardless of the challenges facing a would-be entrepreneur, operating a leisure business can be rewarding and enjoyable. Successful business

entrepreneurs cite that their skill in managing the following elements determined their success when setting up commercial recreation and tourism businesses.

- **Use of business data to make organizational decisions.** Most entrepreneurs use many sources to identify the potential for a business's success. Data from The Roper Center for Public Opinion Research, Harris Interactive Inc., and census sources combined with industry profiles, annual reports, the stock market, and industry publications can reveal trends and solutions. In addition, primary and secondary research can be applied to identify feasibility. Primary research is conducted directly by the company; however, secondary research is that which may have been conducted by others but is still applicable such as census data or product data.

- **Product.** Successful business enterprises market a sound idea or concept to a definitive population.

- **Demographics.** Most successful businesses develop detailed customer profiles (combinations of characteristics) to ensure that they market to the proper target.

- **Management.** Successful leisure services operations are effectively and efficiently run as evidenced by cleanliness, responsive staff, and other factors.

- **Finance.** Successful businesses secure sufficient funding to operate their enterprise. Other aspects of finance include funding sources, financial projections, and ways to organize, all of which can allow a manager to keep track of financial issues.

- **Location.** A favorable site attracts people to it and provides convenient access. When one has conducted a full feasibility assessment, the location properly identified can be key to a successful business.

ORGANIZATIONAL ASPECTS OF COMMERCIAL RECREATION AND TOURISM

We now explore the ways in which commercial recreation and tourism businesses organize, from developing a business plan and establishing the feasibility of starting up or expanding the business, to deciding on how the business will be legally organized, and finally through marketing and financing the service enterprise. We also explore some of the reasons that businesses fail in their first year. Although it is impossible to predict how successful an enterprise will be, steps may be taken to prevent the most obvious failures.

Importance of the Business Plan

The **business plan** is the heart of a business enterprise because it determines the way in which the business will receive and use fiscal resources to gain a profit over a projected period. Embedded within this plan are the marketing and financing projections that become the work plan for the business start-up and continuance. The more thoroughly the business plan is researched, the greater the chances for profit and success.

The first step in establishing a sound business plan is to conduct a **feasibility analysis** to answer the following questions: Is the business plan administratively sound? Will the legal organizational format work? Is the site appropriate? Will the financial plan work? Is the market appropriate? Sometimes the person starting the business will conduct the analysis; more often, however, the entrepreneur seeks assistance from independent consultants, from the corporations that will provide the products, or from financial institutions. The result is a report that lists indicators of the operation's success. If the report does not indicate a green light, the feasibility factors may be reexamined in an attempt to come up with a plan that will work. If the feasibility analysis indicates success, it becomes the blueprint for the business plan used to generate financial support.

Legal Formation of a Business

In developing a business, several legal forms of organizing may be considered:

- **Sole proprietorship.** This is the typical "mom and pop" operation in which the owners take the most financial and legal responsibility for the business. In this situation, one's personal finances are most at risk; however, in an initial start-up, where financial profits are not high, this may be the most feasible way to start.

- **Partnership.** A partnership, either full or limited, involves two or more people who either fully share the financial burden or assign the financial responsibilities to limit liability. In this form, the risk is either fully shared by the partners or divided by agreement.

- **Corporation.** A business may be declared a corporation, which lowers tax liability and personal legal responsibility and assigns it to the corporate entity. This form is usually selected once profits are being earned because the corporate structure is taxed at a lower rate.

- **Franchise.** A franchise is a chain of existing businesses that allow people to buy into the business. McDonald's is an example of a successful franchise. Other examples include Batting Cages, Inc., Yogi Bear Campground, and Putt Putt. This option is often appealing to new business owners, because the parent company makes many resources available for start-up.

Elements of Marketing

The marketing plan is part of the business plan. It must define and outline the ways the business owner will handle the following aspects of marketing:

- **Substitution:** Your plan for handling changes in consumer interests and for preparing your business for new activities to replace those that are no longer popular

The Californias

The Californias campaign in the late 1980s was one of the first launched by the California Office of Tourism, and to this day is one of the most successful. A series of advertisements in print media, a television campaign, and other features comprised a system of distinguishing each of 12 regions of California. By describing the uniqueness of its 12 regions in separate marketing processes, thus marketing the state as a whole instead of relying on individual attractions to market themselves, would-be travelers got a glimpse of California in an entirely new way. The features of each region were described, and the California Raisins were born as an example of the unique offerings in areas where grapes are grown.

- **Niche:** Whatever is unique about your business; the emphasis of your promotion
- **Guerrilla marketing:** An aggressive approach to uncovering new markets and other ways to reach customers
- **Values:** The merit each niche group assigns to various activities that you will emphasize while promoting your services
- **Campaigns:** The long-range and short-range marketing efforts aimed toward increasing volume of visitors in a given community and customers

Financing Basics

It is important to consider major sources of finance when establishing a business plan. The following sources illustrate the range of options. Circumstances such as capacity for funding indicate the level and type of funding that might be available. The amount a business owner may borrow depends on the borrower's character collateral, credit history, and other factors.

- **Venture capital.** This type of funding is granted by companies and investors who are willing to take a risk on a new enterprise that may not have a strong track record. Leisure services are often attractive to venture capitalists because they often produce long-term profitability. Lenders of venture capital funds often charge higher interest rates and expect greater participation in a rate of return.
- **Personal.** A more common source of funding for start-up businesses comes from friends, relatives, and personal savings. These funds are often put up as part of the total investment against loans applied for through small-business investors or banks. For most leisure services operations, 75 percent of the total funding must be available before securing the remaining 25 percent through banks.
- **Commercial loans.** Banks and other sources lend businesses money through many programs and plans. Start-up finance, cash flow funding, inventory funding, and other packages are available through conventional financing or Small Business Administration (SBA) funding.
- **Going public.** A successful business may eventually go public by selling stock to investors. This source of income results in sharing corporate wealth with shareholders who buy stock and receive a return on investment.

The quest for financing may be discouraging at first, especially if the business is perceived to be risky. Therefore, the following alternatives to direct financing may keep the investment to a minimum and prevent the financial risk of overborrowing.

- **Franchises.** In this method, the franchisor may provide a proven product and make low-cost financing and resources available to the franchisee. For example, low-cost loans, marketing assistance, and even operational consulting during start-up may save the business owner a considerable amount of money, allowing him or her to realize a profit sooner. A franchise agreement may also include a way to transfer ownership within the franchise to alleviate the difficulty of trying to end or sell a business.
- **Buying an existing business.** Buying an existing business provides an entrepreneur with collateral and the benefit of goodwill in the community and an established reputation and location. Financing will be easier to secure and the start-up costs may be lower because of the availability of existing decor, inventory, trained staff, and other advantages that reduce financial risk.

- **Incubators.** Many cities provide places where new ideas can be developed through the acquisition of small grants to support product development, feasibility analyses, and other forms of start-up activity. Ideas may be shared with other successful business people, networking secured, and important contacts made before the new business owner must make a major investment in start-up.

- **Extension of an existing business.** Business owners may look for ways to add a feature that will make an existing business more profitable and result in greater success without borrowing money.

- **Public–private cooperative venture.** Close cooperation with local governments may yield a business partnership that involves tax breaks, use of public land instead of buying property, use of buildings under an agreement, and an investment in infrastructure. Many examples of partnerships exist and may be explored. For instance, Great America theme park is a cooperative venture of a local city and a corporation.

Why Businesses Fail

It is estimated that five out of six businesses fail within one year of start-up. These failures are often due to poor planning, impulsive decision making, or organizational conflicts between partners. Of course, in the commercial recreation and tourism field, seasonal fluctuations, threats to travel safety, and other factors can also jeopardize businesses. The following are often cited as reasons that businesses fail.

1. **Undercapitalization.** Start-up financing that fails to cover personal expenses or unanticipated expenses can lead to business failure.

2. **Unanticipated changes in the economy.** Unexpected fluctuations such as changes in leadership or the economy and natural catastrophes may cause a business to flounder.

3. **Poor succession management.** Owners often fail to plan ahead to secure effective leadership as people retire or leave the company.

4. **Poor operational management.** Outmoded business practices, inef-

ficient processes, and poor customer service contribute to business failure.

5. **Inflexibility.** An inability to anticipate and adapt to changing needs may cause a business to fail.

CAREER PATHS IN THE LEISURE INDUSTRY

Career opportunities in the commercial recreation and tourism industries are wide open for those with degrees and professional preparation in recreation and leisure. Jobs within commercial recreation take place at resorts, convention centers, theme parks, sport stadiums, travel agencies, cruise ships, equipment sales companies, and health clubs. Recreation professionals can also work in offices planning business management and hospitality services or marketing any of the recreation services. The following list identifies opportunities that have merit and provide a clear career path.

- **Recreation specialist.** This professional is needed in every significant commercial

A tour guide is just one of many career paths in the leisure industry.

recreation enterprise. The specialist, or programmer, is essential to all leisure experiences regardless of the setting.

- **Meeting manager.** People with a recreation background who possess leadership and programming skills are well suited to organizing conventions and meetings.
- **Event manager.** The same skills required of a meeting manager are required for profes-

sionals who organize events for both small and large groups.

- **Tour guide.** This person coordinates tours for groups with various interests.
- **Administrator.** The path into top management in any of the tourist and commercial recreation segments is available to people with training in recreation and resource administration.

Web Sites to EXPLORE

ActionJobs.com: www.actionjobs.com

Adventures in Hospitality Careers:
www.hospitalityadventures.com

Amelia Island Plantation: www.aipfl.com

American Alliance for Health, Physical Education, Recreation and Dance—CareerLink:
http://member.aahperd.org/careercenter

American Hospitality Academy:
www.americanhospitalityacademy.com

Association of Collegiate Conference and Events Directors International—Jobs: http://acced-i.colostate.edu/imis_web/StaticContent/3/Jobs/job.htm

Athletic Business—Classifieds:
www.athleticbusiness.com/classfieds

AthleticLink.com—Job Seekers: www.athleticlink.com/JobSeekers.asp

Benchmark Hospitality:
www.benchmark.hospitalityonline.com

Big Mountain Resort: http://bigmtn.com

Blue Fox Jobs: www.bluefoxjobs.com

Burr Oak Resort & Conference Center:
www.burroakresort.com

Club Managers Association of America—Executive Career Services: www.cmaa.org/ecs/

Connected International Meeting Planners Association—Career Center: www.jobtarget.com/home/index.cfm

Coolworks: www.coolworks.com

Disney Careers: http://disney.go.com/DisneyCareers

Dornan's: www.dornans.com

Entertainment, Hospitality, Travel & Resort Jobs Page:
www.nationjob.com/hotel

Eventplanner.com—Employment Board: http://eventplanner.com/boards/employment.html

FitnessManagement.com—Classified Ads: www.fitnessmanagement.com/FM/marketplace/classifieds

Flamingo Lodge Marina & Resort Outpost:
www.coolworks.com/everglades/default.htm

Grand Teton Lodge Company: www.gtlc.com

Grand Traverse Resort and Spa:
www.grandtraverseresort.com

Hawk's Cay Resort: www.hawkscay.com

Holiday Inn Job Opportunities: www.holijob.com

Hospitality 1st: www.hospitality-1st.com

Hospitality Online—Job Search:
www.hospitalityonline.com/jobs

Hotel Career Solutions: www.hotelcareersolutions.com

Hotel Jobs Network: www.hospitalityjobs.com

Hueston Woods Resort & Conference Center:
www.huestonwoodsresort.com

International Association for Exposition Mangement—Career Center: http://iaemorg.expoexchange.com/CareerCenter/ccintro.htm

International Association for the Leisure & Entertainment Industry—Classifieds: www.ialei.org/ContentPage.aspx?WebPageId=6163&GroupId=1021

International Association of Amusement Parks and Attractions—Career Opportunities: www.iaapa.org/modules/Careers/index.cfm

International Association of Assembly Managers—Career Opportunities: http://iaam.org/IAAM_News/Pages/NLcareerlist.htm

International Association of Conference Centers—Job Board: www.iaccnorthamerica.org/resources/index.cfm?fuseaction=JobBoard

International Association of Convention & Visitors Bureaus (On-Line Career Opportunities): www.iacvb.org/iacvb/career_center/cbvjobops.asp

International Facilities Management Association—JOBnet: http://jobnet.ifma.org/home/index.cfm?site_id=208

International Festivals and Events Association—Job Bank: www.ifea.com/resources/jobbank.asp

International Health, Racquet & Sportsclub Association—Job Connection: www.ihrsa.org/jobs

International Special Events Society—ISES USA Chapters: www.ises.com/chapters/usa.cfm

Intrawest Resorts: www.wework2play.com

Job Monkey: www.jobmonkey.com

Jobs in Hospitality, Convention and Tourism:
www.unlv.edu/Tourism/jobs.html

Jobs in Paradise: www.jobsinparadise.com

Luxury Hotel Jobs: www.luxuryhoteljobs.com

Maumee Bay Resort & Conference Center: www.maumeebayresort.com

Meeting Professionals International—Job Bank: www.mpiweb.org/resources/jobs

Mohican Resort & Conference Center: www.mohicanresort.com

Monster: www.monster.com

Motecito-Sequoia Lodge: www.mslodge.com

Mountain Resort Community Employment Connection: www.mountainjobs.com

Mpoint.com—Job Board (jobs for planners): http://jobs.mpoint.com

National Intramural-Recreation Sports Association—bluefishjobs: www.bluefishjobs.com

National Recreation and Park Association—Career Center: http://nrpa.jobcontrolcenter.com

Navy's Morale, Welfare, and Recreation Employment Opportunities—Personnel and benefits: www.mwr.navy.mil/mwrprgms/personnel.html

NCAA news online—Employment Opportunities: www.ncaa.org/employment.html

Online Sports Career Center: www.onlinesports.com/pages/CareerCenter.html

Opportunities in Physical Education and Related Areas: www.csufresno.edu/kines/programs/opera

Professional Convention Management Association—Careers: www.pcma.org/resources/careers

Punderson Manor Resort & Conference Center: www.pundersonmanorresort.com

Recreation Resources Service—Job Service Bulletin: www2.ncsu.edu/ncsu/forest_resources/recresource/newjsb.html

Resort and Commercial Recreation Association—Job-Bulletin: www.R-C-R-A.org/RCRAjobbull2.html

ResortJobs.com: www.resortjobs.com

Royal Caribbean Cruises LTD: www.rccl.hcareers.com

Salt Fork Resort & Conference Center: www.saltforkresort.com

Shawnee Resort & Conference Center: www.shawneeresort.com

Ski Resort Jobs: www.coolworks.com

Smuggler's Notch Resort: www.smuggs.com

Society of Independent Show Organizers—Job listings: www.siso.org/App/homepage.cfm?appname=121&linkid=55&moduleid=8

SpecialEventSite.com—Employment: http://specialeventsite.com/IndustryInfo/Employment

Sponsorship.com—Job Bank: www.sponsorship.com/jobbank

Sporting Goods Manufacturers Association—Employment Opportunities: www.sgma.com/jobs/index.html

Sports Event Marketing Information and Links: www.unlv.edu/Tourism/sports.html

Successful Meetings.com—Planning Resources and Industry Links: www.successmtgs.com/successmtgs/business_resources/industry_links.jsp

The Chronicle of Higher Education—Career Network: http://chronicle.com/jobs

The Entertainment Services and Technology Association—Job Board: www.esta.org/jobboard/index.html

The International Association for Exhibition Management—Career Center: http://iaemorg.expoexchange.com/CareerCenter/ccintro.htm

The Meeting Connection: www.themeetingconnection.com

The Meeting Exchange: www.mmaweb.com/meetings/meetingboard

The Meetings Industry Mall—Directory: www.meetingnews.com/meetingnews/mim/directory.jsp

The National Park Service—Employment Information: www.nps.gov/personnel

The Resort at Seabrook Island: www.discoverseabrook.com

Theme Park & Amusement Park Jobs: www.themeparkjobs.com

Theme Park Career Center: www.themedattraction.com/careers.htm

Themed Entertainment Association—Job Board: www.themeit.com/jobs1.htm

Trade Show Exhibitors Association—Career Center: www.tsea.org/careercenter

Tradeshow Week Magazine Classified Bulletin Board: www.tradeshowweek.com/index.asp?layout=classifieds

Travel Jobz: www.traveljobz.com

Traveljobz.net: www.traveljobz.net

United States Army—Morale, Welfare, and Recreation Employment Opportunities: http://mwrjobs.army.mil

United States Office of Personnel Management: www.usajobs.opm.gov

United States Olympic Committee—Jobs: www.olympic-usa.org/12211/htm

Wine and Hospitality Jobs: www.winecountryjobs.com

Winter Park Resort: www.skiwinterpark.com

Women Sport Jobs/Women Sport Services: www.womensportjobs.com

World Leisure Jobs and News: www.worldleisurejobs.com

World Waterpark Association—Classifieds: www.waterparks.com/members_classifieds_new.asp

YMCA of the USA—Employment: www.ymca.net/employment/ymca_recruiting/recruiting_frameset.htm

YWCA—Jobs: www.ywca.org

TRENDS IN THE COMMERCIAL RECREATION AND LEISURE INDUSTRY

Several economic, societal, and environmental trends are emerging that will affect this burgeoning industry in the coming years. This list contains a few that may affect the success or failure of businesses in this sector:

- Baby boomers will generate the highest volume of travel in the United States.
- Travelers will be increasingly willing to pay to protect the environment.
- Worldwide capacity for cruise ships will be reached in the near future.
- Vacation residence ownership will increase.
- A greater emphasis on partnerships with the public sector will increase the number of commercial recreation businesses on public land.
- New or emerging technology will affect the way people experience leisure opportunities and how they will plan for use of facilities and areas (i.e., making reservations over the Internet).
- The effects of terrorism will continue to change the nature of travel for most tourists.

SUMMARY

The leisure industry is composed of organizations that form public, private, and commercial leisure services organizations. Approximately 90 percent of these organizations make up the commercial recreation and tourism industry. In this chapter, you have learned the basic structure of this industry, the way in which business is conducted, and the career opportunities that may present themselves.

Knowing the different segments and characteristics of tourists, tourism, and commercial recreation is essential for success in this industry. Career opportunities are vast and a professional can choose from a wide variety of settings in which to work. In addition, the commercial recreation and tourism industry is a good choice for a student with an entrepreneurial spirit.

CHAPTER 10

Therapeutic Recreation

Frances Stavola Daly and Robin Kunstler

Courtesy of San Jose Parks, Recreation and Neighborhood Services

Growth, joy and friendships come from reaching the heart and soul of an individual, learning what the person needs to help them reach their potential, then continuing to sustain that motivation beyond the aches and pains. Only a therapeutic recreation specialist can attain these lofty goals. They make miracles happen on a daily basis.

Diane Mertz-Hart, associate administrator of Gurwin Jewish Geriatric Center

CHAPTER OBJECTIVES

After reading this chapter, you should be able to do the following:

- Appreciate the scope of therapeutic recreation services
- Define therapeutic recreation
- Understand the importance of philosophy as a foundation for practice
- Identify the benefits of therapeutic recreation
- Analyze the history of therapeutic recreation for its impact on inclusion and contemporary therapeutic recreation services
- Identify key laws affecting therapeutic recreation services
- Evaluate therapeutic recreation practice models
- Analyze the steps in the therapeutic recreation process
- Describe therapeutic recreation interventions
- Explain the components of professionalism
- Understand future challenges for the therapeutic recreation professional

INTRODUCTION

People with illness, disability, or special needs have the same rights to healthy and satisfying recreation participation as anyone else. Limiting conditions such as disease or disability may impose barriers on people's ability to engage in recreation as they would choose to, so professional assistance such as therapeutic recreation (TR) may be required. In fact, most of us can probably recall a situation in which our ability to participate in the things we love to do was impaired by a physical, emotional, or social condition or situation. At these times TR specialists can provide services to facilitate a person's ability to engage in enjoyable recreation. Therapeutic recreation participation can help people to cope with their health problem or disability, "be themselves" in a difficult situation, continue to feel a sense of control and make choices, as well as experiment with new behaviors in a safe and supportive environment. Learning about how therapeutic recreation can help people with special needs is relevant to students and professionals working in any area of recreation and leisure services. People with disabilities and health conditions participate in recreation programs in all types of settings and knowledge of how to support their successful participation is significant for all recreation majors.

You may be wondering how big the field of TR is. The most commonly accepted statistic is that there are 44 million Americans with at least one disability, or approximately one out of every six Americans. The proportion of Canadians with a disability is considered to be about the same

(Bullock & Mahon, 2000). However, only half of the people with a disability consider some aspect of their functioning to be impaired. Another approximately two million people live in nursing homes or residential facilities for people with developmental or psychiatric impairments or other disabling conditions that affect their ability to function adequately in their own homes. Of the 27,000 people employed in TR in 2002, according to the U.S. government, one-third worked in hospitals and one-third in nursing homes, and the remainder were employed primarily in outpatient and day treatment programs (Bureau of Labor Statistics, 2004). We can see that there are huge numbers of people who potentially could benefit from TR services, yet there is a discrepancy between where people with disabilities live (in the community) and where TR specialists are employed (in institutions). The Bureau of Labor Statistics predicts that more jobs will develop in the community-based settings, as opposed to hospital and inpatient treatment facilities, as services develop for people in their local communities. The latest salary survey, conducted by the National Council for Therapeutic Recreation Certification in 2004, found that the average annual salary of certified therapeutic recreation specialists was almost $40,000 U.S. per year. Although entry-level salaries may be less than $30,000 per year for new graduates, earning potential can go as high as $90,000 per year for directors of departments with advanced degrees and experience, depending on setting and location.

This chapter presents the foundations of **therapeutic recreation**, how the field developed, key concepts related to providing TR services, and the scope of TR settings, programs, interventions and populations. A discussion of the therapeutic recreation process outlines the daily duties of a **therapeutic recreation specialist (TRS)**. Important professional issues, trends, and future challenges are examined to provide concrete information that will help you to understand TR and decide on its suitability as a career choice.

DEFINITIONS AND COMMON THREADS OF THERAPEUTIC RECREATION

What exactly is therapeutic recreation? This may be the hardest question you as a student have to answer when family and friends ask, "What is your major?" For TR students, the answer is not simple. Many definitions of therapeutic recreation have been put forth over the years, with slight variations in language and emphasis, leading to a lively debate about what the true definition of TR is. However, all definitions share common themes, which capture the essence of what TR is. These common themes are as follows (Bullock & Mahon, 2000):

1. Purposeful use of recreation activities to reach a goal or **outcome**

2. Enhancement of **functioning** through recreation participation

3. Focus on the whole person or **client** in the context of his or her own environment (known as an ecological perspective), including supports and resources to be provided by the community

4. Long-term improvements in **health,** well-being, and **quality of life** as core concerns

Therefore, a composite definition of TR may be stated as engaging people in planned recreation and related experiences in order to improve functioning, health and well-being, and quality of life, while focusing on the whole person and the needed changes in the optimal living environment.

To fulfill these purposes, therapeutic recreation specialists (TRSs), also known as recreation therapists, use a range of modalities, including traditional recreation activities such as the arts, sports, fitness and exercise, games, crafts, social activities, outdoor recreation, aquatics, and community outings. They also use nontraditional activities such as leisure education, horticulture, volunteerism, adult education, and animal-assisted (pet) therapy. TRSs

may also implement therapeutic interventions such as cognitive stimulation, sensory awareness, assertiveness training, anger management, pain management, stress management, and leisure counseling, depending on the mission and goals of the agency and the needs of the population being served. Complementary and alternative medicine (CAM) is also becoming an area for TR practice. Interventions such as relaxation, aromatherapy, yoga, and tai chi are very popular. TR also addresses the clients' family, environment, or community, advocating for resources and support systems that facilitate successful recreation participation.

Philosophy

Therapeutic recreation is based on a system of beliefs about human nature, needs, and behaviors as well as about the meaning and purpose of leisure, recreation, and play in human lives. A system of beliefs that guide practice is known as philosophy. You might be surprised to learn that recreation students study philosophy. But philosophy helps us understand why we do what we do. Each of us is responsible for developing a philosophy of professional practice based on our readings, reflections, and values that will support our efforts and deepen our understanding of and commitment to our chosen field. This gives meaning and value to our interactions with our clients. Understanding human beings and their development throughout the life span, the variations in human development and experience, the impact of these variations on lifestyle, and the potential contributions of leisure, recreation, and play to healthy human development is essential to informed practice. TR has strong roots in humanistic philosophy, which asserts that people are capable of growth and change, that they strive to meet their needs and goals, and that they are autonomous (capable of making their own decisions and choices and directing their own lives) and inherently altruistic (desire to do good). This means that TRSs believe that, with the help of TR service, people can improve their lives, be it physically, emotionally, mentally, and even spiritually.

One way to understand the power of recreation is to consider that people seek optimal experiences, also known as the zone, a natural high, a peak experience, "flow," or what some call the leisure experience. People in this state experience their true identity, a sense of control over their actions, a heightened sense of awareness, and feelings of competence and mastery. Recreation activities are a major vehicle to attaining this optimal state because they involve challenge, excitement, rewards, choices, concentration, and pure fun. Because recreation activities are pleasurable and satisfying, freely chosen, and autotelic (the satisfaction is gained from actually doing the activity), people are highly motivated to engage in recreation. Therefore recreation can motivate people to change, grow, and improve their health. Recreation has "re-creative" powers; in other words people can renew, restore, and refresh themselves and develop their abilities and skills through participation. In addition, people are social beings—they interact with other human beings and are affected by these interactions. Interaction with others in recreation activities is a strength of TR. For some clients, TR may be their most successful therapy because it is enjoyable and provides opportunities to make choices, set their own goals, and develop feelings of competence and self-confidence in their abilities.

Benefits

To succeed as a TR professional, not only must you be prepared to answer the question "What is TR?"

but also "What are the benefits of TR?" and "Why is TR a valuable service to offer our clients?" TR has many **benefits** and is valuable for many reasons. Understanding the benefits of participation in TR programs helps us to select appropriate TR activities to enable clients to reach their desired goal. An important TR principle is that clients be involved as much as possible in planning the TR services they will receive. By making choices during the planning process, with the assistance of the TRS, clients may feel a sense of control over decisions affecting their care and treatment, thereby maximizing the benefits of TR. We are also required to document the benefits the clients achieve as a result of TR participation. Research on recreation experiences has found that participation provides physical, cognitive, and psychosocial benefits for individuals as well as values for the health care system and society as a whole. This research has been presented by Coyle, Kinney, Riley, and Shank (1991) and is summarized in table 10.1. The benefits research was updated by the National Therapeutic Recreation Society (Broida, 2000).

TABLE 10.1   Benefits of Therapeutic Recreation

Category	Benefits
1. Physical health and health maintenance	Improves general physical and perceptual motor functioning Maintains health Reduces risk of secondary physical complications of the disability Reduces cardiovascular and respiratory risk
2. Cognitive functioning	Improves general cognitive functioning Improves short- and long-term memory Decreases confusion and disorientation
3. Psychosocial health	Improves coping skills and self-control Improves self-concept, self-esteem, and adjustment to disability Improves general psychological health Reduces depression, anxiety, and stress level Improves social skills, socialization, cooperation, and interpersonal interaction Reduces self-abusive and inappropriate behaviors
4. Growth and personal development	Improves communication and language skills Increases age-appropriate behavior Increases acquisition of developmental milestones
5. Personal and life satisfaction	Increases leisure and life satisfaction and perceived quality of life Increases social support, community integration, community satisfaction, and community self-efficacy Increases family unity and communication
6. Societal and health care system	Reduces complications secondary to disability Improves system outcomes Improves follow-through with rehabilitation regimes, satisfaction with treatment, and dedication to treatment Increases outpatient involvement and postdischarge follow-through with treatment plans

Adapted from Bullock and Mahon, 2000.

HISTORY OF THERAPEUTIC RECREATION

How many of you are thinking history is boring? Maybe you haven't considered the reasons for studying history. By studying history we may understand how our profession evolved to its current state and prepare for future challenges. Most students are fascinated to learn that although the therapeutic recreation profession is less than 100 years old, the benefits of participation in recreational activities for people with illnesses and disabilities were recognized thousands of years ago. The ancient Greeks, who believed in a sound mind in a sound body, built curative temples where activities such as walking, gardening, exercise, boating, and music were offered. The Egyptians created a positive environment using music and dance to treat mood disorders. In India, Charaka, a surgeon, had patients play games and drink wine while he operated on them because he knew it would distract them from the pain. However, these enlightened approaches to incorporating recreation alternated over the centuries with cruel treatment of people with certain illnesses and disabilities. The word "handicap" comes from the description of people with disabilities holding a cap in their hand to beg for money or food. History provides few examples of compassionate care for those with disabilities.

In Europe, the Renaissance (1400-1600) and the Age of Enlightenment (1700s) brought a greater concern for the rights of all individuals. The first schools for the deaf and the blind were established in Paris in the late 18th century. In the United States, in the early 19th century, hospitals were built to serve people with mental illness. These hospitals provided recreation activities as part of more humane treatment. During the mid-19th century Florence Nightingale, an English woman considered to be the founder of modern nursing practice, wrote that wounded soldiers should be in beautiful environments or "recreation huts," listen to music, and have visits from family and pets to comfort them and speed their recovery. During the same period as Florence Nightingale, Dorothea Dix in the United States advocated for better treatment of people with disabilities and illnesses in asylums and prisons. The latter half of the 19th century brought many immigrants to North America, leading to the growth of cities, which brought the problems of overcrowding, increased stress, juvenile crime, and problems with health and sanitation. To address these issues, settlement houses, which were community centers providing social services, education, and recreation, were established. The playground movement gathered momentum in response to a growing awareness of the role of recreation in the health and well-being of citizens, including the less fortunate who may have been poor, ill, or disabled.

Recreation services in the 20th century were provided to a variety of populations with special needs. The American Red Cross was one of the first large-scale organizations to promote recreation services to wounded soldiers during and after wartime. During the 1920s, research was conducted in Illinois that demonstrated the value of recreation participation for people with mental retardation. Dr. Karl Menninger, the noted psychiatrist, recognized the vital role of recreation activities in the treatment of psychiatric patients. World War II was a significant event in the history of TR when literally hundreds of thousands of wounded soldiers returned to the United States and Canada. These young men, who had given so much to their country, also had lost physical functioning because of their war injuries. Dr. Howard Rusk, considered the founder of the rehabilitation movement, promoted the value of individual and group recreation in physical rehabilitation. Wheelchair sports were created as a healthy recreation activity for wounded veterans.

The growing prosperity of postwar America and Canada enabled society to pay more attention to the rights of people who were unable to participate fully in the mainstream of everyday life. Public awareness of the importance of recreation for all people increased with the creation of the Special Olympics, new services for senior citizens, the effects of the civil rights movement, and the youth movement of the 1960s with its emphasis on quality of life. Deinstitutionalization, the movement of people with mental illness and cognitive disabilities from large institutions to community-based residences such as group homes, supported residences, and independent apartments, was under way. The first organizations for TR professionals were established during this period to draw attention to the importance of TR, develop standards for practice and personnel qualifications, publish books and journals about TR, and design professional preparation curricula. An era of great accomplishments for people with disabilities and of increased recognition of TR was beginning.

A traditional recreational activity such as aquatics is one modality a therapeutic recreation specialist uses with a client.

Legislation

Effective lobbying resulted in the successful passage of landmark legislation that not only broadened opportunities for people with disabilities but also reflected and promoted a change in more positive attitudes toward people with disabilities by society as a whole. During the 1970s in the United States, the federal government mandated accessibility of buildings and facilities for ease of use by people with disabilities. The U.S. Congress passed Section 504 of the Rehabilitation Act of 1973, which guaranteed equal access to programs funded all or in part by federal funds, and PL 94-142, the Education of All Handicapped Children Act, which provided for a free and appropriate public education for all children. These laws expanded recreation opportunities and services for people of all ages with disabilities, and had a huge impact as people with disabilities became more visible in the community due to increased accessibility, mainstreaming of children from special schools into the least restricted environment, and the normalization movement (Austin & Crawford, 2001). Normalization means giving people with disabilities the opportunities to live a life as close to the patterns and habits of "normal" living as possible. In Canada, the provincial govern-

ments have been more active than the Canadian national government in passing laws related to the rights of people with disabilities. However, the Canadian Charter of Rights and Freedoms, passed in 1982, guaranteed the rights of people with disabilities to equal protection and benefit of the law without discrimination. This has served as the blueprint for the Canadian policy of access to all areas of society including recreation for people with disabilities. Table 10.2 identifies key U.S. and Canadian laws that have significantly affected the lives of people with disabilities, their rights, and access to recreation services.

Society's attitudes toward active participation by people with disabilities in everyday life were changing with the impact of these laws, the effects of the civil rights movement, and the expansion of programs and services. One indicator of the shift in attitudes toward people with disabilities has been the use of "person-first language" or sensitive terminology. Language reflects attitudes. By saying "a person with a **disability**," instead of "the blind person" or "the mentally retarded person," we emphasize that this is a person who happens to have a disability as one of his or her characteristics but that he or she is not defined solely by the disability. Using person-first language denotes

TABLE 10.2 Key Laws of the United States and Canada

UNITED STATES	
Law	**Description**
PL 90-480 Architectural Barriers Act, 1968	Mandated physical accessibility and usability of buildings and facilities
Section 504 of the Rehabilitation Act, 1973	Mandated program accessibility for people with disabilities
PL 94-142 Education for All Handicapped Children Act, 1975	Stated that "all handicapped children" were entitled to a free and appropriate public education in the least restricted environment and may receive recreation as a related service
PL 101-476 Individuals with Disabilities Education Act, 1990	Reauthorization of PL 94-142 that emphasized family involvement, required transition planning, and provided for assistive technology
PL 101-336 Americans with Disabilities Act, 1990	A comprehensive civil rights law intended to eliminate discrimination against people with disabilities in all aspects of American life, including employment, government services, public transportation, public accommodations, and telecommunications; reasonable accommodation must be made to facilitate participation by people with disabilities in these five areas by removing barriers and providing auxiliary aids and services as necessary.
CANADA	
Law	**Description**
Vocational Rehabilitation for Disabled Persons Act, 1962	Provided rehabilitation services for people with disabilities
Canadian Charter of Rights and Freedoms, 1982	Stated that all people have the right to equal protection and benefit of the law without discrimination based on mental and physical disability
In Unison: A Canadian Approach to Disability Issues (government report, not a law), 1998	Provided the basis for asserting equal rights for people with disabilities in order to achieve full integration and access to supports, services, employment, and income

a positive attitude toward people with disabilities and further promotes their rights to participate fully in the lives of their communities.

The Reagan-era cutbacks in funding for social services in the United States led to the 1980s being known as the age of **accountability.** Cost containment became the buzzword of health care. Health professions had to be accountable, or responsible, for documenting that their services actually produced a desired outcome in a cost-effective manner. This prompted a renewed emphasis on the need for efficacy research in TR, which is research that demonstrates that TR can produce the outcomes it claims to produce, and a refinement of TR interventions targeted to specific health care problems and goals. Concurrent with this imperative to demonstrate TR's value in health care was the passage of the Americans with Disabilities Act (ADA) in the United States in 1990 that was the catalyst for the inclusion movement.

Inclusion

Inclusion refers to empowering people with disabilities to become valued and active members of their communities through involvement in socially valued life activities. A key tenet of inclusion is that the community offers supports, friendship, and resources to facilitate equal participation in everyday life by all its members. The result of the inclusion movement has been to broaden the traditional view of TR from focusing solely on the person to encompassing the person in the context of the total environments and settings a person inhabits throughout his or her life span. There is also a growing realization that as health status fluctuates, people require a continuum of treatment, disease prevention, **health promotion,** and opportunities to enhance wellness and improve quality of life. In summary, the sociopolitical movements of the latter half of the 20th century have led to the broader acceptance of people with disabilities, with their rights guaranteed by federal laws and their opportunities expanded in all venues. TR, as did all professions, responded to these forces by developing new approaches and services. Inclusion philosophy and practices evolved from core principles and concepts that are identified in table 10.3 as building blocks of inclusion.

TABLE 10.3   Building Blocks of Inclusion

Building blocks	Definitions
Deinstitutionalization	The move away from large-scale, institution-based care to small-scale, community-based facilities; began in the late 1960s
Accessibility	Equal entry into, and participation in, physical facilities and programs by all people; accomplished through the elimination of architectural, administrative, and attitudinal barriers in order to create a usable environment
Normalization	Making available to people with disabilities the patterns and conditions of everyday life that are as culturally normative as possible
Integration	Physical presence and social interaction of people with and without disabilities in the same setting
Mainstreaming	Movement of people into the activities and settings of the wider community
Least restrictive environment	The environment that imposes the fewest restrictions and barriers on a person's growth, development, and participation in a full life
Supports	Friendships, social networks, assistance, and resources that enable a person to participate in the full life of his or her community
Person-first language	Language that puts the word "person" or "people" first in the sequence of a phrase or sentence to emphasize a positive attitude toward the individual, as in "a person with a disability" rather than "a disabled person"
Inclusion	Empowering people who have disabilities to be valued and active members of their communities by making choices, being supported in daily life, and having opportunities to grow and develop to their fullest potential

New Century Direction

At the beginning of the 21st century, the following trends will continue to shape discussions about health policies and human services, including TR:

- Cultural diversity in North America
- The aging population
- The continued impact of the ADA in the United States and the 1998 report of Canadian governments on disability issues
- People taking personal responsibility for their health and the interest in the relationship of leisure and recreation to health and wellness
- Billions of dollars spent on complementary and alternative medicine
- Ongoing concerns about the cost of health care in the face of the obesity crisis and declining levels of physical activity and fitness
- Technological innovations as well as increased reliance on technology

The populations served by TRSs and the settings in which TRSs work will continue to multiply. To systematically organize and deliver TR services, practice models have been developed that explain the relationships between philosophy and prac-

tice. These models often reflect the political and social realities of the period in which they were developed.

THERAPEUTIC RECREATION PRACTICE MODELS

A model is a visual representation that describes the relationships between philosophy and theory and the real world. A model serves as a guide for practice. The benefits of providing TR services according to an appropriate practice model are that a model directs the types of programs and services offered, communicates TR's purposes and services to other disciplines, and ensures that clients are provided the services and interventions best suited to their needs and goals.

Leisure Ability Model

For many years the primary model of TR services was the leisure ability model, originally developed by Gunn and Peterson. This model was based on earlier work in the field by Edith Ball, Virginia Frye, and Martha Peters among others. According to this model, TR is provided along a continuum encompassing three types of services: functional intervention (previously known as treatment), leisure education, and recreation participation. The recipient of services, known as the client, moves along a continuum of services, gaining more control over his or her decision-making ability and choices as she or he learns new skills, becomes more independent, and participates in a repertoire of healthy recreation activities. The purpose of TR, according to this model, is for clients to develop an appropriate leisure lifestyle. According to Stumbo and Peterson, leisure lifestyle can be defined as follows:

> The day-to-day behavioral expression of one's leisure-related attitudes, awareness and activities revealed in the context and composite of the total life experience. Leisure lifestyle implies that an individual has sufficient skills, knowledge, attitudes and abilities to participate successfully in and be satisfied with leisure and recreation experiences that are incorporated into his or her individual life pattern. (2004, p. 18)

Health Protection and Health Promotion Model

Beginning in the 1980s, the movement to control health care costs prompted the development of the health protection/health promotion model (Austin, 1997). Although similar to the leisure ability model in having three components of services, described as prescriptive activity, recreation, and leisure, the purpose of TR in Austin's model is to achieve optimal health in a favorable environment. This reflected the heightened emphasis on TR's role in health care as a treatment modality, using recreation activities as interventions to address specific health problems as part of the work of the treatment team. For example, the TR specialist could engage a client with depression in an exercise group or sport program for the mood-elevating benefits of physical activity.

Courtesy of Dina Trunzo

A floral design class is one type of intervention a therapeutic recreation specialist might use to improve health and well-being.

TR Services Model and TR Outcome Model

Austin's model was followed closely by the TR services model and TR outcome model, both presented by Carter, Van Andel, and Robb (1996). In designing these models, Van Andel recognized the need for the TR profession to describe the scope and outcomes of TR services. He legitimized leisure experience and quality of life as viable TR goals in the health care arena in addition to the more accepted treatment goals of improving functional abilities and enhancing health status.

Service Model

The service model presents TR as having a potential role in four types of services:

- Diagnosis
- Rehabilitation
- Education
- Health promotion

Similar to the leisure ability model and the health protection/health promotion model, the TR service model provides services along a continuum based on the client's needs and interests, level of functioning and degree of control, and type of setting in which services are received. The TRS may prescribe a single activity that can serve as both a treatment intervention during rehabilitation and as a leisure experience in the health promotion phase, thereby working on both goals simultaneously.

Outcome Model

In the outcome model, Van Andel hypothesized that as functioning and health status improved with the help of TR, so would quality of life. Even if a person had an impairment in one domain, he or she could still experience quality of life (Sylvester, Voelkl, & Ellis, 2001). For example, a person with a terminal illness cannot make gains in physical health but can achieve quality of life as a meaningful outcome through improvements in spiritual and emotional health. This model places the emphasis on the whole person when providing services, not just on one aspect of functioning or health status.

Other Models

Many of the trends in the 1990s such as the increasingly complex world of health care, the inclusion movement, decreased length of stays in hospitals, more services provided in outpatient and day care settings, recognition of the chronic nature of disability over the life span, and people living longer with severe medical problems and disabilities have led to the development of additional models, such as the leisure gyroscope model (Cote, LaPan, & Halle, 1997), the self-determination and enjoyment enhancement model (Dattilo, Kleiber, & Williams, 1998), and the optimizing lifelong health through therapeutic recreation model (Wilhite, Keller, & Caldwell, 1999). The growing cultural and lifestyle diversity of North American society has also brought about a rethinking of the models in light of varying cultural beliefs and practices related to health care and individual responsibility (Sylvester, Voelkl, & Ellis, 2001).

Five Core Themes in the Models

Just as there are common themes in definitions of TR, there are also core themes among the various models, which have been identified as follows (Bullock & Mahon, 2000):

- Services are provided along a continuum of growth and intervention.
- Services are based on a strong belief in the abilities and strengths of the individual.
- The client's freedom and self-determination increase over the course of services.
- Therapist control decreases as the client progresses along the continuum.
- The client's involvement and participation in the natural community increase.

In all models, TR emphasizes the abilities and strengths of the client to overcome or alleviate the disability or illness. People have the right to live in the optimal environment of their choice with appropriate supports provided as needed, and the environment is responsible for providing the needed supports. This ecological perspective recognizes that the person's family, friends, and community are significant factors in their health and well-being.

Applying a Model to Clients and Settings

"How do I know which model is right for me or my clients or my setting?" This is the right question to ask! Having multiple models is a strength of the TR profession because of the diversity of settings and populations. Choosing the appropriate model is based on several factors, including

- agency philosophy, mission, and goals;
- the needs of the clients;
- the regulations of accrediting bodies and government oversight agencies; and
- your own professional philosophy.

Over the course of your career, you should be prepared to adopt the model that best suits your workplace. In Canada, the primary model is the leisure ability model, which reflects this nation's longstanding commitment to integration of people with disabilities into all aspects of society and the recognition that recreation is a part of the vision of full citizenship for all Canadians. Practitioners in the United States also follow the leisure ability model, which is the basis of the philosophical statement of the National Therapeutic Recreation Society. However, the health protection/health promotion model is becoming more widely used in clinical settings.

SETTING FOR THERAPEUTIC RECREATION SERVICES

By now you're wondering, "Where can I work as a TRS?" One of the exciting aspects of the TR profession is the range of settings and populations served by TR specialists. People of all ages, with all types of special needs, are potential recipients of TR services, which can include many types of recreation activities. For students contemplating this profession there are many possibilities ranging from acute treatment in the hospital setting to residential facilities to in-home TR services. TR is offered in any setting where people live or receive services, including hospitals and institutions, nursing homes, hospice programs, rehabilitation centers, prisons, assisted-living facilities, adult day care, partial hospitalization and outpatient programs, drug treatment programs, homeless shelters, group homes, schools, early intervention programs, community recreation centers, camps, and people's homes.

Any person with a physical, psychological, cognitive, or social disability; an illness; an impairment; or a special need can be a recipient of TR services. It should be noted that a particular illness or disability may affect more than one area of functioning. For example, a person with a head injury may experience physical, cognitive, and social deficits. He or she may have trouble walking, behave in a socially inappropriate manner, and be unable to concentrate for long periods of time. Some people have multiple disabilities. A child with cerebral palsy also may be diagnosed with mental retardation, seizure disorder, and a hearing impairment. When designing a TR program, it's important to remember that each person is an individual with a unique set of abilities and limitations. These limitations may impose barriers to the person's ability to function in life activities, including recreation participation. Planning programs that take into account these factors is a key responsibility of the TR specialist. Equally important to remember is that every person with a disability does not necessarily need or want TR services.

Some conditions are congenital, occurring at birth, some manifest in childhood or teenage years, and others are acquired as adults through accident, disease, or the aging process. There are many ways to categorize disabilities and health conditions. Table 10.4 presents specific conditions as categorized by their primary area of disability according to Carter, Van Andel, and Robb (1996). This list has been adapted slightly from their categorization and does not cover all the disabilities and health conditions you may encounter in your career as a TRS.

Job Duties and Responsibilities

"What exactly does a TRS do all day?" The majority of most TRSs' time is spent planning and leading group therapeutic recreation programs. Depending on the setting, the TRS may also provide one-on-one TR activities. To implement an appropriate TR program of activities, the TRS conducts individual assessments, develops treatment plans, plans a schedule of TR programming, motivates clients to participate in TR activities, observes and documents their participation and progress, and attends treatment team meetings (also known as comprehensive care-planning meetings or a similar name) and in-service training. Other duties include maintaining equipment and supplies, supervising volunteers and interns, providing support to family members, and organizing special events and community outings. Management responsibilities may include budgeting, risk management, marketing, and participating in strategic planning and quality assurance projects.

TABLE 10.4   Common Disabilities and Health Conditions

Physical disabilities and conditions	Cognitive impairments	Psychological disorders	Social impairments
• Musculoskeletal—muscular dystrophy, arthritis, spina bifida, amputations, orthopedic • Neurological—cerebral palsy, convulsive disorders, strokes, multiple sclerosis • Circulatory—heart disease, hypertension • Respiratory—chronic obstructive pulmonary disease, tuberculosis, cystic fibrosis • Diabetes • Cancer • Chronic pain and chronic fatigue • Sensory impairments—visual impairment, hearing impairment, deaf, blind • AIDS	• Learning disabilities • Mental retardation • Autism spectrum disorder • Attention deficit disorder and attention deficit hyperactivity disorder	• Anxiety disorders • Mood disorders—depression, bipolar disorder • Personality disorders • Schizophrenia • Eating disorders • Conduct disorders	• Addictions—alcohol, illegal drugs, gambling • Homelessness • Abuse—physical, emotional, sexual, neglect, domestic violence • Criminal and delinquent behavior • At-risk youth

Adapted from Carter, Van Andel, and Robb, 2003.

TR Process

Many of these functions are related to carrying out the TR process, a series of four steps that help fulfill the purposes of TR. A handy acronym for the four steps is APIE: assessment, planning, implementation, and evaluation. The TR process can be applied in any setting where recreation is used with therapeutic intent to help a person achieve specific outcomes. A service setting can range from a traditional clinical setting such as a hospital or rehabilitation center, to a residence such as an assisted-living facility or group home, to a community-based setting such as a school or recreation center. Let's examine the four steps more closely.

Assessment

The first step is assessment, a systematic process of gathering and synthesizing information about the individual client and his or her environment using a variety of methods, including interviews, observation, standardized tests, and input from other disciplines and significant others in order to devise an individualized treatment or service plan. The information the TRS seeks includes the client's level and ability of physical, social, emotional, and cognitive functioning related to two areas: capabil-

ity to participate in different types of TR programs and which functions can be improved through TR participation. The TRS also obtains information related to the client's leisure functioning: interests, needs, perceived problems with leisure, patterns of participation, available leisure partners, planning and decision-making skills, and knowledge of and ability to use leisure resources. Obtaining input from the client, to the best of the client's ability, is highly desirable. Based on the assessment, the TRS specifies goals or outcomes the client will work toward during intervention. These goals can be related both to changing leisure-related behaviors and functional ability.

Planning

Planning refers to the actual development of the client's individual treatment or program plan. This plan is placed in the client's chart as the official record of the TR services the client will receive. The plan includes an assessment summary; the client's goals, specific objectives, or steps to reach the goals; a schedule of the client's planned participation in the TR program; and a discharge plan if required.

Goals and Objectives

Goals are statements that provide direction for the client's treatment. Client goals may be identified

Colleen Wittig, CTRS, Promoting Leisure Activities for Youth

Colleen is a 1995 graduate of Montclair State University in New Jersey with a bachelor's degree in recreation and leisure science with a concentration in therapeutic recreation. Before graduation she had worked for 20 years with people with developmental disabilities. One benefit of her education, she says, is that "the skills a recreation therapist learns in school are directly parallel to those needed to be a successful recreation professional." Her current position is with the Virginia Beach (Virginia) Department of Parks and Recreation PLAY Team, a nationally recognized program of prevention and intervention programs for youth and their families. She plans and implements programs that help young people benefit from participation in activities as she helps them to modify their challenging behaviors. "The distinct difference between these programs and general recreation programs is that the major focus is on positive youth development. Using recreation as the tool, the staff works with the youth on gaining or improving specific skills," she says. Current program offerings include the following:

- Mobile outreach to neighborhoods where there is high crime and high poverty and the youth cannot get to recreation centers easily
- Sports programs with a health education and social etiquette component
- Social skills programs that include skills training in critical thinking, problem solving, decision making, alternatives to violence, celebrating cultural diversity, and planning for their futures
- Intervention programs such as anger management, stress management, and pregnancy prevention

"I believe very strongly in research and devote at least five to eight hours a week to reading updated materials in regard to youth development, successful practices in intervention and program prevention, therapeutic recreation issues, and the latest information on disabilities," Colleen says.

A therapeutic recreation specialist might meet in someone's home to understand the client's family and environment.

by the treatment team for appropriate intervention by one or more disciplines. These goals may include increasing range of motion, attention span, or social interaction. As a member of the treatment team, the TRS may also suggest goals for the client related to leisure-related behaviors such as acquiring knowledge of community resources for recreation participation or learning how to use adapted equipment to enable participation in a particular recreation activity. The TRS also specifies a series of behavioral objectives or measurable goals that are steps toward the overall goal. The achievement of each behavioral objective or measurable goal, in a progression, will lead to accomplishing the overall client goal or goals. It is important to recognize that the terms used to describe the planning process may differ from setting to setting. Some settings use the phrase measurable goals in place of behavioral objectives. The intent and purpose are the same, however, regardless of the exact terminology.

Selection and Scheduling of Activities

A major component of the planning step is the selection and scheduling of specific TR interventions or activities. Recreation activities are the primary means through which TRSs serve our clients, so we need to understand which specific recreation activities produce which outcomes. Just as a doctor knows which medications to prescribe to treat a specific illness, we want to work together with our clients to select the recreation activities with the best chance of producing results. The activities should be chosen with the client to be sure that he or she is interested and willing to participate in them. Through the method of activity analysis, the TR analyzes the components and behaviors that go into doing an activity. You, the TRS, then may prescribe a specific activity or group of activities in the **individual treatment plan,** or care plan. A given activity may help a client progress toward more than one goal, or several activities may address a single goal. Playing computer games can help increase attention span, improve eye–hand coordination, stimulate cognitive functioning, and promote feelings of accomplishment in an elderly nursing home resident with dementia. This resident may participate in a sewing group as well as, or instead of, the computer games, and be working toward the same goals.

The TRS is also responsible for scheduling the duration, frequency, and intensity of the treatment. For example, Mr. Jones has had a stroke resulting in muscle weakness and stiffness. To strengthen his muscles and improve his range of motion, he and the TRS decided he will participate in adapted aquatics three times a week (frequency) for half an hour each time (intensity), for a total of four weeks (duration). This activity selection is based on his previous enjoyment of swimming. He also needs to learn how to use a flotation device that will support him in the pool. The expectation is that at the end of the four weeks he will have made predetermined improvements in his muscle strength, range of motion, and ability to use the flotation device. The TRS has probably worked in conjunction with the physical therapist to plan the interventions and goals. This collaboration will maximize the outcomes for Mr. Jones. The TRS can also identify and indicate in the written plan leadership and therapeutic approaches to use with the client. Mr. Jones may require frequent positive reinforcement, physical assistance, or a demonstration of the appropriate use of the adapted equipment to promote his progress.

When setting up the TR program, you may need to coordinate with other disciplines to schedule use of facilities and to avoid conflicts between services. Clients also may be scheduled for physical therapy or occupational therapy, a meeting with a social worker, or a consultation with a dietitian. Collaboration among disciplines at team meetings can help develop the optimal schedule for the client.

Discharge Planning

Many TRSs are also responsible for developing discharge plans for their clients, especially in treatment or rehabilitation settings. Discharge plans include instructions, guidelines, and resources for the client in order to facilitate his or her continued participation in positive, health-promoting recreation activities back at home or in the next service setting. Mr. Jones' discharge plan could include information and scheduling about an adapted swim program for senior citizens at the local YMCA.

Implementation

The third step in the TR process is implementation. To implement the program, the TRS puts into action the client's individual TR plan. This involves client participation in individual and group TR activities. Implementing a program takes into account the overall facility schedule, available space and resources, needed equipment and supplies, needs of the client, and staffing requirements of programs. Successful implementation may require adjustments to the plan to maximize the benefits to the client.

Evaluation

Evaluation is the final step in the TR process. Evaluation is both formative and summative. Formative evaluation is ongoing during the implementation phase and leads to immediate changes and improvements in the treatment plan. If Mr. Jones was scheduled for aquatics in the morning, but it becomes apparent that he is too tired at that time, moving the program to the afternoon may help. He may be afraid to get into the pool because of his muscle weakness and stiffness and require assistance from two staff members rather than just one, as was originally planned. Summative evaluation occurs at the completion of the program to see if the client's goals were met and if program changes need to be made in order to implement it in the future with other clients. Sometimes a plan may not produce the desired results. This may be due to changes in the client's condition, use of new medications, lack of support from family, important information that was not revealed during the assessment, lack of skill on the part of the TRS, inappropriate leadership approaches, or inconsistency on the part of the team. Determining the factors that may have impeded the client's progress is an important evaluation task.

As the client participates, he will probably achieve the planned outcomes according to the treatment plan. Planned health care outcomes are generally measured in quantitative terms, such as amounts of time spent in activity or increase in the ability to perform a certain task. Mr. Jones may experience some unintended benefits as well. He may express feelings of relaxation as a result of the aquatics and a desire to invite his grandson to participate with him, thereby gaining the benefits of family recreation. These unplanned benefits may be just as significant and are often more subjective, meaning they are unique to the participant and relate to the quality, enjoyment, and personal meaning of the experience for the client. They should not be overlooked when reporting client's progress in TR because they may provide a fuller picture of a client's accomplishments.

Concluding Comments on the TR Process

As you may recall from our discussion of TR models, a TR specialist may begin working with a person at any point along the continuum of services, depending on the person's needs and the department or agency's mission and goals. However, all services begin with an individual assessment and reflect the TRS' knowledge of the TR

process. In some settings, particularly community recreation programs that serve people with disabilities, TRSs may not be required to develop written individualized plans with specific desired behavioral outcomes. General goals of having a positive recreation experience, learning and refining new activity skills, and increasing opportunities for social interaction are more typical in community settings. TRSs may serve as inclusion specialists in community-based programs using their knowledge of disability, accessibility, assessment, and activity analysis to facilitate the participation of people with disabilities in these programs. Thoughtful planning and evaluation of services are also considered best practices in community settings.

THERAPEUTIC RECREATION SPECIALIST

"Do I have what it takes to be a TRS?" Although no one personality type is best suited to being a TRS, people who enter helping professions, such as TR, often possess certain attributes. These attributes are at the heart of being a TR professional. Self-awareness, the desire to learn new things and to communicate with people, taking the initiative, being flexible and able to adapt to change and unexpected events, and having creative ideas, energy, enthusiasm, and compassion for people are highly desirable qualities that facilitate a helping relationship focused on helping the client achieve his or her goals.

Professionalism

What does it mean to be a professional? Being a professional in any field means obtaining an education, possessing the credentials recognized by your profession, adhering to a code of ethical behavior, providing services based on professional standards of practice, continuing your education, updating your professional knowledge through reading and research, and being an active member of professional organizations from the local to the international level. Being a professional entails more than just carrying out your job duties and responsibilities.

Education

The first step in becoming a TR professional is obtaining an education in TR, which will provide you with a philosophical and theoretical foundation related to TR service provision and extensive

OUTSTANDING *Graduates*

Courtesy of Ronald Becker

Background Information

Name: Ronald Becker

Education: Bachelor of arts, community and human services, major in therapeutic recreation, Empire State College; master of science in education in recreation education, therapeutic recreation option, Lehman College of the City University of New York.

Credentials: Certified therapeutic recreation specialist (CTRS), certificate in dementia practice guideline competency, American Therapeutic Recreation Association (ATRA).

Affiliations: New York State Therapeutic Recreation Association (NYSTRA), past president; American Therapeutic Recreation Association (ATRA), member

Career Information

Position: Director of therapeutic recreation services, Coler-Goldwater Specialty Hospital and Nursing Facility, Roosevelt Island, New York, and director of therapeutic recreation services, Gouverneur Nursing Facility, New York City

Organization: As a member of New York City Health and Hospitals Corporation, South Manhattan Network, Coler-Goldwater serves 2,000 beds with 3,300 staff (55 in the therapeutic recreation department). Gouverneur Nursing Facility is also a member of New York City Health and Hospitals Corporation, South Manhattan Network and serves 210 beds. Of its staff of 1,200, 6 work in the therapeutic recreation department.

Organization's Mission: Coler-Goldwater Specialty Hospital and Nursing Facility is a comprehensive care center committed to providing quality medical, rehabilitative, and long-term care services to all New York City residents without regard to source of payment.

Job Description: Oversee the department, including staffing, scheduling, and oversight of all program services, budget, policies, and procedures; oversee all departmental documentation and statistics; organize entertainment, community trips, community outreach and support, and grant proposals; attend interdepartmental and staff meetings; oversee performance improvement through audits and in-service education.

Career Path: I have worked 19 years in the field of recreation, having been director of four nursing homes,

> Working in recreation has changed my life. The rewards of helping others realize the benefits of recreation continually move me forward and reignite my passion for what I do. It has allowed me to move toward my potential as a professional, a student of life, and a server of my community. The opportunity to use my talents and to grow never ends, and the personal and social benefits continue to feed my heart and spirit.

director of the Independent Living Center for the Disabled, which is affiliated with United Cerebral Palsy, and assistant director of Playground for All Children, which serves children with disabilities and those without. While working in the field of recreation, I returned to school to earn my bachelor's and master's degrees, majoring in therapeutic recreation. I served on the board of NYSTRA and attended many conferences and seminars to expand my knowledge. Each move to another facility brought increased responsibilities and opportunity for growth. I accepted my current position because of the creative challenge and opportunity to make a positive impact in leisure services. The variety of populations served, recreational resources available, and administrative support make this organization an excellent environment for creative collaboration that has a positive impact on a client's health and wellness. Auxiliary services provide additional funding to support many programs including music therapy, art therapy, photography, drama therapy, horticultural therapy, and monthly community trips. My original reason for pursuing a master's degree was to become a consultant in the field. However, the challenges and opportunities that inspire me at these facilities create a supportive and rewarding environment, and I see myself here for many years.

Advice for Undergraduates

Therapeutic recreation is the only discipline that can affect all domains in treatment. Be proud of the contribution you can make toward a person's rehabilitation and wellness. Take any opportunity to expand your knowledge base through formal education and experiential growth. Taking risks and experimenting result in new outcomes and knowledge. Advocate for your profession and network with other professionals in the field. Join local, state, or national organizations. Research and document your findings. All of these actions will help you grow as a professional and will help the profession.

knowledge in areas essential to TR practice. Knowledge areas include the nature of illness and disability, the effects of disability on functioning, the role of TR in addressing the limitations imposed by disability, and the procedures and methods used by TRSs in developing treatment plans and implementing TR services. TR curricula may be part of a general recreation degree program or a freestanding degree, ranging from the associate to the bachelor's, master's, and doctoral degree levels. The National Recreation and Park Association (NRPA), in conjunction with the American Association for Leisure and Recreation (AALR), has issued standards for therapeutic recreation content areas as part of its recreation curriculum accreditation standards for United States and Canadian colleges and universities. The value of a sound education in TR cannot be overstated and is a component of requirements for obtaining appropriate professional credentials.

Credentialing

Credentialing is the process by which a profession or government certifies that a professional has met the established minimum standards of competency required for practice. Credentialing is intended to protect consumers as they receive services. The three types of credentialing programs are registration, certification, and licensure. Registration is a voluntary listing of people who practice in a profession, according to established criteria. Certification also requires meeting a set of predetermined criteria and usually includes a written examination. Licensure is a process by which state governments mandate qualifications for practice and administer a licensing program. In therapeutic recreation, the largest credentialing program is administered by the National Council for Therapeutic Recreation Certification (NCTRC). To be eligible for certification as a **certified therapeutic recreation specialist (CTRS)**, according to NCTRC, applicants must meet a combination of education and experience requirements and pass the certification examination.

"You mean after I graduate I still have to pass a test to be certified?" Yes! The credentialing process attests that you have met the standards to practice your profession and that your judgment

Sonia D'Andrea, CTRS, Jewish Home and Hospital, Bronx, NY

Sonia began her education by studying clinical psychology but transferred to Lehman College in New York City and earned her BS and MS degrees in recreation education, with an option in therapeutic recreation. She also is a horticultural therapist who investigated the effect of horticulture therapy on the maintenance of cognitive functioning in nursing home residents with Alzheimer's disease for her master's thesis. For seven years she has worked on the Saul special care unit for people with dementia. The TR room on the unit is virtually an indoor garden full of greenery that opens to an outdoor patio where residents also tend to potted plants and flowers. Sonia's innovative horticulture therapy program provides the benefits of sensory and cognitive stimulation, relaxation, and social interaction in a pleasant environment. Closely related to the horticulture program is the cooking group, which uses the fruits and vegetables grown in the garden to prepare recipes provided by the chef. Even the sewing group has a sensory component; residents have made a sensory blanket with different materials and textures to provide tactile stimulation. Other sewing projects are pillows, walker-bags, and embroidered comforters. Sonia's newest program is aromatherapy, which also makes use of the homegrown plants. The TR room also houses three computers for use in Virtual Mind Games, a program of individual and group activities on the computer including card games, crossword puzzles, and memory games. Sonia has designed these programs to maintain the residents' remaining skills and has documented the following outcomes of participation: improved perceptual motor coordination, increased sensory and visual awareness, increased attention span, and increased self-esteem and feelings of self-worth. "My Hispanic background helps me deal with native Spanish-speaking residents in a comprehensive way, as they are sometimes misunderstood and often classified as being agitated and demented by other health care workers who do not understand them," Sonia says. She spends her free time raising two sons, educating herself, and obtaining additional certifications to better care for her residents. Her work was featured under "Excellence in Alzheimer's and Dementia Care" in *Best Practices* magazine in 2003.

and decision-making skills as a professional are to be trusted. To maintain your credentials, most credentialing programs require TR professionals to participate in continuing education activities in order to update their knowledge and skills for practice. Workshops and conferences that cover a wide range of topics are offered by professional organizations at the local, state, regional, national, and international levels.

Professional Organizations

By becoming a member of a professional TR organization or association, you are joining your peers to promote the value of TR; participate in education, communication, and advocacy; and establish and maintain standards of professional practice and behavior. The national TR organizations include the National Therapeutic Recreation Society (NTRS) and the American Therapeutic Recreation Association (ATRA) in the United States, and the Canadian Therapeutic Recreation Association (CTRA) in Canada. Almost every state and province has either a TR organization or a TR branch of the state or provincial recreation association. Examples include the New York State Therapeutic Recreation Association (NYSTRA) and Therapeutic Recreation Ontario (TRO). Joining professional organizations demonstrates your commitment to advancing the profession. Many TRSs agree that one of the most valued benefits of membership is the interaction with peers through networking, sharing ideas, and forging lasting friendships based on common interests and needs.

Standards of Practice

NTRS, ATRA, and CTRA have developed standards for the practice of TR. Standards of practice define the scope of services provided by TR professionals and state a minimal, acceptable level of service delivery. Adherence to these standards ensures consistent practice across service settings and helps establish the credibility of the profession. Regardless of which set of standards you follow, the following core practices are included: assessment, treatment planning, **documentation,** and management. You will find these standards a valuable guide to designing and implementing quality services and helping to ensure ethical practice and behavior.

Ethics

A hallmark of a true profession is a set of standards for behavior that govern conduct. This is written up as a code of ethics, which describes the established duties and obligations of the professional in order to protect the human rights of recipients of services. Both NTRS and ATRA as well as the provincial Canadian TR associations have issued codes of ethics for TR professionals. Although written very differently, the meaning and intent are the same and cover the four major bioethical principles: autonomy (the client has the right to self-determination, which may conflict with what you, the family, the other staff members, or the agency thinks is best for the client), beneficence (that we only do good for our clients), nonmalfeasance (we use care and skill in service so that we cause no harm), and justice (allocating resources in a fair and equitable manner). Other ethical concerns include confidentiality (the client has the right to control access to information about himself or herself and know who will have access to that information), maintaining a professional relationship with clients (not overstepping boundaries into friendships or personal relationships), and cultural competence (understanding and respecting diverse beliefs and values and how they influence clients' behaviors). Following a code of ethics can guide us in choosing the right course of action in any situation.

Keeping Current in the Profession

The true foundation of a profession is a body of knowledge derived from research. Professionals have the obligation to read and apply relevant research findings and contribute to the body of knowledge in the field by conducting research themselves. You may not feel at this time that you are interested in conducting research. However, a new trend in health care, which started in Canada, uses practitioners' expertise and research findings to select the best programs and services. This trend, known as **evidence-based practice (EBP),** enables practitioners and researchers to collaborate on systematically collecting data to provide evidence of the optimum types of care for clients. EBP is sure to become more widespread because it is a sensible approach to planning and implementing services.

In addition to actively participating in the research process, reading research is vital for a professional. Reading research helps practitioners become more reflective and thoughtful in their work and can enrich their practice as they apply proven techniques. Therapeutic recreation research is published in professional journals such as the *Therapeutic Recreation Journal, Annual in*

Therapeutic Recreation, Journal of Leisurability, and the *American Journal of Recreation Therapy.* Professionals can also contribute to the body of knowledge by authoring books, chapters, and magazine articles for the TR field as well as for publications geared to other professions. Increasing the body of knowledge of TR through research continues to be a major objective of the TR profession.

Being a professional implies a sense of calling to do more than just go to work every day and carry out your assigned responsibilities and duties. Professionalism implies dedication to the beliefs and values of your chosen field, lifelong learning, and commitment to the highest standards of practice. As you explore the TR profession and meet TR practitioners, observe the demeanor and behaviors of people who demonstrate admirable qualities. Can they articulate the meaning and value of TR? Are they enthusiastic and positive about the work they do? Do they demonstrate their love of TR through professional activities outside of work and keep up to date with the latest developments? These are the professional qualities you may wish to emulate in order to have a rewarding and fulfilling career.

Your Future in TR

"Is TR right for me? What can I look forward to if I decide to become a TRS?" Many students are attracted to recreation as a major because of their interest in a particular recreation activity such as sports, fitness, outdoor pursuits, music, or art. Knowledge of a wide range of traditional recreation activities, the ability to implement credible programs, and the initiative to continually learn new activities are essential to continued professional success and satisfaction. Although TRSs must have general knowledge of recreation opportunities, it is also important to be skilled in nontraditional facilitation techniques as well as the increasingly popular wellness and health promotion modalities described at the beginning of the chapter. These may include stress management, assertiveness training, sensory stimulation, and a variety of relaxation techniques. You will learn about many recreation activities as part of your TR curriculum. Attending workshops and conferences is a valuable way to gain exposure to and learn about innovative programs and techniques. Taking noncredit, continuing education or adult education courses helps you to keep up to date on fresh program ideas. Certifications are offered in specialty areas such as adapted aquatics, horticulture therapy, fitness

training, aromatherapy, and yoga. Some jobs may require a driver's license or certification in first aid, CPR, or lifeguard and water safety instruction. Obtaining specialized training and credentials will enhance your qualifications to be a TRS and enrich your job performance. One of the wonderful features of TR is that your personal interests can be incorporated into professional practice. It's important to keep your work interesting and participate with your clients with a sense of joy and fun. If *you* are bored by the programs you lead, think how your clients will feel!

Students will benefit from learning not only new interventions and therapeutic practices but also management and administrative skills as well. The skills of budgeting, grant writing, marketing, public relations, oral and written communication, and the use of technology are essential for TRSs who become supervisors and administrators of TR services. Collaboration skills are needed to work with other disciplines, departments, and agencies in order to maximize resources and services. Cross-cultural competence, the ability to understand, respect, and communicate with diverse people, is essential in the culturally diverse nations of Canada and the United States. Cross-cultural competence is important in interactions with other staff members in addition to interaction with our clients and their families.

Future Challenges

What does the future hold for the TR profession? As we have read, TR is a broad and varied field that operates in numerous settings and with people with all types of special needs and health conditions. Changes in health care, economic pressures, social trends, demographic characteristics, and technological advances are influencing society to focus on health promotion, independent functioning, quality of life, and quality of services. These concerns present both challenges and opportunities for growth and innovation in the therapeutic recreation field. Health promotion and disease prevention, particularly in the areas of obesity and stress-related illness, can be achieved by participation in recreation activities such as exercise, dance, gardening, and sports. Wellness practices such as tai chi, yoga, and aromatherapy are being incorporated into many TR programs. Encouraging people to take responsibility for their health can not only improve health status but also lead to independent functioning. Leisure education, the unique contribution of TR to health care, refers to the process by which people explore their own attitudes toward leisure and recreation, understand the impact of leisure on society and in their own lives, and develop the skills to participate in the recreation activities of their choice. Research into leisure education has documented its effectiveness in achieving the valued outcomes of improved health, functioning, and quality of life and successful community reintegration.

The shift from the institution to the community as the primary residential setting for people with disabilities has opened the doors for TR practice in day programs, group homes, community centers, schools, and people's homes. Emphasis in these settings is on promoting independent functioning and finding joy and meaning in life through recreation participation in the optimal living environment. TRSs have responded to these changes by offering retirement planning, early intervention, family leisure counseling, and community reintegration. The inclusion movement will continue to expand, and opportunities exist for TRSs to function as community inclusion specialists, accessibility consultants,

and trainers in leadership techniques and adaptations for people with disabilities. In the political arena, TR organizations have lobbied to include TR in legislation and regulations affecting health care and disability. There is a movement within the TR profession to explore government-sponsored licensing in order to strengthen the credentialing opportunities for TR practitioners.

"So what are the challenges I should be aware of as I enter this profession?" Although many professionals participate in professional organizations, obtain their credentials, keep current with the latest developments, and continually improve their programs and services, greater involvement in these professional activities is of vital importance for the full recognition of TR as an essential service. Membership in professional organizations at every level does not reflect the number of people who identify themselves as working in TR. Many who are eligible to obtain professional credentials have chosen not to do so. Employers continue to hire people to work in TR positions who do not have a college education in TR. There are also variations among TR curricula in college and university programs. A lack of consistency in using the best practices of the field still exists across TR settings. These challenges need to be addressed by all professionals in order to ensure the most effective and meaningful services for the people we serve.

SUMMARY

As TR faces the challenges of the future, well-educated practitioners will hold the key to ensuring the benefits of therapeutic recreation. We have described the scope and range of clients, settings, and services that make up the TR profession. Learning about TR definitions, models, philosophy, and benefits is essential to fulfilling your role as a recreation professional. If you work in either therapeutic recreation or another area of recreation and leisure services, understanding the TR process and the components of professionalism will help you make your own professional choices and plan for a more satisfying and meaningful career.

Web Sites to EXPLORE

The following Web sites also provide links to national, regional, state, provincial, and local organizations and resources.

American Therapeutic Recreation Association: www.atra-tr.org

Canadian Therapeutic Recreation Association: www.canadian-tr.org

National Council for Therapeutic Recreation Certification: www.nctrc.org

National Recreation and Park Association: www.nrpa.org

National Therapeutic Recreation Society: www.nrpa.org (Click on About NRPA, choose Branches and Sections, then select NTRS)

Therapeutic Recreation Directory: www.recreationtherapy.com

CHAPTER 11

Unique Groups

Robin Mittelstaedt, Brenda Robertson, Kelly Russell, John Byl, Jeff Temple, and Laurie Ogilvie

Canadian Forces Personnel Support Agency

The bow cannot always stand bent, nor can human frailty subsist without some lawful recreation.

Miguel de Cervantes, Spanish writer

CHAPTER OBJECTIVES

After reading this chapter, you should be able to do the following:

- Describe the history and current organization of campus recreation
- Identify trends and career opportunities in campus recreation
- Describe the structure and history of correctional systems in Canada and the United States
- Explain the philosophical shifts in the role of recreation in corrections throughout history
- Describe the goals and types of correctional recreation programming
- Identify current trends and issues affecting correctional recreation
- Understand how to deal with people of faith in a recreation setting
- Understand unique differences within and between faith traditions
- Identify employment opportunities in faith-based recreation
- Describe the history and current conditions of employee recreation
- Identify the principles governing the provision of recreational services within military communities
- Understand the structure and composition of military communities, recognizing the differences between military and civilian environments and the uniqueness of military community needs
- Appreciate the value of recreational opportunities within the military community
- Identify career opportunities in military recreation

INTRODUCTION

In this chapter we discuss the fourth sponsoring sector: unique, or closed, groups. This sponsoring sector provides recreation and leisure activities for people within these groups: Campus recreation serves students and often faculty and staff at universities and colleges, correctional recreation serves the incarcerated population, faith-based recreation serves members of religious groups, corporate recreation serves the employees of a business or corporation, and military recreation serves personnel in the armed forces.

Campus Recreation

Robin Mittelstaedt

For the past 20 years, campus recreation centers have served as the hub of all recreation programs at their respective schools.

Doug Franklin, assistant dean of recreation and wellness at Ohio University

In the United States, at the beginning of the 21st century, "an estimated 2,250 institutions of higher education [ran] intramural programs attracting 12 million participants, resulting in more than 620 million hours of participation each year" (Blumenthal, 2000, p. 40). According to the National Intramural-Recreational Sports Association (NIRSA), more than 1.1 million intramural contests are scheduled each year, and more than 2 million people participate in collegiate sport clubs. Further, more than $1.5 billion U.S. have recently been expended to renovate or build new state-of-the-art collegiate recreational sports facilities (NIRSA, 2005).

A comprehensive **campus recreation** program now includes diverse facilities and programs such as towering climbing walls, high-ropes challenge courses, multipurpose activity courts, specialized fitness areas, special events, intramural and club sports, and outdoor programs that include weekend and even weeklong camping and backpacking trips, outdoor-pursuits rental centers, tennis courts, and perhaps even golf courses. The place of campus recreation "in the center of student life has never been more secure" (Franklin, 2001, p. 85). This section of the chapter covers the history of campus recreation, its status in today's colleges and universities, campus recreation as an area of study and career path, and the types of services campus recreation provides.

HISTORY OF CAMPUS RECREATION

In colonial days, in the United States, the academic and educational spirit and religious beliefs caused people to be critical of and even hostile toward physical education and play (Rice, 1929). Until the late 1800s, sports were deemed by most to have little instructional or educational value.

Early Beginnings

Campus recreation in the United States had its earliest beginnings in competitive sporting events and athletic contests at colleges and universities. According to Mitchell (1939), **intramural sports** in collegiate settings began with student-initiated and student-sponsored athletic contests in which students participated during their leisure time. A boat race between Harvard and Yale in 1852 is the earliest recorded intercollegiate meet. A baseball game in July 1859, between Williams and Amherst at Pittsfield, Massachusetts, is the first recorded baseball game. The eastern colleges also held frequent intramural track meets

from 1870 to 1873 (Rice, 1929). In 1913, the first professional staff members were hired to direct intramural programs for men. The University of Michigan and the Ohio State University led the way by appointing intramural directors to run their programs. The most common intramural sports were football, basketball, baseball, track, and tennis (Mitchell, 1939). Weston believed that, "intramural sports competition developed to fill a need for a competitive program of sports and games for all students" (1962, p. 87).

Growth and Development of Campus Recreation

Over time, intramural programs diversified and participation increased. The recreational values of sports have been widely recognized since 1930. The importance ascribed to athletics in the training camps during World War I had a huge impact on the public school system, and since World War II, several important factors affected the campus recreation movement. Activities of a recreational nature were more in demand than ever before and were gradually accepted by

Intramural programs are just one aspect of a comprehensive campus recreation program.

educators as an important part of the education process. Coeducational activities were added. The period immediately after World War II saw the greatest expansion of intramurals, as colleges and universities experienced a tremendous growth in student enrollment.

Birth of a National Organization

The National Intramural Association (NIA) was formed in 1950, following a meeting of 20 African American men and women intramural directors from 11 historically black colleges. This first Intramural Conference was organized by Dr. William Wasson and convened at Dillard University in New Orleans. NIA evolved into the National Intramural-Recreational Sports Association.

Today, NIRSA is a nonprofit professional organization with thousands of members from colleges, universities, military installations, community recreation departments, corporations, and correctional institutions throughout the United States and Canada as well as other countries. As of 2005, NIRSA had 740 institutional memberships, of which 94 percent represented college and university recreational sports programs. These 740 institutions represented nearly 7 million college students; an estimated 5.5 million of those students participated in recreational programs on their respective campuses (NIRSA, n.d.).

CAMPUS RECREATION IN TODAY'S COLLEGES AND UNIVERSITIES

Any campus recreation program serves a diverse population. Participants might be a typical first-year freshman through senior or graduate student; ages can range from 16 to older nontraditional students. The scope of a campus recreation program can be broad, providing classes, facilities, trips, programs, tournaments, and services, including informal recreation and social events to people of virtually all ages and abilities. Students who are members of a sorority or fraternity take part in many campus recreation program offerings. International students come from around the globe and represent myriad cultures. In addition, college students represent different ethnic, religious, and minority groups. People from various walks of life and with different physical abilities visit campus recreation programs. Participants may include single parents and people with physical disabilities or limitations. Although

it varies from school to school, campus recreation facilities and programs are often available to the faculty and staff, to alumni groups, and even to the local community, including an assortment of special interest or booster clubs.

Campus Recreation: A Working Definition

Campus recreation means different things to different colleges and universities; however, on many campuses, it is defined as a program that uses diverse facilities and programs to promote the physical, emotional, and social growth of people by encouraging the development of lifelong skills and positive attitudes through recreational activities. Recreational programs are viewed as essential components of higher education, supplementing and complementing the educational process by enhancing the students' physical and mental development. Through participation in campus recreation activities, students are encouraged to create new problem-solving strategies, develop critical-thinking skills, sharpen decision-making skills, further develop teamwork and cooperation, learn to challenge themselves in many ways, and to integrate this information and these new skills into all aspects of their lives.

Seven Goals for Campus Recreation

A key organization associated with the campus recreation movement is the National Intramural-Recreational Sports Association. In 1996, NIRSA identified seven primary goals of any campus recreational program as follows (pp. 1-2):

- To provide participation in a variety of activities that satisfy the diverse needs of students, faculty, and staff members, and where appropriate guests, alumni, and public participants can become involved

- To provide value to participants by helping them develop and maintain a positive self-image, stronger social interactive skills, enhanced physical fitness, and good mental health

- To enhance college and university student and faculty recruitment and retention initiatives

- To coordinate the use of campus recreation facilities in cooperation with other administrative units such as athletics, physical education, and student activities

- To provide extracurricular education opportunities through participation in recreational sports and the provision of relevant leadership positions

- To contribute positively to institutional relations through significant and high-quality recreational sport programming

- To cooperate with academic units, focusing on the development of a recreational sports curriculum and accompanying laboratory experiences

Benefits

Many of the goals set by NIRSA in 1996 result in these actual benefits and outcomes, as well as others. Campus recreation programs help attract new students, help retain enrolled students, and help attract new faculty. In *The Strategic Management of College Enrollment,* Don Hossler and John Bean (1990) indicated that recreational sports, which include informal leisure time, relaxation, games, and intramural sports, have been endorsed by institutions for their value in helping students maintain good physical health, enhancing their mental health by providing an important respite from rigorous academic work, and teaching recreational skills that have a carryover effect and translate into people making time for leisure and exercise throughout life.

In addition, "students who participate in recreational sports tend to develop positive self-images, awareness of strengths, increased tolerance and self-control, stronger social interaction skills, and maturity—all gleaned from recreational sports experiences" (Council for the Advancement of Standards in Higher Education, 2004, p.1). Other benefits include feelings of overall health and wellness, improved quality of life, and improved cooperation and teamwork. The broad and diverse benefits of campus recreation programs have been cited in a variety of sources.

CAMPUS RECREATION AS A SPECIALIZED AREA OF STUDY

The modern intramural movement has grown into prominent recreational programs that consider and provide for individual differences and interests. The interest and demand are so great and there are so many diverse employment opportunities that the need to provide avenues for developing the future leaders of these programs has grown. Several institutions have developed programs for campus recreation as a unique and special area of academic study. These programs vary from a few specialized courses (at both the undergraduate and graduate level) with a focus on campus recreation to a full-blown degree program. At Ohio University, one can earn an undergraduate degree in campus recreation, and a few universities, such as Ohio University and Pennsylvania State, offer graduate courses in campus recreation.

DIVERSITY OF SERVICES FOR UNIQUE POPULATIONS: DEMAND AND FUTURE GROWTH

A comprehensive campus recreation program can include as many as 70 intramural activities, more than 30 club sports, dozens of classes, and various special events. Participants find diverse recreational opportunities, including drop-in aerobic fitness sessions, weight training, competitive intramural sports, and pickup basketball games. Swimming and aqua aerobics, challenge-course activities, racquetball, nutrition seminars, wellness programs, individual exercise prescriptions, and informal recreation and social opportunities abound.

Weeklong programs for new students, such as camping, backpacking, or even canoeing and camping trips to the Boundary Waters Wilderness Area are offered at some campuses. Special events can include weekend programs for the younger siblings of enrolled students to visit and enjoy campus life with their older brother or sister. Campus recreation often organizes activities and programs for Mom's Weekend, Dad's Weekend, and events such as a Haunted Halloween, Winterfest, Spring Fling, and the like.

With the many needs and interests associated with college students, faculty, their friends and family members, and the local community, the demand for programs, events, activities, and classes only seems to grow. As we dive into the new millennium, there is a growing interest in health and wellness, in quality of life, in fitness, in recreation and leisure pursuits, and in opportunities to pursue spiritual and mental growth—and the campus recreation movement is responding.

CAREER OPPORTUNITIES

At colleges and universities, the activity, participation, and construction boom has already begun. According to Blumenthal (2000), as more and more Americans [and Canadians] enjoy active and healthy lifestyles and increasing numbers of children participate in recreational sports programs, it is logical to assume that there will be an increased demand for recreational sports activities, services, and facilities from all sectors of the population for the foreseeable future.

According to the United States Department of Labor, recreation and fitness workers held about 485,000 jobs in 2002. About 62 percent were recreation workers; the rest were fitness trainers and aerobics instructors. Overall, employment in the recreation and fitness sector is expected to grow faster than the national average. Between 2002 and 2012, the employment growth in these areas is expected to grow by 21 to 35 percent (U.S. Department of Labor, 2004). The outlook for jobs in the campus recreation arena is bright! A campus recreation professional should be a member of NIRSA and other professional organizations and should be aware of and attain professional certifications in her or his area of expertise (see table 11.1).

According to James Karabetsos (1991), recreation, intramural, and recreational sports programs on college campuses will continue to flourish and grow and will be critical avenues of expression as our society becomes more and more technologically oriented. Campus recreation has grown into a dynamic, exciting area with diverse job and career opportunities. It is a national movement that will serve as a catalyst for promoting and enhancing quality of life, overall health and wellness, fitness, and a more rewarding use of leisure time.

SUMMARY

Campus recreation grew out of intramural sports. Today it provides many benefits and opportunities to college students. Because of the growth of campus recreation, it is a growing field of study in college and offers diverse career opportunities.

Correctional Recreation

Brenda Robertson and Kelly Russell

It is as if our cities had not yet developed a sense of responsibility in regard to the life of the streets, and continually forget that recreation is stronger than vice, and that recreation alone can stifle the lust for vice.

Jane Addams, founder of Hull House

One group within society that is unique in terms of recreation is the **incarcerated** population. Freedom is one of the underling tenants of leisure, yet this group experiences a significant loss in freedom

TABLE 11.1 Associated Professional Organizations and Certifications Available in Campus Recreation

Association	Web site	Certification
American Alliance for Health, Physical Education, Recreation and Dance (AAHPERD)	www.aahperd.org	
Association for Experiential Education (AEE)	www.aee.org	
Association of Outdoor Recreation and Education (AORE)	www.aore.org	
National Swimming Pool Foundation (NSPF)	www.nspf.com	Certified Pool Operator (CPO)
Council for the Advancement of Standards in Higher Education (CAS)	www.cas.edu	
National Association for Campus Activities (NACA)	www.naca.org	
National Association of Sports Officials (NASO)	www.naso.org	
National Intramural-Recreational Sports Association (NIRSA)	www.nirsa.org	Certified Recreational Sports Specialist (CRSS)
National Recreation and Park Association (NRPA)	www.nrpa.org	Aquatic Facility Operator (AFO) Certification Certified Park and Recreation Professional (CPRP)
United States Specialized Sports Association (USSSA)	www.usssa.com	
Wheelchair Sports, USA (WSUSA)	www.wsusa.org	

owing to the nature of their actions. Institutional staff make the decisions about when and how this segment of the population will spend their "free" time. For many, it is their inability to use their free time in ways considered to be socially acceptable that leads to incarceration. However, a significant portion of the population does not support correctional recreation despite the fact that these programs can expose them to more socially acceptable means of spending their free time. As this section illustrates, correctional recreation can also instill within offenders appropriate outlets for emotional expression.

INTRODUCTION TO THE CORRECTIONAL SYSTEM

Both the United States and Canada provide a system of facilities to house **offenders.** These include local facilities, state or provincial facilities, and federally run facilities. The **correctional system** in both countries state similar missions: to protect society and help offenders become law-abiding citizens.

> It is the mission of the [United States] Federal Bureau of Prisons to protect society by confining offenders in the controlled environments of prisons and community-based facilities that are safe, humane, cost-efficient, and appropriately secure, and that provide work and other self-improvement opportunities to assist offenders in becoming law-abiding citizens (Federal Bureau of Prisons, n.d.).

> The Correctional Service of Canada, as part of the criminal justice system and respecting the rule of law, contributes to the protection of society by actively encouraging and assisting offenders to become law-abiding citizens while exercising reasonable, safe, secure, and humane care (Correctional Services of Canada, 2004).

The federal government is responsible for operating the federal **institutions** located throughout the United States and Canada. The most recent 2005 statistics provided by the Bureau of Prisons Web site indicate that at the time this article was comprised, there were 197 institutions located throughout the United States, with a total combined population of 182,153 offenders (Federal Bureau of Prisons, n.d.). This number changes daily, as inmates are being released and new inmates are being booked into custody. In Canada, in the year 2001, there were 53 federal institutions housing 31,600 offenders (Correctional Services of Canada, 2001). This

number may also rise and fall on a daily basis. The security required in these institutions is determined by a combination of their physical features, available technologies, the classification of inmates based on risk factors, and the amount of direct staff supervision. Inmates are sentenced to a specific level of security based on the nature of their crime and on several other factors. For example, those who are able to function with relatively little supervision and do not disrupt the institution's operations or threaten the safety of the staff, other inmates, or the public can be housed in lower-security institutions.

A system of state- or provincial-level institutions is also found in both countries. Each state or province typically runs its institutions differently, but a general concept of care and control is common to all. Detention centers or **jails** are located in cities, counties, and territories and are used primarily as holding facilities for offenders until adjudicated by the courts. The type and length of sentence handed down by a court of law determine where offenders will serve their time. A juvenile, or youth, detention center is a secure facility for housing offenders under the age of 18. In some cases, however, high-risk **juvenile** offenders may be housed in adult facilities. Staff members of community-based correctional facilities such as halfway houses supervise offenders serving their sentences within the community as part of probation, parole, or conditional-sentence orders. Residents of these facilities are expected to obtain employment, pay room and board, and comply with specific treatment orders. The exact number of those housed at a state and local level is difficult to say because it changes daily. Unfortunately, as with federal institutions, trends show that these figures are continually on the rise.

The nature of the facility determines the role of recreation. Local jails where offenders are housed awaiting trial or sentencing generally provide very few if any recreation opportunities. In high-security facilities, the nature of the programs is limited according to various risk factors. In other cases where rehabilitation of the offender is deemed possible, recreation can play a role in that process.

People housed within the correctional system are charged with a wide range of crimes. These people represent all races, backgrounds, origins, physical conditions, and age groups. Some have never been incarcerated, while others are repeat offenders. These factors, along with the size of the facility and the number of staff members available, present the biggest challenges to providing recreation programming.

THE HISTORICAL AND PHILOSOPHICAL FOUNDATIONS OF CORRECTIONAL RECREATION

As you have learned, the parks and recreation movement grew out of concern for youth in the streets of industrial towns and cities throughout North America at the turn of the last century. Life in the urban industrial centers during this period was far from ideal for the working class, who lived in crowded, filthy tenements surrounded by crime, gambling, gang violence, prostitution, and juvenile delinquency (Kraus, 1984). The concern was that if youth had no access to safe places to play, harm would come to them or they would spend their free time engaged in criminal activities. The early recreation pioneers felt that if people had access to appropriate forms of recreation, they would choose those over antisocial behavior.

During colonial times in Canada and the United States, the response to inappropriate behavior was influenced by the British practices of capital and corporal punishment (physical chastisement of an offender such as flogging, mutilation, and branding). Institutionalization was generally only employed to hold offenders awaiting punishment. In the colonies, the community accepted responsibility for both punishing offenders and helping to strengthen community institutions such as the family and churches as a defense against crime. Various factors influenced the development of prisons during the late 1700s and early 1880s. The influence of the European Enlightenment writers who argued that too severe a punishment would serve to perpetuate rather than eliminate criminal behavior was becoming more widespread. As communities grew in size, it became more difficult to accept responsibility for the care and control of deviant people (Ekstedt & Griffiths, 1988).

There was a growing belief that rather than being able to eliminate negative behaviors, community disorder was in fact contributing to them and that offenders were often products of unstable community life. In response, Americans sought to establish a system of **penitentiaries** in which offenders, after being removed from corrupt and unstable communities, were housed and made into useful citizens (Rothman, 1971). In contrast, popular thinking in Canada at the time held that offenders were a dangerous class who posed a threat to the stability and morality of communities and as such must be removed. Penitentiaries

were built as a means of segregating these people (Beattie, 1977).

During the 1930s, interest in exploring the causes of criminal behavior emerged. It was discovered that many people committed crimes leading to incarceration because they did not know how to use free time appropriately. Prevention was considered preferable to treatment, and this became an issue for both correctional officials and the recreation community. Some believed that the root problem was a community's failure to provide adequate recreation facilities and programs.

The contemporary role of corrections is to provide the degree of custody necessary to contain the risk presented by an offender, to provide an environment conducive to personal reformation, and to encourage offenders to adopt acceptable behavior patterns through participation in education, social development, and work-experience programs.

The function of correctional institutions in Canada and the United States has undergone various philosophical shifts in response to societal changes over time. The role that recreation has played within the institutions has taken various forms reflective of the dominant paradigms of the day. The following are philosophical approaches that have been used at various times in both Canada and the United States.

- Given the lack of activity within institutions, labor is considered to be a recreation and those most deserving are granted opportunities to work and therefore opportunities for recreation.

- Although some form of recreation is a right granted to all offenders, participation in most recreation programs is a privilege, and those who earn it have access to opportunities that will serve as an incentive for positive behavior by others.

- Idle minds are susceptible to negative impulses; therefore, active recreation is required to awaken undeveloped and dormant faculties thus occupying the mind.

- Recreation can serve as a mechanism to control the behavior of inmates by granting or denying access to pleasurable pursuits.

- Offenders are incarcerated as their punishment and not for their punishment, and so access to appropriate forms of recreation should not be denied.

- The goal of incarceration is to prepare offenders to pursue a normal lifestyle upon release, and because recreation is part of a normal balanced lifestyle, it must be incorporated into the institutional program.

- Because offenders are completely within their care, institutions have a responsibility to work with the whole person, and that involves providing for their mental, physical, social, and spiritual needs.

The role of recreation within corrections continues to be a topic of debate within the justice system today. There are those who believe that recreation should serve as a control mechanism by dispensing it as a reward for desired behavior within the institution. Others consider recreation to be a valuable component of the rehabilitation process through which offenders gain the knowledge, skills, and attitudes required to make positive and productive use of their free time.

RECREATION PROGRAMMING

It is the responsibility of the many correctional recreation professionals located throughout the United States and Canada to provide the most effective and safe activities possible. These correctional professionals provide recreational activity to offenders in state or provincial facilities, federal correctional institutions and facilities, and in private treatment agencies that provide services to youth and adult offenders. These professionals help offenders develop leisure skills and attitudes to optimize their quality of life within the institution and to prepare the offenders to appropriately use their leisure time upon reentry into society.

Programming Goals

Many positive outcomes can be realized through recreation programs offered in correctional institutions. According to the Federal Bureau of Prisons, correctional recreation programs are expected to keep inmates constructively occupied, to reduce idleness, and to enhance the physical, emotional, and social well-being of inmates. These programs will encourage and help inmates to adopt healthy lifestyle habits through participation in physical fitness and health

education programs and will decrease the need for inmate medical treatment (Federal Bureau of Prisons, n.d.). These positive outcomes are also realized when **leisure education** principles are applied. Leisure education develops the attitudes, skills, and knowledge required for optimal leisure functioning. The components of a typical program include developing the physical and mental skills necessary for participation in recreation activities, gaining a knowledge of leisure opportunities and how to use the required equipment and supplies, developing an understanding of and an appreciation for leisure and its role in quality of life, and providing opportunities to explore and experience a variety of appropriate leisure activities.

The following are goals of correctional recreation programming:

- **Develop acceptable outlets for stress.** Correctional facilities are extremely stressful environments. To survive, inmates must learn to identify and practice socially acceptable ways to relieve stress. For many this is through physical exertion, but for others, cultural pursuits such as music, art, drama, and writing provide positive outlets.

- **Identify activities that serve as alternatives to addictions.** Many people sentenced to correctional facilities experience addictions. Those who participate in treatment programs to address their addictive behaviors often find that they

Correctional recreation programs are expected to keep inmates constructively occupied, to reduce idleness, and to enhance the physical, emotional, and social well-being of inmates.

Courtesy of Kelly Russell

have significantly more free time than they used to. Therefore, substituting recreational pursuits during time previously devoted to the addiction can greatly aid the rehabilitation process.

• **Foster interpersonal skills such as trust, cooperation, and teamwork.** Lack of the basic skills that enable people to live effectively in a community may cause some people to participate in activities generally considered socially unacceptable. Certain forms of recreation can help people identify and develop interpersonal skills.

• **Enhance self-esteem through success.** High self-esteem is a critical component of personal accountability and respect for others, which are important goals of the correctional process. Self-esteem is also at the root of inner confidence that enables people to cope effectively with the challenges of life. Positive recreation experiences can enhance self-esteem.

• **Increase access to new social environments.** People are products of their environment to a large extent and often lack the motivation to alter negative social environments. Adopting new recreation interests can serve as a catalyst to seeking new and potentially more positive social environments.

• **Foster new interests.** Offenders often have a limited leisure-activity repertoire caused in part by a negative attitude toward activities even though they have not experienced the activities firsthand (Robertson, 1993). Recreation programs can help identify the source of the negative attitudes and foster a more positive attitude toward a broader range of leisure pursuits.

• **Negotiate constraints.** Many eople encounter social, psychological, and structural constraints attempting to participate in recreation opportunities such as no one with whom to participate, low self-esteem, and lack of skill or money. Learning how to overcome these constraints can facilitate access to a broader range of activity options, which is desirable when all perceived options have negative consequences.

• **Develop awareness of personal needs and appropriate avenues to satisfy them.** Human behavior is motivated by social, psychological, and biological needs. If certain people are unable to satisfy their needs through socially acceptable means, they turn to delinquent pursuits for satisfaction. Recreation can provide appropriate ways to satisfy specific needs.

• **Develop decision-making and problem-solving skills.** Offenders often have not learned the skills necessary to assess situations and to make decisions that will not harm themselves or others. These skills can be developed and practiced in recreational settings, allowing participants to experience and process the impact of their decisions.

• **Develop new interests that could evolve into a career.** Certain offenders are highly creative and talented, yet vocational programs often fail to recognize or develop these skills. Through recreation, creative skills can be identified and channeled into pursuits such as music, writing, drama, and crafts, which could lead to meaningful employment opportunities.

Types of Programming

Recreation programs in correctional settings can consist of hundreds of activities depending on the nature of the institution and the resources available. When planning an activity for people who are incarcerated, the number one concern is safety, both of the participants and the staff. Before allowing inmates to participate, each activity must be carefully examined to identify potential hazards. Even a board game could present a dangerous situation for inmates and staff if the game pieces could be used for inappropriate purposes. Careful supervision when conducting these activities is required, including accounting for all equipment. It is important to recognize that even though correctional institutions serve as rehabilitation facilities, they can be aggressive and hostile settings, and recreational activities should not agitate offenders. Rather, they should help them focus on the positive aspects of recreation activities: teamwork, cooperation, stress management, and leadership. Teaching offenders to redirect their negative energy in more positive ways, such as involvement in sport, not only serves them while they are incarcerated but can also help them to lead more positive, productive lives on the outside.

Some institutions have extensive recreation facilities, while others are limited. Much of this depends on the type and size of the facility as well as funds that are available and allocated to recreation activities. For example, some institutions are equipped with facilities such as a baseball field, full-length basketball court, weight room, crafts shop, and theater, while others may have only a small multipurpose room.

Active recreation programs offered in institutions include basketball, volleyball, aerobics, handball, hockey, curling, table tennis, pool, baseball, flag football, track and field, shuffleboard, soccer, canoeing, orienteering, and rock climbing. Sports are popular in most institutions. Examples of more passive forms of recreation include drawing, painting, sculpting, crafts, music, journal writing, pet therapy, board games, drama, quilting, knitting, singing, and holiday events.

Pet therapy is an innovative recreation program offered in some institutions. In Bernalillo County, New Mexico, more than 800 juvenile offenders have participated in a program in which they have a chance to pet and play with dogs, ask questions about them and dog behavior, and share stories about their own pets. The youth can also attend ownership classes to address matters of abuse to animals and lessons on humane dog training and treatment. The Nova Institution for Women in Truro, Nova Scotia, has a similar program. Through the canine program, women learn to work with homeless dogs and train them to become family pets for people with physical disabilities. This fosters a sense of responsibility for and nurturing toward the dogs that promote the offenders' self-esteem and provide therapeutic benefits for the women. It also promotes ties to the community by providing a valuable service.

CORRECTIONAL RECREATION PROFESSIONAL

Institutional staff make the decisions about when and how the incarcerated segment of the population spends its "free" time. Staff members can be sworn law enforcement officers or civilian personnel. Most facilities require correctional recreation staff to hold some type of advanced college degree—associate's, bachelor's, or master's degree. Other credentials, such as a certified personal trainer, therapeutic recreation specialist, or certified leisure professional are helpful. All correctional recreation personnel should be certified in first aid and CPR. Candidates interested in applying to a correctional institution are subject to polygraph testing background checks. It is helpful to be fluent in a second language.

Although the specific job titles may vary from facility to facility—recreation officer, recreation specialist, program manager, or program supervisor—the role of correctional recreation personnel is virtually the same throughout the United States and Canada. And these professionals play important roles in the lives of offenders while they are incarcerated. Those with a physical education or recreation background provide valuable experience to the population they serve. People hired for this type of

position receive training related to their specific job as well as the operations of the facility. Much of the focus is geared toward safety and security, the priority when working in a corrections setting, and one must understand that this profession carries with it an inherent risk because of the work environment. But it can also hold great opportunities for learning and understanding. Being part of a correctional setting and working with offenders will not only help someone to develop a strong sense of their own personal safety and boundaries, but it will also help to develop a sense of patience and tolerance in working with the incarcerated population.

TRENDS AND ISSUES

Although often viewed as a large and inflexible governmental machine, correctional institutions are very much affected by societal trends both from the client and administrative perspective. Because of this, they face ever changing and challenging issues such as incarceration rates, budget cuts, philosophical shifts, aging infrastructure, and meeting the needs of the various segments of the incarcerated population based on factors such as age, sex, and race.

A current issue in correctional recreation is the varying perceptions of the role of recreation within correctional settings. Many institutional staff believe that participation in positive forms of recreation is a constructive way for offenders to spend their time during incarceration because it can relieve stress, counter boredom, alleviate frustration, and improve health. However, certain institutions are reluctant to dedicate resources to such programs for fear of recourse from the public who support more punitive approaches to offender treatment. In these cases, basic recreation programs are offered as a means of satisfying legal requirements but lack the developmental components that could aid in offender rehabilitation. But, there appears to be an increasing awareness of the relationship between recreation and crime and an understanding that many people engage in criminal activity as a form of recreation to satisfy individual needs during free time. Research has shown that many of these people lack the knowledge, attitude, skills, or access to opportunities that will facilitate participation in personally satisfying socially acceptable pursuits (Robertson, 1998). As such, the way to rehabilitate them so that they can become law-abiding citizens is to help them develop the appropriate knowledge and skills to pursue alternatives through leisure education–based programs that have a strong developmental component.

SUMMARY

Recreation holds the potential to help correctional institutions, their incarcerated populations, and their staff members achieve the goals of the correctional system. If properly administered, correctional recreation can help foster an institutional environment in which offenders can develop knowledge and skills that will enable them to live more productive lives both behind prison walls and once they return to community settings.

Faith-Based Recreation

John Byl

The city streets will be filled with boys and girls playing there.

Zechariah 8:5

Teach boys swimming, horsemanship, and archery.

Muhammad Sallallāhu 'alayhi wa Sallam, Islamic prophet of Muhammad, messenger of Allah

People of faith often engage in recreational activities through their religious institutions. In the United States in 2001, 81 percent of those 18 and older identified with a religious group (Kosmin, Mayer, & Keysar, 2001). Therefore, we can see why "religious organizations should be recognized as legitimate providers of recreation activities in the leisure service delivery system" (Emard, 1990, p. 146). It is important to recognize and understand the role that religious institutions play in providing satisfying recreational opportunities within their communities.

DEALING WITH PEOPLE OF FAITH IN A PUBLIC SETTING

Although this section focuses on recreation in faith-based settings, we first briefly consider the role of inclusion in a public setting. For example, some recreation providers say, "We provide services for everybody." But then they don't permit Muslim women to wear track suits under their team uniforms or do not prevent males from gazing at these women as they participate in active recreation. Both of these practices exclude many Muslim women from participation because they may expose limited amounts of skin and not be in a situation where males view them. Some Christians do not participate in sport on Sundays, and some Jews and Seventh Day Adventists do not participate in sport on Saturdays. Recreation providers often include only current participants in their definition of "everybody." Seven of the largest religious groups in the United States are shown in table 11.2. One needs to ask, how well do recreation providers meet the needs of religiously committed people? If a recreation provider suggests that "we provide services for everybody," and yet does not pay attention to the unique needs of religious groups within their community, that provider may informally exclude people from their programs.

TABLE 11.2 United States Religious Identification

Group	Population of those 18+	Percentage
United States	207,980,000	100
Christian	159,030,000	76.5
Jewish	2,831,000	1.3
Muslim	1,104,000	0.5
Buddhist	1,082,000	0.5
Hindu	766,000	0.4
Unitarian/Universalist	629,000	0.3

Adapted from B. Kosmin, E. Mayer, and A. Keysar, 2001.

The challenge for recreation providers is to encourage people from diverse cultures to participate in settings that serve various cultures and religions, while avoiding using public institutions to promote a specific religion. In the United States, "Congress shall make no law respecting an establishment of religion, or prohibiting the free exercise thereof" (First Amendment to the U.S. Constitution). As interpreted by the courts, this amendment has legal implications (not all of which encourage diversity), and it means, for example, that in public schools, student-led prayers before events are unconstitutional, while in the area of clothing "Muslim girls may wear a hijab over their hair and long pants under their shorts, Jewish boys may wear yarmulkes, and Sikh boys may wear turbans. Furthermore, observance of clothing customs, coupled with rules regulating physical contact and modesty in coeducational settings, may preclude some students from participating in activities such as swimming and dance" (Kahan, 2003b, p. 12).

In the United States, the federal government is committed to fitness as outlined in their initiative called Healthy People 2010. The federal government "challenges individuals, communities, and professionals—indeed, all of us—to take specific steps to ensure that good health, as well as long life, are enjoyed by all" (Office of Disease Prevenention, 2005). Canadian federal and provincial governments have set a goal of increasing Canada's physical activity levels by 10 percentage points in provinces and territories by the year 2010. If these physical activity goals are to be achieved, recreation providers must understand barriers that limit people of different faiths from participating in certain activities. Developing solutions is an important step in including them in fuller activity. Furthermore, more work is needed if sport is to be used as a tool for bringing people together. One study concludes, "intergenerational recreation is an excellent means of fostering positive change and better relations between Israeli Arabs and Jews" (Leitner & Scher, 2000). But let's turn now to the faith-based communities themselves.

FAITH TRADITIONS ENGAGING, DISENGAGING, AND REENGAGING IN RECREATION

Different faith traditions have been engaged or disengaged in recreational involvement at different times in their history. For example, in their book on *Muscular Christianity: Evangelical Protestants and Development of American Sport,* Tony Ladd and James Mathisen trace the path of the calls by muscular Christians to manliness, character development, and healthful living that occurred within the framework of an evangelical Protestant ethos that called for personal salvation as well as development (1999). But the path has gone through different stages at different times. The first path, labeled as **engagement,** occurred in the late 1800s through the efforts of leaders like Dwight Moody and Amos Alonzo Stagg, who wanted leaders to persuade the souls of men as well as their bodies. The movement was especially strong in organizations such as the YMCA and the many new colleges and universities springing up throughout North America at the time. The second path, **disengagement,** started in the early 1900s and was promoted by men like Billy Sunday. Sunday was a star professional baseball player who converted to Christianity. A few years later he began to view baseball and Christian work as mutually exclusive endeavors. On the earlier path, Christians had appreciated the physical and spiritual benefits of sport and engaged in sport, and on the second path they saw their faith and sport involvements as conflicting activities and disengaged from sport. The third path, **reengagement,** began in the late 1940s through the work of evangelist Billy Graham. Graham invited the American mile champion Gil Dodds to join him at his crusades. Once again, sport and **Christianity** were seen as positive and symbiotic organizations, and many churches and Christian organizations actively united sport and faith (Ladd & Mathisen, 1999).

Differences Within Faith Traditions

Ladd and Mathisen's important work painted trends with a wide brush. However, they did recognize that religious groups are not necessarily one homogeneous unit. Some of these differences are fostered because of different ways of thinking about their beliefs, and some of these differences are fostered because of different ethnic roots. For example, compare two protestant Christian groups: the Christian Reformed Church (CRC), which was started by Calvinists of Dutch background, and the Canadian Mennonite Brethren (MB), which was started by Anabaptists of Germanic background. A study looking at the main journals for each group determined that for the CRC, "enjoying one's leisure time was highly encouraged, especially if the recreation called for a combination of active, stewardly, and playful participation in God's creation" (Byl, 1999, pp. 318-319). One writer from this community described camping as "almost like sneaking back into paradise while the angels aren't looking" (Witvoet, 1988, p. 11). However, they had little interest in organized church camps for evangelistic purposes. However the Mennonites valued church camps for two purposes: "one, showing young Christians how to live a Christian life, and two, leading people to Christ" (Byl, 1999, p. 320). The CRC sees recreation primarily as a way to experience God's creation, while the MB views recreation primarily as a teaching and evangelistic tool.

The study demonstrates that two Christian groups can hold significantly different views about the purpose of recreation; the study also indicates that within each denomination members hold different views (Byl, 1999). Some of the differences between religious groups relate to individual commitments and ethnic backgrounds. Some people's religious beliefs intentionally and fully shape their recreation choices, while others express beliefs that unintentionally and partially shape their recreation choices. Nationality also shapes unique differences between religious groups. The intersection of nationality and religious beliefs encourages some to recreate with people with similar interests, background, religious affiliation, and language. Being in this comfort zone within a subculture and being shaped by the subcultural values are referred to as **selective acculturation** in leisure (Shaull & Gramann, 1998).

Differences Between Faith Traditions

There are many religious groups in North America, but looking at three faith groups provides insight into how different traditions value and engage in recreation. We look at Muslims as an emerging faith group in North America, Christians as a group with a long-standing history, and Jews as the second-largest faith group in the United States.

Islam

Nearly 20 percent of the world's population follows **Islam,** a way of life lead by the teachings of Muhammad. Although most Muslims live in Middle Eastern countries, Muslims are the fastest growing religious group in the United States (Kosmin, Mayer, & Keysar, 2001). Their numbers doubled in the United States from 1990 to 2000. Because many of these Muslims are recent immi-

grants to North America, because they immigrated from a variety of countries, and because they live in various socioeconomic groups, it is difficult to consider all Muslims as being the same. In general terms, however, Muslims follow the teachings laid out in the Koran and Hadith.

According to Islamic teachings, both men and women should learn to ride horses, shoot a bow and arrow, swim safely, fence, run, and wrestle. In part, these sports are encouraged as a means to personal well-being, and in part they are a means to being well prepared in case of war (Anahar, Becker, & Messing, 1992). Because participation in sport must comply with Islamic teaching, a Muslim may not participate in sport for personal financial benefit or for personal fame, nor can he or she ignore religious practices concerning prayer, modest clothing, and men spectating at sporting events for women or women watching men (Fleming & Khan, 1994; Kamiyole, 1993). There must be opportunity for prayer in the morning, at 7:30 in the evening, as well as three other times during the day. The Ramadan requirements of daily fasting from dawn until sunset during the ninth month of the Muslim year must be taken into consideration (Taylor & Toohey, 2001/2002). Recreation also must not interfere with family responsibilities such as watching over siblings, performing household duties, or doing school work (Carrington, Chivers, & Williams, 1987; De Knop, Theeboom, Wittock, & De Martelaer, 1996; Fleming, 1993).

Clothing can present Muslim women (and consequently recreation providers) a major barrier to becoming involved in active recreation. In strict Muslim circles, women are not permitted to publicly show more of their body than their face and hands. Typically, women cover their head with a hijab in public (Jalili, 1994), but all this clothing does not encourage active participation in sport. Some Muslim women join private health and fitness facilities for women only in order to meet their religious considerations (Taylor & Toohey, 2001/2002).

Certainly a key to helping Muslims become more physically active is to understand their religious customs (Benn, 1996). David Kahan, assistant professor in the department of exercise and nutritional sciences at San Diego State University, has recently begun studying factors that facilitate and inhibit physical activity in adolescents from religions that include clerical and scriptural proscriptions against and prescriptions for exercise. Kahan, in an insightful article on "Islam and Physical Activity: Implications for American Sport and

Physical Educators," outlines eight suggestions for providing a more inviting physical-activity culture that respects Islamic boundaries.

1. Muslims must have more opportunities to voice their concerns about combining religious customs with physical activity.

2. Physical education and recreation providers must engage in dialogue with Muslim clergy and parents to attain advice for advancing participation. These providers also speak with their participants about sensitivity to Muslim needs.

3. Young people need more Muslim role models that excel in physical education and sport as instructors, organizers, and elite athletes.

4. Physical activity providers must ask more questions from and about Muslims to better understand their faith tradition.

5. Recreation providers need to be aware of prayer times, daylong fasts during Ramadan, and other important holidays such as Id al-Fitr and Id al-Adha and be aware that these holidays occur at different times from year to year because the Muslim calendar is based on a lunar cycle.

6. Those responsible for program design must realize that Muslims come from a tradition rich in activities such as badminton, field hockey, and folk games. However, coed activities where there is a potential for body contact, such as basketball or touch football, or activities that require exposing large amounts of the body, such as swimming or gymnastics, cannot be considered. Ways to deal with minor physical contact include separating females and males during games or let females guard females and males guard males as in a sport like korfball (a version of basketball played with a soccer ball popular in Europe).

7. Legal rulings have consistently supported people from specific religious groups who wear clothing required by their religious convictions (Kahan, 2003b). In the case of Muslims, this means females must wear clothing that covers all but their face and hands, and males must wear clothing that covers the area between the navel and the knees. Public nudity is also forbidden in Islam. Showers must be made optional or shower stalls provided for showering and changing.

© Photodisc

Camps are a popular activity for faith-based organizations.

8. Muslims should encourage the development of Muslim-specific clubs and organizations (Kahan, 2003a).

Reprinted, by permission, from D. Kahan.

In a conversation with a Muslim, I learned that in Canada, each mosque is governed by a mosque council, which oversees a variety of concerns, including a sport council. The sport council organizes recreation events for men and women including ball hockey, volleyball, golf, and bowling, and it offers sport clinics for youth and day- and weeklong sport camps. These activities are a means to building community, encouraging healthy lifestyles, and providing opportunities to those otherwise unable to afford recreational events. Islamic standards are applied to these events, accommodating prayer times, modesty in clothing, and restricting the opportunities for males gazing on females or females gazing on males. Community recreational facilities are rented to accommodate activities such as swimming exclusively for females. The recreation events are organized exclusively for members of the mosque or for other Muslims. The recreation activities are not used to evangelize or recruit people to the Islamic faith.

Christianity

Since the beginning of the Christian church, living in community with fellow believers has been valued. The Bible states that in the early church nearly 2,000 years ago, "they broke bread in their homes and ate together with glad and sincere hearts" (Acts 2:46 New International Version). During the past 100 years, togetherness as a congregation has been enjoyed in church fellowship halls through coffee socials, boys and girls clubs, annual church picnics, dances, and competitive leagues with teams from similar congregations. Table 11.3 indicates the wide selection of recreational activities offered and what percentages of Canadian churches offer these activities. The purpose of this recreation is to enhance a sense of community between people of the same faith. With the reengagement of Christianity and sport, as discussed by Ladd and Mathisen, U.S. churches, particularly Baptist churches in the South, began to enhance their recreation programs with a significant focus on ministering to people's needs and recruiting new members (Popke, 2001a).

Typically, church programs, particularly those for kids, include a refreshment break that provides an opportunity for leaders to speak briefly about

TABLE 11.3   Recreation Programs Offered in Small-Town Ontario Churches

Activity	Percentage of churches offering this activity
Social recreation	93
Study and discussion groups	84
Fund-raising activities	73
Music and drama	59
Arts, crafts, and hobbies	51
Film nights	48
Game nights	44
Outdoor activities	42
Retreats	39
Excursions	37
Physical activities	36
Vacation Bible school	31
Organized team sports	31
Day camp	14
Dances	14

Adapted, by permission, from M. Emard, 1990, "Religion and leisure: A case study of the role of the church as a provider of recreation in small Ontario communities." Unpublished master's thesis, University of Waterloo.

following Christian principles of living or to share a personal testimony and to invite participants to accept Jesus as savior of their life. Special kids' programs like KidsGames are modeled after the Olympics and take place during church summer camps during the years when the Summer Olympics and World Cup of Soccer occur. Competitions are held in various sport events, Bible knowledge, poster design, and answering an essay question. KidsGames began in Barcelona in 1985 as an evangelical Christian program in preparation for the Olympic Games in that city and is now worldwide (Bynum, 2003).

In addition to kids' programs, many Christian churches organize adult church sport leagues. These leagues generally do not permit alcohol use at games, and they include time for prayer, fellowship, and talking with others about their relationship with God. These leagues try not to overemphasize the importance of sport by limiting the number of weekly practices and games (Popke, 2001a). In Canada, at least in small-town churches in Ontario, sport is one of the activities ranked lowest in current offerings. Many churches in the United States have built large fitness centers to serve their members as well as to serve and reach out to others in the community. In these fitness centers Christian music is often played, and during breaks in the activity people can share a personal testimony and pray.

Several for-profit companies have organized to fill a niche in the fitness market for Christian fitness centers that train both the body and soul. The Lord's Gym was founded in Florida in 1997 and now has more than 15 locations. Its membership is open to all people regardless of religious background, but a dress code is enforced, Christian music and television stations are played, and 10 percent of all member fees are given to charities (Popke, 2001b). Another company is Angel City Fitness, which offers classes in yoga, Pilates, kick fit, stretching, and self-defense. Other amenities include personal trainers and a cafe.

An organization that helps churches use sport and recreation programs to reach out to their communities is the Association of Church Sports and Recreation Ministers (CSRM). CSRM provides "a way for these church leaders to come together as a profession to learn from each other, to find support for their chosen ministry field, to meet others working in churches, and to share resources" (Association of Church Sports Web site: www.csrm.org). CSRM's motto is "Helping churches use sport and recreation programs to reach out to their communities."

Judaism

People of Jewish background are discussed here for two reasons. First, those who identify themselves as Jewish form the second-largest religious group in the United States (Kosmin, Mayer, & Keysar, 2001). And second, although Christians and Muslims see all of life as affected by their religious commitments, Jews distinguish between sacred and secular activities, therefore providing an alternative perspective on faithful living in one's recreation.

For Jews, religion affects what happens in the synagogue and in personal and family devotional life but not what happens on the soccer pitch or boxing ring. However, something that binds Jews together, regardless of religious affiliation, is their nation, Israel. Therefore, some recreation activities are based more on national commitments than on Jewish faith commitments. For example, the quadrennial Maccabiah Games is held in Israel the year following the Olympic Games. According to Maccabi Canada, the purpose of the Maccabiah Games is "to promote the Jewish identity and traditions through athletic, cultural, social and educational activities for both youth and adults alike and to promote a bond with the State of Israel, both domestically and abroad" (Maccabi Canada, 2005).

The Maccabi World Union was set up in 1921 at the Zionist Congress to coordinate the activities of the various Jewish sport clubs and sports organizations operating around the world. The Zionist Congress first met in 1896 for purposes of establishing a Jewish State. The term "Maccabi" is a name to remember Judah Maccabi who led a band of Jewish patriots against the Syrian invaders. The Maccabi World Union developed the idea of holding a sort of Jewish Olympiad every four years in Israel. The first Maccabiah Games was held in 1932. In addition, the Pan American Maccabi Games is held every four years in various South American cities. The JCC Maccabi Games, sponsored by the Jewish Community Centers, is held annually in the United States. These Olympic-style sporting competitions are held each summer in North America and comprise the largest organized sports program for Jewish teenagers in the world (Jewish Community Centers Maccabi Games, 2005).

Some argue that the establishment of the Maccabiah Games was political and believe that throughout the 1950s and '60s, according to an American Jewish historian, George Eisen, speaking during a radio program titled "Muscular Judaism" on a 2001 broadcast of "The Sports Factor with Amanda Smith," Jews were "using sport, to say that the newly formed Israeli State, created in 1948, was here to stay" (Smith, 2001). This priority is reflected on the Canadian Maccabi Web site, which states, "Our main goal at Maccabi Canada is to bring as many young Jews as possible to Israel so that we can expose them to their religion, their traditions, and most of all, give them an 'Israel Experience'" (Maccabi Canada, 2005). These games provide an Israeli experience but not necessarily a faith-based experience. It is important to many Jews to support and visit Israel, and the Maccabiah Games provides a way to do both.

Another important influence on the recreation habits of Jews in the United States and Canada was the establishment of organizations to help recent immigrants adapt to their new surroundings. During the late 1800s and early to mid-1900s Jewish settlement houses, immigrant aid institutions, and Young Men's and Young Women's Hebrew Associations were established in cities like Boston, New York, and Chicago. The Young Women's Associations offered programs in calisthenics, basketball, baseball, track and field, tennis, physical culture, domestic education, aquatics, "religious work, gymnastics, social work, and educational work to promote social and physical welfare for Jewish families" (Borish, 1999, p. 248). These centers were concerned with the Americanization of Eastern European immigrants (Borish, 1999).

These organizations provided places where Jews could participate in new activities and learn about North American culture without losing their Jewish culture. For example, "With basketball as its center, both at Jewish community centers, public schools, and settlement houses, they learned American values, tried out new identities, thought new thoughts, challenged their routes and made choices—all within Jewish-bounded space. Their stories demonstrated the possibilities for living in the United States as Americans in ways that do not deny a real Jewish presence and a fierce pride in being Jewish" (Levine, 1992, p. 137).

During an interview, a director of a Jewish community center said that there is nothing religious in the recreation center program. The recreation program is "completely secular." The centers cater mostly to Jewish people but are open to others. Some programs that focus on Jewish culture, such as Jewish writers, are also open to non-

Jews. The membership at this particular center is approximately 75 percent Jewish; however, of those attending the center's recreation programs, approximately 50 percent are not Jews. The Web site of the Jewish Community Centre of Greater Vancouver illustrates the inclusiveness of Jewish community center programming. The site notes that the organization offers "exceptional cultural, educational, recreational and social programs, the Centre is more than a community centre. The home of many of our leading organizations including Jewish Federation and Jewish Family Services Agency, the Centre is more than an office building. Over the generations, thousands of people have made the Centre what it is today, yet the Centre is more than its members, volunteers and donors. The Centre is the heart of our community. It is our gathering place, reflecting and accommodating our many and diverse needs. No wonder it's simply referred to as the *Centre*" (Jewish Community Centre of Greater Vancouver, 2005).

The Jewish Community Centers Association of North America guides the Jewish community centers across North America. This organization states that it is a movement "leading the way to a vibrant future by establishing cooperative ventures with local and national Jewish organizations, by supporting Jewish culture, community, and education, and by encouraging and enabling Jews of all ages and backgrounds to engage in the joys of Jewish living" (Jewish Community Centers of North America, 2005). These centers, like the Maccabiah Games, are concerned with "Jewish living," not **Judaism** as a religion.

Why do Jews recreate? Christians and Muslims see recreational choices as ways to glorify their God. Christians might use a Biblical text to explain this conviction, quoting from Romans 12:1, which states, "Present your bodies a living and holy sacrifice, acceptable to God, which is your spiritual service of worship." However, Jews participate in recreation for other reasons.

"Historically, education has been the number one priority for Jews, which has led to the misconception that Jews don't participate in sports, as George Eisen, a Jewish sport historian, pointed out during the 2001 Australian Broadcasting Corporation radio talk show, "The Sports Factor with Amanda Smith," "there's a creative tension between Jews perceiving themselves as people of the book, or as people of muscle . . ." (Smith, 2001). I spoke with a teacher from a Jewish school, and she noted that physical education and sport received little attention in her school. However, according to Anthony Huges, an Australian historian who appeared on the same broadcast, "there were physically active Jews throughout the [20th] century. When we see the rise of a Jewish middle class, following the emancipation of Jewry throughout Europe, that coincides with the rise of organized sport, the revival of the Olympic Games by Pierre de Coubertin, and the institution of the Zionist movement . . . in 1898 at the Second Zionist Congress in Basel in Switzerland, Max Nordau, who was one of Theodore Herzl's lieutenants in the Zionist movement, came up with this idea of the muscular Jews, and it really became a potent symbol for the Zionist movement" (Smith, 2001). Theodore Herzl was the author of *Der Judenstaat*, a book that encourages the establishment of a Jewish State. In 1897, he convened the First Zionist World Congress.

Athletes took the idea of the muscular Jew to heart. In 1950, the Canadian press named Fanny "Bobbie" Rosenfeld the Canadian woman athlete of the half-century. She was "one of the consummate female athletes of the 20th century, but also was the greatest Canadian Jewish athlete of the modern Olympic movement. [She was] inducted into the International Jewish Sports Hall of Fame in 1981" (Levy, Rosenburg, & Hyman, 1999).

Another reason some Jews participate in sport is to counteract perceived anti-Semitism in such things as various immigration laws and previous entrance requirements at Harvard that limited the number of Jews that were eligible to immigrate or enroll. Robert Cohn, a middleweight champion boxer from Princeton, "cared nothing for boxing, in fact he disliked it, but he learned it painfully and thoroughly to counteract the feeling of inferiority he'd felt on being treated as a Jew at Princeton" (Smith, 2001).

On the same broadcast, Ramona Koval, a former javelin thrower, explained, "In my mind this was quite a useful thing to do if you really needed to defend yourself, to be able to throw a javelin and aim it right into the heart of the enemy. That's how I was brought up, you never knew where or when an attack was going to come" (Smith, 2001). For Hemingway's Cohn and for Koval, sport was an opportunity to prove their superiority, at least not inferiority, over others, as well as an opportunity to defend themselves from harm. In some ways, sport had to do with survival.

There was another way that Jews used sport and recreation as a tool of survival. Anthony Hughes, who has written extensively on Jewish-Australian sport, notes, "Jewish communities in Sydney and Melbourne were very worried about exogamy, about the disintegration or the loss of their community through young people marrying outside the Jewish faith, and they really did see sport as a way to get young people together to preserve their community" (Smith, 2001). Although this quote speaks about Australian Jews, we can draw similar arguments for North America. Once again, sport and recreation serve as ways to keep an ethnic community together (Schneller, 1998).

Just as there is diversity in the beliefs and practices of Christians and Muslims, recreation and sport are not universally valued among Jews. A daughter of a holocaust survivor spoke about her mother's thoughts on participation in sports. "I think she felt that the Jews were the losers, and especially after the Holocaust . . . So she had suspicions of groups, and she thought that it was better that you just kept your head down and be quiet, and not get involved with team sports" (Smith, 2001).

These examples illustrate that the anti-Semitic stereotypes of Jewish physical incompetence are inaccurate (Vertinsky, 1994). However, sport and recreation have not been highly valued within the Jewish culture. What is valued more highly is the state of Israel and the ethnic identity of being Jewish. Religious practices are distinct from secular activities like recreation, and therefore, there are only occasional relationships between Jewish religion and recreation.

EMPLOYMENT IN FAITH-BASED RECREATION

Professionals in faith-based recreation must meet three requirements. One, a passionate commitment to the faith is central and is the first entry point into any position. Although, for the Jewish leaders faith is not critical but a positive disposition to Jewish culture is important. Two, although some people with ecclesiastical training are hired, most have training in recreation and leadership. The academic training may consist of a recreation diploma from a college, or a recreation, physical education, or leadership degree from a university. Three, a faith-based recreation leader must nurture the faith, or the culture in the case of the Jewish leaders, through recreation in people of various backgrounds. Although some of this nurturing involves specific spiritual instruction, the nurturing may also be primarily focused on encouraging friendships within the group.

Web Sites to EXPLORE

Angel City Fitness: www.verizonsupersite.com/
   angelcityfitnessmdrcom/door/
Association of Church Sports and Recreation Minis-
   ters: www.csrm.org
Best Catholic Links: www.catholicity.com/links/
   categories.html?catid=29
Canadian Jewish Congress: www.cjc.ca
Christian Camping International Canada:
   http://ccicanada.gospelcom.net
Germantown Baptist Church: www.gbconline.net/
   templates/cusgermantown/Details.asp?id=20898
   &PID=39131&RID=39120
Islamic Circle of North America: www.icna.com
Islamic Society of North America: www.isna.net
Jewish Community Centers Maccabi Games:
   www.jccmaccabi.org/index_home.php
Jewish Community Centers of North America:
   www.jcca.org

Jewish Community Centre of Greater Vancouver:
   www.jccgv.bc.ca
KidsGames: www.kidsgames.com
Lord's Gym and Fitness Centers:
   www.lordsgymbirmingham.com
Maccabi Canada: www.maccabicanada.com
Maccabi USA: www.maccabiusa.com
Machers—your gateway to the Jewish community:
   www.machers.com/Default.aspx?tabid=393
Muslim Students Association of the United
   States and Canada: www.unl.edu:2020/alpha/
   Muslim_Students_Association_of_the_US_and_
   Canada.html
Peachtree Presbyterian Church:
   www.peachtreepres.org/ministries/
   recreation.html
Penn State Holy Day Observance Letter and Calen-
   dar: www.psu.edu/advising/calendar.htm, then
   click on "Holy Day Letter and Calendar."

SUMMARY

Most North Americans identify with some form of religion. Each ideology presents clear and unique ramifications on the way followers engage in recreation. Religious institutions play an important role in advising their members on the importance of recreation and, in many cases, in providing opportunities for their members and those from the broader community to take advantage of recreational activities.

Employee or Corporate Recreation and Wellness

The provision of employee services, or life style benefits, including recreation activities and programs, does much to improve employee morale, can help reduce employee turnover, and can go a long way to increasing employee productivity—and the resulting improved bottom line.

> *Roger A. Lancaster, general manager of the U.S. Department of Agriculture Employee Services and Recreation Association, past president of the Employee Services Management Association, and a member of its board of directors.*

For many in the workforce, trying to balance work, personal and family life, and recreation presents a constant juggling act. Because people spend the greater part of their day at work, employers and corporations have realized the important role that exercise, sports, fitness, recreation, and wellness play in the lives of their employees and how these factors are necessary for corporate wellness, too.

HISTORY

Corporate, or employee, recreation and wellness is not a new concept. In the late 19th century, the Pullman Company, manufacturer of Pullman sleeping train cars, was one of the first companies in America to implement an employee recreation and fitness program and later went on to form a company athletic association.

In that same era, John H. Patterson, president of the National Cash Register Company, invited employees to accompany him on predawn horseback rides before the workday. A decade later Patterson introduced morning and afternoon exercise breaks for his workers and later established a 325-acre (131.5 hectare) company recreation park.

The trend of companies implementing recreational programs for employees continued. In

1941, the National Industrial Recreation Association (NIRA) formed. The NIRA continued to expand employee and corporate fitness and wellness until it became the Employee Services Management (ESM) Association in 2000. The ESM Association is the only international association in its field and represents more than 5,000 corporations and 22 million employees by keeping members abreast of trends and assisting them in their implementation of corporate health, fitness, and recreation programs. ESM services include publications, research, consultation, a reference library, conferences and workshops, program awards, certification, merchandise discounts, travel programs, and internships in employee services (Employee Services Management Association, 2004). Although ESM is comprehensive in nature, its top 10 program areas include sports leagues and special-interest clubs, special events, and wellness for member corporations.

The association offers those responsible for administering employee services and recreational activities in government and private industry an opportunity to exchange ideas, knowledge, and expertise in order to develop programs that are beneficial to employers, improve their company's bottom line, and solve problems facing those in the employee services profession (Employee Services Management Association, 2004).

EMPLOYEE RECREATION BENEFITS AND SERVICES

Corporations across the United States and Canada have realized the importance of healthy employees. At the heart of employee recreation is the belief that active employees will benefit corporate wellness through an increase in productivity. Participants, through involvement in sports and special interest clubs, develop new or enhance their skills and leadership. On a personal level, employees benefit from weight management, athletic achievement, long-term disease prevention, and personal confidence and a sense of well-being. These benefits result in a decrease in sick leave and injury rates, which in turn creates decreased health insurance premiums and saves lives (Recreation, Health and Exercise Consultants, Inc., n.d.).

Employee recreation sites include small and large corporations, nonprofit organizations,

government and health care–based work environments (Staying Fit in 2004). For example, the U.S. Department of Agriculture (USDA), at its Washington, DC, site, operates four fitness centers, serving 16,000 employees. Nationwide, the USDA Employee Services and Recreation Association (USDA/ESRA) serves 110,000 field employees throughout the nation (Browning, 2003).

Beyond on-site fitness and sports, other employee recreation programs include hobby clubs and special interest groups. Lockheed Martin Recreation Association, located in Ft. Worth, Texas, offers employees 23 recreation activities and facilities that include sports, jewelry making, a stained-glass shop, and photography courses and a darkroom. One of the most successful programs has been a facility for model trains, which has grown significantly since its inception 21 years ago and has won numerous corporate awards (Higby, 2003).

In addition to implementing fitness and recreation services in-house, these activities can be provided by outside organizations. For example, parks and recreation districts offer corporate fitness programming. Other opportunities for outsourcing recreation services include companies that provide specialized recreation support through team-building programs, recreation adventures, recreational activities to celebrate events, and the hosting of special corporate events.

TRENDS IN EMPLOYEE RECREATION

In a 2004 ESM survey, softball and golf topped the list of sports programs that companies offer employees, but other recreational activities are on the rise. With the growing health risks from obesity, employees, insurers, and corporations are focusing on physical activity and fitness. Employee programs in sports and fitness—indoors or outdoors, in employee fitness facilities or in the community—can support a healthier and more productive workforce. On-site indoor facilities predominately focus on fitness programs; sports programs such as volleyball and basketball are the next most common. Some companies have outdoor facilities such as softball fields, tennis courts, and fitness trails. Programs for bowling and indoor soccer are gaining in popularity.

Outstanding Employee Recreation Program

Recreation and Fitness

SAS Institute, a business software design company, believes that employees' health can be improved and stress reduced by offering employees and their families excellent facilities and programs for fitness, wellness, and recreation. The recreation and fitness program is company sponsored and is available to all employees. In 2003, use of the Recreation and Fitness Center jumped to 145,000 visits logged by more than 3,400 employees and their family members.

The company opened its 26,000-square-foot on-site Recreation and Fitness Center (RFC) in December 1985. An expansion in 1998 increased the size of the facility to nearly 35,000 square feet (3,251 square meters), and a 17,000-square-foot (1,579-square-meter), 10-lane natatorium opened in 1999. The RFC is equipped with a gymnasium, a weight room, racquetball courts, locker rooms, an aerobic exercise room, and a meeting place. The RFC develops fitness activities, programs for wellness and leisure, and special recreational events. Outdoor facilities include soccer fields, softball fields, golf putting green, walking and jogging trails, and tennis courts. Ninety percent of the company's employees use the RFC, and 70 percent use it on a regular basis. Employees in the regional offices may join a local fitness center at the company's expense.

The RFC continues to increase employee interest and involvement by providing diverse programs such as fitness counseling, one-to-one prenatal exercise, aerobics, and competitive sports. Employees can receive personal training and nutrition counseling. The RFC's incentive program encourages and rewards participation in RFC programs. Beginners and those already involved in a regular exercise routine may choose to participate in one or several motivational and reward systems.

The RFC works in conjunction with the Health Care Center to develop wellness programs of interest and value to the more than 4,000 employees at the Cary, North Carolina, headquarters. The RFC publicizes all recreational and leisure events and activities in the *Recreation and Fitness* newsletter, on bulletin boards, in the company cafe, and on the Intranet.

A special events calendar offers employees a variety of activities. Employee trips to ski resorts in the United States and Europe are coordinated by the RFC. Each year the RFC organizes a white-water rafting trip, a bus trip to the North Carolina Zoo, a golf tournament, a fishing rodeo, and outings to area baseball games to offer warm-weather relaxation to employees and their families. Discount tickets are available through the RFC to area movie theaters; Disney World and other southeast amusement parks; the Biltmore Estate in Asheville, North Carolina; and area events as they are scheduled.

The RFC's programs have helped the company win the North Carolina Governor's Award for Fitness and Health in Business for three consecutive years, and three Eastwood Awards from the National Employee Services and Recreation Association.

Wellness Program

SAS Institute values employee health, well-being, and personal and professional growth, and believes that an extensive wellness program will help its employees to lead healthier lives. The Health Care Center staff works in conjunction with the recreation and fitness staff to develop wellness programs of interest and value to all employees. A full-time wellness coordinator joined the recreation and fitness staff in 1991 to work directly with the Health Care Center and the work life department to coordinate these programs.

Wellness programs are usually offered as lunchtime seminars and are available to all employees and their families at no cost. Programs are designed to help employees lead a healthier, richer, less stressful, and more enjoyable life. Each month, four to six different wellness programs are offered to employees on topics that fall into one of five wellness categories: physical, psychological, nutrition, social, and fitness. A member of the Health Care Center or Recreation and Fitness Center staff or an outside expert administers the wellness activities. Titles of recent seminars include "Preventing Marital Atrophy," "Climbing the Activity Pyramid," "Burn Prevention," "Taking Control of Your Financial Life," "Surgery for Better Sight," "Cross-Cultural Relationships," "Computer Vision Syndrome," and "Stress, Anxiety, and Panic—Where's the Tiger?"

Programs for expectant mothers and parents including classroom instruction in prenatal health and fitness are available on an ongoing basis. For instance, Pre-Natal to Cradle, a program started in 1993, offers comprehensive one-to-one counseling on fitness, nutrition, and other health issues to the company's expectant mothers. The U.S. Senate and Childhelp USA have recognized SAS for its prenatal wellness program.

In 1995, on-site massage became available by appointment through the Wellness Center. Employees choose from a list of nine contractual, certified massage therapists for a full massage or a 20-minute chair massage at the Wellness Center. Fees are payroll deducted.

SUMMARY

The top priority for recreation programs is to help employees stay fit and adopt healthy lifestyles through mind and body exercises and functional fitness opportunities in an attempt to lower health care costs for the employee and the employer.

Recreation in the Armed Forces

Jeff Temple and Laurie Ogilvie

"Serving Those Who Serve" is not just a motto; it's a commitment to ensuring that the members of the Canadian Forces are fit, focused and operationally ready. Provision of recreational opportunities for them and their families is a key part of that commitment.

Major General Langton, CEO Canadian Forces Personnel Support Agency

We are dedicated to providing support and leisure services that are as outstanding as the people we serve.

United States Army Morale, Welfare and Recreation

Recreation programs in the Canadian and the United States armed forces are based on two basic philosophies: that members of the military and their families are entitled to the same quality of life as is afforded the society that they protect and that quality recreation programs have a direct impact on mission readiness and retention. Recreation programs are designed to maintain a positive quality of life that leads to a sound mind and body, a productive community, and a strong family environment. Recreation programs for the Canadian and U.S. armed forces have unique requirements that set them apart from other public-sector programs. These programs must support military personnel and their families at their home stations as well as in deployed environments at remote sites around the world.

HISTORY

Recreation and other **morale and welfare** programs have existed in both Canada and the United States for hundreds of years. Recreation and other morale and welfare type programs have existed in the United States Army for hundreds of years. Organized programs started on the battlefields of the Revolutionary War where "sutlers" were assigned the responsibility of providing for the personal needs of the soldiers. These sutlers were the premise for what we now see as the Army Air Force Exchange Service, and a portion of their profits were returned to the units. These unit funds were the early structure under which our current recreation program is funded, and the funds were used for a variety of leisure-type activities to include reading libraries, financial assistance programs, bands, and school projects. In fact, the "fife and drum corps" was the earliest organized recreation program in a wartime environment.

By the Civil War, sutlers had made themselves extinct by pricing themselves out of business, and their roles were assumed by "Canteen Associations," which became the essential social club for the unit and were authorized by Congress in 1893. According to the Office of the Secretary of Defense, "these activities had naturally become centers for command sponsored social events and were recognized as important for promoting esprit de corps" (Potter, 2001). Organized programs started on the battlefields of World War I, where the Salvation Army and Red Cross members ministered to the needs of soldiers as the forerunners of today's recreation specialists.

In 1940, at the beginning of World War II, the U.S. Morale Division, later named Special Services, was established in the U.S. Army. Between 1946 and 1955, core recreation programs were established and staffed by a combination of active-duty military personnel and civilians. Until the mid-1980s, active-duty personnel held occupational specialties in Special Services at every level of command. As those specialties were discontinued, civilians continued to operate programs with military oversight as the program requirements grew and the senior commanders came to understand the value of recreation in readiness and retention.

In Canada, it has long been recognized that the success of the Canadian military depends on the physical, emotional, and spiritual well-being of the **military community.** Throughout the history of the Canadian military, morale and welfare programs have been available to all serving members and their families with the goal of enhancing the quality of life of the military community and contributing to the **operational readiness and effectiveness** of the armed forces. In 1996, the **Canadian Forces Personnel Support Agency** was created with the mission of providing the military community with morale and welfare programs and services.

Today, in both Canada and the United States, recreation programs within the military environment are broad in scope, evolving constantly to meet the ever changing needs of the military community. The United States' morale and welfare service departments use the common acronym **MWR** for **Morale, Welfare and Recreation** to refer to these programs, while in Canada, the **PSP Division,** or the **Personnel Support Division** of the Canadian Forces Personnel Support Agency, is the key provider of recreational services within the military environment.

The Canadian military community recreation program is similar to the recreational agenda of the United States Armed Forces, although the scope and service delivery processes vary slightly. Overall, the goal of military recreation in both Canada and the United States is to maintain and enhance the morale and welfare of military members and their families, such that the operational readiness and effectiveness of the armed forces are assured. How this goal is achieved is formalized differently in each country. Specifically, the oversight for providing recreation services in the United States is governed by specific agencies within each branch of the military. In Canada, one agency oversees recreation for each of the three branches of the military.

MWR and PSP programs play an important role in the military community. MWR and PSP provide support through community-development activities, events, and celebrations, uniting and strengthening the military community. MWR and PSP focus on building a community through programs that promote social and personal growth, fellowship and networking, strong cooperative relationships, and, ultimately, a strengthening of the military esprit de corps.

Recreation programs are key factors in personal and professional growth. **Military service members** continually train to build skills and stay sharp, promoting personal growth, self-enrichment, learning, and discovery. Recreation programs comprise a significant part of the military community's safety net by promoting personal and family stability while providing peace of mind while engaging in challenging and difficult missions. Being a member of today's armed forces is tough and demanding. Soldiers need balance and time to recover from a hard day's work and to relax, recharge, renew, and rejuvenate. According to Rear Admiral James B. Hinkle, U.S. Navy, assistant chief of naval personnel for personal readiness and community support, this can be accomplished through MWR:

> MWR's principal mission is to provide a varied program of wholesome, constructive off-duty recreation and leisure opportunities that promote the mental, physical, and social well-being of sailors and their families. These programs enhance readiness and retention by fostering teamwork, fitness, a positive mental outlook, improved morale, and a healthy alternative to substance abuse (www.house.gov/hasc/testimony/105thcongress/98-3-12Hinkle.htm).

MILITARY VERSUS CIVILIAN RECREATION

Military recreation departments are administered similarly to civilian recreation departments. Many of the programs, such as swimming lessons, leadership certifications, and recreation club activities are conducted in partnership with, or modeled on the products of, civilian agencies. Like their civilian counterparts, military recreation departments also employ many operational tools to more efficiently manage and profile programs and services. From recreation management software to online recreation brochures, military recreation strives to encourage participation, increase patronage, and enhance the benefits of recreational participation.

Although military recreation is modeled after civilian recreation programs, the unique environment and requirements of the military community result in several distinct differences between the two services providers. One of the key differences is the transient nature of the client. Military families relocate frequently. Programs and services based on the expressed need of the military community one year may be quite different the next as the families who make up the community relocate. Recreation professionals must constantly survey the military community, aware of the changing needs and interests of military families.

Secondly, many military communities are located in remote or unstable places around the world. Recreation opportunities are as important to the serving members in isolated or combat environ-

ments as they are to members and their families at the home station. Recreation professionals must be prepared and willing to provide services under difficult and sometimes dangerous conditions.

A third difference between civilian and military recreation is the scope of the recreation department. Civilian recreation departments provide service to the residents of their community and other interested users. Military recreation departments are exclusive, providing service to military members, their families, and other members of the military community.

Lastly, volunteer management can be challenging within the military community. Volunteers are a key contributor to the success of the military community recreation program. Without volunteers, many programs would be unsustainable, but with the high turnover of military families, managing volunteers is often difficult. MWR and PSP have developed viable volunteer management programs, striving to develop, support, and nurture the involvement of volunteers in recreational programs.

UNITED STATES ARMED FORCES

The United States Department of Defense provides a variety of recreation programs that, although tailored to each specific branch, improve the morale of its personnel and provide incentives for retention. Defense leadership firmly believes that recreation programs are a vital factor in maintaining each force's ability to fight and win its nation's wars. They also believe that their fighting forces need a balance of work and leisure in order to be ready to fight when needed. As well, the defense leadership believes that families left behind during a deployment must be cared for so that the soldier can fight without worrying about those left at home. Although each branch uses a different acronym and the scope of each program may vary, the mission is the same: to provide quality recreation programs to the United States' fighting forces, both at home and abroad.

Department of Navy

The U.S. Navy Morale, Welfare and Recreation Division, located in Memphis, Tennessee, administers a varied program of recreation, social, and community-support activities at U.S. Navy facilities worldwide. These programs provide active-duty, reserve,

OUTSTANDING *Graduates*

Courtesy of John Powell

Background Information

Name: John Kelly Powell

Education: Bachelor of science and master of science, Indiana University, School of Health, Physical Education, and Recreation

Special Awards: Indiana University, Lebert H. Weir Award for the Outstanding Graduate Student; Department of Navy Meritorious Civilian Service Award; Secretary of Defense Certificate of Appreciation; Department of Defense Award for Excellence; Indiana University Eppley Distinguished Alumni Award

Special Affiliations: Athletic Business Advisory Board, member

Career Information

Position: Head of Mission Essential Branch of the Morale, Welfare and Recreation Division for the United States Navy, Memphis, Tennessee

Organization: The Mission Essential Branch of the Morale, Welfare and Recreation (MWR) headquarters employs 10 staff members. It is estimated that more than 3.2 million active-duty personnel, dependents, and retired patrons out of a total authorized population of 3.5 million used MWR fitness programs, services, and facilities this past year.

Organization's Mission: Our branch is responsible for providing policy and guidance for the administration of the following programs: Fleet Readiness (Fleet Recreation and Liberty-Recreation Center for Young Sailors) , Navy Fitness (fitness, recreational sports, health promotions, aquatics, physical readiness, and nutrition programs), and Navy Sports (all-navy, armed forces, national, and international competitions).

Job Description: To meet the needs of the navy community, we have approximately 1,018 personnel working in MWR fitness and sports programs worldwide. Oversee approximately 200 MWR personnel providing Liberty programs and services worldwide. Oversee 32 fleet recreation coordinators and 18 afloat recreation specialists and 10 afloat fitness directors in direct support of deploying units.

Advice to Undergraduates

Always do your *very best* on every task you are given or assigned. There is no room for anything less than your best effort.

---

and retired Navy personnel and their families with sports and physical fitness activities, child development and youth programs, and a variety of food and beverage services. The mission is to provide quality support and recreational services that contribute to the retention and readiness and the mental, physical, and emotional well-being of sailors.

The navy serves the needs of its members around the world at installations and on board ships at sea, while ensuring a consistent level of high-quality service. Civilian recreation specialists carry out this mission work on installations in the United States and overseas and are assigned on board most of the navy's larger ships to manage MWR programs and services.

United States Marine Corps

The Marine Corps manages the MWR program through its headquarters in Quantico, Virginia, and provides fitness and recreation programs, personal

services, and business activities to directly support individual and family readiness and retention. The vision of the Marine Corps MWR program is to "make a difference in the lives of marines, sailors, and families by doing the right things the right way." The Semper Fit Branch "develops plans and policies and provides resources to sustain and enhance recruitment, retention, and operational readiness and improve the quality of life for marines and their families around the world," in peacetime and in war. The MWR teams strive to provide marines and their families with programs that promote optimal health, quality of life, and operational readiness.

Department of Army

The U.S. Army administers an MWR program through its headquarters office of the Community Family Support Center (CFSC) in Alexandria, Virginia, and supports the following mission:

To serve the needs, interests and responsibilities of each individual in the Army community with support and leisure services designed to enhance the quality of their lives for as long as they are associated with the Army, no matter where they are. MWR programs are designed to meet the needs of all active, Reserve, and Guard soldiers, civilian employees, retirees, and family members by informing them of and connecting them to a broad range of programs—from family, child and youth services to recreation, sports, entertainment, travel and leisure activities. MWR programs maintain service quality, which ensures that all programs deliver real value, are truly enjoyed and have adequate participation to guarantee their availability when needed.

MWR provides leisure products and services in the belief that these programs directly contribute to recruiting, sustaining, and retaining the ready force, providing the same quality of life as that of the society the soldiers are pledged to defend. Army MWR provides a significant benefit that not only supports soldiers and their families but is also a major element in the enlistment and retention of the new recruits. The unique challenge to the army is the requirement to provide the same level of support to troops around the world regardless of the existence of a viable base (location can vary from an actual military post in the United States to a tent in the desert).

Department of Air Force

The U.S. Air Force operates MWR programs through its headquarters office in San Antonio, Texas, under the title of Services Squadron. The following is the mission of the Air Force's MWR program:

Canadian Forces members at CFB Trenton engaging in physical training.

Canadian Forces Personnel Support Agency (1999)

To contribute to readiness and improve productivity through programs promoting fitness, esprit de corps and quality of life for Air Force People. Provide policy and direction for the worldwide Services program, which includes fitness, peacetime and wartime feeding, mortuary, lodging, child development and youth programs, a wide spectrum of recreation activities, and business operations like golf, bowling and clubs to help sustain AF mission.

Although not normally considered recreation programs, the air force has included activities such as mortuary services and wartime feeding under the umbrella of MWR services, which makes its program delivery broader than those of the other service branches.

Department of Homeland Security

Since 2002, the U.S. Coast Guard has been aligned under the newly established Department of Homeland Security and no longer falls under the umbrella of the Department of Defense. However, the Coast Guard, as part of the armed forces of the United States, provides recreation programs to its members worldwide. Although it is the smallest of the service branches, it offers a critical element in the quality-of-life programming for its members and their families. The mission of the Coast Guard MWR program, operating out of Chesapeake, Virginia, is to uplift the spirits of the Coast Guard family and be an essential element of Coast Guard mission readiness and retention through customer-owned and driven MWR programs and services around the world.

CANADIAN ARMED FORCES

The mission of the **Canadian armed forces,** or the Department of National Defense, is to protect Canada, defend North America in cooperation with the United States, and to contribute to peace and international security. The Department of National Defense is one of the few Canadian institutions that reside exclusively under the authority of the federal government, with a presence in every Canadian province and territory, and represents the cultural, linguistic, and regional diversity of Canada. The Canadian Department of National Defense represents the many values that unite Canadians, such as helping those at home and abroad, peacekeeping, and protecting Canada.

The Department of National Defense is made up of more than 100,000 Canadians including members of the regular force, the reserve force, the Canadian Rangers, and civilian employees of defense. Within the Canadian Department of National Defense are three Environmental Commands: the Maritime Command, the Land Force, and the Air Command and numerous support divisions.

- **Maritime Command.** The goal of Canada's navy is to conduct surveillance operations to protect the sovereignty of Canadian coasts and to defend Canadian waters against illegal fishing and ecological damage. The navy also supports international initiatives for peace and humanitarian assistance.

- **Land Force Command.** The mission of Canada's army is to perform and support peacekeeping, combat operations, and disaster recovery missions at home and abroad. In times of crises, the army delivers assistance and helps civil authorities restore public order.

- **Air Command.** Canada's air force provides surveillance and control of Canada's airspace, provides air transport of Canadian military personnel and equipment throughout the world, and supports army and navy operations. As with the other commands, the air force assists with humanitarian relief operations.

- **Military Community.** The Department of National Defense is made up of more than the navy, army, and air force members. Supporting departments, civilians, and military families contribute to the ongoing operations and continuity of the military community. Today, the military is present in more than 3,000 communities across Canada, with military members and their families representing more than half a million of the Canadian population.

Support for the Canadian armed forces' morale and welfare programs is administered through the Canadian Forces Personnel Support Agency's headquarters, located in Ottawa, Ontario. The mission of the Canadian Forces Personnel Support Agency is "to enhance the quality of life of the military community and contribute to the operational readiness and effectiveness of the Canadian Forces" (www.cfpsa.com/en/NewsCentre/index.asp, 2005).

Canadian Morale and Welfare Programs

Throughout Canada and locations around the world, the Canadian Forces Personnel Support Agency delivers morale and welfare programs, facilities, and instruction to maintain military physical fitness and health. Physical education, leisure, and recreation opportunities are key components of the Canadian military morale and welfare program. Physical education programs are the primary means of ensuring that military personnel maintain required levels of physical fitness, while recreation programs make a positive contribution to a stable military environment and contribute to high levels of morale and operational efficiency.

In each military community, the Canadian Forces Personnel Support Agency offers a variety of fitness, recreation, sport, leisure, and special-interest programs and services to military members and their families. Gyms, field houses, swimming pools, golf courses, bowling alleys, meeting places for hobby clubs, sport fields, and arenas make up some of the facilities available in almost all Canadian military communities.

Recreation is a key component of the Canadian Forces Personnel Support Agency's mission to enhance the morale and welfare of the Canadian military. A well-balanced recreation program helps maintain total fitness, while reducing mental fatigue, tension, and frustration, all of which can develop within the military operational setting. In addition to the benefits of recreational participation for the military member, the well-being of the military family is a main consideration of the recreation mandate. Because of operational requirements, many military families live in remote communities, relocate frequently, and often live without the military member at home because of operational deployments. A comprehensive, varied, and universal recreation program gives military members assurance that their family is well cared for in their absence, and provides the military family with opportunities to engage in the community while maintaining or enhancing their personal morale and welfare.

Canadian Military Recreation Principles

The military recreation program is founded on seven governing principles, which support numerous recreation program components. The governing principles serve to

- provide inclusive, creative, and diversified recreation opportunities for the military community;
- address the physical, emotional, and social characteristics, interests, and needs of all members of the military community equally and consistently;
- operate according to the needs and interest of the military community, making optimal use of supporting resources;
- provide opportunities for leadership development;
- create opportunities for individual and group growth and development through responsibility, accountability, and leadership in the planning and operating of recreational activities;
- nurture partnerships with recognized recreational agencies for the provision of high-quality, responsive recreational services; and
- ensure that recreational services are governed in accordance with Canadian military financial, operating, and management policies.

MILITARY RECREATION PROGRAM AREAS

In both Canada and the United States, the recreation mandate operates to serve a variety of MWR and PSP program offerings. These are sports and fitness, skill development, libraries, outdoor recreation, child and youth activities, recreation centers, special events and entertainment, business activities, recreation clubs, and private organizations.

Sports and Fitness

At the heart of every recreation program is the sports and fitness program. Because of the need to maintain a strong and healthy force, sports and fitness programs have long been recognized by military leadership as a key to mission readiness and have become the centerpiece of every MWR and PSP organization. These programs offer state-of-the-art gymnasium and fitness facilities as well as organized sports competitions from intramural to competitive levels.

Skill Development

A staple of the military recreation program's inventory is skill development through instructional classes. Instructional classes are organized in response to a community's interest in skill development and leadership opportunities. Instructional classes include specialty cardio workouts and aerobics, arts and crafts, camps, swimming lessons, weight training for youth, sport clinics, and leadership development. Programs are available for all ages and interests and are developed and implemented in consultation with members of the military community.

Libraries

Libraries remain a vital part of most MWR programs in areas where the local communities cannot provide adequate or convenient services to the military population. Libraries vary in size and offerings but generally provide standard recreational reading inventories, reading programs, educational studies, research materials, Internet and e-mail services, and support services. Library programs have become especially crucial in supporting troops in deployed locations and on ships at sea around the world where no local civilian resources are available.

Outdoor Recreation

Outdoor recreation programs provide outdoor equipment and access to campgrounds, parks, beaches, and lakes as well as adventure programs and other activities that promote the care and protection of our natural resources. Because of the huge land masses placed under the care of military installations, myriad outdoor recreation opportunities are available. Military organizations are entrusted with the care and preservation of valuable natural resources and that responsibility provides the opportunity for military personnel to develop new skills while preserving and enjoying natural resources around the world.

Child and Youth Activities

Child and youth programs and services are offered at all military locations where family support is offered. Programs offer various levels of support that include child development centers, youth centers, and youth activities such as skill development and sports programs. All programs are age appro-

priate and offer activities that focus on supporting transition, easing the stress of relocation, building and sustaining meaningful relationships, and developing a sense of belonging within the community. Activities that provide universal access to information, tools, resources, and services that support youth; activities that focus on the promotion of healthy and fulfilling life choices; and activities that encourage the development of leadership and assets in youth (40 assets developed by the Search Institute, www.search-institute.org) are also central to the recreation mandate.

Recreation Centers

Each military community offers a variety of drop-in opportunities for casual participation in unorganized recreation. Access to facilities and recreational services is available to military members as well as their families and provides a safe and comfortable environment for self-directed activities as well as for designed programs.

Special Events and Entertainment

Each military community offers a variety of special events annually to profile military community activities and accomplishments, while honoring the contributions of volunteers and community partners. Many services host worldwide concert series tours, which provide live entertainment to troops, while others focus on local events and festivals.

Business Activities

A variety of pay-as-you-go activities geared toward leisure and fitness pursuits are available at most military locations. Theaters, golf courses, special-interest clubs, restaurants, night clubs, and bowling centers are popular activities enjoyed by military families. The operation of these types of commercial services are generally offered when no local off-base resources are readily available. These operations provide military members the type of services available in most civilian communities and provide a revenue source to support other morale and welfare activities.

Recreation Clubs and Private Organizations

Recreation clubs or private organizations are self-governing and self-funded entities operated for and by specific-interest groups in accordance with established constitutions and bylaws. Recreation club constitutions and bylaws are military directives that outline club operating principles and member codes of conduct. All recreation clubs are managed by a volunteer executive council and governed by its membership. Examples of recreation club activities include specialty arts, scuba, running, wood hobbies, sailing or marinas, martial arts, gymnastics, swimming, figure skating, and dancing and activities for auto and motorcycle, saddle, and rod and gun enthusiasts. These organizations are authorized when the MWR or PSP program cannot carry out programs in a viable manner because of resource limitations or when a special-interest group is willing and able to operate a self-directed program.

EMPLOYMENT OPPORTUNITIES

Military recreation provides vast employment opportunities because of the thousands of civilian employees around the world that make up the various MWR and PSP organizations. MWR employs more than 100,000 people in the United States and overseas. People entering employment in military recreation programs generally begin in a specialty such as outdoor recreation, club manager, or child development specialist and then move into general management positions within the personnel system. The personnel system may be paid for with federal tax dollars (appropriated funds) or paid for with funds generated in the field (nonappropriated funds); both systems are parallel and considered civil service with portability between each. Careers in MWR are varied but generally start out at the entry level with progressions to the top of the civil service advancement ladder.

MWR assigns people to a variety of locations: from the beaches of California to the sands of the Afghan desert to the icy rivers of Alaska and the high seas of the Atlantic. The variety of both the job and the location means there's little opportunity for boredom in the business of providing recreation programs to the armed forces. MWR employees work hard so that others can have fun and enjoy life, and they do it seven days a week, sometimes 24 hours a day. The benefits of a career in MWR range from the great potential for upward mobility to the opportunity to travel and live abroad. See Web Sites to Explore for Internet links for employment within United States Armed Forces recreation programs.

Web Sites to EXPLORE

Air Force: www.nafjobs.com
Army: http://mwrjobs.army.mil
Coast Guard: www.uscg.mil/mwr/
Marine Corps: www.usmc-mccs.org/employ/index.cfm
Navy: www.mwr.navy.mil

In Canada, the Canadian Forces Personnel Support Agency is the largest employer of physical education, human kinetics, and leisure study graduates. The variety of positions and the potential for mobility between Canadian military locations contribute to the attractiveness of a career in the Canadian military recreation field. Most recreation positions within the Canadian Forces Personnel Support Agency require an undergraduate degree or college diploma plus specific qualifications, such as lifeguarding and first aid certifications or volunteer management certificates to match the position's requirements. Some senior management and director positions require postgraduate degrees and specialty knowledge and experience in the field of military morale and welfare. Furthermore, in recognition of Canada's linguistic diversity, most positions with the Canadian Forces Personnel Support Agency require proficiency in both French and English.

Each Canadian military recreation department is composed of a recreation director and various program-specific support staff, for example, an aquatics supervisor, a youth programmer, or an administration coordinator. Part-time staff, such as lifeguards, camp staff, and youth center monitors also provide programs directly to the military family. Throughout Canada, the Canadian Forces Personnel Support Agency employs more than 5,600 staff to deliver and support morale and welfare programming.

For more information on a career with the Canadian Forces Personnel Support Agency, contact www.CFPSA.com.

SUMMARY

Nearly everyone, if not all, in the profession of armed forces recreation would tell you that they feel that they make a valuable contribution to the mission of the armed forces and are very proud to serve those who serve. Armed forces recreation professionals work around the world and strive to improve the quality of life for sailors, soldiers, airmen, marines, and coast guardsmen and their families serving their countries in difficult and challenging times.

Armed forces recreation professionals are proud to support their country's military mission because they believe in the importance of what they do for the armed forces and understand the impact that they have on mission readiness and, ultimately, the defense of their country. Much like their counterparts in the civilian sector, military recreation professionals must strive to ensure that the programs they provide are beneficial.

CHAPTER 12

Leisure and Recreation Across the Life Span

Laura L. Payne and Lynn A. Barnett

Courtesy of San Jose Parks, Recreation and Neighborhood Services

People do not cease to play
because they grow old;
people grow old because
they cease to play.

George Bernard Shaw, playwright

CHAPTER OBJECTIVES

After reading this chapter, you should be able to do the following:

- Describe the developmental characteristics for each life stage that are the most relevant to the design and delivery of leisure and recreation services
- Explain how these developmental characteristics affect leisure and recreation programs
- Describe model programs from different leisure and recreation sponsoring sectors that effectively address developmental characteristics through their program content and format

INTRODUCTION

The leisure and recreation industry is one of the largest in the world and increasingly plays a prominent role as a social and behavioral force. The role of leisure and recreation is recognized in national imperatives to improve physical and mental health; decrease risky behaviors such as substance use, sex, and vandalism among youth; and foster valuable social relationships among community members. As the industry has grown, there has been a corresponding shift in the overall mission of leisure and recreation services from fun and games to a focus on benefits that can be achieved through leisure and recreation engagement. This philosophical shift emphasizes that the activity itself is not the end point but rather the activity is the vehicle by which outcomes such as challenge, accomplishment, self-efficacy, self-expression, and enjoyment are accomplished. When programmers carefully consider how to manage the components of the leisure experience (facility, equipment, leadership) and appropriately address the developmental characteristics of the target audience, they greatly increase their ability to facilitate a leisure experience among participants. In short, becoming an excellent recreation program planner or supervisor hinges on your ability to design the program from the participant's perspective, keeping their characteristics, abilities, needs, and interests in mind.

Developmental psychologists generally describe development from three perspectives: **physical abilities** (physical growth, motor development, and sensory and perceptual development), **cognitive abilities** (thinking, reasoning, learning, memory, intelligence, and language), and **socioemotional characteristics** (personality, emotional and moral development, self-concept, identity, and social relationships). These three categories are used to discuss the nature of development within the seven life stages: **infancy** (birth to 2 years), **early childhood** (3 to 6 years), **middle and late childhood** (7 to 12 years), adolescence (13 to 19 years), **early adulthood** (20 to 39 years), **middle adulthood** (40 to 59 years), and **late adulthood** (60 years and older). For each of these stages, developmental highlights are presented, key points for programming are offered, and examples of programs from various service sectors are discussed. This discussion of developmental characteristics and programming considerations is by no means intended to be comprehensive. Instead, the authors wish to introduce and familiarize you with some of the ways in which development shapes leisure engagement, and affords an important perspective from which to generate leisure opportunities and services.

INFANCY: FROM BABY TO TODDLER

Infancy is the time from birth until approximately 2 years of age. Rapid change occurs over this two-year period that affects how the infant or toddler functions and interacts with the world around her. Physical, cognitive, and socioemotional milestones of this developmental stage are presented, followed by considerations for programming and examples from various leisure services sectors.

Developmental Highlights

During this first stage of life infants make large gains in gross (large muscle) motor skills such as sitting up, rolling, and crawling. Cognitively, infants begin to grasp the concept of cause and effect, recognition, and memory. The beginning of infancy is also marked by the need to feel secure, but in the second year of life, as motor and cognitive skills develop, toddlers begin to realize their uniqueness, express their individuality, and initiate interactions with toys and peers. The major physical, cognitive, and socioemotional characteristics associated with this life stage are as follows.

Physical Abilities

The infant's physical development in the first two years is extensive and remarkable. New motor skills are the most dramatic and visible changes that occur in the first year of life, and they significantly increase the ability of infants to move and control their bodies. At birth, infants have little ability to coordinate their trunk or arms, but by their first birthday they can typically walk on their own, and they become increasingly independent in the second year. The age at which infants develop **gross motor skills** varies, but the sequence of these accomplishments remains fairly consistent.

Fine motor skills (small body movements) are more difficult for the toddler to master than gross motor skills because they require the more precise coordination of complex muscle groups. These skills develop in small steps, unlike some gross motor skills that seem to emerge quite suddenly, like standing up. The improvement of fine motor skills over the first two years of life is a reflection of the toddler's increasing eye–hand coordination. The age at which a particular baby first displays a particular motor skill depends on the interaction between inherited and environmental factors. Each infant has a genetic timetable for maturation, which can be faster or slower than that of other infants from other ethnic groups, from the same ethnic group, and even from the same family. The importance of early environmental experiences in the development of motor skills has been demonstrated in several research studies. Child development experts believe that motor activity during this stage is vital to the child's physical and **psychosocial development** and that few restrictions, except for safety reasons, should be placed on their motor escapades.

Cognitive Abilities

It is truly astounding that the infant began life as a single cell and nine months later is born with a brain and nervous system that contains about 100 billion neurons. The newborn's brain at birth is about 25 percent of its adult weight, but by its second birthday it has grown to be about 75 percent of its adult weight. The brain's areas do not mature uniformly: Some areas, such as the primary motor areas, develop earlier than others, such as the primary sensory areas. Shortly after birth, a baby's brain produces trillions more connections between neurons than it can possibly use, and the brain eliminates the connections that are seldom or never used throughout the first 10 years of life.

Before birth, genetic factors primarily direct how the brain establishes basic wiring patterns, but after birth, environmental experiences are important in the development of the brain.

Cognitive development in the first two years of life is extensive. During their first six months, infants have the ability to recognize the properties of objects and are able to mentally sort them into categories. The ability to understand cause-and-effect relationships develops slowly in the first few months of life, and toward the end of the first year, this leads to early problem-solving abilities. By their first birthday, most infants are able to set simple goals for themselves, and they have the knowledge and ability to achieve them. In their second year, toddlers actively experiment with actions and objects and thus find new ways to accomplish their goals. Toward the end of the second year, they are able to mentally manipulate images of objects and behaviors, they can pretend, and they can remember what they saw several days before and then reenact it.

Socioemotional Characteristics

A newborn has a relatively stable and characteristic style of responding to the environment, which can be shaped and modified by later experiences. Research (Chess & Thomas, 1977; Rothbart & Putnam, 2002) has shown that infants have characteristic temperaments. One infant might be cheerful and happy much of the time, while another baby might cry a lot and display a negative mood consistently more often. Infants show their unique personalities by differing from one another in their emotional responses to similar situations. Central to the development of the infant's personality are issues related to trust and independence. The first year of life is characterized by a critical period in which the infant comes to regard the world as a secure place, where basic needs will be readily satisfied, or instead, as an unpredictable place where needs are met only after much crying and sometimes not even then. The development of this sense of security inspires trust and confidence to explore and interact within the world with a minimal amount of fear and apprehension about the future.

In the second year of life, infants are able to recognize themselves and see themselves as having a distinct and unique appearance. Along with this developing sense of self, independence also becomes a more central theme in the toddler's life. Building infants' developing mental and motor abilities and the sense of pride they feel in their new accomplishments, toddlers seek autonomy. If their desire to do things themselves is met with encouragement rather than annoyance and constraints, they will develop a sense of confidence in their abilities. This sense of autonomy felt during the toddler years later gives adolescents the courage to be independent people who can choose and guide their own future.

Infants show clear, unambiguous signs of interest in other infants even during the first few months of life. Babies make efforts to communicate with one another, and by their second year they show elementary signs of peer play. The amount and variety of communication between peers is extensive by the middle of the second year of life: Children show their toys to one another, offer and give one another toys, invite peers to play with them, protest a playmate's actions, and in general, communicate their feelings effectively to one another. As communication becomes more sophisticated in the second year, early signs of cooperative play can be seen.

Considerations for Program Design

Play takes several forms during infancy, and these should be considered when designing programs for even the youngest participant. Much of the play in the first few months of life is **sensorimotor** in nature and meant to stimulate and engage infants because they cannot yet grasp toys or other objects. Infants enjoy vivid colors, bright pictures and sounds from rattles, noisemakers, mobiles, and music boxes. By six months, infants develop the ability to grasp, and they should be given objects to put in their mouth, squeeze, and so on, such as soft balls and blocks, cloth books, and teething toys. At this age, toys that react to an infant's movements by making noise or some other action are preferred by infants because they will be played with longer, and reactive toys tend to engage several senses. For example, a stuffed pig that oinks when a baby touches it and rattles when he shakes it is more interesting than a stuffed animal that does nothing. Between 6 and 12 months, gross

Courtesy of San Jose Parks, Recreation and Neighborhood Services

Toddlers make efforts to communicate with one another, and by their second year they show elementary signs of peer play.

motor skills become more developed, so activities enabling infants and toddlers to throw balls, stack blocks, and fill containers will be popular. During the second year of life, toddlers become much more aware of how objects should be used. For example, rather than banging on a toy lawn mower with a spoon, a child is likely to push the toy lawn mower around a room. Dolls, hand puppets, and stuffed animals are objects toddlers become attached to and use for pretend play. They use boxes or pots and pans as drums and later, close to 2 years old, objects take on more abstract properties. For example, sticks may be used as swords.

Examples From Recreation and Leisure Services Sectors

Public parks and recreation agencies usually offer a variety of programs and services for infants and toddlers. Many programs pair the caregiver with the infant for programs that feature music and movement because they are fun and facilitate motor skill, language, and sensory development. The following are examples of programs offered by the Schaumburg (IL) Park District (Schaumburg Park District, 2004) designed specifically for infants and toddlers:

- **Wiggles, Giggles, and Fun.** This program develops coordination through art, music, and play.
- **Tot Rock.** This program focuses on the development of fine motor skills, refinement of gross motor skills, social development, and sensory stimulation. Activities include songs, group games, and manipulation of rhythm instruments.
- **Infant Chat and Play.** Music and simple toys and play equipment are used to help infants learn the skills of rolling, sitting, and crawling.

Infancy is a time of rapid change and development that acquaint infants with people and objects in their environment. This is also a time when gross motor skills develop and recognition of people, places, and objects occur. Programs should foster development and prepare the infant for the next stage of life: early childhood.

EARLY CHILDHOOD: PRESCHOOL YEARS

Early childhood is the time between the ages of 2 and 6 years. Significant changes occur as toddlers grow taller and stronger and increase their energy level as well as their attention span. Developmental characteristics and programming considerations are presented for preschool children, along with examples from leisure services.

Developmental Highlights

During this time there is significant improvement in fine motor skills, and gross motor skills continue to be refined. Cognitively, children's attention span increases, and they begin to engage in mental reasoning and symbolic thought. Symbolic thinking means that the child is able to think about objects even when the objects are not physically present. In this stage, they have strong desires to explore, take initiatives, and interact with their peers. Pretend play and construction play are the dominant forms of play behavior.

Physical Abilities

During the preschool years, boys and girls slim down as the trunks of their bodies lengthen and body fat decreases. For the first time, sex differences in body type become apparent: Girls have more fatty tissue than boys, and boys have more muscle tissue. Gross motor development during these years improves dramatically as a result of bodies that are slimmer, stronger, and less top-heavy and as brain maturation permits greater control and coordination of the extremities. Children between the ages of two and six move with greater speed and grace, and they become much more capable of directing and fine-tuning their movements.

Fine motor skills also show significant improvement. Although 3-year-old children have had the ability to pick up the tiniest objects for some time, they are still somewhat clumsy at doing so. By the end of this period children can construct buildings with blocks, draw colorful pictures of family members, and use scissors to cut paper with some accuracy. The difficulty that many preschool children experience with tasks requiring fine motor skills is due to the fact that the central nervous system is not yet fully developed.

Cognitive Abilities

The brain continues to grow in early childhood, but it does not grow as rapidly as it did in infancy. Children's emerging cognitive abilities stem from the increasing maturation of the brain combined with enhanced opportunities to experience an increasingly vast and more complicated world. Research has shown that during early childhood, the most rapid growth takes place in the areas of the brain involved in maintaining attention to tasks and in the planning and organizing of new actions (Anderson, Lorch, Field, Collins, & Nathan, 1985; Vurpillot, 1968).

Preschool children's thoughts are determined more by their subjective views of the world than by reality. For example, at 3 years old, children believe that wishes usually come true and that inanimate objects have lifelike qualities and are capable of action. This type of imaginative thinking eventually declines by the later preschool years, thus allowing children the ability to take into account the actions and feelings of others in what they do and say. In other words, children begin to see things from others' perspectives and possibly adapt their behavior accordingly. Early childhood is also a time when mental reasoning emerges, reflecting a transition from primitive to more sophisticated use of symbols. The prevalence of pretend play during this age is a good example of the child's newfound ability to engage in symbolic thought.

The child's ability to pay attention changes significantly during the preschool years. Toddlers wander around, shift attention from one activity to another, and seem to spend little time focused on any one object or event. By comparison, the preschool child is able to spend much longer periods of time on a play episode or watching a video or television program. In addition, as children age, the speed and efficiency with which they can process information increase.

Socioemotional Characteristics

During early childhood, children combine their increasing perceptual, motor, cognitive, and language skills to make things happen. They have a surplus of energy that allows them to venture in new directions and to take new initiatives—even if they seem dangerous. It is during these adventures that they begin to hear their inner voice guiding and judging their activities. This inner voice is an early indication that young children can regulate their actions by considering possible consequences. Their initiatives and enthusiasm may bring them rewards or punishments. Initiatives are supported when children's questions are answered, when they are given the freedom and

As a result of their increased fine motor skills, preschoolers can construct buildings with blocks.

opportunity to initiate motor play, and when they are not derided or inhibited in their fantasy or play activities. In contrast, if children are made to feel that their motor activity is bad, that their questions are a nuisance, or that their play is silly or foolish, they will likely develop a sense of guilt over self-initiated activities that may persist through life's later stages.

As children grow older, peer relationships consume an increasing amount of their time and energy. One of the most important functions of these same-age peer interactions is to provide children a source of information and comparison. At this stage, children are able to compare themselves to others and thus achieve greater understanding of themselves and where they fit in relation to their peers. Research has shown that there is significant value to play with peers: It releases tension, advances cognitive development, increases exploration, promotes attachments with others, helps children deal with problems and traumatic events, and provides a safe haven in which to engage in potentially dangerous behavior (Barnett, 1991). The preschool years are generally recognized as the golden years of pretend, or make-believe play; at no other time in life is a human being so thoroughly involved in the world of fantasy. The ratio of activities involving make-believe to all episodes of free play increases significantly from the age of 3 to the age of 6. Pretend play comprises approximately two-thirds of all of the play of preschool children.

Considerations for Program Design

During this stage of life, children have fairly well-developed large motor skills; thus, activities should afford opportunities for running, kicking, throwing, and catching large soft balls. Memory is also developing rapidly; therefore, games with simple rules can be enjoyed. However, preschool children have limited skills for understanding complex rules, so simpler games such as Tag and Red Light, Green Light work well. In addition, programmers should also be aware that children in this age range are energetic, and their energy often comes in bursts because their endurance is not as developed as that of older children. Young children are capable of sharing with peers, but in a structured program setting, it is best to have enough supplies such as tape, paper, toy cars, and so on for all children so that they do not become jealous, bored, or frustrated.

Examples From Recreation and Leisure Services Sectors

Destination resorts generally offer younger children camp programs to give parents a break for a couple of hours so that they can play tennis or golf or relax by the beach. The following are ideas for specific activities that effectively incorporate developmental characteristics into resort camp programs.

- **Matching memory games.** The memory of younger children is improving at a fast pace, and kids can identify and differentiate between objects. Therefore, matching card games such as Memory are a hit with younger children.

- **Shadow Tag.** This is a simple but fun way to develop coordination, and the only requirement is a sunny day. Take a group of children to a sunny open area, and talk to the group about shadows and how they move when you move. To play the game, all players run and try to tag each other by stepping on one another's shadow. When a player is tagged, he or she is frozen until freed by an untagged person. Once untagged, players run and try to tag another person. The game continues as long as the children are interested in it.

- **Songs.** Children love music, and in early childhood they are becoming adept at learning songs. Songs with actions are also well received by this age group.

Early childhood is a time when children take the initiative to test new skills and abilities. Whether it is gross motor skills, memory, attention, or symbolic play, children in this stage actively use leisure to facilitate their growth and development and further refine skills to carry over into middle childhood and beyond.

MIDDLE AND LATE CHILDHOOD: ELEMENTARY SCHOOL YEARS

Children 7 to 12 years old are in the stage termed middle and late childhood. The developmental tasks of this stage are more sophisticated as cognitive and motor skills become more complex and refined. Physical, cognitive, and socioemotional tasks associated with this stage of development are discussed, and considerations for program planning are presented.

Developmental Highlights

Although physical growth is slower and more consistent during middle and late childhood than in other life stages, cognitive and physical changes improve dramatically. Middle and older children can skillfully manipulate objects, pay attention for longer periods, and think logically. Friendships and being accepted by peers also become important during this stage.

Physical Abilities

During the elementary school years, physical growth is slow and consistent. Improved muscle tone results as muscle mass gradually increases. Children double their strength capabilities during these years, and lung capacity expands, so with each passing year children can run faster and exercise longer. During this period, children's motor development becomes much smoother and more coordinated than it was in early childhood. As children move through the elementary school years, they gain greater control over their bodies and can sit and attend for longer periods. However, children in this age range are far from reaching their physical maturity, and they need to be active.

Fine motor skills continue to improve and are refined during middle and late childhood. Children can use their hands more steadily and more adroitly than they were able to in earlier years. At 10 to 12 years old, children begin to show a level of skillful manipulation similar to the abilities of adults. The intricate, precise, and complex movements needed to produce fine-quality crafts or to play a difficult piece of music can be readily mastered.

Cognitive Abilities

A 9- or 10-year-old has very different thought processes from that of a preschool child. Not only do older children know more, they also use their minds much more skillfully and effectively when they must solve a problem or remember information. Their thought processes involve considering evidence, planning ahead, thinking logically, and formulating alternative hypotheses, and they try to incorporate these abilities into their own reasoning. One of the most important cognitive achievements of middle childhood is the ability to reason logically about things and events. Children acquire an understanding of logical principles, and they know how to apply them in specific, concrete situations. Children's logical thinking, acquisition of knowledge, and ability to communicate clearly and persuasively with others illustrate major develop-

mental differences between children of preschool and elementary school ages.

Socioemotional Characteristics

Several noted theorists such as Freud and Erikson have posited that middle childhood is a quiet or relatively uneventful period emotionally because changes in emotional development are not as dramatic as those in early childhood or adolescence. During this period, children are interested in learning how things are made and how they work, and they struggle to master cultural values such as social norms. Based on their degree of success, children come to view themselves as either industrious or inferior, competent or incompetent, productive or failing, and a "winner" or a "loser." When adults encourage children in their efforts, a sense of industry increases, but when their efforts are viewed as "mischief" or "making a mess" a sense of inferiority results. Children's social worlds beyond their parents and family also contribute to attaining a sense of industry or inferiority.

During middle and late childhood, children spend more and more time with their peers, which leads to the child's sense of self-competence. In middle childhood, children tend to become more dependent on each other not only for companionship but also for self-validation and advice. When school-aged children play together, they develop patterns of interaction that are distinct from those of adult society and culture. They have special norms, vocabulary, rituals, and rules of behavior that flourish without the approval, or sometimes even the knowledge, of adults.

Although acceptance by the peer group is valued, personal friendships are even more important. Research has identified six functions of children's friendships at this age and provided evidence of the importance of each to the child's healthy development (Gottman & Parker, 1987). These functions are

- **companionship** (providing a partner and playmate who will spend time and join in collaborative activities),
- **stimulation** (providing interesting information, excitement, and amusement),
- **physical support** (offering time, resources, and assistance),
- **ego support** (providing the expectation of support, encouragement, and feedback, which helps the child maintain an impression of himself or herself as competent, attractive, and worthwhile),

- **social comparison** (providing information about where the child stands in relation to others and whether the child is "okay"), and

- **intimacy and affection** (offering a warm, close, trusting relationship with another in which sharing and self-disclosure take place).

The importance of these functions of friendship in the child's life cannot be overemphasized. Researchers are in general agreement that during this age, peers play a more central role in socializing the child than the parents, primarily because of these functions of friendship. In addition, children who have been rejected by peers or who have grown up socially isolated are at risk for depression and later drug and alcohol abuse. It thus becomes important to recognize the critical value of social interactions for the developing school-aged child in the design and delivery of leisure programs and services.

Considerations for Program Design

Programming for youth in this stage is relatively easy compared to programming for other stages because of the more developed and integrated cognitive and physical skills. At this age, children can consider multiple aspects of a situation simultaneously, and in the face of challenge, they tend to persevere rather than become frustrated and give up easily. Nonprofit organizations such as Boy Scouts and Girls Scouts, theater, recreational sports, and other special interest clubs are appealing to youth in this age range because they offer opportunities to affiliate with a social group as well as be active and express creativity. Also, clubs provide opportunities to develop physical skills such as eye–hand coordination, balance, speed, and intellectual skills such as understanding procedures and rules and developing strategy. Programs such as day camps are popular with elementary school–age children because of the variety of activities such as sports, games, and arts and crafts offered and the opportunities to socialize with others.

Examples From Recreation and Leisure Services Sectors

Summer Daze is a youth recreation program administered in rural Illinois communities and strives to meet the needs and interests of youth through a variety of activities. Park district staff

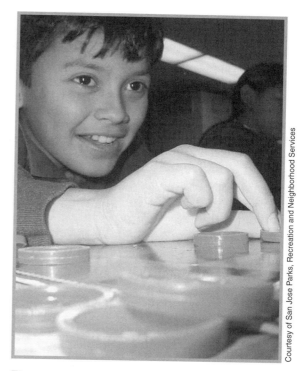

Courtesy of San Jose Parks, Recreation and Neighborhood Services

Elementary school–age children enjoy games that develop their intellectual skills such as understanding rules and developing strategy.

adhere to the following principles in designing their recreation programs.

- **Learning new skills.** Activities involving sport clinics, advanced arts and crafts, brain teasers such as word jumbles and crossword puzzles, model planes and trains, and musical instruments are appealing to kids in this age group. In addition, they build on the child's desire to use and further develop the more sophisticated cognitive and motor skills they are rapidly acquiring.

- **Mastering rules and competition.** Children ages 7 to 12 are eager to use their cognitive reasoning and analytical skills in many types of sports and games. Competitive recreational sports, physically active games such as Tag and Capture the Flag, and board games are effective because they facilitate rule mastery and social interaction.

- **Competition versus cooperation.** At this stage, games can emphasize communication, cooperation, and teamwork. Team-building games, such as the Human Knot, which emphasizes intragroup cooperation to solve a problem, are generally new to youngsters. And team-building games require both cognitive problem-solving skills and physical skills, enabling youth with different strengths to contribute to the solution. Both the variety of required skills and the nontraditional nature of the activities are important to ensuring that all participants can feel a sense of contribution and accomplishment to the larger group.

Compared to other life stages, this is a fairly easy age group for which to design programs. Children in this age group have a wide variety of skills and interests, have longer attention spans, and interact well with other children. Therefore, the programmer has many options when designing and implementing activities.

ADOLESCENCE: TEENAGE YEARS

Adolescence occurs between the ages of 13 and 19 years. During this time, boys and girls experience the full ravages of puberty, although its onset might have occurred a few years earlier, become more independent from their parents, and begin to form intimate friendships and romantic relationships. These and other developments present implications for programming.

Developmental Highlights

Adolescence is highlighted by significant socioemotional change focused on developing self-concept and identity. Moreover, physical maturation occurs as teens experience changes associated with puberty. The cognitive processing and memory of teenagers increase significantly, and they can consider hypothetical situations more effectively than younger children can.

Physical Abilities

A noticeable growth spurt occurs in adolescence—a sudden, uneven, and somewhat unpredictable jump in the size of almost every part of the body. While their bones lengthen, adolescents eat more and gain weight more rapidly than before, primarily to provide energy for the many changes taking place. A height spurt follows soon after the start of the weight increase, burning up some of the stored fat and redistributing some of the rest. In the following one to two years, muscle mass increases, and as a result, the pudgy and clumsy appearance typical of early puberty generally disappears.

Adolescence has been regarded as a period of transition from childhood to adulthood. A rapid physical maturation involving hormonal and bodily changes occurs with puberty. This often plunges adolescents into a preoccupation with their body and a perception of what their body is and should be like. Early and late maturation, social comparisons with peers, and differing amounts of peer attention contribute to emerging sexual feelings and the formation of sexual identity.

Cognitive Abilities

Adolescent thought is qualitatively different from a child's thought. Cognition is different and more advanced—the result of improvements in cognitive processing and memory as well as exposure to a new type and culture of learning in school. The single most distinguishing feature of adolescent thought is the capacity to think of possibilities, not just reality or practicalities (Keating, 1990). This ability to think in terms of possibility allows adolescents to fantasize, speculate, and hypothesize more readily and on a far grander scale than children, who are still tied to the tangible reality of the here and now, can. Teenagers are in a position to make personal decisions and independent choices that could have far-reaching consequences for their future. They can decide, for example, what and how diligently to study, whether and where to go to college, whom to befriend, what career to pursue, whether to become sexually active, whether to use drugs, and whether to take a part-time job. Because they think about possibilities, not practicalities, few adolescents actually decide these issues in a rational manner (Keating, 1990).

Socioemotional Characteristics

This period is primarily the story of developing an identity: Adolescents find out who they are, what they are all about, and where they are headed in life. Although identity formation is a gradual process beginning in infancy and lasting into old age, adolescence is the first time physical, cognitive, and social development is advanced to the point that the person can reflect on past experiences and construct a feasible path toward adult maturity. It is important at this age that adolescents actively experiment with the numerous roles and identities they draw from the surrounding culture. A person who develops a healthy identity is flexible, adaptive, and open to changes in society, in relationships, and in careers. Adolescents who do not successfully experiment with and commit to an identity can become confused and may withdraw, isolating themselves from peers and family, or they may lose their identity in a crowd (Bosma & Kunnen, 2001).

Adolescents enjoy hanging out with each other. Peer relationships become increasingly important.

Adolescents become increasingly dependent on friends to satisfy several of their basic needs such as secure attachment, playful companionship, social acceptance, intimacy, and sexual relations; thus, their experiences with friends increasingly shape their sense of well-being. In particular, the need for intimacy intensifies during adolescence, motivating teenagers to seek close friends and significant others. Teenagers with superficial relationships, or no close friendships at all, report feeling lonelier and more depressed, and they have a lower self-esteem, compared to teenagers with intimate friendships (Berndt, 2002; Yin, Buhrmester, & Hibbard, 1996). As peers gain in importance and influence, young adolescents conform to peer standards; this conformity to peer pressure in adolescence can be positive, for example, doing charity work as part of a group, or negative, for example, stealing, vandalizing, using foul language, or ridiculing others.

Teens spend a considerable amount of time either dating or thinking about dating. In many cultures, dating is a form of recreation, a source of status and achievement, and a setting for learning about close relationships. Early romantic relationships serve as an arena for adolescents to explore how they should romantically interact with someone, how attractive they are, and how all of this appears to their peer group. The **socio-cultural** context exerts a powerful influence on the functions of adolescent dating as well as on dating patterns. Values and religious beliefs of people in various cultures often dictate the age at which dating begins, how much freedom in dating is allowed, whether dates must be chaperoned by adults or parents, and the different roles of males and females in dating.

Considerations for Program Design

Teenagers present a significant challenge to recreation programmers. Teens often experience boredom, which can impede healthy development. Boredom can lead to engaging in risky behaviors, such as substance use, sexual behavior, and vandalism. For years, programmers have struggled with how to get teens actively involved in recreation programs. Teenagers need consistent staff to whom they can relate, look up to, and from whom they will model appropriate (e.g., cooperation, respect) behaviors. Young adults are old enough to be an authority figure and respected but young enough to be considered good role models for teens—someone they want to be seen with in the community, rather than being embarrassed to be seen.

Programmers should engage teens in the process of program planning; forming a teen advisory board is one way to involve teenagers. When developing a teen advisory board, it is wise to select a cross section of teens that are viewed as leaders and associate with different social groups. A teen advisory board composed of people from only one social group limits program success because attendees will likely be from the social group with which the board is associated. Teens should be afforded opportunities to offer input into the design of the environment in spaces such as teen and community centers; for example, they could select and place the artwork, arrange the furniture, and create a conducive ambiance. The environment should feel to them as though it is free from parental control or influence as they try to differentiate themselves from parents and family. Common amenities include the teens' style of music, low lighting, video games, dart boards, and pool table along with comfortable chairs for socializing and hanging out, and of course, a snack bar.

When planning program formats and content, keep in mind that this age group appreciates opportunities for casual social interactions that develop both individual identity and group identity. Hanging out and talking on the phone are two of the most popular teen leisure activities. Teens also want to engage in activities that demonstrate their competence by consistently accomplishing tasks. It is also important to remember that not all teens are adept or interested in athletics. Thus, when planning programs, remember to cater to numerous skills and interests.

Examples From Recreation and Leisure Services Sectors

A midwestern public parks and recreation agency has reengineered its teen programs by using an empowerment approach to programming. First, the agency created a board of teens to advise program offerings. Teen boards are common and beneficial because teens feel like they are the producers of

their own leisure time by shaping programs, and they develop ownership of the programs that they are interested in participating in. Once the board was formed, the park district staff learned that the teens in the community wanted a place to hang out rather than a series of structured programs. However, the park district staff didn't promote the facility as a "teen center" for fear that the name would stigmatize the site. The label "teen center" might be perceived as uncool among members of this age group. The staff allowed the teen advisory board to decide the types and locations of seating areas and types of games to stock, thereby determining how the space would be used. The facility was staffed by college students whom the teens generally looked up to and did not consider their presence to be constraining or threatening.

Adolescence is a time for teens to explore their identities, experiment with different roles, and explore romantic relationships. During this time, teens become more autonomous and desire more control over their activities and environments. Therefore, it is important for recreation programmers to provide flexible and appealing environments and activities that facilitate this exploration in an active and healthy manner.

EARLY ADULTHOOD: 20s AND 30s

Early adulthood is the time between ages 20 and 40. Many significant changes occur as young adults begin careers and make important choices about relationships and marriage. The physical, cognitive, and socioemotional characteristics of young adulthood are presented along with considerations for planning recreation programs for this age group.

Developmental Highlights

Early adulthood is focused on developing a career path and looking for a significant other with which to share the joys and challenges of life. Physical performance and health are at their peak during this time and much of leisure tends to center on social and physical pursuits.

Physical Abilities

It is in early adulthood, particularly between the ages of 19 and 26 that most people are healthiest and reach their peak physical performance. Young adults have fewer colds and respiratory problems than they did when they were children, and very few have chronic health problems. Young adults can draw on these physical resources for a great deal of physical activity and pleasure, often bouncing back easily from physical stress and abuse. However, there is a hidden danger: This physical exhilaration can lead them to push their bodies too far. The negative effects of abusing one's body may not show up in the first half of early adulthood but probably will surface later in early adulthood or in the middle-adulthood years.

Not only do young adults reach peak physical performance during early adulthood, but it is during the latter half of this age period that they also begin to decline in physical performance. About the age of 30 or shortly thereafter, muscle tone and strength usually begin to show signs of decline, the body's fatty tissue increases, the lens of the eye loses some of its elasticity and becomes less able to change shape and focus on near objects, and hearing begins to deteriorate. Many of these changes can be improved by reducing the incidence of certain health-impairing lifestyles, such as overeating, and by engaging in health-improving lifestyles that include good eating habits, regular exercise, and not abusing alcohol or drugs.

Cognitive Abilities

Some developmental psychologists believe that it is not until adulthood that many people consolidate their thinking skills. Adolescents may begin to plan and hypothesize about intellectual problems, but people become more systematic and sophisticated at this as young adults. Young adults engage in more reflective judgment when solving problems, they think deeply about many aspects of politics, their career and work, relationships, and other areas of life. They also become more skeptical about whether there is a single truth and often are not willing to accept an answer as final. As young adults move into the world of work and begin to face many of the constraints imposed by reality, the idealism they held as adolescents declines.

Socioemotional Characteristics

Friendships and romantic relationships are the primary means by which people seek to form intimate relationships with others in early adulthood. At the same time that they are seeking intimacy, adolescents pursue independence and freedom. It has been said that socioemotional development in early adulthood involves an intricate balance of intimacy and commitment on the one hand and independence and freedom on the other. An inability to develop meaningful relationships with others results in feelings of isolation and can harm a person's personality. It may lead people to reject, ignore, or attack those who discourage them.

Childhood is a time when people have idealistic fantasies about what they want to be when they grow up (superhero, skilled athlete, movie star). As they move through their high school years, they have typically begun to think about careers on a less idealistic, although wishful, basis. In their late teens and early 20s, career decision making has usually turned more serious as people explore different career possibilities and focus on the career they want to enter. By their early and mid-20s, many people have completed their education or training and entered a full-time occupation. From this time through the remainder of early adulthood, people often seek to establish their emerging career in a particular field—they may work hard to move up the career ladder and improve their financial standing.

A wide range of lifestyles can be found in early adulthood. There has been a dramatic rise in the percentage of adults in their 20s and 30s who choose to remain single. A growing number of people choose cohabitation instead of marriage. The past decade has witnessed a significant increase in both the number of adults who engage in this lifestyle and the acceptance of what once was considered an unconventional choice. Researchers have found that gay and lesbian relationships are similar in their satisfactions, loves, joys, and conflicts to heterosexual relationships (Hyde & DeLamater, 2003; Peplau & Beals, 2002). Increasingly, gay and lesbian couples are creating families that include children. Although this is controversial to many heterosexual people, research has shown that children growing up in gay or lesbian families are just as popular with their peers and are no different in adjustment and mental health than children raised in heterosexual families (Hyde & DeLamater, 2003; Patterson, 2002).

Considerations for Program Design

Developmental tasks during young adulthood focus on career development and establishing personal relationships. Leisure activities reflect these issues because they are often centered on networking and socializing. Because physical abilities also peak in young adulthood, and health is usually optimal compared to other life stages, physically challenging activities are also sought. Many young adults have entered the workforce but haven't necessarily taken on significant financial demands such as a house or children, so disposable income is more available. Thus, travel and cultural activities such as concerts, plays, and fine dining tend to be affordable for this age group.

Competitive, physically active recreation is popular among young adults for many reasons: Team sports tend to be social, sports provide a physical outlet for diffusing work-related stress, and they provide opportunities to develop and refine physical skills. Young adults are drawn to exercise and fitness and outdoor recreation activities because in general, they desire social opportunities, possess the cognitive and physical skills necessary to engage, and have the disposable income to invest in specialized recreation equipment. Networking and social events are important to young adults as they work to expand and develop friendships beyond those they made in high school and college. Volunteerism is another form of networking: Young adults connect with others by volunteering with charitable organizations and attending charitable events.

Because of the diversity in lifestyles seen during these years, programmers must be sensitive to the needs and interests of different groups. The content, timing, and environmental requirements of recreation programs must be tailored to the lifestyles of the participants, often requiring a range in both how and when programs are offered and staffed. The proportion of traditional dual heterosexual–parent families is on the decline, and both public and private recreation providers must be aware of the changing demographics of their clientele.

Examples From Recreation and Leisure Services Sectors

Chicago Sport and Social Club is a commercial recreation organization that specifically targets young adults. Members must be 21 or older, and the average age range of members is 21 to 35. This organization offers members many program opportunities. These include intramural sports such as soccer, football, softball, volleyball, basketball, and kickball; games such as billiards, cards, and darts; and adventure recreation and exercise classes including yoga, kayaking, rock climbing, and dancing. The club also sponsors social events and parties, trips, and volunteerism opportunities such as charity events. The organization recognizes that young adults vary widely in their recreation needs and motivations; thus, it offers courses and leagues at different skill and competition levels. In addition to these programs, the organization also serves as a resource for young adults to identify other special interest sport and recreation clubs, such as the Chicago Area Runners Association. Moreover, the organization has a message board on its Web site where members can chat, exchange information, announce social gatherings, and find players for intramural sports teams. The club aims to be a friendly and upbeat organization that helps people connect through activities that they naturally enjoy.

© Photodisc

Young adults are drawn to exercise and fitness and outdoor recreation activities because in general, they desire social opportunities, possess the cognitive and physical skills necessary to engage, and have the disposable income to invest in specialized recreation equipment.

Young adults are drawn to active pursuits that challenge them physically, creatively, and intellectually. In addition, social networking is important; therefore, events such as parties, charity events, sport leagues, and festivals are popular among young adults. However, the demographics and recreation preferences of this age group are diverse, so recreation programmers must consider this in their program design and delivery.

MIDDLE ADULTHOOD: 40s AND 50s

Middle adulthood is the time between the ages of 40 and 59. Although this is the stage where physical aging becomes more noticeable, cognitively, middle adults are still developing. Thus, the developmental characteristics of middle adulthood and programming considerations are discussed.

Developmental Highlights

During middle adulthood, people begin to show signs of their age, and their risk of developing chronic disease increases significantly. People in this stage have the benefit of life experience that enhances reasoning and problem solving. During this life stage adults seek to evaluate the impact they are making on others and society through work, raising a family, and other activities.

Physical Abilities

Physical changes in middle adulthood are usually gradual. Although everyone experiences physical changes during midlife, the rate of aging varies considerably from one person to another. One of the most noticeable signs of bodily changes in middle adulthood is physical appearance. The skin begins to wrinkle and sag because of a loss of fat and collagen in underlying tissues. Small, localized areas of pigmentation in the skin produce aging spots. Hair becomes thinner because of a lower replacement rate and grayer because of a decline in melanin production. Muscle strength decreases noticeably by the mid-40s, and many people experience joint stiffness and more difficulty in movement because the cushions for surrounding bones become less efficient. From middle adulthood on, there is a progressive loss of bone; the rate of this bone loss begins slowly but accelerates in the 50s. People also lose inches in height during middle age, and many gain weight. Obesity increases the likelihood of several ailments, among them hypertension and digestive disorders. For people who are 30 percent or more overweight, the probability of dying in middle adulthood increases by about 40 percent.

Changes to the sensory organs and cardiovascular system are also observable in middle adulthood. Hearing may no longer be as acute, and the ability of the eye to focus and maintain an image experiences its sharpest decline during this period. Cardiovascular disease increases considerably in middle age. Blood pressure usually rises as people move into their 40s and 50s. The linings of the blood vessels show increased fatty deposits and scar tissue slowly accumulates, gradually reducing blood flow to various organs, such as the heart and brain. Regular exercise, weight control, and a diet rich in fruits, vegetables, and whole grains can often help to stave off many cardiovascular problems in middle adulthood.

The appearance and onset of a chronic illness during middle adulthood are determined largely by genetic makeup and lifestyle factors. At some time during this age range, women usually reach menopause. The changes women in midlife experience caused by the decline in certain hormones, especially estrogen, progesterone, and testosterone, and cessation of menstruation and ovulation are problematic for only a minority of women.

Cognitive Abilities

Many have wondered whether there are similar declines in cognitive abilities along with the decline in physical characteristics in middle adulthood. Longitudinal research examining people's intellectual abilities through the adult years has found that four of six areas of mental functioning actually reach their highest level during the middle adulthood years (Schaie, 1994, 1996). Vocabulary (understanding ideas expressed in words), verbal memory (encoding and recalling meaningful words), inductive reasoning (recognizing and understanding patterns and relationships in a problem and using this understanding to solve other instances of the problem), and spatial orientation (visualizing and mentally rotating stimuli in two- and three-dimensional space) show peak performance during the middle adulthood years. For only two of the six cognitive areas—numerical ability (performing simple mathematical computations) and perceptual speed (quickly and accurately making simple discriminations in visual stimuli)—are there declines in middle adulthood.

Practical problem solving often increases through the 40s and 50s as people accumulate practical experience. People become more adept at handling real-world problems, the result of employing strategies to address these issues. Expertise—having an extensive, highly organized knowledge, and an understanding of a particular topic or domain—often increases in the middle adulthood years.

Socioemotional Characteristics

For middle-aged adults, having a positive identity has been linked with **generativity**—people's desire to leave a legacy of themselves to the next generation, thereby achieving a sense of immortality—in middle age. Through generativity, middle-aged adults seek to promote and guide the next generation by parenting, teaching, leading, and doing things that benefit the community. In contrast, when people sense that they have done nothing for the next generation, a sense of **stagnation** may result.

Middle adulthood has been viewed as a time of life when people question how their time should be spent and often reassess their priorities. Midlife can be a time of evaluation, assessment, and reflection in terms of the work people do and want to do in the future. One common outcome of this reconsideration of working life is additional emphasis placed on leisure. Leisure can be an especially important aspect of middle adulthood because of the changes many people experience during this time. For many people, middle adulthood is the first time they have the opportunity to diversify their interests. By middle adulthood, more money is usually available, and there may be more free time and paid vacations. These changes typically produce expanded opportunities for leisure. Adults at midlife may also begin preparing psychologically for retirement. Constructive and fulfilling leisure activities in middle adulthood have been shown to be an important part of this preparation (Mannell, 2000). If an adult develops leisure activities that can be continued into retirement, the transition from work to retirement can be less stressful.

One important event in a family is the launching of a child into a career or his/her own family. This typically creates a disequilibrium in the family of origin and requires new adjustments be made to the child's absence. The term "empty nest syndrome" has been given to the situation where the departure of the children may create feelings of emptiness or unrest because the satisfaction the parents felt from their children wanes as the children leave the "nest." This may create a decline in marital and/or life satisfaction, particularly for parents who lived vicariously through their children. For many other parents, however, with their children gone they have the time to pursue career interests and share more time and experiences together.

Considerations for Program Design

Middle adulthood is a time in life when people wrestle with generativity and stagnation. Generativity can be fostered through leisure, especially through activities that focus on self-expression and self-exploration and activities that replace roles lost from the "empty nest" experience or the death of parents. Midlife is a time when physical changes caused by aging become more visible. Thus, it is important to emphasize vitality during this stage of life.

Examples From Recreation and Leisure Services Sectors

The public, nonprofit, and private for-profit sponsoring sectors all have much to offer those in middle adulthood. From country clubs, to parks and recreation agencies, to specialized athletic clubs, the follow programming ideas are relevant to a variety of service sectors.

- **Physical activity and movement.** In middle age, interests may change from more strenuous physical forms of exercise such as aerobics and running to more expressive and social forms of physical activity such as yoga, Pilates, dance, water aerobics, and hiking and walking. In addition to being aerobic, these activities often include a social component that fosters the development of social support networks and friendships.

- **Expressive activities.** People in their 40s and 50s often have more discretionary time and greater interest in beginning or renewing hobbies they had placed on hold while caring for their families or pursuing a career. Creative activities in the fine arts such as pottery, painting, and photography and in the performing arts such as dance and theater are popular, as are hobbies such as woodworking, gardening, poetry, model building, and bird-watching. These activities provide for fellowship, quiet contemplation, challenge, a sense of accomplishment, and enjoyment.

- **Volunteerism and citizenship.** Midlife is also a time when adults seek to make contributions to the community. Volunteering at church, serving on the local park district board of commissioners, coaching a youth sport, or serving as a big brother or big sister are all examples of volunteerism that people find challenging, rewarding, and enjoyable.

OUTSTANDING *Graduates*

Background Information

Name: Christina Vugteveen (nee Hogeterp)

Education: Bachelor of science, Redeemer University College, Ancaster, Ontario, biology and physical education double major

Credentials: Senior first aid and CPR certificates; class 4 drivers license; National Coaching Certification Program (NCCP), level 1; Lifesaving Society Bronze Medallion

Special Awards: Female Scholar Athlete of the Year (1995-1996)

Career Information

Position: Program manager, YMCA of Greater Vancouver; youth and adult program manager, Tong Louie Family YMCA, Surrey, British Columbia

Organization: The YMCA is a charitable organization whose programs are accessible to everyone. The YMCA of Greater Vancouver has been at the center of the community for more than 100 years. It is composed of seven divisions encompassing 42 child care centers, community and international services, three family YMCA centers, a residence, three outdoor education and camping sites, and an English-language college. All of the programs offered are values based and are designed to build strong kids, strong families, and strong communities.

Organization's Mission: The YMCA is a charitable association dedicated to the development of people in spirit, mind, and body as well as the improvement of local, national, and international communities.

Job Description: Market programs. Supervise program directors, who directly oversee and implement programs and help recruit, train, and supervise more than 500 volunteers per year and more than 60 staff members per year. Supervise strategic planning, budgeting, staff and volunteer training, program and policy development, and customer service; this includes dealing with unhappy program participants. Organize, coordinate, and supervise all small- and large-scale programs such as summer day camps (3,200 campers), youth sports leagues (800 players), and programs for seniors, adults, and youth. Organize large special events. Serve as liaison with community groups. Plan and implement large staff and volunteer training events. Develop and manage $1 million Canadian budget. Maintain responsibility for all program administration, promotional designs, and program marketing. Serve on several community committees. Pursue and maintain partnerships within the community.

Courtesy of Christina Vugteveen

Career Path: During summer breaks from school I worked as a day camp supervisor at the YMCA. During the school year I volunteered my time as a basketball coach and worked as a basketball referee and babysitter-training instructor. As I finished my schooling, I became a full-time program director in the summer of 1998, managing camps, youth sports leagues, and other activities for youth in the community of Langley. In early 2001, as a result of restructuring, I became the community programs manager for the communities of Langley and Surrey, managing the same programs but more of them. When the Tong Louie Family YMCA opened in 2003, I became responsible for youth and adult programming in that facility in addition to my other responsibilities as program director.

Likes and Dislikes About the Job: I love the different people that I meet and mentor, particularly youth who are training to get further experience that will lead to career choices. I also love the administration work. I love that I work for an organization with a mission to make a difference in people's lives. I get frustrated that there is so much that could be done and not enough resources to make it happen.

Advice to Undergraduates

It is incredibly rewarding to work in this field. If you are looking for a career where you can make a positive difference in people's lives, you certainly can do it here. Expect to work many hours, especially during most people's downtime (holidays, weekends, and evenings).

> Recreation and leisure are great tools that provide steps along the path to wellness for individuals, families, and communities. In such a broken world, playing a small part in the pursuit of wellness is an incredibly rewarding and humbling experience, and it is an honor to be a part of it.

Midlife is a time when adults find that volunteering satisfies an important need to contribute to society and support the development of youth.

Volunteerism may satisfy an important need to contribute to society and further support the development of an organization or younger person.

Programming in middle adulthood is focused on self-expression, physical activity, and volunteerism. Expressive activities such as hobbies are popular, especially for people who have experienced empty nest syndrome, because they are challenging, fulfilling, and satisfying. Volunteering provides a sense of contribution, and moderate physical activity should be undertaken or continued to maintain health.

LATE ADULTHOOD: SENIOR YEARS

People who are 60 years old or older are considered older adults. Health status and functional ability vary greatly among people in this stage of life. Current literature about aging now focuses on the positive aspects of growing older—a departure from the long-held perception that older adults are in a constant state of decline. "Successful aging" means that the older adult is satisfied with life, is able to adapt to changing levels of skills and abilities, and maintains relationships to lead an emotionally fulfilling life. One key to aging successfully is to continue to stay engaged physically, cognitively, and socioemotionally. In this section the developmental characteristics of later life are presented, and programming considerations are discussed.

Developmental Highlights

Although older adulthood is often associated with physical decline, engaging in physical activity and good nutritional practices can optimize health. Also, some aspects of cognitive function decline while other aspects improve with age. Social contact is important to older adults because the support received from others can help them face the challenges associated with aging.

Physical Abilities

During late adulthood, functions slow, from speed of walking to speed of thinking, from reaction time to reading time, and from speech to heart rate. This overall slowdown is a universal result of aging. Virtually every bodily system becomes less efficient during late adulthood: The heart pumps less blood per beat, the arteries harden, the digestive organs become less efficient, the lungs lose capacity, sleep becomes less sound, and sexual responses become slower. Although many of these changes occur over several decades, the pace speeds up in later life. A general slowing of movement in older adults has been found in everyday tasks such as reaching and grasping and moving from one place to another and in continuous movement such as walking.

In late adulthood, visible changes in physical appearance become more pronounced, most noticeably in the form of wrinkles and age spots. People also get shorter because of bone loss in the vertebrae. Weight also usually drops after the age of 60, most likely caused by loss of muscle mass, which gives bodies a "sagging" look. Exercise and appropriate weightlifting can help reduce the loss of muscle mass and improve the appearance of an older person's body.

For many healthy elderly people, the most troubling aspect of aging is not how they appear to others but how they connect with the outside world. This connection depends primarily on their senses, all of which lose sharpness with each passing decade. The decline in vision that began for most people in early or middle adulthood becomes more pronounced in late adulthood. Night driving is especially difficult, and older people take longer to recover their vision when going from well-lit rooms to semidarkness. Although hearing impairment can begin in middle adulthood, it usually does not become an impediment until late adulthood. It has been estimated that 15 percent of the population over the age of 65 is legally deaf, usually because of degeneration of the cochlea, the primary neural receptor for hearing in the inner ear (Olsho, Harkins, & Lenhardt, 1985). Most older adults lose some of their sense of smell or taste or both and often prefer highly seasoned foods (sweeter, spicier, saltier) to compensate for their diminished taste and smell. Change in touch is also associated with aging: People detect touch less in the lower extremities than in the upper extremities. Older adults are less sensitive to pain and suffer from it less than younger adults.

Compared to earlier ages, chronic diseases become much more common in late adulthood. People's lifestyle choices and social and psychological factors are linked with health status in older adults. Engaging in physical activity, developing good eating habits, and maintaining a network of people who provide emotional and physical support have all been linked to better functioning and recovery from illness in older people (Lee, Manson, Hennekens, & Paffenbarger, 1993; Pruchno & Rosenbaum, 2003; Singh, 2002).

Cognitive Abilities

In late adulthood, some dimensions of cognitive functioning decline, while others remain stable or even improve. The "hardware" of the mind is termed **cognitive mechanics** and reflects the **neurophysiological** structure of the brain. Cognitive mechanics refers to the speed and accuracy of the processes involved in many cognitive abilities: sensory input, attention, visual and motor memory, discrimination, comparison, and categorization. Because of the strong influence of biology, heredity, and health on cognitive mechanics, it is highly likely that these processes will decline with age. In contrast, **cognitive pragmatics** refers to the culturally based "software programs" of the mind. Cognitive pragmatics includes cognitive abilities such as reading and writing skills, language comprehension, educational qualifications, professional skills, and also the practical and personal types of knowledge about the self and life skills. Because of the strong influence of culture on cognitive pragmatics, their improvement into old age is possible for many people. Thus, certain types of cognitive abilities may decline during old age, while others may improve.

Socioemotional Characteristics

This final stage of development is a time when older adults reflect on the past and review their own life experiences and integration within the broader community. If these retrospective glances and reminiscences provide a positive picture of a life well spent, the older adult will be satisfied and feel a sense of integrity. But if he or she found this retrospective to be negative, despair will result from the belief that time is now too short to attempt to remedy events or try alternate life paths (Erikson, 1968). The individual conducts a "life review"—looking back at one's experiences and evaluating and interpreting (and often reinterpreting) them. Sometimes this life review proceeds quietly, while with other individuals it may be intense, often requiring considerable effort to achieve some sense of reconciliation. As the past marches before the individual, the older adult observes it and reflects on it. The individual often reconsiders previous experiences and what they mean, and there might be an expanded understanding that takes place (Cully, LaVoie, & Gfeller, 2001).

This reorganization of the past may provide a more meaningful picture for the individual and result in a new and significant meaning to one's life. It may also help prepare the individual for death, and in the process reduce the fear of confronting one's own impending mortality (Butler, 1996).

Research has shown that self-esteem often drops significantly when people reach their 70s and 80s. Several explanations have been suggested, including deteriorating physical health and negative societal attitudes toward older adults, although research has not fully confirmed how strong an influence these factors exert (Robins, Trzesniewski, Tracey, Potter, & Gosling, 2002) . Self-esteem is also related to personal control—the extent to which people believe that they control what they do, rather than feeling controlled by their environment. The term "self-efficacy" has been used to describe perceived control over the environment and the ability to produce positive outcomes (Bandura, 2000). Successful aging involves feeling that one is in control over his/her environment and the feeling of a sense of self-efficacy (Bertrand & Lachman, 2003). Researchers have found that many older adults are very effective in maintaining a sense of control and

having a positive view of themselves (Brandstadter, Wentura, & Greve, 1993).

Social support is important to the physical and mental health of older adults. It is linked to a reduction in the symptoms of disease and to the ability to meet personal health care needs. Social support also decreases the probability that an older adult will be institutionalized, and it is associated with a lower incidence of depression (Antonucci, 1990; Joiner, 2000). The importance of social integration—maintaining and fostering close ties with others—cannot be overemphasized. Being part of a social network is related to longevity; both women and men who actively participate as members of organizations live longer than their counterparts who participate less (House, Landis, & Umberson, 1988; Mannell & Dupuis, 1996; Tucker, Schwartz, Clark, & Friedman, 1999).

Considerations for Program Design

The biggest challenge to serving the older-adult population is yet to come with the aging of the baby boomers. This group will be more diverse in terms of abilities and interests, and is likely to

Programming choices for older adults should allow for more than the traditional activities such as playing cards and bingo. Programmers must also offer fitness activities to optimize health.

cause major changes in the way recreation programming is designed and delivered. The following are characteristics of effective programming for older adults.

- **Involvement.** Older adults should be involved in developing program ideas to the greatest extent possible. An advisory board or needs assessment survey provides valuable information to the programmer about what these adults want to do and how and where they want to do it.

- **Diversity.** Health status and cognitive and physical function vary greatly among people in the 65-to-74, 75-to-84, and 85-and-older age groups, as well as among people within each of these groups. Recreation professionals must remember that individual differences, especially for those over the age of 60, are pronounced. The error in assuming that senior programs are appropriate for and enjoyed by everyone within this age group could be serious.

- **Choice and variety.** The traditional senior activities of long ago—chair exercises, playing cards, and bingo—may be suitable for only a few older adults. Instead, a range of recreational opportunities such as dancing, art, cultural activities, and exercise should be available.

- **Social connectedness.** Intergenerational activities are popular with people of all ages and are important because they help refute the stereotypes associated with ageism and expose younger generations to the wisdom and abilities of older adults. These activities can include social gatherings, Senior/Junior Olympics, dancing, and arts and crafts. In planning activities, it is important to remember that older adults generally prefer to participate in exercise and physical activity classes with people their own age because they feel more comfortable with people they can relate to in terms of body image, stage of life, and performance. Older adults also tend to prefer not to exercise with children, whom they might consider noisy and unpredictable.

Examples From Recreation and Leisure Services Sectors

One public park and recreation agency in Colorado is positioning its programs to accommodate the diverse needs and abilities of older adults. Active Options is an exercise-based wellness program that incorporates physical, emotional, and social components of wellness to take a more holistic approach toward health promotion. Members pay a fee for access to facilities and movement-oriented classes such as tai chi, yoga, balance ball, water walking, aquacize, moving for life, strength training, and dance. This program takes into account the abilities and needs of this age group in several ways:

- **Chronic-disease training.** All Active Options instructors are certified through the American Council on Exercise or a comparable organization and receive training on common chronic diseases associated with later life, their symptoms, and strategies for managing symptoms.

- **Peer instructors.** The park district makes an effort to hire and train older people as course instructors. Class participants are often more motivated when led by a peer rather than a young person in a tight-fitting outfit.

- **Health and wellness seminars.** In addition to classes, Active Options offers members a series of health seminars on topics that vary from financial management to reflexology, nutrition, and homeopathy, thus providing resources that serve the whole person.

- **Social activities.** Active Options members participate in a group orientation before starting the program to become acquainted with program features and goals, familiarize new members with the staff, and facilitate social interaction among new members. In addition, staff members periodically hold group luncheons and picnics to encourage social interaction.

- **Trips and outings.** Many older adults maintain a strong interest in traveling; however, declining vision and slower reaction time can make traveling and day trips challenging. Group trips provided by the recreation agency are highly popular for many reasons: transportation is provided, the itinerary is planned, there are many people to socialize with while traveling, and there is a perception of safety when participating in a group tour.

Older adults comprise a diverse population, and recreation programmers will be challenged to effectively meet their needs. However, common preferences include the need for social interaction and physical activity that is light to moderate in intensity.

SUMMARY

The importance of leisure and recreation in the lives of people of all ages is well-established. Leisure experiences may serve different functions

Web Sites to EXPLORE

Afterschool Alliance: www.afterschoolalliance.org
This organization is an advocacy group for developing after-school
recreation and enrichment programs.

American Camp Association: www.acacamps.org
This organization provides resources, education, and training for
anyone who works with residential and day camps.

Discovery Channel: www.discoverychannel.com
This site provides numerous arts and crafts and game ideas for youth.

National Recreation and Park Association: www.nrpa.org
This organization offers members several resources for programming
for different populations.

Senior Fitness Association: www.seniorfitness.net
This Web site is a terrific resource for people who want to be involved
in senior physical activity and fitness activities.

at different ages and stages and in different circumstances of life, but leisure is a fundamental contributor to happiness and effective functioning. The ways in which people use their discretionary time and the many choices available for individual expression provide glimpses into the ways that people live in their world and the desires and preferences they have for optimal interaction. Leisure affords people of all ages with unique opportunities for enjoyment, fun, pleasure, affiliation, movement, and skill and personal development.

The leisure professional is thus entrusted with a significant and overwhelming responsibility. Providing opportunities in which people can express themselves through recreation and leisure programs, facilities, and resources is an awesome challenge. As such, recreation professionals must be closely attuned to the developmental characteristics of people at different ages as well as sensitive to the diversity within each of these life stages. The highlights of each stage of development across the life span have been presented, and considerations for how these characteristics can be incorporated into leisure programs and services have been offered. It is our hope that you have gained insight into the *process* of applying the knowledge of these characteristics to design, program, and implement recreational opportunities for people across the life span.

PART III

Recreation and Leisure Service Areas

CHAPTER 13

Program Delivery and the Many Modes of Recreation

Maureen Glancy

© Photodisc

> To the eagle the best appointed cage will not replace the free heavens, nor will the warrior soul be born of office drudgery.
>
> *Joseph Lee, "father" of the playground movement and one of the founders of the National Recreation Association*

CHAPTER OBJECTIVES

After reading this chapter, you should be able to do the following:

- Identify several career paths that the field of recreation offers
- Explain the role of program planning in the field of recreation
- Discuss the variety of leisure activities that recreation offers to participants
- Illustrate the concept that recreation choices reflect lifestage developmental needs for growth or adjustment
- Describe the five program formats and provide examples of activities for each format
- Imagine what kind of career path might attract you to professional work in recreation
- Envision recreation programs and services as a force for inclusion of all people

INTRODUCTION

The words spoken by Joseph Lee at the National Playground Association conference a century ago remain true today. Speaking of the plight of working- and middle-class Americans caught up in the peak of industrial production and unaccustomed to the routinized way of life work demanded a century ago, Lee was an advocate of the inherent human need for personal freedom to seek challenge and discover things on one's own. Despite all the advances enjoyed today by so many people living in economically developed regions of the world, slavish attachment to work and its reward, money, still does not fill the wellsprings of the heart or inspire exploration beyond what offers tangible payoffs or ease of accomplishment. In the mid-1900s, youth (boys) worried about getting good enough jobs to rise economically above their fathers. Parents wanted to see their children do better than they did. Nowadays, too many people are overworked, working multiple jobs, unemployable, or are workaholics and are depressed, bored, or unhappy with their lives. Children of this century (boys and girls) observe their parents' singular focus on getting and keeping well-paying jobs and worry that they, too, will lead the same, meaningless life as their parents. Work (and money), touted as the prescription for happiness, is now being recognized the source of physical, social, and emotional ills. It was mainly Lee's visionary leadership that prompted the organization of recreation leadership and services as a preventive and remedy for the American lifestyle that was rapidly reforming into one centered on work. In this chapter, we discuss the types of program services recreation professionals provide and the paths people take in the profession with the purpose of helping people find meaning in their lives.

Included in this chapter are stories of the paths several people have taken within the field of recreation. As you read about their experiences, remember that these people cannot represent every opportunity for a career in such a broad field of service, but they can stimulate you to think creatively about your *self* in your search for the right career path.

This chapter also briefly explains the characteristic that makes recreation unique from every other profession—**programming.** Programs are created so people can participate recreationally in activities that match their leisure interests. Our discussion of recreation and programming includes the following activity groups: recreational sport, fitness and wellness, outdoor and adventure, and arts and culture. Web addresses are provided for most organizations and many of the examples mentioned in this chapter. More specific information about each of these topics is included in chapters 14 through 17. This information should provide an understanding of the recreation services and professional paths for delivering those services.

PERSONAL STORIES TRACING CAREER PATHS

I often find myself telling students how I ended up teaching in a department of recreation and leisure studies and why it is so important to me. As my story goes, "I do this because of Girl Scout cookies." That is, at age 10 I sold enough cookies to be awarded two weeks at one of the nation's oldest Girl Scout camps, Camp Hoffman in Rhode Island. By the end of my stay, I was crying because I had to go home. The magical experience at camp made up my mind that I wanted to grow up to be a camp director. My years of scouting led to counselor training, volunteering with children's and senior citizen's groups at the YWCA, playing basketball for the YWCA in the city recreation league, being president of the Y Teen club at my high school, representing teens in the Providence YWCA at a national staff conference, serving as day and resident camp counselor for the YWCA and Girl Scouts, discovering a college major with three camping courses, and taking a memorable social recreation course in my junior year.

This last part is significant because I had no idea that recreation was a course of study, but when Dr. "Cat" Allen introduced me to social recreation, I was captivated. Dr. Allen was one of the many *great* women leaders who served in World War II, providing leadership in the United Service Organization (USO), which provides services for military personnel away from home, including social recreation. Dr. Allen labeled me as "one of hers," meaning I was meant to be in recreation, and I knew in my heart she was right. To make this long story short, I went into recreation leadership through the YWCA, being paid more than I thought any professional ought to be paid who loved and learned as much as I did—$4,000 a year in 1961! I advanced in positions and responsibilities until I was state director of physical recreation and camping for the YWCAs of Greater Rhode Island. I loved the challenges, what I was learning, and what I was accomplishing: event planning, teaching all age groups, marketing, and even hosting a regular spot on a local TV show teaching Danish gymnastics for home exercise. I thrived on the challenge of helping people discover their potentials and expand their life experience. To my way of thinking, through personal growth, people were living more fully; they were re-creating themselves into competent, happier, and more self-satisfied people with the challenges their recreation choices offered.

Eventually I realized I could expose more people to the rewards of lives fully lived by teaching college students majoring in recreation. My first teaching job was with my mentor, Catherine Allen, who had become dean of our college and started a recreation major curriculum. Since then, I have earned my master's and doctoral degrees, held teaching positions around the country, offered the first for-credit wilderness camping course in the United States, co-founded a residential environmental center, volunteered as a youth camp accreditation visitor for the American Camp Association and a recreation curriculum accreditation visitor for the National Recreation and Park Association, and

have researched the social organization of people interacting in small groups for recreation. What an unbelievable ride. I truly love my life, even the bumps and scrapes.

STARTING TO THINK ABOUT YOUR STORY

My career, then, began with Girl Scouting and involved more than one key mentor and role model all from recreation beginning in my youth: Girl Scout camp staff (55 years later, I still turn to Grace Donnelly [now president of her own business, BIO-SPEC, related to workplace hazards] for environmental and risk-management advice, and we still enjoy birding, although infrequently). Charlotte Steen and Regina Bouin, both YWCA professionals, recognized my teenaged need to feel appreciated for my accomplishments. Charlotte allowed me to take on more and more responsibility in the Teen Program Department, so eventually, when she left, I was called upon to train her successor even though I was still in high school. At the same time, Regina challenged me to develop more teaching and leadership skills, building on my Girl Scout Counselor-In-Training program. Under Regina's tutelage, I taught water safety and swimming to frail, elderly women and became the supervisor of a Saturday children's program.

I already mentioned Dr. Allen from my college and professional years, but there were also several special colleagues I met at professional conferences or in one job or another who shared their knowledge freely and helped me fit in when job changes moved me into different circles of professionals and required different ways of thinking. There was Pat Magee (in the YWCA), who taught me the art of building programs by creating relationships with the participants; Jan Adams, a private camp owner, who taught me that sharing what was in my heart was motivating to campers and staff; Jay Kroll, a TV personality in Rhode Island who invited me to do a weekly exercise program for the station and taught me to draw upon capabilities to engage the public; Roy Buck, my doctoral minor advisor, who taught me to think in systems and to realize that certain people had control of the formal systems (He also said, "There's always more than one way to skin a cat." That idea has never let me down!); Chris Howe, who taught me how to revise my first article that was published and was my "cheer-leader" for many years; Nick DiGrino, my chair at Western Illinois University, who reminded me to think positively and never give up; and Marshall Kaplan, president of an aerospace engineering consulting company that employed me while I was finishing my doctorate (in recreation!), who taught me to write multimillion-dollar complex proposals for funding and the strategy of "no lose" thinking. What variety! How could I fail with people like this leading me? Each of the people whose impact I felt as an uncertain teenager and developing adult and professional had a way of stirring me to reflect on myself. These are significant memories because of the personal growth that happened. I think of these as precious moments during which I was fully present to personal discovery. Now as a mentor myself, I try to be aware of moments when students, younger colleagues, or friends are able to be open to new ways of thinking.

All this leads to the point that there is no more important time in life than the "precious present" moment. It is a moment when you might meet or seek out a mentor. Over the years, I have learned that students who ask faculty and professionals to be their mentors are more confident about their future plans and what they must do to accomplish them. Thinking reflectively about your day's experiences allows you to mentor yourself or prepare to ask specific questions of mentors. The idea is to be tuned in to each moment, whether recreating, studying, engaging in class, or talking with mentors or friends, to *your* fullest extent possible with your mind open to everyone and everything around you. It is when you engage the present moment with your full concentration and zest for discovering what thoughts might occur in your mind that you find out more about yourself and truly enjoy life. So, now, just to appease me, think about some of the "precious" moments in your life. How did they happen, and why are they precious to you? Do you have a personal story you can trace moment by moment?

What thoughts came to mind? My guess is some of your best memories and discoveries about yourself included precious people, your mentors. Oftentimes, you may have been recreating, doing something that spelled fun, novelty, or challenge to you. Whatever you consider to be your precious moments, these are clues as to what might be a good career path for you. Add to these personal insights as you continue to read, reflecting upon the ideas in the chapter as if you were the actor doing them.

DELIVERY SYSTEMS FOR RECREATION OPPORTUNITIES

Recreation takes many forms and enters our lives from many directions. Of course, the original source for recreation is always with us. It exists instinctively at birth and grows with the mental *self* we construct with every choice we make, every moment of each day. A German anthropologist who studied play, Johan Huizinga (1950), wrote that play is inborn in the human mind, and it is always there. Perhaps today we would say we are genetically disposed to play. How people play is similar across societies even though what games or other fun activities we do may differ. Thus, as you engage in play and recreation, you are creating yourself. As your own original source for recreation, some of you choose to read, shoot a few hoops, or design a page in your journal. Others wander through a mall to watch people or see what's new, and still others may decide to go out and pick berries if the season is right. When you were young, you absorbed yourself by using your imagination to create and re-create experiences and to observe and explore your surroundings. I remember spending hours watching ants ply their trade as they scavenged for bits of leaves, flowers, and other bugs and trekked along secret trails only they could see on the concrete and forest floor. For most children and adolescents, the school years lead to exploring a wider range of opportunities. Many, but not nearly all, young people spend out-of-school time in organized or **programmed** recreation like piano lessons, painting class, band practice, or dance class; swim lessons, soccer practice, or judo club; Camp Fire, 4-H, or Scout groups; or afternoon drop-in programs at school or at the local recreation center.

Historically, organizations that offer recreation have been founded on religious tenets, others have been voluntary organizations of socially conscious citizens, and some have been realized through **public agency.** For example, the Reverend Gunn started the first organized camping trip for boys who wanted to test their mettle by living like the soldiers they had heard about in the war just ended—the Civil War. The camp was repeated for several years. News of it spread rapidly, and within 25 years, summer camps for youth could be found throughout the East and were spreading westward.[1] Camping is just one example of

---

[1] To learn about the impact of summer camp, read Michael Eisner's (2005) book *Camp.* He found that his years as a camper and counselor taught him the essential skills he needed to become the CEO of Disney.

The school years provide adolescents a time to explore a wider range of recreation opportunities such as dance class.

organized recreation provided through a variety of agents: religious institutions, volunteer or youth-serving organizations, schools and colleges, community services, the military, employers for employee groups, organizations that serve tourists, and private businesses.

By the end of the first quarter of the 20th century, all sponsoring sectors of recreation services **delivery systems** had emerged: public, nonprofit, and commercial (private for-profit), and these sectors continue today. Although clearly distinguished by mission and program offerings in their early days, many recreation programs today may be better distinguished by their source of funding. No matter the source of funding, the network of recreation services allows people to pick and choose among the organizations to fulfill their own personal needs in satisfying ways. It is common for people who pursue their leisure passions (passion-driven interests) in more than one sector of recreation. Think of the adults who play softball in the municipal recreation league,

a private league, and work out at a commercial softball facility. The same variety of opportunity is sought by people who love the arts and other forms of recreation. For example, someone may recall loving dramatic games at Boys and Girls Club summer camp, writing scripts for skits and plays as a counselor in a religious day camp, taking acting classes in college, and now be an actor in the local community theater who also teaches a drama class for at-risk youth in an after-school recreation program. Just such continuity of interests led to a challenging career in recreation for one young man who loves the water. Read Cary Smith's story to see how his career evolved from his choices for seeking challenge, fun, and social groups. Although he now works for a government agency, he has worked in private clubs and associations, nonprofit organizations, resorts, and municipalities. He sees his work as serving and benefiting people and the natural environment, and there is nothing better for him than that.

Career Path to Ranger (on the Water)

Cary Smith, deputy harbormaster, Pillar Point Harbor, California

On the day my mother gave birth to me, she swam in the ocean, and I have been near the water ever since then. I have lived mainly on the California coast, but for several of my teenage years, I also spent summers in Nahant, Massachusetts, on the North Shore near Boston. As a youngster, I went with my mother and her friends almost daily to the beach at Santa Barbara, so the beach was my playground. My first memory of being wowed was when I was about 4 years old. One of my mother's friends worked for Sea World. As a trainer working with the whales and porpoises, he took me on a behind-the-scenes tour that convinced me I would grow up to work around the water. At age 5, I was already a swimmer, and when I spent the summer with my grandma, I swam every day at a public swimming pool because it was so hot where she lived. There I began racing in the under-8 competitions and didn't stop competitive swimming until I was finished with junior college. As a teenager, I played water polo and swam for my high school and junior college teams. During my summers in Massachusetts, I learned to sail, fish, row, and take "death-defying leaps" from cliffs on the small islands a bunch of us used to swim around for sport. When I was at home in Santa Cruz, I learned to surf. All I ever wanted to do was to be around the water.

Courtesy of Maureen Glancy

Having passed the state lifeguard test, I was able to earn money for school by lifeguarding during the summer for Santa Cruz Parks and Recreation. Because I was a student-athlete, I could teach college and children's swim classes and lifeguard for the community college during the school year. Up until this point, I had felt sort of directionless because I couldn't think how to turn my passion into year-round work. Then I attended the California Surf Lifesaving Association meeting and met a group of people who were older than I was and doing just what I wanted to do: They wore shorts all year and worked around the water! This was a great opportunity to meet people who felt like I did. One, Kia Weisser, took me under his wing. His operation impressed me. At Santa Cruz, we operated 5 lifeguard towers during the summer; at Huntington Beach, he had 25 towers with lifeguards working year-round.

That same year, I won the National Lifeguard Championship and was sent by the U.S. Lifesaving Association to New Zealand as the California exchange lifeguard for six months and learned that I loved the lifestyle that permanent guards live. There was tremendous camaraderie; it felt like an international brotherhood and sisterhood. Lifeguards everywhere in the world, except in the United States, are volunteers. In New Zealand, they are provided with bunkhouses for sleeping, and social clubs adopt their beach team. When I returned to the United States, I spent the winter using my Emergency Medical Technician (EMT) skills in ski country and learned about ski operations.

In the spring, I returned to my community college to take a recreation course. I could not believe that every assignment was something I was familiar with: leadership, programming classes and special events, and safety. Inspired, I went to San Jose State University and found myself a home: recreation and leisure studies. By the end of my course work, the department faculty trusted me to go to Guam to work at a resort for my internship; that was the icing on the cake. I taught small craft, surfing, and swimming and planned special events for the clientele.

After graduating, I returned to lifeguarding in Santa Cruz, but that was only seasonal work. In my third year of trying to fulfill my career dream, I was invited back to New Zealand as a paid instructor to teach rescue and safety techniques to lifeguards. On my return, I was hired by the harbor patrol at Santa Cruz—year-round! I found my dream career. As deputy harbormaster, now in Pillar Point Harbor, I do the things that my recreation education and personal experience have prepared me to do: supervision and enforcement, special-event planning, service provision for the fishing and sailing public, and personnel training in personal watercraft. In fact, if you are interested in surfing, you know that the biggest competition in the mainland United States is here at Maverick Beach, and the water safety plan and media and public services are part of my job.

The recreation course of study taught me the professionalism that recreation and tourism organizations and personnel in leadership must have. I have been rewarded, receiving two Officer of the Year awards, the first for a night rescue of two brothers whose boat had overturned and been lost for almost eight hours and the second for rescuing three boaters whose boat had overturned in 16- to 18-foot seas. I am proud to have been associated with establishing state policies for personal watercraft training and for being selected to work on developing national policies. I have been professionally active with the California Boating Safety Officers Association and currently serve as its president.

EVERYONE NEEDS PERSONAL INTERESTS AND OPPORTUNITIES FOR CHOICE

The term "recreation" suggests doing what is needed to re-create, uplift, or heal the human spirit. This implies a "spirit-full" experience during which you *enjoy yourself.* Generally, then, recreation ought to be something that raises your spirits and makes you feel good about yourself. Exactly what makes something recreational is, therefore, a matter of personal experience and learned preference. A variety of activity areas are likely sources for recreation: sports, fitness and wellness activities, outdoor and adventure endeavors, and arts and cultural activities. Recreation choices will vary according to culture, geography or climate, gender, social class, and religion. Although in North America, you might not like to think of recreation as being class based, cultural upbringing still influences both the opportunities at hand and the choices you make.

Many social changes have occurred, however, even in my lifetime. I recall having to defend to my executive director offering tennis and golf classes to a mill-working clientele and having to try to quell the fears of local residents when I included an African American child in swimming with his fellow campers in a backcountry pond. Now I am thrilled to learn from a graduate student that her team won an ice hockey championship in a tournament in Canada, and another student goes hang gliding in his wheelchair despite his quadriplegia. We must understand that recreation is the most important, if not the only, choice we have control over in everyday life. Work, although stimulating to many people, is neither awe-inspiring nor a rewarding creative challenge to most people who go to work day-in and day-out following the same or similar routines. For those of us who recognize its importance and have opportunities from which to choose, recreation may be our only reliable source for feeling good about ourselves. How sad it is to realize that recreation may not be an option for some people because they are different from others. Therefore, do not assume that everyone has the same set or an equally desired set of opportunities for recreation; as you will see from the story in the sidebar on page 260, we are still evolving toward being an authentically inclusive society.

Marty Turcios' story illustrates how it is possible to combine passion for an activity with unique personal circumstances to forge a rewarding career. Marty, a well-qualified recreation therapist, started life with people seeing his disabilities rather than his abilities. He conquered several barriers in sport and education and wants others to recognize him as the fully able professional he is. He is working through professional associations, private clubs, and public schools with a goal to bring golf for people with physical disabilities to all golf venues in the United States.

Career Path to Therapeutic Recreation

Marty Turcios, MS, CTRS

How did I end up in recreation? That's easy. Three recreational experiences (golf, camp, and a girl I was dating) led me to where I am now as a recreation therapist specialist in golf and associated with the PGA.

Being born with a developmental disability, cerebral palsy, my ability to do anything physical was discounted by others, and I was often perceived as being mentally incompetent. Perhaps that's why I developed a determined streak when challenged by difficult situations. My first success in golf was when I was watching my father and uncle practicing on the putting green at Nicholl Park in Richmond, California, and being absolutely sure that at age 5 or 6 I could do what they were doing. They both laughed at my childish demand to be allowed to play, but my dad relented and let me try. I took one putt at five feet from the hole, and it went in. They called it a "lucky shot." From then on, I played in the backyard with sticks and, eventually, old wooden golf clubs cut down to my size. Golf became my ambition, my life, my soul's path. By age 10, I was sneaking onto a nearby private golf club to play a hole or two. (I think the staff chose to ignore me because I stayed out of the way of other players.) In my early teens, my older brother worked as a caddy; he let me join him and his friends when they were allowed to play the course on Mondays. At home, we developed our own course in a construction site near our house; it had lots of great hazards. To me, every little success was a motivating reward.

In college, I played a lot of golf with two or three guys and on my own, but I tired easily at first. Eventually I was able to play 18 holes at a time. Accomplishing this filled me with the zeal to challenge myself with more goals. One story I often tell when speaking to groups is about the time I hit the best shot in my life. I hit a perfect shot from 50 to 60 yards out right into the cup! No one saw me do it, but I can still feel the "glory" of it as if I had won the Olympics. This is the leisure experience, **optimal experience** at its best, because it's indelibly imprinted in my memory and feelings about myself. When I teach people to play golf, my goal is for them to learn where the thrill is in the moment-to-moment game or practice and play.

During my first year or so at college, I was one of those undecided students trying a psychology major. When the woman I was dating told me she was changing her major to recreation therapy, I followed her. As you might guess, I fell in love with recreation and recreation therapy, and the girl and I are still good friends.

As a child, I went to a summer camp operated by the Easter Seals Society. Camp made me proud of myself because I learned to fish, and I became the Easter Seals poster child. I went back a couple of years later with my hand in a cast, which, of course, caused problems. Even when I fell into a small stream and ruined the cast, no one threatened to send me home. Camp gave me a sense of freedom. No one told me what to do; I could make my own decisions and was allowed to do everything. This taste of freedom was exhilarating! Sixteen years later, I went back as a counselor specialist with my certification in therapeutic recreation. I found myself being respected—what a wonderful feeling that was!

Although I have worked hard for everything I have accomplished, I am still discounted because I have a disability. To other people, I don't appear to move easily. I don't speak clearly, but I have a good mind, a master's degree in recreation, and am developing a theoretical model to improve community and school recreation services for people with disabilities. My life is exciting and rewarding because I am able to bring the opportunities to play golf to people who are usually discounted because of what appears to be a disabling condition.

OPTIMAL RECREATION: WHEN THE AHA AND WOW HAPPEN

Marty's story makes me realize why he is thrilled with his *AHA* moments of success and his ecstatic *WOW* that marks accomplishment. I have never had to work as hard mentally, physically, and emotionally as he does with everything in life, but I certainly can relate to his jubilance. He reminds me that when I overcome any challenge, I am rewarded with the *AHA* of discovering how to do something and I recognize the power of my accomplishment by thinking (or yelling) *WOW*! Sometimes Marty's *AHA* is gained by reducing barriers that conventions for participation create. For example, golfers must move rapidly through the course or move aside to allow following players to pass. For Marty, physical movement is not as straightforward as it is for me, and the more he tries to rush, the more erratic his movement becomes. It took him years to master his frustration and worry on the golf course to move as efficiently as he possibly could. Marty's diligent analysis of golf and himself has allowed him the reward of many *AHA* moments, and in the long run, his mastered techniques result in *WOWs* that provide great personal reward. I am awed when watching what he does with his body to drive the ball and that he makes the ball fly straight down the fairway.

What Marty's story also suggests is that people discover an interest, work at becoming good at it, and enjoy themselves immensely when they do it. Recreation professionals learn to assist people in these experiences by designing programs for people to learn, to show off, to share with others, and to test themselves in the spotlight.

What does this mean in the scope of the search for self through recreation? It means that, if you enter whole heartedly into doing things that challenge you and work to master them, you will make discoveries about yourself and the thing you are trying to master, and you will be *WOWed* by what you can do. You are also likely to be an interesting person who has friends who enjoy sharing what you like to do, and they will attend your photo exhibit, go to your recital, or cheer at your game.

RECREATION PROGRAMMING DEVELOPS THE SELF

At this point, you have read several personal accounts of the paths that others have followed through recreation. Clearly, their childhood choices and adult careers have been rewarding. Now the question is to analyze just why recreation choices are such powerful factors in leading people to recognize their personal and career potentials. Here is a way to understand the hidden potential of recreation: If what you are doing turns out to be a challenge well met, you are exhilarated. In Csikszentmihalyi's [chick-sent-me-hi] (1990) terms, you have had an *optimal experience,* you have been in a mental state of *flow,* loving what you have been doing, forgetting about everything else, enjoying yourself immensely, and developing your *self* in the process.

Not only does Csikszentmihalyi say that *what* you choose is important because it must offer a challenge to whatever level of skill you bring to the action, but developmental psychologists Rappoport and Rappoport (1975) determined that your **life stage** is a significant frame of reference in all choices you make. It is as if you hold the things you need to learn at each stage in life in the "back of your mind," and these ideas silently guide your perceptions about what would be a good thing to do.

For example, the baby picks up objects and turns them over and over in his or her hands, sucks on them, and thereby forms an image of the objects in the mind. At age 4 or 5, the need is to expand one's visual focus and begin to imagine what cannot be seen, so the toddler loves guessing "which hand" holds the cookie and will ask the clown who reaches out and pulls a quarter from behind his or her ear to repeat the act over and over. These youngsters are easily mesmerized by puppet shows (even the simple ones performed by older children!) and will sit for stories so long as they can see the pictures and answer questions that use their language skills and show their ability to be "good boys and girls" (that is, to please adults by doing the right thing).

Since older children need to master new skills, knowledge, and courage, they love to build things, act dramatically, or take on dares to prove their agility, speed, or dexterity. They can spend hours making a hydroelectric generator out of a coffee can turned by a stream; perfecting a sport, music, or dance skill; or performing the hardest jump-rope rhymes without a miss.

The adolescent, focused on preparing to enter adulthood, needs to come to terms with her or his identity in respect to sexuality, future career, capabilities, and values. Thus, being able to "hang out" at a teen center, plan and hold dances, belong to interest groups, volunteer for special community

©Jim West—Theatre Production

Youth theater holds an attraction for adolescents as they come to terms with their own identity and prepare for adulthood.

or forming new partnerships following separation or loss; and learning from others about ways of handling decisions about the future, which include saving for children's college, investing for retirement, coping with aging parents, and becoming an interesting individual in midlife.

As we complete the aging cycle, needs vary, but often, recreation becomes a vehicle allowing seniors to continue exploring their interests and potential abilities and to meet with specialists and practitioners. In community and nonprofit agencies, healthy seniors often come for morning classes, stay for lunch, enjoy each other's company at bridge or poker or dancing, and find ways of raising funds to support their programs. Seniors with more focused interests, and expendable funds, join museum or art guilds, tennis or golf clubs, travel clubs, or political and social-activist groups and use their last active years participating in Elder Hostel, taking personal development seminars, or learning and investing in those things that time now allows. Frail elderly are less apt to be participating in recreation independently, but they enjoy maintaining the same regimen of activities within their household or in supported and assisted-living facilities.

Without their preferred recreational interests, adults (of any age) feel a loss of identity, as if they are being forced into a lifestyle that is unrewarding and meaningless. You can judge by these examples how important recreation is to people throughout their lives and that their choices reflect the stages of life. Perhaps recreation is the most important vehicle for growing and adjusting in life simply because of the vast potential for choice and the fact that the expectations and rewards are controlled by each individual, not by school standards or by an employer.

THE INTERACTIVE NATURE OF RECREATION

With every choice you make, recreation forces you to interact mentally with what you are doing and where you are directing yourself in the process, thus revealing information about yourself and the thing you are doing. Rossman (1995) makes the point that you interact with three sources of mental stimulation: other people or ideal models

events, and join team-centered enterprises such as sports, bands, youth theater, or start a fund-raising business holds great appeal for teens.

Young adults look for opportunities to meet socially through recreation because their need is to settle into a community and find a life partner. Social activity clubs that offer a variety of choices along with shared meals are ideal, but since keeping the body beautiful is also important, individual exercise programs can be modified with the addition of juice bars, lite-meal dining, or social activity such as bowling or chess. Actually, young adults are attracted to the small social groups formed around particular interests such as bicycle riding, scrapbooking, walking or hiking, kayaking or the like.

Later, the adult is concerned with the aging process and long-term security, so recreation is a means of developing healthy living practices; engaging with one's partner in shared interests whom you seek to emulate, the objects you are using in your recreative experience (equipment and supplies), and perhaps a leisure or specialized environment that you use such as your living room, an indoor gymnasium, a pottery shop, a weaving studio, a garden, an ice rink, or a stage. Your interactions suggest ways for you to adjust your actions or your goals. While you are engaging in your recreation (or recalling it in reverie), your mind fills with memories, deeper understanding of the experience, and opportunities for new action. These thoughts underlie what is called meaningful life experience.

Recreation, then, provides a context for interactive opportunities that you perceive as optimal challenges whereby you can discover, fulfill, and develop your potential (see figure 13.1). Note that, if the mind is not activated and you are not feeling a sense of satisfaction or enjoyable excitement with yourself, probably whatever you are doing is not important. You may just be filling (killing) time. Thus, the recreation professional is concerned with creating contexts for participation with lifestage–appropriate challenges that children and adults can grow on. We call this recreation programming.

PROGRAMMING: BRIEFLY

The fundamental building block in the field of recreation is programming, that is, designing experiences for people to come together, engage in challenges, and have fun in the interactive process. Recreation programs take five forms: instruction, drop-in, club, competition or exhibition, and special event (Farrell & Lundegren, 1983). You have probably participated in all five forms, so the following examples will help you think of your own experiences that correspond to the **program formats**.

- Instruction (to learn or practice with guidance): fencing class, Red Cross swim program, photography class, watercolor painting class

- Drop-in (to pursue one's own challenges): open swim, open tennis court, after-school games and crafts, open gym for basketball

- Club (to share interests and accomplish common goals): Girl or Boy Scouts, model railroaders club, drama club, Golden Agers club, teen club

- Competition (to perform, demonstrate, or exhibit ability): recreation league sports, in-class tournaments, juried art shows, state lifeguard or martial arts tests, swim meets, end of instruction demonstration for parents and friends

- Special event (to celebrate, honor, commemorate, or experience novelty): Fourth of July celebration, father–daughter dance, pancake breakfast, recitals, concert in the park

- Multiple format (combines more than one format): summer camp, trips, workshops, conferences, training, special events

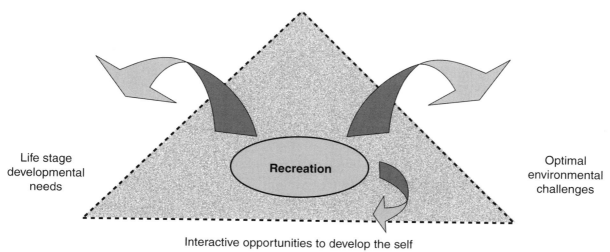

FIGURE 13.1 Key elements in recreation programming: interaction, the developing self, and challenges.

A parade is just one example of special event programming.

Programming is the combination of knowledge and practiced skills that differentiates recreation leaders and managers from professionals in athletics, education, business, entertainment, and other organized-group situations. The purpose of programming is to design opportunities in which people can interact with others, the recreative objects, and a leisure environment to derive a rewarding sense of meaning and self-worth. The question is "With what do you create programs in each of the formats?" Although the answer is "Almost anything that people want to do for the simple reward of doing it," for the purposes of teaching the principles and opportunities of programming, the broad realm of recreation activity is divided into program areas: recreational sport, fitness and wellness, outdoor and adventure, and arts and culture. These program areas can be combined when designing some programs. For example, on a camping trip, you might plan for people to engage in hiking (club), journal writing (instruction then drop-in), woodland games (instruction or competitive), swimming (drop-in), carving memory sticks (instruction), cooking (instruction or competitive, i.e., performance, and cleanup), campfire singing and skits (special event),

and campsite chores (club). Programmers will plan each activity separately as they organize each of the five days, *envisioning* what might happen as people come together and use the camping environment as a context for self-discovery, self-expression, personal growth, learning, sharing, and enjoyment. Through the envisioning process, the program plan is created, edited, revised, and mentally perfected (Rossman [1995] suggests students learn to do this with eyes closed, making mental corrections as they go through the experience). Using the mental imaging technique, the programmer tries to foresee what may occur at every stage in the recreation experience, and he or she makes changes to improve the plan before presenting it to participants. I believe this technique led to an accident-injury-free summer when I worked as a swimming pool director, responsible for instruction, swim club, competitions, drop-in swim, and family night events. Every evening, I went home and visualized what had gone on at the pool. In the process, I often imagined new ways for swimmers to cause themselves injury or accidents that could result in drowning. Based on these thoughts, I made improvements in procedures, safety rules, and pool maintenance. I don't believe there was any training course or pool manual that covered all the problems that I realized were possible.

Recreational Sport

Recreational sport includes individual and team activities, organized group games, and technically ruled sport. They take place in indoor, field, and natural land and water environments. Sport and games begin with teaching skills to participants who can advance into organized systems for play. Instruction could include teaching a 6-year-old to anticipate danger while playing checkers, keep alert in London Bridge Is Falling Down, watch the ball in Kickball, or to swim safely by learning to float in a swimming pool; whereas, teaching a college student to take the *en garde* stance in fencing with a saber and showing a middle-aged adult how to feel the weight of the lure being cast into a fishing pool might represent skills learned after childhood. Sport and games can be a part of every program format. For example, to reach the Olympic games, an athlete's abilities are developed through a system that most likely includes some combination of instruction, coached club practice and play, drop-in practice perhaps with coaching, and lead-up competitions. We can say that the Olympians, at least most from the United States and Canada, are amateurs at the peak of their development. As such, they are involved in recreational sports and games. In contrast, you or some of your classmates may be college athletes or band musicians or you may know a professional athlete or dancer. Generally speaking, the amateurs are focused on the experience and how each event makes them feel or grow; whereas, the contracted performer is focused on doing what the coach, choreographer, or owner expects, and the paycheck outweighs the personal growth as a reward. Whenever people play for the fun of challenging themselves rather than for a paycheck, a scholarship, a trophy, or to be named the winner, you can view it as recreational. Marty and Cary are examples of recreational players.

Fitness and Wellness

Fitness and wellness activities have become popular since the President's Council on Physical Fitness found in the 1950s that the nation's youth were unfit for national service. In truth, fitness and wellness have been part of the values and practices of social groups and nation-states for thousands of years. Just as certain practices rise and fall in popularity in the United States and Canada, the value of fitness and wellness has risen and declined historically. Scientific and medical advances for preventive, treatment, and rehabilitative procedures have encouraged healthier lifestyles globally, and cross-cultural information exchange has deepened our knowledge of and broadened the variety of health-maintenance opportunities. Thus, it is not surprising that recreation organizations offer a variety of weight-loss, stress-reduction, and muscle-toning programs. Demand for these programs has boosted the expansion of spas, health resorts, and meditation and yoga centers. These programs are also prevalent in public and nonprofit organizations.

Outdoor and Adventure

Outdoor and adventure activities often seem to cross tracks with sport and games, but this is true of many program activities. You can create a program for learning how to paint landscapes while camping in the countryside or a program for winter trekking up mountains to compete in ski races. And won't both of these ideas result in health-and-fitness rewards for the participants? However, when the outdoor environment is necessary for the experience and participating expands knowledge of the environment, then the activity is assigned to the outdoor and adventure program area. One way to help classify an activity is to determine whether the environment can be constructed or must it be naturally occurring. To what program area would you assign SCUBA training and diving: recreational sport or outdoor and adventure? Beginning rock climbers can start on a manufactured indoor or outdoor climbing wall, then challenge themselves by tackling a natural rock formation. The challenges can increase as the climbers develop more knowledge and skill through instruction and experience until they are able to join an international expedition, climbing in Nepal.

Since the 1960s, great growth has been realized in outdoor recreation through programs for camping, fishing, boating, and hiking; outdoor sport using the natural environment for orienteering, sailing, and skiing; and challenge courses using natural and constructed facilities. However, there is nothing better in many people's minds than a peaceful afternoon on the beach basking in the sun with a few friends, listening to the waves and the seagulls, talking while sipping something cold, and finishing the afternoon with a stroll down the beach looking for something the waves turned up.

Arts and Culture

Arts and culture, like the other program areas, is indistinct in many ways. You hear about the art of juggling or that fitness trekking is part of the Swiss and German cultures. What is essential in the concept of art is that the person is developing an aesthetic understanding or knowledge and, if directly participating, developing performance skills. Thus, what is considered art can range from crafts such as sewing, sculpting, and designing stained glass to fine arts such as painting, drama, music, and formal dance disciplines. Other categories include popular culture, consisting of current music, dance, art, or literature and folk arts, which maintain traditions such as ethnic dance, batik, and basket weaving.

Again, assigning categories is difficult. If the main goal of an activity relates to developing or appreciating the aesthetic essence of something, it fits in with arts and culture. In the 1800s, the Chautauqua was invented to bring art and culture to people living in rural and undeveloped parts of the United States. People traveled for miles to camp out and attend the lectures, debates, readings, plays, dances, musical performances, and sing-alongs and to learn what was new and unusual in the world. Remnants of the Chautauqua movement exist today in some parts of the country. On Nantucket Island in Massachusetts, some homes are built on tent platforms used in the summer meetings, and in Ashland, Oregon, the Shakespeare Festival's Elizabethan Theater incorporates part of a wall from the old Chautauqua hall. This suggests that traces of recreation from one era can exist in the present day and not always in the form we would imagine. What program might you establish that

Career Path Into Public Recreation

Oralethea Davenport, recreation supervisor for the Lan-Oak Park District in Illinois

As a child, I was always out playing in the neighborhood with the other kids. If we weren't climbing fences and trees, we were riding our bikes to the park to play there. Of course, we loved sidewalk games like double-Dutch jump rope. Whatever was a challenge was fun. I don't think any of us thought that what we were doing was recreation then. We were just a bunch of kids playing, taking risks to outdo the others, and having a good time. At the end of my senior year in high school, I needed to earn money for college, so I got a job with the Chicago Park District as a camp counselor. I liked this work because it was a good job and it would be there every year while I was in college. I still did not put two and two together—that my summer job could be a career opportunity—until I had tried five different majors in college, in subjects as diverse as criminal justice and agriculture! After several people told me to look into the recreation major, I tried the introductory course (probably like the one you are taking right now). I definitely liked what I was reading and hearing, so I did some career research on my own. The job descriptions, responsibility, pay, and opportunities sounded right for me. I also realized I had already been "in training" for leadership in the field with my summer camp work.

My major provided lots of on-the-job experience with internships and projects, so I knew I was on the right track. I worked at a YMCA, the Chicago Park District, and several other recreation organizations. I am now a recreation supervisor, and I *love* my job. I work with all age groups, from prenatal to seniors, doing regular programming, special events, and staff supervision. I have even planned our huge Fourth of July celebration and intergenerational events for grandparents and grandchildren. What fun! I am also proud to say that I have been elected as the Ethnic Minority Society representative to the Illinois Park and Recreation Society Board of Directors.

One thing I want you to know is that it is easy to think that nobody knows what we are doing, that nobody is really watching us, but that is not true. I was shocked one day when the local newspaper contacted me to say I had been selected as the community member to be in their spotlight feature article. From this I learned that it meant something to the parents and others who found me in my office working long hours or who realized I knew the names of every one of the 120 preschoolers in the program. People do notice, never forget that.

would take root and foster creativity and expression of aesthetic values?

Dreaming up programs is an exciting part of leisure services, one a new professional shared with her career story. Oralethea's story is about discovering her passion in life: programming. She has just started her career and is learning what her constituents value, and she is absolutely sure she's on the right path.

IS THIS THE LIFE FOR YOU? TYPES OF SERVICE AND CAREER PATHS

To the uninformed, choosing a career in recreation is so unimaginable, it can be tantamount to announcing a plan to join a band of Martians. Fortunately, with a little education, family and friends change their attitudes from disbelief to envy. Parents of students confirm their change of heart every year at graduation. Imagine working to improve the quality of life for people and their communities. Because of the scope of job opportunities, either existing or to be invented, you need to experience a variety of possibilities and gain self-understanding to find your niche.

Although the field of recreation is vast and varied, job titles can provide clues to the professional responsibilities. Table 13.1 lists common titles in each of the program areas. Two levels are shown: jobs comprising work directly with clientele or **resources** and jobs primarily consisting of managing the system or organization.

Most recreation professionals developed their interest in the field because of their firsthand experiences, perhaps playing on a recreational sport team, taking swim or acting lessons, or joining an interest group or club. In fact, many organizations offer leadership or counselor training for teens, and that leads some young people to think about staying in recreation as a career. With their accrued knowledge, opportunities for volunteer and paid teaching or leading become available, and these young people reap the rewards of helping others find their passion and enjoy themselves. For this reason, many professionals try to remain in the face-to-face leadership roles as much as possible.

In the administrative ranks, specialized knowledge of the program area is needed, but administrators take on responsibilities such as scheduling, funding, budgeting, marketing, public relations, training, and acting as liaison with other departments or organizations. Many administrative

TABLE 13.1   Sample Job Titles Associated With Each Program Area

Recreational sport	Fitness and wellness	Outdoor and adventure	Arts and culture
DIRECT-SERVICE POSITION TITLES			
Coach	Coach	Coach or facilitator	Artist
Leader or instructor	Instructor	Leader or instructor	Coach
Programmer	Leader	Interpreter	Leader
Trainer	Therapist	Therapist	Teacher
Scheduler	Trainer	Trainer	Therapist
ADMINISTRATIVE-POSITION TITLES			
Administrator	Coordinator	Administrator	Administrator
Coordinator	Director	Coordinator	Producer
Manager	Manager	Manager	Director
Head or lead	Programmer	Ranger	Manager
Supervisor	Supervisor	Supervisor	

Program areas can have administrative positions that are similarly described. For example, large organizations could have any of the following lists of departmental tasks and more. Typical areas of special responsibility: advertising, finance, human resources, programming, public relations, resource management, risk management.

personnel fulfill their desire to work directly with participants by continuing to teach or lead on a limited basis. However, it is more common for administrators to satisfy their passion to serve others directly by working with personnel, committees, task forces, and boards and by training future leaders.

One career opportunity in high demand in all sectors is planning and managing festivals, events, and parades. As you have read, those responsibilities are part of Cary's and Oralethea's jobs. But specialists with event programming and management skills are also sought by small and large businesses for tradeshows, member or clientele development and services, and for entertainment. These positions can be found in nearly every large corporation and association, and event planners form their own businesses for weddings and other celebrations.

When investigating recreation jobs, be aware that although job responsibilities may be similar, job titles may differ. For example, ranger is a typical title for personnel working in parks and forests; however, people who are classified as rangers may also be called watershed keepers and harbormasters. Those performing the duties of scouting's professional scouts would be called program coordinators or supervisors in other organizations, so don't let the titles fool you.

Read job descriptions to see if the work interests you. Within kindred organizations, titles and jobs are similar, but between different types of organizations, the titles and responsibilities vary. For example, if you compare public recreation and

Web Sites to EXPLORE

American Camp Association: www.acacamps.org

American Red Cross (water safety services): www.redcross.org/services/hss/aquatics/

American Society of Association Executives: www.asaenet.org

Adventures in Wild California (Maverick Beach at Pillar Point): www.wildca.com/wild-stories/wild-locations.htm

Boy Scouts of America: www.scouting.org

Boys and Girls Clubs of America: www.bgca.org

Beautiful Nauvoo (Mormon historic site and tourist recreation): www.beautifulnauvoo.com/site/default.asp

California Boating Safety Officers Organization: www.cbsoa.org

California Surf Lifesaving Association: www.cslsa.org

Canadian Red Cross (water and boating safety): www.redcross.ca/main.asp?id=000278

The Civil War Reenactors: www.cwreenactors.com

Eastern Amputee Golf Association: www.eaga.org

Easter Seals Society Canada: www.easterseals.ca

Easter Seals recreation & camping: www.easterseals.com/site/PageServer?pagename=ntl_camping_recreation&s_eslocation=serv_cr

Ethnic Dance Chicago: www.EthnicDance.net

Girl Scouts: www.girlscouts.org

History of Chautauqua movement: www.campuschool.dsu.edu/myweb/history.htm

Huntington Beach, California: http://surfcityusa.com

Illinois Parks and Recreation Association: www.il-ipra.org

Indiana Easter Seals Society (Bradford Woods Camp Riley for kids with physical disabilities): www.indianaesa.org/camp-riley.htm

Jewish Community Center of Greater Washington: www.jccgw.org

Lan-Oak Park District: http://lanoakparkdistrict.org

Montgomery County Recreation Department: www.montgomerycountymd.gov/content/rec/index.asp

National Association of YWCA Executives: www.naye.org

National Audubon Society: www.audubon.org

National Intramural-Recreation and Sports Association: www.nirsa.org

National Recreation and Park Association: www.nrpa.org

NRPA (Joseph Lee Memorial Library and Archives): www.nrpa.org/content/default.aspx?documentId=513

New Life in the Fast Lane (Christian recreation information): www.newlifeinthefastlane.com/recreation.htm

New Old Time Chautauqua: www.chautauqua.org

Outward Bound of Canada: www.outwardbound.ca

Outward Bound USA: www.outwardbound.org

Sacred Heart High School Catholic Youth Organization (Lynn, Massachusetts): www.lynnyouth.com

Sea World: www.seaworld.com

United States Adaptive Golf Association: www.usagas.org

United States Lifesaving Association: www.usla.org

United Service Organizations: www.uso.org

What Is Enlightenment magazine (article about Mihalyi Csikszentmihalyi and the flow theory): www.wie.org/j21/csiksz.asp

YMCA of USA: www.ymca.net

YWCA of the USA: www.ywca.org

Career Path Into Organizational Leadership

Kent Blumenthal, PhD, CAE, executive director of the National Intramural-Recreational Sports Association

I was the lowest-paid lifeguard working at the Montgomery County (Maryland) Recreation swimming pool when I started my first job. As I continued through high school, I remained an employee of Montgomery County Recreation as playground leader, director of a playground program, and then summer camp director. The work was satisfying and rewarding in many respects. It never occurred to me that I might want a career in recreation, so I majored in sociology. After graduating from college, I went to Israel and experienced a profound awakening. I met a guy who was a reserve officer in the Israeli Defense Forces and a student at the Israel Institute of Technology in Haifa. He had a part-time job working with emotionally disturbed young adults. What he was doing with these young people totally impressed me. As soon as I returned to the United States I learned that over here we call it therapeutic recreation, and I enrolled in a master's degree program in therapeutic recreation at the University of Maryland.

Now this is where my life takes on the feeling of a fairy tale. While at Maryland, I met several professors who were considered leaders in the field. Fred Humphry, chair of the recreation department (a mentor and early leader in professional education), recommended me to U of M's Summer Programs Office where I was hired (at age 23!) to plan and supervise all campus recreation facilities and the full- and part-time staff for the university's summer recreation programs. I still can't believe I did that! Another professor, Charlotte Leedy, a former USO leader during World War II, took me under her wing and arranged for me to work as a research assistant part-time for the National Recreation and Park Association (NRPA) on a C.S. Mott Foundation community education grant. Along with that work, I was hired to work full-time at NRPA, and I slowly completed my master's degree. Meanwhile, I continued working part-time in community therapeutic recreation with several special populations: people with developmental disabilities, emotional disabilities, and physical disabilities. I always felt appreciated when doing therapeutic recreation. I had only been finished with my master's for a couple of years when Dr. Humphrey encouraged me to start the doctoral program to study recreation administration. In 1990, while still working with the NRPA, I finished my doctorate. All totaled, I spent 19 unbelievable years at NRPA, changing jobs within the organization every three to five years, from assistant to the deputy director and director of the information system division to acting director of governmental affairs in President Reagan's Commission on Americans Outdoors, with many other positions in between. It was easy to stay with the organization because I was constantly learning new things; it was never routine and never became boring.

At the point when I was considering going into college teaching, someone suggested that I apply for the position of western region director of NRPA, in Colorado. I held that job for five years and realized that I had learned a great deal about association management through all my experiences with the national association. Again, I was approached to apply for a job (quite an honor), this time to head the National Intramural-Recreational Sports Association (NIRSA). Whew! I went from a staff of 2 to a staff of 15 full-time and 6 part-time employees at NIRSA. I have loved the challenges of building NIRSA from a little-known organization with a proud history to one that reaches 7.13 million college students with members on college campuses throughout the United States. I am proud to say that I have just passed the national exam to become a certified association executive (CAE) through the American Society of Association Executives.

In retrospect, I realize that I was mentored by some of the best leaders in our field. In exchange for making myself available to them to do their work and to engage with them often, I was introduced to other organizations and opportunities, given challenges for personal and professional growth, and have never had to wonder where my next job would come from. I can also say that some of my most memorable and rewarding experiences have been working as a therapeutic recreation specialist. The impact that recreation had on clients was immeasurable, and it made me feel that every little thing I did was worthwhile. I would add that I have felt very dynamic as a professional in this field; it has been a good fit with my personality and temperament. With my constant need to learn, I have always been interested in my jobs, and I have been able to see my progress and growth through what I have done. Every day is different, with new challenges that are not always easy, but there is a great sense of accomplishment in solving problems and applying innovative and creative thinking every day.

parks organizations from city to city, you are likely to find that more of the face-to-face leadership jobs are part-time, and professionals tend to be coordinators, supervisors, or administrators. In nonprofit organizations like the YMCA, YWCA, Girl Scouts and Boy Scouts, Boys and Girls Clubs, and religious institutions, professionals are usually involved in more direct leadership and take on administrative duties as they demonstrate capability. For-profit enterprises are more likely to combine the levels, doing multiple functions, since the business often provides less direct leadership to participants. You can see this pattern in fitness clubs, community theater, and event-planning businesses, for example.

The following personal story provides an example of a career path that went from face-to-face leadership; to coordinator, event planner, and manager; and finally to the national directorship of a nonprofit organization. Kent Blumenthal's story exemplifies why you should look for role models and good mentors every moment, wherever you are. Be alert for the "precious present."

SUMMARY

The chapter started with the words of Joseph Lee. His idea was that without opportunities that light you up on the inside, or worse, without opportunities at all, life will be unsatisfying. Therefore, when programming recreation, effective professionals try to gain the perspective of their clients, understand their growth needs, and see the world as they see it and experience it. By seeking various perspectives you will include more participants, and inclusion is at the heart of recreation. After all, there are few other activities in which people are free to interact with one another and strengthen their communities through shared experience and mutual understanding and respect.

When people's lives are totally encumbered by work, whether by lack of knowledge that there are other options besides putting work at the center of life or because of economic necessity, people are not living fully. To dissuade people from lives centered on work, income, and material acquisition, tantalizing opportunities are needed lure them to add a recreational dimension to their daily routine. As Lee aptly realized, with the routine specialization and organization associated with rapidly advancing society, the human dimension of life is easily compromised. Thus, the job of recreation programming and leisure services delivery is central to the health and happiness of people living today. The freedoms in recreational choices are numerous—join, practice, change, or quit—most of us can't do that freely in our jobs. Recreation is not an obligation; it is a choice for happiness.

Now that you have a broad understanding of recreation programming and the opportunities for personal discovery and reward, the next few chapters go into more detail about each of the program areas. As you learn about each area, let your imagination run free as you explore rewarding career choices that allow you to help others participate in creating meaningful lives.

CHAPTER 14

Recreational Sport Management

Craig M. Ross

Sports for all means sports for all ages, all racial and ethnic groups, all ability levels, all genders, and all social strata.

Andre Carvalho,
chief of the programme development
and operations group, United Nations

CHAPTER OBJECTIVES

After reading this chapter, you should be able to do the following:

- Understand the foundation of recreational sport management
- List the broad scope of recreational sport activities and events
- Describe the trends affecting recreational sport management
- Understand the scope of participation in recreational sport
- List career opportunities in recreational sport management

INTRODUCTION

It is evident that sport in American society has experienced tremendous change and increased popularity over the past several decades. Today sport and physical activity are as much a part of American culture as other institutions such as work, marriage, and the family. Levels of sport interests and participation from all sectors of society are reaching unprecedented levels. Once considered a diversion from work and a tool for recreation, sport has grown to a multibillion-dollar industry. This evolution of sport has been described as a dominant influence in American society (Parkhouse, 1996). Another recreation scholar suggests that for a growing number of Americans, sport almost is a religion (Kraus, 2000).

Sport has not only had an impact in the United States, but its popularity is also seen in Canada. In 1998, 34 percent of Canadians 15 years of age or older (8.3 million) participated regularly in one or more sports (Statistics Canada, 2003).

These changes and beliefs have had a significant impact on the way sport and leisure services have been delivered in the past and will continue to be delivered in the future. On the one hand, sport has become very entertainment and spectator oriented, and record numbers of people are attending professional sporting events. Professional athletes are considered folk heroes and are paid astronomical salaries. On the other hand, when sport participation is viewed as an "experience," it is considered leisure (Kelly & Freysinger, 2000). In this regard, sport has become participant oriented, involving diverse populations in a variety of programs and activities. The growth of sport in some form in modern society cannot be questioned. "Sport has a major role in modern society as an element of the economy, a spectacle with symbolic meanings, an arena of development for the young, and in the leisure lives of many individuals" (Kelly, 1996, p. 226).

Recreational sport is a popular and appealing form of leisure and recreation to many American adults. And levels of participation in youth sports programs have risen to all-time highs (Cordes & Ibrahim, 2003). **Recreational sports** participation far surpasses all other types of recreational activities (Edginton, Jordan, DeGraaf, & Edginton, 2002; Kraus, 2000; Shivers & de Lisle, 1997). Sixty-nine percent of Americans who are 6 years old or older participate in some type of sport, fitness, and outdoor activities (Sporting Goods Manufacturers Association [SGMA], 2004). Robinson and Godbey (1997) in their book *Time for Life* have even described sports and fitness activities as "mainstays in the lifestyles of large numbers of Americans" (p. 186).

IDENTITY: LOOKING AT SPORT MANAGEMENT FROM A RECREATIONAL PERSPECTIVE

The discipline that manages sport programs has been referred to by experts in a variety of different terms and titles over the years. Although there is no consensus on the name of the field, the term "sport management" is generally the umbrella term used to identify the administration and management of a large number and variety of sports, fitness and wellness, and recreation programs (Stier, 1999). Traditionally, sport management has focused on the "business enterprise" side of sports, specifically professional sports marketing, sales, public relations, promotions, sporting goods, media relations, and fund-raising. Mull, Bayless, Ross, and Jamieson (1997) suggest that sport management is the "total process of structuring the business or organizational aspects of sport" (p. 7). More recently, sport management has begun to emphasize the leadership and management of people and resources in a variety of participatory or recreational settings. In this delivery, the key principle of "active" sport participation is represented by various degrees of competitive activity within many sectors. These sectors include collegiate, municipal parks and recreation, commercial, corporate, correctional, and military recreation to name just a few.

From this perspective, recreational sport is a major component of a person's lifestyle, as either a participant in or spectator of sports during leisure (Mull, Bayless, & Jamieson, 2005). These authors provide a leisure sport management model (see figure 14.1) that illustrates the concepts of participation and being a spectator in sport programming, ranging from **educational sports** at the lowest level to **professional sports** at the highest.

A large number of participants, ranging from youth to seniors, actively participate in sport at the educational or instructional and recreational levels. Then, as participants progress upward in the model toward the apex, participation in the leisure experience shifts from being actively involved in the activity to involvement as a spectator watching the event. For example, at the professional level of sport, the leisure experience of most people consists of watching professional athletes perform and compete rather than being actively involved in the sport.

DEFINING RECREATIONAL SPORT

Traditionally, recreational sport has been described as intramural sport, physical recreation, physical activity, nonvarsity athletics, open recreation, intramural athletics, and so on. However, none of these accurately reflects what recreational sport actually is. The basis of recreational sport is the involvement during leisure time either as an active participant or as a spectator at one of the levels of the leisure sport hierarchy. The major characteristic of recreational sport management that separates it from other sport disciplines is its focus on sport participation for the masses. Recreational sport programs are designed to give *everyone* an active role regardless of sport interest, age, race, gender, or athletic ability. It truly is sport for all. Because recreational sport programs are participant driven, sport programmers and managers put significant effort into defining and meeting participants' wants and needs. The increasing complexity and magnitude in recreational sport management are more than likely a result of societal demands for more and better services, targeting mass participation in recreational sport.

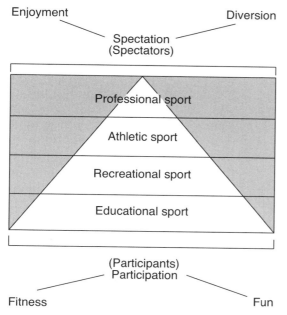

FIGURE 14.1   Leisure sport management model.

FIVE PROGRAMMING AREAS OF RECREATIONAL SPORT MANAGEMENT

Five basic program delivery areas comprise the recreational sport spectrum: instructional sports, informal sports, intramural sports, extramural sports, and club sports. **Instructional sports** are the recreational sport activities that teach skills, rules, and strategies in a noncredit or academic environment; **informal sports** involve self-directed participation with an individualized approach focused on fun and fitness; intramural sports involve structured sports in the form of leagues, tournaments, and contests conducted within a particular setting; **extramural sports** consist of structured sport activities between winners of various intramural sport programs; and **club sports** are undertaken by groups of participants that organize because of a common interest in a sport.

Instructional Sport

Most traditional recreational sport programs are based on sport competition, and they appeal primarily to people who are already familiar with a particular sport or have some degree of skill and involvement with sports. The instructional sport program area focuses on an even larger segment of the population that needs to learn basic sport skills and how to incorporate the physical activity and fitness components of sport into daily life. This program area was developed to encourage participants to gain the core skills in various levels of sport activities and to provide a way for people to have fun and enjoy the many benefits of participating in the sport activity. The primary emphasis, then, is on participant skill development, enjoyment, and learning how to play the game.

Years ago, instructional sport was offered only through educational settings, such as physical education classes and varsity athletics. But with the increased interest and popularity in recreational sport participation, instructional sport has expanded into nonacademic settings such as the YMCAs, YWCAs, Boys and Girls Clubs, municipal parks and recreation, commercial recreational sports, and the armed forces recreation sector. Practically every setting (campus, military, municipal, youth, and so on) now offers instructional sports that teach individuals or groups through classes, lessons, clinics, and workshops and usually at three instructional levels: beginning, intermediate, and advanced. Examples of instructional sports include exercise and conditioning, gymnastics, martial arts, swimming, golf, bowling, tennis, racquetball, and squash.

Informal Sport

Informal sport, probably one of the most misunderstood and misrepresented program delivery areas in recreational sport management, is self-directed sport participation for fun and fitness. This program area is at the other end of the spectrum from structured intramural sports and possesses the least structured. Informal sport activities include backyard volleyball or softball at the family picnic, pickup basketball games at the local park, an early-morning swim or lunchtime run, or lifting weights in the weight room of a fitness facility. This program area emphasizes self-directed participation. The participant designs and develops the specific personal program and goals, and the recreational sport staff facilitates the involvement or experience through appropriate and available facilities and equipment. In most sectors (municipal parks and recreation, armed forces recreation, educational recreation), informal sport involves the largest number of participants. Because informal sports are the least structured, sport takes place whenever there is an available facility or interest in the activity. For recreational sport programmers, many elements go into informal sport programming and management. Because the primary goal is to facilitate sport participation, perhaps the biggest concerns for informal sports programmers are facilities and equipment management and scheduling. Having available and accessible facilities and equipment is essential to creating a satisfying and positive experience for all participants.

Although the benefits of fitness and wellness are part of all of the program delivery components, managing specific fitness and wellness programs has become a special programming area in informal sports over the past decade. Group exercise programs such as step aerobics, trekking, indoor cycling, and mind and body activities such as Pilates, yoga, and tai chi are especially popular with women. These programs help participants enhance or achieve overall well-being through sport and fitness activities and play an integral role in the overall management of recreational sport.

Intramural Sport

Intramural sport is structured participation *within* a specific setting such as leagues, tournaments, and matches. The word "intramural" is derived from the Latin words "intra" (within) and "mural" (walls). Intramural sports, then, are structured activities between teams and individuals within an agency's limits or boundaries such as city limits, university campus, YMCA branch, and so on. Intramural sports are generally limited to participation among the participants served by a

Group fitness programs have become a special programming area in informal sports.

particular agency and should provide opportunities for men, women, and mixed competition with a variety of rule modifications to meet the particular needs and interests of the participants in that setting. Intramural sports can include the following:

- **Individual sports.** Events that generally allow people to participate alone (e.g., fishing, golf, swimming, diving, trap and skeet, cycling, hunting, boxing, and archery)

- **Dual sports.** Events that require at least one opponent (e.g., badminton, table tennis, tennis, squash, handball, and racquetball)

- **Team sports.** Events that require a specific number of players who play as a team of either men, women, or mixed intramural divisions (e.g., baseball, basketball, softball, kickball, lacrosse, field hockey, rowing, soccer, volleyball, wallyball, water polo, and flag football)

- **Meet sports.** Separate events occurring within a larger event and usually conducted over a period of one or two days (e.g., swimming, gymnastics, diving, wrestling, golf, and track and field)

- **Special events.** Nontraditional activities usually not practiced regularly by the participants (e.g., Wacky Olympics, sports all-nighters and festivals, and superstar competitions)

Intramural sports are typically the "signature" program or mainstay of recreational sport agencies. In many instances, they provide the basic sport opportunities from which agencies build and expand their overall program offerings. This is because of the familiarity and high-profile nature of traditional sport programs, the large participation base, a well-organized and highly structured program delivery, competitive (but wholesome!) atmosphere, and the recognition and awards for participants and teams who excel.

Historically, the term "intramural sports" has been associated with recreational sport programs at colleges and universities. However, municipal and community recreation departments, churches, YMCAs, military bases, elementary and secondary schools, industries, and private clubs now offer a variety of sport events that are very similar to collegiate recreational sport but with a different participant than the typical 18- to 22-year-old college student. These events, although not thought of as "intramural sports," in fact meet the definition of sport played "within the walls" of a particular agency.

Extramural Sport

Extramural sports refer to structured recreational sport participation that provides participants with an opportunity to compete against participants from other agencies or organizations. Competition takes place between winning teams from several programs. Extramural sports include sport programs and activities in which participants and teams from winning programs are extended an invitation to represent their home agency and compete for an overall championship. The Little League Baseball World Series is an extramural sport event. Other examples are a navy basketball team representing its base Morale, Welfare and Recreation (MWR) department playing in the local municipal parks and recreation tournament or a collegiate intramural flag football championship team from one university playing against other collegiate champions for "national champion" recognition. Many times, the extramural sport program fills the gap between varsity athletics and intramural sports and provides additional opportunities for many higher-skilled athletes to compete.

Club Sport

Club sports involve any group that organizes to further its interest or skill level in a specific sport activity. These interests range from very competitive club teams that travel and play in various high-level competitions to the recreational, social, and instructional clubs that conduct activities such as basic-skill instruction and tournaments among themselves.

The history of club sports is long. It is believed that club sports are the forerunners of college athletics, intramural sports, and formal physical education classes. The main purpose of a club

sport program is to provide various degrees of interaction and sport participation to its members. In many instances, a club sport is formed for the social aspects that incorporate practices, informal get-togethers, and philanthropic functions. Other clubs offer instruction and skills development for beginning to advanced skill levels, and others organize for the sole purpose of competition and tournaments. Because clubs are not limited to the college setting, they can be found in the public, military, commercial, private, and correctional settings. Club sport programs have become popular because they generally operate with fewer administrative resource needs such as staffing, facilities, referees, and so on than other types of organized recreational spot programming. Many clubs are self-sufficient and generate all needed funding.

The nature of club sports allows members to direct their interests both within and outside of the recreational agency. Characteristics that distinguish club sports from intramural sports, informal sports, and extramural sports include the following:

- They are self-administered and regulated to some degree with participant-developed operating policies.
- Members are able to conduct their club sport without substantial administrative support from the agency.
- Members seek opportunities for regular and ongoing year-round participation.
- Club sports offer a more structured design than informal sport participation.
- Unlike the staff-structured intramural sports program, club sport members develop, operate, and administer the club.

Recreational sports provide diverse sport programs, facilities, equipment, and services that promote and enhance a greater appreciation for a lifelong involvement in sport and fitness. Over the years, there has been a significant increase in the interest and the need for broad-based recreational sport programming that meets the needs and interests of *all* participants regardless of age, race, gender, religion, or athletic ability. It is important to identify and understand the components of recreational sports and the role they play in the realm of sport management.

OUTSTANDING *Graduates*

Courtesy of Matthew Vanderkamp

Background Information

Name: Matthew Vanderkamp

Education: Bachelor of education and human services, Western Illinois University, major in recreation, parks, and tourism administration, minor in management

Credentials: Provisional park and recreation professional (PPRP); National Youth Sports Coaches Association (NYSCA) and Parents Association for Youth Sports (PAYS), certified instructor

Special Affiliations: Illinois Parks and Recreation Association (IPRA), member; National Recreation and Park Association (NRPA), member; IPRA, Athletic Committee, member

Career Information

Position: Youth athletic supervisor at Gurnee Park District in Gurnee, Illinois

Organization: The Gurnee Park District, a municipal governing agency, was established for the primary purpose of providing parks, recreational facilities, and programs for the residents within the Gurnee Park District. The park district is governed by five elected commissioners who set the general policies of the district.

Organization's Mission: The Gurnee Park District, through its facilities, programs, services, and personnel, seeks to enhance the quality of life and the environment; to acquire, conserve, and protect natural resources; and to provide leisure-time opportunities for the benefit of its current and future citizens.

Job Description: Plan, organize, budget, and supervise youth athletic programs and leagues. Report to the superintendent of recreation.

Career Path: This is my first job in the recreation field. I have been with the Gurnee Park District since September 2002.

Likes and Dislikes About the Job: It's funny, but my main like and dislike are the same thing: working with the public. Working with the public is always exciting and never boring. And if it weren't for them, I would not have a job in the public sector of the recreation field.

> When Ray Berry coached the New England Patriots, he took pictures of all the ball boys who assisted the team. At a team meeting, he distributed the photos and told each player to learn the boys' names. "The boys know who you are," Berry told the team. "I want you to know them. Everyone's important."

Advice to Undergraduates

Be flexible, open minded, and a team player. In most cases you will not have a 9-to-5 job; you will work evening hours and weekend hours as well. When you're working with the public, no two days will be the same; there will always be new challenges and obstacles.

SCOPE OF PARTICIPATION IN RECREATIONAL SPORT

Participation in recreational sport has grown steadily over the past several decades. Millions of people participate in team, individual, or dual sports in municipal parks and recreation programs, campus recreational sport programs, nonprofit agencies such as the YMCA and Boys and Girls Clubs, employee recreation programs, private clubs, commercial recreational sport facilities and programs, and armed forces MWR programs around the world. The following brief descriptions of participation in recreational sport programs and facilities provide an overview of the scope of participation that should meet the needs of most people who want to participate in recreational sports.

Active Participation Choices

Active participation, as discussed earlier, is a much more integral part of recreational sport management than it is of varsity **athletic sports** and professional sports. The key principle of active participation is the person's choice to participate in either structured sports (instructional, intramural, extramural, or club) or self-directed sports (informal) and the broad spectrum of degrees of participation. This broad spectrum of recreational sport, which should be afforded to *all,* is the distinguishing feature that differentiates it from athletic and professional sports.

Participants

It is essential for recreational sport programmers to recognize whom they provide service to in order to better meet the needs and interests of the participants. Recreational sport management is intended for the enjoyment of all age groups. These groups include children, youth, adolescents, adults, and senior citizens.

Location

Very simply, participation in recreational sport occurs in both *indoor* and *outdoor* sport facilities. Indoor recreational sports facilities may include bowling centers; handball, racquetball, and squash courts; gymnasiums for volleyball, basketball, badminton, and floor hockey; billiard rooms; roller- and ice-skating rinks; aquatic centers; strength and conditioning weight rooms; and exercise rooms. Outdoor recreational sport facilities may include softball and baseball diamonds; golf courses; trap and skeet ranges; fields for soccer and flag football; tennis courts; and outdoor aquatic centers. Outdoor facilities may also include natural facilities such as white-water rivers and streams, caves, lakes, and mountains.

Sport Settings

Recreational sport management is programmed in a variety of sport settings. These include the following:

Recreational sport can take place indoors in a tennis facility or outdoors on the basketball court.

- Recreation departments on armed forces installations around the world
- Boys and Girls Clubs
- Churches
- City and community parks and recreation departments
- Commercial recreational facilities such as racket clubs, bowling centers, and roller- and ice-skating rinks
- Correctional institutions (city, county, state, and federal)
- Educational institutions (public and private elementary, secondary, and higher education)
- On-site industrial and corporate recreational sport facilities
- Private clubs (country clubs and fitness and health clubs)
- YMCAs and YWCAs
- Vacation resorts (hotels, motels, and cruise ships)

These settings represent thousands of employment positions in recreational sport programming and open the door to numerous job opportunities for those wanting a career in this field.

Benefits

Recreational sport participation can provide one of the most important sociocultural learning environments in our society, and it provides a substantial range of benefits for participants and the community, organization, or agency that sponsors them. While active participants gain many health and physical benefits, the community or agency can also benefit from an economical or environmental perspective. By providing sport opportunities and by encouraging participation, recreational sport programs can develop participant interests, knowledge, and skills to enable participation in recreational sport and fitness activities that can last a lifetime.

Personal Benefits

For the person who regularly participates in recreational sport activities, improved health, physical fitness, and self-esteem can be gained. However, the benefits from recreational sport are not only physical. Although physical benefits are easy to

detect, active participation can also provide positive and enjoyable experiences that can decrease stress and psychological tension. Recreational sport activities provide participants the opportunity to "burn" excess energy and emotional stress not released in other aspects of their lives. These activities also create a positive social environment where people can relax and enjoy the company of others.

Competition and winning and losing help many people learn how to control their emotions and express aggression in a positive way. Cooperation is fostered because people must work together to achieve a goal. By working with others, people gain interpersonal skills, learn to tolerate differences, and learn time management and goal-settings skills. People can develop integrity by establishing their own values and behavior patterns, and then by testing those against the values and behaviors of others.

Community Benefits

By providing opportunities for social interaction, recreational sport programs can help increase community cohesion and encourage community interaction by engaging different sections of the community in wholesome sporting activities, regardless of age, race, ethnicity, or gender. Participation can also help deter antisocial behavior, including vandalism, gang violence, and crime. Communities can benefit economically from well-planned and well-managed sport facilities. These economic benefits include direct and indirect employment in recreational sport programs, income from sales of recreational sporting goods and services, and the revenue generated from holding local, city, state, regional, or even national recreational sports tournaments and events. Tourism-related activities, through the promotion of recreational sport opportunities and the quality of sporting facilities, can contribute significantly to the local economy.

Agency, Organization, or Setting Benefits

Participation in recreational sport programs can have a direct effect on the agency, organization, or setting that provides the activities. The following are examples:

- The Employee Services Management (ESM) Association suggests that recreational sport leagues and special-interest clubs allow employees to develop a broader range of skills, learn to be leaders,

Participation in recreational sport can benefit the individual as well as the community. Individuals can boost self-esteem and decrease stress, and the community can see economic benefits from a large event as well as increase community cohesion.

and enjoy coming to work (ESM, 2001). Recreational sport programs can deliver tangible benefits in terms of workplace safety and improved productivity from happier and healthier employees.

• Studies conducted by the National Intramural-Recreational Sports Association (NIRSA) report that in the collegiate setting, active engagement in recreational sport and fitness programs is a key determinant of college satisfaction, success, recruitment, and retention (NIRSA, 2004).

• Navy MWR fleet recreational sport programs and equipment support the quality of life of more than 200,000 men and women on land and at sea on board navy ships. These mission-essential MWR programs consist of voluntary fitness and recreational sport activities conducted for the purpose of promoting morale and physical and mental combat readiness (Navy Morale, Welfare and Recreation, n.d.).

• Through the YMCA mission of "putting Christian principles into practice," recreational sport, a mainstay of the YMCA offerings, emphasizes teamwork and cooperation over winning at any cost, and developing solid values over developing the next superstar (YMCA, n.d.).

TRENDS IN RECREATIONAL SPORT MANAGEMENT

To be able to fully plan and make projections properly, it is essential to examine current issues and concerns. Examining current challenges and problems and forecasting their impact on the future are

of great value to any profession, and recreational sport management is no exception. By identifying and studying future trends, professionals and practitioners in the field can prepare and explore many aspects of their current programs and activities. Although it is not possible to predict exactly what will occur, observing and identifying future trends might allow us to redefine the nature of what we do and how we do it.

Young and Ross (2000) conducted a research study with a panel of recreational sport management experts in order to identify possible trends affecting the delivery of recreational sport programs until 2015. Experts in the study identified 31 trends having the greatest potential for impact, with the majority of these trends emerging from funding, legal aspects, sport facilities, technology, personnel, and programming areas.

Funding

One of the top trends in recreational sport management is income generation for sport programs and facilities. Most recreational sport administrators are not surprised by this trend because most programs have been forced to reduce budgets during the past few years because of the sluggish economy. A new role for recreation administrators is that of an entrepreneur who seeks creative, resourceful ways to use scarce funds to obtain additional resources (Crompton, 1999, p. 10). Experts agree that commercial sponsorships, concessions, and licensing will become even more widely accepted methods of generating revenue to supplement the more traditional sources of recreational sport income such as fees and charges and tax-based revenue (Sawyer & Smith, 1999).

Legal Aspects

It is imperative for recreational sport administrators to educate not only themselves in various legal aspects but also their staffs and participants. Recreational sport administrators must become responsible for developing sound risk management plans and programs that reduce the likelihood of accidents and injuries that might lead to participant lawsuits against the agency. Administrators should become familiar with the laws of their state that apply to recreational sport programs and facilities. Effective risk management planning is essential for reducing losses and avoiding lawsuits. Well-prepared risk management plans and thorough reporting, record keeping, facility inspections, training, event supervision, and emergency procedures will help reduce the potential for lawsuits.

Sport Facilities

Facility construction is a growth area in recreational sport management. Over the past few decades, recreational sport programs, in a variety of sectors, have witnessed tremendous growth in the number of new sport facilities being constructed. Collegiate recreational sport is leading the way in the number of new recreational sport complexes on campuses across the country. Experts believe that participants will continue to demand larger and more specialized recreational sport facilities resulting in even more new construction well into the 21st century. It has been suggested that as the sport industry continues to change and expand to meet the demands of current and future participants, the chances of a sport manager becoming involved in a construction project are very likely (Sawyer & Smith, 1999, p. 219).

Technology

In the past 10 years, computing technology has significantly affected the way businesses and government agencies deliver services, making delivery more efficient and services more competitive. This trend is also occurring in the management of recreational sport programs. Selecting appropriate technology may have the biggest impact on improving the efficiency of a sport program. Although technology is not the panacea for a

quality recreational sport program, it is clear that using technology, including hardware and software components, is an important trend and tool that can improve the quality and speed of daily operations. It can also provide valuable information to assist in administrative decision making. Recreational sport management managers, however, must stay current with the changes in technology (Toh & Jamieson, 2000).

Personnel

Because technology is ever changing and its use is growing, recreational sport managers must hire additional staff to maintain current applications. "Recreational sport administrators are realizing the benefits and necessity of technology and are now hiring more full-time and part-time computer support staff to develop and sustain current levels of computer use" (Ross & Forrester, 1999, p. 80). In addition, with the increase in the technological benefits of local area networks (LANs) and recreational sport agency–owned servers, there will also be an increase in the number of part-time computer generalists and full-time LAN and network administrators joining the traditional recreational sports programming staff.

Because recreational sport programs have become so diverse and are rapidly expanding in terms of programs and facilities to meet the growing needs of participants, marketing has become a core activity for recreational sport management. Recreational sport staffs now include marketing specialists with the skills, experience, and dedicated time to plan and implement marketing strategies to support the sport programs and services. These staff members have a significant impact on the success of the agency.

Programming

Sports Participation in America: Participation Trends in Fitness, Sports and Outdoor Activities (SGMA, 2004) covers 103 athletic activities in the United States and describes a variety of participation trends in recreational sport programming. The following are several facts listed in the report:

- Women represent more than 60 percent of participants in fitness activities such as stretching, fitness walking, aerobic dance, yoga, tai chi, exercise to music, elliptical motion trainer, water exercise, Pilates, and cardio kickboxing.

- Health club memberships have almost doubled since 1990, to 39.4 million.
- Baseball participation grew nearly 5 percent between 2002 and 2003.
- Racquetball players participated an average of 34 days per year in 2003 compared to 18 days in 1990.
- Combined, billiards and bowling attracted more than 95 million players in 2003.
- Since 1990, extreme sports participation has skyrocketed.

Recreational sport and fitness programs are immensely popular and usually attract large numbers of participants. Countless millions of Americans partake in a variety of recreational sport and outdoor recreation activities throughout the year. Tables 14.1 and 14.2 provide the estimated number of participants in several recreational sport activities as listed in the U.S. Census Bureau, Statistical Abstract of the United States for 2003. Table 14.3 illustrates the popularity of recreational sports in Canada. Golf, hockey, baseball, and swimming are the sports of choice for Canadians.

As illustrated in table 14.1, exercise walking, camping, swimming, and exercising with equipment rank among the top series I recreational sport activities in which Americans participate. (Series I and II are categories used by the U.S. Census Bureau.) Table 14.2 reflects the top series II recreational sport activities in which Americans

TABLE 14.1 Estimated Number of Participants in Top 10 Series I Recreational Sport Activities: 2002

Rank	Activity	Participants (million)
1	Exercise walking	82.2
2	Camping	55.4
3	Swimming	54.7
4	Exercising with equipment	50.2
5	Fishing (net)	44.2
6	Bowling	43.9
7	Bicycle riding	41.9
8	Fishing (fresh water)	38.5
9	Billiards	35.3
10	Hiking	30.5

Statistical Abstract of the United States: 2004-2005. U.S. Census Bureau. www.census.gov/prod/2004pubs/04statab/arts.pdf

TABLE 14.2 Estimated Number of Participants in Top 10 Series II Recreational Sport Activities: 2002

Rank	Activity	Participants (million)
1	Working out at a club	28.9
2	Boating (motor or power)	26.6
3	Target shooting	18.9
4	In-line skating	18.8
5	Mountain biking (on road)	15.3
6	Scooter riding	13.4
7	Darts (soft tip)	11.0
8	Darts (metal tip)	9.9
9	Skateboarding	9.7
10	Mountain biking (off road)	7.8

Statistical Abstract of the United States: 2004-2005. U.S.Census Bureau. www.census.gov/prod/2004pubs/04statab/arts.pdf

TABLE 14.3   Most-Played Sports by Canadians (Aged 15 and Older): 1998

Rank	Activity	Participants
1	Golf	1.8 million
2	Ice hockey	1.5 million
3	Baseball	1.3 million
4	Swimming	1.1 million
5	Basketball	787,000
6	Volleyball	744,000
7	Soccer	739,000
8	Tennis	658,000
9	Downhill skiing	657,000
10	Cycling	608,000

Adapted from Statistics Canada Web site: www.40.statcan.ca/101/cst01/arts16.htm

participate: working out at a club, boating, target shooting, and in-line skating.

CAREER OPPORTUNITIES

When considering the growing popularity of recreational sport programs and the trends in the field discussed earlier, it's clear that there will be a significant demand for competent professionals, both full-time and part-time, who are capable of delivering and overseeing recreational sport programs and services in diverse employment settings. The number of positions and job responsibilities will vary depending on the setting.

Four Levels of Positions

With this growth and interest in recreational sport programs, there have been increased opportunities for employment ranging from leadership positions working face to face with participants to top administrative positions. Four general levels of personnel are commonly found in settings providing recreational sport management: administrative staff, program administrative staff, program staff, and auxiliary staff (Mull, Bayless, & Jamieson, 2005).

Administrative Staff

The administrative staff personnel are the ultimate authority and provide the overall direction and leadership for the entire recreational sport program and its resources including staff, budget, facilities, and equipment. Specific duties of the administrator are to determine the nature, scope, and direction of the program; evaluate overall program efficiency in terms of goals and standards; provide guidelines, establish priorities, and determine schedules for the acquisition and construction of recreational sport facilities; and explain policy and major program changes to staff and the public. Typical job titles at this level are administrator, director, or executive director. Because of the wide range of recreational sport programs and the need for experience in decision making, top administrators usually hold a master's degree and have a minimum of 10 years of experience.

Program Administrative Staff

The program administrative staff are full-time professionals who support the administrator. In addition, they help formulate and administer policies, guidelines, and resources while monitoring programs, facilities, and program staff. People in this role also serve as a liaison between the top administrator and the program staff in day-to-day decision making. Job titles are often specific to the sport setting, but general titles at this level include associate director, program director, fitness director, public relations director, operations director, facility manager, and sports coordinator or director. People in these positions usually hold a bachelor's degree and many hold a master's degree in recreation, sport management, or a related field and have a minimum of five years of programming-related experience.

Program Staff

Program staff member is the entry-level position in this field and refers to many positions within an organization. Work responsibilities require specialized skills and training in organizing and conducting various sport programs. People in this role may initiate publicity and promotion, purchase and inventory equipment, and implement policies for safety, participant control, and governance. The program staff is also responsible for recruiting, hiring, training, and scheduling support staff including sport officials, lifeguards, and supervisors. Typical job titles are assistant director, marketing assistant, coordinator, building manager, personal trainer, pool operator, leader, and activity specialist. Many of these positions require a bachelor's degree, but many employers prefer candidates with a master's degree.

Auxiliary Staff

The auxiliary staff consists of part-time, hourly wage or volunteer positions that engage in face-to-face contact with the program participants. The auxiliary staff primarily consists of seasonal or part-time positions such as officials, scorekeepers, supervisors, aerobics and group exercise leaders, equipment room attendants, aquatics instructors, fitness consultants, facility entry attendants, lifeguards, maintenance crews, and youth sport coaches. Although this is the level at which many program staff members gain experience, people seeking employment at this level usually do not

Recreational Sport Management Professional Certifications

Many opportunities exist for recreational sport professionals to gain certification; however, the most frequently obtained certifications by recreational sport practitioners are the following:

General Programming

Certified recreational sports specialist (CRSS)—Certified by National Intramural-Recreational Sports Association (NIRSA)

Certified park and recreation professional (CPRP)—Certified by National Recreation and Park Association (NRPA)

Certified pool operator (CPO)—Certified by National Swimming Pool Foundation (NSPF)

Health and Fitness Certification Programs

Certified aerobics instructor—Certified by Aerobics and Fitness Association of America (AFAA)

Physical fitness specialist—Certified by the Cooper Institute for Aerobics Research (CIAR)

Certified group fitness instructor—Certified by American Council on Exercise (ACE)

Certified personal trainer—Certified by American Council on Exercise (ACE)

Certified clinical exercise specialist—Certified by American Council on Exercise (ACE)

Various health and fitness certifications—Certified by American College of Sports Medicine (ACSM) and YMCA of the USA

Youth Sport Coaching Certification Programs

Gold Level Certified Coach—Certified by National Alliance for Youth Sports (NAYS)

Coaching Principles Bronze Level—Certified by American Sport Education Program (ASEP), a division of Human Kinetics

Miscellaneous Certification Programs by the American Red Cross

Water safety instructor (WSI)

Emergency first aid (EFA)

Cardiopulmonary resuscitation (CPR)

have a degree but may hold some type of specialized sport credential such as first aid, water safety instructor, CPR, sport official certification, or youth sport coaching certification.

Job Outlook

Finding a career in recreational sport management is a promising prospect for those willing to pursue it. There are various levels of recreational sport management positions in thousands of for-profit and nonprofit institutions throughout the United States. These institutions support recreational sport programs that serve millions of people of all ages. In many settings, the demand for qualified recreational sport management specialists far exceeds the supply, which provides great job opportunities for students interested in this field. Employment opportunities include the following:

• The Amateur Athletics Union's (AAU, n.d.) philosophy of "sports for all, forever," is shared by nearly 500,000 participants and more than 50,000 volunteers in the United States. The AAU is divided into 57 distinct associations that annually sanction more than 34 sport programs, 250 national championships, and more than 10,000 local events across the country and provide employment opportunities involving sport facilities, programming, and operations.

• Armed forces recreation supports 215,000 full-time employees with 10 million users at more than 900 locations within the United States and 360 overseas locations. Sport programmers and sport directors provide various services to all branches of the U.S. military. PSP Division, or the Personnel Support Division of the Canadian Forces Personnel Support Agency, is the key provider of recreational services within the military environment.

• Boys and Girls Clubs of America (2005) serve more than 4.4 million youth in more than 3,700 clubs in the United States and is one of the fastest growing youth services agencies with nearly 44,000 full-time professional staff members. There are over 100 Boys and Girls Clubs of Canada (2004) that serve 150,000 children and youth in 700 community-based locations nationwide.

• Association of Church Sports and Recreation Ministers (CSRM) serves a network of church recreation and sports ministry professionals.

• In Canada in 2003, about 161,000 nonprofit and voluntary organizations were operating across the country in a wide variety of areas. The largest group of organizations (21%) operate in the area of sports and recreation (Statistics Canada, 2004).

• The collegiate and campus setting offers a variety of recreational sports career opportunities across the United States.

• Commercial sports offer thousands of job opportunities in country clubs, bowling centers, theme parks, health and fitness spas, racket clubs, tennis centers, ski resorts, golf courses, aquatic centers, hotels, and natural settings for boating, rafting, and fishing.

• Correctional recreation programs are staffed by practitioners at the federal, state, and local levels, working in juvenile, medical, and community-based facilities. A growing emphasis in this specialty is on promoting inmate health and fitness and providing sport opportunities.

• Employee recreational sports provide career opportunities for sport programmers in business, commercial, and industrial employee recreational sport programs.

• Fitness club membership in the United States at the end of 2003 was estimated at approximately 38 million people (18 percent of adults 18 years old and older).

• Municipal parks and recreation departments in the United States staff approximately 3,000 positions in sports programming.

• State games festivals are organized by the State Games of America (2005), a property of the National Congress of State Games (NCSG), which is a membership organization composed of 40 summer state games and 14 winter state games organizations and a community-based member of the United States Olympic Committee. Job opportunities are available at the national and state levels for full-time sport directors and event management coordinators as well as thousands of volunteers needed to conduct these large, multisport events across the United States.

• The 2,500 YMCAs and 302 YWCAs in the United States employ approximately 20,000 full-time professionals. Of these positions, 4,000 are related to recreational sport. YMCA Canada (2005) is a federation of which all 61 YMCAs and YMCA-YWCAs in Canada are a member. Each of the 61 clubs is independent and hires its own staff and volunteers. Over 14,000 people are employed in this setting.

• In the United States, Big Brothers Big Sisters (2004) serves more than 225,000 children, ages 5 through 18, in 5,000 communities across all 50 states in after-school sport programs and other recreational activities. Big Brothers Big Sisters of Canada (n.d.) is the leading child- and youth-serving organization in Canada with over 170 local agencies.

Professional Organizations

It is essential for recreational sport professionals to remain current in theoretical and practical concerns in the field. Many recreational sport practitioners hold active memberships in a variety of professional organizations that sponsor a wide range of continuing education courses, institutes, workshops, regional and national conferences, and other in-service training for people working in this field. The professional organizations most closely associated with recreational sport management are listed in table 14.4. Professional organizations provide practitioners and students with opportunities for conferences, workshops, seminars, and management schools that help them stay abreast

TABLE 14.4 Recreational Sport Management Professional Organizations

Acronym	Association	Fields and professionals served
AAHPERD	American Alliance for Health, Physical Education, Recreation and Dance www.aahperd.org	Educators (primary, secondary, postsecondary) in health, physical education, recreation, and dance
ACA	American Camp Association (formerly American Camping Association) www.acacamps.org	Camping
ACSM	American College of Sports Medicine www.acsm.org	Provides educational and practical exercise and fitness applications
ASEP	American Sport Education Program www.asep.com	Sports administrators, volunteers, coaches, officials, and parents
CAHPERD	Canadian Association for Health, Physical Education, Recreation and Dance www.cahperd.ca	Educators (primary, secondary, postsecondary) in health, physical education, recreation, and dance in Canada
CPRA	Canadian Parks and Recreation Association www.cpra.ca	Public parks and recreation in Canada
ESM	Employee Services Management Association (formerly National Employee Services Recreation Association) www.esmassn.org	Employee and corporate recreation
IAAM	International Association of Assembly Managers www.iaam.org	Facility, stadium, and arena management
IHRSA	International Health, Racquet and Sportsclub Association www.ihrsa.org	Commercial and private recreational sports
NAGWS	National Association for Girls and Women in Sport www.aahperd.org/nagws	Educators promoting interest in girls' and women's sports
NASPE	National Association of Sport and Physical Education www.aahperd.org/naspe/template.cfm	Educators in sport and physical education (branch of AAHPERD)
NASSM	North American Society for Sport Management www.unb.ca/web/SportManagement/nassm.htm	Sport management educators
NCRA	National Correctional Recreation Association www.strengthtech.com/correct/ncra/ncra.htm	Correctional and penal recreation
NIRSA	National Intramural-Recreational Sports Association www.nirsa.org	Campus recreational sports, military recreational sports, correctional recreation, and public recreation
NAYS	National Alliance for Youth Sports www.nays.org	Youth sports administrators, volunteers, coaches, officials, and parents
NRPA	National Recreation and Park Association www.nrpa.org	Armed forces recreation and parks and recreation practitioners and educators
NYSCA	National Youth Sports Coaches Association www.nays.org/IntMain.cfm?Page=1&Cat=3	Youth sports administrators, volunteers, coaches, officials, and parents
RCRA	The Resort and Commercial Recreation Association www.r-c-r-a.org	Commercial recreation and resorts

Professional Journals and Publications

American Fitness—Aerobics and Fitness Association of America

Athletics Administration—National Association of Collegiate Directors of Athletics

Athletic Business

CAHPER Journal—Canadian Association for Health, Physical Education, Recreation and Dance

Club Business International—International Health, Racquet and Sportsclub Association

Fitness Management

Journal of Physical Education Recreation & Dance—American Alliance for Health, Physical Education, Recreation and Dance

Journal of Sport and Exercise Psychology

Journal of Sport Management—North American Society for Sport Management

Journal of Sport and Social Issues—In association with Northeastern University's Center for the Study of Sport in Society

Journal of Sports Sciences—On behalf of the British Association of Sport and Exercise Sciences

Parks & Recreation—National Recreation and Park Association

The Physical Educator—Phi Epsilon Kappa

Recreational Sports Journal—National Intramural-Recreational Sports Association (formerly *NIRSA Journal*)

Scholastic Coach

Web Sites to EXPLORE

Agency and Setting-Specific Web Sites

Collegiate Recreational Sports

National Intramural-Recreational Sports Association: http://nirsa.jobcontrolcenter.com/search/results (jobs posted on bluefishjobs.com)

Canadian Association for Health, Physical Education, Recreation and Dance: www.uregina.ca/kinesiology/campusrec/

Nonprofit Organizations

Boys and Girls Clubs of America: www.bgca.org/careers

YMCA: www.ymca.net/index.jsp

YMCA Canada: www.ymca.ca/

Public Recreation and Government

Canadian Parks and Recreation Association: www.cpra.ca/

Cool Works: www.coolworks.com

General Pay Plan Schedule: www.usajobs.opm.gov/B5A.asp

Govtjobs.com: govtjobs.com

National Recreation and Park Association: www.nrpa.org

OPM Job Announcements: www.usajobs.opm.gov

Commercial Recreation

Resort and Commercial Recreation Association: www.r-c-r-a.org

Cruise Line Jobs: www.cruiselinejobs.com

Club Managers Association of America: www.cmaa.org/who/index.htm

Bally Total Fitness: www.ballyjobs.com

Exercisejobs.com: www.exercisejobs.com

Sportsplex Operators and Developers Association: www.sportsplexoperators.com

General Web Sites

Athleticlink.com: www.athleticlink.com/Default.asp

Canadian Sport Centre Job Postings: www.cscatlantic.ca/e/jobs/index.htm

GolfingCareers: www.golfingcareers.com

The Riley Guide (hospitality, sports, and recreation): www.rileyguide.com/hosp.html

Sports Careers: www.sportscareers.com

Women Sports Jobs: www.womensportsjobs.com

WorkInSports.com: www.workinsports.com/home.asp

of trends and practices and their implications for program delivery in the rapidly changing recreational sport management field.

SUMMARY

The role of recreational sport as an integral part to human enjoyment and vitality is well established and recognized. Participation in sport for fun and fitness is a very popular leisure-time pursuit among Americans and Canadians. Active participation in recreational sports is an important part of day-to-day existence for many people and involves an individual's choice of participating in either structured sports (instruction, intramural, extramural,

club) or self-directed sports (informal) at a multitude of sport settings. These settings, ranging from municipal parks and recreation, campus recreation, YMCA, and military installations to youth service organizations, offer recreational sport programs and events that provide mental, physical, social, and emotional benefits to all participants.

With the increasing interest in recreational sport participation and fitness activity for all age groups, there has arisen a need for broad-based recreational sport programming that reflects these needs and interests. In turn, this will continue to spur the growth of recreational sport management, providing a variety of exciting and fulfilling job opportunities in diverse settings.

CHAPTER 15

Health, Fitness, Wellness, and Livability

Kathy Spangler and Ellen O'Sullivan

Many of us think of health only as an absence of illness. It is much more than that. It is a state of being, which extends beyond just "feeling good" and enters the "plus" margin of physical, mental, and social well-being.

*Charles Brightbill,
pioneer in parks and recreation*

CHAPTER OBJECTIVES

After reading this chapter, you should be able to do the following:

- Recognize the shift in the medical world from treatment to prevention
- Identify both the current and emerging roles for parks and recreation related to health
- Recognize wellness outcomes inherent in recreation activities
- Distinguish between the various approaches to leisure facilitation
- Explain the important role that environment plays in healthy lifestyles
- State the importance of parks and recreation to the coming health crisis

INTRODUCTION

In 1996, the U.S. Surgeon General issued a report similar in significance to the one issued decades previously on the hazards of cigarette smoking (U.S. Department of Health and Human Services, 1996). This report, however, focused on a new health threat: lack of leisure-time physical activity. This recognition by the Surgeon General signaled the beginning of a renewed emphasis on the relationship between leisure time and health. Parks and recreation professionals and programs are now central players in 21st century health and well-being in Canada and the United States. The industry assumes this role in a variety of ways and across myriad settings and contributes to three major components of the health and well-being of individuals and communities: wellness, leisure facilitation, and livability.

1. **Wellness** refers to the many desirable outcomes associated with health and well-being that are the natural results of participation in physical endeavors, including parks and recreation activities.

2. **Leisure facilitation** is the process of providing information, developing skills, and supporting opportunities for people to pursue health and well-being and in the end, adopt a healthier lifestyle.

3. **Livability** reflects environmental and economic factors that support community access and opportunities for individuals, families, and neighborhoods to pursue healthy lifestyles.

MAJOR SHIFT: FROM TREATMENT TO PREVENTION

A person born at the beginning of the last century lived to his or her mid-40s; we would now consider this middle aged. Today, the average life expectancy for people living in the United States is closer to 77 than 47. The increased longevity is due to improvements in living standards and scientific developments during the last century. One hundred years ago, the leading causes of death were infectious diseases such as tuberculosis, pneumonia, and diarrhea. Today, a little more than 100 years later, the leading causes of death have changed also. Data from the Centers for Disease Control and Prevention (CDC) identify the leading causes of death in the United States as heart attack, cancer, stroke, and chronic lower-respiratory diseases. In fact, the top two leading causes of death, heart attack and cancer, are responsible for more than 50 percent of all deaths in the United States. The dramatic shift in causes of death may best be illustrated by the report that the death rate from infectious diseases has dropped by more than 700 percent since the start of the 20th century (U.S. Department of Health and Human Services, 1997).

The study "Actual Causes of Death in the United States, 2000," which appeared in the March 2004 issue of *The Journal of the American Medical Association,* found that 400,000 deaths in the United States in 2000, or 17 percent of all deaths, were related to poor diet and physical inactivity. Only tobacco use caused more deaths but only by an additional 35,000. Most of the major preventable causes of death showed declines or little change since 1990, but the deaths caused by poor diet and physical inactivity increased 33 percent (Mokdad, Marks, Stroup, & Gerberding, 2004). Life expectancy for men and women in Canada is 76.0 and 81.5 years, respectively. When adjusted for death rates due to contracting these diseases, the life expectancy drops to 67.9 years for men and 71.1 years for women. Cancer represents the greatest burden of disease in the Canadian life expectancy projections, and eliminating it would increase men's life expectancy to 79.6 years and women's to 85.1

years (Manuel, Luo, Ugnat, & Mao, 2003). As in the United States, infectious disease is no longer the leading cause of death. Table 15.1 provides data that illustrate the current causes of death in the United States. With the exception of influenza and pneumonia, none of the current leading causes of death are due to infectious diseases, and the remaining causes in many instances are related to lifestyle behaviors.

Just as health trends are changing, so is the way we approach health care. In general, there are three approaches to health care: treatment, environmental risk reduction, and prevention. The evolution of each of these approaches has been caused by the growing cost of health care and the prevalence of lifestyle-related diseases and conditions.

The medical approach to health involves doctors, nurses, hospitals, and remedies such as prescription medicine and surgery. Its focus is on treating illness, disease, disability, and discomfort. Another approach to maintaining or restoring health focuses on the natural environment and addresses the health risks associated with water contamination, food poisoning, airborne diseases, and other occurrences in the environment. Societal forces that influence socioeconomic status, which also determine health risks, are also addressed by this approach. The third approach to health has evolved the most recently and directs resources toward prevention rather than treatment. Monitoring leading causes of death and determining the contributors to those deaths gave rise to the prevention model. This model recognizes that preventing lifestyle-related diseases such as heart attack, cancer, stroke, and chronic lower-respiratory diseases rather than treating the condition after a person has already developed it is a more effective approach. The treatment mode remains in use, but the prevention model is gaining popularity.

EXPANDED INDUSTRY OF HEALTH AND THE ROLE OF PARKS AND RECREATION

Existing industry segments with either direct or less-apparent ties to health are evolving to meet the challenges of the prevention model. In addition, new businesses and specializations are addressing the unique opportunities afforded by this approach. What then is the relationship between medicine, public health, and parks and recreation? How is parks and recreation similar and how is it different from other professional areas such as the world of medicine, where the traditional focus is upon treating or trying to cure diseases? What role will parks and recreation play in the evolving and emerging areas of wellness, fitness, and health promotion?

Medical providers are encouraged and often influenced by insurance companies to practice the prevention model with an emphasis on "wellness" rather than the absence of disease. Hospitals provide a variety of healthy lifestyle alternatives and opportunities through wellness centers or community outreach specialists. Although parks and recreation personnel do not provide medical advice or services, they are conversant in various wellness areas and often work in partnership with local physicians and hospitals in addition to providing recreation activities complete with wellness outcomes of their own.

Public health organizations are charged with protecting the community's well-being by directing its resources toward natural and man-made environmental issues. Societal threats to disease-carrying mosquitoes would be an example of a natural issue while problems with waste disposal facilities would illustrate a man-made condition. Achieving parity in health status for everyone in the community is also a long-held priority of this field. Public health organizations have augmented their activities to include health promotion and increasingly emphasize leisure-time physical activity. Parks and recreation professionals are forming partnerships with health departments to improve environmental and social access to leisure-related

TABLE 15.1   Ten Leading Causes of Death in the United States: 2001

Cause	Percentage of all deaths
1. Heart disease	29.0
2. Cancer	22.9
3. Cerebrovascular disease	6.8
4. Chronic lower-respiratory disease such as emphysema, chronic bronchitis	5.1
5. Unintentional injuries	4.2
6. Diabetes mellitus	3.0
7. Influenza and pneumonia	2.6
8. Alzheimer's disease	2.2
9. Nephritis and nephrosis (kidney disease)	1.6
10. Chronic liver disease	0.1

From National Vital Statistics Report, Vol. 52, Nov. 9, 2003.

aspects of health promotion. If people do not have a public park or safe walking area within a reasonable walking distance from their home, this would be considered an environmental access issue. In a similar manner, an individual's inability to afford a youth sports league due to costs of uniforms, equipment, and parental involvement results in a social access issue.

Another recreation field related to the "prevention era" is physical education. Physical education, recently eliminated or reduced in some public schools, historically focused on physical skill development and physical fitness such as the President's Physical Fitness Tests in the 1960s and 1970s. However, two shifts have occurred within this profession. The last decades of the 20th century witnessed the transformation of traditional physical education curricula in colleges and universities being renamed and becoming more focused upon an emphasis on human physical performance as a means for assessing a person's physical condition with an aim of prevention or rehabilitation. The other change that has happened over the past few years has been the recognition and the reemphasis on lifetime skills as a critical outcome of physical education. Parks and recreation programs do not provide skill instruction in as structured a setting as schools but supplement opportunities for additional skill development and other physical activity during the nonschool hours.

The medical model, with its focus on treating illness and disease, has little direct connection with parks and recreation. However, the environmental and the prevention models are closely aligned with the role and purpose of parks and recreation. The environmental model of addressing natural forces and societal factors that potentially affect the health of a community is a role assumed by public parks and recreation. Parks and recreation programming has always focused on the environment. In addition to its efforts to preserve and protect open space, which includes a strong wellness connection, parks and recreation facilities are the community leaders in providing widespread access to places and spaces for play and physical activity. The baseball and soccer fields that line the roadways throughout North America contribute to that access. The recreation centers with swimming pools and adjacent tennis courts are also part of the infrastructure. Parks and recreation is an essential component of the "livability" of communities and society overall.

In addition to providing physical spaces and places, parks and recreation programs have long been concerned with another aspect of the environment: societal factors that shape and influence people's ability to access and participate in leisure-time physical activity. Parks and recreation departments throughout Canada and the United States strive to retain affordable opportunities for basic recreation activities such as youth sports and swimming. It is primarily the public sphere of parks and recreation that is challenged to protect the right of all people to participate in recreational activities regardless of socioeconomic status or circumstances.

Parks and recreation has always been a player in the "prevention" approach to health and well-being. Frederick Law Olmsted, best known as the founder of American landscape architecture, was not only the designer of Central Park but had earlier assumed a role serving as the Executive Secretary of the U.S. Sanitary Commission. Joseph Lee created play spaces so that children would have someplace safer than the streets to play in. In current practice, parks and recreation assumes a role in health promotion. The health promotion and wellness approaches practiced by the medical and public health community are closely tied to the facilities, programs, services, and philosophy of parks and recreation. Preschool and youth activities have always been based on a human growth and development model that addresses the "whole child." Mentoring programs for teens, midnight basketball, and adventure outings are components of leisure services that provide alternatives to gang membership or drug use. Cruise lines, health spas, and hiking trails are just a few leisure services directed toward reducing the stress on today's adults. Some of these activities are modified and directed toward older adults as a way to maintain overall well-being and physical, social, emotional, and intellectual skills, enabling them to remain independent members of their communities.

RECREATION'S ANSWER TO PREVENTION: WELLNESS

The parks, recreation, and leisure field offers activities, programs, services, memberships, opportunities, and experiences of many kinds. The underlying philosophy of these numerous and varied offerings is positive growth and development of the "whole person." Parks and recreation programs have been part of the wellness movement before these efforts became known as the wellness movement. Although there is no one universally accepted definition of "wellness," there are several constructs that appear common to many of the definitions. These include the belief that wellness is focused on optimal well-being across multidimensional aspects of life. The key concepts are "optimal" rather than just "well" or "not sick," which reflects parks and recreation's philosophy and activities directed toward supporting the highest quality of life possible. The "multidimensional" reference has been incorporated into the holistic human growth and development model of parks and recreation since its earliest inception.

Dimensions of Wellness

Different organizations and individuals share many of the same beliefs about wellness, and they universally concur that various subsegments of wellness exist within its holistic, multidimensional nature. The dimensions of wellness featured here include physical, intellectual, emotional, social, spiritual, and environmental.

Parks and Recreation Across the Dimensions

Physical wellness enables a person to attain and maintain the optimal physical condition of the body. Many areas go into creating and then maintaining optimal physical functioning. Many experts believe that many factors contribute to the growing levels of preventable lifestyle-related diseases such as heart disease and strokes. The Surgeon General of the United States (U.S. Department of Health and Human Services, 2001) identifies two of the more significant causes as lack of physical activity and poor dietary habits. More leisure services providers are recognizing their role in their participants' nutritional choices and are taking steps to improve them. For example, youth programs are substituting healthier foods for less-nutritious afternoon snacks. And organizations are replacing vending machine choices that are high in sugar and fat with healthier alternatives.

Physical wellness facilities, activities, services, and programs take place in nearly all segments of parks and recreation. The public walking track or hiking trail, the swimming pool at the YMCA, the cardio classes at the health club, the climbing wall on a cruise ship, and medical screenings held on site in any of these settings provide physical wellness options and opportunities.

Intellectual wellness is a state of having an active and healthy mind. An active mind moves a person along the continuum to optimal health and well-being by supporting an enriched existence. Lifelong learning, for example, enables people to keep pace with the ever changing world in which they live as well as enriching their lives. Mental stimulation in the form of challenging games or activities, even dancing, helps people to "use it" rather than "lose it." Lifelong learning and mental stimulation create a healthy attitude that is open: open to new people, ideas, experiences, adventures, and the unfamiliar. When our lives become so mundane that we can move through the day without consciously thinking, an open mind and attitude can serve as an antidote.

Although parks and recreation organizations do not primarily hold formal education sessions, they do provide myriad learning opportunities. A long list of leisure learning classes and opportunities enable people to learn how to use a computer, acquire a foreign language, or create pottery. The field also serves as a primary provider of mental stimulation and opportunities to meet new people, go different places, and experience adventure. Children may acquire critical-thinking skills by planning winning strategies. For some adults, learning to surf the Net could be considered an enriching, intellectual experience.

Emotional wellness develops and helps maintain a positive emotional and mental state with the optimal outcome of being able to enjoy life and cope with challenges. Self-efficacy (the power to produce an effect), self-esteem, feeling in control, resiliency, and motivation are among the desirable outcomes of emotional wellness. All of these are necessary for people to be able to set and reach goals and live life to the fullest. Daniel Goleman (1995) coined the term emotional intelligence, which suggests one's ability to understand and deal with one's own emotions as a way of being able to function in life may be even more critical to success than the more traditional measure of IQ. This concept suggests that one's ability to motivate one's self and being able to empathize with other people are contributors to overall wellness. Motivation, a factor identified within emotional intelligence, has received renewed interest and attention from educators recently with the emerging concept of emotional intelligence and the supposition by some experts that emotional intelligence may be more critical to success than IQ.

In what ways does or can parks and recreation play a role in emotional wellness? Through recreation, people are able to accomplish goals. Hitting a home run, acting in a theater production, and reaching the ranger station by foot are just a few examples. Many traditional parks and recreation experiences enable people to reach goals and develop a greater sense of self-esteem and self-efficacy. However, other parks and recreation activities more directly address emotional development. The wide range of adventure and developmental programs including trust-building exercises, climbing treks, and white-water rafting specifically target elements within emotional wellness.

Social wellness incorporates a person's ability to interact with others and be comfortable in group settings as a means to achieving intimacy and a sense of belonging. Caring connections with other people are recognized as an essential part of optimal well-being. Some of the indicators of social wellness include healthy relationships with others and the ability to perform and assume social roles.

Although leisure can be experienced in solitude, many parks and recreation programs and services involve some type of interaction with others. In fact, some of the intended outcomes of many of the programs are to develop social skills. Preschool programs often focus on tumbling or other physical games even though one of the more important outcomes is socialization. Helping children learn to play side by side, share toys, and wait their turn all support social development.

Some aspects of the industry are specifically social in nature. Drop-in programs where people can participate in an activity and meet others with a common interest are popular for singles and people new to a community. Teaching families simple line dances enables them to be more fully involved at social functions and celebrations. Community bands, choral groups, and, of course, community concerts are opportunities to create and experience the bonds of being part of a community.

The importance of social well-being has experienced a resurgence recently. This is evident in the efforts of the California Park and Recreation Society's VIP project plan. This strategic plan for the industry identified creating community as the

Courtesy of Craig Ross

Accomplishing a goal, such as reaching the top of the wall, helps develop self-esteem and self-efficacy and builds emotional wellness.

most unique and essential role of parks and recreation. The "We Create Community Through People, Parks, and Programs" mission statement appears in community brochures and Web sites throughout the state, while the intent and outcomes of programs and services are shifting to incorporate this desirable aspect of the field (California Park and Recreation Society, 1999).

Spiritual wellness does not necessarily mean belonging to or believing in an organized religion, although that may be the case. Spiritual wellness is, however, a core element of existence that provides people with meaning, purpose, and value in life. This aspect of wellness manifests itself in many different ways, determined by individual makeup. For some people, spiritual wellness would be achieved through membership and regular participation in organized religion. For others, it might manifest itself as contemplation, volunteer work to help others, or communing with nature and reflecting on the natural and human balance of the world. The Wellness Center at Santa Clara University in California addresses all dimensions of wellness. The following description of spiritual wellness from its Web site illustrates the many elements within this one dimension.

> When we are in tune with our spiritual selves, we can find meaning in life events, comfort when things aren't going well, the beauty in life, the ability to be compassionate towards others, and individual purpose. Many factors play a part in defining spirituality: religious faith, beliefs, values, ethics, principles, and morals. Spirituality allows us to find the inner calm and peace needed to get through whatever life brings. (Santa Clara University, 2004)

Environmental wellness emerges as an expanded dimension of wellness. Recognizing elements or aspects of your own personal environment and taking steps to create an environment that better supports your health and well-being are aspects of this dimension. Some health clubs and community centers are addressing aspects of personal environment in the design of and practices within their facilities. Some beach and park areas restrict cigarette smoking, some locker rooms ban video-enhanced cell phones, and quiet areas are being incorporated into building design.

Although it can address the qualities of a broader, personal environment whether it be school, workplace, or community, environmental wellness is also an appreciation of and preservation of the natural environment. The more traditional view of environmental wellness relates to the natural world. Many parks and recreation organizations make recycling an essential part of the way in which they operate to serve as an example for others. The broader picture of preservation of the natural environment and access to open space for both Americans and Canadians has long been the central role played by national, provincial, state, and local parks.

Interconnectedness of the Wellness Dimensions

It is critical to note and remember that these six dimensions of wellness are linked and interact continually. People's needs cannot always be segmented into one specific area and in a similar manner neither can activities that support well-being. The need for stress reduction is tied not only to emotional health and well-being but to physical and social health as well. Yoga can take on both the physical and spiritual aspects of wellness. Youth sports address physical skill and motor development as well as the socialization that comes from being part of a team. Both intellectual and emotional well-being are components of that same youth soccer league–building self-efficacy and critical thinking skills. There is rarely an instance when a particular wellness activity does not incorporate more than one dimension of wellness.

Some of the studies listed below reflect the interconnectedness of some of these wellness dimensions.

- When comparing vigorous physical activity among first-year university students during their first two months of college versus their last two months of high school, Bray and Born (2004) found a significant decline in the average frequency of vigorous physical activity from 3.32 sessions per week during the last two months of high school compared to 2.68 sessions per week during the transition to university. Students who were active during the transition period reported higher levels of vigor and lower levels of tension and fatigue than insufficiently active students.

- A research study conducted at the Duke University Medical Center with adults 65 years of age and older found that those who prayed, read scriptures, and attended services regularly were 40 percent less likely to have a stroke or heart attack than subjects who were not religious (Goldberg, 2003).

- A study conducted at the Human-Environment Research Laboratory at the University of

Illinois determined that green space present in inner-city neighborhoods resulted in the development and maintenance of stronger social ties among residents (Kuo, Sullivan, Coley, & Brunson, 1998).

- A Centers for Disease Control and Prevention survey of 4,000 high school students indicated that a low level of activity (less than two days of light exercise and no days of hard exercise in the past 14 days) was associated with various risk behaviors: tobacco and pot use, lower fruit and vegetable consumption, greater TV watching, failure to wear a seat belt, and lower perception of academic performance.

- Scientists from the University of Illinois have drawn the conclusion that parklike areas contribute to increased safety within the neighborhood by relieving mental fatigue and that feelings of violence and aggression can occur because of fatigue (American Planning Association, 2003a).

- A national study on aging and creativity and its potential benefit for people 65 years of age and older is under way in San Francisco, New York, and Washington, DC. The intent of the research is to determine if participation in arts and creative programming results in less health deterioration among the elderly. Early results have exceeded expectations; participants in the arts and creative programming reported falling less often, feeling less depressed and lonely, requiring fewer medications, and becoming more active than the comparison group (Kornblum, 2004).

- Contact with nature such as plants, animals, pleasing landscapes, and wilderness areas contributes to several health benefits including lower blood pressure and lower cholesterol levels, more rapid recovery from surgery, and lower self-reported stress (American Planning Association, 2003b).

Play: An Essential Wellness Component

Without play—without the child that still lives in all of us—we will always be incomplete. And not only physically, but creatively, intellectually, and spiritually as well.

George Sheehan, cardiologist, avid runner, and author

Play is a potentially powerful pursuit. The excitement of the first time a human connects a bat with a moving ball or the surge of adrenaline brought about by a trip down a zip line is an example of the power of the play experience. Although play has long been recognized as integral to parks and recreation, some segments of the industry are more cognizant than others of the critical nature of play to one's human growth and development and well-being over the life span.

The renewed emphasis on health and holistic well-being is the driving force that bolsters a stronger recognition of the power of play for children and adults. Play's essential role in addressing the multiple dimensions of wellness is reflected in the variety of outcomes inherent within the leisure-time play experience as cited in the Sheehan quote. There is a natural tendency to regard play as an activity of childhood and indeed, it is. However, play, with its unique characteristics, is critical to the optimal well-being of humans at all ages. It is those unique characteristics of play that create a challenge to arriving at one definition. One definition that is widely recognized and encompasses many of these attributes is attributed to Richard Kraus (1990) who defines play as:

> A form of human or animal behavior, self-motivated and carried on for intrinsic purposes. It is generally pleasurable, and is often marked by elements of competition, exploration, and problem solving, mimicry or role-taking. It may appear both in leisure and in work, and may be marked either by freedom and lack of structure, or by a set of rules and prescribed actions.

Children learn to wait their turn, an important construct of both emotional and social wellness, from simple games such as the old standard, Duck, Duck, Goose. Families on a day hike can walk and talk and enjoy nature while spending what society has come to call "quality time." An adult teaching chess at an after-school youth program contributes to his intellectual, social, and spiritual wellness just through the act of teaching, interacting, and sharing. The founder of the Institute for Play, Stuart Brown, a physician by training, believes that play is as "important for humans as vitamins or sleep," and maintains that play is how homo sapiens adapt and survive throughout the world (www.instituteforplay.com/13stuart_brown.htm). The rapid and nonstop change indicative of life in the 21st century reinforces the importance of play for children and adults.

For a long time, most public parks and recreation departments distanced themselves from the play concept, but that has changed. The Canadian

OUTSTANDING *Graduates*

Background Information

Name: Meghan Rita Wagner

Education: Bachelor of science in leisure services management, Kent State University, Kent, Ohio; master of science in parks and recreation, North Carolina State University

Credentials: Aerobic and Fitness Association of America, certified aerobic instructor; American Red Cross, CPR, automated external defibrillator (AED), and first aid for the professional rescuer certificates; American Red Cross, lifeguard and water safety instructor; Aqua Exercise Association, certified instructor; FiTOUR, kickbox certification; Johnny G Spinning, instructor; Academy of Educational Development National Training Institute for Community Youth Work—Building Exemplary Systems for Training (BEST), certified youth worker trainer; Boston BEST, certified youth worker and certified supervisor; YouthBuild USA, Diversity Leadership: Healing and Dealing; YouthBuild USA, Leadership Development in Youth Work: A Key Pathway for Youth Development and Social Change

Special Awards: Mary Manchester Award—Superior Scholarship, Outstanding Leadership, Constructive Citizenship, Kent State University (KSU); Virginia P. Harvey Award—Outstanding Senior in Leisure Studies, KSU; Student Leadership Excellence Award, KSU; All-American Scholar; Who's Who Among Students in American Colleges and Universities

Special Affiliations: Girls' Coalition of Greater Boston, member; South End/Lower Roxbury Youth Workers' Alliance, member; Strong Women, Strong Girls Board of Directors, member; Team EnVision (women's triathlon team), member; USA Triathlon, member

Career Information

Position: Program associate, The Medical Foundation, Boston, Massachusetts

Organization: The Medical Foundation (TMF) is a nonprofit public health organization with 43 staff members serving primarily the underserved populations of Greater Boston and other parts of Massachusetts and New England. Working with institutions, organiza-

tions, and communities in New England and around the country, TMF offers a variety of training, development, management, and communication services.

Organization's Mission: For more than 40 years, The Medical Foundation has been a leader in public health, consistently at the forefront of efforts to improve the health of individuals and communities. Its mission is to help people live healthier lives and create healthy communities through prevention, health promotion, and research.

Job Description: Serve as project coordinator for Healthy Girls, Healthy Women, a youth osteoporosis and obesity prevention project that provides education about nutrition, physical activity, and disease prevention to groups of teenage and young adult women. Organize the public health campaign to reach other girls and young women in Greater Boston through materials such as transit advertising, Web sites, and brochures. Develop and present workshops and facilitated discussions throughout the Greater Boston community on diversity, overweight youth, body image, respect, and communication. Coordinate the Boston Area Youth Tobacco Awareness Group, an adolescent peer leader anti-tobacco advocacy program. Serve as a trainer at the Youth Development Training Institute.

> I do not let others demean my work and my career choices. Not everybody can do leisure and recreation; it is not easy all the time. I have studied and trained hard, and I will always strive to complete my work with strong ethics and values, constantly looking for the next challenge.

Career Path: While working on my master's degree in parks and recreation, I held a graduate assistantship in the intramural and recreational sports department. I completed an internship at the Cary YMCA in Raleigh, North Carolina, and served as department manager of the aquatics and fitness department at YWCA Boston for two years.

Likes and Dislikes About Your Job: I love my job! I love working with young people, training and facilitating in front of groups, sharing knowledge, and writing curricula and training agendas. I love working with others with similar passions and commitments. Sometimes it is challenging to be "on" in front of groups all day. The pay is good for nonprofit youth work. When working with youth, working hours can be during weekends and nights, but that's how it is in recreation too; I'm used to it!

(continued)

Outstanding Graduates *(continued)*

Advice to Undergraduates

1. Travel for your internship; it's wonderful to experience a new place. Use your internship to decide if this is what you want to be doing. I completed an internship in commercial recreation at the Marriott in Hilton Head. I loved going to Hilton Head but ended up not liking commercial recreation. I served a different population than the one I serve now. Vacationers are tough and challenging. Besides investigating the type of work you want to do, make sure you know who and how you want to serve. Understand that it is primarily a service field (unless you get into research or academics) and know whether or not you can provide that service day in and day out.

2. Try to work a bit in the field before going on to graduate school. I would have chosen a different graduate program had I worked for a while. However, all experiences (and time lines) are good experiences!

3. Love what you are doing all the time. If you are not, don't worry about changing jobs so early in your career. Life is too short to be involved in work that becomes unhealthy for you because you do not truly enjoy it.

Logo from Come Out and Play First Week, a national celebration encouraging people to become more active in their leisure time.

Parks and Recreation Association (CPRA) and the International Play Association (IPA) Canada (www.cpra.ca) of Canada have partnered with Sunlight Laundry Detergent to sponsor the Sunlight National PlayDay Program (www.cpra.ca/cpra-new/playday/e/index.htm). A PlayDay is an innovative event held in larger communities throughout Canada that focuses on supervised but spirited play for children, families, and communities. Another community event celebrating play is Come Out and Play First Week, an event cosponsored by the National Recreation and Park Association and Leisure Lifestyle. This event coincides with the beginning of the new calendar year, a time when people tend to be more open to and interested in lifestyle changes. It's an opportunity for community departments to showcase the range of facilities and programs provided as well as introduce residents to leisure skills and alternatives.

LEISURE FACILITATION: AWARENESS, EDUCATION, COACHING, AND COUNSELING

Western culture is standing on the threshold of a new era. Never before has such an abundance of free time been coupled with such an array of choices. For centuries we have adapted to a world where work predominated and all our efforts focused on this world of work. Suddenly, within the last two decades, we have had to adapt to an unforeseen world that has completely reversed itself to the degree that life away from work often now predominates to an extensive degree. This abrupt reversal has caught us unaware and precipitated a multitude of difficulties for those trying to adapt constructively to this change.

Leoni and Berbling (1980)

These sentences are an excellent summary of the current situation and the challenges that lie ahead for parks, recreation, health, wellness, and livability. However, the irony is that this information is from a 1980 Illinois Parks and Recreation publication titled, "Leisure Coaching." It is true that over the last few years an "unforeseen world" revolving around work has arrived. That world finds some people with too much leisure time or even enforced leisure while others have very limited discretionary time. Enforced leisure may be the challenge faced by people unemployed or underemployed; latch key children instructed by their parents to remain inside the house during after-school hours; or individuals with physical or other types of limitations that create periods of enforced leisure. Considering the challenges of obese children, stressed adults, and the growing popularity of legalized gambling, people need more information, direction, and support in order for leisure time to contribute to a healthy lifestyle. Make way for leisure facilitation.

Leisure facilitation differs from wellness, the first recreation application for health cited in this chapter. Wellness is naturally a part of recreation activities and programs. And although health and well-being are derived from participation in these activities and programs, those positive outcomes are often overlooked or unrecognized. Leisure facilitation includes intentional efforts by leisure providers to encourage positive growth, development, and optimal well-being and consists of information, assistance, and support provided at different times and at various levels. Levels of leisure facilitation include awareness, education, coaching, and counseling.

Leisure awareness is directed toward raising people's appreciation for the many positive attributes and effects of leisure-time activity. Free time is growing increasingly limited and people don't always know how to make the best and most positive use of this valuable commodity. Therefore, the benefits movement was started in Canada in the early 1990s and later adopted in the United States to help people identify the important personal, community, environmental, and economic values and benefits of parks and recreation services. This movement represents one of the first efforts by the industry to build leisure awareness.

A more recent endeavor in raising the awareness of the role that parks and recreation plays in the health of individuals and communities is the National Recreation and Park Association's national health promotion campaign deployed in 2004 that uses the tag line Healthy Lifestyles. Livable Communities. *It Starts in Parks!* Parks and recreation supports both individual participation and environmental factors associated with healthy living and livable communities. This bold, but accurate, positioning effort addresses the need for places and spaces for people to be physically active.

Leisure education reflects the learning aspects of leisure facilitation and includes skill development as well as exposure to a variety of leisure-time experiences. The VIP Project, a strategic plan for the industry of parks and recreation undertaken by the California Park and Recreation Society (CPRS) referred to leisure education as one of its market opportunity areas for the industry. The reference to leisure education in the plan calls for "Programs aimed at increasing education skills or enrichment programs; intersession programs; summer programs; before-, during-, and after-school programs; preschool development; literacy programs; facilities; staff training; parenting skill development, and family and child leisure education" (CPRS, 1999, page 57, paragraph 2).

One such leisure education initiative with a specific focus on health was Hearts N' Parks. The National Recreation and Park Association (NRPA) along with the National Heart, Lung, and Blood Institute (NHLBI) of the Institutes of Health (2001) embarked on a 52 community field test to document and demonstrate the roles of information and instruction in a recreation setting.

The first two years of the Hearts N' Parks project demonstrated that parks and recreation programs can affect individual health through physical activity and nutrition. Comparison of pretest and posttest questionnaires completed by program participants across 48 sites showed that participation in the program significantly increased knowledge of and positively changed attitudes toward heart-healthy behaviors. NRPA and NHLBI reported the following results (National Institutes of Health, 2003):

- When asked whether participants would choose healthier foods over less-healthy foods, children's scores improved 14 percent and adolescent scores improved 15 percent.

- All age groups reported increasing their physical activity levels, with adults significantly improving this behavior by 15 percent.

- Adults reported reducing the number of hours per week spent in sedentary activities, such as watching TV, by two to four hours.

Leisure coaching is the third form of leisure facilitation. Leoni and Berbling (1980) suggested that leisure coaching is a "structured self-help technique which draws on the individual's own resources and potential" (1980, p. 2). Think of a traditional sports team coach—that person provides specific guidance but it is up to the person to put it into practice. Leisure coaching is a growth area within the industry. The 29th National Wellness Conference of the Wellness Institute featured several sessions and one

This ad was part of a series of advertising messages promoting the values of parks and recreation under the tag line, *It Starts in Parks!*, that appeared in *Sports Illustrated* magazine.

full-day workshop on coaching skills for wellness. Wellness is a core component of life coaching. Life coaching has become popular in the last decade as individuals often living away from friends and families facing increasingly more challenging situations contract with a life coach that assists them in identifying, clarifying, and dealing with specific goals and challenges. Life coaching can focus upon career or promotional opportunities, parenting challenges, or personal goals. Since wellness incorporates all facets of a person's life, wellness coaching is a natural application of life coaching and paves the way for the advent of leisure coaches.

A nationwide approach to leisure counseling is illustrated by the overwhelmingly successful Canadian social-marketing and health-communication campaign, ParticipACTION. This program focused on the behavioral determinants of healthy lifestyles and created the Canadian movement for personal fitness. It was a structured program that helped a nation to draw on existing local resources and citizens' potential for activity. This marketing and communications effort used the five Ps of marketing (product, place, price, promotion, and positioning) to creatively reach an audience to promote physical activity participation. Even though the ParticipACTION national campaign ended in 2001 after 30 years, 85 percent of Canadians still recognize the ParticipACTION brand and message (Knox, 2004).

ParticipACTION'S Marketing Mix

Product: An active, healthy lifestyle and a fit nation

Place: Being active at home, while traveling to and from school and work, while enjoying the outdoors, and in your neighborhood and community

Price: Being active is easy, fun, accessible, and inexpensive. Benefits include health, appearance, and well-being.

Promotion: Public service advertising, public relations, personal selling, community events, educational resources; channels of distribution included mass and targeted media sponsor messages; the Internet; workplaces; schools; universities; communities; events; point of purchase in supermarkets and pharmacies and recreation, fitness, and sport venues; educational material (films, posters), health professionals; dietitians; and community leaders.

Positioning: The Canadian movement for personal fitness (Edwards, 2004)

Leisure coaching is closely related to leisure counseling. The exact role and parameters of leisure counseling remain subject to a variety of definitions and outcomes. Both leisure coaching and leisure counseling hold lifelong pursuit of a positive leisure lifestyle (where an individual voluntarily pursues activities that result in overall well-being) as a desirable outcome, but the approaches vary. Leisure counseling generally takes a more organized and structured approach than does leisure coaching and focuses on changing attitudes and breaking down barriers to participation. Leisure counseling will experience growth in the coming years because of the growing emphasis on health and wellness and the opportunities afforded by the growth of personal and life coaching.

LIVABILITY

Recent research by the U.S. Department of Health and Human Services (2001) and decades of public health practice have demonstrated that integrating physical activity into daily routines may be a more effective public health strategy than participating in structured exercise programs. Therefore, providing an environment conducive to physical activity—promoting community livability—is now a necessity rather than a nice thing to do. Community livability reflects environmental and economic factors that support access and opportunities for individuals, families, and neighborhoods to pursue a healthy lifestyle. A livable community is defined as one in which people can live safely, secure employment, acquire essential services, and gain access to a variety of leisure experiences. This livability does not involve just one segment of a community. It is a critical but challenging undertaking. Components of community livability that include roles for the parks and recreation industry include community mobilization, land-use planning, park accessibility, and public policy.

Community Mobilization

Communities working to enhance the quality of life for their citizens engage public, private, and nonprofit sectors in partnership with community-based, educational, clinical, and business stakeholders. Each community is different and may have a different set of values and beliefs, but increasingly, communities are consulting these often disparate voices to identify issues of livability, allowing communities to leverage each sector's individual strengths and improve their capacity to support healthy lifestyles.

Mobilizing communities to support livability issues requires strategic planning, community engagement, and vibrant leadership. Every sector of the community has a role to play in fostering livability. Leadership can and should come from any segment within the community, but essential support must be gained from the public sector through advocacy and policy implementation. Clinical, educational, and community-based institutions must join the public sector and citizens in a comprehensive commitment to change.

The Millennium Park bicycle garage is just one facet the Chicago Park District developed to increase livability and encourage wellness and fitness.

The role that parks and recreation can serve in community mobilization is both as a catalyst and facilitator for livability and healthy lifestyles. Hearts N' Parks is an example of a community mobilization effort. This initiative identified five areas of concentration (National Institutes of Health, 2001):

1. **People.** People both inside and outside of the organization, to advance the health promotion effort

2. **Programs and practices.** Additional efforts within current program offerings that promote health improvements

3. **Public visibility.** Strategies for gaining public attention for the health-related benefits of parks and recreation resources

4. **Partnering.** Techniques for attracting unique and nontraditional partners to support improved health outcomes

5. **Performance indicators.** Measuring, documenting, and demonstrating the impact of parks and recreation services

Additionally, a sixth area has been identified to support community mobilization:

6. **Policy interventions.** Environmental indicators and policies that promote healthy lifestyles and livable communities

The success of the program was evident in statistically significant increases in heart-healthy knowledge, skill, and attitudes. However, the involvement of partners will have a more far-reaching and long-lasting impact on community health. For example, Springfield, Missouri, formed a group representing all segments of health-related services within the community in order to make better use of existing resources and to improve the health of residents. The city of Las Vegas partnered with the University of Nevada at Las Vegas where a Hearts N' Parks class was established to provide opportunities for nutrition majors to hone their skills in the city's after-school programs. South Bend, Indiana, received a funding grant from a local hospital. The range and diversity of partners and resources mobilized were quite extensive.

The Active Living by Design Project funded by the Robert Wood Johnson Foundation is a part of the School of Public Health at the University of North Carolina. This program establishes and evaluates innovative approaches to increase physical activity through community design, public policies, and communications strategies. Community partnerships form the basis for these 25 Active Living by Design (n.d.b) communities that have been funded to develop, implement, and sustain collaboration among a variety of organizations in public health and other disciplines such as city planning, transportation, architecture, recreation, crime prevention, traffic safety, and education and among key advocacy groups concentrating on land use, public transit, nonmotorized travel, public spaces, parks, trails, and architectural practices that advance physical activity.

For example, the residents of the Upper Valley regions of Vermont and New Hampshire benefited from community partnership that included the Upper Valley Trails Alliance, National Park Service Rivers and Trails Program, Dartmouth Medical School, Dartmouth Hitchcock Medical Center, and the Lebanon Parks and Recreation Department. These partners promote increased physical activity by expanding the use of a trails network. Promotional strategies target employers and schools to build awareness and expand trail usage (Active Living by Design, n.d.b).

Land-Use Planning

Land-use planning is among one of the recognized contributors to livability and has increasingly become more vital to designing a livable community. After WWII large numbers of people moved from cities to suburbs, and these communities were largely designed for automobile use, which has inadvertently engineered physical activity out of daily living. For instance, although people moved to the suburbs, they often commuted back to the cities for employment. The initial attraction of the suburbs was the opportunity to own single family homes with a private piece of lawn that contributed to the distances between places and spaces. Smart growth refers to a philosophy

of planning and development that supports both the economy and the environment as well as the social and life quality of a community. The smart growth movement has developed a sprawl index that quantifies how urban sprawl affects common livability issues such as access to bike paths and trails, density of housing, lack of neighborhood centers, and poorly connected networks such as cul de sacs and highways and overpasses dividing neighborhoods.

The current focus on land use and livability centers on early 20th-century community design in which communities were designed as compact spaces where schools, stores, businesses, and other amenities were within easy walking. This traditional style of development and planning for "livability" has sparked numerous efforts to improve quality of life through effective community land-use efforts. In 1991, a group of land-use planners convened to discuss forms of community planning and design that focus on sustainable design elements to enhance livability. Sustainable design refers to construction of communities that sustain and support the quality of life over time such as self-contained communities where people can walk to work, school, and shopping rather than contributing to air pollution by automobile use or preservation of open space as a way to protect and maintain natural watersheds for drinking water. The result was the Ahwahnee Principles, which have been used as a benchmark for planning in communities nationwide. The preamble to these principles states the intent of this approach to land use:

> Preamble: Existing patterns of urban and suburban development seriously impair our quality of life. The symptoms are: more congestion and air pollution resulting from our increased dependence on automobiles, the loss of precious open space, the need for costly improvements to roads and public services, the inequitable distribution of economic resources, and the loss of a sense of community. By drawing on the best from the past and the present, we can plan communities that will more successfully serve the needs of those who live and work within them. (Calthorpe, Corbett, Duany, Moule, Plater-Zyberk, & Polyzoides, 1991).

Active Living by Design, a project funded by the Robert Wood Johnson Foundation located at the University of North Carolina, supports community design projects intended to enhance opportunities for physical activity. One such program involves a Federal grant to the Health Communities Initiative in Buffalo, New York to make the streets supportive of increased physical activity by adding bike lanes, widening sidewalks, and increasing street lighting. Another land-use planning project in conjunction with Active Living by Design occurs in Santa Ana, California that includes a collaboration with law enforcement and the YMCA to create a connected walking trail in a heavily urban setting that will result in access to community and school facilities (Active Living by Design, n.d.a).

Community Description:

- Because law enforcement is often the biggest item in a city budget, neighborhoods should be designed to be self-policing.

- Require common space in new developments such as pocket parks, community gardens, community centers, and neighborhood schools.

- Retrofit existing neighborhoods with community spaces such as community gardens and community centers. Share facilities with neighborhood schools.

- In dense multifamily housing, provide semi-private courtyards shared by no more than 30 people.

Land-use planning and development will receive even greater attention in the next decade as the obesity epidemic continues to grow and the need to curtail urban and suburban sprawl becomes an even greater priority.

Park Accessibility

Access to parks, recreation facilities, bike paths, and trails is essential to community livability and the health and well-being of its residents. As the health field has begun examining environmental factors that may influence the growing obesity crisis in the United States and Canada, parks and the facilities and opportunities associated with park areas have been included in this research. The results of the research examining proximity and accessibility to parks and open space have revealed the following:

- People who report having access to sidewalks are 28 percent more likely to be physically active, and people who report having access to walking and jogging trails are 55 percent more likely to be physically active (Humpel, Owen, & Leslie, 2002).

- In a Missouri survey (Brownson, Housemann, Brown, Jackson-Thompson, King, Malone,

& Sallis, 2000), 55.2 percent of people using trails reported an increase in walking since they began using the trails. Women and people with a high school education or lower were more than twice as likely to have increased their amount of walking since they began using the trails. This study (Brownson, Baker, Housemann, Brennan, and Bacak, 2001) also found that walking trails may be beneficial in promoting physical activity among women and people in lower socioeconomic groups.

- People with access to recreational facilities were twice as likely to get the recommended levels of physical activity (Huston, Evenson, Bors, & Gizlice, 2003).

- People with the best access to a variety of built and natural facilities were 43 percent more likely to exercise 30 minutes most days than those with poor access (Giles-Corti & Donovan, 2002).

- People living in areas with few public outdoor recreation facilities were more likely to be overweight (Catlin, Simoes, & Brownson, 2003).

It is apparent from reviewing even this concise list of research findings that accessibility to parks, facilities, and trails significantly supports physical activity and health.

Public Policy

Receiving funds to construct roads is a result of public policy. Federal budgets passed without reinstating funding for the Land and Water Conservation Fund to secure additional park space is also a result of policy or lack of policy. The Land and Water Conservation Fund was a fund created by Congress for the expressed purpose of purchasing parks and open space and developing appropriate areas and facilities for citizens' use. The critical role assumed by public policy affects livability. The Centers for Disease Control and Prevention's Active Community Environments Initiative (ACES) promotes walking, bicycling, and the development of accessible recreation facilities. The initiative encourages environmental and policy interventions that will affect increased levels of physical activity and improved public health (Centers for Disease Control and Prevention, 2005). An activity-friendly environment, one in which it is easy for people to be physically active, can be supported in the following ways:

- Encourage the development of environments that are friendly to pedestrians and bicycles.
- Promote active forms of transportation like walking and bicycling.
- Disseminate information about active community environments.

These recommendations by the CDC lead to the development of an active community environment, a community where people are afforded safe, convenient, and pleasant places and spaces to walk and ride bicycles. Friendly pedestrian and bicycle environments are ones where there are wide sidewalks or bike lanes available as well as overpasses or underpasses where people can safely cross busy intersections or highways.

These practices must be transformed into policy initiatives to ensure that livable communities are widespread rather than the exception to the rule in the United States and Canada. Otherwise, people will continue their sedentary habits, leading to further increases in health care spending and the continuation of the medical model's approach to health care. The shift to the prevention model, which includes community mobilization of resources as well as land-use planning, requires policy development and public advocacy.

These environmental factors such as neighborhood parks and bike trails also serve as an economic stimulus for business relocation, community development, and tourism. Communities incorporating trail systems for hiking and walking trails for exercise can turn to an increasing number of scientific studies to reinforce policy recommendations and public investment. The role of the parks and recreation professional is to understand the elements of community design and their impact on the planning, provision, and sustainability of a parks and recreation system. It will be through collaboration with other disciplines and services that parks and recreation will become an essential factor in creating livable communities.

The role of the parks and recreation community is to serve as catalyst and facilitator in order to advance public health strategies that change the way communities envision health. Parks and outdoor environments are designed to provide health and social benefits and, along with a holistic approach to community design, are increasingly viewed as an essential public resource that fosters healthy lifestyles and livable communities.

CAREER OPPORTUNITIES

Attention to and concern for health is a growth area of the economy in both Canada and the United States. The revenue in the United States generated by health clubs was $14.1 billion U.S. in 2003 (International Health, Racquet and Sportsclub Association, 2003). Health spending in the United States continues to grow with estimates of expenditures approaching $3 trillion dollars by 2011 according to a forecast by the Centers for Medicare and Medicaid Services (Mercola, 2002). Canada spends more on health care than any other comparable industrialized country with expenditures representing 11.7 percent of its gross domestic product (The Fraser Institute, 2002). Parks and recreation professionals in this growth area work with any and all age groups; work in public, nonprofit, private, and commercial settings; and often focus on outdoor adventure or therapeutic recreation.

Career opportunities are likely to require either a degree in parks and recreation or a degree in a support field. The first option involves securing a degree in parks, recreation, or leisure. The focus within these degree programs is shifting from programs and activities to facilitating and supporting health through wellness programs, leisure facilitation, and community mobilization.

The second option is a degree in a field other than parks and recreation such as physical education, public health, exercise physiology, health education, or community planning. A minor or concentration in parks and recreation because of its close connection to these various disciplines and their related philosophies will augment your education. The following are examples of related specializations:

Public health careers including health education and promotion. American Public Health Association: www.apha.org

Fitness, human performance, or physical education careers. American Alliance for Health, Physical Education, Recreation and Dance: www.aahperd.org

Community planning or park design in the public or private sector. American Planning Association: www.planning.org

Health and wellness–related careers in a recreation or park setting. National Recreation and Park Association: www.nrpa.org; Canadian Parks and Recreation Association: www.cpra.ca

Health promotion and disease prevention through physical activity. Coalition for Active Living: www.activeliving.ca

Professions that focus on wellness in the school, community, or corporate sector. National Wellness Institute: www.nationalwellness.org

Military wellness and fitness. Executive Business Media: www.ebmpubs.com; or contact a specific branch of the military

Careers that incorporate play into wellness and recreation. The American Association for the Child's Right to Play: www.ipausa.org; Association for Play Therapy: www.a4pt.org; Canadian Association for Child and Play Therapy: www.cacpt.com

SUMMARY

The Brightbill quote that introduced this chapter reminds us that health is not just about the absence of sickness and even goes beyond "feeling good." Health refers to the "plus" margin. The parks, recreation, and leisure industry in all its forms and serving numerous groups of people is central to optimal quality of life, or the plus margin.

Our industry plays two related but divergent roles in promoting health and well-being. One role is directed toward individuals or small groups of people and focuses on attaining wellness through recreation activities or by building awareness and providing education, coaching, or counseling. These recreation programs and activities and the

---

Web Sites to EXPLORE

American Alliance for Health, Physical Education, Recreation and Dance: www.aahperd.org

American Planning Association: www.planning.org

American Public Health Association: www.apha.org

Athletic Business: www.athleticbusiness.com

California Park and Recreation Society: www.cprs.org

Canadian Parks and Recreation Association: www.cpra.ca

Institute for International Medical Education: www.iime.org

National Recreation and Park Association: www.nrpa.org

National Wellness Institute: www.nationalwellness.org

---

information that supports leisure facilitation focus on people and their behaviors.

The second role played by parks and recreation in promoting health addresses communities and societal norms. As the prevention model of health care began gaining acceptance, we began to understand the importance livability—the role of the environment in the overall health and well-being of communities and society. Environmental concerns such as land use, community mobilization, and access to parks and recreation are essential to community livability, and parks and recreation serves a vital and visible role in promoting these concerns.

CHAPTER 16

Outdoor and Adventure Recreation

Randy J. Virden

© Photodisc

We simply need that wild country available to us, even if we never do more than drive to its edge and look in. For it can be a means of measuring our sanity and ourselves as creatures, a part of the geography of hope.

Wallace Stegner, writer and environmentalist

CHAPTER OBJECTIVES

After reading this chapter, you should be able to do the following:

- Provide an overview of outdoor recreation in North America
- Summarize the history of outdoor recreation in North America
- Understand the social, economic, psychological, and cultural importance of outdoor recreation
- Identify the organizations related to and careers available in outdoor recreation
- Provide an overview of the outdoor adventure and experiential education movement

INTRODUCTION

During the second half of the 20th century, outdoor recreation has emerged as an important component of the American and Canadian lifestyle. A recent Roper public opinion poll (The Recreation Roundtable, 2004) indicated that 87 percent of Americans participated in an outdoor recreational activity in 2003. The same study indicated that 32 percent of Americans visited national parks; Parks Canada (2002) reported that 35 percent of Canadians had visited national park sites in Canada within the previous year. Over the past 50 years, there has been a dramatic increase in both the total number of outdoor recreation visits and in the per capita consumption of outdoor recreation experiences (see table 16.1). The United States Department of State estimates 900 million outdoor recreation visits to national parks, forests, historical refuges, reservoirs, and lands. State parks contribute another 800 million visitors. There are no comprehensive estimates of overall outdoor recreation use in either Canada or the United States. However, if one assumes that more outdoor recreation occurs in local parks and natural areas that are closer to home than in national or state-level resources, it is likely that several billion outdoor recreation visits occur annually in North America. Canada and the United States also have a shared history of providing outdoor recreation opportunities for their citizens and for international visitors as well. Both countries have a comprehensive system of public lands, parks, forests, rivers, trails, wilderness, and developed facilities that help to meet the demand for outdoor recreation and nature-based tourism.

On one level, outdoor recreation can be viewed as the simple pleasure of enjoying a shared leisure experience in a natural setting. At the same time, outdoor recreation has been shown by scholars to be a complex social phenomenon that has myriad relationships with cultural, economic, environmental, and political systems. Beginning with the Outdoor Recreation Resource Review Commission (ORRRC) Report in 1962, the outdoor recreation phenomenon has been increasingly studied in a systematic and focused way for the past 40 years (Manning, 1999).

This chapter provides an overview of the outdoor recreation phenomenon in North America. The introduction reviews key outdoor recreation–related concepts and a brief discussion of the North American meaning of nature. It also reviews the history of outdoor recreation, both in terms of its emergence as a mass form of leisure and the social and political movements that have protected our forests, parks, and other natural resources. This is followed by a discussion of outdoor recreation demand in light of historical social forces, current participation trends, and economic impact as well as a discussion of the social–psychological explanations for this phenomenon. The chapter also presents outdoor recreation providers and the types of contemporary professional opportunities available in Canada and the United States. And finally, the area of adventure programming and experiential education is discussed as a separate and important

TABLE 16.1 Historical Visitation to U.S. National Parks and National Forests

Agencies	1925	1950	1975	2000
National Park Service	2,054,562	33,252,589	190,390,827	285,891,275
U.S. Forest Service (RVDs)	5,622,200	27,367,800	199,200,800	341,204,000 (1996)

Note: The last year that recreation visitor days (RVDs) were estimated was 1996.

From visitation documented by the National Park Service and the U.S. Forest Service.

component of service delivery within the outdoor recreation field.

CONCEPTS RELATED TO OUTDOOR AND ADVENTURE RECREATION

To establish a common nomenclature to clarify the meaning of outdoor recreation and related concepts, it is necessary to define important terms. The following section discusses and defines these terms.

Outdoor Recreation

The term "recreation" generally refers to a broad array of activities and experiences that are voluntarily engaged in during free time and are motivated by the internal enjoyment or satisfaction derived by the participant. **Outdoor recreation** is the array of recreation behaviors, activities, and experiences that occur in or depend on the natural environment for their fulfillment. The type of natural setting or degree of naturalness can vary

considerably and still be considered outdoor recreation. For example, both a wilderness backpacking trip or a round of golf is considered outdoor recreation, although the former is more dependent on a pristine natural environment and the latter on a designed or constructed natural setting. This relationship with nature is what separates outdoor recreation from other forms of leisure.

Nature-Based Tourism and Ecotourism

A significant amount of outdoor recreation behavior or participation is intertwined with tourism. According to the World Tourism Organization, tourism comprises the activity of people traveling to and staying in places outside their usual environment for not more than one year for leisure, business, and other purposes. More specifically, tourists travel at least 100 miles and spend one or more nights away from home, for pleasure, business, or personal affairs. A significant portion of tourism includes travel to natural-resource attractions, such as national parks, national forests, historical

Participating in an environmental education class is just one of the outdoor recreation opportunities available to children.

sites, beaches, and other nature-based attractions. **Nature-based tourism** is travel behavior that depends to some degree on the natural environment. It is common for managers in federal and state public land agencies and professionals in the tourism industry to refer to outdoor recreationists or tourists as "visitors" and to track "visits" or "visitor days" as a measurement of production. Both ecotourism and adventure tourism are considered to fall within the broader domain of nature-based tourism. Ecotourism is "responsible travel to natural areas that conserves the environment and improves the well-being of local people" (The International Ecotourism Society, 2004).

Environmental Interpretation

Environmental interpretation can be traced back to Enos Mills, a naturalist from Rocky Mountain National Park who wrote *Adventures of a Nature Guide*. Interpretation is most tied to the development of the National Park Service and is now commonly found in all natural-resource land agencies (as well as in private and nonprofit visitor centers) that provide outdoor recreation opportunities to visitors of public lands, and historical and cultural sites. "**Environmental interpretation** is an educational activity that aims to reveal meanings about our cultural and natural resources" (Beck & Cable, 1998, p. xi).

Adventure Recreation and Adventure Tourism

Outdoor recreation spans a broad array of activities and a set of diverse motivations that drive participation in those activities. Over the past 35 years, there has been a special interest in **adventure recreation,** which are outdoor activities that are perceived by the participant to include elements of danger and adventure. Common forms of adventure recreation include skiing, white-water rafting, rock climbing, mountaineering, caving, ocean kayaking, and mountain biking; these activities often carry desires on the part of the participants for risk taking, challenge, sensation seeking, achievement, competence, and testing one's skills. As with outdoor recreation, adventure recreation often happens during tourism outings or trips. Tourism that includes either organized or dispersed adventure recreation is considered **adventure tourism.** In addition to public land agencies that provide recreation and tourism

opportunities, the tourism industry and outdoor equipment companies are also major promoters of adventure recreation and tourism.

Adventure Programming and Experiential Education

The largest segment of participation in outdoor recreation occurs in the autonomous context of families, friends, and individuals freely choosing to engage in certain activities in a particular setting or favorite outdoor site. This same trend also holds for adventure recreation, where the majority of participation occurs outside the supervision of qualified trained instructors. However, during the last 50 years, youth educators, camps, and outdoor schools have emerged to provide outdoor leadership and programs focused on teaching adventure recreation activities in a safe environment under qualified instruction. Adventure programming goes beyond adventure recreation to include other forms of outdoor recreation and outdoor and environmental education. For the purposes of this chapter, **adventure programming** includes the broad base of philosophies, theories, and leadership techniques used in the fields of outdoor leadership, experiential education, and adventure education.

Experiential education is closely tied to adventure programming but emphasizes a learning philosophy based on direct experience in an outdoor setting. **Experiential education** is a philosophy and methodology in which educators purposely engage with learners in direct experience and focused reflection in order to increase knowledge, develop skills, and clarify values. Experiential education engages the learner directly as an active participant in the education process. Both adventure programming and experiential education require trained outdoor leaders who understand how nature can contribute to personal and social growth opportunities.

MEANING OF NATURE AND SPECIAL PLACES

For many, the desire to engage in outdoor recreation and nature-based tourism is inextricably linked to a strong attraction to the natural world. Nature, especially the physical component of the natural environment appears on the surface to be a straightforward and clear concept. The natural sciences have accomplished much over the past centuries to improve and enrich our understanding of the natural world. Before the European influence, the nature of North America was inexplicably intertwined with the lifestyle, the perceived natural order of the universe, and religion of Native American cultures. The arrival of the European explorers, colonists, and traders brought along new conceptions of nature: nature as an obstacle to progress, a more economic or utilitarian view of nature. Other more favorable views and meanings were expressed toward the natural environment of the New World by mystics, grand tourists, romantics, artists, and writers.

The noted American historian William Cronon argues that "nature is a human idea, with a long and complicated cultural history which has led different human beings to conceive of the natural world in very different ways" (Cronon, 1996, p. 20). For many Americans and Canadians, nature has long held an allure that is interwoven into the desire to visit natural places and settings. In other words, the meanings that we attach and hold toward nature explain in part our desire to

recreate and be outside. The meaning of nature in North America is uniquely tied both to the frontier experience and the subsequent abuse of natural resources. Aldo Leopold, considered the father of wildlife ecology, noted that "when the end of the supply is in sight [do] we discover that the thing is valuable" (Nash, 2001, p. 189). Nash argues that our sadness and concern for the abuses of the North American frontier ultimately led to the efforts to protect forests, and cultural and natural wonders. This same frontier experience created a new romance and mythology of North American nature with characters like Leatherstockings, Buck, and Paul Bunyan and places like the Klondike, Yukon, Yellowstone, and Niagara Falls.

In addition to the shared cultural meanings held toward nature in general, outdoor recreation and nature-based tourism often are focused on specific meanings attached to a particular place or setting. For example, certain national parks, such as Yosemite, Banff, and Yellowstone have tremendous symbolic and personal appeal that attracts visitors to these special places. Additionally, many Americans

National parks, such as Yosemite, have tremendous symbolic and personal appeal that attracts visitors to these special places.

and Canadians have spent portions of their youth, family time, and personal time in special outdoor settings that have become important over the years. The experiences and memories shared with other people add to the personal meaning and value that people assign to summer homes, cabins, lodges, campgrounds, summer camps, lakes, forests, beaches, and other natural places. The shared meanings of nature and the personal meanings of these special places must be recognized as an important part of outdoor recreation and nature-based tourism behavior. Some people tend to focus only on the outdoor recreation activities themselves as the draw, without realizing that the meaning that nature has for Americans and Canadians strongly drives these behaviors and our tradition in the outdoors.

HISTORY OF OUTDOOR RECREATION

Outdoor recreation is closely tied to our past, but it has also been enhanced and accelerated through postindustrialization and modernity. This section provides an overview of the history of outdoor recreation in North America, both in terms of its emergence as a mass form of leisure and the social and political movements that have protected our forests, parks, and other natural resources.

History of Outdoor Recreation in North America (1500 to 1890)

Outdoor recreation has deep historical and cultural roots in both the United States and Canada. The Native American tribes that inhabited North America before the first Europeans arrived engaged in many activities that relate to current expressions of outdoor recreation. Fishing, hunting, canoeing, outdoor celebrations, gathering berries and medicinal plants, and recognizing the connection between spirit and nature are Native American practices that share traditions with modern-day outdoor recreation. The manner in which Native American religions and cosmologies were connected and intertwined with the natural world demonstrates an ethic of respect, sacredness, and acceptance of nature. Although our cultures are different, this connection and appreciation of nature are tied to values in modern-day environmentalism and the appreciation of nature.

The early European explorers and colonists brought many things with them to the New World, including new forms of technology, new lifestyles, and new ways of thinking about nature. These early immigrants brought a wealth of opinions and beliefs about nature from European folklore such as Hansel and Gretel and classic mythology such as Beowulf. For example, in Hansel and Gretel, the forest is portrayed as a foreboding environment containing an evil witch who disliked children. Often wild animals and humans (e.g., wolves, bears, werewolves, trolls, Pan, wild men) were infused in European folklore with hostile, fearful, and sinister images of wild country: Roderick Nash (2001) discusses many examples in detail in his chapter titled "Old World Roots of Opinion" in *Wilderness and the American Mind*. In addition to these shared stories, the early settlers' and colonists' views were also deeply influence by the Judeo-Christian tradition. Early Puritan writing often used the contrast between light and dark imagery to express that wilderness was ungodly and sinister. After all, the wilderness was a harsh place, especially for the early settlers who confronted a hostile environment and inhabitants. Nash (2001) argues that a natural bias or antipathy emerged against the wilderness, especially in Puritan New England, where Native Americans were viewed as heathens or godless. Puritan pioneers often believed they were engaged in a moral war or regeneration process to turn the "ungodly and useless into a beneficent civilization" (p. 43). It was all too easy to cast the wilderness in terms of something that had to be conquered or subdued.

Along with the focus on early survival, other European conventions such as a system of laws, private land ownership, and colonial capitalism reinforced the utilitarian value system that emerged in North America where nature was valued more for its development potential and natural resource commodities. Domestic animals, new crops, guns, saws, fishing nets, plows, and other tools of early settlers brought other changes to the environment and frontier. Farther north and west in the heart of the continent, fur trappers and traders slowly explored and harvested a growing fur trade based on the pelts of beaver and otters. These early French and English trappers were the advance agents of European and Anglo culture, and they traveled into the heart of North America. Much like Native and first Americans, they traveled by foot and canoe and later by horseback into the rivers, lakes, and mountains of the New World and among the native inhabitants. The outdoor lifestyles, modes of travel, and places that these early trappers explored are all important parts of the romantic outdoor recreation heritage and attractions enjoyed by Americans and Canadians today.

As settlers advanced westward, so did the sawmills, steam engines, and clearing of forests and land for farming. Most rural Americans and Canadians relied on hunting, fishing, and sustenance agriculture for survival until well into the 19th century. The destruction of the eastern forests and wildlife and erosion and flooding that resulted from deforestation were a wake-up call for many Americans in the last half of the 19th century. At the same time, wildlife such as the bison was disappearing, and the plains and mountain Indian nations were being reduced and forced onto reservations. Nash points out that the growing urban population began to recognize and mourn the loss of what had been perceived as an infinite North American frontier. The new awareness was strongest in the growing urban areas of the East and Northeast and led to public support for protecting places like Niagara Falls, Yellowstone, and urban parks.

Alfred Runte (1997) and Roderick Nash (2001) both note that 19th- and early 20th-century North Americans shared nationalistic and romantic notions of nature and the diminishing wilderness. In Canada, the Voyageurs were legendary French Canadian fur trappers who used canoes to traverse across central Canada, the northwestern United States, and the Great Lakes. The early Rocky Mountain explorers and the Royal Canadian Mounties were all part of the emerging romance of the early Canadian frontier experience. In the United States, writers like James Fennimore Cooper and Jack London created characters such as Leatherstockings and White Fang and brought pioneer adventure stories of moving west to a growing national audience. Protecting places like Banff, Yellowstone, Niagara Falls, Yosemite, and the Grand Canyon grew in popularity as the public began to consider the frontier, wildlife, and forests as important and valuable national symbols.

History of Outdoor Recreation in North America (1890 to Present)

In 1890, the U.S. Census Bureau (2004) recognized for the first time that there was no longer a frontier line; for all practical purposes, the North American continent had been subdued. By 1900, a little more than 40 percent of North Americans lived in cities, and urbanization and industrialization were in full bloom. American President Theodore Roosevelt personified the love of nature that was widespread in urban America at the turn of the century. President Roosevelt was an avid hunter, hiker, horseback rider, and adventurer. He helped found the Boone and Crockett Club, a men's organization devoted to hunting and conservation. During his presidency, Teddy Roosevelt helped to establish 150 national forests, the first 51 federal bird reservations, 5 national parks, the first 18 national monuments, the first 4 national game preserves, and the first 21 reclamation projects. During the first decades of the 20th century, Americans and Canadians were flocking to lakes, forests, and new national parks. Summer camps for children began to emerge in the rural areas closest to the emerging eastern cities. Youth organizations that focused on the outdoors, such as the Boy Scouts, Girls Scouts, Boy Pioneers, and Campfire Girls, started during this period. The Appalachian Mountain Club in the East and the Sierra Club in California took their primarily urban members into the newly protected forests and mountains. The National Park Service in the United States was established in 1916. Nash coined the term *wilderness cult* to describe the enthusiasm and popular interest in outdoor recreation that emerged in the United States during this period (Nash, 2001, p. 141).

Conservation efforts continued into the 1930s, and automobiles made their grand entrance into national parks and forests between 1910 and 1920. By the late 1920s more people visited national parks by automobile than by train. The accessibility of the automobile also led to what was termed the first "golden age of tourism" in North America, and many tourists wanted to visit natural attractions and scenic areas. Then as quickly as this new outdoor recreation boom appeared, the Depression put an end to the affluence and discretionary income that had fueled it. The depression years deflated the demand for outdoor recreation and nature-based tourism in Canada and the United States. World War II further suppressed outdoor recreation and tourism as national energy increasingly focused on the war effort.

By 1950, the Canadian and American populations once again focused on domestic issues and rebuilding the economy. As postwar economic production flourished, products like the automobile, housing, food, and outdoor recreation consumer goods became affordable and accessible to the masses. Most families now had access to reliable personal transportation, and systems were soon planned for a cross-national (interstate and interprovincial) highway system across North America. War-based

OUTSTANDING *Graduates*

Courtesy of Eric Baldin

Background Information

Name: Eric Baldin

Education: Bachelor's of environmental studies (1999) and masters of environmental studies (2003), University of Waterloo, Waterloo, Ontario, faculty of environmental studies

Career Information

Position: Land management research technician at Credit Valley Conservation (CVC), Mississauga, Ontario

Organization: CVC is one of 36 conservation authorities operating in Ontario. It employs more than 60 people under the guidance of a board of directors and serves more than 600,000 residents of the Credit River watershed daily. Conservation authorities are community-based environmental organizations originally formed by an act of provincial government and dedicated to conserving, restoring, developing, and managing natural resources within the watershed. CVC is a partnership of the 12 local and regional municipalities within the Credit River watershed. In 2004, Credit Valley Conservation celebrated 50 years of working to protect the natural environment within the 386 square miles (1,000 square kilometers) drained by the 55-mile-long (90-kilometer-long) Credit River and its 932 miles (1,500 kilometers) of tributaries. This watershed is located in a part of Canada that is being urbanized rapidly. It is adjacent to the Greater Toronto Area and includes parts of the municipalities of Mississauga and Brampton. The river's headwaters are located above the Niagara Escarpment, a World Biosphere Reserve, and are the source of four rivers: the Credit, Humber, Etobicoke, and Nottawasaga. A small section of the Oak Ridges Moraine and several other moraines are located within the boundaries of the watershed.

Organization's Mission: CVC believes that watershed management must focus on the future. CVC intends to continue to be visionaries in watershed management and provide leadership to ensure a healthy environ-

> Natural heritage planning and source-water protection provide exciting and satisfying opportunities that will only increase as they become more important to society and their momentum grows.

ment for future generations. CVC's work is guided by three principles: to look at the long term, to look at prevention by dealing with problems before they happen rather than trying to deal with the consequences of poor decisions, and to look at the cumulative impact of decisions and actions. CVC also practices adaptive environmental management (AEM). This means that our methods of managing the Credit River watershed respond to changes, to new data, and to the most current understanding of effective watershed management.

Job Description: Develop management plans for conservation areas and other CVC-owned properties. Develop and implement CVC's Greenlands Securement Strategy, a watershed approach to securing key greenlands. Develop land securement proposals, manage property, and do research for natural heritage planning.

Career Path: I took parks management courses at university and served as a natural heritage and planning research technician at Toronto and Region Conservation (TRC).

Likes and Dislikes About the Job: I take pride in seeing the benefits of good environmental management take hold at a conservation area that I helped manage. To take that one step further, I can identify properties that would enhance our system of existing conservation areas and work with CVC staff and our partners to secure and protect those properties from future development.

Advice to Undergraduates

Don't let a job description predetermine your attitude toward the job. In many cases these descriptions are created as a necessity for a job posting. If you are ambitious, willing to learn, and willing to make mistakes, you will be given the chance to make the job whatever you want it to be.

technology brought a new set of outdoor recreation toys such as jeeps, aluminum trailers, boats and canoes, inflatable rafts, and army surplus camping gear. The 1950s and early 1960s saw phenomenal interest and participation in outdoor recreation visits to national parks, provincial and state parks, forests, lakes, oceans, and other outdoor resources. In 1962, the U.S. Congress established the Outdoor Recreation Resource Review Commission (ORRRC) to study the demand for and supply of outdoor recreation for the next 40 years and to make recommendations to accommodate those needs.

World War II also contributed to the emergence of adventure outdoor programming. Outward Bound was established to give British sailors the skills and experience to survive the bitter cold of the North Sea if their ships were torpedoed by German U-boats. Kurt Hahn, a German educator, and Lawrence Holt, helped develop an outdoor-based curriculum to provide young sailors the confidence and ability to cope with demanding challenges. The early programs were based in Wales, and the program was eventually brought to North America in the 1960s.

The late 1960s and 1970s also brought a new idealism and political commitment to the environmental movement in the United States and Canada; much of this support came from the post–World War II baby boom generation. The Wilderness Act was passed in 1964 followed by the Land and Water Conservation Fund Act in 1965. The later piece of legislation led to the establishment of the Bureau of Outdoor Recreation and monies for comprehensive national and state-level outdoor recreation planning and funding. Since the 1970s, participation in outdoor recreation, nature-based recreation, and adventure recreation has continued to grow. The past 30 years have also seen significant changes to park and public land agency organic acts (legislation that provides an agency's mission) and an increased supply of parks, wilderness, protected areas, river protection, and heritage and historical preservation.

OUTDOOR RECREATION DEMAND

Next we examine the components and forces that determine the demand for and supply of outdoor recreation opportunities. The emergence and sustained popularity of outdoor recreation are driven by modern social forces, contemporary trends and lifestyles, economic behavior, socialization, and psychological forces. Together, these forces tell the story of outdoor recreation demand.

Historical Social Forces

This section presents and discusses some of the more important social forces that have influenced the demand for outdoor recreation in Canada and the United States over the past 125 years.

Population Growth

Many of the social forces that drive outdoor recreation participation and behavior are shared with leisure behavior of society in general. In 2004, the World Fact Book (Central Intelligence Agency, 2004) estimated Canada's population at 32.5 million and the United States' at 293 million. Both countries share a similar history of explosive population growth caused by healthy-birth rates and immigration over the past 200 years. The land area for both countries is similar: 37.3 million square miles (96.6 million square kilometers) for Canada and 38.6 square miles (99.9 square kilometers) for the United States, meaning that the population density is much less in Canada than in the United States. Table 16.2 provides population estimates for both countries from 1900 and projected through 2050. The population growth rate for both counties from 1900 to 2000 was more than a 600 percent increase. These population trends have had and will continue to have a significant effect on outdoor recreation because more people translates into more demand for outdoor recreation

TABLE 16.2 Past and Future Population Estimates

Year	United States (millions)	U.S. urban**	Canada (millions)
1900*	76.1	40%	5.3
1950	152.3	60%	14.0
2000	282.3	80%	31.3
2050	420.1	n/a	41.4

*1901 for Canada
** Percentage of population living in urban areas of 50,000 or more

and more competition for natural resources to support a growing North American population.

Urbanization

A related phenomenon to population growth is the influence of urbanization and the needs associated with an urban lifestyle. Going back to the eastern cities of the mid-1800s, the desire to escape to city parks, youth facilities, summer camps, and natural places and attractions has fueled many of the early social and conservation efforts. Central Park in New York City and Mount Royal Park in Montreal were both designed by Frederick Law Olmstead for growing urban populations that desired constructed nature in an urban setting. Table 16.2 also provides a glimpse of the urbanization trend from 1900 through 2000 in the United States, where more than 80 percent of the population now lives in metropolitan areas with populations of 50,000 or more. Although similar data are not available for Canada, the 2001 Canadian census reveals that a similar 79.4 percent of Canadians currently live in urban areas. Urban life has moved people away from rural landscapes, while increasing people's need to reconnect to those same landscapes during leisure and vacations. Open space, public-land access, parks, and outdoor recreation opportunities in close proximity to major urban centers are especially important.

Increased Ethnic and Racial Diversity

Ethnic and racial diversity has exerted and will continue to exert a strong influence over the changing population profile and outdoor recreation participation in both countries. The United States has grown increasingly diverse in recent decades, with several states, including California, Hawaii, and New Mexico, having a majority Hispanic population, with Texas and other states along the Sun Belt soon to follow. According to the 2000 census, Hispanics now comprise the largest minority population in the United States with more 35 million residents, followed by 34.6 million African Americans, 10.2 million Asians, and 2.5 million American Indians and Alaskan Natives.

Both Canada and the United States have experienced significant immigration influxes over the past 20 years. In the United States, Latino and Asian immigrants dominate population increases. In Canada in the 2001 census, the proportion of foreign-born residents was the highest in 70 years at 18 percent of the total population. The Latino (215,000) and Black (660,000) populations in Canada are smaller than in the United States. The

visible minority population in Canada reached 4 million (13.5 percent of the population) in 2001, a three-fold increase over the 1981 census. The largest minority group is Chinese (more than 1 million), followed by South Asian (915,000) and Black. Toronto, Vancouver, and Montreal attracted almost three-quarters of Canada's decade of the 1990's new immigrants. Additionally, the population reporting Aboriginal identity in Canada reached nearly 1 million in 2001.

Outdoor recreation preferences and ways of relating to nature differ depending on the cultural group. The USDA Forest Service has dedicated considerable research funding to studying the new visitors that are increasingly frequenting national forests and wilderness areas close to urban areas in California, Arizona, and the southern states. A more diverse population means that outdoor recreation professionals must understand a variety of cultural groups in order to provide the outdoor recreation opportunities that they desire. International tourists make up a growing visitor segment at many Canadian and American national parks and historic and cultural sites. Increasingly, outdoor recreation managers, interpreters, and planners must think strategically about communicating and serving this growing international clientele (USDA Forest Service, 2004a).

Increase in Leisure and Income

The increase in both leisure time and discretionary income has contributed to the growth of outdoor recreation over the past 50 years. The three-day weekend and paid vacations have become a part of the working lives of most Canadians and Americans. Weekend, winter, and summer travel to cabins, resorts, and hotels close to outdoor attractions is pervasive in modern life. In addition to time, growth in discretionary income allows most Canadians and Americans to afford the equipment, travel, and transportation costs associated with outdoor recreation activities. According to the U.S. Department of Labor, personal income (after controlling for inflation) more than doubled between 1967 and 2000 (U.S. Department of Labor, 2004b). Similar trends in Canada suggest that the average citizen has more income available for discretionary spending, including outdoor recreation and nature-based tourism.

Technology

Technology is another factor that has made an enormous impact on outdoor recreation in the last 50 years. The World War II technologies mentioned earlier gave rise to camping trailers, aluminum boats, lightweight army backpacking gear, off-road vehicles, and rubber rafts. Air transportation and a highly specialized road system ranging from interstate highways to countless logging roads have been constructed over the past 50 years. During the 1960s, backpacks and tent materials became lighter and more compact. High-tech metals, plastics, and electronics have revolutionized almost every outdoor recreation pursuit, including navigation, downhill skiing, hunting, angling, hiking, water skiing, boating, rock climbing, rafting, and kayaking. Backcountry and outdoor clothing have become a multimillion-dollar industry with a plethora of new fabrics, outdoor apparel, and footwear. Perhaps the technology with the biggest impact on outdoor recreation access and the environment is in new vehicle designs and products: SUVs, four-wheel drive vehicles, motorcycles, ATVs, snowmobiles, recreation vehicles, travel trailers, boats, personal watercraft, mountain bikes, and aircraft. These

All-terrain vehicles allow people more access to the backcountry, but their use can also cause considerable impact to the environment.

modern vehicles allow many more people access to places in the backcountry than was available in previous generations. Additionally, the growth and popularity of these vehicles can cause considerable impacts to soil, wildlife habitat, wetlands, grasses, forests, and air and water quality. Also increases in motorized recreationists have resulted in social conflicts with nonmotorized recreationists, as these two types of users often seek different outdoor experiences.

Participation and Trends in Outdoor Recreation

Demand in outdoor recreation can be illustrated through recent national and regional surveys that provide a snapshot of the outdoor recreation participation and preferences of the general population. The first United States National Recreation Survey was conducted in 1960. This study has evolved and been replicated several times in the last 40 years. The current version is called National Survey on Recreation and the Environment (NSRE) and is conducted regularly by the USDA Forest Service (USDA Forest Service, 2004b). The most recent NSRE data were collected from September 1999 through February 2004. Table 16.3 provides a statistical overview of outdoor recreation in the United States by reporting the percentage and number of American adults (age 16 and older) who participated in at least one of 37 different activities. The list includes both general tourism-related activities such as viewing natural scenery, visiting nature centers, and driving for pleasure, as well as more specialized activities, such as boating, day hiking, and mountain biking. The activities with the highest percentage of growth between 1994 and 2004 were kayaking, snowboarding, jet skiing, viewing or photographing fish, snowmobiling, ice fishing, sledding, viewing wildlife, backpacking, day hiking, bicycling, horseback riding, and canoeing.

Another national study is the January 2004 Outdoor Industry Foundation Consumer Outreach Report prepared by Harris Interactive that focused on human-powered outdoor recreation. The study found that 57 percent of the general population (145.7 million Americans) participated in at least one human-powered outdoor activity. Since 1998, participants in human-powered outdoor activities are slightly younger (median age 35 years), more racially diverse (20 percent nonwhite), and have families (Outdoor Industry Foundation, 2004). Hiking, bicycling on paved roads, and camping

TABLE 16.3   Outdoor Recreation Participation in the United States: 2002

Outdoor activity	Percent participating	Participants (million)
Viewing and photographing natural scenery	70.6	151.2
Visiting nature centers	63.5	135.9
Driving for pleasure	61.2	130.9
Viewing and photographing other wildlife	58.2	124.6
Viewing and photographing wildflowers and trees	57.0	122.0
Visiting beaches	56.9	121.8
Swimming in lakes and streams	54.2	116.1
Visiting historical sites	53.1	113.6
Picnicking	52.4	112.1
Boating	44.2	94.6
Viewing and photographing birds	39.8	85.2
Day hiking	38.0	81.3
Bicycling	37.6	80.5
Fishing (all types)	37.5	80.3
Visiting wilderness or primitive areas	33.6	71.9
Viewing and photographing fish	32.1	68.7
Camping (developed area)	31.1	66.5
Freshwater fishing	30.9	66.1
Motor boating	30.3	64.9
Snow and ice activities	29.2	62.4
Driving (off road)	22.5	48.1
Visiting prehistoric and archeological sites	21.6	46.2
Mountain biking	19.8	42.5
Camping (primitive)	15.5	33.1
Rafting	15.5	33.1
Jet skiing	13.4	28.7
Hunting	13.1	28.1
Coldwater fishing	13.0	27.7
Canoeing	12.6	26.9
Backpacking	12.1	25.8
Horseback riding (general)	8.9	19.1
Horseback riding on trails	7.1	15.2
Kayaking	7.0	15.0
Downhill skiing	6.8	14.5
Snowmobiling	6.3	13.5
Snowboarding	5.9	12.6
Cross-country skiing	2.7	5.7

From USDA Forest Service, National Survey on Recreation and the Environment.

were the most popular and the most accessible outdoor activities to the general public. Table 16.4 presents the percentage of participation (for the general population and the motor-powered population) and the percentage of the motorized populations who claim that activity as their favorite. Human-powered outdoor recreation activities are those that require human physical exercise for movement rather than an activity that is dependent on a motorized vehicle during participation.

In Canada, Alberta Community Development has tracked the favorite recreation activities of Albertans for more than 20 years. Table 16.5 pro-vides the results of the past five studies conducted from 1981 to 2000. Although the data do not show the number of participants, they do provide a look

TABLE 16.4 Percentage of General U.S. Population and Human-Powered Population Participation in Human-Powered Activities

Activity	General population participation	Human-powered population participation	Favorite activity motorized population
Backpacking and hiking	28	55	18
Camping	25	46	13
Bicycling (road)	28	50	13
Bicycling (off road)	10	18	6
Bird-watching	5	11	5
Cross-country skiing	2	8	3
Fly-fishing	4	9	5
Paddle sports	15	32	16
Trail running	6	12	4
Climbing	5	11	4
Snowshoeing	2	7	2
Downhill skiing and snowboarding	7	14	9

Data provided by the Outdoor Industry Foundation, 2004.

TABLE 16.5 Favorite Recreation Activities of Albertans

Activity	Rank 2000	Rank 1996	Rank 1992	Rank 1988	Rank 1981
Walking for pleasure	1	1	1	2	6
Golfing	2	2	3	3	2
Camping	3	3	2	1	1
Bicycling	4	n/a	4	6	15
Crafts and hobbies	5	10	10	8	n/a
Gardening	6	8	27	13	26
Swimming	7	6	6	5	8
Reading	8	5	7	7	7
Hiking and backpacking	9	13	16	19	23
Fishing	10	4	5	4	4
Running and jogging	11	9	21	25	16
Downhill skiing and snowboarding	12	14	17	11	3
Performing arts	13	32	19	37	n/a
Ice hockey	14	27	8	9	5
Aerobics, fitness, and aquasize	15	7	11	12	n/a
Softball and baseball	16	11	9	14	12
Curling	17	17	12	10	10
Soccer	18	29	n/a	54	35
Dancing	19	16	13	18	13
Hunting and shooting	20	20	15	16	11
TV and movies	20	31	n/a	41	21

From Alberta Community Development (2000).

at total demand (including latent preferences) and trends over time. Latent demand or preferences would refer to activities that people would like to engage in but some barrier or constraint keeps them from doing so. Eleven of the top 15 favorite activities are outdoor recreation activities. Although golf has maintained a high ranking, either second or third, over the past 20 years, other outdoor activities have gained considerably in popularity over the past 20 years. These include bicycling, gardening, hiking and backpacking, and running and jogging. Outdoor activities that have decreased in popularity include fishing, downhill skiing, ice hockey, and curling. Participation rates for hunting, one of the more traditional outdoor recreation activities, have decreased in both Canada and the United States over the past three decades. Some forms of angling, such as fly-fishing and saltwater fishing, have increased, while other forms, such as freshwater fishing, have shown decreases (U.S. Fish and Wildlife Service, 2004b).

Economics of Outdoor Recreation

North Americans spend a substantial amount of money on outdoor recreation; however, outdoor-related expenditures are not comprehensively documented by recreation researchers, policy makers, or economists. Therefore, it's difficult to measure the economic impact of outdoor recreation Part of the problem is the disjointed nature of the public-sector agencies and private for-profit enterprises that provide outdoor recreation and nature-based tourism products and services. Perhaps the best systematic attempts to quantify the economic impact of outdoor recreation–related expenditures have occurred in the angling, hunting, and sporting goods areas. For example, the U.S. Fish and Wildlife Service has commissioned a series of national studies on angling and hunting in the United States. The 2001 National Survey of Fishing, Hunting, and Wildlife-Associated Recreation estimated that 82 million U.S. residents 16 years old and older either hunted (13 million), fished (34.1 million), or watched wildlife (66.1 million). Wildlife-related expenditures for 2001 were estimated at $108 billion U.S. or about 1.1 percent of the gross domestic product (GDP). This data can be broken down in two ways. First, of the $108 billion U.S. total, $28 billion U.S. was for trips, $64 billion U.S. for equipment, and $16 billion U.S. for other items. These same people spent a total of $36 billion U.S. on fishing, $21 billion U.S. on hunting, $16 billion U.S. on items used both in hunting and

fishing, and another $38 billion U.S. on wildlife-watching trips, equipment, and other items.

The hunting, fishing, wildlife viewing, and birding data contained in table 16.3 show that these activities represent a small portion of the overall participation in outdoor recreation in the United States. The boating, downhill skiing, sporting goods, outdoor apparel, and camping industries are all formidable and well established. Nature-based travel to beaches, forests, national parks, lakes, and mountains is a major element of the tourism systems in both countries. Tourism generated a total of $51.2 billion Canadian and $557 billion U.S. in 2002. Perhaps 30 to 40 percent of those expenditures were for nature-related tourism and travel. If one considers other organizations such as summer camps, churches, scouting organizations, conservation groups, and outdoor leadership schools (e.g., Outward Bound), the economic implications of outdoor recreation are mind-boggling. A conservative estimate of all outdoor recreation–related expenditures (equipment, clothing apparel, travel, vehicles, boats and other durable goods, government expenditures) in North America (Canada and U.S.) is in the range of $300 to $400 billion annually. This translates to somewhere from 2.5 to 3 percent of the GDP of Canada and the United States combined.

A Social–Psychological Phenomenon

Although outdoor recreation participation rates provide valuable information to those who plan outdoor recreation activities, their usefulness is limited. A basic understanding of the social psychology that drives behavior and participation in outdoor recreation is important for providing meaningful nature-based recreation opportunities. Outdoor recreation behavior for both groups and individuals has been studied extensively over the past 35 years (Manning, 1999) by leisure, natural resource, and tourism scholars in the United States and Canada. Our knowledge has improved significantly in the areas of psychology, consumer behavior, and visitor management and in understand constraints to outdoor recreation participation.

Demand for Experiences

What is the meaning of outdoor recreation behavior? Students and professionals who plan to work in the outdoor recreation–related fields need a basic understanding of outdoor recreation behavior in order to provide the kinds of experiences and settings that are desired by their customers. Unlike other areas of natural resource management (e.g., timber, water, mining, and grazing), the product for outdoor recreation is an experience. This places professionals who provide outdoor recreation opportunities in the service sector. One way of thinking about outdoor recreation experiences is within the attraction and escape framework. The attraction principle argues that outdoor behavior is the result of a desire to connect with the natural setting and the many attributes that that setting offers. In this case, the personal and social rewards of visiting a favorite natural setting "attract" or "pull" outdoor enthusiasts and tourists into natural settings and environments. The escape principle focuses more on what drives a person away from his or her everyday living and working environment into a natural setting. From this perspective, outdoor recreation serves as an escape from the stress, environments, and roles that people deal with daily. You probably recognize some truth in each perspective because both the attraction and escape principles can operate at the same time.

Other factors besides attraction and escape drive outdoor behavior. Achievement and challenge are important components of many outdoor pursuits, especially skill-based activities and adventure recreational pursuits. The desire to socialize and bond with friends and family is another key goal of most outdoor recreation experiences. These examples are useful for showing the diversity of needs that are fulfilled through the recreation and tourism experiences that people seek in the outdoors. This needs-based behavioral model views outdoor recreation as goal-directed behavior and the outdoor recreationist as an active participant in creating the kinds of experiences he or she desires. These desired experiences reflect human needs and have been studied extensively in a variety of different settings over the past 30 years. Many of the motivations that drive outdoor recreation behavior are exhibited in figure 16.1.

It is important to note that several goals or motives can operate at the same time when participating in an activity. In other words, "bundles" of motives make up the typical recreation experience. Research has found that people participating in the same activity tend to share similar motivational profiles (compared to people participating in other activity categories) (Manning, 1999). Even within an activity such as camping, there are *activity styles* such as tent camping, RV camping, backcountry camping in which participants share a common motive profile, setting preferences and expectations for similar recreation experiences.

Outdoor Recreation Motivations

- Achievement
- Stimulation and excitement
- Autonomy (freedom)
- Risk taking
- Equipment (*Note:* Many recreationists are into using and acquiring equipment [e.g., anglers, rock climbers, backpackers, hunters, photographers, four-wheel drivers, etc.])
- Family togetherness
- Socializing and sharing
- Meeting new people
- Learning
- Enjoying nature
- Introspection
- Creativity
- Nostalgia and recollection
- Physical fitness
- Physical rest and relaxation
- Escape from personal and social pressures
- Social security
- Escape from family
- Teaching and leading others
- Risk reduction
- Temperature (*Note:* Climate [e.g., in Arizona residents flock to mountain areas for cool weather in the summer—in the winter folks flock to Arizona])

FIGURE 16.1 By understanding and identifying the types and importance of motives, the goals and meanings behind nature-based recreation and tourism can be better understood.

Because the "product" of outdoor recreation is an experience, monitoring the quality of that product becomes important. The extent to which the expectations and desired experiences are fulfilled determines to a large extent how satisfied outdoor recreationists and nature-based tourists are with their experience. Consequently, it is useful for outdoor recreation managers, leaders, and service providers to inventory, market, and monitor the types of experience desired and achieved by their visitors and customers.

Human–Environment Interaction

The definition of outdoor recreation draws attention to the unique importance of the natural environment to recreation experience. For students who may have an interest in this area, environmental psychology offers considerable insight into human–environment interaction. If the natural environment is important to outdoor recreation and nature-based tourism, then it is critical to understand how the setting influences behavior. The recreation opportunity spectrum (ROS) is an outdoor recreation management tool used by outdoor recreation planners to help provide better outdoor recreation opportunities (USDA Forest Service, 1979). The ROS places outdoor settings along a continuum with six classes ranging from primitive to semiprimitive and roaded to urban (see table 16.6). One assumption behind the ROS is that different people prefer different natural settings and by offering a diverse range of settings and opportunities, we increase the likelihood of people finding the type of environment they enjoy.

Many people feel a special connection with the majestic grandeur and natural setting of a national park like Banff or Yosemite. Some of the attributes that draw people to natural settings include beauty, colors, water, wildlife, forests, scene complexity, and light shading. However, the environmental setting is more than just the physical environment; it also includes the social environment and managerial environment. For example, in the social setting, the presence or absence of other people affects our recreation experiences, as well as our behavior. The ROS also identifies the managerial environment as a key to visitor satisfaction and enjoyment. Outdoor recreation managers and service providers are an important component of the recreation experience. For example, high-quality maps and information, well-prepared guides, well-maintained restrooms, and posted park rules to protect the resource and experience are all ways that managers affect outdoor recreation behavior. Consequently, the physical, social, and manage-

TABLE 16.6 Recreation Opportunity Spectrum Categories

ROS class	Description
Primitive	Area is characterized by an essentially unmodified natural environment of fairly large size. Interaction between users is very low and evidence of other users is minimal. The area is managed to be essentially free from evidence of human-induced restrictions and controls. Motorized use within the area is not permitted.
Semiprimitive, nonmotorized	Area is characterized by a predominantly natural or natural-appearing environment of moderate to large size. Interaction between users is low, but there is often evidence of other users. The area is managed in such a way that minimum on-site controls and restrictions may be present but are subtle. Public motorized use is not permitted.
Semiprimitive motorized	Area is characterized by a predominantly natural or natural-appearing environment of moderate to large size. Concentration of users is low, but there is often evidence of other users. The area is managed in such a way that minimum on-site controls and restrictions may be present but are subtle. Motorized use is permitted.
Roaded natural	Area is characterized by predominantly natural-appearing environments with moderate evidence of the sights and sounds of humans. Such evidence usually harmonizes with the natural environment. Interactions between users may be low to moderate, with evidence of other users prevalent. Resource modification and utilization practices are evident but harmonize with the natural environment. Conventional motorized use is allowed and incorporated into construction standards and design of facilities.
Rural	An area that is characterized by a substantially modified natural environment. Resource modification and utilization practices are to enhance specific recreation activities and maintain vegetative cover and soil. Sights and sounds of humans are readily evident, and the interaction between users is often moderate to high. A considerable number of facilities are designed for use by a large number of people. Facilities are often provided for special activities. Moderate user densities are present away from developed sites. Facilities for intensified motorized use and parking are available.
Urban ROS Class	Area is characterized by a substantially urbanized environment, although the background may have natural-appearing elements. Resource modification and utilization practices are to enhance specific recreation activities. Sights and sounds of humans are predominant on site. Large numbers of users can be expected, both on site and in nearby areas. Facilities for highly intensified motor use and parking are available.

Source: USDA Forest Service (1979). Recreation Opportunity Spectrum Users Guide.

rial environment are all important components in the interaction between humans and nature.

So, not only do outdoor recreationists and nature-based tourists choose the types of experiences in which to participate, they also have preferences for certain kinds of settings. Some kinds of outdoor experiences are more dependent on a certain setting or place than others. For example, an Outward Bound instructor in Quetico Provincial Park in Ontario likely knows of specific places where her students can best learn white-water and rock-climbing skills. In this case, experience has taught the instructor where students can best gain the kinds of experiences and skills that they desire.

A final topic related to natural-setting interaction is the concept of attachment to place. For personal, social, or cultural reasons, people become attached to special places. The example in the previous paragraph illustrates how the rock wall or white-water rapids are unique in Quetico. Consequently, visitors who want to participate in certain types of activities that require special settings depend on those settings. Rock climbing and base jumping are examples. This type of place attachment is referred to as place dependence. A second type of place attachment has to do with how people relate to or identify with a place. For example, your grandparent's lake cabin or the beach house that your family has visited for years might be a special place and part of your family's place identity. The recreation experience consists of more than just the motivations sought, it also includes the meaning of the places where people recreate. Therefore, outdoor recreation providers must be sensitive to the meaning of places and settings.

Roles of Socialization and Experience

In the late 1960s and early 1970s, outdoor recreation research examined how hunters, anglers, and campers learned about their activities. Childhood experience was identified in several studies as an important factor in explaining adult participation in outdoor recreation (Manning, 1999). Because many outdoor recreation activities involve skill development and unique social worlds (skiers, surfers, hikers, rock climbers, snowboarders), the processes of leisure socialization take on special importance. For example, there is a rock climbing culture (social world) that supports the activity of rock climbing. This culture shares experiences, jargon, and clothing styles and provides identity, knowledge, and

skill development focused on rock climbing. As a rock climber evolves from a novice to a more experienced climber, this culture plays an important role in the development process.

Leisure socialization can be defined as the lifelong process of learning leisure attitudes, roles, norms of behavior, skills, and preferences. Leisure socialization often begins in childhood and is affected by parents, family members, schools, recreation, religious and youth leaders, and friends. The nonprofit associations and private for-profit enterprises also play a significant role in leisure learning. For example, golf courses, climbing gyms, and ski resorts offer lessons and skill-appropriate recreation opportunities to help participants at different levels of development.

Hobson Bryan identified the principle of *recreation specialization* to capture the socialization stages that an enthusiast might go through in becoming specialized within an activity (Manning, 1999). He argues that every recreation activity has a range of participants (a continuum of behavior) from novices to highly specialized recreationists. He first identified this phenomenon within fishing, but over the past 25 years, researchers have studied specialization in canoeing, hiking, boating, bridge, mountaineering, rock climbing, river running, camping, mountain biking, and hunting. As a person becomes more specialized, the importance of that activity increases in the person's life. Highly

Skiers inhabit a unique social world where they share experiences, jargon, and clothing styles.

specialized recreationists share motive profiles, prefer specific types of settings, process greater skills and knowledge, and enjoy interacting with other highly specialized participants.

We have seen that demand can be expressed for activities, experiences, and settings; however, a fourth type of demand has received attention in recent years as well: the desire for actual benefits. A benefit can be defined as improved conditions that result from outdoor recreation and nature-based tourism. For example, backpacking in Grand Teton National Park can improve mental and physical health by getting one's mind off the stresses of work and exercising the body. At the same time it can increase family solidarity by allowing a family to spend intimate time together and bond in ways that do not happen in the city. And backpackers can bring economic benefits to the regional tourism economy. People who study recreation benefits categorize them into four categories: personal benefits, social and group benefits, economic benefits, and environmental benefits.

In summary, outdoor recreation can be framed as goal-directed behavior in which people choose to engage in certain activities and experiences in certain settings in order to meet needs. Recreation presents the opportunity to act on or fulfill needs that cannot be met during the more constrained times of life. The meaning of outdoor recreation can best be understood by identifying the types of goals sought. One recreation experience or activity can produce a bundle of desired outcomes (motives) that operate concurrently. The experience desired also influences the type of setting the participant chooses. Consequently, a visitor or recreationist arrives on site with a generalized set of expectations, then satisfaction is subsequently determined, at least in part, by the degree to which the expectations and needs are fulfilled. One's past socialization and experience level can also exert powerful influences on the kinds of activities, experiences, and environmental settings preferred.

TYPES OF OUTDOOR RECREATION RESOURCES, PROVIDERS, AND CAREERS

Because both Canada and the United States are rich in natural resources, both countries offer amazing and diverse opportunities for outdoor recreation and nature-based tourism. Outdoor recreation–related careers can be found in the public, private for-profit, and nonprofit sectors. The missions of many of the public-sector agencies are broad and involve understanding other disciplines like ecology, forestry, wildlife management, hydrology, or fire management. Many private-sector career opportunities in outdoor recreation are tourism based or guide and outfitter based. Finally, the nonprofit sector offers a broad array of career opportunities including such diverse fields as environmental advocacy, youth camps, and adventure programming.

Parks, Wilderness, and Preserves

Parks, wilderness, and nature preserves receive the highest level of protection of all the natural-resources reservation categories. In general, these types of resources can be managed by the national, provincial, state, or local government or by nonprofit associations. These agencies focus their recreation and tourism opportunities on interpreting the natural, historical, and cultural stories that are connected with these special places. The recreation activities in these preserves are usually more restricted than those in national forests or public lands in order to protect the resource, nature experience, habitat, and wildlife. Motorized travel is usually restricted to paved access areas or trailheads that serve as entrances to the more protected areas of these resources. It is important for the professionals who work in these types of environments to understand both natural resources and visitor management.

Forests, Grasslands, Deserts, and Wetlands

Forest management has a longer history in both Canada and the United States than grasslands, desert, or wetland management. However all four types of resources have a history of abuse in North America. Although a small portion of the most pristine forests, grasslands, deserts, and wetlands are protected as parks, wilderness, and nature preserves, the vast majority of these resources have either passed into private ownership or are managed by government organizations as multiuse or mixed-use resources. Consequently, understanding agriculture, timber management, wildlife management, grazing, watershed management, mining, and development issues is needed. The policies, laws, and political consideration often determine how these types of resources are managed. Recreational use of these resources can range from backcountry human-powered activities to motorized forms of travel and enjoyment. It is common for professionals and recreationists to encounter problems related to conflicting resource uses and to balancing motorized and nonmotorized forms of recreation.

Water-Based Resources

Both Canada and the United States possess incredible water resources—both coastal and inland fresh and salt water. Water features, whether oceans, bays, estuaries, lakes, rivers, streams, canals, wetlands, or a desert oasis, all hold tremendous value as recreation and tourism resources. Water-based resources also are important natural resources that serve as waterways, watersheds, and important habitat as well as provide recreation opportunities. In both countries there has been considerable financial and political capital invested in protecting natural water-based ecosystems and habitat over the past 25 years. Water-based recreation, particularly boating, fishing, hunting, birding, camping, sunbathing, swimming, and river running, is a major component of the outdoor recreation and tourism system.

U.S. Federal Land Agencies

Outdoor recreation has grown in importance as a public land use in the United States since World War II. At the federal level in the United States, four natural-resources agencies and three water-resource agencies provide outdoor recreation opportunities to the public. It is common for employees who want to enter the federal workforce to begin their careers as seasonal employees.

The National Park Service (NPS) is responsible for a variety of recreation resources that include national parks, national monuments, national historical sites, and national recreation areas (see table 16.7). The NPS was the pioneer agency in developing outdoor and environmental interpretation. Park interpretation is one of the unique park ranger skill sets within this agency; the entry-level position is a park ranger. Today park rangers and other NPS employees are involved in visitor management, resource protection, interpretation, law enforcement, and park maintenance. Another career track in the NPS is in planning; most NPS planning is done through the Denver Service Center where special skills in planning, public participation, landscape architecture, and research methods are valued.

TABLE 16.7   U.S. National Parks, 2000

Classification	Federal acreage	Units	Visitor use
National battlefields	11,940 (4,832 ha)	11	1,515,034
National battlefield parks	8,060 (3,261 ha)	3	2,124,140
National historical parks	115,566 (46,767 ha)	36	26,625,827
National historical sites	20,138 (8,149 ha)	72	10,214,814
National lakeshores	145,744 (58,979 ha)	4	3,619,755
National memorials	8,041 (3,254 ha)	26	26,330,618
National military parks	35,640 (14,423 ha)	9	5,348,379
National monuments	1,881,500 (76,1402 ha)	76	23,811,367
National parks	49,839,065 (20,168,777 ha)	51	66,074,921
National parkways	164,100 (66,408 ha)	4	33,998,215
National preserves	21,492,411 (8,697,508 ha)	14	1,689,066
National recreation areas	3,406,267 (1,378,442 ha)	18	49,964,115
National reserves	10,933 (4,424 ha)	2	66,255
National rivers	311,143 (125,913 ha)	6	4,297,272
National seashores	478,290 (193,553 ha)	10	18,920,188
National wild & scenic rivers	72,913 (29,506 ha)	9	938,755
Other parks	37,723 (15,266 ha)	11	10,352,557
Total	78,039,474 (31,580,864 ha)	366	285,891,278

Statistics from the National Parks Service, 2000.

The USDA Forest Service also has a long history of involvement in recreation management. It currently manages 155 national forests and 20 national grasslands (see figure 16.2). This legally recognized multiple-use agency has incorporated recreation in its services since its establishment in 1905. Recreation-related careers in the USDA Forest Service include outdoor recreation planning and wilderness management. The agency has been deeply involved in pioneering research and management tools for addressing outdoor recreation. For example, the recreation opportunity spectrum (see table 16.6) was developed to help guide planning decisions about the diverse types of nature-based experiences and settings desired by the public. Seasonal and part-time positions in both the Forest Service and National Park Service are common entry points for students seeking to work for the federal government (USDA Forest Service, n.d.).

The Bureau of Land Management (BLM) currently manages the most federal lands of any agency, 261 million acres (106 million hectares),

located primarily in 12 western states (see table 16.8). Similar to the USDA Forest Service, BLM is a multiple-use agency with recreation playing an increasingly important role as the population of the western states continues to grow and urbanize (National Wilderness Institute, 1995). The BLM public lands provide visitors with many recreational opportunities. These include hiking, hunting, fishing, boating, hang gliding, camping, off-highway vehicle driving, mountain biking, birding, and visiting national monuments and cultural heritage sites. Entry-level positions can be found as outdoor recreation planners and in field operations and law enforcement (U.S. BLM, 2005).

The U.S. Fish and Wildlife Service manages a system of wildlife refuges, fish hatcheries, and bird sanctuaries. As traditional hunting activities such as bird and big-game hunting have declined, new recreational pursuits like photography, fly-fishing, and bird-watching have emerged as fast-growth wildlife-based activities. Programs focused on viewing wildlife, interpretive facilities, and edu-

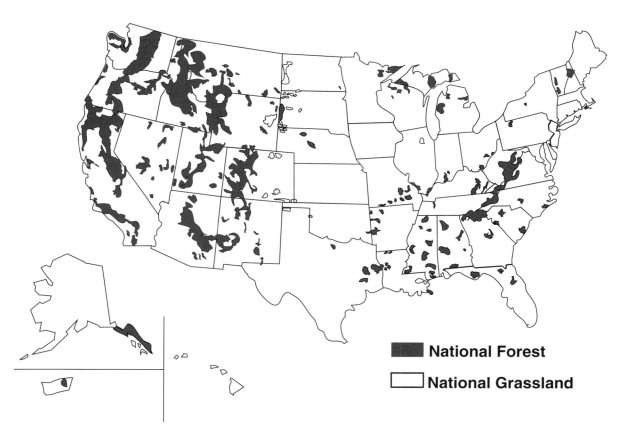

National Forest

National Grassland

FIGURE 16.2   National forests and grasslands.

From Federal Land Agencies, www.fs.fed.us/recreation/map/finder.shtml.

TABLE 16.8   U.S. Land Agencies, 2003

Surface-managing agency	Acres (million)	Percentage of total acres
BLM	261 (106 ha)	40.7
Forest Service	191 (77 ha)	29.8
Fish & Wildlife Service	93 (38 ha)	14.5
National Park Service	84 (34 ha)	13.1
Dept. of Defense U.S. Army Corps of Engineers	12 (5 ha)	1.9
Total	641 (260 ha)	100

From U.S. Bureau of Land Management.

Photo courtesy of Randy Virden

The Army Corps of Engineers operates Albeni Dam, which forms Lake Pend Oreille in Northern Idaho. The lake provides water-based recreation opportunities such as boating, fishing, water-skiing, and tubing.

cational programs offer recreation-related career opportunities.

The Army Corps of Engineers operates a large system of reservoirs and inland and coastal waterways across the United States. Army Corps of Engineers projects include more than 2,500 recreation areas, much of them providing water-based recreation opportunities. This organization employs many field-level and recreation-planning personnel who provide water-based recreation and camping opportunities at these areas. The Tennessee Valley Authority (TVA) and Bureau of Reclamation are water-resource agencies with a regional presence.

The TVA is concentrated in the southern states and is responsible for a series of dams and reservoirs that have grown into popular water-based recreation areas. The Bureau of Reclamation was created to provide water for agriculture and development to the arid western states. All three federal water-based agencies employ outdoor recreation professionals as well as seasonal personnel.

Canadian Land Agencies

The Canadian system of national and provincial parks provides a rich and diverse system of natural, historical, and cultural resources for Canadians and visitors. The first national park in Canada was set aside in 1885: Rocky Mountains Park, now Banff National Park. Parks Canada is the leading national agency in protecting and managing nationally significant cultural and natural heritage parks. Its mandate is to "protect and present nationally significant examples of Canada's natural and cultural heritage, and foster public understanding, appreciation and enjoyment in ways that ensure the ecological and commemorative integrity of these places for present and future generations" (Parks Canada, 2003). The agency manages 41 national parks, 150 national historic sites, and two national marine conservation areas.

Parks Canada also works with other levels of government such as provincial park agencies and with private organizations to provide programs focused on parks, historical sites, cultural resources, Canadian heritage rivers, heritage railway stations, and international heritage conservation. Parks Canada and the provincial agencies offer a variety of unique and challenging careers such as park wardens, interpreters, historians, management officers, and planners.

State and Provincial Outdoor Recreation Agencies

In Canada and the United States, the provincial and state governments play a major role in providing outdoor recreation and nature-based tourism opportunities to their citizens and visiting tourists. Niagara Falls is an early example of a significant natural resource protected by a state and provincial cross-border partnership in the late 1800s. Today, both Ontario and New York have developed extensive park systems in their respective province or state that provide diverse outdoor opportunities and employment to hundreds of employees.

In Canada, the provincial governments in British Columbia, Alberta, Saskatchewan, Manitoba, Ontario, Quebec, Newfoundland and Labrador, New Brunswick, and Nova Scotia, and the territorial governments in Northwest Territories and the Yukon all have park and preserve systems. In the United States, 758 million visitors frequented state parks in 2002 (see table 16.9) across all 50 states. As visitation rates have increased, so too has the need for park rangers, interpreters, trail and river managers, historical and cultural specialists, and law enforcement personnel.

Local and County Governments

Municipal and county parks and recreation agencies provide a significant number of outdoor opportunities in parks, nature preserves, rivers, and trail systems that are close to where visitors live. Many county parks systems provide large regional parks with a complement of services including camping, boating, and trails systems. Municipal governments provide an array of outdoor recreation–related employment opportunities including adventure recreation programming and park management and planning. Career positions related to outdoor recreation in county and local governments include outdoor programmer, outdoor recreation coordinator, park manager, park ranger, urban park ranger, interpretive coordinator, and environmental educator. There are also many part-

TABLE 16.9   U.S. State Park Statistics

	1980	1990	2002
State park units	4,512	4,599	5,655
Acreage (millions)	9 (3.6 ha)	10 (4.0 ha)	13 (5.2 ha)
Day visitors (millions)	467	664	758
Overnight visitors (millions)	68	60	67
Full-time staff	11,192	15,739	21,148
Part-time staff	21,168	25,981	35,482
Operating expenditures (millions)	$495 U.S.	$1,060 U.S.	$1,800 U.S.
Fixed capital outlay (millions)	$490 U.S.	$435 U.S.	$665 U.S.

Data from The National Association of State Park Directors.

time and seasonal positions available through local and county governments such as outdoor leaders, trip leaders, camp counselors, and parks and recreation aides.

Private Sector

The private sector plays an important role in the provision of outdoor recreation and nature-based tourism opportunities. Examples of private-sector providers include full-service nature-based resorts, marinas, commercial recreation businesses, outdoor tour operators, rafting and river-running companies, equipment rentals, private camps, and outdoor instructors and schools. The numbers of guide services, outdoor schools, and tour enterprises have grown considerably over the past 25 years. Many of these enterprises hire outdoor guides for river running, canoeing, scuba diving, backcountry hiking, mountain biking, and horseback riding. Aside from the direct provision of outdoor instruction, guiding, and programming, many of these businesses require expertise in marketing, accounting, and management.

The outdoor retail industry is also large in the United States and Canada. In 2000, human-powered recreation alone generated more than $17 billion in the United States. Major outdoor retailers like Recreation Equipment, Inc. (REI), Eastern Mountain Sports, Mountain Equipment Co-op, LL Bean, Bass Pro Shops, Cabela's, and Campmor provide not only equipment but also retail destinations that attract residents and tourists to an outdoor lifestyle theme. Many jobs are available in the outdoor retail industry where specialized outdoor recreation knowledge and skills can often be converted into sales, trip planning, and marketing positions.

Nonprofit Associations

The nonprofit sector began its involvement in the outdoors with youth-serving agencies like the Boy Scouts, YMCA, Girl Scouts, and Campfire in the early 1900s (see chapter 8). Many of these youth-serving agencies still provide outdoor recreation and education opportunities to youth and, therefore, provide a developed career path. Many nonprofit and church-related camps offer outdoor experience and programming to youth, usually in the summer. Camp directors and administrators often hold year-round full-time positions that offer

a unique career opportunity that often begins as a camp counselor.

Environmental and conservation organizations are another important part of the nonprofit sector. Examples include Project for Public Places, Sierra Club, the Trust for Public Lands, The Nature Conservancy, National Parks and Conservation Association, and National Audubon Society. Most of these organizations are involved in environmental advocacy that may focus on specialized natural resource or environmental issues such as wildlife, national parks, or environmental education.

A final area of career opportunities in the nonprofit sector is outdoor programming and leadership schools. For example, Outward Bound is a nonprofit education organization devoted to providing adventure-based programming to inspire self-esteem, self-reliance, and concern for others and the environment. Other similar programs are the National Outdoor Leadership School, Project Adventure, and the Wilderness Education Association. Hundreds of local and regional outdoor adventure programs run as nonprofit or nongovernmental organizations in North America. These types of nonprofits also offer careers related to education and programming in the outdoors. Once again, many students begin as a participant and then move into a part-time or seasonal position.

ADVENTURE PROGRAMMING AND EXPERIENTIAL EDUCATION

Adventure programming and experiential education have developed into a maturing subfield under the broader umbrella of outdoor recreation. Youth educators, camps, and outdoor schools have emerged over the past 50 years to provide outdoor leadership and programs focused on teaching adventure recreation activities in a safe environment under qualified instruction. Adventure programming is defined as the broad base of philosophies, theories, and leadership techniques used in the fields of outdoor leadership, experiential education, and adventure education. Unlike most outdoor recreation in which participants orchestrate their experience, adventure programming involves a leader or facilitator who designs an outdoor program with specific participant outcomes or benefits in mind.

Brief History of Adventure Recreation

Although the early scouting movement in England and the United States could be loosely considered a form of adventure programming, Kurt Hahn's development of the Gordonstoun School (1934) in Scotland and Outward Bound program (1941) in Wales along with Lawrence Holt is generally regarded as the beginning of the adventure programming movement. Outward Bound continued to grow and in 1962 opened its first school in North America at Marble, Colorado. In 1965 a former Outward Bound instructor, Paul Petzoldt, established the National Outdoor Leadership School (NOLS) in Lander, Wyoming. The NOLS program was more focused on training and preparing outdoor leaders and instructors. NOLS offers courses in six North American locations and in Mexico, Patagonia, Australia, New Zealand, and India.

Project Adventure was founded in 1971 to provide educational and curricular leadership in adventure learning. Project Adventure grew out of the Outward Bound movement but focused more on bringing adventure learning into the school system and corporate world. By 1976, Paul Petzoldt was again looking for a new vehicle for outdoor leadership training through universities. In 1977, he and several educators established the Wilderness Education Association (WEA). Also that year, the Association for Experiential Education (AEE) was formed. Today AEE has grown into the largest international organization for promoting professional development, conferences, and research in adventure programming and experiential education.

Programming

Adventure programming and experiential education both use the natural environment as an interactive participant in creating leisure and educational experiences for participants. Recreation programming in general is a goal-oriented process of facilitating beneficial outcomes for participants. Priest and Gass (2005) present a philosophy of adventure programming based on behavioral, cognitive, and experiential learning theories. The experiential component in particular takes unique advantage of the holistic, interactive, and responsive characteristics of the natural environment as an educational setting.

Priest and Gass identify four general applications for adventure programming: recreation, education, development, and therapy. Recreation-focused programs seek to provide enjoyable outdoor recreation experiences often while teaching new skills and activities. These types of programs are often found at summer camps and may be offered by municipal parks and recreation agencies. Education-focused programs, such as Project Wild or the Outdoor Living Skills program sponsored by the American Camping Association, seek to increase outdoor knowledge and generate environmental awareness. A development-focused program targets various aspects of human development by promoting leadership and communication skills and social competence often aimed at specific age or gender groups. The final application, therapeutic adventure programming, is aimed at rehabilitating or changing dysfunctional behaviors. Common therapeutic adventure programs deal with alcohol and drug abuse, low self-esteem, physical or sexual abuse, or addressing dysfunctional behaviors. River Rampage is a therapeutic-based outdoor adventure program in Arizona for young people who face significant life challenges. It's coordinated by the City of Phoenix Parks and Recreation Department.

Outdoor Leadership

Leadership is a key component of adventure programming and experiential programming. Not only do outdoor leaders have to be familiar with the educational, developmental, and philosophical components of outdoor adventure and experiential education, but they also have to be familiar with the management, safety, and liability aspects of being an outdoor leader. Priest and Gass have outlined practical and organizational skills for outdoor leaders. These include technical outdoor skills, safety skills, environmental-appropriate skills, trip-planning skills, and knowledge of liability and risk management procedures. Outdoor leaders must understand instructional and facilitation methods. Experience, sound judgment, ethics, communication, and leadership ability also play important roles in creating effective outdoor leaders.

Outdoor Adventure Schools and Associations

Hundreds of outdoor schools provide adventure and experiential education programs in North

America. Many of these programs are small in scale and occur at summer camps, college campuses, and private and nonprofit schools. However, the following three organizations are key international players in the adventure programming and experiential education movement.

1. The Association for Experiential Education (AEE) reports more than 1,600 members in 30 countries. Its mission "is to develop and promote experiential education. The Association is committed to support professional development, theoretical advancement, and evaluation of experiential education worldwide" (Association for Experiential Education, 2005a). AEE is the foremost international professional organization for experiential education; it provides a clearinghouse for publications and jobs, regional and international conferences, professional leadership training, and accreditation for adventure programs and schools. AEE currently has five recognized professional groups within its structure. They include experience-based training and development (EBTD), schools and colleges (S&C), therapeutic adventure (TAPG), women in experiential education (WPG), and natives, Africans, Asians, Latino(a)s, and allies (NAALA) (Association for Experiential Education, 2005b).

2. The Wilderness Education Association (WEA) was founded in 1977 and promotes wilderness safety and conservation by training qualified outdoor leaders. The focus is on training and educating outdoor leaders who can take their skills and knowledge to recreation programs, camps, schools, and guide services. The national-standard program is a 21- to 35-day course for people with minimal outdoor experience who want to become a certified outdoor leader. WEA also offers a short course for professional outdoor leaders who want an expedited national-standard certification. WEA is affiliated with several universities in North America and around the world that provide WEA training and certification.

3. Outward Bound International is an umbrella nonprofit organization with licensed affiliates in more than 40 schools worldwide. Outward Bound courses are open to all people regardless of race, religion, physical or mental strength, and educational background. Outward Bound USA serves more than 60,000 participants annually in four wilderness schools (Outward Bound West, Hurricane Island, Voyagers, and North Carolina), two urban centers, and a primary/secondary school-reform program. Through Outward Bound, students develop teamwork, self-confidence, responsibility, compassion, and environmental and community stewardship (Outward Bound USA, n.d.). Outward Bound Canada has graduated more than 80,000 people since 1969. The Canadian Outward Bound courses take place in diverse settings including the coast of British Columbia, the Canadian Rockies, Ontario's boreal forest, and the rivers of the Yukon (Outward Bound Canada, n.d.).

OUTDOOR RECREATION CHALLENGES AND TRENDS FOR THE FUTURE

Outdoor recreation as a mass social phenomenon has matured since the Second World War. As the population of North America continues to grow and as urbanization and development continue to put pressure on open space and natural areas, the demand for outdoor recreation will continue to grow. Increased demand, new technologies and modes of travel, and more diverse social and cultural groups converging on a limited resource mean that managing conflicts between groups will become more and more important.

Undoubtedly, the future is bright for those who seek careers in the outdoor recreation, nature-based tourism and adventure programming fields. Public agencies will continue to have the largest responsibility in managing the outdoor-resource base. However, nature-based tourism and private-sector services should continue to grow as the postindustrial economy continues to mature in Canada and the United States. Adventure tourism, ecotourism, and cultural-based tourism are three of the fastest growing areas of the tourism market. Nonprofit organizations have been one of the fastest growing sectors, especially related to environmental advocacy and providing outdoor education and adventure recreation opportunities.

SUMMARY

Outdoor recreation has a long and rich history in North America. Canadians and Americans are active outdoor enthusiasts, and both countries have a strong tradition of setting aside protected areas for their recreation, cultural, and environmental values. Both countries have a comprehensive system of public lands, parks, forests, rivers,

Web Sites to EXPLORE

Alberta Community Development: www.cd.gov.ab.ca/
Army Corps of Engineers: www.usace.army.mil/recreation/
American Camping Association: www.acacamps.org/
Bureau of Land Management: www.blm.gov/nhp/index.htm
Bureau of Reclamation: www.usbr.gov/
Association for Experiential Education: www.aee2.org/customer/pages.php?pageid=28
International Ecotourism Society: www.ecotourism.org/
GORP Resource for Outdoor Recreaction: http://gorp.away.com/index.html
National Association of State Park Directors: http://naspd.indstate.edu/
National Outdoor Leadership School: www.nols.edu/
National Park Service: www.nps.gov/
Outdoor Industry Association: www.outdoorindustry.org/
Outward Bound Canada: www.outwardbound.ca/
Outward Bound USA: www.outwardbound.org/
Outdoor Recreation Research: www4.ncsu.edu/~leung/recres.html
Outdoor Recreation in America: www.funoutdoors.com/
Parks Canada: www.parkscanada.ca/
Recreaction.gov: www.recreation.gov/
Sierra Club of Canada: www.sierraclub.ca/
Sierra Club: www.sierraclub.org/
U.S. Fish and Wildlife Service: www.fws.gov/
U.S. Forest Service: www.fs.fed.us/
Tennessee Valley Authority: www.tva.gov/
Wilderness: www.wilderness.net/
Wilderness Education Association: www.weainfo.org/

trails, wilderness, and developed facilities that help to meet the demand for outdoor recreation and nature-based tourism. Domestic and international nature-based tourism also contributes significantly to the economies of both countries. The provision of outdoor recreation has evolved into a variety of professions and careers related to outdoor recreation in the public, nonprofit, and private sectors. Current trends suggest that the demand for outdoor recreation and tourism will continue to expand as will the need for educated professionals to plan, develop, and manage the diverse opportunities and services desired by the public. The 21st century will continue to bring new opportunities and challenges to people who choose a career in this exciting field.

CHAPTER 17

Arts and Culture

Gaylene Carpenter

Courtesy of Philadelphia Department of Recreation

In recreation, experiences in the arts are one of the most sought after opportunities in which people may rediscover themselves and their relationships within a family and community.

Nellie D. Arnold, author, The Interrelated Arts in Leisure

CHAPTER OBJECTIVES

After reading this chapter, you should be able to do the following:

- Develop an understanding and awareness of arts and cultural experiences
- Explain the importance of providing arts and cultural experiences in North America
- Identify components in the arts and cultural program area
- Describe the meanings and benefits realized by organizations and individuals through arts and cultural experiences
- List the social and community benefits associated with arts and cultural programs
- Describe the evolution of arts and cultural programming in parks and recreation, public education, and private enterprise
- Understand the number, type, and breadth of arts and cultural experiences available
- Discuss programs provided by public agencies and nonprofit arts organizations that address contemporary needs and demonstrate contemporary practices

INTRODUCTION

Not long ago, I was surprised by an unanticipated **arts** experience called PDX in Bloom (PDX is the acronym for the Portland International Airport). A baby grand piano sat in a busy central location in the airport near the security check-in area that led to the terminals. A pianist was replacing the white noise and hustle of the airport with delightful, relaxing melodies. As I began to board my flight, the airport public-address announcer mentioned that a dulcimer performance would be beginning shortly. The idea of airports as performing arts venues was new to me, yet in retrospect, this experience was indicative of the rapid growth in arts and cultural programming opportunities across North America.

The provision for arts and cultural experiences has been a long tradition in recreation and leisure settings. Fifty years ago, Meyer and Brightbill (1956) advocated that arts and crafts, dancing, dramatics, literary activities, and music activities be standard in a comprehensive recreation program. Arts and cultural recreation opportunities continue to be both a part of public agencies' responsibilities to their citizens and viable offerings in self-support programs.

In addition to programs in recreation and leisure, arts managers working in a variety of for-profit and nonprofit arts and cultural organizations provide a wide array of arts and cultural opportunities that offer benefits to individuals and societies. Participation in the arts occurs in a variety of contexts including museums, galleries, community arts centers, art fairs and festivals, and performance venues. The **arts and cultural sector** has become more visible in part because of administrative initiative to provide arts and cultural experiences, and in part because arts managers have been responsive to the desires people have for more choices of things to do during their discretionary time. In addition, successful arts participation–building efforts have resulted from restructuring efforts undertaken by small nonprofit and community-based arts organizations and large nonprofit and commercial arts institutions (McCarthy & Jinnett, 2001), and have contributed to the growth.

Economic impact studies show the importance of arts and cultural activities to communities throughout North America. Information generated by various studies shows that when community leaders invest in the arts, they also invest in the economic health of their local communities. According to the president and CEO of Americans for the Arts, Robert L. Lynch, the nonprofit arts industry generates $24.4 billion U.S. in federal, state, and local government revenues annually, and that by comparison, they collectively provide less than $3 billion U.S. in support for the arts each year. Private-sector businesses and organizations also benefit from activity-related spending by attendees for eating, transportation, and overnight lodging. The National Governors Association states the following benefits:

> Cultural activities attract tourists and spur the creation of ancillary facilities such as restaurants, hotels, and the services needed to support them. Cultural facilities and events enhance property values, tax resources, and overall profitability for communities. In doing so, the arts become a direct contributor to urban and rural revitalization. (Americans for the Arts, 2002, p. 11)

The Americans for the Arts (2002) and Statistics Canada (2000) report findings associated with the economic impact of arts and culture participation. For Canada, although government spending on culture varies, monies to support cultural-sector objectives are made available at the municipal, territorial, provincial, and federal levels. During the last three years of the last decade, modest increases in cultural spending were reported at the provincial and federal levels. In contrast, in the United States, there have been significant cuts at the state level, modest cuts at the local level, and only small increases to the National Endowment for the Arts for grants. In spite of these funding concerns, economic figures and participation patterns in arts and culture seem to be holding steady. What follows are examples of the economic impact associated with arts and cultural participation for the United States and Canada.

- The total economic activity in the nonprofit arts industry in the United States was $134 billion U.S., which included the total spending by organizations ($53.2 billion) and spending by arts audiences ($80.8 billion).

- Two-thirds of American travelers included a cultural, arts, heritage, or historic activity or event while on a trip of 50 miles (80 kilometers) or more, one-way. Cultural tourists spend more and stay longer than other types of U.S. tourists.

- Nonlocal U.S. arts patrons attending performances, festivals, and so on spend almost twice as much as local attendees.

- In 2002, 39.4 percent of American adults attended at least one of the following types of live arts events: jazz or classical music performance, opera, musical, play, ballet, or art museum exhibit.

- There has been a 22 percent increase in the number of nonprofit performing arts companies (theater, music, dance, opera) across Canada through the last decade. Figures indicate that the total number of theater, music, dance, or opera companies exceeds 600. In addition, there are more than 2,300 organizations designated as heritage institutions. These include museums, art galleries, archives, and historic sites.

- Tourists spent an estimated $760 million Canadian on cultural activities while visiting Canada during 1998.

- Canadian festivals experienced a 12 percent decrease in government contributions yet generated $86.2 million Canadian in 1997 to 1998.

- From 1997 to 1998, 52,000 Canadians listed their occupation as part of the visual arts (painting, sculpting, drawing, crafts, photography), and another 89,000 listed themselves as artistic designers and workers in related occupations. In the same year, the Canadian government spent $57.6 million Canadian for the creation and production of works of visual arts and crafts, presumably for those not employed in the visual arts sector.

Arts and cultural activities not only provide recreation and leisure opportunities, but they also make solid contributions to the economic health of communities. Thinking about the value of providing arts and cultural opportunities for improving peoples' lives, livelihoods, and communities can be extended further. Many believe that the arts attract educated workers to geographic regions and the companies that seek to hire them, with the result being even greater positive economic benefits to communities and local government and business enterprises (Florida, 2002).

This chapter discusses arts and cultural leisure experiences and the organizations that offer them. The importance of providing arts and cultural experiences along with their inherent benefits is examined. Contemporary programs are provided throughout in order to highlight specific arts and cultural programs.

ARTS AND CULTURE AS PART OF RECREATION AND LEISURE

It is helpful for us to clarify terms that will be used throughout this chapter. As we've mentioned, those involved in the arts and culture sector represent nonprofit, for-profit, public, and private organizations. Broadly defined, arts and culture can be thought of as an identifiable sector present in every community and understandable in both economic and quality-of-life terms (Godfrey, 2002). The definition of arts and culture also lies in two contexts: social interaction and cultural anthropology. We explore both briefly.

Congdon and Blandy (2003) describe a direct relationship between arts and culture as everyday life that includes the myriad ways in which people assemble, work, and act together for a variety of

Taiko drummers share their music to bring people closer together.

political, aesthetic, economic, familial, religious, and educational purposes. The authors believe that participating in the culture of everyday life through art—broadly conceived of as *folklife*—is something all of us do. Within this context, then, the inclination to make and appreciate art is so ordinary that it is often overlooked for the extraordinary contribution it makes to such commonplace activities as cooking, fishing, keeping house, gardening, computing, and the multitude of other endeavors required in daily life (Congdon & Blandy, 2003, p. 177).

The arts and cultural sector in America is a large, heterogeneous set of individuals and organizations engaged in the creation, production, presentation, distribution, and preservation of and education about aesthetic, heritage, and entertainment activities, products, and artifacts (Wyszomirski, 2002). Some see the arts industry, or sector, at the very center of a circle of circles made up of cultural industries (Chartrand, 2000). Sixteen cultural industries make up Chartrand's well-regarded conceptualization of the arts industry and include parks and recreation, leisure, education, tourism, antiques and collectables, cosmetics, cuisine, funeral, furniture and fixtures, gaming, multicul-

turalism, native culture, official languages, physiotherapy and psychotherapy, sports, and religion. As can be seen, organizational contexts such as parks and recreation, leisure education, and tourism are all viewed as part of the arts and culture sector in America. Other components in the sector suggest leisure behaviors (antiques and collecting, cuisine) and pursuits (gaming, sports). As such, leisure organizations and behaviors are considered part of the contemporary arts and culture sector.

Within the literature on recreation and leisure, the arts have been categorically identified. Traditionally, the arts consist of a variety of visual, performing, folk, and ethnic activities as well as specific sports, home economics, and horticultural practices (Arnold, 1976). Popular art, a term suggested by Arnold (1978) as a way to categorize arts experiences, includes 11 content areas. These areas are illustrated in table 17.1. Arnold's categories were the first definitions of the various arts experiences found in parks and recreation programs.

As depicted in table 17.1, the arts are often defined by activity descriptors. McCarthy and Jinnett (2001) remind us that defining what we mean by the arts can be challenging because many

TABLE 17.1 Categories for Popular Arts

Category	Description
Horticulture arts	Parks, gardens, houseplants, growing scenes
Home economic arts	Weaving, crafts, cooking, fabrics, decorating, design
Athletic arts	Martial arts, display arts of gymnastics, fencing, exhibitions
Folk arts	Participatory level of arts in fairs, festivals, and circus
Cultural arts	Arts participated in by people of various cultures, which are distinguishable by their geographic location
Ethnic arts	Performance or exhibition of cultural arts by performing groups
Fine arts	Visual-arts expressions in painting, sculpting, photography, and architecture
Performing arts	Ballet, opera, theater, symphonies performed on stage
Communication arts	Theater arts for television, radio, speech, some modern dance, children's theater, extemporaneous theater, and improvisational works
Sensual arts	Arts experiences designed to provide exploratory use of the senses: touch, taste, sight, smell, hearing
Child art	Children's interpretation and experimentation with life

Adapted, by permission, from N.D. Arnold, "Pop art: The human footprint in infinity," *Journal of Physical Education, Recreation and Dance* (Reston, VA: AAHPERD).

Courtesy of City of Eugene Recreation Services

Many people classify hip-hop into the more popular arts. Arnold's categories help recreation professionals further categorize popular arts.

make a distinction between what has been called the classic arts (opera, ballet, dance, theater, classical music, painting, sculpture, literature), the more popular arts (rock and roll, hip-hop, graffiti murals), and entertainment enterprises (film, radio, television, computers). It seems reasonable, however, to conclude that the arts include notions associated with auditory, visual, movement, and experiential factors. Over the years, Arnold's categories have proven useful to recreation professionals.

Meanings of Arts and Culture: Organizations and Participants

Arts and culture is meaningful within the context of recreation and leisure in contemporary society. Some experts predict that changes related to time and subtle shifts in workplaces, leisure activities, communities, and peoples' everyday lives are developing creative class economies (Florida, 2002). According to Florida (2002), the creative class is made up of artists, engineers, architects, musicians, computer scientists, writers, entrepreneurs, entertainers, and creative professionals in business, finance, law, health care, and related fields.

Through the various program offerings, recreation organizations have contributed greatly to the general population's knowledge about arts and cultural opportunities. In doing so, not only have they assisted in educating the public about leisure options in the arts sector, but they have also played a key role in defining and perhaps establishing social values that reinforce the idea that creative opportunities for all is a good thing.

In recent years, state and provincial representatives from organizational settings such as folklife and heritage, historic preservation, visual and performing arts, and other culture-based groups have formed alliances and written position papers exalting the values of policies designed to enhance public support for arts and culture (Dwyer & Frankel, 2002). Recreation and leisure organizations are well positioned to be among those who advocate for, offer arts and cultural experiences to, and partner with organizations that make up the broader arts sector. Many recreation and leisure organizations already participate in these ways; examples are given later in this chapter.

The National Endowment for the Arts (1997) Survey of Public Participating in the Arts reported that 63 percent of Americans personally participated in the arts. This figure is important because it represents both those who do the art and those who attend arts events as part of an audience, and in recreation settings, professionals tend to develop programs for both groups. Both the organizational mission and organizational resources influence how arts and cultural programs are provided for children, youth, and adults. The American Assembly issued a highly influential report titled "The Arts and the Public Purpose" (1997). The report noted that virtually all Americans participate in arts and culture of some kind.

An earlier analysis found that 65 percent of adult Americans watched or listened to the arts primarily produced or presented by nonprofit arts organizations through the media by watching television or listening to the radio, 58 percent created or produced these arts themselves, and 43 percent experienced these arts in person. The report noted that electronic arts experiences, such as those experienced through the media, a computer, or a portable digital music player such as an iPod, had become the dominant form of participation in the arts. Many people experience art outside of any organizational context. The media was the primary means of distribution for both for-profit and nonprofit agencies (The American Assembly, 1997).

Benefits of Arts and Cultural Recreation Opportunity

Because of the widespread public participation in arts-related activities, we need to know more about how people come to devote part of their leisure time to the arts (Orend, 1989). Our understanding can be increased by the following passage taken from the report issued by the American Assembly:

> The arts in our country celebrate and preserve our national legacy in museums, concert halls, parks, and alternative spaces; they also inhere in the objects and buildings we use every day, and in the music we listen to in our cars, workplaces, homes, and streets. They calm us and excite us, they lift us up and sober us, and they free our spirit from the relentless mill of daily obligations; they entertain as well as instruct us; they help us understand who we are as individuals, as communities, and as a people. Their beauty or rage can fill us with emotion. In grief or celebration, and also in the subtler modes of irritation, amusement, sexiness, or depression, in great works or in the humblest objects or diversions, they tell our personal and national stories. (The American Assembly, 1997, pp. 4-5)

Next we explore benefits associated with arts and culture participation in recreation. In doing so, we rely on the wisdom of author and philosopher David Gray. Gray wrote a seminal paper in 1984 titled "The Great Simplicities." Simply put, these are the workings of the human mind, moral imagination, and the value of people and their capacity for growth. In his paper, Gray challenged recreators to negotiate the maze of organizational complexity, budgets and bargaining woes, and bureaucratic channels in order to find these three great simplicities and the real meaning and value of the recreation experience for individuals, groups, and communities. Clearly, our understanding of the benefits of arts and cultural experiences can be examined within the contexts of individuals, groups, and communities.

Individuals

The ways in which people in a free society choose to spend their discretionary time has been of interest to professionals whose jobs are to develop and conduct arts and cultural programs. The benefits people realize from arts and cultural participation vary by individual and by actual type of experience. We know that leisure is characterized by feelings of individual freedom and choice. Central to the nature of creative activity is freedom (Kelly & Freysinger, 2000). We also know that repeat participation in certain leisure is, in part, because individuals receive unique benefits from participation. The same experience, such as singing in a choral group, will produce different benefits for different people. One person may find joy in the music, and another may find joy in the friendships that singing with others facilitates.

Research tells us a good deal about typical benefits people realize during leisure engagement, and this information is useful for parks and recreation professionals. Estes and Henderson (2003) remind us that parks and recreation professionals would do well to remember that the unique thing we do best is provide people with opportunities for enjoyment.

> Happiness . . . may . . . be found in full engagement in the present through involvement in creative endeavors, or may occur in repose or quiet peacefulness. To become happy, one needs to open oneself to the delights of pleasure and the many wonderful things to enjoy in the world, such as food, art, poetry, music, science, and adventure. (Estes & Henderson, 2003, p. 24)

The arts add excitement and joy to our lives, and arts-related experiences are said to create an understanding of and appreciation for the arts that will lead us to participate more as adults (Orend, 1989). Over the years, studies have shown that older people who have consistently participated in a core of leisure activities throughout their lives display positive attitudes toward their leisure over time and lead a more balanced life (Kelly, 1997; Kleiber, 1999).

Knowing oneself is another benefit of participation in arts and culture. Csikszentmihalyi (1990) reminds us that when involved in expressive activity, we feel in touch with our real self. Use of our creative abilities and potential is also reason to participate in arts and cultural experiences. Even when someone is not able to feel very expressive, engaging in a creative experience can still be important. Kelly and Freysinger (2000) noted that there is something uniquely satisfying in the creative process even when it is strenuous, demanding, frustrating, and exhausting.

> When creativity is in full fire, people can experience what athletes and performers call the "white moment." Everything clicks. Your skills are so perfectly suited to the challenge that you seem to blend with it. Everything feels harmonious, unified, effortless. (Goleman, Kaufman, & Ray, 1992, p. 46)

Groups

Activities that involve others can be beneficial in forming and validating friendships and relationships that revolve around shared passions for arts and cultural experiences. Shared experience is a common ingredient of many recreation events (Gray, 1984) and often brings people together who might not share other interests or relationships. Take, for example, the popular concert in the park programs that take place across North America. People from all walks of life converge in New York City's Central Park for free, open-air concerts or in Albany, Oregon, for their outdoor summer concert series in Monteith Riverpark just to sit together and enjoy the *same* musical performance at the *same* time.

Leisure is an ongoing learned behavior (Kelly, 1996). We not only learn how to engage in activities and interact with others in leisure settings, but we also learn culture-specific values and orientations for our leisure (p. 42). Family, schools, recreation and arts organizations, and peer groups and friendships provide contexts in which our early creative interests are developed. Our propensities for arts and cultural experiences are found and nourished within group situations.

The family unit typically presents people with their first group. This group is important because arts participation by adults can influence participation by their children. If parents enjoy playing music, for example, it is more likely that their children will find similar activities challenging (Csikszentmihalyi, 1990). We know that early exposure to recreation experiences will establish roots from which future recreation pursuits reemerge during adulthood (Iso-Ahola, 1980; Kleiber, 1999).

In his studies on creativity, Csikszentmihalyi (1996) noted that the role of the parent should be one of providing opportunities, taking seriously the child's interest after it shows itself, and then supporting the child's involvement. Csikszentmihalyi acknowledged that motivational, personality, and cognitive factors contribute to creativity. In addition, he urges parents and educators (to which we would add recreators) to encourage opportunities for both solitude and gregariousness and for

Courtesy of City of Eugene Recreation Services

Group situations nourish our arts and cultural experiences. Not only are we influenced by peer groups and friendships, but we also influence others.

flexibility in gender roles. Group-oriented arts and cultural experiences can enable people to be both inward and outgoing. For example, a music-oriented program that encourages individuals to write songs and then share them with the group would foster both.

The concept of *serious leisure* is often viewed as group activity and has relevance in understanding arts and cultural leisure experiences. Stebbins (1992) studied and wrote about serious leisure because of his personal avocation as an amateur musician. Stebbins found that serious leisure is the systematic and determined pursuit of an activity by an amateur, hobbyist, or volunteer that eventually leads to a career in the activity (p. 3). Arts and cultural activities, whether participated in alone or in a group, easily lend themselves to the pursuit of serious leisure. When a person starts to earn money for the pursuit, it shifts from leisure to a vocation. Work for pay examples include professional musician or a person who gets hired after having "worked" as a volunteer.

Amateurs include musicians, dancers, and other performing artists. Hobbyists include collectors (rare books, violins, paintings), makers and tinkerers (furniture and toys, classic cars), and activity participants (social dancing, video games). Volunteering is a serious leisure pursuit that is gaining increased importance in arts and cultural agencies (Stebbins & Graham, 2004). Volunteering affects both participants and arts and cultural organizations because volunteers donate hours and expertise to advance an organization's missions and programs, and volunteering also serves as a leisure experience for the individual. Stebbins' (2005) exploration of **project-based leisure** contributes to an understanding of group behavior that may relate to shared arts and cultural activities. Many times, project-based leisure is experienced in a group. Examples include short-term projects that are beneficial to the larger community, which is explored next.

Communities

Arts and cultural recreational experiences are socially significant because these types of experiences, either when people participate in them or attend them, build communities. Researchers in the city of Philadelphia found that local **cultural activity** has a dramatic influence on neighborhoods (Stern & Seifert, 2002). Their findings showed that

- cultural activity draws new residents into communities, reducing poverty and increasing population;

- cultural participation and diverse communities are mutually reinforcing and tend to promote gradual growth rather than rapid gentrification;

- cultural activity creates a positive social environment resulting in greater civic participation, lower truancy rates, and lower delinquency rates; and

- cultural participation builds bridges across neighborhood, ethnic, and class divisions in ways that many other forms of civic engagement do not.

Shared recreational pursuits are based on kinship, work, and neighborhood (Gray, 1984) and friendship or special interest groups—contexts in which we build a sense of community with others. Pioneering work in the benefits of recreation and leisure was done in Canada by a team of professionals and educators under the auspices of the Parks and Recreation Federation of Ontario and the Ontario Ministry of Tourism and Recreation (1992). This work produced a catalog of benefits associated with personal, social, economic, and environmental leisure. The social benefits that contribute to building community follow:

- Leisure provides leadership opportunities that build strong communities.

- Community recreation reduces alienation, loneliness, and antisocial behaviors.

- Community recreation promotes ethnic and cultural harmony.

- Recreating together builds strong families, the foundation of a stronger society.

- Leisure provides opportunities for community involvement and shared management and ownership of resources.

- Integrated and accessible leisure services are critical to the quality of life of people with disabilities and disadvantaged people.

- Leisure opportunities, facilities, and the quality of the local environment form the foundation of community pride.

- Leisure services enrich and complement protective services for latchkey children through after-school and other recreational services.

The social benefits of community festivals have recently become an area of interest and lend additional credence to the importance of the individual, group, and community in arts and culture (Delamere, Wankel, & Hinch, 2001). Parks and recreation agencies often produce large-scale public festivals, and many arts organizations hold art fairs and festivals in their major promotional and fund-raising efforts. Agency staff motivated by their desire to be able to measure the social impact of community festivals can help arts and culture advocates bring intangibles associated with these kinds of leisure experiences into policy-driven discussions. Knowing the intangible benefits, along with economic impact benefits, allows staff to bring more information to agency decision making.

Delamere (2001) developed a scale to measure residents' attitudes toward the positive and negative social impacts of community festivals. The scale has been used by the Cloverdale community of Edmonton, Alberta, and the Edmonton Folk Music Festival. Because the scale provides substantial information in four categories—community benefits, cultural and educational benefits, quality-of-life concerns, and community resource concerns—organizers can identify and promulgate positive factors associated with their events and address negative factors. For example, participants' beliefs about the social benefits of a festival may include an enhanced image of the community, a sense of community well-being, or the ability to experience a variety of cultural experiences. These positive effects can be weighed against social costs such as reduced community privacy, overcrowding, and increased noise levels during the festival.

EVOLUTION OF ARTS AND CULTURAL PROGRAMMING

Both the public and private sectors have played significant roles in the evolution of arts and culture. Parks and recreation agencies have had much to do with the number and variety of arts and cultural opportunities that abound in contemporary society. Historically, parks and recreation has made access to art for citizens of all ages a public responsibility. The public schools have also contributed greatly by providing children and youth with learning opportunities in a range of arts- and culturally based experiences. Private businesses have created arts and cultural options based on public demand for these experiences. Because institutional constraints on businesses are often less confining than those on public organizations, businesses are often able to offer experiences more quickly, and these endeavors become cost effective as patrons demonstrate their willingness to pay for experiences. We examine recreation, schools, and business contributions next.

Role of Parks and Recreation in Arts and Culture

One of the pioneers in parks and recreation, Jane Addams, along with Ellen Gates Starr, established the first settlement house in Chicago in 1889 (Russell, 2005). Called the Hull House, settlement houses became community centers where a variety of recreation programs were provided for the urban poor, immigrant, and undereducated people living in urban cities. At Hull House, music, dance, and drama were part of the total program (Kraus, 1978). Since those early beginnings, we can trace the attention paid to arts and cultural programming through textbooks on program theory published in leisure studies. This review shows the developing emphasis placed on providing arts and cultural programs during the preparation of recreation and parks professionals.

Meyer and Brightbill (1956) discussed what they called the field of activities in recreation: arts and crafts, dancing, dramatics, literary activities, and music. Later, Butler (1967) devoted entire chapters of introductory textbooks to arts and crafts, music, and drama. He also introduced the idea of cultural activities in which recreation agencies cooperated with several community organizations, for example, the Oakland Education Association. Tillman (1973) included arts and crafts, dance, music, and drama in a category that he called cultural programming.

Kraus (1966, 1979, 1985) was a prolific author in parks and recreation. His textbooks in programming, administration, and leadership extensively cover programming for the arts. His early texts devote entire chapters to performing arts and to recreational arts and crafts and include specific examples about how to develop and lead arts experiences. Although Kraus' how-to approach has been followed by other authors, new lines of thinking about arts and cultural programming have emerged. For example, Farrell and Lundegren

(1978, 1983, 1991) presented art, crafts, dance, drama, and music along with four other categories—environmental activities, sports and games, volunteering, and social recreation—in a chapter identified as program areas. Corbin and Williams (1987) included individual chapters on drama, arts and crafts, dance, and music; they also included mental and linguistics as its own type of art.

Although not strictly a program theory text, Arnold's 1976 book, *The Interrelated Arts in Leisure*, provides an in-depth examination of arts and culture in parks and recreation. Referred to earlier in this chapter, Arnold's categorization of arts and cultural activities continues to guide recreation professionals producing arts and cultural programs. As an artist, arts manager, and professor of leisure studies, Arnold provides an informed overview of arts programming in public recreation settings.

Changes in textbooks on program theory were seen in the mid-1980s and early 1990s. Howe and Carpenter (1985) broke from the tradition of in-depth discussions of specific program areas and instead presented a program theory that emphasizes procedures associated with needs assessment, program development, implementation, evaluation, and modification. Up to that time, the idea of cultural programs had not been addressed in detail. Kraus (1966) mentioned cultural activities briefly in discussing arts and crafts, music, dance, and drama. One of the patterns in leisure programs that Howe and Carpenter identified and discussed was the cultural program pattern. This type of programming included festivals and celebrations, excursions to see musical or theatrical performances, culinary events, multicultural activities, and historic reenactments.

Rossman (1989, 1995, 2000) also broke from the tradition of examining specific program areas. Instead, he focused on program theory with the underlying assumption that whatever the program was (music or sports), the programmer's task was to facilitate individuals' engagement in leisure experiences based on their understanding of how leisure was experienced, how best to structure programs to facilitate leisure realization, and the purpose of their particular organizational context.

Edginton, Hanson, and Edginton (1992) and Edginton, Hudson, Dieser, and Edginton (2004) delineated the arts in detail. Included were the performing arts (dance, music, drama, visual arts), new arts (photography, computer-generated animation), and literary activities along with other programming areas (self-improvement and education activities; sports, games, athletics; aquatics; outdoor recreation; wellness hobbies, social recreation; volunteer services; travel and tourism). This format was maintained in subsequent texts (see Edginton, Hanson, Edginton, & Hudson, 1998; Edginton et al., 2004), although in 1998, the idea of culturally based programming to address the needs of diverse groups was included; the authors indicated that arts and crafts, festivals, and special events that reflected participants' cultural backgrounds were program opportunities (Edginton et al., 1998). Historically, parks and recreation agencies have made significant contributions to arts and culture over time. In responding to their missions, which emphasize providing recreation opportunity for all, arts and cultural activities have been frequently included in professional preparation and delivered to the public at community, state, regional, and national levels.

Role of Public Education in Arts and Culture

Schools have traditionally contributed greatly to citizens' knowledge of arts and culture and appreciation for and aptitudes in the many forms of artistic and cultural expression. Arts educa-

tion in the schools dates back to the late 1800s and typically included music, dance, theater, and visual arts at the elementary and secondary levels. Arts education was based on the desire to pass on the cultural achievements of a civilization to new generations, and the arts represented these achievements (Webster, 2003).

Over the years, efforts in arts education have varied and included cycles of interest and neglect, often depending on budget constraints. Webster (2003) noted that these cycles have spawned school and community interest in the arts.

> As these cycles evolved, partners outside of the school setting emerged alternately to support, stimulate, or restore the loss of school arts programs. This has resulted in the expansion of the field of arts education to include school as well as community-based efforts, and those working in it to comprise arts specialists, generalists, artist, and arts groups. (p. 154)

More recently, many schools have had to reduce or eliminate music, dance, and visual arts experiences from their curriculums. For many elementary schools, arts specialists are a thing of the past (Dreeszen, 2003). Increasingly, public educators

Broader cultural events can provide education for children that are no longer provided for in their schools.

Courtesy of City of Eugene Recreation Services

must look outside the schools to community-based arts organization programs and services for specialists. More and more, school districts must rely on the efforts of nonprofit and public organizations and regional arts councils and associations to send staff, artists, and volunteers to schools to teach the various arts. Larger arts and cultural organizations frequently employ staff designated to conduct arts education. Other times, students are invited to attend agencies' rehearsals or previews. These arts experiences give students an opportunity to view performance art and to interact with some of the artists and performers. The budgetary challenges that schools face in offering arts experiences to students add to the challenge of arts managers and program specialists who are highly motivated to share the arts with young audiences but often don't have the financial resources to do all they want to do.

Webster (2003) identified two important ways that local arts agencies are supporting arts education in the schools: partnership building and community cultural planning. She noted that partnering with other cultural, civic, social, or governmental agencies that share similar goals occurs with the public schools and in other community settings. In addition, Webster (2003) sees that community cultural planning, which includes arts education, is expanding the role of local arts agencies and helping to reveal the community's desire for increased opportunities for young people and adults to engage in the arts in both school and community settings.

In the past, parks and recreation arts and culture programs have been viewed as supplementing the educational opportunities students were gaining through their public education. These days, it may be that students' first and only arts experiences are those that occur through partnerships with public recreation and other local arts organizations, making these types of experiences even more important to individual and community development.

Role of Private Enterprise in Arts and Culture

Businesses and industries also add to the number and variety of art and cultural opportunities for people of all ages. From Disneyland to Las Vegas, from a children's birthday gathering at a local pizza parlor to a specially prepared culinary event for adults seeking a unique dining experience, private enterprises can take risks to pursue new markets and new arts and cultural experiences. Entrepreneurs have devised many ways for people to spend their discretionary money during their free time.

Entertainment choices abound, particularly in large urban areas, and in part because of the initiative of entrepreneurs. Through private exchange, the cost of participating in certain arts and cultural experiences is passed on to the consumer. Historically, those who could afford it, could buy it; others did without. Today, we see more of what is called democratization in arts and culture where certain experiences are theoretically accessible to everybody. This democratization occurred in part because of the commercialization of leisure experiences. So as more arts-related leisure experiences become accessible to more people, the choices and opportunities multiply and in turn, more people are able to participate in more experiences.

The growth of the middle class, commercialization of leisure, and cultural assimilation have spawned new entertainment choices along with new concepts we associate with arts and cultural experiences. Ideas linked to popular culture, high culture, and mass culture also add entertainment choices. Even though these terms are related, there are subtle distinctions. Popular culture is the commercialized everyday pastimes of a majority of people in a social group (Russell, 2005). An example is the Deadheads, thousands of fans who followed the Grateful Dead around the country attending their concerts. High culture generally refers to classical music, theater, poetry, and the fine arts (Kando, 1975). And the culture that is widely disseminated through the mass media is known as mass culture.

Commercial recreation organizations function within the business and industry sector operating leisure experiences that people are willing to purchase. Commercial organizations offering arts and cultural experiences include operations that directly sell entertainment and others that use entertainment in attracting or keeping patrons (music halls, casinos, movie theaters); organizations that disperse popular culture and media-based forms of entertainment including computers, television, and magazines; theme parks and amusement centers and businesses that sell food and drink; and operations that provide shopping opportunities such as malls and estate sales.

Another role played by private-sector businesses is that of supporting public and nonprofit organizations through sponsorships. Seen as positive advertising strategies, businesses provide money to organizations that in turn help to support arts or cultural offerings. Sponsorships are a way for businesses to support the arts and to align themselves with respected arts organizations in the community. Arts managers and recreation and public school professionals have become more and more skilled in securing sponsorships and therefore are able to plan and implement a wider variety of arts experiences for the general public. And businesses have learned that it is good for business to contribute to their communities in this way.

TYPES OF ARTS AND CULTURAL ORGANIZATIONS

Adding to the mix found in the public and private sectors are the vast number of nonprofit arts and cultural organizations in existence today. With the increased number of nonprofit and for-profit organizations producing a wide variety of cultural and arts experiences, the public is afforded wider choices, including dance, theater, visual and performing arts, and culinary and literary arts. The increased number of arts organizations contributes to the increasing number of arts participants (National Endowment for the Arts, 1997), and this in turn increases the variety of arts experiences made available to the public.

By all accounts, these numbers have grown in the last decade. This growth is in part due to the interest in arts and cultural opportunities and to the additional number of programs offered by long-established arts organizations. The kinds of arts and cultural organizations that function today include community arts centers, art museums, performing arts organizations, art commissions and councils, historic sites, museums and reenactments, folklore associations, libraries and literary organizations, arts and cultural festivals, and youth organizations offering special arts and cultural programs. In addition, nonprofit organizations like Elderhostel offer arts and cultural programs for older adults. Frequently partnering with arts organizations, Elderhostel helps promote and publicize unique activities associated with a festival or event.

The vast numbers of these arts and cultural organizations are nonprofit or quasi-public organizations, each having its own mission and resources for meeting its goals. These organizations typically have both professional and volunteer staff. In addition, they work with professional and amateur performers, artists, crafters, teachers, and facilitators to offer arts and cultural experiences.

To illustrate the types of arts and cultural organizations operating in North America today, table 17.2 lists jobs recently acquired by graduates of the University of Oregon's master's program in arts and

TABLE 17.2 Examples of Professional Positions in Arts and Cultural Organizations

Museums	Performing arts	Community arts	Events
Manager of teacher and school programs, Seattle Art Museum	Program manager, the Hult Center for the Performing Arts, Eugene, Oregon	Program director, Zimmerman Community Center, Portland, Oregon	Managing director, Portland Jazz Festival
Director of Jacobs Gallery, Eugene, Oregon	Executive director, Altoona Symphony Orchestra, Pennsylvania	Development associate, Southwestern Assoc. for Indian Arts, New Mexico	Assistant event manager, Mondavi Center for the Performing Arts, UC Davis, California
Project coordinator, University of Oregon Museum of Natural and Cultural History	Director of information systems, Oregon Ballet Theatre	Executive director, Interstate Firehouse Cultural Center, Portland, Oregon	Recreation program supervisor, Eugene, Oregon
Curatorial assistant, Portland Art Museum, Oregon	Development director, Oregon Mozart Players	Director, community development, Idaho Commission on the Arts	Director of development and major gifts, Oregon Festival of American Music
Program coordinator, Van of Enchantment, Museum of New Mexico	General manager, Lord Leebrick Theatre, Eugene, Oregon	Cultural affairs coordinator, Minneapolis	
Director of education, Frederic Remington Museum, New York			

administration. Jobs are categorized by type, and most positions are in arts and cultural organizations, not parks and recreation agencies. These professionals work in a variety of museum and performing arts settings, and the programs are sponsored by the public, nonprofit, and for-profit sectors. The positions depicted are typical of options available to a graduate of a master's program that emphasizes arts and culture. The diversity of positions illustrates the growth in arts and cultural organizations.

CONTEMPORARY PRACTICES IN ARTS AND CULTURE

Next we examine contemporary practices for providing arts and cultural experiences and programs in the parks and recreation setting. We begin by giving examples of best practices from public parks and recreation agencies.

Each example demonstrates comprehensive arts and cultural programs. The first example describes a statewide program from the northwestern United States. The second illustrates what's possible in a major urban city. And the third example describes the arts and cultural programs of the only national park for the performing arts in the United States. After reviewing current practices, we examine contemporary management practices associated with the delivery of arts and cultural programs. These examples not only cross many organizational boundaries in order to show the various ways organizations work and plan together, but they also show programs that address the unique interests of various user and lifestyle groups.

Arts and Cultural Programs in Parks and Recreation: Best Practices

In the last few years, and in spite of challenging economic times, Oregon is experiencing growth in the number and type of opportunities for citizens to participate in arts and cultural programs. In this state of less than 3 million residents, an increasing number of nonprofit and for-profit organizations have been producing a wide variety of cultural and arts experiences including dance, theater, visual and performing arts, and culinary and literary arts. In addition, the public sector plans and implements programs. Recreation professionals have long been aware that the social and psychological benefits derived from recreation participation include those associated with arts participation. Therefore, as public organizations with a mission to provide

recreation opportunities to all citizens in their service areas (cities, special districts, regions), public agencies are in a unique position to provide arts opportunities to a wide range of people.

Because the extent to which Oregon recreation organizations were providing arts and cultural programs was not clear, a project was undertaken to find out. Selected members of the Oregon Recreation and Park Association (ORPA) were invited to participate in a study designed to identify the number and types of arts and cultural programs taking place throughout the state. The purpose of this study was to identify the number and type of arts and cultural programs offered during the summer of 2003 (Carpenter, 2004). What follows is a brief overview of the findings.

- Most organizations provided arts opportunities for both youth and adults throughout the summer months. The majority of these offerings were visual arts programs, followed by performing arts programs. The most popular visual arts programs were a wide variety of arts and crafts experiences. Performing arts programs included dance, movement, music, and theater experiences.

- Special events that included arts and cultural experiences were offered in nine cities, five districts, and two regional organizations.

- In three of the cities, programs took place in visual or performing arts centers. Eight of the cities conducted visual or performing arts camps that ran for at least one week throughout the summer months. Proportionately more cities than special districts held summer concert series (9 of the 12 cities, 1 of the 6 special districts).

- Nontraditional program offerings included literary and culinary arts experiences and culturally based touring opportunities. Three of the cities, two of the districts, and both of the regional organizations offered literary arts programs. Five of the cities and two of the districts offered culinary arts programs. Five of the cities and three of the districts offered culturally based touring opportunities with those serving adults far more often than youth.

The city of Philadelphia alone, with just half as many residents as the entire state of Oregon, offers a wide array of arts and cultural experiences for its 1.4 million citizens. The Philadelphia Department of Recreation was organized around the turn of the 19th century. The department has a long and well-developed arts and cultural program that includes historic buildings such as the

Courtesy of Gaylene Carpenter

Arts and crafts is vital to the growth of youth and is also one of the most popular visual arts programs.

Atwater Kent Museum, Betsy Ross House, Camp William Penn, and Olde Fort Mifflin and recreation programs that include arts and cultural activities in after-school programs, camps, teen centers, programs for people with physical or mental disabilities, and activities for senior citizens. The department also provides cultural and performing arts programs such as dance classes, dance festivals, music classes, neighborhood concerts, and young performers theater camps, and visual arts programs in arts and crafts, ceramics, painting, and pottery and events such as art shows and art camps. Although the Philadelphia Department of Recreation (www.phila.gov/recreation/) offers arts and cultural experiences most people expect to see if interest and resources are adequate, these programs also include several innovative features:

- After-school programs include the arts at 130 sites, five days a week, and serve 2,800 children.
- The senior art camp provides opportunities to learn painting, drawing, and paper sculpture and culminates in the final-day celebration and exhibit.

- Teen center cultural activities include photography, ceramics, jewelry making, movie nights, and special events.
- Phil-A-Kid History Camp, held at Olde Fort Mifflin, is a fun, entertaining, and educational five-day camp where children assume identities of past Philadelphians and discover people's everyday lives through various activities.

In addition to traditional activities, the department also offers unique programs. One of these is the Creative Resolution Theatre program that uses interactive theater to help children and adults move from conflict to creative resolution in a fun, safe, and supportive environment. The Mural Arts program has created more than 2,300 indoor and outdoor murals throughout the city. The program involves city residents in the creative process, offering art education programs at recreation centers, homeless shelters, and other sites around the city (Mural Arts Program, 2002). The Mummers Parade that takes place on New Year's Day each year is one of America's oldest folk art traditions. More than 15,000 Philadelphia Mummers *strut their stuff* up Broad Street dressed as comics, fancies, string bands, and fancy brigades (Mummers.com, 2005). Robin Hood Dell East amphitheater has 5,800 reserved seats and lawn space for 2,500, and offers diverse musical performances throughout the summer months.

Many do not realize the extent to which the National Park Service (NPS) is involved in arts and culture in the United States. Although most of its 83 million acres (34 million hectares) are prized natural and scenic lands, two-thirds of the NPS sites are historical or cultural in nature and accounted for more than 90 million recreation visits in 2002—a third of the park system's total (Noonan, 2004). What began as a gift to the American people from Catherine Filene Shouse, the Wolf Trap National Park for the Performing Arts, has evolved into a showcase of both parks and arts in one locale. Wolf Trap's comprehensive programs and services in arts and culture mirror the best practices of what most other local recreation agencies and arts organizations are only able to offer in smaller segments. Located in Virginia, not far from the Capital Beltway, Wolf Trap manages two performance venues, an opera company, and education program, all of which produce a variety of arts and cultural activities in addition to public performances (see figure 17.1).

Contemporary Management Strategies That Enhance Arts and Cultural Opportunities

Contemporary management practices in arts and culture include using high-profile events to promote awareness and entertain the public, collaborating and forging partnerships, planning cultural events, addressing youth interests, associating with tourism initiatives, responding to lifestyle shifts, and creating art experiences in public places. In this last portion of the chapter, we present several best practices that emphasize these contemporary management strategies in providing arts and cultural experiences. Recreation professionals interested in promoting arts and cultural experiences should become involved with other organizations, members of their staff, and key arts advocates in their communities in order to find ways to initiate innovative programs.

High-Profile Events

High-profile arts and cultural events are popular strategies for promoting ongoing programs,

---

Arts and Cultural Programs at the Wolf Trap National Park for the Performing Arts

Performance Venues

Filene Center
- Face of America
- Musical Theatre
- National Symphony Orchestra
- Jazz and Blues Festival
- Preperformance Previews

The Barns at Wolf Trap
- The Discovery Series
- Center Stage from Wolf Trap

Children's Theater in the Woods

Education
- Center for Education at Wolf Trap
- Institute for Early Learning Through the Arts
- Classes at the center
- Internships
- Master classes

Wolf Trap Opera Company
- Performances
- Filene Young Artists
- Outreach

Interpretive Programs
- Backstage tours
- Nature walks
- Junior ranger program

FIGURE 17.1   Wolf Trap's programs demonstrate its major commitment to its performing arts and education mission.

Source: National Park Service, U.S. Department of the Interior, Wolf Trap www.nps.gov/wotr.

---

entertaining the public, and generating income. By high profile, we are referring to large public events that are promoted to wide markets outside of the regional area in which the promoting organization resides. Fringe festivals are a good example because their uniqueness draws arts-friendly attendees from all around North America to see nonjuried performers and emerging artists in a festival-like environment, usually lasting several days. During its run, the Winnipeg Fringe Theatre Festival, member of the Canadian Association of Fringe Festivals, boasts 23 venues, 134 performing companies, 1,168 shows, 800 volunteers, two full-time staff members, and another 50 hired during the festival (C. Couldwell, personal communication, July 29, 2004). The following are examples of other high-profile events that draw attendees regionally:

- Once a year the city of Portland, Oregon, dumps 100 cubic yards of sand in a downtown square for all ages to engage in sand sculpting.

- One of the top arts festivals in North America, the Cherry Creek Arts Festival, takes place in Denver over the Fourth of July weekend.

- The Charlottetown Festival on Prince Edward Island is recognized as the top event in Canada by the American Bus Association.

- Plate and Pitchfork dinners, featuring gourmet meals and fine wines, are held (in Canby, Sherwood, and Troutdale, Oregon) in agricultural fields as a way to bring city folk and farm folk together to support farm awareness.

- Thousands of classic car collectors and enthusiasts travel to towns across North America to participate in events such as the Concour d' Elegence or hot rod cruises.

- The Hemingway Days Festival takes place in Key West, Florida.

Collaboration and Partnerships

We are seeing more and more collaborative efforts and partnerships among public and nonprofit agencies to offer arts and cultural programs. Partnering with organizations that have similar missions in order to accomplish goals for the greater good is increasing throughout North America. Ninety-one percent of local arts agencies in a recent survey collaborate or have formed a partnership with at least one other public or community agency such as a school district, parks and recreation department, social service, economic development organization, or chamber of commerce, and 78 percent participate in three or more ongoing collaborations (Americans for the Arts, 2004). Collaborating not only makes sense in terms of using limited

By partnering with a museum, a school district can expand its arts education to students.

human resources, but it also enables organizations to provide arts and cultural experiences. Several examples illustrate this growing strategy.

The state of New York's innovative Urban Cultural Park/Heritage Area program is a joint venture between the New York State Office of Parks, Recreation and Historic Preservation and 22 historically significant communities around the state. Kingston is one of these areas and has benefited from this partnership by creating a series of outreach history and educational programs, local history exhibits created with school-age youngsters, celebrations and festivals, band concerts on the waterfront, and even a reenactment of the story of the British trying to rid Kingston of rebels during the Revolutionary War.

Collaborations between universities and arts organizations can create learning opportunities for college students and provide arts opportunities for the public. The Kamloops Art Gallery and the University College of the Cariboo in Kamloops, British Columbia, supported by a Community–University Research Alliance grant, are involved in a collaborative effort to find out how cultural and arts organizations work together in a small city setting. ArtsBridge America is a national network of universities that work in partnership with public schools in their communities. Their efforts have brought arts education back to many public schools. The ArtsBridge America program demonstrates that having the arts in education is valuable, promoting interdisciplinary knowledge while enhancing students' appreciation of and contributions to **culture** (ArtsBridge, n.d.). In Los Angeles, the housing authority police, city and county recreation and parks departments, and California State University at Dominguez Hills partnered to offer a comprehensive program that emphasizes the development of self-confidence, cultural awareness, and constructive social interactions of young girls through personal exploration and guided group activities (Cappel, 1995).

Government grant support can encourage arts organizations to engage in collaborative efforts. For example, the Canada Council for the Arts was created by Parliament almost 50 years ago to foster and promote the study and enjoyment of and the production of works in the arts. One of these programs, Artists and Community Collaboration Fund, offers grants in support of diverse artistic activities.

Emphasis on Cultural Planning

Local arts agencies typically lead efforts for community cultural planning, and in communities with a cultural plan, local government arts funding grows at a significantly faster rate than communities without a plan (Americans for the Arts, 2004). The city of Edmonds, Washington, is located about 15 miles (24 kilometers) from Seattle. You would expect residents to access arts and culture in that large, metropolitan city, but through cultural planning, arts-related organizations in Edmonds have found ways to meet residents' interests locally. This pattern may well become the norm as more and more professionals with interest in the arts and the desire to live and work in less urban areas look around at the cultural amenities in their own backyard. The Edmonds Community Cultural Plan includes goals related to increasing the visibility of the arts; positioning the arts as a focus for economic development; creating links with arts, business, education, heritage, tourism, city beautification, and recreation; broadening community involvement in the arts; and developing work, performance, exhibition, and retail space for artists and gathering places for the public. Cultural planners represented arts organizations, the city of Edmonds, the state, private businesses, local nonprofit organizations, and local festivals and museums. Recreation professionals should be involved when community-wide cultural planning takes place and may even want to initiate such efforts if they are not already being undertaken.

Addressing Youth Interests

Youth and young adults often have special interests in arts and cultural activities that occur outside the typical organizational contexts. It is important to keep in mind that many youth and young adults are attracted to community arts experiences, but it is also important to recognize that many others are not. Two innovative, nonagency-based practices that many youth and young adults find interesting are the DIY movement and creating and reading zines. DIY refers to doing it yourself: making and promoting music without major record label backing and without a great level of "selling out." Zines are low-volume, periodic publications distributed to satisfy the publisher's whim rather than to produce profit. Two additional examples that address youth and young adult interests in arts and culture that do occur within an organizational context are discussed next.

Filling a desire of girls who had an interest in rock music but few opportunities to engage, Rock 'n' Roll Camp for Girls (RRCG) took hold in Portland, Oregon, in 2001 (Jones, 2002). Designed for girls and young women, RRCG is a weeklong day camp that includes musical education, technical instruction, forums to discuss and explore creativity and self-expression, and role models and examples for promoting motivation, self-reliance, and empowerment through music. Camp culminates with a public showcase on the last night.

Totally Cool Totally Art (TCTA) is a program for youth run by the Austin (Texas) Parks and Recreation Department. Austin, known for its comprehensive parks and recreation arts and cultural programs, which include outdoor sculpture, murals, public art, and museum and cultural heritage, responded to a city council initiative to help the community deal with teen issues. Some eight years later, TCTA objectives include promoting arts education, a sense of belonging, new experiences, teamwork and communication, and respect and trust.

> TCTA's philosophy is based on a process-oriented educational method, emphasizing the process of art making instead of the product. Through the creative process, each participant has opportunities to enhance creativity, promote self-esteem, and foster respect for others. (Austin Parks and Recreation Department, 1995)

Associating With Tourism Initiatives

Recreation agencies and arts organizations offering arts and cultural programs should routinely associate with their local convention and visitors bureaus (CVB). CVBs can assist programmers by including the arts and cultural opportunities in tourism initiatives. They also have tools and systems in place to help professionals conduct economic impact studies to determine when arts programs bring visitors to a region. And because CVBs are part of strategic tourism planning, they recognize ways that organizations can partner to offer better and more inclusive and exciting arts and cultural programs.

The city of Hamilton, Ontario, for example, designed and offers walking tours that go beyond the traditional historic overview to include topics with clear cultural connections related to the evolution of the city. Tours like "The Man Who Knew Lincoln" and "Pardon My Lunch Bucket Industrial Heritage Tour" are available to tourists. And the European Festival Network created and markets a FestPass Guide to help tourists not only find and get to the various festivals but also to encourage them to stay in the area for a few days at a time, thus boosting visitor spending in local regions. Arts organizers can also lobby with their local CVBs to create a familiarization tour. "Fam" tours help organizations publicize their programs and services to others in the city or region. Arts and cultural organizations, whether public and nonprofit agencies or private businesses, should nurture public awareness whenever possible.

Responding to Lifestyle Shifts

Those creating and promoting arts and cultural experiences are better served when paying close attention to lifestyle and popular culture changes. The idea that one size does *not* fit all is one that arts organizers must continue to embrace. Peoples' contemporary lifestyles influence what they do with their free time and discretionary money, and their choices represent their values. Many times, these values emerge in expressions associated with arts and culture and therefore have relationships to management strategies. Take, for example, recent research on the informal arts.

Researchers are intrigued by what they call the intersection between arts and everyday life (Wali, Marcheschi, Severson, & Longoni, 2001). Their discoveries not only have implications for cultural planning, but they also address lifestyle issues because they are finding that vast numbers of people experience the arts in an informal manner. The researchers have found that the **informal arts** are characterized and distinguished by their overall accessibility as vehicles for artistic expression, by the self-determining nature of people's participation, and by the generally noncommercial nature of the activities (Wali et al., 2001). They describe their motivation to start their inquiry from observing the following activities.

> On any given evening around the city of Chicago, you are likely to encounter people singing, dancing, rehearsing lines of a play, working on a painting, or writing poems. A sense of intense engagement, of dedication, and of enjoyment permeates the spaces in which these activities take place. At a drumming circle in the park, a young man rises and moves into a fluid dance, an expression of ecstasy on his face. In a church basement, a director painstakingly rehearses the actors in their lines, while the stage crew works late into the evening painting the set. At a weekly rehearsal of a south Asian music ensemble, a chemist, a computer engineer, an executive secretary, and a music student lead the group through a composition. Everyone is intensely concentrating on everyone else's playing, trying to stay on beat. (p. 215)

Informal arts were found to be taking place in park district facilities (painting and folk dancing classes), branch libraries (poetry workshops and readings), in neighborhoods (storefront theater and performance-related groups), and faith-based institutions (choral groups). Next we present lifestyle-related factors that have the potential to continue to define new forms of informal arts.

- As people continue to move from older, industrial cities, places such as Detroit, Pittsburg, and Baltimore have focused on recent revitalization, and new projects are creating trendy areas that attract young professionals wanting to be close to work and nightlife (Armas, 2004).

- Sundays are changing and becoming days that programs can be, and increasingly are, offered to the public. For example, laws supporting liquor sales exist in 31 states, Sunday sales are commonplace, and a New Jersey–based bank recently designed its entire promotional campaign around doing business on Sundays (Anthony, 2004).

- As time scarcity continues to be challenging for so many people, what has been called **leisure episodes** will remain relevant. Fairs, festivals, and special events in particular have properties that appeal to people with limited time (Carpenter, 1995). Other arts and cultural experiences may need to be designed with leisure episodes in mind.

- As the baby boomers grow older, they may develop interest in reengaging in activities they participated in as children, and if so, many activities are likely to be related to the arts. Many in this population are moving to downtowns, drawn to urban cultural attractions such as performing arts, museums, and gourmet food (Sutel, 2004).

Creating Arts Experiences in Public Places

Making arts available in public places is a long-standing practice. Parks and recreation organizations often coordinate public arts design, selection, and placement. Although these types of programs emphasize visual arts, this discussion also includes performance arts. Places for public arts and culture can include certain sections of our towns and cities that temporarily become arts places, such as increasingly popular arts walks in busy sections of towns. Space can be set aside for arts and cultural events in settings designed for something else: for example, bringing musicians or magicians into shopping malls, using public parks to turn soccer fields into arts festivals, or creating rose gardens in outdoor movie theaters during the summer. Busi-nesses can support the arts by offering late-night poetry slams to small groups in clubs after the larger groups have left or letting musicians practice in a neighborhood restaurant after it closes.

Another way to create public spaces for arts experiences is to renovate rather than bulldoze abandoned buildings. The Dia Art Foundation renovated an abandoned Nabisco carton-making plant along the Hudson River in Beacon, New York, to create the Dia:Beacon museum that houses its contemporary art collection. Reexamining decisions that would allow for the development of public spaces to serve as appropriate venues or centers for a variety of arts and cultural experiences, instead of practices that favor demolition of unused private buildings, could be cost effective ways to increase the number of program sites and offerings. Those with an interest in arts and culture must continually remain open to new ways of bringing these experiences to unanticipated public places, for example, finding a pianist in PDX as I did and described earlier in the chapter.

SUMMARY

Opportunities in arts and cultural recreation represent a multifaceted area of recreation programming. Ample evidence indicates its importance throughout the history of the parks and recreation movement. Our professional literature offers numerous examples of how professionals can provide arts and cultural leisure experiences to the public. Many people have not only enjoyed the arts through recreation services over the years but have also developed an appreciation for and skill in leisure pursuits that have lasted a lifetime. It is important for recreation professionals with an interest in promulgating arts and cultural experiences not only to be aware of the many arts and cultural programs provided today but to find ways to associate with and partner with other arts enthusiasts in their communities. The benefits derived from arts and cultural experiences contribute not only to individual growth and the development of leisure interests but also to building our communities through shared experiences. There is every reason to believe that arts and cultural experiences will continue to be vital experiences that define our time and communicate our social values.

Web Sites to EXPLORE

Organizations

Americans for the Arts: ww3.artsusa.org/

The American Assembly: www.americanassembly.org

ARTSBRIDGE: www.artsbridgeonline.org/

National Recreation and Park Association: www.nrpa.org/

University of Oregon Arts and Administration Program: http://aad.uoregon.edu

Univeristy of Oregon Festival and Event Management: www.center.uoregon.edu/festivalevent/

National Endowment for the Arts: www.nea.gov/

Wolf Trap National Park for the Performing Arts: www.nps.gov/wotr

Statistics Canada: www.statcan.ca/

Cultural Future of Small Cities: www.tru.ca/smallcities/index.htm

Programs

Rock 'N' Roll Camp for Girls: www.girlsrockcamp.org/about.htm

Austin Totally Cool Totally Art: www.ci.austin.tx.us/tcta/

Illinois Arts Alliance: www.artsalliance.org/

National Arts Centre: www.nac-cna.ca

Fringe Festival: www.fringefestival.org/

CHAPTER 18

The Nature of Recreation and Leisure As a Profession

Mary G. Parr, Mark E. Havitz, and Andrew T. Kaczynski

Courtesy of Craig Ross

How we choose to use our leisure time as opposed to how we choose to trudge to work tells us an enormous amount about a culture or an individual. That's very valuable in human life. So, the people who say, "Oh my God, it's a game!" and giggle nervously haven't thought very long about the role these activities play in an individual's or a society's life.

A. Bartlett Giamatti, president of Yale University (1978-1986), commissioner of Major League Baseball (1989)

CHAPTER OBJECTIVES

After reading this chapter, you should be able to do the following:

- Identify the criteria used to define a profession
- Discuss the diverse roots of professional preparation in leisure services
- Describe the benefits approach to leisure and discuss its use to the leisure services profession
- Describe factors limiting public recognition of the value of recreation and leisure services
- Describe the historic foundations of our professional education programs
- Understand the various degrees normally used for admission to and advancement in the leisure services profession
- Describe the respective roles of academic journals, professional magazines, and books in advancing professional knowledge related to leisure services delivery
- Identify the purposes of accreditation
- Identify the purposes of certification
- Describe the role and purpose(s) of professional associations and identify specific organizations that serve the leisure services profession
- Discuss the purpose of a code of ethics and its value to the leisure services profession

INTRODUCTION

If I hire a window washer to clean my windows, I have an expectation that my windows will be cleaned more effectively (cleaner) and more efficiently (quicker) than I can do the job. Is the window washer a professional simply because I'm willing to pay him to do a job that is too much "work" for me? Is a teenager who is paid to mow grass for several of her neighbors a professional? Are the employees of a landscaping company that mow the grass of several others in the neighborhood professionals because they do it full-time?

As you can see from these examples, defining a profession or who is a professional is a precarious task. When people think of a professional, they may envision a business suit, a briefcase, or perhaps a large paycheck. They might also think of someone who is highly skilled, who is committed to his or her job, who does quality work, and who conducts him- or herself in an ethical manner. One professor who has extensively studied the professionalism of recreation and leisure has stated " . . . professions are unique in that their members have special knowledge, perform a specialized role and *have control over their occupation's structure, function, practice and destiny*" (Sessoms, 1991, p. 249). In addition, it is generally agreed that professional status is contingent upon the public's acceptance of the profession's expertise. That is, we accept that medical doctors, lawyers, and accountants, just to name a few, have expertise that the general public does not, and we seek them out when faced with a particular problem or issue.

This chapter explores various issues related to professionalism and whether leisure services qualify as a profession. After a brief introduction to the leisure services profession, six major criteria that define a profession are discussed, and the field of parks, recreation, and leisure services is measured against these indicators.

EVALUATING THE LEISURE SERVICES PROFESSION

Most would agree that the leisure services field does not meet the strict criteria of a profession along the lines of law, education, or medicine. Part of the issue is a difficulty in defining leisure services—what is the encompassing field of professional services and its core body of knowledge common to all of the areas outlined in this text? As you have seen, each of the leisure services areas has unique service components, knowledge, skills, abilities, clients, and so forth. As pointed out later in this chapter, some of these services areas have made attempts to develop a distinct professional identity.

For example, the Cleveland Metroparks, a park district located in northeast Ohio including 14 reservations with over 20,000 acres of land, employs 660 full-time and part-time workers and has a seasonal workforce of 600 additional members. Table 18.1

TABLE 18.1 Cleveland Metroparks Positions, 2004

Office or department	Positions
Executive Director's Office	Administrative Assistant—Executive Director's Office Executive Assistant Executive Director/Secretary Law Director Legal Assistant/Legal Secretary Risk Manager
Treasurer's Office	Accounting Assistant Accounting Manager Accounts Payable Specialist Associate Information Systems Manager Buyer Helpdesk Support Specialist Information System Manager Payroll/Fringe Benefits Specialist Purchasing Clerk Purchasing Manager Revenue and Internal Audit Administrator Technology Support Specialist Treasurer
Marketing and Golf Clubhouse Services	Administrative Assistant—Marketing Associate Manager of Design Associate Manager of Production Director of Marketing and Golf Clubhouse Services Exhibit Specialist Exhibits Coordinator Golf Professional/Clubhouse Manager Golf Professional/Instruction and Special Events Manager Golf Specialist Manager of Marketing and Public Relations—Parks Manager of Research and Program Evaluation Manager of Visitor Services Manager of Visual Communications Marketing Associate Marketing Assistant Marketing Specialist—Publications Print Specialist Technician (Union) Senior Graphics Designer Senior Graphics Designer/System Administrator Senior Technician (Union) Senior Visitor Services Specialist Visitor Services/Marketing Assistant Visitor Services Assistant Visitor Services Representative Visitor Services Specialist Visual Communications Specialist
Planning, Design and Natural Resources	Administrative Assistant—PDNR Aquatic Biologist Architect Chief of Natural Resources Chief of Park Planning Director of Planning, Design and Natural Resources Engineer Technician Fisheries Biologist Landscape Architect Manager of Field Research—Natural Resources Natural Resources Area Manager Real Estate and Contract Manager Regional Park Planner and GIS Manager Secretary—PDNR

(continued)

TABLE 18.1 *(continued)*

Office or department	Positions
Planning, Design and Natural Resources *(continued)*	Senior Civil Engineer I Senior Civil Engineer II Surveyor Wildlife Manager
Park Operations	Administrative Assistant—Park Operations Aquatic/Facility Manager Assistant Building Trades Manager Assistant Forestry Manager Assistant Site Construction Manager Budget Records and Input Technician Building Trades Manager Chief of Administrative and Recreation Services Chief of Operations Resources Chief of Outdoor Education Chief of Parks Cultural History Interpreter Director of Park Operations Education Specialist Facilities/Concessions Manager Facilities/Food Services Specialist Field Contract Manager Fleet Manager Forestry Manager Historical Interpreter/Naturalist Information Specialist Look-About Lodge Manager/Naturalist Management Trainee—Operations Manager of Nature Shops Natural Landscape Specialist Naturalist/Artist Naturalist I Naturalist II Nature Center Manager Outdoor Adaptive Recreation Specialist Outdoor Recreation Manager Outreach Manager Park Manager Park Operations Analyst Safety and Environmental Manager Secretary—Park Operations Senior Service Worker (Union) Senior Technician (Union) Service Worker (Union) Site Construction Manager Technician (Union) Technology Support Specialist Visitor Center Manager Youth Outdoors Manager Youth Outdoors Recreation Specialist
Golf-Turf	Chief Superintendent of Golf—Turf Golf Course Manager Manager of Golf Course Construction Senior Service Worker (Union) Service Worker (Union) Technician (Union)
Rangers	Administrative Assistant/Information System Specialist Captain—Field Operations Captain—Special Operations Chief Ranger Deputy Chief Public Information Manager

Office or department	Positions
	Ranger
	Ranger Division Lieutenant
	Ranger Lieutenant—Administrative
	Ranger Lieutenant—Communications (TAC)
	Ranger Sergeant—Mounted Unit
	Records Administrator and Court Liaison
	Sergeant (FOP)
	Secretary—Rangers
Zoo	Admissions Manager
	Animal Care Manager
	Animal Keeper (Union)
	Animal Registrar
	Assistant Animal Care Manager
	Associate Research Curator
	Associate Veterinarian
	Curator of Conservation and Science
	Curator of Education
	Curator of Zoological Programs
	Curator of Rainforest, Mammology, and Ornithology
	Director of Cleveland Metroparks Zoo
	Education Scheduling Coordinator
	Education Specialist/Volunteer Coordinator
	Education Specialist I
	Group Sales Manager
	Group Sales Representative
	Guest Services Administrative Assistant/Training Coordinator
	Guest Services Operations Specialist
	Horticulturist (Union)
	Lead Animal Keeper (Union)
	Lead Horticulturist (Union)
	Lead Maintenance Engineer (Union)
	Lead Mechanic (Union)
	Interactive/Electronic Technician (Union)
	Manager of Guest Services
	Manager of Zoo Buildings and Facilities
	Manager of Zoo Grounds and Services—Days
	Manager of Zoo Grounds and Services—Nights
	Manager of Zoo Horticulture
	Manager of Zoo Marketing and Public Relations
	Marketing Specialist—Media and Publications
	Marketing Specialist—Partnerships and Support
	Marketing Specialist—Special Events
	Secretary—Facility Operations
	Secretary—Zoological Programs
	Senior Education Specialist
	Service Maintenance Level I
	Service Maintenance Level II
	Superintendent of Zoo Facility Operations
	Veterinarian
	Zoo Animal Health Technician
	Zoo Education Assistant
	Zoo Executive Secretary
	Zoo Guest Services Secretary
	Zoo Hospital/Medical Records Administrator
	Zoo System and Records Administrator
Human Resources	Director, Human Resources
	Diversity Consultant
	Human Resources Assistant
	Manager, Compensation, Benefits and Continuous Learning
	Manager, Employee Relations
	Manager, Human Resource Administration
	Manager, Recruitment and Retention
	Manager, Volunteer Services
	Senior Recruitment and Diversity Specialist

From Cleveland Metroparks.

contains a list of positions at the Metroparks for 2004 (Cleveland Metroparks, personal communication, 2004). As you can see from the table, it takes a wide variety of skills and positions to run a park district. A brief survey of the list demonstrates the wide variety of knowledge, skills, and abilities required to operate a large leisure services agency. Some of these positions would be considered professional, such as law director, accounting manager, fisheries biologist, aquatic facility manager, and golf professional and clubhouse manager, and some would not, for example, purchasing clerk, attendance counter, janitor, and service worker. However, as we can see from the list, a professional working for a "leisure services" agency doesn't necessarily qualify as a "leisure services" professional.

Several criteria have been identified as defining a profession (Kraus, 2001; Sessoms, 1991). The remainder of the chapter builds on earlier work in specific sections that address six criteria that help determine whether recreation and leisure services qualify as a profession:

1. Social value and purpose
2. Public recognition
3. Specialized professional preparation
4. Specialized body of knowledge
5. Quality assurance through accreditation, certification, and professional associations
6. Professional code of ethics

SOCIAL VALUE AND PURPOSE

If you ask someone what they like to do on the weekend or how they want to spend their retirement years, chances are the response you get will contain a reference to leisure. Different people might mention fishing off the dock at the cottage, volunteering as a kids' soccer coach, or pursuing a hobby, such as quilting, with more passion and effort. It is no secret that most people enjoy their leisure time, and although some may not admit it, they may even attach greater importance to these pursuits than to their work roles. Perhaps this suggests that recreation and leisure has social value and serves a purpose in today's society, and accordingly, that the people who facilitate this value and purpose are leisure professionals.

Until the past 20 years, efforts to document and describe the value of recreation and leisure were sporadic and ill conceived. Although many people suspected that our services were "more than just fun and games," the assertions about recreation's impact on society were mostly intuitive. For example, a 1986 report from the President's Commission on American Outdoors argued that:

The total value of the outdoors for recreation is difficult to describe, let alone price . . . price denotes short-term value . . . a sunset, a rainbow, an ocean wave, a 500-year-old tree are priceless commodities . . . the real value of the outdoors lies in its vitality . . . the way it enhances our lives. When a sport program keeps a teenager away from drugs, when a neighborhood park offers a friendly

By helping young children realize the value of their own community, a leisure professional provides a social purpose.

Courtesy of San Jose Parks, Recreation and Neighborhood Services gathering place for older people, when families learn to appreciate each other on a camping trip, when a jogger adds years to his or her life, how do we place a price on it? The value is life itself. (as cited in Jordan, 1991, p. 367)

These types of arguments make a strong appeal for the intrinsic value of leisure and recreation in the outdoors, and a similar case could be made for music programs in a long-term care facility or a group of coworkers' participation in a softball league, just to name a few examples. However, although participation in recreation for its own sake is a laudable goal, what is it about leisure opportunities that makes them so valuable to the people who participate in them? And beyond the benefits to actual participants, could other benefits from these activities and facilities extend to the larger community or country? Some of the answers to these questions may arise from examining the field's professional mandate.

Our Professional Mandate

Groups of individuals usually earn the designation of a profession based on the important service they provide or the crucial role they play in society. For example, Sessoms (1992) notes that

> One of the characteristics of a profession is that it has a social mandate. That mandate is grounded in meeting a fundamental need of society, whether it be a concern for its health, system of justice, literacy, or quality of life. Without a mandate, there is no soul, no sense of purpose, no sustaining will, which attracts people to the cause. . . . (p. 47)

Although recognition of the value of leisure extends back to ancient Greece, the field's professional mandate has not always been clear. Plato advocated for children's involvement in leisure so that they could "grow up to be well-conducted and virtuous citizens" (1930), a notion not so dissimilar from later arguments for leisure's significance. Even the Puritans of the 1600s, famous for their work ethic, tolerated purposeful recreation on Sunday if it contributed to their health and vitality during the workweek (Cross, 1990). More modern accounts of leisure's roots begin in the early 1900's with the Playground Movement and its emphasis on children's play as the basis for moral and healthy development. Still others around that same time fought for the creation of urban park spaces, such as New York's Central Park and Nova Scotia's Halifax Common, as sanctuaries in the growing cities. In more recent times, there has been greater recognition of the economic contributions of recreation and leisure, such as its ability to stimulate tourism and its contributions to making communities more attractive to businesses and their employees (Crompton, 1999). In summary, several theoretical contributions of leisure have been identified over the years, but to many, a precise professional mandate has yet to be defined. Although different opinions exist about the role recreation and leisure should play in society, efforts to demonstrate the field's significance have improved dramatically in recent years. This is the focus of the next section.

Benefits Approach to Leisure

Starting in the late 1980s, researchers and managers began to recognize the need to better document and communicate the benefits of parks, recreation, and leisure services and amenities. The various efforts have been subsumed under the mantra of the **benefits approach to leisure** (Driver & Bruns, 1999). In Canada, the charge was led by the Parks and Recreation Federation of Ontario (1992), which published its catalogue titled *The Benefits of Parks and Recreation*. In the United States, Dr. Bev Driver and associates coordinated a conference of researchers and professionals that culminated in the book *Benefits of Leisure* (Driver, Brown, & Peterson, 1991), which contained 21 "state-of-knowledge" chapters on the positive impacts of leisure. Although there may be other contributions that could be added, the extensive list in Figure 18.1 represents the most complete and up-to-date compilation of the personal, psychological, physiological, social and cultural, economic, and environmental benefits attributed to leisure in various publications.

It has been argued that the benefits approach to leisure (BAL) "is not only a *philosophy* about the roles of leisure in society and how leisure service delivery systems should be managed, but also a *system* for directing leisure research, instruction, policy development, and management" (Driver & Bruns, 1999, p. 349). In this view, the BAL is not just a way of thinking about and studying recreation and leisure, but it is also a practical tool designed to help researchers and managers advance our field of work and practice. Several reasons exist for adopting a benefits approach to guide the profession.

First, information about the outcomes of participation in various activities can help the people

I. Personal Benefits

  a. Psychological

    1. Better mental health and health maintenance
- Holistic sense of wellness
- Stress management (prevention, mediation, and restoration)
- Catharsis
- Prevention of and reduced depression, anxiety, and anger
- Positive changes in mood and emotion

    2. Personal development and growth
- Self-confidence
- Self-reliance
- Self-competence
- Self-assurance
- Value clarification
- Improved academic and cognitive performance
- Independence and autonomy
- Sense of control over one's life
- Humility
- Leadership
- Aesthetic enhancement
- Creativity enhancement
- Spiritual growth
- Adaptability
- Cognitive efficiency
- Problem solving
- Nature learning
- Cultural and historic awareness, learning, and appreciation
- Environmental awareness and understanding
- Tolerance
- Balanced competitiveness
- Balanced living
- Prevention of problems to at-risk youth
- Acceptance of one's responsibility

    3. Personal appreciation and satisfaction
- Sense of freedom
- Self-actualization
- Flow and absorption
- Exhilaration
- Stimulation
- Sense of adventure
- Challenge
- Nostalgia
- Quality of life and/or life satisfaction

FIGURE 18.1 Positive outcomes attributed to parks, recreation, and leisure.

Reprinted, by permission, from B.L. Driver and D.H. Burns, 1999, Concepts and uses of the benefits approach to leisure. In *Prospects for the twenty-first century* (State College, PA: Venture Publishing), 352-353.

- Creative expression
- Aesthetic appreciation
- Nature appreciation
- Spirituality
- Positive change in mood or emotion

  b. Psychophysiological
    1. Cardiovascular benefits, including prevention of strokes
    2. Reduced or prevented hypertension
    3. Reduced serum cholesterol and triglycerides
    4. Improved control and prevention of diabetes
    5. Prevention of colon cancer
    6. Reduced spinal problems
    7. Decreased body fat and obesity and/or weight control
    8. Improved neuropsychological functioning
    9. Increased bone mass and strength in children
    10. Increased muscle strength and better connective tissue
    11. Respiratory benefits (increased lung capacity, benefits to people with asthma)
    12. Reduced incidence of disease
    13. Improved bladder control of elderly
    14. Increased life expectancy
    15. Management of menstrual cycles
    16. Management of arthritis
    17. Improved functioning of the immune system
    18. Reduced consumption of alcohol and use of tobacco

II. Social and Cultural Benefits
  a. Community satisfaction
  b. Pride in community and nation (pride in place and patriotism)
  c. Cultural and historical awareness and appreciation
  d. Reduced social alienation
  e. Community and political involvement
  f. Ethnic identity
  g. Social bonding, cohesion, and cooperation
  h. Conflict resolution and harmony
  i. Greater community involvement in environmental decision making
  j. Social support
  k. Support democratic ideal of freedom
  l. Family bonding
  m. Reciprocity and sharing
  n. Social mobility
  o. Community integration
  p. Nurturance of others
  q. Understanding and tolerance of others

FIGURE 18.1 *(continued)*

r. Environmental awareness, sensitivity

s. Enhanced world view

t. Socialization and acculturation

u. Cultural identity

v. Cultural continuity

w. Prevention of social problems by at-risk youth

x. Developmental benefits of children

III. Economic Benefits

a. Reduced health costs

b. Increased productivity

c. Less work absenteeism

d. Reduced on-the-job accidents

e. Decreased job turnover

f. International balance of payments (from tourism)

g. Local and regional economic growth

h. Contributions to net national economic development

IV. Environmental Benefits

a. Maintenance of physical facilities

b. Stewardship and preservation of options

c. Husbandry and improved relationships with natural world

d. Understanding of human dependency on the natural world

e. Environmental ethic

f. Public involvement in environmental issues

g. Environmental protection

1. Ecosystem sustainability

2. Species diversity

3. Maintenance of natural scientific laboratories

4. Preservation of particular natural sites and areas

5. Preservation of cultural, heritage, and historic sites and areas

FIGURE 18.1   *(continued)*

we serve to make informed decisions about their leisure choices. For example, knowing that participation in baseball improves eye–hand coordination and hockey is associated more with cardiovascular fitness may help parents decide which activity is right for their child. Second, benefits research helps managers to educate policy makers and the general public about the value of their services and, if necessary, to defend their programs and employees from budget cuts. Third, documenting leisure benefits for legislators provides them with information on which they can base funding decisions. In the absence of information on the positive impacts of leisure for individuals and the community, politicians have little motivation or justification to allocate more public resources to parks and recreation concerns.

Another rationale for adopting the benefits approach is its consistency with a marketing orientation, which has been embraced by many recreation organizations over the past 20 years. Recreation and leisure services marketing is centered on identifying the needs of participants and segmenting them into groups so that these needs might be fulfilled efficiently and effectively. According to most marketing scholars, the primary variable in segmenting is the "benefits sought" by participants (Crompton & Lamb, 1986; Kotler, 2000). To effectively meet people's needs, we need to know which leisure pursuits provide the benefits they seek. In this way, the benefits approach provides a useful vehicle for facilitating successful marketing efforts.

Although our understanding of leisure's value to individuals and communities has drastically increased in recent times, we should not be fooled into thinking that the benefits of recreation are infinite. Although the list in figure 18.1 may look long, it would be unrealistic to suggest that, in any one locale, all of the outcomes can be achieved through leisure. Indeed, some advocates have suggested that parks and recreation agencies will gain greater public support by clearly "positioning" their services to focus on the specific issues that are important to the people in their local communities (Crompton, 1993). Moreover, the outcomes of our programs and services are not always positive. In our push to promote health and fitness, some participants have taken the message too far and have turned to steroids and other harmful substances to enhance their body and their performance. Similarly, excessive exercising and eating disorders may be two of the negative by-products of recreation activities that reinforce body image issues, especially among women (Shaw, 1991). Outwardly fun activities, such as mountain biking and snowmobiling, are pursued without sufficient consideration for the environmental degradation they might cause. As Dustin, McAvoy, and Schultz (1990) caution, the search for pleasure and other benefits of recreation experiences must be balanced with preserving the natural environment and protecting our collective health. In addition, some have argued that focusing on the benefits reduces leisure to its instrumental value, thereby implying that leisure in and of itself is less valuable than the outcomes it produces (Hemingway & Parr, 2000). This goes against the basic tenets of leisure proposed by the ancient Greeks: that leisure is valuable for its own sake and that when it is used to serve some other purpose, it ceases to be leisure.

PUBLIC RECOGNITION

The previous section described the numerous positive impacts of parks, recreation, and leisure services, and therefore, you might tentatively conclude that our field has significant social value and purpose in today's society. A second indicator of a field's level of professionalism is the level of public recognition it receives. Unfortunately, it appears that recreation and leisure does not rate as highly on this criterion. As Driver and Bruns (1999) stated, "Obviously there is a paradox: while leisure is the leading economic sector and the most important social service sector, the scope and magnitude of the benefits of leisure are not recognized and appreciated" (p. 351). These same authors note that, at the start of the 21st century, neither Canada nor the United States had federal policies to "broadly recognize, protect, and promote leisure as a significant business and social service." This provides some indication of our inability to convince the general population of leisure's significance. Although we have tended to focus on only the public sector when gauging our field's public recognition level, the conclusions of research in this area suggest that much remains to be done to improve our image.

However, the news may not be all bad. In one national U.S. telephone survey, more than 60 percent of respondents said that their community benefited "a great deal" from local parks (Godbey, Graefe, & James, 1993). It was found that the personal and social benefits, such as getting to know people and community awareness, accruing from recreation programs provided by local governments were perceived to be high. What is discouraging, however, is that economic and environmental benefits were mentioned much less frequently. Therefore, although our field is viewed positively for its contributions to personal and community wellness, in the many communities where economic or environmental concerns are more prominent on the public agenda, the importance afforded to parks and recreation services may be disturbingly low.

A different way of measuring public recognition is to look at the size of a public service area's budget. In a municipality, for example, all of the available funds from property taxes, parking tickets, and other user fees are divided up each year by elected officials and are allocated to different departments in the city. If the "piece of the pie" that parks and recreation receives each year increases, we might infer that recognition of the importance of our services is improving. Indeed, Crompton and Kaczynski (2003) conducted an analysis using expenditure data for all local governments in the United States from 1964-65 to 1999-2000. They concluded that, "in the broad context of the United States as a whole, park and recreation interests have been relatively successful in fending off disproportionate cuts in their budgets in difficult times, but have been less successful in securing proportionate increases in budgets when economic conditions improve" (p. 133). Connolly and Smale (2001/2002) came to a similar conclusion in Canada. Overall, these data suggest that public parks and recreation are valued enough for their funding levels to be sustained but that when extra money is available, it is generally allocated to other departments in the city. This conclusion is somewhat encouraging, but it suggests that our level of public recognition is low relative to most other government services, and this does not bode well for our ability to augment our services or our impact on the community.

Potential Reasons for Recreation and Leisure's Poor Public Profile

That's not to say that the value of leisure and recreation is completely minimized in Canada and the United States. In the United States, July is National Recreation Month, which is declared by the president. Nevertheless, most people in the field would agree that the public's perception of recreation and leisure leaves something to be desired. At least four factors might help explain why this situation exists.

The first factor, and one you may have already encountered, is that recreation and leisure is sometimes disregarded as a serious area of study or employment. Far too often, people confuse the act of studying or working with the object of their study or work (Cooper, 1999). For example, just as all criminologists don't commit crimes as part of their job, most leisure services professionals don't get paid to play. The general public seldom recognizes the difficulty and complexity of managing facilities, preserving parkland, or creating quality leisure experiences. This confusion may result from a simple lack of awareness about our profession, and for that we may be as much to blame as anyone. Indeed, in a study done with university recreation students about the field's public perception problem (McChesney, Everett, & Gerkin, 2002), one student commented, "it is *our* responsibility to inform the public about what we do and the importance of recreation that directly impacts their quality of life" (p. 53, emphasis added).

A second factor is that hard facts about the benefits of parks and recreation to society are hard to come by. In contrast, medical personnel make a rather concrete contribution, saving lives, and so they are afforded our respect and an almost unquestioned professional status. As you have seen, however, leisure services can also provide substantial benefits to individuals and communities. The problem is that the social merits of leisure are often not adequately articulated to the general public and decision makers. Instead, organizations too often resort to declaring how many people swim in their pools or how many acres of parkland they manage, rather than focusing on the positive outcomes that these resources produce (Driver & Bruns, 1999). Advances in our understanding of marketing and the benefits approach to leisure have helped to combat this inward-looking mentality, but much work remains to be done in increasing the general public's awareness of the impacts of our field.

A third and related factor surrounds the professional mandate for our field. Although the previous section described numerous benefits that parks and recreation can confer, for most established professions that have solidified an image and reputation among the general public, the list of their contributions would likely be more defined. The diversity of backgrounds and mandates has enabled us to affect multiple areas of social and economic concern in society, but it may also serve to create a complicated or fuzzy image of the field, especially among people who do not regularly use our services.

A final factor (though there are undoubtedly others) is the emphasis placed on work in North American society. It is revealing that when people first meet at parties, they usually initially introduce themselves according to their area of employment. Although the remainder of the conversation may center on common leisure interests, this small example is representative of our society's work-first orientation, which likely is a remnant of the Protestant work ethic.

Efforts to Improve the Public's Perception of Recreation and Leisure

Several steps are being taken to improve the way the public views our field. First and foremost, there is greater awareness of the need for even more research on the positive contributions that our programs and facilities make to individuals and communities. And it is not only professors who bear the responsibility for exploring the benefits of parks, recreation, and leisure services. Recreation professionals, too, are challenged with not only delivering services but also with documenting and communicating the outcomes of their efforts.

Some have suggested that economic arguments will resonate more with policy makers, but it seems that any rigorous outcome-related research will help to further advance public recognition of the benefits of leisure.

Another advancement in the efforts to raise recreation and leisure's public profile is the idea of **repositioning.** Repositioning is the process of changing the perceptions of stakeholders, such as citizens and elected officials, so that parks and recreation is perceived to be a significant contributor to important community concerns (Kaczynski & Crompton, 2004b). In that sense, repositioning focuses primarily on the community-wide outcomes produced by leisure services in order that even nonparticipants will better understand how they benefit from having their tax dollars invested in leisure programs and facilities. Advocates of repositioning suggest that a parks and recreation department cannot and should not attempt to convince the public and politicians that it provides all of the benefits described in the previous section. Instead it should focus its efforts and resources on affecting only a select set of community issues that are most important to the people it serves (Kaczynski & Crompton, 2004a). For example, if high numbers of at-risk youth are a concern in the community, the local parks and recreation department may be wise to adopt youth development and crime prevention as its "position." As efforts in the area of the benefits approach and repositioning continue to improve, recognition of the social and economic value of leisure services should also continue to grow.

SPECIALIZED PROFESSIONAL PREPARATION

Another characteristic of a profession is that its members have completed specialized, formal education and training through an **academic discipline.** A historical examination of our profession reveals that our roots are diverse. Recreation professionals generally trace their history to the appalling conditions that faced working adults and their children as the United States and Canada became more industrialized and urbanized. Likewise, our interest in parks and protected areas evolved as a direct result of the environmental degradation that accompanied industrialization and urbanization. Along the same lines, profound changes related to working hours, life span, income, and technology spurred the growth of the tourism industry. Some of those same changes, coupled with evolving political policy and religious movements, paved the way for participation in organized sport and made sport spectatorship more socially acceptable (Cross, 1990).

Not surprisingly, therefore, recreation and leisure studies are multidisciplinary in nature. Our parent disciplines include psychology, sociology, geography, economics, planning, philosophy, political science, history, marketing, and management science. There is no single appropriate "home" for a recreation and leisure studies program within a college or university setting. That said, most of our academic programs can trace their roots to one of three basic areas. Most recreation and leisure programs evolved from broader physical education programs, whereas outdoor recreation evolved from broader forestry and resource development programs, and many tourism and sport management programs reflect the growing specialization occurring in business-based education.

On the surface, college and university programs in recreation and leisure studies may seem old and well established. Sessoms and Henderson (1994) stated that "as early as 1911, short courses and training manuals for instruction of playground workers were being prepared" (p. 295). Specialized education in recreation, at the university level, was offered by Harvard University in 1912. From the mid-1920s to the mid-1930s, the National Recreation Association offered a nine-month, postgraduate course in recreation, but no special college degree was granted upon completing the course. Michigan State College (now University) offered parks management courses within its forestry curriculum in 1935. In 1937, the first College Conference on Training Recreation Leaders was convened at the University of Minnesota. This and later conferences focused on curriculum development and establishment of recreation as a major course of study at institutions of higher education.

The first independent undergraduate program in parks and recreation was established at the University of Minnesota in 1937 (Dustin & Goodale, 1999). The University of Illinois pioneered graduate studies in recreation by offering its first course in 1939 and establishing a master of science degree in 1953 (Sapora, 1996). By 1960, 62 American colleges and universities had recreation and leisure programs (Sessoms, 1961). In Canada, undergraduate leisure studies–related courses were offered at Western Ontario University and the University of Toronto in the 1940s, but neither program exists today. A recreation curriculum was developed at the University of British Columbia in 1954 (McFarland, 1970). Programs at the University of Ottawa and the University of Waterloo, both founded in 1968, have served as the model for many of the contemporary Canadian university leisure studies programs (Karlis, 2004).

The greatest growth to date in the establishment of recreation and leisure studies programs occurred in the 1960s and 1970s (Sessoms & Henderson, 1994). By 1980 more than 400 university and college recreation and leisure studies programs were operating in North America, but that number dropped to approximately 260 by 1990 (Society of Park and Recreation Educators [SPRE], 1992). As of 2003, 115 American programs and 3 Canadian programs were accredited by the National Park and Recreation Association (NRPA) in the United States. In addition, there are more than 125 master's programs and more than 20 doctoral programs (Houghton, 2002). Traditionally, less than half of the existing programs have been accredited, so it seems likely that there are more than 300 undergraduate programs in existence. The number of actual programs is difficult to determine and is relatively fluid because our roots are diverse and because programs are constantly being added, merged, and eliminated. For example, Karlis (2004) noted that Canada alone had 30 universities and 40 community colleges with some form of recreation or leisure studies program. However, only three of those programs were included in the aforementioned Society of Park and Recreation Educators catalogue.

In terms of student numbers, the 118 recreation and leisure programs listed in the SPRE catalogue (2002-2003) enrolled more than 16,000 undergraduates, more than 1,600 master's students, and about 300 doctoral students. As noted, these numbers substantially underestimate the number of students studying leisure, recreation, and allied disciplines because only a fraction of existing North American programs are accredited by NRPA. For example, relatively few of those focusing on tourism and sport management are represented on this list. Although the number of students seems large, it is not overwhelming relative to the thousands of professional positions in the public, nonprofit, and commercial sector agencies, organizations, and businesses in our field.

Although there is substantial evidence that this is a maturing discipline in terms of both the number of academic programs and the amount and quality of specialized knowledge that they produce, the relative volatility of the number of academic programs also suggests that recreation and leisure studies have not yet reached the professional or disciplinary stature of some fields.

Some examples of high-profile North American recreation and leisure studies programs that have been eliminated from their respective campuses in recent years include those at the University of Maryland, the University of Oregon, and the University of North Carolina. In the first two cases, programs at the bachelor's, master's, and doctoral level were lost. Many programs have changed names or focus or both because of mergers or various external administrative pressures or threats. Many others have changed their names for more positive reasons, such as repositioning themselves to better reflect their changing roles as envisioned by the faculty, students, and graduates of the program.

Community college programs are normally two years long, preparing graduates primarily for entry-level and frontline positions. As a general rule, it is easier to transfer credits from community colleges into universities in the United States than it is in Canada. The systems in the United States are normally set up to allow relatively seamless transitions, whereas the Canadian college and university systems have historically been more distinct. Most four-year undergraduate programs provide a broad liberal education with a goal of producing generalists. The National Curriculum Conference on Parks and Recreation held in Salt Lake City, Utah, in 1997 concluded that the highest priority for undergraduate university education in recreation and parks was to graduate a "well-educated" person. Specifically, the conference report noted the following:

> The aims of this education are traditionally found in liberal education with depth and breath [sic], which encourages students to acquire a solid grasp of one subject, and a broad exposure to a variety of other fields. . . . It is centered in the humanities, social sciences, and natural sciences. Specific learning should result from studies in literature and the arts, history, social analysis, moral reasoning, biological sciences, physical sciences, behavioral sciences and diverse and foreign cultures. (National Curriculum Conference, 1997, p. 23)

By contrast, a master's program usually takes one to two years to complete and focuses on "leisure concepts and philosophy, applied research, and preparing professionals for the eventuality of becoming mid-level managers in a specialty area within the field" (p. 27). Finally, doctoral programs, which usually take three to four years to complete, emphasize research and broad philosophical understanding of the discipline. Doctoral degrees normally lead to academic positions at the university level or to research-oriented positions in government or the private sector.

Numerous authors have, over the years, critiqued the state of our academic programs. For example, Burdge (1985) argued that the tension between the relatively theoretical emphasis of leisure studies and the relatively applied emphasis of the recreation profession would make long-term union untenable. His prediction has not, to date, come to pass. Nevertheless, he articulated concerns that have shadowed our professional development since the field's inception. Reflecting on the origins of our profession and on the developments of, especially, the latter part of the 20th century, Dustin and Goodale (1999) discussed more than a half dozen major challenges facing higher education related to leisure studies. They challenged the fragmentation of the field, cautioned against overemphasis on practical application at the expense of broader theoretical understanding, and criticized the bottom-line mentality currently driving many decisions. They concluded by championing the "cultivation of socially responsible" graduates as a potential unifying principle of our diverse programs, and stated that "when we do our best work we lift people up and out of their self-absorption to reveal the beauty, complexity, and mystery of the larger world" (p. 485).

A professional's success in the field depends upon the published knowledge developed as part of the profession.

SPECIALIZED BODY OF KNOWLEDGE

Although more than 150 years of "professional" history exists in Canada and the United States, the published knowledge related to our understanding of leisure and parks and recreation management was, before 1960, not extensive. It was limited to a small number of textbooks, a few professional magazines, and sporadically published proceedings from various research symposia.

Most of the professional magazines in our field began publication in the early to middle part of the 20th century (see table 18.2). Perhaps the most common type of article published in professional magazines are case studies wherein a professional describes how a particular agency deals with a challenging issue or how they develop programming to meet a specific need. Also common are summary papers that synthesize existing mate-

rial on a particular topic. For example, articles might summarize what we know about leisure constraints, pricing strategies for recreation facilities, or park design. Professional magazine articles normally are just a couple of pages long. They normally do not include discussion of the theory or research method supporting the article, how the data (if any) were collected, and whether the case in question is similar to circumstances in other places or contexts. The articles in professional journals are normally edited for style and length but are not usually externally critiqued on the basis of content.

Buoyed by unprecedented levels of demand for various leisure services, increasingly organized professional organizations, and by the growing number of college and university academic programs that support the field calls for more systematic "scientific" inquiry into leisure and

TABLE 18.2   Selected English Language Leisure and Recreation Professional Magazines

Name of journal	Published in	Published since
Journal of Physical Education, Recreation and Dance	United States	1931
Parks and Recreation Canada	Canada	1943
World Leisure and Recreation Journal	Canada	1958
Parks and Recreation Magazine	United States	1965 (1902)
Parks and Recreation Business	United States	2001

recreation behavior became common. Within this era, 1962 represented a watershed year because the report of the Outdoor Recreation Resources Review Commission (ORRRC) was published in the United States. This commission, created by an act of Congress in 1958, was charged with answering three questions:

1. What are the recreation wants and needs of the American people now, and what will they be in the years 1976 and 2000?

2. What recreation resources of the nation are available to fill those needs?

3. What policies and programs should be recommended to ensure that the needs of the present and future are adequately and efficiently met? (ORRRC, 1962, p. iii)

The ORRRC reports produced, for the first time, a relatively comprehensive inventory of organized recreation activity. Although much of the material included in the ORRRC reports was generated by scholars at colleges and universities, primary responsibility for producing ongoing data of this type has been borne by government agencies, especially at the state and provincial level. Academic research, by contrast, evolved rather rapidly to focus on "why, what, and how" type questions: Why do men participate more frequently in a particular activity than do women? What is the maximum number of visitors this national park site can hold before quality of experience begins to decline because of overcrowding? How do flow experiences and leisure satisfaction impact well-being? How do recent immigrants to Canada define leisure compared to those from the dominant Anglophone and Francophone cultures?

It is not surprising, therefore, that the vast majority of scientific inquiry into leisure, sport, tourism, and recreation has occurred since 1960. The number of academic journals, professional magazines, and professional books has expanded exponentially in the last 45 years. Although not intended to be a comprehensive inventory, tables 18.3 and 18.4 list some of the research journals most commonly referenced by North American leisure services professionals. One noticeable fact emerging from these figures is that all of the journals commenced publication after 1965. Although the 1960s may seem like ancient history to someone who wasn't born until the 1980s or 1990s, it is sobering to consider that little of the academic literature related to our profession is more than 35 years old and that virtually all of it has been created in the lifetimes of the parents of most contemporary university students. Imagine that you are a leisure services professional, perhaps not yet retired when this textbook was published, who completed a bachelor's degree in 1968. Only one of the research journals listed in these figures even existed during your undergraduate career! This is one noticeable difference between the leisure services profession and others based on older disciplines such as accounting, medicine, physics, chemistry, biology, and the like. Each of those professions can trace scholarly literature back for hundreds of years.

Research journals are critical to a profession's development because "new" knowledge is usually first published in academic journals. The research presented therein is rigorously planned, theories are considered and developed, questions are carefully crafted, and data meticulously collected and rigorously analyzed. Submitted papers normally go through a "double-blind" peer review process. This means that, before papers appear in print, they are critiqued by several other professionals but that the reviewers do not know who wrote the paper and the author or authors do not know who reviewed the paper. This represents one way that academic journals maintain their credibility. Indeed, it is not uncommon for certain journals to reject more than

TABLE 18.3   Selected English and French Language Leisure and Recreation Research Journals

Name of journal	Published in	Published since
GENERAL LEISURE		
Journal of Leisure Research	United States	1969
Leisure/loisir (formerly JARR)	Canada	1999 (1971)
Leisure Sciences	United States	1977
Loisir & Société (Society & Leisure)	Canada	1978
Leisure Studies	United Kingdom	1982
THERAPEUTIC RECREATION		
Therapeutic Recreation Journal	United States	1967
Leisurability	Canada	1974*
Annual in Therapeutic Recreation	United States	1990
RECREATION AND SPORT MANAGEMENT		
Journal of Park & Recreation Administration	United States	1983
Journal of Sport Management	United States	1987
Managing Leisure	United Kingdom	1995
Sport Marketing Quarterly	United States	1992
Sport Management Review	Australia	1998

* Ceased publication in 2000.

TABLE 18.4   Selected English Language Tourism, Parks, and Resource Management Research Journals

Name of journal	Published in	Published since
TOURISM		
Annals of Tourism Research	United States, United Kingdom, Korea, Japan	1974
Journal of Travel Research	United States	1962
Journal of Travel and Tourism Marketing	United States	1992
Journal of Hospitality and Leisure Marketing	United States	1994
Tourism Analysis	United States, Germany	1997
International Journal of Hospitality & Tourism Administration	United States	2000
PARK AND RESOURCE MANAGEMENT		
Journal of Environmental Psychology	Netherlands, United Kingdom, United States, Japan, Singapore	1981
Society and Natural Resources	United States	1988
Biodiversity and Conservation	United Kingdom	1992
Sustainable Tourism	United Kingdom	1993
Journal of Ecotourism	United Kingdom, Canada	2002

half of the papers that they receive! It often takes at least a year or two for a researcher to bring an idea from the conception stage, through data collection, analysis, and write-up before he or she sees the research paper in print.

Books allow space for a more thorough exploration of specific issues than do professional magazine articles or academic journal papers. The number of recreation, leisure, sport, and tourism textbooks has also grown exponentially in recent years (figure 18.2). In addition to our professional organizations, at least two independent North American publishers, Sagamore and Venture, focus exclusively or primarily on leisure- and recreation-related topics. Other independent publishers, such as Human Kinetics, Waveland, Allyn & Bacon, Idyll Arbor, and George Allen & Unwin, have fairly large recreation and leisure divisions, and still other companies publish recreation texts from time to time. It is important to recognize, however, that information in books is often relatively dated compared to information in professional magazines and academic journals. This is because book authors must synthesize information from multiple sources and because it normally takes a year or two to put together a book. Given the lead time necessary to produce primary sources of

information such as magazines and journals, much of the data in even the most current textbook are at least several years old.

There is some debate regarding what knowledge a leisure services professional has as a result of education, training, and experience that others do not possess. Several studies have attempted to identify the content of the knowledge base used by those employed in the field. However, the knowledge, skills, and abilities used by practitioners may not be exclusive to leisure services professionals. For example, Smale and Frisby (1992) surveyed more than 500 Ontarian municipal recreation managers and produced a list of managerial functions based on four traditional categories—planning, organizing, influencing, and controlling—that are relevant to our field but are quite similar to those mentioned by professionals in an entirely different profession. Similarly, a study by Hammersley and Tynon (1998) analyzed the job competencies required of entry-level resort and commercial recreation professionals. They found the following competencies to be most important: communication; leadership; guest services; programming; supervision; regulations, rules, and standards; promotion and publicity; maintenance; and retail operations. These were similar to competencies required of public parks and recreation employees but with a greater emphasis on guest services and retail operations. Other studies of recreational sport and sport management competencies also reveal a strong emphasis on business and management competencies. In the end, the unique component of leisure services professionals' education may be a thorough understanding of recreational activities and program areas, including, and perhaps most important, the value and benefits of leisure for individuals, communities, and the environment (Dustin & Goodale, 1999; Schreyer & Driver, 1989).

FIGURE 18.2 The volume of published work in our profession is now sufficient to keep a professional library well stocked with current material.

QUALITY ASSURANCE THROUGH ACCREDITATION, CERTIFICATION, AND PROFESSIONAL ASSOCIATIONS

Professional status and professionalism are associated with high quality. When we hire a professional to do a job, we expect quality because of the person's expertise and experience. Members of a profession work together to establish a standard of quality that will communicate to the public at large and members of the profession what is, or can be, expected from individuals and agencies providing leisure services. Accreditation and certification are formal processes of quality assurance and are discussed in the following sections.

Accreditation

Accreditation is a process whereby an agency's ability to provide quality, standardized services is evaluated. Those agencies or service providers meeting the standard earn accredited status. According to the National Recreation and Park Association (NRPA), accreditation of curricula in parks, recreation, and leisure serves to assure academic program quality and to provide a means of self-study and evaluation by external reviewers (academicians and practitioners) in order to facilitate improvement (www.nrpa.org). Although graduation from an accredited program cannot guarantee the quality of any one person, it does provide some assurance for employers that the graduates have been exposed to a standardized body of knowledge.

Currently, academic degree programs in recreation, parks, and leisure services are eligible to apply for accreditation through the American Association for Leisure and Recreation's Council on Accreditation, which is sponsored by the National Recreation and Park Association. The accreditation status is awarded based, in part, on a program's core curriculum required of all majors. In addition, an academic program may seek accreditation status for one or more of the following subspecialties: leisure services management, natural resources, recreation management, leisure and recreation program delivery, and therapeutic recreation.

Academic programs in sport management at the undergraduate, master's, and doctoral levels in both the United States and Canada are reviewed and may be approved by the Sport Management Program Review Council (SMPRC). The council operates in conjunction with several professional organizations related to sport and physical activity including the American Alliance for Physical Education, Recreation and Dance (AAPHERD), the National Association for Sport and Physical Education (NASPE), and the North American Society for Sport Management (NASSM). At the time of this writing, there are no existing accreditation standards for academic programs in travel and tourism or resort and commercial recreation.

Certification

Certification is usually granted by a professional organization representing the field to individual practitioners who meet or exceed standards of performance. Common purposes of certification, regardless of the professional specialty, are to recognize qualified professionals, to raise the status of the given profession, and to establish high performance standards for its practitioners. Currently, certification in most branches of leisure services is voluntary and serves to communicate to employers and the general public the commitment on the part of the individual to upholding the values of the profession. However, to practice therapeutic recreation, certification is almost always a required qualification for employment.

To become certified, a candidate must submit his or her credentials to the governing body including documentation of specialized education, practical experience, and in some cases, passage of a certification examination. NRPA grants the following certifications: certified park and recreation professional (CPRP), provisional park and recreation professional (PPRP), and associate park and recreation professional (APRP). More information about qualifications and the application procedure can be found at NRPA's Web site: www.nrpa.org. The Resort and Commercial Recreation Association (RCRA) and the Employee Services Management (ESM) Association also offer certification programs.

Professional Organizations

A professional organization or association represents practitioners working in a given field. "Professionals" may be members of the profession by virtue of their employment status. That is, they serve clients through the agency they work for in an exemplary fashion. In addition, they may be members of a group of professionals. The purpose of the "group" is to serve the profession itself. An association serves the profession in two ways: professional development of its members and communication to the general public (including citizens and politicians at the national, state, provincial, regional, and local levels) of the value of the services provided by its members. This is accomplished through any or all of the following activities: sharing information among members regarding best practices, providing continuing education opportunities, facilitating

Meeting with peers is an essential aspect of professional development.

the generation and sharing of new knowledge in the field, providing program resources, setting standards of quality, and evaluating agencies and practitioners against those standards (accreditation and certification). These activities are usually accomplished through Web sites, e-mail listserves, conferences, and publications such as magazines and journals. Many national organizations also have state or provincial chapters. For example, the Ohio Parks and Recreation Association and Michigan Recreation and Park Association are affiliated with the National Recreation and Park Association. Likewise, the Recreation Nova Scotia and Parks and Recreation Ontario are associated with the Canadian Parks and Recreation Association. Table 18.5 provides a partial list of professional and honorary associations related to recreation, parks, and leisure services.

PROFESSIONAL CODE OF ETHICS

Another component of professional status is a code of ethical practice, or **code of ethics.** "Ethic," in its simplest form, means "the right thing." So to behave in an ethical manner is to "do the right thing," thus conforming to some moral standard. The standards by which actions are judged to be right or wrong are products of both individual and cultural morals and values. We often hear

of a person who has a "strong work ethic." This implies that the person believes in and puts into practice the notion that hard work is "the right thing to do"; it is valued and desirable, and will lead to certain rewards both for the individual and the community. Less common, but perhaps just as important, is a "strong leisure ethic."

As was pointed out in earlier chapters, freedom is a major component of the leisure experience. Leisure activities are freely chosen, during time that is relatively free from obligation, and allow a person to freely express his or her identity. What is lacking in this definition is any sort of moral or ethical component. Choosing among available opportunities and choosing what is right are not always the same thing. For example, two teenagers have chosen to participate in two different activities and they both experience a sense of accomplishment, exhilaration, enjoyment, and social acceptance. This sounds good, until we learn that one teenager is spray painting graffiti on picnic tables in the park and the other is participating in a soccer match. Which teenager is "doing the right thing"? What are the criteria used for judging either of these activities to be right or wrong? As a leisure services professional, you may be asked to make these kinds of judgments when deciding what kind of services to offer, to whom, when, and where.

Because of differences in the values of various constituent groups, the absence of a moral

TABLE 18.5 Partial List of Professional and Honorary Associations Related to Recreation, Parks, and Leisure Services

Association acronym	Association name	Web site
ALS	The Academy of Leisure Sciences	www.academyofleisuresciences.org
AALR	American Association for Leisure and Recreation	www.aahperd.org/aalr/template.cfm?template=main.html
AAPHERD	American Alliance for Physical Education, Recreation and Dance	www.aapherd.org
AAPRA	American Academy for Park and Recreation Administration	www.rpts.tamu.edu/AAPRA
ACA	American Camping Association	www.acacamps.org
ACUI	Association of College Unions International	www.acui.org
ANZALS	Australian and New Zealand Association for Leisure Studies	www.staff.vu.edu.au/anzals
ATRA	American Therapeutic Recreation Association	www.atra-tr.org
CALS	Canadian Association for Leisure Studies	www.eas.ualberta.ca/elj/cals/home.htm
CPRA	Canadian Parks and Recreation Association	www.cpra.ca
ESM	Employee Services Management Association	www.esmassn.org
IAAM	International Association of Assembly Managers	www.iaam.org
IFEA	International Festivals and Events Association	www.ifea.com
NASPE	National Association for Sport and Physical Education	www.aahperd.org/naspe/template.cfm
NASSM	The North American Society for Sport Management	www.nassm.com
NIRSA	National Intramural-Recreational Sports Association	www.nirsa.org
NRPA	National Recreation and Park Association	www.nrpa.org
NRPA Branches	AFRS—Armed Forces Recreation Society	
	APRS—American Park and Recreation Society	
	CB—Citizen Branch	
	NAB—National Aquatic Branch	
	NSPR—National Society for Park Resources	
	NTRS—National Therapeutic Recreation Society	
	SPRE—Society of Park and Recreation Educators	
	SB—Student Branch	
NRPA Sections	CRTS—Commercial Recreation and Tourism Section	
	LAS—Leisure and Aging Section	
RCRA	The Resort and Commercial Recreation Association	www.r-c-r-a.org
TIA	Travel Industry Association of America	www.tia.org
TTRA	Travel and Tourism Research Association	www.ttra.com
WLRA	World Leisure and Recreation Association	www.worldleisure.org

or ethical component in a definition of leisure may create challenges for agencies charged with providing recreational activities that promote the well-being of individuals, communities, and the environment. For example, outdoor resource managers may have to formulate policies that allow snowmobilers to coexist with cross-country skiers, while preserving the natural environment from overuse by both groups. Whenever decisions about right and wrong are to be made, values come into play. Individuals consider their personal values and the dominant cultural values to which they ascribe when making decisions about their actions, including leisure. But the larger questions are who decides what is to be considered right and wrong? Which groups' values are accepted as the standards? How do parks, recreation, and leisure services professionals mediate among differing and sometimes conflicting standards?

Many professional groups adopt standards of ethical practice that serve as guidelines for "doing the right thing." For example, the American Medical Association, a professional group representing physicians, publishes and maintains the *Code of Medical Ethics*. As stated earlier, professional associations are charged with policing their members to ensure quality products and services. If a professional engages in unprofessional or unethical behavior, he or she risks being expelled from the professional association. In the medical professions, practitioners are legally required to be certified and licensed to practice, and so they also run the risk of losing their license and thus the ability to legally practice.

In the case of leisure services, with the exception of therapeutic recreation in the United States, there are no licensure requirements to practice. Currently, Utah is the only state that requires a license to practice therapeutic recreation. Practitioners in Utah who violate the standards of professional and ethical conduct are at risk of losing their license and thus the ability to practice in that state. However, most agencies do require therapeutic recreation specialists to be certified as a condition of employment. Although most professional associations related to leisure services have no power to limit the practice of unqualified individuals, many associations have adopted a code of ethics to communicate to its members and the public what the organization believes is the standard. These codes of ethics are developed by the associations' membership and represent their agreed upon values against which "right" and "wrong" may be judged.

For example, the National Therapeutic Recreation Society (NTRS) code of ethics is divided into six sections: obligation of professional virtue, obligation of the professional to the individual, obligation of the professional to other individuals and to society, obligation of the professional to colleagues, obligation of the professional to the profession, and obligation of the professional to society (Note: NTRS is a branch of the National Recreation and Park Association, and their entire code of ethics can be found via the NRPA Web site.) The National Recreation and Park Association asks its members to agree to the following:

- Adhere to the highest standards of integrity and honesty in all public and personal activities to inspire public confidence and trust
- Strive for personal and professional excellence and encourage the professional development of associates and students
- Strive for the highest standards of professional competence, fairness, impartiality, efficiency, effectiveness, and fiscal responsibility
- Avoid interest or activity that is in conflict with the performance of job responsibilities
- Promote the public interest and avoid personal gain or profit from the performance of job duties and responsibilities
- Support equal employment opportunities

Leisure services professionals are frequently faced with ethical decisions. The outcomes of recreation participation may be positive and beneficial for an individual but at the same time may be detrimental to the larger community, as in the example of the two teenagers previously mentioned. Sometimes leisure services professionals must make decisions based on the greatest good for the greatest number, while still protecting the rights and freedoms of individuals. A professional code of ethics can assist professionals in making these decisions, providing a consistent, high-quality, image of the parks, recreation, and leisure services profession.

SUMMARY

This chapter discusses what it means to be a member of a profession, a professional working in leisure services. Although leisure services may not meet the strict criteria of a profession along the lines of law or medicine, it is clear that both informal and formal processes are in place that will continue to enhance the status of parks, recreation, and leisure services. Opportunities to experience recreation, leisure, and play are critical to human development, and leisure services professionals are in a unique position to facilitate that development.

Six criteria were identified that define a profession, and the leisure services profession was measured against these criteria. Clearly, leisure services has the potential to contribute significant social value, although the general public does not always associate value with leisure services. Continued research and application of the benefits of leisure will most likely aid in enhancing the positive image of parks and recreation. The college- and university-based programs that train leisure services professionals have progressed over the last four decades. However, professional education in our discipline is still maturing relative to more established disciplines. The professional body of knowledge is constantly evolving and is reflected in the movement toward accreditation of agencies and academic programs and certification of practitioners. Overall, the reach of leisure services extends into multiple societal domains, but with this impact comes a great deal of responsibility for professionals in our field to act ethically and consider the impact of their actions on participants, the larger community, and the environment. Being a professional in leisure services can be challenging, but with that challenge comes the potential for an exciting and rewarding career.

APPENDIX

Accreditation Standards

STANDARDS FOR BACCALAUREATE PROGRAMS IN RECREATION, PARK RESOURCES, AND LEISURE SERVICES ESTABLISHED BY THE COUNCIL ON ACCREDITATION (COA)

The COA is co-sponsored by the National Recreation and Park Association (NRPA) and the American Association for Leisure and Recreation (AALR). The NPRA/AALR Council on Accreditation has established professional competencies for all students. The standards listed are ones the authors believe they have addressed in part in their chapters. The chapter numbers for each standard are in parentheses.

8.01 Understanding of the conceptual foundations of play, recreation, and leisure. (Chapters 1, 13, and 14)

8.02 Understanding of the significance of play, recreation, and leisure in contemporary society. (Chapters 1, 2, 3, 4, 15, and 16)

8.03 Understanding of the significance of play, recreation, and leisure throughout the life span. (Chapters 1, 3, 4, 13, and 15)

8.04 Understanding of the interrelationship between leisure behavior and the natural environment. (Chapters 6, 12, and 14)

8.05 Understanding of environmental ethics and its relationship to leisure behavior. (Chapter 16)

8.06 Understanding of the following as they relate to recreation, park resources, and leisure services: (Chapters 2, 7, 8, 10, 11, and 18)

8.06:01 History and development of the profession (Chapters 2, 6, 7, 8, 10, 11, 13, 16, and 18)

8.06:02 Professional organizations (Chapters 2, 6, 7, 8, 10, 15, 11, and 18)

8.06:03 Current issues and trends in the profession (Chapters 7, 8, 10, 11, 15, and 18)

8.07 Understanding of ethical principles and professionalism. (Chapters 3, 4, 7, 10, 11, and 18)

8.08 Understanding of the importance of maintaining professional competence and the available resources for professional development. (Chapters 7, 8, 10, 14, 11, and 18)

8.09 Understanding of the roles, interrelationships, and use of diverse delivery systems addressing recreation, park resources, and leisure. (Chapters 11 and 14)

8.10 Understanding of the importance of leisure service delivery systems for diverse populations. (Chapters 3, 4, and 11)

8.11 Understanding of inclusive practices as they apply to: (Chapters 7, 11, and 14)

8.11.01 Operating programs and services (Chapters 7, 8, 10, and 13)

8.12 Understanding of the roles, interrelationships, and use of diverse leisure delivery systems in promoting: (Chapter 7)

8.12.01 Community development (Chapter 7)

8.13 Understanding of the variety of programs and services to enhance individual, group, and community quality of life. (Chapters 7, 10, 11, 12, and 13)

8.14 Ability to implement the following principles and procedures related to program/event planning for individual, group, and community quality of life: (Chapters 11 and 12)

8.14:01 Assessment of needs (Chapter 10)

8.14:02 Development of outcome-oriented goals and objectives (Chapter 10)

8.14:03 Selection and coordination of programs, events, and resources (Chapter 10)

8.14:06 Implementation of programs/events (Chapter 10)

8.14:07 Evaluation of programs/events (Chapter 10)

8.15 Understanding of group dynamics and processes. (Chapter 11)

8.16 Ability to use various leadership techniques to enhance individual, group, and community experiences. (Chapters 10 and 14)

8.18 Understanding of the fundamental principles and procedures of management. (Chapter 7)

8.21 Understanding of the principles and procedures of budgeting and financial management. (Chapter 14)

8.25:05 Knowledge of the following principles and procedures of developing areas and facilities: operations and maintenance. (Chapter 16)

8.26 Understanding of the following related to recreation, park resources, and leisure services: (Chapter 18)

8.26:01 Legal foundations and the legislative process (Chapter 18)

7B.05 Understanding of the relationship of business, society, the environment, and the economy, including the role of the entrepreneur. (Chapter 6)

9B.01 Understanding of the history and development of natural resources recreation policies and their implications for recreation resources management. (Chapter 6)

9B.10 Understanding of the social, economic, cultural and environmental impacts associated with multiple uses of natural resources. (Chapter 6)

9D.01 Understanding of and ability to analyze and apply health care and therapeutic recreation delivery models, theories, and concepts. (Chapter 11)

9D.02 Understanding of the psychological, sociological, physiological, and historical significance of therapeutic recreation. (Chapter 11)

9D.06 Understanding of the role of the therapeutic recreation professional as an advocate for leisure and human rights and services for individuals with illnesses and disabilities. (Chapter 11)

9D.13 Understanding of and ability to apply leisure education content and techniques with individuals, families, and caregivers. (Chapter 11)

APPENDIX

Accreditation Standards

COMMISSION FOR ACCREDITATION OF PARK AND RECREATION AGENCIES

There are 155 minimal standards of excellence divided into 10 categories that are recognized by park and recreation professionals. The standards are a guide for agencies to gauge just how well the organization is performing. The standards listed are ones the authors of chapter 7, pages 109-130, believe they have addressed in their chapter.

1.1.1 Source of authority

1.1.1.1 Public authority/policy body

1.5 Relationships

1.5.2 Operational coordination and cooperation (agreements)

1.5.3 Interagency relationships with counterpart agencies (liaisons)

1.5.4.1 Public and social service agencies

1.5.4.2 Local government agencies

Reprinted with permission from the Commission for Accreditation of Park and Recreation Agencies sponsored by the National Recreation and Park Association and the American Academy of Park and Recreation Administrators.

Glossary

21st Century Community Learning Centers—Centers in schools or other community facilities that provide after-school and evening community education activities. These were funded through the United States federal government between 1996 and 2002.

academic discipline—A field of study. Leisure studies is often referred to as an interdisciplinary field because it is generally approached from a variety of disciplinary perspectives.

accountability—Being responsible for providing services that produce results as efficiently and effectively as possible.

accreditation—A process by which agencies or academic programs are certified as meeting particular standards.

adolescence—The ages 13 through 19 when people make the transition from childhood to adulthood. One of seven life stages.

adventure programming—A broad base of philosophies, theories, and leadership techniques used in the fields of outdoor leadership, experiential education, and adventure education.

adventure recreation—Outdoor activities that the participant perceives to include elements of danger and excitement.

adventure tourism—Travel behavior that includes organized or unstructured outdoor activities that the participant perceives to include elements of danger and excitement.

Air Command—The name for the Canadian air force.

amusement—Pleasure-seeking activity that Aristotle judged to be inferior to leisure.

arm's length provider—One of the five roles that governments can take in delivering public services; the government creates a special-purpose agency, such as a museum, that operates outside the regular apparatus of government.

arts and cultural sector—A large, heterogeneous set of individuals and organizations engaged in the creation, production, presentation, distribution, and preservation of and education about aesthetic, heritage, and entertainment activities, products, and artifacts (Wyszomirski, 2002).

arts—A wide variety of visual, performing, folk, and ethnic arts as well as specific sports, home economics, and horticultural practices (Arnold, 1976).

Athenian ideal—The well-rounded ideal of the ancient Greeks, which was a combination of soldier, athlete, artist, statesman, and philosopher.

athletic sports—Sport activities undertaken with the desire to achieve excellence.

benefits approach to leisure (BAL)—A philosophy about the roles of leisure in society and how leisure services delivery systems should be managed; a system for directing leisure research, instruction, policy development, and management.

benefits—Things that contribute to or enhance well-being.

biosphere reserves—A biosphere reserve is a designated geographic area where people exemplify various ways to sustain local economies and resource use while also conserving the biological diversity (biodiversity) found in different kinds of ecosystems. As of April 1999, there were 356 biosphere reserves in 90 countries.

building-centered setting—One of four settings for recreation and leisure services; examples include YMCA and YWCA facilities, Boys and Girls Clubs, athletic clubs, recreation centers, museums, and commercial businesses.

business plan—An outline of how a start-up business will receive and use fiscal resources to gain a profit over a projected period.

campus recreation—A program that uses diverse facilities and programs to promote the physical, emotional, and social growth of a college or university's students, faculty, and staff and sometimes community members by encouraging the development of lifelong skills and positive attitudes through recreational activities.

Canadian armed forces—A part of the Canadian Department of National Defense composed of three environmental commands: the Maritime, Land, and Air Commands.

Canadian Forces Personnel Support Agency—An organization that manages morale and welfare programs for the military community.

caste system—A system of classification in which social position is ascribed at birth.

cause-related marketing—A marketing approach in which businesses and charities, or causes, form a partnership to market an image, product, or service for mutual benefit. The charity receives a percentage of the sale as a donation; the business receives an image boost and often a significant increase in sales.

certification—A process by which practitioners are evaluated and judged to possess desired qualifications (such as particular knowledge, skills, and abilities).

certified therapeutic recreation specialist (CTRS)—An individual who has successfully met the requirements of the National Council for Therapeutic Recreation Certification (NCTRC), has been granted the CTRS credential, and maintains his or her certification in accordance with the regulations of NCTRC.

charities—The most readily identifiable form of nonprofits that represent diverse organizations that often serve the most vulnerable of populations for free or for reduced fees. Charities in the United States are organized under the 501(c) (3) Internal Revenue Service code.

charter boat—An entire boat that is rented and typically has six anglers or fewer, similar to a taxi, to go offshore fishing.

Christianity—A religious faith that follows the teachings of Jesus, laid out in the Bible.

class system—A system of classification in which social position is earned by wealth, power, and status.

client—A recipient of services.

closed group—The sponsoring sector consisting of unique groups, such as students of a college, employees of a specific industry, or members of a religion-affiliated organization.

club sports—Sport activities organized because of a common interest in a sport.

code of ethics—A set of principles or rules of conduct used by a group to guide practice.

cognitive abilities—One of three perspectives used by developmental psychologists to describe development. These abilities include thinking, reasoning, learning, memory, intelligence, and language.

cognitive mechanics—The "hardware" of the brain; the speed and accuracy of the processes involved in many cognitive abilities such as sensory input, attention, visual and motor memory, discrimination, comparison, and categorization.

cognitive pragmatics—The culturally based "software programs" of the mind; abilities such as reading and writing, language comprehension, educational qualifications, professional skills, and knowledge about the self and life skills.

commercial recreation and tourism—The businesses that provide recreation-related products and services by private enterprise for a fee with the long-term intention of being profitable.

commercialized public recreation—The businesses that provide recreation-related products and services by a government or nonprofit organization, with much or all of the costs covered by fees, charges, or other nontax revenues.

community education—A concept, philosophy, and practice that focus on community participation in planning, developing, and offering activities and programs that strengthen and benefit individuals, families, and communities.

community schools—Centers, located in school buildings, in which the community participates in planning, developing, and offering after-school and evening classes, events, and activities that benefit all members of the community.

consequence-based ethics—An ethical theory used to resolve moral dilemmas by weighing outcomes. Typically, consequence-based ethical analyses aim to maximize the greatest good for the greatest number of people.

conservation—Using natural resources such as trees, water, or rangeland in a wise, regulated, or planned manner so that it is not destroyed but can be used and renewed indefinitely.

correctional system—The treatment and rehabilitation of offenders through a program involving penal custody, parole, and probation.

cultural activity—People's behavior that reflects their arts and cultural interests.

culture—The knowledge and values shared by a social group.

deinstitutionalization—A process by which people with disabilities are moved from large hospitals and institutions back into the community.

delivery system—Refers to an organized set of work activities for the purpose of providing recreation programs and resources to clients. (The 4-H delivery system is implemented by the state extension service and usually has one regional professional staff member with a recreation degree or other relevant degree who assists volunteer adults with training and in organizing and developing youth club programs, special 4-H events, and county fair competitions.)

direct provider—One of the five roles that governments can take in delivering public services; the government department or agency develops and maintains leisure facilities, operates programs, and delivers services using public funds and public employees.

disability—A physical or mental impairment that substantially limits one or more life activities.

disengagement—A movement in the early 1900s in which Christian leaders believed that sport involvement conflicted with their faith and, therefore, disengaged from sport.

documentation—Written records of the actions taken by, for, and with the client; part of official and legal record of client services.

duty-based ethics—An ethical theory used to resolve moral dilemmas by determining what obligations must be satisfied.

early adulthood—One of seven life stages; from 20 to 39 years old.

early childhood—One of seven life stages; from 3 to 6 years old.

economic benefits of parks and recreation—The extensive impact of direct, indirect, and associated monetary benefits attributed to the diverse offerings within the field.

ecotourism—Responsible travel to natural areas that conserves the environment and improves the well-being of local people.

educational sports—Teaching sport skills for the purposes of education and improvement.

emotional wellness—A positive emotional and mental state, enabling one to enjoy life and cope with challenges.

enabler and coordinator—One of the five roles that governments can take in delivering public services; the government identifies organizations and agencies that produce leisure services and helps coordinate their efforts, resources, and activities.

engagement—A movement in the late 1800s in which Christian leaders attempted to address the souls of men as well as their bodies.

entrepreneurial recreation—The businesses that take advantage of emerging trends and changes in recreation habits to provide new recreation-related services and products.

environmental benefits of parks and recreation—The accomplishments of parks and recreation in sustaining human life by protecting the ecosystem.

environmental interpretation—An educational activity that aims to reveal meanings about our cultural and natural resources.

environmental wellness—A state of supporting and respecting one's personal environment as well as the larger societal and natural environments.

ethical dilemma—A situation in which two basic moral choices must be made, neither of which appears desirable.

ethics—The philosophic study of morality and moral justification.

ethnicity—Possessing distinctive cultural characteristics.

evidence-based practice (EBP)—The selection of the best available treatment based on research findings and professional expertise.

experiential education—A philosophy and methodology in which educators purposely engage with learners in direct experience and focused reflection in order to increase knowledge, develop skills, and clarify values.

extramural sports—Structured sport activities between winners of various intramural sport programs.

family—Two or more people living together in one household.

feasibility analysis—A report that looks at various factors to determine the likelihood that a business will be successful. These factors include the legal format of the business, the appropriateness of the site, availability of financing, and marketing.

fine motor skills—Movements of the small muscles of the body such as writing, cutting, and picking up small objects.

foundations—Types of nonprofits organized as private, operating, or community foundations with the expressed purpose of amassing resources and providing grants or direct programs for the public good.

functioning—The ability to perform specific functions in each of the five domains of health: cognitive or mental, physical, psychological or emotional, social, and spiritual.

gender—The social characteristics that a society considers proper for males and females that include attitudes, expectations, and expressions of masculinity and femininity.

general community—One of four settings for recreation and leisure services; examples include community centers and most public recreation settings.

generativity—People's desire to leave a legacy of themselves to the next generation, thereby achieving a sense of immortality.

gross motor skills—Movements of the large muscles of the body such as throwing, walking, crawling, and sitting up.

head boat—Also known as a party boat. The boat typically has from 12 to 60 (larger boats may have more than 100) anglers on it to go near-shore or offshore fishing. Each angler buys a ticket, similar to a bus.

health promotion—Engaging in healthy lifestyle practices to promote health and wellness.

health—The state of complete physical, mental, and social well-being, not merely the absence of disease.

hedonism—A philosophy that focuses on pleasure as the ultimate goal.

hospitality—The businesses that cater to travelers and the special needs of residents by providing accommodations, food and beverages, and other amenities.

human-service agency—A type of nonprofit organization, often referred to as a voluntary agency that provides services to its members, which are often a targeted population with specific needs. These agencies rely heavily on volunteers and receive funding from the United Way, limited membership fees, and donations.

improved condition—Use of parks and recreation to ameliorate (make better or more tolerable) a human, natural, or economic factor not functioning at full capacity or functioning in a deleterious (harmful) manner.

incarcerated—To be put in prison and subjected to confinement.

inclusion—The degree to which a person with a disability participates in community life. The range includes segregated programs, parallel inclusion, supported inclusion, and independent inclusion.

individual and personal benefits of parks and recreation—The ways in which a person's life can be enriched and enhanced or even extended by various leisure pursuits.

individual treatment plan—A written course of action to be taken by, for, and with the client, based on assessment; part of a client's record.

infancy—One of seven life stages; the time from birth to approximately 2 years old.

informal arts—Arts characterized and distinguished by their overall accessibility as vehicles for artistic expression, by the self-determining nature of people's participation, and by the generally noncommercial nature of the activities (Wali et al., 2001).

informal sports—Self-directed participation in sports with an individualized approach focused on fun and fitness.

institutional setting—One of four settings for recreation and leisure services; examples include facilities for closed populations, and colleges, industries, churches, and military bases.

institution—An established organization or corporation, especially of a public character.

instructional sports—Sport activity that emphasizes skills, rules, and strategies in a noncredit environment.

intellectual wellness—A state in which the mind is active and able to support decision making and an enriched life.

intramural sports—Structured sport activity in the form of leagues, tournaments, and contests conducted "within the walls" of a particular setting.

intrapreneurial recreation—Businesses that provide new recreation-related services and products within an organization.

Islam—A religious faith that follows the teachings of Muhammad, laid out in the Koran and hadith.

jail—A place under the jurisdiction of a local government for the confinement of people awaiting trial or those convicted of minor crimes.

Judaism—A religious faith that follows the teaching of God as laid out in the Torah.

juvenile—A young person; a young person resembling an adult except in size and reproductive activity.

Land Force Command—The name for the Canadian army.

land tax—Land in a municipality is taxed each year. The landowners pay according to the value and uses of the land and mill rate assigned by the municipality. Also known as a real-estate tax.

late adulthood—One of seven life stages; 60 years old and older.

legislator and regulator—One of the five roles that governments can take in delivering public services; the government passes laws that leisure services providers and consumers must abide by.

leisure awareness—Activities or actions directed toward raising people's appreciation for the many positive attributes and effects of leisure-time activity.

leisure coaching—A "structured self-help technique which draws on the individual's own resources and potential" (Leoni & Berbling, 1980).

leisure education—The process of acquiring the knowledge, attitude, and skills necessary for positive leisure functioning.

leisure episode—Brief incidents or occurrences of leisure that require minimal commitment or time to experience (Carpenter, 1995).

leisure facilitation—The process of providing information, developing skills, and supporting opportunities for people to pursue health and well-being and in the end, adopt a healthier lifestyle.

leisure—Originally defined by the ancient Greeks as the most worthy activity that humans could engage in. For Plato and Aristotle, leisure consisted of philosophic contemplation.

life stage—The stages of growth and maturation during a person's life span. Changes occur mentally, physically, emotionally, and socially as a result of biological, genetic, and social factors prompting adjustment by the individual. Successful adjustment is generally considered necessary to be ready to cope with the demands of subsequent stages. The stages are infancy, early childhood, middle and late childhood, adolescence, early adulthood, middle adulthood, and late adulthood. Recreation programs should be tailored to accommodate the needs of a person's life stage.

livability—Reflects environmental and economic factors that support community access and opportunities for individuals, families, and neighborhoods to pursue healthy lifestyles.

local commercial recreation—The businesses that provide recreation-related services to residents and tourists and provide entertainment.

mainstreaming—An educational movement in which students with disabilities participate in classrooms with their peers without disabilities.

Maritime Command—The name for the Canadian navy.

middle adulthood—One of seven life stages; from 40 to 59 years old.

middle and late childhood—One of seven life stages; from 7 to 12 years old.

military community—The military service members, their families, and supporting partners that sustain the military environment.

military service members—Personnel in service of the nation in the armed forces. This term includes active-duty personnel, national guardsmen, reservists, and their families.

morale and welfare—Within a military community context, morale and welfare refers to the quality of life and operational ability of military service members, individually and globally.

Morale, Welfare and Recreation (MWR)—Key provider of recreational, fitness, family, and community services to U.S. military members and their families.

multiple-use management—Managing natural areas for a variety of uses concurrently, such as outdoor recreation, wildlife and fish habitat, range grazing, timber production, watershed protection to control pollution, and erosion and allocation of water uses.

national park—A protected area managed mainly for ecosystem protection and recreation. It is a natural area of land and/or sea, designated to protect the ecological integrity of one or more ecosystems for present and future generations; excludes exploitation or occupation inimical to the purposes of designation of the area; and provides a foundation for spiritual, scientific, educational, recreational, and visitor opportunities, all of which must be environmentally and culturally compatible.

natural environment—One of four settings for recreation and leisure services; it includes local, state, and national parks; forests; and water bodies. Resident camps and adventure and challenge activities and trips also take place in the natural environment.

nature-based tourism—Travel behavior that depends to some degree on the natural environment.

neurophysiological—Relating to the physiology of the nervous system.

nonprofit association—The sponsoring sector in which human-service agencies and private nonprofit associations provide services to their members. A recreation provider with a "tax-exempt" status; the expectation is that its services will be rendered to its clientele without making a profit. When funds accrue in nonprofit organizations, they are used for capital (large-cost) improvement of existing resources such as buildings or private roads or for capital expenditures on acquisition of large-cost items (new heating system), new construction, or land.

nonprofit organization—An organization with a tax-exempt status under the U.S. Internal Revenue Code or by Revenue Canada. These organizations are tax exempt, and contributions to them are tax deductible. A nonprofit is governed by a volunteer board of directors and operated for public benefit, and its business is not conducted for profit. Organizations of this type are said to belong to the nonprofit, or third, sector.

nonprofit sector—The segment of society composed of organizations that are private and nongovernmental and seek to serve the public good without the motivation of profit.

offender—One convicted of an offense.

operational management—Recreation and leisure professions concerned with the administration of service modalities, including risk management, safety and security, public relations and marketing, business management, and facility facilitation, design, and operation.

operational readiness and effectiveness—The mental, physical, emotional, and social conduct of military service members steering their ability to be prepared for and perform in combat, peacekeeping, and military operational settings.

optimal experience (flow)—A term coined by Csikszentmihalyi to refer to the alert, flowing (thinking clearly), and positive state of mind a person experiences when fully challenged and learning to work successfully with the conditions at hand. The result is personal growth, pride, and sense of accomplishment.

ORV site—Off-road vehicle areas for all-terrain vehicles (ATVs) such as dune buggies, jeeps, motorcycles, four-wheel drive vehicles, dirt bikes, and snowmobiles whose drivers engage in activities such as mudslinging, trail rides, rallies, and generally challenge rugged terrains with their machines, often denuding and eroding landscapes in the process; however, it is very popular in some areas.

outcome—The observed changes in a client's status as a result of intervention.

outdoor recreation—The broad array of leisure behaviors, activities, and experiences that occur in or depend on the natural environment for their fulfillment.

penitentiary—A public institution in which offenders against the law are confined for detention or punishment; a state or federal prison in the United States.

person visit—The statistic of one person visit is one person entering the park once.

Personnel Support (PSP) Division—Division of the Canadian Forces Personnel Support Agency that delivers recreational, fitness, family, and community services to Canadian military members and their families.

philanthropy—Voluntary action for the public good through acts of giving (time, money, and know-how) by individuals and organizations to causes that they care about.

philosophy—Literally, the "love of wisdom." Originally, the term philosophy applied to all academic studies.

physical abilities—One of three perspectives used by developmental psychologists to describe development. Characteristics include physical growth, motor development, and sensory and perceptual development.

physical wellness—A state in which the functional operation of the body enables a person to reach and maintain optimal physical condition.

play—A pleasurable, spontaneous, creative activity associated with recreation, games, music, and theater.

playground movement—Development beginning in the late 1800s and early 1900s in Canada and the United States with the purpose of providing safe places for children to play in order to prevent delinquency and promote healthy development.

population segment—One of the four delivery systems for recreation and leisure services. It is based on the age of the group served or the type of needs the group faces.

preservation—Protecting a natural area—wildlife and ecosystem—in a relatively undisturbed natural state (different from conservation).

prevention of a worse condition—Use of parks and recreation to stem further erosion or deterioration of a human, natural, or economic condition.

primary group—A group based on intimate, long-term association such as family and close friends.

private for-profit enterprise—The sponsoring sector in which business and commercial enterprises and tourism focus on profit and emphasize marketing and consumerism in offering a product or service to customers for a price. A recreation provider that expects to earn a profit by offering programs or services; the profit can be used to reward an owner or investors or for improvement or expansion of services or infrastructure. Investing profit back into the business reduces the amount of taxes the profit-making enterprise will pay.

private nonprofit association—A type of nonprofit organization that provides specific services to members who pay to join and receive these services.

professional and trade associations—Nonprofits organized to promote the business interests of a community, industry, or profession. They generally qualify for tax exemption under Section 501(c) (6) of the U.S. Internal Revenue Service tax code.

professional organization—Agency that provides support for recreation programs and promotes the importance of recreation and leisure for health and well-being.

professional sports—Sport events that place emphasis on entertainment and generating money.

program fields—Categories of activities (services modalities) provided by recreation and leisure professionals.

program format—The general purpose that frames organization of participant experience. (Instructional format offers opportunities to learn or practice with guidance from an instructor or coach.)

program, programmed, programming—As a verb, to program means to create a plan that brings people together to interact in a leisure setting, engaging in leisure interests and objects.

project-based leisure—Short-term, moderately complicated, either on-shot or occasional, though infrequent, creative undertaking that is carried out during one's free time (Stebbins, 2005).

Protestant work ethic—The idea that work is virtuous and is the most important activity in an individual's life.

provincial park—Parks designated and managed by the host province in Canada, usually containing a wide diversity of landscapes and outdoor recreation activities. The parks, called provincial parks in Canada, are usually classified as national parks according to the IUCN categories of national parks and protected areas.

psychosocial development—The aspect of human development that includes the development of emotions, temperament, personality, and social skills, and reflects the influences of family, friends, culture, and the larger society.

public agency—The sponsoring sector in which municipal, county, state, provincial and federal governments; schools; and other institutions sponsored by the government provide community recreation and leisure services.

purple leisure—Questionable activities that bring pleasure to participants but may harm society.

quality of life—The subjective assessment of psychological and spiritual well-being, characterized by feelings of joy, satisfaction, contentment, and self-determination.

quasi-public—An entity that is organized privately to promote public ideals.

race—Inherited physical characteristics that distinguish groups.

Ramsar Convention—An international agreement and convention monitored by UNESCO to protect wetlands designated as internationally important under the Convention on Wetlands (www.ramsar.org, 1971). These wetlands are commonly known as *Ramsar Sites*. Globally in 2005, there are 146 Contracting Parties to the Convention, with 1,459 wetland sites, totaling 125.4 million hectares, designated for inclusion in the Ramsar List of Wetlands of International Importance.

realization of a psychological experience—Pursuit of the intrinsic values afforded through a park, recreation, or leisure experience such as stress reduction, sense of control, spirituality, and so on.

recreational sports—Direct involvement in a sport activity for the sake of fun, fitness, and participation.

recreation—The use of leisure time to refresh oneself for work.

reengagement—A movement starting in the late 1940s, in which Christian leaders, churches, and organizations actively united sport and faith.

religion—Beliefs and practices that separate the profane from the sacred and develop a community of believers.

resources—The environment and supplies for recreational activities such as trails, woods, lakes, parks, facilities, and equipment and the things that support recreational activities such as funding, personnel, information, and programs.

schole—Ancient Greek concept of having time for oneself, being occupied in something for its own sake such as music, poetry, and visiting, and embracing the experience and not the outcome.

secondary group—A larger (compared to a primary group), formal, and impersonal group based on a shared interest.

Section 501(c) (3)—A U.S. Internal Revenue Service classification for qualifying nonprofits that gives such organizations a tax-exempt status in order to operate for purposes of the public good. Most U.S.-based nonprofits operate under this tax-exempt category.

selective acculturation—A process by which one chooses to form relationships with people with similar interests, background, religious affiliation, and language and allows this subculture to shape his or her values.

sensorimotor—Functioning in both sensory and motor aspects of bodily activity.

serious leisure—A type of leisure that is characterized by a high degree of commitment, sacrifice, skills development, and an extended period of involvement.

service modality—One of the four delivery systems for recreation and leisure services. It is based on the type of service provided.

setting—One of the four delivery systems for recreation and leisure services. It is based on the location in which recreation and leisure activities take place, such as the natural environment, the community as a whole, or a building.

sex—The biological characteristics that distinguish males and females.

social and community benefits of parks and recreation—The opportunities for success and enjoyment afforded by interacting with others in parks and recreation settings; these encounters can be positive and enriching for individuals, small groups, and society overall.

social capital—The network of social contacts that people develop to support them in times of difficulty and enhance the quality of their lives.

social welfare organizations—Nonprofits involved in advocacy, lobbying, and political campaign activities under the U.S. 501(c) (4) IRS code.

social wellness—A state of being able to interact with others and being comfortable in group settings as a way to secure intimacy and a sense of belonging.

society—People who share a culture and a territory.

sociocultural—Relating to or involving a combination of social and cultural factors.

socioemotional characteristics—One of three perspectives used by developmental psychologists to describe development. These characteristics include personality, emotional and moral development, self-concept, identity, and social relationships.

solitary leisure—Activities undertaken without the physical presence of another person.

special recreation association—An intergovernmental agreement between two or more communities or park districts, established to provide recreational services to people with special needs.

special recreation—A recreational service that takes place in a public, community setting, offered to people with special needs. Its purpose is to provide enjoyment, challenge, and enrichment rather than to provide a treatment modality.

spiritual wellness—A state of being able to discover one's core element of existence that provides meaning, purpose, and value in life.

spirituality—A person's private beliefs about the relationship between humans and something greater than oneself.

sponsoring sector—One of the four delivery systems for recreation and leisure services. It is based on who provides services, such as a public agency, nonprofit association, or private for-profit enterprise.

stagnation—A person's sense that he or she has done nothing for the next generation.

state park—Parks designated and managed by the host state in the United States, usually showcasing an area of historical or representative natural environment for that state (e.g., prairie in Illinois, beaches in Florida).

supporter and patron—One of the five roles that governments can take in delivering public services; the government provides support to existing organizations that produce public leisure services.

system plan for parks—A plan for the identification and establishment of parks within an overall strategy.

therapeutic recreation (TR)—Engaging people in planned recreation and related experiences in order to improve functioning, health and well-being, and quality of life, focusing on the whole person and the needed changes in the optimal living environment.

therapeutic recreation specialist (TRS)—A person with the appropriate education and experience to carry out the duties and responsibilities of therapeutic recreation practices.

three-sector model—The economic (business sector), political (government sector), and social (nonprofit sector) segments found in most societies in which individuals and organizations act and interact within their environments. Recreation organizations are found across all three sectors.

Title IX—Legislation enacted in 1972 that directed educational institutions to develop parity for men's and women's sports.

tourist—Someone who travels for business or pleasure and spends at least one night away from home.

travel services—The businesses that move people and services.

virtue-based ethics—An ethical theory used to resolve moral dilemmas by appealing to one's conscience and character.

visitor day—A visitor day of recreation is one day of recreation for one person. This unit of measurement is used internationally so that park systems all over the world can collect and report tourism use data according to a standard.

walk-in area—Areas that can only be accessed by foot and where there is no motorized access (some may allow horses or pack animals).

wellness—The many desirable outcomes associated with health and well-being that are the natural results of participation in physical endeavors, including parks and recreation activities.

wilderness—Large areas left in an entirely natural condition, usually without roads or motorized vehicles, and without buildings or utilities.

wildlife refuge—Lands, wetlands, and waters that are primarily managed as wildlife or fish habitat or protected areas (although some allow regulated hunting and fishing) by fish and wildlife agencies, usually at the state or federal level. Limited recreational use compatible with wildlife management is permitted in most (not all) refuges.

wise-use philosophy—This philosophy holds that the earth's resources were meant to be exploited for human gain and profit, typically with more of a short-term focus. Wise use tends to be promoted by the extractive industries such as mining and lumber companies who lobby politicians to influence the multiple-use agencies such as the Forest Service and Bureau of Land Management toward more of a so-called wise-use orientation.

work—A productive, purposeful activity that was disliked by the ancient Greeks, but that is assigned great importance in modern societies.

World Conservation Union—An international body that coordinates conservation and sustainable development activities worldwide. It is also known by its old acronym, IUCN.

World Heritage Site—A specific site (such as a forest, mountain range, lake, desert, building, complex, or city) that has been designated within the international World Heritage Convention administered by UNESCO. The World Heritage List in 2005 includes 788 properties forming part of the cultural and natural heritage, which the World Heritage Committee considers as having outstanding universal value. These include 611 cultural, 154 natural, and 23 mixed properties in 134 countries.

References

Active Living by Design. (n.d.a). *ALbD community partnerships*. Retrieved June 7, 2005 from www.activelivingbyd esign.org/cgi-bin/albd.org/view_services.cgi?request = sh ow_public_home&dept_id = 120 [June 28, 2005].

Active Living by Design. (n.d.b). *About Upper Valley*. Retrieved July 29, 2004 from www.activelivingbydesig n.org/cgi-bin/albd.org/view_services.cgi?request = show _public_home&dept_id = 123 [June 28, 2005].

Active Living by Design. (n.d.c). www.activelivingbydesig n.org [June 28, 2005].

Adirondack State Park Agency. (2003). *About the Adirondack Park*. Retrieved June 28, 2005 from www.apa.state.ny.us/ About_Park/index.html.

Alabama State Parks. (2005). *Welcome to Cheaha State Park*. Retrieved June 4, 2005 from http://cheahastpark.com/ [June 28, 2005].

Alberta Community Development. (2000). 2000 Alberta recreation survey (A look at leisure #41). Edmonton, AB: Sport and Recreation Branch.

Alberta Recreation and Parks Association. (1992). *Careers in recreation and parks*. Retrieved September 1, 2004 from www.lin.ca/resource/html/car.htm [June 28, 2005].

Allison, M. (1981). *Competition and co-operation: A sociocultural perspective*. Westpoint, NY: Leisure Press.

Allison, M. (1982). Sport, ethnicity, and assimilation. *Quest, 34*(2), 165-175.

Allison, M. (1988). Breaking barriers: Future directions in cross-cultural research. *Leisure Sciences, 10*(4), 247-259.

Amateur Athletic Union. (n.d.). *About AAU*. Retrieved on May 25, 2005 from http://aausports.org/ default.asp?a = pg_about_aau.htm [June 28, 2005].

America's Public Parks Centennial Celebration, *A centennial salute,* July, 1998.

American Alliance for Health, Physical Education, Recreation and Dance. (n.d.a). *About*. Retrieved August 9, 2004 from www.aahperd.org/aahperd/template.cfm [June 28, 2005].

American Alliance for Health, Physical Education, Recreation and Dance. (n.d.b). *Mission statement*. Retrieved August 9, 2004 from www.aahperd.org/aahperd/temp late.cfm?template = mission_statement.html [June 28, 2005].

The American Assembly. (1997). *The arts and the public purpose*. Retrieved July 13, 2004 from www.americanassembly.org/ index.php [June 28, 2005].

American Planning Association. (2003a). *City parks forum briefing papers: How cities use parks to create safer neighborhoods* [Electronic version]. Retrieved on August 1, 2004 from www.planning.org/cpf/pdf/createsaferneigh borhoods.pdf [June 28, 2005].

American Planning Association. (2003b). *City parks forum briefing papers: How cities use parks to improve public health* [Electronic version]. Retrieved on August 1, 2004 from www.planning.org/cpf/pdf/improvepublichealth.pdf [June 28, 2005].

American Planning Association. (2003c). *How cities use parks to help children learn*. Retrieved June 4, 2005 from www.naturalearning.org/helpchildrenlearn.html [June 28, 2005].

American Society of Association Executives. (2004). *Number of associations in the United States*. Retrieved September 1, 2004 from www.asaenet.org/asae/cda/index/ 1,,ETI10471,00.html [June 28, 2005].

Americans for the Arts. (2002). *Arts and economic prosperity*. Retrieved July 13, 2004 from www.AmericansForTheA rts.org [June 28, 2005].

Americans for the Arts. (2004). *Arts facts: Local arts agencies*. Retrieved July 13, 2004 from www.AmericansForTheA rts.org [June 28, 2005].

Anahar, H., Becker, U., & Messing, M. (1992). Scholastic sport in the context of an Islamic country. *International Journal of Physical Education, 29*(4), 32-36.

Anderson, D.R., Lorch, E.P., Field, D.E., Collins, P.A., & Nathan, J.G. (1985, April). Television viewing at home: Age trends in visual attention and time with TV. Paper presented at the biennial meeting of the Society for Research in Child Development, Toronto.

Anderson, R.N., & Smith, B.L. (2003, November). Deaths: Leading causes for 2001. *National Center for Health Statistics, 52*(9). Retrieved June 7, 2005 from www.cdc.gov/ nchs/data/nvsr/nvsr52/nvsr52_09.pdf [June 28, 2005].

Anthony, T. (2004, July 18). Sunday shifts into day for sundry fun. [The Associated Press] *The Register-Guard,* pp. A1, A12.

Antonucci, T.C. (1990). Social supports and relationships. In R.H. Binstock & L.K. George (Eds.), *Handbook of aging and the social sciences*. San Diego: Academic Press.

Armas, G. (2004, 24 June). *People motoring out of Motor City and other older, industrial communities*. New York: Associated Press, 1.

Arnold, N.D. (1976). *The interrelated arts in leisure*. St. Louis: Mosby.

Arnold, N.D. (1978). Pop art: The human footprint infinity. *Leisure Today,* 24-25.

ArtsBridge. (n.d.). *ArtsBridgeAmerica.* Retrieved July 20, 2004 from www.arts.uci.edu/artsbridge [June 28, 2005].

Association for Experiential Education. (2005a). *About AEE.* Retrieved February 28, 2005 from www.aee2.org/customer/pages.php?pageid=24 [June 28, 2005].

Association for Experiential Education. (2005b). *AEE professional groups.* Retrieved February 28, 2005 from www.aee2.org/customer/pages.php?pageid=22 [June 28, 2005].

Association of Church Sports and Recreation Ministers: www.csrm.org [June 28, 2005].

Austin Parks and Recreation Department. (1995). *Totally cool totally art.* Retrieved July 20, 2004 from www.ci.austin.tx.us/tcta/ [June 28, 2005].

Austin, D. (1997). *Therapeutic recreation: Processes and techniques* (3rd ed.). Champaign, IL: Sagamore.

Austin, D., & Crawford, M. (2001). *Therapeutic recreation: An introduction* (3rd ed.). Needham Heights, MA: Allyn & Bacon.

Bandura, A. (2000). Self-efficacy. In A. Kazdin (Ed.), *Encyclopedia of psychology.* Washington, DC: American Psychological Association.

Barnett, L.A. (1991). Developmental benefits of play for children. In B.L. Driver, P.J. Brown, & G.L. Peterson (Eds.), *Benefits of leisure* (pp. 215-247). State College, PA: Venture Publishing.

Beattie, J.M. (1977). *Attitudes toward crime and punishment in upper Canada, 1830-1850: A documentary study.* Toronto: Centre of Criminology, University of Toronto Press.

Beaubier, D. (2004). Athletic gender equity policy in Canadian universities: Issues and possibilities. *Canadian Journal of Educational Administration and Policy,* 34, 49-59.

Beck, L., & Cable, T. (1998). *Interpretation for the 21st century.* Champaign, IL: Sagamore.

Belasco, W.J. (1979). *Americans on the road: From autocamp to motel, 1910-1945.* Baltimore: Johns Hopkins Press.

Benn, T. (1996). Muslim women and physical education in initial teacher training. *Sport, Education and Society,* 1, 5-21.

Bernard, S. (2002, July 19). They've got game. *New York,* 35(28), 20-27.

Berndt, T.J. (2002). Friendship quality and social development. *Current Directions in Psychological Science,* 11, 7-10.

Bernstein, P. (2004). *Hispanic and Asian Americans increasing faster than overall population.* U.S. Census Bureau. Retrieved July 27, 2004 from www.census.gov/Press-Release/www/releases/archives/race/001839.html [June 28, 2005].

Berry, L. (2000). When pray mixes with play. *Athletic Management,* 12(4), 22-30.

Bertrand, R.M., & Lachman, M.E. (2003). Personality development in adulthood and old age. In I.B. Weiner (Ed.), *Handbook of psychology, vol. VI.* New York: Wiley.

Big Brothers Big Sisters. (2004). *About us.* Retrieved on June 1, 2005 from www.bbbsa.org/site/pp.asp?c=iuJ3JgO2F&b=14600 [June 28, 2005].

Big Brothers Big Sisters of Canada. (n.d.). *About us.* Retrieved on June 1, 2005 from www.bbbsc.ca/english/index.shtml?about.inc [June 28, 2005].

Black, H. (2000) Environmental and public health: Pulling the pieces together. *Environmental Health Perspectives,* 108. Retrieved August 1, 2004 from http://ehp.niehs.nih.gov/docs/2000/108-11/spheres.html [June 28, 2005].

Blumenthal, K.J. (2000). The new century. *Athletic Business,* 24(1), 35-41.

BoardSource. (2002). *Major subcategories of the U.S. nonprofit sector.* Retrieved January 15, 2005 from www.boardsource.org/FullAnswer.asp?ID=82 [June 28, 2005].

Borgmann, A. (1984). *Technology and the character of contemporary life: A philosophical inquiry.* Chicago: University of Chicago Press.

Borish, L. (1999, Summer). Athletic activities of various kinds: Physical health and sports programs for Jewish American women. *Journal of Sport History,* 26(2), 240-270.

Bosma, H.A., & Kunnen, E.S. (2001). *Identity and emotion.* New York: Cambridge University Press.

Boys and Girls Club of America. (2005). *Who we are: The facts.* Retrieved on May 15, 2005 from www.bgca.org/whoweare/facts.asp [June 28, 2005].

Boys and Girls Club of Canada. (2004). *About us.* Retrieved on May 15, 2005 from www.bgccan.com/content.asp?L=E&DocID=1 [June 28, 2005].

Braden, D.R. (1988). *Leisure and entertainment in America.* Dearborn, MI: Henry Ford Museum and Greenfield Village.

Brandstadter, J., Wentura, D., & Greve, W. (1993). Adaptive resources of the aging self: Outlines of an emergent perspective. *Journal of Behavioral Development,* 16, 323-349.

Bray, S.R., & Born, H.A. (2004). Transition to university and vigorous physical activity: Implications for health and psychological well-being. *Journal of American College Health,* 52, 181-188.

Brightbill, C. (1963). *The challenge of leisure.* Englewood Cliffs, NJ: Prentice-Hall.

Broida, J. (2000). *Therapeutic recreation—The benefits are endless . . . Training and resource guide.* Ashburn, VA: National Therapeutic Recreation Society.

Brown, D. (1970). *Bury my heart at Wounded Knee: An Indian history of the American west.* New York: Henry Holt & Company.

Brown, S. (n.d.) *The Institute for Play.* www.instituteforplay.com/13stuart_brown.htm [June 28, 2005].

Browning, T. (2003, February). ESM/NCR President. *ESMA Capital Edition,* 1(1).

Brownson, R. (2000). Promoting physical activity in rural communities: Walking trail access, use, and effect. *American Journal of Preventive Medicine,* 18(3).

Brownson, R.C., Baker, E.A., Housemann, R.A., Brennan, L.K., & Bacak, S.J. (2001). Environmental and policy determinants of physical activity in the United States. *American Journal of Public Health,* 91, 1995-2003.

Brownson, R.C., Housemann, R.A., Brown, D.R., Jackson-Thompson, J., King, A.C., Malone, B.R., & Sallis, J.F. (2000). Promoting physical activity in rural communities: Walking trail access, use, and effects. *American Journal of Preventive Medicine, 18,* 235-241.

Bullock, C., & Mahon, M. (2000). *Introduction to recreation services for people with disabilities: A person-centered approach.* Champaign, IL: Sagamore.

Bultena, G., & Field, D. (1978). Visitors to national parks: A test of the elitist argument. *Leisure Sciences, 1,* 395-409.

Burdge, R.J. (1985). The coming separation of leisure studies from parks and recreation education. *Journal of Leisure Research, 17,* 133-141.

Bureau of Labor Statistics. (2004). *U.S. Department of Labor, occupational outlook handbook, recreational therapists.* Retrieved August 10, 2004 from www.bls.gov/oco/ocos082.htm [June 28, 2005].

Bureau of Land Management. (2002). *Annual Report Bureau of Land Management: FY 2002.* Retrieved June 12, 2005 from www.blm.gov/nhp/info/stratplan/AR02.pdf [June 28, 2005].

Bureau of Land Management. (2003). *What is the Bureau of Land Management (BLM)?* Retrieved June 12, 2005 from www.blm.gov/nhp/faqs/faqs1.htm#1 [June 28, 2005].

Bureau of Reclamation. (2005). *Bureau of Reclamation.* Retrieved June 6, 2005 from www.usbr.gov [June 28, 2005].

Burton, T.L., & Glover, T.D. (1999). Back to the future: Leisure services and the reemergence of the enabling authority of the state. In E.L. Jackson & T.L. Burton (Eds.), *Leisure studies: Prospects for the twenty-first century.* State College, PA: Venture.

Butler, G.D. (1967). *Introduction to community recreation.* New York: McGraw-Hill.

Butler, R.N. (1996). Global aging: Challenges and opportunities of the next century. *Aging International, 21,* 12-32.

Byl, J. (1999). Calvinists and Mennonites: A pilot study on shepherding Christianity and sport in Canada. In J. Byl & T. Visker (Eds.), *Physical education, sport, and wellness: Looking to God as we look at ourselves* (pp. 311-326). Sioux Center, IA: Dordt College Press.

Bynum, M. (2003). The little flock. *Athletic Business, 27*(5), 36-40.

California Park and Recreation Society. (1999). *VIP project plan, creating community in the 21st century.* Retrieved August 1, 2004 from www.cprs.org/creating-action.htm [June 28, 2005].

Calthorpe, P., Corbett, M., Duany, A., Moule, E., Plater-Zyberk, E., & Polyzoides, S. (1991). *Ahwahnee principles for resource-efficient communities.* Retrieved on July 29, 2004 from www.lgc.org/ahwahnee/principles.html [June 28, 2005].

Campbell, P. (1997). *Population projections: States, 1995-2025.* Current Population Reports. Retrieved July 26, 2004 from www.census.gov/prod/2/pop/p25/p25-1131.pdf [June 28, 2005].

Canada. (1938). *Final report of the National Employment Commission.* Ottawa, ON: King's Printer.

Canada. (1943). *The National Physical Fitness Act.* Ottawa, ON: King's Printer.

Canada. (1947). *Letters patent of the Parks and Recreation Association of Canada.* Ottawa, ON: Secretary of State for Canada.

Canada. (1961). *Fitness and Amateur Sport Act.* Ottawa, ON: Queen's Printer.

Canada. (1982). *Constitution Act.* Retrieved June 6, 2005 from http://laws.justice.gc.ca/en/const [June 28, 2005].

Canada. (2003). *Physical Activity and Sport Act.* Retrieved June 28, 2004 from http://laws.justice.gc.ca/en/p-13.4/92297.html [June 28, 2005].

Canadian Association of Health, Physical Education, Recreation and Dance (n.d.). *Canadian Association of Health, Physical Education, Recreation and Dance.* Retrieved June 30, 2004 from www.cahperd.ca/ [June 28, 2005].

Canadian Biosphere Reserve Association (CBRA). (2005). *Homepage.* Retrieved July 11, 2005 from www.biosphere-canada.ca/home.asp [June 28, 2005].

Canadian Broadcasting Corporation. (2000). *ParicipACTION packing it in?* Retrieved August 7, 2005 from http://archives/cbc.ca/IDC-1-41-615-3312/sports/fitness/clip10.

Canadian Forces Personnel Support Agency. (2005). *About CFPSA.* Retrieved June 28, 2005 from www.cfpsa.com/en/NewsCentre/index.asp [June 28, 2005].

Canadian Heritage. (2004). *Welcome.* Retrieved September 1, 2004 from www.canadianheritage.gc.ca/index_e.cfm [June 28, 2005].

Canadian Parks and Recreation Association. (1997). *The benefits catalogue.* Ottawa, ON: Canadian Parks and Recreation Association.

Canadian Parks and Recreation Association. (2004). *Sunlight National Play Day.* Retrieved August 1, 2004 from www.cpra.ca/cpra-new/playday/e/index.htm [June 28, 2005].

Canadian Parks and Recreation Association. (n.d.a). *CPRA history.* Retrieved June 30, 2004 from www.cpra.ca [June 28, 2005].

Canadian Parks and Recreation Association. (n.d.b). *About CPRA.* Retrieved June 30, 2004 from www.cpra.ca [June 28, 2005].

Canadian Public Health Association. (2004). *ParticipACTION: The mouse that roared. A marketing and health communications success story.* Retrieved June 28, 2004 from www.cpha.ca/english/inside/mediarm/newsrel/mouse_e.htm [June 28, 2005].

Cappel, M.L. (1995). Sista-2-sista: A self-empowerment program. *Leisure Today,* 19-21.

Carlson, R.E., Deppe, T.R., & MacLean, J.R. (1968). *Recreation in American life.* Belmont, CA: Wadsworth.

Carpenter, G. (1995). The appeal of fairs, festivals, and special events to adult populations. *World Leisure & Recreation, 37*(1), 14-15.

Carpenter, G. (2004). Assessing arts and cultural programming in Oregon's recreation organizations. *CultureWork, 8*(4), 1-6. Retrieved July 22, 2004 from http://aad.uoregon.edu/culturework/culturework.html [June 28, 2005].

Carrington, B., Chivers, T., & Williams, T. (1987). Gender, leisure and sport: A case-study of young people of South Asian descent. *Leisure Studies, 6,* 265-279.

Carter, M., Van Andel, G., & Robb, G. (1996). *Therapeutic recreation: A practical approach* (2nd ed.). Prospect Heights, IL: Waveland Press.

Catlin, T.K., Simoes, E.J., & Brownson, R.C. (2003). Environmental and policy factors associated with overweight among adults in Missouri. *American Journal of Health Promotion, 17,* 249-258.

Cavallo, D. (1981). *Muscles and morals: Organized playgrounds and urban reform, 1880–1920.* Philadelphia: University of Pennsylvania Press.

Centers for Disease Control and Prevention. (2005). *ACES: Active Community Environments Initiative.* Retrieved June 7, 2005 from www.cdc.gov/nccdphp/dnpa/aces.htm [June 28, 2005].

Central Intelligence Agency. (2004). *World fact book.* Retrieved September 6, 2004 from www.cia.gov/cia/publications/factbook/ [June 28, 2005].

Chape, S., Blyth, S., Fish, L., Fox, P., & Spalding, M. (compilers). (2003). *2003 United Nations list of protected areas.* IUCN, Gland, Switzerland and Cambridge, UK and UNEP-WCMC, Cambridge, UK.

Chartrand, H.H. (2000). Toward an American arts industry. In J.M. Cherbo & M.J. Wyszomirski (Eds.), *The public life of the arts in America* (pp. 22-49). New Brunswick, NJ: Rutgers University Press.

Chavez, D.J. (2002). Adaptive management in outdoor recreation: Serving Hispanics in southern California. *Western Journal of Applied Forestry, 17*(3), 129-133.

Chess, S., & Thomas, A. (1977). Temperamental individuality from childhood to adolescence. *Journal of Child Psychiatry, 16,* 218-226.

Christian, K. (n.d.). Get fit. *Ocala Magazine Online.* Retrieved July 1, 2005 from www.ocalamagazine.com/getfit_story.html [June 28, 2005].

Chubb, M., & Chubb, H. (1981). *One third of our time: An introduction to recreation behavior and resources.* New York: Wiley.

CMG Worldwide. (n.d.). *The official site of Bob "Bullet" Feller.* Retrieved May 25, 2005 from www.cmgworldwide.com/baseball/feller/fastfacts.htm [June 28, 2005].

Congdon, K.G., & Blandy, D. (2003). Administering the culture of everyday life: Imagining the future of arts sector administration. In V.B. Morris & D.B. Pankrantz (Eds.), *The arts in a new millennium* (pp. 177-188). Westport, CT: Praeger.

Connecticut Trust for Historic Preservation. (2005). *Towngreens.com.* Retrieved June 4, 2005 from www.towngreens.com [June 28, 2005].

Connolly, K., & Smale, B.J.A. (2001/2002). Changes in the financing of local recreation and cultural services: An examination of trends in Ontario from 1988 to 1996. *Leisure/Loisir, 26*(3-4), 213-234.

Cooper, W. (1999). Some philosophical aspects of leisure theory. In E.L. Jackson & T.L. Burton (Eds.), *Leisure studies: Prospects for the twenty-first century.* State College, PA: Venture.

Corbin, H.D., & Williams, E. (1987). *Recreation: Programming and leadership* (4th ed.). Englewood Cliffs, NJ: Prentice-Hall.

Cordes, K.A., & Ibrahim, H.M. (2003). *Application in recreation and leisure for today and the future.* Boston: McGraw-Hill.

Correctional Services of Canada. (2001). *Basic facts about federal corrections, 2001 edition.* Retrieved June 28, 2005 from http://epe.lac-bac.gc.ca/100/201/301/basic_facts_fed_corrections/e.pdf-basic.

Correctional Services of Canada. (2004). *Organization.* Retrieved June 28, 2005 from www.csc-scc.gc.ca/text/organi/organe01_e.shtml [June 28, 2005].

Corwin, M.R. (2001, September). Guess who I am? *Parks & Recreation,* 168.

Cote, L., LaPan, B., & Halle, A. (1997). *Modele normatif d'animation-loisirs en centre d'hebergement pour la creation d'un milieu de vie anime [Normative model for the leisure/animation in long-term care centers to enhance quality of life]* (pp. 1-23). Quebec, Canada: Publication for the Federation Quebecoise du Loisir en Institution.

Council for the Advancement of Standards in Higher Education. (2004). *The role of recreational sports: CAS standards contextual statement.* Retrieved July 5, 2004 from www.nirsa.org/about/cas.htm.

Coyle, C., Kinney, W., Riley, B., & Shank, J. (Eds.). (1991). *Benefits of therapeutic recreation: A consensus view.* Philadelphia: Temple University Press.

Crompton, J.L. (1993). Repositioning recreation and park services: An overview. *Trends, 30*(4), 2-5.

Crompton, J.L. (1999). *Financing and acquiring park and recreation resources.* Champaign, IL: Human Kinetics.

Crompton, J.L. (2000). *The impact of parks and open space on property values and the property tax base.* Ashburn, VA: National Recreation and Park Association.

Crompton, J.L., & Kaczynski, A.T. (2003). Trends in local park and recreation department finances and staffing from 1964-65 to 1999-2000. *Journal of Park and Recreation Administration, 21*(4), 124-144.

Crompton, J.L., & Lamb, C.W. (1986). *Marketing government and social services.* New York: Wiley.

Cronon, W. (Ed.). (1996). *Uncommon ground: Rethinking the human place in nature.* New York: Norton.

Cross, G. (1990). *A social history of leisure since 1600.* State College, PA: Venture.

Crossley, J., Jamieson, L., & Brayley, R. (2001). *Introduction to commercial recreation and tourism.* Champaign, IL: Sagamore.

Csikszentmihalyi, M. (1990). *Flow: The psychology of optimal experience.* New York: Harper & Row.

Csikszentmihalyi, M. (1996). *Creativity.* New York: HarperCollins.

Cuff, G. (1990). First on the agenda: Last on the budget. *Recreation Canada, 48*(2), 32-34.

Cully, J.A., LaVoie, D., & Gfeller, J.D. (2001). Reminiscence, personality, and psychological functioning in older adults. *The Gerontologist, 41*(1), 89-95.

Curtis, J. (1979). *Recreation: Theory and practice.* St. Louis: Mosby.

Daigle, J. (1982). *The Acadians of the maritimes.* Moncton, NB: Centre d'études acadiennes.

Dare, B., Welton, G., & Coe, W. (1987). *Concepts of leisure in western thought: A critical and historical analysis.* Dubuque, IA: Kendall/Hunt.

Dattilo, J., Klieber, D., & Williams, R. (1998). Self-determination and enjoyment enhancement: A psychologically based service delivery model for therapeutic recreation. *Therapeutic Recreation Journal, 32*(4), 258-271.

Decker, L., & Decker, V. (Guest Eds.). (2004). *Community Education Journal, XXVIII*(1&2).

DeGraff, J., Wann, D., & Naylor, T.H. (2001). *Affluenza: The all-consuming epidemic.* San Francisco: Berrett-Koehler.

Degrazia, S. (1963). *Of time, work and leisure.* Garden City, NJ: Doubleday.

De Knop, P., Theeboom, M., Wittock, H., & De Martelaer, K. (1996). Implications of Islam on Muslim girls' sport participation in Western Europe: Literature review and policy recommendations for sport promotion. *Sport, Education and Society,* 1, 147-164.

Delamere, T.A. (2001). Development of a scale to measure resident attitudes toward the social impacts of community festivals, part II: Verification of the scale. *Event Management,* 7, 25-38.

Delamere, T.A., Wankel, L.M., & Hinch, T.D. (2001). Development of a scale to measure resident attitudes toward the social impacts of community festivals, part I: Item generation and purification of the measure. *Event Management,* 7, 11-24.

Department of Health, Education and Welfare, U.S. Office of Education. (1980). *Community education managing for success.* Washington, DC: U.S. Government Printing Office.

Doran, J. (2004, July/August). Trends in recreation. *ESM magazine.* Elmhurst, IL: ESM Association.

Dreeszen, C. (Ed.). (2003). *Fundamentals of arts management.* Amherst, MA: Arts Extension Service.

Driver, B. (1998, February). The benefits are endless . . . but why? *Parks & Recreation,* 26.

Driver, B.L., Brown, P.J., & Peterson, G.L. (Eds.). (1991). *Benefits of leisure.* State College, PA: Venture.

Driver, B.L., & Bruns, D.H. (1999). Concepts and uses of the benefits approach to leisure. In E.L. Jackson & T.L. Burton (Eds.), *Leisure studies: Prospects for the twenty-first century* (pp. 349-369). State College, PA: Venture.

Dustin, D.L., & Goodale, T.L. (1999). Reflections on recreation, park, and leisure studies. In E.L. Jackson & T.L. Burton (Eds.), *Leisure studies: Prospects for the twenty-first century* (pp. 477-486). State College, PA: Venture.

Dustin, D.L., McAvoy, L., & Schultz, J. (1990). Recreation rightly understood. In T. Goodale & P. Witt (Eds.), *Recreation and leisure: Issues in an era of change.* State College, PA: Venture.

Dwyer, M.C., & Frankel, S. (2002). Policy partners: Making the case for state investments in culture. RPM Research Corporation. Funded by The Pew Charitable Trusts.

Eagles, P.F.J. (2005). *Ontario Provincial Park Budgets, 1982-2003.* Guelph, ON: Parks Research Forum of Ontario.

Eagles, P.F.J., McLean, D., & Stabler, M.J. (2000). Estimating the tourism volume and value in parks and protected areas in Canada and the USA. *George Wright Forum,* 17(3), 62-76.

Edgington, C., Jordan, D., DeGraff, D., & Edgington, S. (1998). *Leisure and life satisfaction: Foundational perspectives.* Boston: WCB/McGraw-Hill.

Edginton, C., Hanson, C., & Edgington, S.R. (1992). *Leisure programming* (2nd ed.). Dubuque, IA: Brown & Benchmark.

Edginton, C., Hanson, C., Edgington, S.R., & Hudson, S.D. (1998). *Leisure programming* (3rd ed.). Dubuque, IA: Brown & Benchmark.

Edginton, C., Hudson, S.D., Dieser, R.B., & Edgington, S.R. (2004). *Leisure programming* (4th ed.). Dubuque, IA: Brown & Benchmark.

Edgington, C.R., Jordan, D.J., DeGraaf, D.G., & Edgington, S.R. (2002). *Leisure and life satisfaction: Foundational perspectives* (3rd ed.). Boston: McGraw-Hill.

Edwards, H. (1973). *Sociology of sport.* Homewood, IL: Dorsey Press.

Edwards, P. (2004). No country mouse: Thirty years of effective marketing and health communications. *Canadian Journal of Public Health,* 95, 58.

Ehrlich, G. (2000). *John Muir: Nature's visionary.* Washington, DC: National Geographic.

Ekstedt, J.W., & Griffiths, C.T. (1988). *Corrections in Canada: Policy and practice* (2nd ed.). Toronto: Butterworths.

Emard, M. (1990). Religion and leisure: A case study of the role of the church as a provider of recreation in small Ontario communities. Unpublished master's thesis, University of Waterloo.

Employee Services Management Association. (2001). *Ten components of employee services.* Retrieved on June 1, 2005 from www.esmassn.org/tencomponents.htm#recreation [June 28, 2005].

Employee Services Management Association. (2004): www.esmassn.org.

Erikson, E.H. (1968). *Identity: Youth and crisis.* New York: W.W. Norton.

Eschleman, J., Cashion, B., & Basirico, L. (1993). *Sociology: An introduction* (4th ed.). New York: Harper Collins College Publishers.

Estes, C., & Henderson, K. (2003, February). Enjoyment and the good life. *Parks & Recreation,* 22-31.

Farrell, P., & Lundegren, H. (1978). *The process of recreation programming: Theory and technique.* New York: Wiley.

Farrell, P., & Lundegren, H. (1983). *The process of recreation programming: Theory and technique* (2nd ed.). New York: Wiley.

Farrell, P., & Lundegren, H. (1991). *The process of recreation programming: Theory and technique* (3rd ed.). State College, PA: Venture.

Federal Bureau of Prisons. (n.d.) *Mission and vision.* Retrieved June 28, 2005 from www.bop.gov [June 28, 2005].

Finlay, J., & Sprague, D. (2000). *The structure of Canadian history* (6th ed.). Scarborough, ON: Prentice-Hall Canada.

Fleming, S. (1993). Schooling, sport and ethnicity: A case study. *Sociology Review,* 3, 29-33.

Fleming, S., & Khan, N. (1994). Islam, sport and masculinity: Some observations on the experiences of Pakistanis in Pakistan and Bangladeshis in Britain. In P. Duffy &

L. Dugdale (Eds.), *HPER: Moving toward the 21st century* (pp. 119-128). Champaign, IL: Human Kinetics.

Florida, R. (2002). *The rise of the creative class.* New York: Basic Books.

Floyd, M. (1998). Getting beyond marginality and ethnicity: The challenge for race and ethnic studies in leisure research. *Journal of Leisure Research,* 30(1), 3-22.

Foot, D.K. (1998). *Boom, bust and echo 2000.* Toronto: Macfarlane Walter & Ross.

Foot, D.K. (2002, March 21). Boomers blow up census. *The Globe and Mail,* p. A17.

Foster, J. (1978). *Working for wildlife: The beginning of preservation in Canada.* Toronto: University of Toronto Press.

Francis, R.D., Jones, R., & Smith, D. (1988). *Origins: Canadian history to confederation.* Toronto: Holt, Rinehart, and Winston of Canada.

Franklin, D. (2001, October). The entrepreneurial challenge. *Athletic Business,* 25(10), 85-91.

The Fraser Institute. (2002). *Canada spends the most on health care among OECD countries but ranks low on key health indicators.* Retrieved on August 1, 2004 from www.fraserinstitute.ca/shared/readmore.asp?sNav = nr &id = 475 [June 28, 2005].

Frumkin, H. (2001). Beyond toxicity: Human health and natural environment. *American Journal of Preventive Medicine,* 20(3), 237.

Gerbner, G. (1999, March). The stories we tell. *Peace Review,* 11(1).

Giles-Corti, B., & Donovan, R.J. (2002). The relative influence of individual, social, and physical environment determinants of physical activity. *Social Science Medicine,* 54, 1793-1812.

Glendening, J. (1997). *The high road: Romantic tourism, Scotland, and literature, 1720-1820.* New York: St. Martin's Press.

Godbey, G. (1997). *Leisure and leisure services in the 21st century.* State College, PA: Venture.

Godbey, G., Graefe, A., & James, S. (1993). Reality and perception: Where do we fit in? *Parks and Recreation,* January, 76-83, 110-111.

Godfrey, M.A. (2002, September). *National and local profiles of cultural support executive summary.* Retrieved July 14, 2004 from www.pewtrusts.com/pubs/pubs_item.cfm?content_item_id = 1294&content_type_id = 8&page = p3 [June 28, 2005].

Goldberg, P. (2003). *The spirit of wellness.* Retrieved August 1, 2004 from http://healthy.net/scr/column.asp?PageType = Column&id = 558 [June 28, 2005].

Goldman, S., Nagel, R., & Preiss, K. (1995). *Agile competitors and virtual organizations.* New York: Van Nostrand Reinhold.

Goleman, D. (1995). *Emotional intelligence: Why it can matter more than IQ.* New York: Bantam Books.

Goleman, D., Kaufman, P., & Ray, M. (1992). *The creative spirit.* New York: Penguin Books.

Goodale, T., & Godbey, G. (1988). *The evolution of leisure.* State College, PA: Venture.

Gottman, J.M., & Parker, J.G. (1987). *Conversations of friends.* New York: Cambridge University Press.

Gray, D. (1984, April). The great simplicities. Paper presented at the J.B. Nash Scholar Lecture, Anaheim, CA.

Gruneau, R. (1999). *Class, sports, and social development.* Champaign, IL: Human Kinetics.

Gulick, L.H. (1920). *A philosophy of play.* New York: Scribners.

Hall, M., & Banting, K.G. (2000). *The nonprofit sector in Canada: An introduction.* Kingston, ON: McGill-Queen's University Press.

Hamilton, E., & Huntington, C. (Eds.). (1961). *The collected dialogues of Plato.* Princeton, NJ: Princeton University Press.

Hammersley, C.H., & Tynon, J.F. (1998). Job competency analyses of entry-level resort and commercial recreation professionals. *Journal of Applied Recreation Research,* 23, 225-241.

Hansmann, H. (1987). Economic theories of non-profit organizations. In W.W. Powell (Ed.), *The nonprofit sector: A research handbook.* London: Yale University Press.

Harnick, P. (2000). *Inside city parks.* Washington, DC: Urban Land Institute.

Harper, J., Neider, D., Godbey, G., & Lamont, D. (1996). *The use and benefits of local government recreation and park services in Edmonton, Alberta.* Winnipeg, AB: Health, Leisure and Human Performance Institute, University of Manitoba.

Harrington, M. (1996). Women's leisure and the family in Canada. In N. Samuel (Ed.), *Women, leisure and the family in contemporary society: A multinational perspective* (pp. 35-48). Wellingford, UK: CAB International.

Hemingway, J. (1988). Leisure and civility: Reflections on a Greek ideal. *Leisure Sciences,* 10, 179-191.

Hemingway, J. (1996). Emancipating leisure: The recovery of freedom in leisure. *Journal of Leisure Research,* 28(1), 27-43.

Hemingway, J.L., & Parr, M.G. (2000). Leisure research and leisure practice: Three perspectives on constructing the research-practice relation. *Leisure Sciences,* 22(3), 139-162.

Henslin, J.M. (1993). *Sociology: A down-to-earth approach.* Boston: Allyn & Bacon.

Higby, C. (2003, May/June). *ESM magazine.* Elmhurst, IL: ESM Association, p. 25.

Hiller, J.K. (1998). *The treaty of Utrecht.* Memorial University of Newfoundland. Retrieved June 7, 2005 from www.heritage.nf.ca/exploration/utrecht.html [June 28, 2005].

The Holy Bible: New International Version. (1978). Grand Rapids, MI: Zonderven Bible Publishers.

Horna, J. (1994). *The study of leisure: An introduction.* Toronto: Oxford University Press.

Hossler, D., & Bean, P. (1990). *The strategic management of college enrollment.* San Francisco: Jossey-Bass.

Houghton, J. (Ed.). (2002). *SPRE curriculum catalog: Recreation and park education, 2002-2003.* Ashburn, VA: National Recreation and Park Association.

House, J.S., Landis, K.R., & Umberson, D. (1988). Social relationships and health. *Science,* 241, 540-545.

Howe, C.Z., & Carpenter, G.M. (1985). *Programming leisure experiences: A cyclical approach.* Englewood Cliffs, NJ: Prentice-Hall.

Hudson, B.J. (2001). Wild ways and paths of pleasure: Access to British waterfalls, 1500-2000. *Landscape Research, 26*(4), 285-303.

Huizinga, J. (1950). *Homo ludens.* Boston: Beacon Press.

Humpel, N., Owen, N., & Leslie, E. (2002). Environmental factors associated with adult's participation in physical activity. *American Journal of Preventive Medicine, 22,* 188-199.

Hunnicutt, B. (1990). Leisure and play in Plato's teaching and philosophy of learning. *Leisure Sciences, 12,* 211-227.

Huston, S., Evenson, K., Bors, P., & Gizlice, Z. (2003). Neighborhood environment, access to places for activity and leisure time physical activity in a diverse North Carolina population. *American Journal of Health Promotion, 18,* 58-69.

Hyde, J.S., & DeLamater, J.D. (2003). *Understanding human sexuality* (8th ed.). New York: McGraw-Hill.

Ibrahim, H. (1979). Leisure in the ancient world. In H. Ibrahim & J. Shivers (Eds.), *Leisure: Emergence and expansion* (pp. 45-78). Los Alamitos, CA: Hwong.

Ibrahim, H. (1991). *Leisure and society: A comparative approach.* Dubuque, IA: Brown.

Illinois State Museum. (2000). *The Illinois society: Recreation.* Retrieved January 15, 2000 from www.museum.state.il.us/muslink/nat_amer/post/htmls/soc_rec.html [June 28, 2005].

Imagine Canada. (2005). www.imaginecanada.ca [June 28, 2005].

Independent Sector. (2004). *Giving and volunteering in the United States 2001.* Retrieved September 1, 2004 from www.independentsector.org/programs/research/gv01main.html [June 28, 2005].

The International Ecotourism Society. (2004). *What is ecotourism.* Retrieved February 28, 2005 from www.ecotourism.org/index2.php?what-is-ecotourism [June 28, 2005].

International Health, Racquet and Sportsclub Association. (2003). *The scope of the US health club industry (industry estimates).* Retrieved August 1, 2004 from http://cms.ihrsa.org/IHRSA/viewPage.cfm?pageId=804#graph2 [June 28, 2005].

International Peace Garden. (2005). *The International Peace Garden.* Retrieved June 6, 2005 from www.peacegarden.com [June 28, 2005].

Interprovincial Sport and Recreation Council. (1987). *National recreation statement.* Retrieved June 30, 2004 from www.lin.ca/resource/html/statemen.htm [June 28, 2005].

Ipson, N., Mahoney, E.M., & Adams, J.H. (1999). Public relations, marketing, and customer service. In B. van der Smissen, M. Moiseichik, V.J. Hartenburg, & L.F. Twardzik (Eds.), *Management of parks and recreation agencies.* Ashburn, VA: National Recreation and Parks Association.

Irwin, P., Gartner, W., & Phelps, C. (1990). Mexican American/Anglo cultural differences as recreation style determinants. *Leisure Sciences, 12,* 335-348.

Iso-Ahola, S.E. (1980). *The social psychology of leisure and recreation.* Dubuque, IA: Brown.

Jackson, A., Fawcett, G., Milan, A., Roberts, P., Schetagne, S., Scott, K., & Tsoukalas, S. (2000, November). *Social cohesion in Canada: Possible indicators—Highlights.* Ottawa, ON: Canadian Council on Social Development.

Jalili, G. (1994). Moslem students and physical education. *Active and Healthy, 1*(1), 9-10.

Jensen, L.C. (1985). *Adolescence: Theories, research, implications.* St. Paul, MN: West Publishing Co.

Jewish Community Centers Maccabi Games. (2005). www.jccmaccabi.org/index_home.php [June 28, 2005].

Jewish Community Centers of North America. (2005). www.jcca.org [June 28, 2005].

Jewish Community Centre of Greater Vancouver. (2005). www.jccgv.bc.ca [June 28, 2005].

Johnson, C.Y., Bowker, J.M., English, D.B.K., & Worthen, D. (1997). *Theoretical perspectives of ethnicity and outdoor recreation: A review and synthesis of African-American and European-American participation.* General Technical Report SRS-11. Ashville, NC: USDA Forest Service, Southern Research Station.

Johnson, R., & McLean, D. (1994). Leisure and the development of ethical character: Changing views of the North American ideal. *Journal of Applied Recreation Research, 19*(2), 117-130.

Joiner, T.E. (2000). Depression: Current developments and controversies. In S.H. Qualls & N. Abeles (Eds.), *Psychology and the aging revolution.* Washington, DC: American Psychological Association.

Jones, M.L. (2002, July 21). Girls band together. *Oregonian,* pp. B1, B4.

Jordan, C.R. (1991). Parks and recreation: More than fun and games. In B.L. Driver, P.J. Brown, & G.L. Peterson (Eds.), *Benefits of leisure.* State College, PA: Venture.

Journal of Leisurability. (2000). *Leisure education as a rehabilitative tool for youth in incarcerated settings.* Retrieved from www.lin.ca/lin/resource/html/vol27/sp0044.pdf [June 28, 2005].

Kaczynski, A.T., & Crompton, J.L. (2004a). An operational tool for determining the optimum repositioning strategy for leisure service departments. *Managing Leisure, 9,* 127-144.

Kaczynski, A.T., & Crompton, J.L. (2004b). Development of a multi-dimensional scale for implementing positioning in public park and recreation agencies. *Journal of Park and Recreation Administration, 22*(2), 1-26.

Kahan, D. (2003a). Islam and physical activity: Implications for American sport and physical educators. *Journal of Physical Education, Recreation and Dance, 74*(3), 48-54.

Kahan, D. (2003b). Law review: Religious boundaries in public school physical activity settings. *Journal of Physical Education, Recreation and Dance, 74*(1), 11-12, 14.

Kamiyole, O. (1993). Physical educators' albatross in African Muslim societies. *International Journal of Physical Education, 30*(2), 29-31.

Kando, T.M. (1975). *Leisure and popular culture in transition.* St. Louis: C.V. Mosby Company.

Karabetsos, J.D. (1991, Winter). Campus recreation: Future direction. *NIRSA Journal, 15*(2), 10-16.

Karlis, G. (2004). *Leisure and recreation in Canadian society: An introduction.* Toronto: Thompson Educational.

Karlis, G., & Dawson, D. (1990). Ethnic maintenance and recreation: A case study. *Journal of Applied Recreation Research,* 15(2), 85-99.

Karlis, G., & Dawson, D. (1995). Ethnicity and recreation: Concepts, approaches and programming. *Canadian Ethnic Studies,* 27(2), 167-180.

Karlis, G., & Dawson, D. (1996). Native culture and recreation: A preliminary inquiry. *Native Studies Review,* 1192, 121-129.

Keating, D.P. (1990). Adolescent thinking. In S.S. Feldman & G.R. Elliott (Eds.), *At the threshold: The developing adolescent.* Cambridge, MA: Harvard University Press.

Keene, A. (1994). *Earthkeepers: Observers and protectors of nature.* New York: Oxford University Press.

Kelly, J., & Godbey, G. (1992). *The sociology of leisure.* State College, PA: Venture.

Kelly, J.R. (1987). *Freedom to be: A new sociology of leisure.* New York: Macmillan.

Kelly, J.R. (1996). *Leisure* (3rd ed.). Boston: Allyn & Bacon.

Kelly, J.R. (1997). Activity and aging: Challenge in retirement. In J.T. Haworth (Ed.), *Work, leisure and well-being* (pp. 165-179). London: Routledge & Kegan Paul.

Kelly, J.R. (1999). Leisure and society: A dialectical analysis. In E.L. Jackson & T.L. Burton (Eds.), *Leisure studies: Prospects for the twenty-first century.* State College, PA: Venture.

Kelly, J.R., & Freysinger, V.J. (2000). *21st century leisure: Current issues.* Boston: Allyn & Bacon.

Kentucky State Parks. (2005). *The Lake Barkley State Resort Park.* Retrieved June 6, 2005 from http://parks.ky.gov/resortparks/lb/index.htm [June 28, 2005].

Killan, G. (1993). *Protected places: A history of Ontario's provincial park system.* Toronto: Dundurn Press.

Kleiber, D.A. (1999). *Leisure experience and human development.* New York: Basic Books.

Knox, M. (2004). ParticipACTION: The mouse that roared. *Canadian Journal of Public Health,* 95, 5.

Knudson, D.M., Cable, T.T., & Beck, L. (1999). *Interpretation of cultural and natural resources.* State College, PA: Venture.

Kornblum, J. (2004, June 17). Arts help seniors age gracefully; And with improved health, early research suggests. *USA Today,* p. D04.

Kosmin, B., Mayer, E., & Keysar, A. (2001, December). *American religious identification survey: Profile of the U.S. Muslim population.* Retrieved June 6, 2005 from City University of New York, Graduate Center Web site: www.gc.cuny.edu/studies/aris.pdf.

Kotler, P. (2000). *Marketing management: The millennium edition.* Upper Saddle River, NJ: Prentice-Hall.

Kraus, R. (1966). *Recreation today: Program planning and leadership.* New York: Meredith.

Kraus, R. (1971). *Recreation and leisure in modern society.* Glenview, IL: Scott, Foresman and Company.

Kraus, R. (1978). *Recreation and leisure in modern society* (2nd ed.). Santa Monica, CA: Goodyear.

Kraus, R. (1979). *Social recreation: A group dynamics approach.* St. Louis: Mosby.

Kraus, R. (1984). *Recreation and leisure in modern society* (3rd ed.). Dallas: Scott Foresman.

Kraus, R. (1985). *Recreation program planning today.* Glenview, IL: Scott Foresman.

Kraus, R. (1990a). *Leisure in modern society.* Boston: Addison-Wesley.

Kraus, R. (1990b). *Recreation and leisure in modern society* (4th ed.). Glenview, IL: Scott, Foresman and Company.

Kraus, R. (2000). *Leisure in a changing America: Trends and issues for the 21st century.* Boston: Allyn & Bacon.

Kraus, R. (2001). *Recreation and leisure in modern society* (6th ed.). Sudbury, MA: Jones & Bartlett.

Kraus, R.G., & Curtis, J.E. (1990). *Creative management in recreation, parks, and leisure services* (5th ed.). St. Louis: Times Mirror/Mosby College.

Krumpe, E. (2004). *Fall 2004 professional foundations of recreation resources and tourism.* Retrieved on September 6, 2004 from http://images.google.com/imgres?imgurl=http://www.cnr.uidaho.edu/rrt287/images/ROS.gif&imgrefurl=http://www.cnr.uidaho.edu/rrt287/lecture_slides.htm&h=162&w=200&sz=9&tbnid=2Pl6NunHq84J:&tbnh=80&tbnw=99&hl=en&start=5&prev=/images%3Fq%3Drecreation%2Bopportunity%2Bspectrum%2B(ROS)%26hl%3Den%26lr%3D%26safe%3Doff%26sa%3DN [June 28, 2005].

Kubey, R., & Csikzentmihalyi, M. (1990). *Television and the quality of life: How viewing shapes everyday experience.* Hilsdale, NJ: Lawrence Erlbaum.

Kuo, F., Sullivan, W., Coley, R., & Brunson, L. (1998). Fertile ground for community inner-city neighborhood common spaces. *American Journal of Community Psychology,* 26(1), 823-851. Retrieved June 5, 2005 from www.tpl.org/pforp [June 28, 2005].

Ladd, T., & Mathisen, J. (1999). *Muscular Christianity: Evangelical Protestants and the development of American sport.* Grand Rapids, MI: Baker Books.

Landrum, N.C. (2004). *The state park movement in America: A critical review.* Columbia, MO: University of Columbia Press.

LaPierre, L. (1992). *Canada, my Canada: What happened?* Toronto: McLelland & Stewart.

Lee, I.M., Manson, J.E., Hennekens, C.H., & Paffenbarger, R.S. (1993). Body-weight and mortality: A 27-year follow-up. *Journal of the American Medical Association,* 270, 2823-2828.

Lee, J. (1911). *Play as an antidote to civilization.* Reprinted from *The Playground,* July 1911. New York, NY: Playground and Recreation Association of America.

Leitner, M., & Scher, G. (2000). A follow-up study to peacemaking: The positive effects of intergenerational recreational recreation programs on the attitudes of Israeli Arabs and Jews. *World Leisure and Recreation* (Lethbridge, AB), 42(1), 33-36.

Leland, J. (2004, July 26). Airports carry excess baggage as cookie-cutter, postmodern metropolises. [New York Times News Service], *The Oregonian,* B1, B3.

Lenski, G., & Lenski, J. (1987). *Human societies: An introduction to macrosociology* (5th ed.). New York: McGraw-Hill.

Lenski, G., Nolan, P., & Lenski, J. (1995). *Human societies: An introduction to macrosociology* (7th ed.). New York: McGraw-Hill.

Leoni, E., & Berbling, M. (1980). *Leisure coaching: A common sense approach.* Retrieved August 1, 2004 from www.lib.niu.edu/ipo/ip800726.html [June 28, 2005].

Levine, P. (1992). Basketball and community: Assimilation and the American Jewish experience. *North American Society for Sport History, Proceedings & Newsletter,* 136-137.

Levy, J., Rosenburg, D., & Hyman, A. (1999, Summer). Fanny "Bobbie" Rosenfeld: Canada's Woman Athlete of the Half Century. *Journal of Sport History,* 26(2), 392-396.

Lyons, R.F. (1981). Profile of municipal leisure services for special populations in Canada. *Journal of Leisurability,* 8(4), 14-24.

Maccabi Canada. (2005). www.maccabicanada.com [June 28, 2005].

MacIntosh, D., Bedecki, T., & Franks, C.E.S. (1988). *Sport and politics in Canada: Federal government involvement since 1961.* Kingston, ON: McGill-Queen's University Press.

Malloy, D.C., Nilson, R.N., & Yoshioka, C. (1993). The impact of culture upon the administrative process in sport and recreation: A Canadian perspective. *Journal of Applied Recreation Research,* 18(2), 115-130.

Mannell, R.C. (2000). Older adults, leisure, and wellness. *Journal of Leisurability,* 26, 3-10.

Mannell, R.C., & Dupuis, S. (1996). Life satisfaction. In J.E. Birren (Ed.), *Encyclopedia of gerontology [Vol. 2].* San Diego: Academic Press.

Manning, R.E. (1999). *Studies in outdoor recreation: Search and research for satisfaction* (2nd ed.). Corvallis, OR: Oregon State University Press.

Manuel, D.G., Luo, W., Ugnat, A.M., & Mao, U. (2003). Cause-deleted health-adjusted life expectancy of Canadians with selected chronic conditions [Electronic version]. *Chronic Disease in Canada,* 24, 108-115.

Markham, S. (1992). Our leaders speak up. *Recreation Canada,* 50(2), 15-19.

Markham, S. (1995). The early years: 1944 to 1951. *Recreation Canada,* 53(3), 6-16.

Markham, S.E. (1988). *The development of parks and playgrounds in selected Canadian prairie cities: 1880-1930.* Edmonton, AB: University of Alberta, Edmonton.

Markham, S.E. (1991a). Editorial. *Recreation Canada,* 49(4), 4.

Markham, S.E. (1991b). Rural recreation: The quintessential partnership. *Recreation Canada,* 49(4), 12-14.

Markham, S.E. (1998). Mabel Peters. In *Dictionary of Canadian biography* (Vol. XIV, pp. 836-838). Toronto: University of Toronto Press.

Marty, S. (1984). *A grand and fabulous notion: The first century of Canada's parks.* Toronto: NC Press.

Mason, D. (1999, November 5). [Address on accepting ARNOVA's Award for Distinguished Lifetime Achievement]. Speech presented to the Association for Research on Nonprofit Organizations and Voluntary Action, Washington, DC.

McCarthy, K.F., & Jinnett, K. (2001). *A new framework for building participation in the arts.* Santa Monica, CA: RAND.

McChesney, J., Everett, C., & Gerkin, M. (2002). Public Image, Ltd.: Students say their future field is misunderstood by the public. *Parks & Recreation,* 37(10), 51-53.

McFarland, E. (1982). The beginning of municipal park systems. In G. Wall & J. Marsh (Eds.), *Recreational land use: Perspectives on its evolution in Canada.* Ottawa, ON: Carleton University Press.

McFarland, E.M. (1970). *The development of public recreation in Canada.* Ottawa, ON: Canadian Parks and Recreation Association.

McKeon, R. (Ed.). (1941). *The basic works of Aristotle.* New York: Random House.

McLean, A.D., Hurd, A.R., & Rogers, N.B. (2005). *Kraus' recreation and leisure in modern society.* Sudbury, MA: Jones and Bartlett.

Mendelsohn, D. (2004, August 8). What Olympic ideal? *The New York Times Magazine,* pp. 11-13.

Mercola, J. (2002). *Nearly 3 trillion dollars in U.S. health spending is projected.* Retrieved June 7, 2005 from www.mercola.com/2002/mar/30/health_spending.htm [June 28, 2005].

Meyer, H.D., & Brightbill, C.K. (1956). *Community recreation: A guide to its organization.* Englewood Cliffs, NJ: Prentice-Hall.

Mill, R. (1986). Tourist characteristics and trends. *Literature review: The President's Commission on Americans Outdoors.* Washington, DC: Government Printing Office.

Miller, C. (2004). *Gifford Pinchot and the making of modern environmentalism.* Washington, DC: Island Press.

Minzey, J.D., & LeTarte, C.E. (1979). *Community education: From program to process to practice.* Midland, MI: Pendell.

Missouri State Parks and Historic Sites. (2005). *The history of Missouri's state park system.* Retrieved January 16, 2005 from www.mostateparks.com/history.htm#ccc [June 28, 2005].

Mitchell, E.D. (1939). *Intramural sports.* New York: Barnes.

Mokdad, A.H., Marks, J.S., Stroup, D.F., & Gerberding, J.L. (2004). Actual causes of death in the United States, 2000 [Electronic version]. *The Journal of the American Medical Association,* 291, 1238-1245.

Moore, L. (1992). Community education and educational reform: Where the states are now. In L. Decker & V. Romney (Eds.), *Educational restructuring and the community education process* (pp. 75-83). Charlottesville, VA: University of Virginia.

Mull, R.F., Bayless, K.G., Ross, C.M., & Jamieson, L.M. (1997). *Recreational sport management* (3rd ed.). Champaign, IL: Human Kinetics.

Mull, R.F., Bayless, K.G., & Jamieson, L.M. (2005). *Recreational sport management* (4th ed.). Champaign, IL: Human Kinetics.

Mummers.com. (2005). The Philadelphia mummers New Year's Day parade. Retrieved July 23, 2004 from http://mummers.com [June 28, 2005].

Mural Arts Program. (2002). *About us.* Retrieved July 23, 2004 from www.muralarts.org/about [June 28, 2005].

Nanus, B., & Dobbs, S.M. (1999). *Leaders who make a difference: Essential strategies for meeting the nonprofit challenge.* San Francisco: Jossey-Bass.

Nash, J. (1953). *Philosophy of recreation and leisure.* Dubuque, IA: Brown.

Nash, R. (1982). *Wilderness and the American mind* (3rd ed.). New Haven, CT: Yale University Press.

Nash, R. (2001). *Wilderness and the American mind* (4th ed.). New Haven, CT: Yale University Press.

National Assembly of Health and Human Service Organizations. (2004). Retrieved September 1, 2004 from www.nassembly.org/nassembly/members.html#11 [June 28, 2005].

National Association of State Park Directors. (2004). Retrieved September 28, 2004 from http://naspd.indstate.edu/statistics.html [June 28, 2005].

National Curriculum Conference. (1997). Proceedings of the National Curriculum Conference on Parks and Recreation, Salt Lake City, UT, October 27-November 1, 1997.

National Endowment for the Arts. (1997). *1997 survey of public participation in the arts. NEA Research Division Report 39.* Retrieved July 14, 2004 from www.arts.gov/pub/Survey/SurveyPDF.html [June 28, 2005].

National Endowment for the Arts. (2002). *National Endowment for the Arts releases details of latest arts participation survey.* Retrieved July 29, 2004 from www.nea.gov/news/news04/SurveyAnnounce.html [June 28, 2005].

National Geographic News. (2004). *U.S. national parks told to quietly cut services.* Retrieved June 4, 2005 from http://news.nationalgeographic.com/news/2004/03/0319_040319_parks.html [June 28, 2005].

National Heart, Lung, and Blood Institute of the National Institutes of Health. (2001). *Hearts N' Parks: Community mobilization guide.* NIH Publication No. 01-1655.

National Institute on Out-of-School Time. (2003). *Making the case: A fact sheet on children and youth in out-of-school time.* Retrieved June 5, 2005 from www.niost.org/publications/Factsheet_2003.pdf [June 28, 2005].

National Institutes of Health. (2001). *Hearts N' Parks: Community mobilization guide.* Retrieved June 6, 2005 from www.nhlbi.nih.gov/health/prof/heart/obesity/hrt_n_pk/hnp_resg.htm [June 28, 2005].

National Institutes of Health. (2003). *Reducing nationwide obesity starts in neighborhoods.* Retrieved June 5, 2005 from www.nhlbi.nih.gov/new/press/03-07-03.htm [June 28, 2005].

National Intramural-Recreational Sports Association. (1996). *General and specialty standards for collegiate recreational sports.* Corvallis, OR: Author.

National Intramural-Recreational Sports Association. (2004). *The value of recreational sports in higher education: Impact on student enrollment, success, and buying power.* Champaign, IL: Human Kinetics.

National Intramural-Recreational Sports Association. (2005). *NIRSA highlights.* Retrieved June 3, 2005 from www.nirsa.org/about/cd_history/history.htm [June 28, 2005].

National Intramural-Recreational Sports Association. (n.d.). *About NIRSA.* Retrieved May 27, 2004 from www.nirsa.org/about/index.htm [June 28, 2005].

National Marine Sanctuaries. (2005). *National Marine Sanctuaries.* Retrieved June 6, 2005 from www.sanctuaries.nos.noaa.gov [June 28, 2005].

National Outdoor Leadership School. (2004). *NOLS courses.* Retrieved September 6, 2004 from www.nols.edu/courses [June 28, 2005].

National Park Service. (2000). *Visitation statistics.* Retrieved on September 6, 2004 from www2.nature.nps.gov/stats/visitbody.htm [June 28, 2005].

National Park Service. (2003). *A brief history of the National Park Service: National park service created.* Retrieved June 12, 2005 from www.cr.nps.gov/history/online_books/kieley/kieley4.htm [June 28, 2005].

National Park Service. (2004). *Careers: Park rangers.* Retrieved June 13, 2005 from www.nps.gov/personnel/rangers.htm [June 28, 2005].

National Park Service. (2005a). *Rethinking the national parks for the 21st century.* Retrieved July 20, 2005 from www.nps.gov/policy/report.htm [June 28, 2005].

National Park Service. (2005b). *State Land and Water Conservation Fund.* Retrieved June 4, 2005 from www.nps.gov/lwcf [June 28, 2005].

National Park Service. (2005c). *Wild and scenic river system: Wild rivers list.* Retrieved June 4, 2005 from www.nps.gov/rivers/wildriverslist.html [June 28, 2005].

National Park Service, Office of International Affairs. (2005). *Office of International Affairs.* Retrieved June 4, 2005 from www.nps.gov/oia [June 28, 2005].

National Recreation and Park Association. (n.d.). *About us.* Retrieved July 21, 2004 from www.nrpa.org [June 28, 2005].

National Wilderness Institute. (1995). *State by state government land ownership.* Retrieved on September 6, 2004 from www.nwi.org/Maps/LandChart.html [June 28, 2005].

Navy Morale, Welfare and Recreation. (n.d.). *Navy MWR fleet recreation.* Retrieved on June 1, 2005 from www.mwr.navy.mil/mwrprgms/fleetrec.htm [June 28, 2005].

Nebraska Game and Parks Commission. (n.d.). *Eugene T. Mahoney State Park.* Retrieved June 6, 2005 from www.ngpc.state.ne.us/parks/guides/parksearch/showpark.asp?Area_No = 273 [June 28, 2005].

Newman, D. (1999). *Sociology of families.* Thousand Oaks, CA: Pine Forge Press.

Noonan, D.S. (2004, June). *A political economy of cultural national parks.* Paper presented at the meeting of the Association for Cultural Economics International, Chicago, IL.

Office of Disease Prevention and Health Promotion, U.S. Department of Health and Human Services. (2005). *Healthy People.* www.healthypeople.gov [June 28, 2005].

Olsho, L.W., Harkins, S.W., & Lenhardt, M.L. (1985). Aging and the auditory system. In J.E. Birren & K.W. Schaie (Eds.), *Handbook of the psychology of aging* (2nd ed., pp. 332-377). New York: Van Nostrand Reinhold.

O'Neill, M. (2002). *Nonprofit nation: A new look at the third America.* San Francisco: Jossey-Bass.

Online Newshour. (1997, May 19). *Gender parity in sports: The pros and cons of Title IX.* Retrieved June 16, 2005 from www.pbs.org/newshour/forum/may97/title9_5-19.html [June 28, 2005].

Orend, R.J. (1989). *Socialization and participating in the arts.* Princeton, NJ: Princeton University Press.

Osborn, L.D., & Neuremeyer, M.H. (1933). *The community and society: An introduction to sociology.* New York: American Book.

O'Sullivan, E. (1996). *The benefits of parks and recreation.* Alexandria, VA: National Recreation & Park Association.

O'Sullivan, E. (1999). *Setting a course for change: The benefits movement.* Ashburn, VA: National Recreation & Park Association.

Outdoor Industry Foundation. (2004, January). *Exploring the active lifestyle: Consumer outreach report.* [HarrisInteractive survey]. Retrieved October 11, 2004 from www.outdoorindustry.org/MediaExecSummary.pdf [June 28, 2005].

Outdoor Recreation Resources Review Commission. (1962). *Public outdoor recreation areas: Acreage, use, potential.* Washington, DC: U.S. Government Printing Office.

Outdoor Recreation Resources Review Commission. (1963). *Outdoor recreation for America.* Washington, DC: U.S. Government Printing Office, Superintendent of Documenters.

Outward Bound Canada. (n.d.). *What is Outward Bound?* Retrieved February 28, 2005 from www.outwardbound.ca/whatis.asp [June 28, 2005].

Outward Bound USA. (n.d.). *Outward Bound, a brief history.* Retrieved February 28, 2005 from www.outwardbound.org/about.html [June 28, 2005].

Parkhouse, B.L. (1996). *The management of sport: Its foundation and application* (2nd ed.). St. Louis: Mosby.

Parks and Recreation Association of Canada. (1947). *Charter.* Toronto, ON.

Parks and Recreation Federation of Ontario. (1992). *The benefits of parks and recreation: A catalogue.* Ottawa, ON: Ontario Ministry of Tourism and Recreation.

Parks and Recreation Ontario. (n.d.). *About PRO.* Retrieved June 30, 2004 from http://216.13.76.142/PROntario/about.html [June 28, 2005].

Parks Canada. (2002). *Annual report 2001-2002: Visitor impacts.* Retrieved October 11, 2004 from www.pc.gc.ca/docs/pc/rpts/RP-PA2001-2002/index_e.asp [June 28, 2005].

Parks Canada. (2003). *The Parks Canada charter.* Retrieved October 11, 2004 from www.pc.gc.ca/agen/chart/chartr_E.asp [June 28, 2005].

Parks Canada. (2005). *World heritage.* Retrieved July 11, 2005 from www.pc.gc.ca/progs/spm-whs/index_e.asp [June 28, 2005].

Parks Canada Agency. (2002). *Parks Canada mandate.* Retrieved June 30, 2004 from www.pc.gc.ca/agen/index_E.asp [June 28, 2005].

Parks Canada Agency. (n.d.). *Parks Canada agency.* Retrieved June 30, 2004 from www.pc.gc.ca [June 28, 2005].

Parson, S.R. (1999). *Transforming schools into community learning centers.* Larchmont, NY: Eye on Education.

ParticipACTION Archive. (n.d.) *The early years: TV, radio and print media.* Retrieved October 12, 2005, from www.usask.ca/archives/participaction/english/motivate/theearlyyears.html.

Patterson, C.J. (2002). Lesbian and gay parenthood. In M.H. Bornstein (Ed.), *Handbook of parenting* (2nd ed.). Mahwah, NJ: Erlbaum.

Payton, R.L. (1988). *Philanthropy: Voluntary action for the public good.* New York: American Council on Education and Macmillan.

Peplau, L.A., & Beals, K.P. (2002). Lesbians, gays, and bisexuals in relationships. In J. Worell (Ed.), *Encyclopedia of women and gender.* San Diego: Academic Press.

Peters, M. (1913). Annual report of the committee on vacation schools and supervised playgrounds. In National Council of Women of Canada (Ed.), *The yearbook containing the report of the twentieth annual meeting of the National Council of Women of Canada* (pp. 53-48). Toronto: National Council of Women of Canada.

Philadelphia Department of Recreation. (n.d.). *The Philadelphia Department of Recreation.* Retrieved July 26, 2004 from www.phila.gov/recreation [June 28, 2005].

Phillip, S. (2000). Race and the pursuit of happiness. *Journal of Leisure Research, 32*(1), 121-124.

Pieper, J. (1998). *Leisure: The basis of culture* [R. Scruton, Trans.]. South Bend, IN: St. Augustine's Press.

Plato. (1930). *The republic* [P. Shorey, Trans.]. Cambridge, MA: Harvard University Press.

Poliakoff, M. (1993). Stadium and arena: Reflections on Greek, Roman and contemporary social history. *Olympika: The International Journal of Olympic Studies, 2,* 67-78.

Popke, M. (2001a). Spread the Word. *Athletic Business, 25*(10), 55-61.

Popke, M. (2001b). Spiritual profit. *Athletic Business, 25*(10), 58.

Potter, C. (2001). OSD history narrative used by permission by interview on February 27, 2005.

Pratt, M., Macera, C., & Guijing, W. (2000). Higher direct medical costs associated with physical inactivity. *The Physician and Sportsmedicine,* retrieved June 5, 2005 from www.physsportsmed.com/issues/2000/10_00/pratt.htm [June 28, 2005].

Prebish, C. (1993). *Religion and sport: The meeting of sacred and profane.* Westport, CT: Greenwood Press.

Preiss, K., Goldman, S., & Nagel, R. (1996). *Cooperate to compete: Building agile business relationships.* New York: Van Nostrand Reinhold.

Priest, S., & Gass, M. (2005). *Effective leadership in adventure programming* (2nd ed.). Champaign, IL: Human Kinetics.

Pruchno, R., & Rosenbaum, J. (2003). Social relationships in adulthood and old age. In I.B. Weiner (Ed.), *Handbook of psychology, Vol. VI.* New York: Wiley.

Putnam, R. (2000). *Bowling alone.* New York: Simon & Schuster.

Putney, C. (2001). *Muscular Christianity: Manhood and sports in protestant America, 1880-1920.* Cambridge, MA: Harvard University Press.

Rails to Trails Conservancy. (2005). *Welcome to the Rails to Trails Conservancy.* Retrieved June 4, 2005 from www.railstrails.org [June 28, 2005].

Rainwater, C. (1992). *The play movement in the United States.* Chicago: University of Chicago Press.

Ramsar. (2005). *Canada names new Ramsar site in British Columbia.* Retrieved July 11, 2005 from www.ramsar.org/wn/w.n.canada_columbia.htm [June 28, 2005].

Rappoport, R., & Rappoport, R.N. (1975). *Leisure and the family life cycle.* London: Routledge & Kegan Paul.

Recreation, Health and Exercise Consultants, Inc. (n.d.). http://vanity.qwestdex.com/rhec/Page2.html [June 28, 2005].

Recreation Nova Scotia. (n.d.). *Recreation Nova Scotia.* Retrieved June 30, 2004 from www.recreationns.ns.ca [June 28, 2005].

The Recreation Roundtable. (2004, January). *Outdoor recreation in America 2003: Recreation's benefits to society challenged by trends.* [RoperASW survey]. Retrieved October 11, 2004 from www.funoutdoors.com/files/ROPER%20REPORT%202004_0.pdf [June 28, 2005].

Revenue Canada. (2004). *Definition of a nonprofit organization.* Retrieved September 1, 2004 from www.cra-arc.gc.ca/tax/nonprofit/menu-e.html [June 28, 2005].

Rice, E.A. (1929). *A brief history of physical education.* New York: Barnes.

Ritvo, H. (2003). Fighting for Thirlmere: The roots of environmentalism. *Science, 300*(5625), 1510-1511.

Robertson, B. (1998). Issues in leisure education for persons in correctional systems. In J. Mundy (Ed.), *Leisure education theory and practice.* Champaign, IL: Sagamore.

Robertson, B.J. (1993). *An investigation of leisure in the lives of adolescents who engage in delinquent activity for fun, thrills, and excitement.* Unpublished doctoral dissertation, University of Oregon, Eugene.

Robins, R.W., Trzesniewski, K.H., Tracey, J.L., Potter, J., & Gosling, S.D. (2002). Age differences in self-esteem from 9 to 90. *Psychology and Aging, 17,* 423-434.

Robinson, J.P., & Godbey, G. (1997). *Time for life: The surprising ways Americans use their time.* University Park, PA: Penn State University Press.

Ross, C.M., & Forrester, S.A. (1999). Tracking computer trends of the 1900s in collegiate recreational sports. *Athletic Business, 23*(10), 79-81.

Rossman, J.R. (1989). *Recreation programming: Designing leisure experiences.* Champaign, IL: Sagamore.

Rossman, J.R. (1995). *Recreation programming: Designing leisure experiences* (2nd ed.). Champaign, IL: Sagamore.

Rossman, J.R. (2000). *Recreation programming: Designing leisure experiences* (3rd ed.). Champaign, IL: Sagamore.

Rothbart, M.K., & Putnam, S.P. (2002). Temperament and socialization. In L. Pulkkinen & A. Caspi (Eds.), *Paths to successful development.* New York: Cambridge University Press.

Rothman, D.J. (1971). *The discovery of the asylum.* Toronto: Little, Brown.

Runte, A. (1997). *National parks: The American experience* (3rd ed.). Lincoln, NE: University of Nebraska Press.

Runte, A. (1998). *Trains of discovery: Western railroads and the national parks* (4th ed.). Lanham, MD: Roberts Rinehart.

Russell, B. (1960). *In praise of idleness: And other essays.* London: George Allen & Unwin.

Russell, R.V. (2002). *Pastimes: The context of contemporary culture* (2nd ed.). Champaign, IL: Sagamore, pp. 308-309.

Russell, R.V. (2005). *Pastimes: The context of contemporary leisure* (3rd ed.). Champaign, IL: Sagamore.

Rutherford, P. (Ed.). (1974). *Saving the Canadian city: The first phase, 1880-1920.* Toronto: University of Toronto Press.

Ryan, J. (1992). Life support: Conserving biological diversity. *Worldwatch Paper 108.* Washington, DC: Worldwatch Institute.

Rybczynski, W. (1999). *A clearing in the distance: Frederick Law Olmsted and America in the nineteenth century.* New York: Scribner.

Salamon, L. (1999). *America's nonprofit sector* (2nd ed.). New York: Foundation Center.

Salamon, L.M. (Ed.). (2002). *The state of nonprofit America.* Washington, DC: Brookings Institution Press. Published in collaboration with the Aspen Institute.

Salamon, L.M., & Anheier, H.K. (1996). The international classification of nonprofit organizations: ICNPO-revision 1. *Working Papers of the Johns Hopkins Comparative Nonprofit Sector Project,* no. 19. Baltimore: The Johns Hopkins Institute for Policy Studies.

Santa Clara University. (2004). *The wellness center.* Retrieved August 1, 2004 from www.scu.edu/wellness/Spiritual-Wellness.cfm [June 28, 2005].

Sapora, A.V. (1996). *The origin and early development of professional preparation in recreation (leisure studies) at the University of Illinois-Urbana.* Retrieved May 27, 2005 from www.leisurestudies.uiuc.edu/history.htm [June 28, 2005].

SAS Institute. (n.d.a). www.sas.com [June 28, 2005].

SAS Institute. (n.d.b). www.sas.com/news/preleases/042805/news2.html [June 28, 2005].

Saskatchewan Parks and Recreation Association. (n.d.a). *What is the SPRA?* Retrieved June 30, 2004 from www.spra.sk.ca/about.htm [June 28, 2005].

Saskatchewan Parks and Recreation Association. (n.d.b). *SPRA history.* Retrieved June 30, 2004 from www.spra.sk.ca/history.htm [June 28, 2005].

Saunders, A. (1998). *Algonquin story* (3rd ed.). Whitney, ON: Friends of Algonquin Park.

Sawyer, T. (2002). Law review: Legal rights of community groups' use of school facilities. *Journal of Physical Education, Recreation and Dance, 73*(7), 8-10.

Sawyer, T.H., & Smith, O. (1999). *The management of clubs, recreation, and sport.* Champaign, IL: Sagamore.

Schaie, K.W. (1994). The life course of adult intellectual abilities. *American Psychologist, 49,* 304-313.

Schaie, K.W. (1996). *Intellectual development in adulthood: The Seattle Longitudinal Study.* New York: Cambridge University Press.

Schaumburg Park District. (2004). *Schaumburg Park District 2004 summer brochure.* Retrieved June 28, 2005 from www.parkfun.com/dir/publications/progcat/progcat.html [June 28, 2005].

Schneller, R. (1998). From anti-leisure to controlled leisure-culture in the Jewish Ultra-Orthodox community in Jerusalem. *World Leisure and Recreation, 40*(1), 26-29.

Schor, J. (1998). *The overspent American.* New York: Basic Books.

Schreyer, R., & Driver, B.L. (1989). The benefits of leisure. In E.L. Jackson & T.L. Burton (Eds.), *Understanding leisure and recreation: Mapping the past, charting the future* (pp. 385-419). State College, PA: Venture.

Schrodt, B. (1979). *A history of Pro-Rec: The British Columbia provincial recreation programme: 1934-1953.* Unpublished dissertation, University of Alberta, Edmonton.

Searle, M., & Brayley, R. (1993). *Leisure services in Canada: An introduction.* State College, PA: Venture.

Sears, J. (1980). *Sacred places: American tourist attractions in the nineteenth century.* Amherst, MA: University of Massachusetts Press.

Seibel, G.A. (1995). *Ontario's Niagara Parks, Niagara Falls.* Niagara Falls, ON: Niagara Parks Commission.

Sellars, R.W. (1999). *Preserving nature in the national parks.* New Haven, CT: Yale University Press.

Sessoms, H.D. (1961). Recreation education in American colleges and universities today. *American Recreation Journal, 1*(7), 28.

Sessoms, H.D. (1991). The professionalization of parks and recreation: A necessity? In T.L. Goodale & P. Witt (Eds.), *Recreation and leisure: Issues in an era of change* (3rd ed.). State College, PA: Venture.

Sessoms, H.D. (1992). Lessons from the past. *Parks and Recreation,* February, 46-53.

Sessoms, H.D., & Henderson, K.A. (1994). *Introduction to leisure services* (7th ed.). State College, PA: Venture.

Shaffer, M.S. (2001). *See America first: Tourism and national identity, 1880-1940.* Washington, DC: Smithsonian Institution Press.

Shaull, S., & Gramann, J. (1998). The effect of cultural assimilation on the importance of family-related and nature-related recreation among Hispanic Americans. *Journal of Leisure Research, 30*(1), 47-63.

Shaw, S.M. (1991). Body image among adolescent women: The role of sports and physically active leisure. *Journal of Applied Recreation Research, 16,* 349-367.

Sherer, P.M. (2003). *Why America needs more city parks and open spaces.* Retrieved June 5, 2005 from www.tpl.org/pforp [June 28, 2005].

Shivers, J.S., & deLisle, L.J. (1997). *The story of leisure: Context, concepts, and current controversy.* Champaign, IL: Human Kinetics.

Simo, M.L. (1988). *Loudon and the landscape.* New Haven, CT: Yale University Press.

Singh, M.A.F. (2002). Exercise comes of age: Rationale and recommendations for a geriatric exercise prescription. *Journal of Gerontology: Medical Sciences, 57A,* M262-M282.

Smale, B.J.A., & Frisby, W. (1992). Managerial work activities and perceived competencies of municipal recreation managers. *Journal of Park and Recreation Administration, 10*(4), 81-108.

Smith, A. (2001, July 20). *Muscular Judaism. The Sports Factor with Amanda Smith.* [Radio broadcast transcript]. Sydney: Australia Broadcasting Corp. Retrieved June 6, 2005 from www.ausport.gov.au/fulltext/2001/sportsf/s332335.htm [June 28, 2005].

Society of Park and Recreation Educators. (1992). *SPRE curriculum study.* Arlington, VA: National Recreation and Park Association.

Sosteck, A. (2004). Giving big-league sports a run for the money. *Governing,* July, 27.

Sporting Goods Manufacturers Association. (2004). *Sports participation in America: Participation trends in fitness, sports and outdoor activities.* North Palm Beach, FL: SGMA.

Standeven, J., & DeKnop, P. (1999). *Sport tourism.* Champaign, IL: Human Kinetics.

State Games of America. (2005). *About us.* Retrieved May 20, 2005 from www.stategames.org/sga/overview.html [June 28, 2005].

Statistics Canada. (1999). *Characteristics of dual-earner families.* Retrieved July 5, 2004 from http://dsp-psd.pwgsc.gc.ca/collection-R/Statcan/13-215-x1B/13-215XIB-e.html.

Statistics Canada. (2000). *Canadian culture in perspective: A statistical overview.* Retrieved July 12, 2004 from www.statcan.ca [June 28, 2005].

Statistics Canada. (2002). *2001 census: Age and sex profile: Canada.* Retrieved June 30, 2004 from www12.statcan.ca/english/census01/Products/Analytic/companion/age/Canada.cfm [June 28, 2005].

Statistics Canada. (2003). *For the love of it.* Retrieved on May 15, 2005 from http://142.206.72.67/02/02f/02f_009b_e.htm [June 28, 2005].

Statistics Canada. (2004). *The Daily: National survey of non-profit and voluntary organizations.* Retrieved on May 15, 2005 from www.statcan.ca/Daily/English/040920/d040920b.htm [June 28, 2005].

Statistics Canada. (2005). *Estimated population of Canada, 1605 to present.* Retrieved October 11, 2004 from www.statcan.ca/english/freepub/98-187-XIE/pop.htm [June 28, 2005].

Staying Fit in 2004. (2004, January/February). *ESM magazine.* Elmhurst, IL: ESM Association.

Stebbins, R.A. (1992). *Amateurs, professionals, and serious leisure.* Montreal: McGill-Queen's University Press.

Stebbins, R.A. (2005). Project-based leisure: Theoretical neglect of a common use of free time. *Leisure Studies, 24*(1), 1-11.

Stebbins, R.A., & Graham, M. (2004). *Volunteering as leisure/leisure as volunteering: An international assessment.* Cambridge, MA: CAB International.

Stern, M.J., & Seifert, S.C. (2002). *Culture builds community evaluation summary report.* Retrieved July 23, 2004 from www.ssw.upenn.edu/SIAP [June 28, 2005].

Stier, W.F. (1999). *Managing sport, fitness, and recreation programs: Concepts and practices.* Boston: Allyn & Bacon.

Strong-Boag, V.J. (1976). *The parliament of women of Canada, 1893-1929.* Ottawa, ON: National Museums of Canada.

Stumbo, N., & Peterson, C. (2004). *Therapeutic recreation program design: Principles and procedures* (4th ed.). San Francisco: Pearson Education.

Sutel, S. (2004, July 6). *Suburban flight: Empty-nesters flock to hip downtown areas.* New York: Associated Press, 1.

Sylvester, C., Voelkl, J., & Ellis, G. (2001). *Therapeutic recreation programming: Theory and practice.* State College, PA: Venture.

Tate, A. (2001). *Great city parks.* New York: Routledge.

Taylor, A.F., Kuo, F.E., & Sullivan, W.C. (2001). Views of nature and self-discipline: Evidence from inner city children. *Journal of Environmental Psychology, 22,* 49-63.

Taylor, T., & Toohey, K. (2001/2002). Behind the veil: Exploring the recreation needs of Muslim women. *Leisure/Loisir, 26*(1-2), 85-105.

Tennessee Valley Authority. (n.d.). *Recreation.* Retrieved June 6, 2005 from www.tva.gov/river/recreation/index.htm [June 28, 2005].

Tillman, A. (1973). *The program book for recreation professionals.* Palo Alto, CA: Mayfield.

Toh, K.L., & Jamieson, L.M. (2000). Constructing and validating competencies of sport managers (COSM) instrument: A model development. *NIRSA Journal, 23*(2), 38-55.

Top4x4sites. (2005). *Top4x4sites.* Retrieved June 12, 2005 from www.top4x4sites.com [June 28, 2005].

Totten, W.F. (1970). *The power of community education.* Midland, MI: Pendell.

Tucker, J.S., Schwartz, J.E., Clark, K.M., & Friedman, H.S. (1999). Age-related changes in the associations of social network ties with mortality risk. *Psychology and Aging, 14,* 564-571.

UNESCO. (2005a). *Biosphere reserves.* Retrieved July 19, 2005 from www.unesco.org/mab/brlistEur.htm [June 28, 2005].

UNESCO. (2005b). *World heritage.* Retrieved June 12, 2005 from http://whc.unesco.org/en/about [June 28, 2005].

United Nations Environment Programme. (2004). *Protected area and world heritage programme: Parks for peace.* Retrieved June 12, 2005 from www.unep-wcmc.org/protected_areas/transboundary/somersetwest/somersetwest-24.html [June 28, 2005].

United Nations Environment Programme. (2005). *UNEP-WCMC and world heritage.* Retrieved June 12, 2005 from www.unep-wcmc.org/index.html?http://www.unep-wcmc.org/protected_areas/transboundary/somersetwest/somersetwest-24.html ~ main [June 28, 2005].

U.S. Army Corps of Engineers. (2002). *Services for the public.* Retrieved June 6, 2005 from www.usace.army.mil/public.html#Recreation [June 28, 2005].

U.S. Bureau of Land Management. (2003, April 4). *Surface acreage managed by BLM.* Retrieved September 6, 2004 from www.blm.gov/nhp/facts/acres.htm [June 28, 2005].

U.S. Bureau of Land Management. (2005). Retrieved February 28, 2005 from www.blm.gov/nhp/index.htm [June 28, 2005].

U.S. Census Bureau. (2004). *Historical national population estimates: July 1, 1900 to July 1, 1999.* Retrieved October 11, 2004 from www.census.gov/population/estimates/nation/popclockest.txt [June 28, 2005].

U.S. Census Bureau. (2004-2005). *Statistical abstract of the United States.* Retrieved on June 28, 2005 from www.census.gov/prod/www/statistical-abstract-04.html [June 28, 2005].

U.S. Census Bureau. (2005). *IDB: Rank countries by population 1950-2050.* Retrieved September 28, 2004 from www.census.gov/ipc/www/idbrank.html [June 28, 2005].

USDA Forest Service. (1979). *Recreation opportunity spectrum users guide.* Washington, DC: Author.

USDA Forest Service. (2001). *Recreation facts: USDA Forest Service.* Retrieved June 12, 2005 from www.fs.fed.us/recreation/programs/facts/facts_sheet.shtml [June 28, 2005].

USDA Forest Service. (2002). *National and regional areas summary.* Retrieved June 12, 2005 from www.fs.fed.us/land/staff/lar/LAR02/table1.htm [June 28, 2005].

USDA Forest Service. (2004a). *National visitor use monitoring program.* Retrieved September 28, 2004 from www.fs.fed.us/recreation/programs/nvum [June 28, 2005].

USDA Forest Service. (2004b). *2005 national survey on recreation and the environment: A partnership.* [Study in conjunction with NOAA, University of Georgia, and University of Tennessee]. Retrieved on October 11, 2004 from www.srs.fs.usda.gov/trends/Nsre/NSRE2005.ppt [June 28, 2005].

USDA Forest Service. (2004c). *Recreational activities: Find national forest and grasslands.* Retrieved September 6, 2004 from www.fs.fed.us/recreation/map/finder.shtml [June 28, 2005].

USDA Forest Service. (2005). *Recreation, heritage and wilderness programs: 2002 national visitor use report.* Retrieved June 5, 2005 from www.fs.fed.us/recreation/programs/nvum/ [June 28, 2005].

USDA Forest Service. (n.d.). *Working for the great outdoors.* Retrieved October 11, 2004 from www.fs.fed.us/fsjobs [June 28, 2005].

U.S. Department of Health and Human Services. (1996). *Physical activity and health: A report of the Surgeon General.* Atlanta: Centers for Disease Control.

U.S. Department of Health and Human Services. (2001). *The Surgeon General's call to action to prevent and decrease overweight and obesity.* Retrieved June 7, 2005 from www.surgeongeneral.gov/topics/obesity/calltoaction/cover.htm#citation [June 28, 2005].

U.S. Department of Health and Human Services, Centers for Disease Control and Prevention, National Center for Health Statistics. (1997). *Summary of notifiable diseases.* Retrieved June 6, 2005 from www.cdc.gov/mmwr/preview/mmwrhtml/00039679.htm#00001409.htm [June 28, 2005].

U.S. Department of Labor. (2004a). *Recreation and fitness workers.* Retrieved July 6, 2004 from http://bls.gov/oco/ocos058.htm [June 28, 2005].

U.S. Department of Labor. (2004b). *Bureau of Labor Statistics.* Retrieved September 28, 2004 from ftp://ftp.bls.gov/pub/special.requests/cpi/cpiai.txt [June 28, 2005].

U.S. Department of the Interior. (n.d.). *Bureau of Indian Affairs*. Retrieved June 6, 2005 from www.doi.gov/bureau-indian-affairs.html [June 28, 2005].

U.S. Fish and Wildlife Service. (2004a). *Annual report of lands under control of the U.S. Fish and Wildlife Service.* Retrieved June 5, 2005 from www.fws.gov/realty/PDF_Files/2004_lands.pdf.

U.S. Fish and Wildlife Service. (2004b). *National survey of fishing, hunting and wildlife-associated recreation.* Retrieved October 11, 2004 from http://fa.r9.fws.gov/surveys/surveys.html [June 28, 2005].

Vancouver Board of Parks and Recreation. (2005). *Sunset Community Centre.* Retrieved June 6, 2005 from www.city.vancouver.bc.ca/parks/cc/sunset [June 28, 2005].

VanDoren, C., & Hodges, L. (1975). *America's park and recreation heritage: A chronology.* Washington, DC: U.S. Department of the Interior, Bureau of Outdoor Recreation.

Veblen, T. (1998). *The theory of the leisure class.* Amherst, NY: Prometheus Books. (Original work published 1899).

Vennum, Jr., T. (2005). *Native American history of lacrosse.* Retrieved January 17, 2005 from www.laxhistory.com/history/index.htm?/history/vennum.htm ~ laxmain [June 28, 2005].

Vertinsky, P. (1994). The Jew's body: Anti-Semitism, physical culture and the Jew's foot. *NASSH Proceedings*, pp. 12-13.

VH1 Save the Music Foundation. (n.d.). *Who we are.* Retrieved March 5, 2005 from www.vh1.com/partners/save_the_music/who_we_are/success_stories.html [June 28, 2005].

Vileisis, A. (1997). *Discovering the unknown landscape: A history of America's wetlands.* Washington, DC: Island Press.

Virden, R.J., & Walker, C.J. (1999). Ethnic/racial and gender variations among meanings given to, and preferences for, the natural environment. *Leisure Sciences*, 21(3), 219-239.

Virginia State Parks. (2005). *History of Virginia state parks.* Retrieved January 17, 2005 from www.dcr.state.va.us/parks/his_parx.htm [June 28, 2005].

Vurpillot, E. (1968). The development of scanning strategies and their relation to visual differentiation. *Journal of Experimental Child Psychology*, 6, 632-650.

Wagner, L., Orvananos de Rovzar, M., & Imdieke, B. (2003). International perspectives on fund raising. In H.A. Rosso & Associates, & E.R. Tempel (Eds.), *Hank Rosso's achieving excellence in fund raising* (pp. 442-455). San Francisco: Jossey-Bass.

Wali, A., Marcheschi, E., Severson, R., & Longoni, M. (2001). More than a hobby: Adult participation in the informal arts. *The Journal of Arts Management, Law, and Society* 31(3), 212-230.

Wals, A.E.J. (1994). Nobody planted it, it just grew! Young adolescents' perceptions and experiences of nature in the context of urban environmental education. *Children's Environment*, 11(3), 1-27.

Weber, M. (1958). *The protestant ethic and the spirit of capitalism* [T. Parson, Trans.]. New York: Scribner's (Original work published 1930).

Webster, M. (2003). Arts education: Defining, developing, and implementing a successful program. In C. Dreeszen (Ed.), *Fundamentals of arts management* (pp. 151-198). Amherst, MA: Arts Extension Service.

West Virginia Division of Natural Resources. (2005). *Pipestem Resort State Park.* Retrieved June 4, 2005 from www.pipestemresort.com [June 28, 2005].

Westland, C. (1979). *Fitness and amateur sport in Canada: The federal government's programme: An historical perspective.* Ottawa, ON: Canadian Parks and Recreation Association.

Weston, A. (1962). *The making of American physical education.* Englewood Cliffs, NJ: Appleton-Century-Crofts.

Wetherell, D.G., & Kmet, I. (1990). *Useful pleasures: The shaping of Alberta, 1896-1945.* Regina, SK: Canadian Plains Research Centre.

Wetlands International. (2005). *Introduction to Ramsar sites information service.* Retrieved June 12, 2005 from www.wetlands.org/RSDB/default.htm [June 28, 2005].

Wilderness Society. (2005a). *Explore wilderness data.* Retrieved June 12, 2005 from www.wilderness.net/index.cfm?fuse=NWPS&sec=advSearch [June 28, 2005].

Wilderness Society. (2005b). *Wilderness fast facts.* Retrieved June 12, 2005 from www.wilderness.net/index.cfm?fuse=NWPS&sec=fastFacts [June 28, 2005].

Wilhite, B., Keller, M.J., & Caldwell, L. (1999). Optimizing lifelong health and well-being: A health enhancing model of therapeutic recreation. *Therapeutic Recreation Journal*, 33(2), 98-108.

Williams, D., Patterson, M., Roggenbuck, J., & Watson, A. (1992). Beyond the commodity metaphor: Examining emotional and symbolic attachment to place. *Leisure Sciences*, 14, 29-46.

Wisconsin Department of Public Instruction. (2004). *Community education 1911.* Retrieved March 5, 2005 from www.dpi.state.wi.us/dpi/dltcl/bbfcsp/ce1911.html [June 28, 2005].

Witt, P.A. (1973). Are municipalities serving the needs of the handicapped? *Recreation Canada*, 31(5), 25-27.

Witt, P.A., & Crompton, J.L. (1996). The at-risk youth recreation project. *Journal of Park and Recreation Administration*, 14(13), 1-9.

Witt, P.A., & Ellis, G. (1982). Status of municipal recreation services for special groups: A comparison of two studies. *Journal of Leisurability*, 9(2), 39-41.

Witvoet, B. (1988). My favourite vacation. *Calvinist Contact*, 22 April, 11.

Wolf Trap National Park for the Performing Arts. (n.d.). *National Park Service, U.S. Department of the Interior, Wolf Trap.* Retrieved July 26, 2004 from www.nps.gov/wotr [June 28, 2005].

World Playground Industry. (2005). *The world playground, parks & recreation products and services Web directory: Parks and recreation associations.* Retrieved June 13, 2005 from www.world-playground.com/ParkRecreation.htm [June 28, 2005].

Wright, J.R. (1983). *Urban parks in Ontario, part I: Origins to 1860.* Toronto, ON: Ministry of Tourism and Recreation.

Wyszomirski, M.J. (2002). Arts and culture. In L.M. Salamon (Ed.), *The state of nonprofit America* (pp. 187-218). Washington, DC: Brookings Institution.

Yin, Y., Buhrmester, D., & Hibbard, D. (1996, March). *Are there developmental changes in the influence of relationships with parents and friends on adjustment during early adolescence?* Paper presented at the meeting of the Society for Research on Adolescence, Boston.

YMCA. (n.d.). *About the YMCA.* Retrieved on June 1, 2005 from www.ymca.net [June 28, 2005].

YMCA Canada. (2005). *YMCA jobs.* Retrieved on June 1, 2005 from www.ymca.ca/eng_jobs.htm [June 28, 2005].

Young, S.J., & Ross, C.M. (2000). Recreational sports trends for the 21st century: Results of a Delphi study. *NIRSA Journal, 24*(2), 25-38.

Young, T. (2004). *Building San Francisco's parks, 1850-1930.* Baltimore: Johns Hopkins University Press.

Zaslowsky, D., & Watkins, T.H. (1994). *These American lands: Parks, wilderness and the public lands.* Washington, DC: Island Press.

Zbicz, D.C. (1999). *Transfrontier ecosystems and internationally adjoining protected areas.* Durham, NC: Duke University Press.

Zinser, C.I. (1995). *Outdoor recreation: United States national parks, forests and public lands.* New York: John Wiley & Sons.

Index

Note: Tables and figures are indicated by an italicized *t* or *f,* respectively.

About the Contributors

Robert F. Ashcraft, PhD, is director of the Center for Nonprofit Leadership and Management and an associate professor in the School of Community Resources and Development at Arizona State University. He has nearly 30 years of experience working in nonprofit leadership and management roles and in teaching students the theory and practical elements behind that work. Ashcraft served for 10 years on the national board of the YMCA of the USA and served as the youngest executive director of a local chapter in the American Red Cross. Ashcraft serves on the board of trustees of the NRPA and is a board member of the Nonprofit Academic Centers Council. He has served as director and in many other capacities for American Humanics, Inc., an undergraduate nonprofit management education program based in Kansas City.

Lynn A. Barnett, PhD, is an associate professor in the Department of Recreation, Sport, and Tourism at the University of Illinois at Urbana-Champaign, where her research has focused on the play of children and young adults and the contribution of play to development. Barnett is the author of numerous theoretical and empirical chapters and articles about play as an essential quality of human experience, learning, and development. She has translated this research into the design of toys and play structures and programs. For many years she has been teaching an upper-division course called Leisure and Human Development, which chronicles the course of play and leisure across the life span. Barnett is the author of numerous chapters and articles theorizing about play. She is a member of Play Research International and the National Recreation and Park Association (NRPA).

John Byl, PhD, is a professor of physical education at Redeemer University College in Ancaster, Ontario. Byl has taught recreation and physical education and has coached for more than 25 years. He has authored, coauthored, or edited 10 books related to recreation, physical education, and games. He has a keen interest in understanding the impact of faith on one's daily life. Byl is president of CIRA Ontario and of Ontario's Active Living Rewards online program.

Gaylene Carpenter, EdD, is an associate professor and director of the Arts & Administration Program at the University of Oregon. She has taught leisure program theory for nearly 30 years at five different universities and has written numerous journal articles about arts and cultural programs for the past seven years. An active advocate of arts and cultural programs, she is the academic coordinator for the Festival & Event Management Certificate Program at the University of Oregon. Carpenter received an Ovation Award for Lifetime Achievement from the Oregon Festivals and Events Association, and has also received awards for teaching innovation and excellence from the Society of Park & Recreation Educators. She is a member of the NRPA and the International Festivals & Events Association (IFEA).

Frances Stavola Daly, EdD, CTRS, CPRP, is an associate professor at Kean University in New Jersey, where she coordinates the recreation administration program and the gerontology certificate program. A past president of the National Therapeutic Recreation Society (NTRS), Daly is on the board of trustees of the NRPA and has served on the NTRS board for since 1998. She has presented at more than 30 national, state, and local conferences on various topics. She has been president of the Metropolitan New York Recreation and Park Association, the public policy chair for the New Jersey Therapeutic Recreation section, and a cochair of the New Jersey Governor's Advisory Commission on Recreation for Individuals with Disabilities. Daly was selected as the 2004 Distinguished Professional of the Year by the New York State Therapeutic Recreation Association and 2003 Supervisor of the Year by the New Jersey Recreation and Park Society.

Paul F.J. Eagles, PhD, is a professor specializing in environmental planning the University of Waterloo in Canada. His primary appointment is in the Department of Recreation and Leisure Studies. He is also cross-appointed to the School of Planning. Over the last 30 years Eagles has worked on a variety of planning projects with an emphasis on the planning and management of parks and protected areas. He has undertaken work in nature-based tourism in more than 25 countries. Since 1996 he has been chair of the Task Force on Tourism and Protected Areas for the World Commission on Protected Areas and of the World Conservation Union, based in Switzerland. Eagles has authored more than 300 publications in tourism, planning, management, and related areas, including coauthoring the book, *Sustainable Tourism in Protected Areas: Guidelines for Planning and Management.*

M. Rebecca Genoe, MA, is a PhD student in recreation and leisure studies at the University of Waterloo. She received her master's degree from Dalhousie University in Halifax, Nova Scotia, where her focus was on older men's leisure across the life span. Genoe has served as a research assistant at Mount Saint Vincent University in Halifax, where she has explored rural Canada's supportiveness to seniors. Her interests are in leisure, aging and gender, and she hopes to pursue research in this area.

Maureen Glancy, PhD, has worked and taught in the field of recreation since she was a teenager. She received her doctorate in parks and recreation from Penn State University. Glancy has worked in nonprofit agencies, private organizations, and universities doing general programming, environmental education and adventure camping, management and marketing, and teaching all aspects of undergraduate and graduate education. As a professor, Maureen's special interest in research revolves around understanding how people organize their recreation and share the deeper meanings of the common leisure experience with others. Now retired, Maureen lives on the California coast building gardens, publishing the club newsletter for the Northern California Norwich and Norfolk Terrier Club, and training and showing Scarlett and Arlie (her two Norwich terriers) in breed shows, Agility, Earthdog, and obedience trials. Because of her love of teaching, she continues to mentor graduate students and faculty, and she volunteers as a curriculum accreditation visitor for the NRPA.

B.J. Grosvenor, MS, is a lecturer and undergraduate coordinator in the department of recreation and leisure studies at San Jose State University in San Jose, California. As the primary instructor for the department's introductory course, she is well versed in the breadth and depth of material that needs to be covered in an introductory course and has developed strategies to facilitate knowledge acquisition in the classroom. Grosvenor has served on various boards for the California Park and Recreation Society and the California Board of Recreation and Park Certification. She has presented more than 35 various topics at regional and national conferences. Grosvenor received the 2004 Lifetime Achievement Award from the Therapeutic Section of the California Park and Recreation Society and the 2003 Distinguished Alumni Award from the department of recreation and leisure studies of the College of Applied Sciences and Arts at San Jose State University. She received a citation in 1998 for passage of SB 1347 State of California, Therapeutic Recreation Title Protection Act, awarded by the Therapeutic Section of the California Park and Recreation Society.

Mark E. Havitz, PhD, is a professor in the department of recreation and leisure studies at the University of Waterloo in Ontario, Canada. He has more than 30 years of professional and academic experience with some of the top municipal recreation agencies in the United States and universities in the United States and Canada. He is a coauthor of *The Diverse Worlds of Unemployed Adults: Consequences for Leisure, Lifestyles, and Well-Being,* the first systematic exploration of leisure and unemployment in north America. Havitz is a member of the NPRA, the Society of Park and Recreation Educators (SPRE), and the Canadian Association for Leisure Studies (CALS). He is an elected fellow in the Academy of Leisure Sciences (ALS).

Sara Hensley, MSA, is director for the department of parks, recreation and neighborhood services for San Jose, California. She has served in similar positions in Virginia Beach, Virginia, and Champaign, Illinois, and has spearheaded numerous projects in various cities to enhance more than 300 neighborhood parks and facilities. She also directed the development of national training facilities for the US Field Hockey Association and led the efforts for Virginia Beach in being selected as a Magnet Center for Sports Strategy by the NRPA. She has received multiple honors from the American Academy for Park and Recreation Administration (AAPRA) and many other honors from local and state associations, most recently the David E. Clark Distinguished Professional Award. A member of the NRPA since 1988, she has held numerous positions in various park and recreation organizations at the regional, state, and national levels, and has served as coeditor of various publications for the NRPA.

Jane Hodgkinson, MS, is the executive director of the Western DuPage Special Recreation Association, which has won two National Gold Medal Awards for its special recreation programs. She has spent more than 24 years heading special recreation associations in Illinois, and for two years she was the head of the Southern Illinois Special Olympics. Hodgkinson has also taught for two years at Southern Illinois University. She is the author of *Guide for Running a Local Special Olympics Program,* which explains how to run a local event. She is a recipient of the 1999 Robert Artz Award, the 1989 Illinois Park and Recreation Association's Professional of the Year Award, the Outstanding Woman Leader Award from DuPage County. Hodgkinson is a founding board member of the Illinois Special Olympics and past president of the Illinois Park and Recreation Association. She is a member of the Illinois Park and Recreation Association, the NRPA, and the AAPRA.

Stephen M. Holland, PhD, is an associate professor and department chair in the department of tourism, recreation and sport management at the University of Florida. He has worked as a National Park Service ranger and has taught undergraduate and graduate classes on outdoor recreation and ecotourism for 20 years. Holland has conducted more than $1 million of funded research on parks, beaches, and outdoor recreation behavior activities. He is a 17-year leader of the National Outdoor Recreation and Rural Tourism Consortium held at Smoky Mountain National Park each September. Holland is a board member for the National Society for Park Resources and a member of the NRPA. He has published numerous articles and conducted research in five national park service areas, nine state parks, two national wildlife refuges, and public beach access locations. He has been awarded the William Penn Mott, Jr. Award for Excellence and a Service Award for board of director service by the National Society for Park Resources.

Lynn M. Jamieson, ReD, is chair and full professor in the department of recreation and park administration at Indiana University. Previously she served as curriculum coordinator of the recreation administration program at California Polytechnic State University and spent 12 years in administrative positions as a recreation administrator, with special emphasis on recreational sport management. She has coauthored four texts and more than 50 articles about various aspects of management in leisure services. Her special interests include sport and leisure policy development and violence in sports.

Andrew T. Kaczynski, MSc, is a PhD candidate in the department of recreation and leisure studies at the University of Waterloo in Ontario. His academic and professional interests focus on the marketing, financing, and management of park and recreation services and particularly on the use of these techniques and resources to facilitate social and economic benefits for communities and the individuals therein. His research has been published in the *Journal of Park and Recreation Administration*, *Managing Leisure*, and *Leisure Sciences*. Kaczynski is a member of the NRPA, the Society of Park and Recreation Educators (SPRE), the Canadian Association for Leisure Studies, the American Association for Leisure and Recreation (AALR), and Parks and Recreation Ontario.

Douglas Kennedy, EdD, CPRP, is professor and chair of the department of recreation and leisure studies and associate dean of campus recreation at Virginia Wesleyan College in Norfolk, Virginia. He has taught a course on history, philosophy, and trends of recreation and leisure for 17 years. He has spoken at numerous professional events nationally and internationally, addressing the critical events in the development of the recreation profession. Kennedy is a past chair of the NRPA/AALR Council on Accreditation, a past president of the Virginia Recreation and Park Society, and a delegation leader of the Uzbekistan National Youth Democracy Education Project. As part of that project, Kennedy wrote a series of documents that facilitated democracy education in Uzbekistan though work with local teachers on integrating principles of democracy in grade-school curricula. He is a member of SPRE and the Virginia Recreation and Park Society.

Robin Kunstler, ReD, CTRS, is a professor at Lehman College of the City University of New York. She has been a professor of therapeutic recreation for 24 years and has been in the field for more than 30 years. She wrote some of the first articles in therapeutic recreation on entrepreneurship (1983), the homeless (1991), the naturally occurring retirement community (2001), and hepatitis C (2004). Kunstler has taught therapeutic recreation courses on every population and aspect of therapeutic recreation. She is coeditor of the Practice Perspectives section of the *Therapeutic Recreation Journal.* Kunstler is a member of the Society of Park and Recreation Educators, National Therapeutic Recreation Society, and the American Therapeutic Recreation Association.

Susan Markham-Starr, PhD, is an associate professor in the School of Recreation Management and Kinesiology at Acadia University in Wolfville, Nova Scotia. She has experience as a researcher about the history of the development of recreation and parks services in Canada and as a practitioner and consultant in recreation and parks planning. She is the former president of the Canadian Association for Leisure Studies (CALS) and served as chair for both the Canadian Parks and Recreation Association (CPRA) editorial committee and the Wolfville Recreation Commission. Markham-Starr wrote the CPRA Research Policy and coedited its 50th-anniversary publication. She also wrote the first City of Halifax Recreation Master Plan and is a member of CALS and World Leisure.

Donald J. McLean, PhD, is an associate professor in the department of recreation, park, and tourism administration at Western Illinois University–Quad Cities in Moline, Illinois. He has been teaching ethics classes since 1989. His interest in this area was spurred by practical experience gained through 12 years of coaching competitive rowing and founding rowing programs and clubs at the varsity, campus recreation, and community levels. He has presented papers on applied ethics at national conferences and served as guest editor for a special issue on applied ethics of the *Journal of Applied Recreation Research.* In his own leisure time, he enjoys golfing, traveling, and boating.

Robin Mittelstaedt, PhD, joined the recreation studies program faculty at Ohio University in 1991. She has served as coordinator of both the undergraduate and graduate recreation studies programs since 2001. Her research interests include the social psychology of leisure behavior, leisure research methods, and topics related to women's leisure. She has served as a reviewer for eight scholarly journals and as associate editor of *Leisure/Loisir* for six years. She has worked in numerous recreation positions, including being codirector of Summit Expedition, a mountaineering school in California; director of Parks and Recreation in California; naturalist for Los Angeles County Outdoor School; program director of a private summer camp in the San Juan Islands; director of summer day camps in California; and director of Camp Adventure in Yokosuka, Japan, at the Navy base.

Ellen Montague, EdM, is a communications manager at the Willamette Education Service District in Salem, Oregon. She has been involved in the field of community education since graduating from the University of Oregon in 1980. Montague has held leadership positions at the local, state, and national level and has written successful grants that brought on new programs and further developed existing community education programs in Oregon and Alaska. She is a member of the Oregon Community Education Association and the National Community Education Association.

Laurie Ogilvie, MA, is a national recreation and youth services manager with the Canadian Forces Personnel Support Agency, where she manages the policy and strategic implementation of recreational services in the Canadian forces.

Ellen O'Sullivan, PhD, CPRP, is president of Leisure Lifestyle Consulting and professor emeritus at Southern Connecticut State University, where she was a professor in recreation and leisure studies and in public health. She has written two books on parks and recreation topics and coauthored another book. She also has developed curriculum for the NRPA and served as the first chair of the Wellness Coalition at Southern Connecticut State University. She is a member of the American Academy for Park and Recreation and of the NRPA, from whom she received a National Distinguished Professional Award. She also served as lead trainer for Hearts N' Parks, a project that she helped develop in North Carolina that led to a nationwide program for the National Institutes of Health.

Mary G. Parr, PhD, is an associate professor in leisure studies at Kent State University in Kent, Ohio. Her scholarship is focused on the link between knowledge of leisure, leisure services practice, and the professional identity of leisure services. She has published numerous articles in the *Journal of Leisure Research*, *Leisure Sciences*, and *Schole* and is a regular presenter at NRPA's Leisure Research Symposium, the Canadian Congress for Leisure Research, and the Society of Park and Recreation Educators' Teaching Institute. She is a member of the NRPA, the Society of Park and Recreation Educators (SPRE), and the Ohio Parks and Recreation Association.

Laura L. Payne, PhD, is an assistant professor of recreation, sport and tourism at the University of Illinois. She is also the director of the Illinois Rural Recreation Development Project, which helps rural communities develop sustainable local parks and recreation programs and services that have a positive effect on the quality of rural life. Payne has worked in community recreation, nonprofit association management, resort recreation, and public relations. She has taught courses in leadership and group dynamics, recreation programming, leisure service administration, leisure and aging, introduction to leisure, and leisure and human development. She also has examined the role of recreation and leisure services in community development and the relationship between leisure lifestyle and health of older adults with chronic conditions. Other areas of research include the role of local parks and recreation agencies in the promotion and maintenance of health and the relationship between nature-based leisure experiences and health.

Brenda Robertson, PhD, is an associate professor in the School of Recreation Management and Kinesiology at Acadia University in Wolfville, Nova Scotia. She has studied youth crime and correctional recreation for the last 15 years and focused her PhD research on why youths commit crime for fun. Her research and teaching focus on the leisure behavior, marginalized populations, and leisure education. She has presented her work on youth crime throughout Canada and the United States as well as in Europe and Africa, and she has produced 25 publications on leisure and youth crime and related topics. She published *The Interface Between Leisure Education Delivery Models and Youth Justice Renewal,* a report that examines the role of leisure education in correctional settings. She has served on the Board of the National Correctional Recreation Association and the Canadian Association of Leisure Studies, and as director of the Centre of Leisure Studies. She currently serves as a Citizens Advisory Committee Chair for Correctional Services of Canada.

Craig M. Ross, ReD, is an associate professor in the department of recreation and park administration at Indiana University. He has written 60 professional articles, including nearly 40 refereed articles, many of them published in the National Intramural-Recreational Sports Association journal. He has received nearly two dozen awards for his writing, teaching, research, and service. In addition, he has coauthored three editions of *Recreational Sport Management* for Human Kinetics and has served as associate director at Indiana University with primary responsibilities in the campus intramural sports program. Ross has given presentations at the local, state, national, and international levels in recreational sport management.

Kelly Russell, CTRS, is the senior recreation specialist at the Jefferson County Sheriff's Office in Golden, Colorado, where she has expanded the program at the facility to serve more than 1,300 inmates, hired a second recreation specialist, and improved the overall quality of the recreation facilities and the programs that are provided. She was a member of the National Correctional Recreation Association and is currently a member of the National Recreation and Parks Association and the Colorado Parks and Recreation Association. Russell is a certified therapeutic recreation specialist.

Jerome Singleton, PhD, has been employed by the School of Health and Human Performance at Dalhousie University in Halifax, Nova Scotia, since 1981. Singleton is cross-appointed to the School of Nursing, Sociology and Anthropology at Dalhousie and to the école de Kinésiologie et Récréologie, Université de Moncton. Singleton has also been cross-appointed to the department of community health and epidemiology and the School of Social Work, both at the University of Toronto. He has been involved with Therapeutic Recreation and Older Adults for the past 24 years. Singleton has published articles in numerous journals and has presented at various professional conferences. He also has coproduced a video titled "Therapeutic Recreation Assessment of Persons With Alzheimer's."

Kathy Spangler, CPRP, joined the NRPA as the Northeast regional director in 1987 and has served in a variety of capacities for that association, including fitness and wellness director, American Park and Recreation Society staff liaison, and marketing director. In her current role she is national partnerships director. She spearheaded the creation of a national programs department in 1998 and has been responsible for advancing NRPA's external partnership and public visibility profile including the landmark campaign Healthy Lifestyles, Livable Communities . . . It Starts in Parks!, which was featured in *Sports Illustrated* and *Fitness* magazine. Recently, Spangler was appointed to serve on the National Park Service Advisory Board Committee for Recreation and Health. As a certified park and recreation professional, Spangler has made numerous presentations and contributed many articles and publications in a variety of areas related to health, wellness, and recreation. She has received many awards from state and national organizations. The University of Maine at Presque Isle, which recognized her as Alumni of the Year in 1998, conferred on her an honorary doctorate in 2004.

Jeff Temple is a 25-year veteran of Armed Forces Morale, Welfare and Recreation (MWR) and has been an active-duty sailor, a military family member, and an MWR civilian employee with both the Navy and the Army. After graduating from the University of Maryland with a BA in business management, Temple worked with the Navy and held several positions in Italy before becoming the first MWR director at the Naval Support Activity in Souda Bay, Crete. Temple also spent several years at Pt. Mugu, California, and in the Northwest as the leisure service director at SUBASE Bangor before accepting a position with Army Europe as the recreation chief in Giessen, Germany. He then served for three years as the MWR director in Schweinfurt, Germany, and as the chief of community recreation and business programs at Aberdeen Proving Ground, Maryland. He is presently the Liaison Officer, Quality of Life Programs, U.S. Army Europe in Heidelberg, Germany. He has served as an officer of the Armed Forces Recreation Society (AFRS) Board of Directors for more than 12 years. Jeff was appointed to the board in 1992 as a regional representative serving in that capacity in both the Northwest and in Europe and was then elected as president in 1998. Jeff currently serves the military recreation community as the AFRS representative to the NRPA National Forum.

Betty van der Smissen, ReD, JD, is professor emeritus of recreation and parks at Michigan State University and visiting professor in the Division of Leisure, Youth, and Human Services at the University of Northern Iowa. Van der Smissen has maintained memberships in many organizations and has been active in the fields of recreation, camping, environmental education, and adventure and challenge for nearly 50 years. The national organizations in these and several related fields have recognized van der Smissen's professional contributions by honoring her with their highest awards for service as well as naming certain awards in recognition of her service. These include a leadership award, a research grant, and a conference scholarship. Van der Smissen is noted for her extensive work, beginning in the early 1960s and continuing to date, in the development, implementation, and revision of the four major accreditation programs in her fields: academic curriculum, organized camping, adventure and challenge programs, and recreation and park agencies. She has served more than one term on the national accreditation body (council commission board) of each of these four programs.

Randy J. Virden, PhD, is an associate professor and the director of the School of Community Resources and Development at Arizona State University. Dr. Virden teaches courses related to the management of outdoor recreation resources and research methods. He earned a PhD in recreation resource management from the College of Natural Resources at Utah State University in 1986. His primary areas of academic interest are the application of social science knowledge to natural resource planning and policy, recreation and tourism behavior, and visitor management. Research projects include grants with the U.S. Forest Service, Bureau of Land Management, National Park Service, Arizona State Parks, and Maricopa County Parks and Recreation Department. Dr. Virden currently serves on the ASU Center for Environmental Studies Faculty Advisory Council and on the board for the ASU Center for Nonprofit Leadership and Management. He is chairman of the Maricopa County Parks & Recreation Commission.

Daniel G. Yoder, PhD, is a professor in the recreation, park and tourism department at Western Illinois University in Macomb. In his research and teaching his focus is on leisure and sociology. In his position as a parks and recreation director in Colorado, he observed and organized activities for a diverse group of people and faced practical leisure and sociological issues on a daily basis. He coauthored *Issues in Recreation and Leisure: Ethical Decision Making* with Don McLean for Human Kinetics, and he was presented an Outstanding Teacher Award in 2004 for his teaching at Western Illinois. Yoder is a member of the NRPA and the Illinois Parks and Recreation Association.